THOU SHALT KILL

THOU SHALT KILL

REVOLUTIONARY TERRORISM

IN RUSSIA, 1894–1917

ANNA GEIFMAN

PRINCETON UNIVERSITY PRESS

PRINCETON, NEW JERSEY

Copyright © 1993 by Princeton University Press
Published by Princeton University Press, 41 William Street,
Princeton, New Jersey 08540
In the United Kingdom: Princeton University Press,
Chichester, West Sussex
All Rights Reserved

Library of Congress Cataloging-in-Publication Data

Geifman, Anna, 1962–
Thou shalt kill : revolutionary terrorism in Russia,
1894–1917 / Anna Geifman
    p.   cm.
Includes bibliographical references and index.
ISBN 0-691-08778-4 (cloth)
ISBN 0-691-02549-5 (paper)
1. Terrorism—Russia—History—20th century.
2. Terrorism—Russia—History—19th century.
3. Russia—Politics and government—1894–1917.
4. Russia—History—1801–1917. I. Title.
HV6433.R9G45 1993   363.3'2'0947—dc20   92-46314

This book has been composed in Adobe Times Roman

Princeton University Press books are printed
on acid-free paper and meet the guidelines for
permanence and durability of the Committee on
Production Guidelines for Book Longevity
of the Council on Library Resources

Second printing, and first paperback printing, 1995

Printed in the United States of America
by Princeton Academic Press

10 9 8 7 6 5 4 3 2

To S. L. and L. A. Shur

CONTENTS

LIST OF ILLUSTRATIONS

*Gosudarstvennyi Arkhiv Rossiiskoi Federatsii (Moscow)

ACKNOWLEDGMENTS

WITH great pleasure, I wish to convey my gratitude to the many teachers, colleagues, and friends without whose help this book would not have been written. First, I would like to express my profound appreciation to Norman Naimark, who inspired and guided my first steps in the study of Russian history, and to Richard Pipes, who did so much to stimulate and encourage my interest in the field. Their high scholarly standards proved invaluable to me, and I will always be grateful for their unfailing support throughout my studies, and their wise and perceptive advice through the course of completing this book.

I am also much indebted to the following colleagues for their sharp and thoughtful comments, criticisms, and suggestions after reading the manuscript along the way: Vladimir Brovkin, Franklin Ford, William Fuller, William and Rheta Keylor, Michael Melancon, Martin Miller, and Philip Pomper. I also owe much to Yuri Felshtinsky for his advice and substantial help with the initial research. My research in Moscow was significantly facilitated by the able assistance of Dmitrii Oleinikov at the Russian Academy of Sciences' Institute of Russian History. In addition, Nikolai Baratov's advice and help with the illustrations for this book, and Fedor Larionov's expert work on the index are gratefully acknowledged.

I must express special appreciation to Linda Montgomery for her friendship and ever-helpful editorial assistance and counsel. Her expertise and endless patience during our years of working together have been indispensable. James Montgomery's knowledge of computers and Daniel Montgomery's clerical assistance have also been invaluable. This book has also benefited from Tanya Wolfson's able translation of political anecdotes and other examples of early twentieth-century Russian humor.

To all of these people I owe a substantial debt for their remarkable generosity with their time, constructive advice, and kind encouragement, which have helped me enormously in making this book a reality. Any errors of judgment, fact, or scholarship are of course my own responsibility.

Most of my initial research for this book was conducted in Stanford and Amsterdam with financial assistance from Harvard University: a Department of History Summer Fellowship, the Frederick Sheldon Traveling Fellowship, and the Foreign Language and Area Studies Fellowship. Additional research was supported by a grant from the International Research and Exchanges Board (IREX), with funds provided by the Andrew W. Mellon Foundation, the National Endowment for the Humanities, and the U.S. Department of State. Generous financial support for completion of the book came from the John M. Olin Foundation in the form of a Faculty Fellowship. None of these organizations is responsible for the views expressed.

I am also sincerely grateful for the assistance of the librarians at Harvard's Widener Library, and the archival staffs of the Hoover Institution on War, Revolution and Peace at Stanford University in California, the International Institute of Social History in Amsterdam, and the State Archive of the Russian Federation (Gosudarstvennyi Arkhiv Rossiiskoi Federatsii, or GARF) in Moscow, where Z. I. Peregudova was especially generous in sharing her time, attention, and knowledge of the sources.

Last, but certainly far from least, I am always thankful to my family and friends for their patience, support, and love.

THOU SHALT KILL

INTRODUCTION

FROM APRIL 1866, when former student Dmitrii Karakozov made the first unsuccessful attempt on the life of Tsar Alexander II, through July 1918, when Lenin and his closest associate, Iakov Sverdlov, ordered the assassination of Tsar Nicholas II, and soon thereafter proclaimed a general policy of Bolshevik "red terror," a half-century of Russian history was blood-stained by revolutionary terrorism. While it is essential to study the origins of terrorism and its early development in the 1870s and 1880s, this book undertakes an examination of terrorist activity in the Russian Empire during its most explosive stage, from the period just prior to the turn of the twentieth century through the revolution of 1917, focusing on the turbulent years of the first Russian revolution, 1905–1907. The primary objective of this study is to analyze the extent and significance of the sudden and unprecedented escalation of terrorism after approximately twenty years only incidentally disturbed by gunfire and the explosion of dynamite.

This task has been significantly facilitated by the existence of a number of studies dealing with Russian terrorism in the nineteenth century. Soviet scholars in the post-Stalin era were permitted and indeed encouraged to investigate the early history of the Russian revolutionary movement, and particularly what is known as its heroic period, 1878–1881, when the Party of the People's Will (Narodnaia Volia) dominated the radical camp.[1] Western historians have also been concerned with this group, the first modern terrorist organization in the world.[2] In addition, an important work by contemporary scholar Norman Naimark deals in part with the advocates of terrorist tactics in the years between the early 1880s, when the government succeeded in crushing the People's Will, and the mid-1890s, when isolated revolutionary groups of various orientations began to seek ways to consolidate their strength in larger political organizations.[3]

Still, in these years acts of political violence were relatively infrequent: from the 1860s through approximately 1900 there were no more than one hundred casualties from terrorist attacks.[4] Although the threat of terror, often overstated in police reports, did instill fear and distract the government from experimenting with reforms, this terrorist campaign hardly shook the foundation of the political regime or disrupted the normal flow of life in the empire, perhaps with the sole exception of the assassination of Alexander II in 1881. It was merely a prelude to the enormous escalation of terrorist activity in the country in the first decade of the twentieth century—a topic entirely neglected in the existing scholarly literature on the period. Not a single monograph has yet been written dealing specifically with the new wave of Russian terrorism in the reign of the last tsar, Nicholas II, 1894–1917.[5]

Several factors have contributed to this absence of concentrated discussion of the period's terrorist practices. First of all, in the years following the Bolshevik takeover in October 1917, the tendency was for official Soviet historians to focus their attention primarily on Lenin and the Bolshevik faction, which was by then in full control of the first socialist state. Scholars have also tended to neglect the losers—all the other political parties, including in particular the parties that did not belong to the Social Democratic (SD) camp, such as the Party of Socialists-Revolutionaries (PSR), whose members are commonly referred to as the "SRs," and the anarchists, who were primarily responsible for the terror in Russia. After failing to gain the upper hand in the revolution, these parties were relegated by Soviet historians to secondary status and considered to have been doomed to failure from the day of their formation.[6] This tradition continued even in the post-Stalin period, when scholarly discussion of terrorist activity was no longer expressly prohibited, as in the previous twenty-five years, though still implicitly discouraged. As a result, until very recently Soviet scholars have failed to make any significant contribution to an understanding of Russian terrorism in the early twentieth century.

Western historians have also neglected the topic, since for years they relied on Soviet historiography and tended to view the Socialists-Revolutionaries, the anarchists, and terrorist activity in general through Bolshevik eyes. Recently, however, scholars in the United States and Western Europe have begun to concern themselves with topics that touch at least in passing on the question of revolutionary terrorism in Russia. A number of studies have appeared on the PSR, the organization most notorious for its terrorist practices. There have also been several illuminating Soviet and Western studies of the 1905 revolution—a period when terror was particularly widespread.[7]

And yet, perhaps because of the still significant influence of Marxist class analysis in Soviet scholarship, and also because of the current emphasis on social history in the West, these works are primarily concerned with mass movements and mass violence, that is, peasant uprisings, workers' strikes, military and naval mutinies, student disorders, and armed demonstrations. Recent studies on these topics pay little or no attention to the fact that every day newspapers throughout the Russian Empire recorded dozens of individual assassination attempts, bombings, ideologically motivated robberies (or, as the radicals preferred to call them, "expropriations," usually shortened to "ex's"), incidents of armed assault, kidnapping, extortion and blackmail for party purposes, and vendettas based on political issues. By their sheer quantity and devastating impact on the life of an entire society, these and other forms of violence that fall within the definition of revolutionary terrorism[8] represent not only a powerful, but also a unique social phenomenon. On the basis of new research it seems justifiable to argue that the multitude of individual and usually premeditated acts against set targets—the most extreme form of radicalism and the main emphasis of this study—played a primary role in the crisis of 1905–1907 and in early twentieth-century Russian revolutionary history in general.

In every section, this book seeks either to provide the reader with new information based on sources hitherto unavailable or neglected by historians, or to reevaluate currently accepted assumptions and interpretations about the Russian extremists. The first chapter, which examines the extent and significance of revolutionary terrorism in Russia, establishes the general context in which the rapid intensification of radical activity took place, and surveys the immediate reasons for the escalation of violence throughout the empire after the turn of the century. It then seeks to analyze the available statistics on terrorist acts, demonstrating that by 1905, terror had indeed become an all-pervasive phenomenon, affecting every layer of society. In addition, this section of the book includes a discussion of the situation in the border regions of the empire, such as the Caucasus, Poland, and the Baltics, as well as the areas within the Jewish Pale, all of which were particularly affected by the escalating terror. An attempt is also made to place Russian terrorism within the general European context, an approach warranted by the fact that the perpetrators of violence were not confined in their actions by the borders of the Russian Empire, and instead expanded their practice of political assassination and expropriation abroad. Finally, the initial chapter demonstrates the tremendous impact of terrorism, which became part of everyday life, on the Russian government and the population at large.

The primary objective of the next three chapters is to examine the extent to which various political groups and parties in the antigovernment camp were responsible for the spread of revolutionary terror. Of all the organizations that openly advocated terrorist tactics, the most formidable political foe of the tsarist regime was the Party of Socialists-Revolutionaries, to which the second chapter is devoted. The PSR provided the new generation of radicals a fresh justification for their deeds by adapting the old terrorist ideas of the People's Will to the basic principles of "scientific Marxism," by then dominating socialist thought. A substantial part of this chapter is dedicated to demystification of the SR Combat Organization (Boevaia Organizatsiia), a conspiratorial terrorist body within the party set up specifically for the purpose of undermining the foundations of the tsarist regime by a series of centralized political assassinations. The Combat Organization operated primarily in the capitals, and, at least in its choice of targets and methods, was a direct heir of the Executive Committee of the People's Will.

In contrast to the leadership of the People's Will, however, the founders of the PSR did not predominantly confine their organization to centrally controlled terror, and allowed its members to exercise terrorist initiative freely in the periphery. It is to these decentralized operations, as well as to the terrorist activity of the Maximalists, radical defectors from the PSR, that the balance of the second chapter is devoted, modifying several common assumptions about the SRs and their tactic of "propaganda by deed."

The third chapter presents a reevaluation of party policy vis-à-vis political assassination on the parts of various representatives of the revolutionary Marxist trend, a relatively coherent grouping that includes such members of the Russian Social Democratic Workers' Party as the Bolsheviks, the Mensheviks, the Jewish Bund, and the Latvian and Polish Social Democrats, as well as independent Social Democrats from Lithuania and Armenia. Here again the study is at odds with the still prevalent traditional view that the very essence of their ideological convictions prevented the Russian Marxists from participating in individual terrorist acts.

While the second and third chapters deal with formal political organizations and their practical policies with regard to terrorism, the fourth chapter is concerned with the anarchists and various obscure terrorist groups, none of which were part of any unified movement. Each of these radical circles, scattered throughout the empire, acted independently and was not controlled by or accountable to any central leadership. It was primarily among these extremists that the classic type of early twentieth-century Russian terrorist developed.

In generalizing about patterns of terrorist activity in the initial decade of the century, the study puts much emphasis on what a prominent Russian liberal thinker and publicist of that era, Petr Struve, appropriately termed a *"new type of revolutionary* that developed unnoticed by society . . . in the prerevolutionary years and finally emerged during 1905–1907." This new type of radical was "a blending of revolutionary and bandit [marked by] the liberation of revolutionary psychology from all moral restraints."[9] Initial signs of this tendency, already present in the nineteenth century, were perceptively noted by Dostoevsky and depicted in *The Devils*. The process reached its apogee in the post-1905 period when the combat practices of increasing numbers of radicals qualified them as the "new type of terrorist." By then the phenomenon was evident not only to attentive observers, but also to the general public, which quickly incorporated it into popular humor: "When does a murderer become a revolutionary? When, browning [pistol] in hand, he robs a bank. When does a revolutionary become a murderer, then? In the same way!"[10]

These radicals came to differ significantly from most of their revolutionary predecessors who had operated between the 1860s and the 1880s, except, of course, for a few pathological types such as the infamous Sergei Nechaev, father of the new type of extremism in Russia, upon whom Dostoevsky based the sinister Petr Verkhovenskii.[11] The new extremists exhibited a considerably lower level of intellectual and ideological awareness, as well as less inclination toward selfless idealism and dedication to the cause, and comparably limited discrimination in selection of the targets for their attacks. Indeed, for these individuals terrorism became "so addictive that it was often carried out without even weighing the moral questions posed by earlier generations."[12] Many radicals themselves recognized that terror now "extended beyond the boundaries of a narrow circle of people totally devoted to the cause of liberation," and also that the revolutionary organism was infected with Nechaevism (nechaevshchina), a "terrible disease . . . the degeneration of the revolutionary spirit."[13] Largely due to the nature of their creed, the anarchists and members of the obscure extremist groups perpetrated the new type of terrorism more frequently than any other radicals; robbing and killing not only state officials but also ordinary citizens, randomly and in mass numbers, they bore primary responsibility for the pervading atmosphere of fear and chaos in the empire.

Throughout, the book also deals in detail with the "lower depths" of the revolution, an essential aspect that for the most part remains obscured from historiography, despite the fact that its careful consideration allows for the construction of an original and largely revisionist picture of the new phase of Russian revolutionary tradition prior to 1917. Contrary to the tendency of many historians to concentrate their attention on the elevated and idealistic rhetoric of the antigovernment camp, accepting at face value what its members chose to reveal about themselves, this study seeks to demystify and deromanticize the Russian revolutionary movement, and consequently the revolution itself and its participants, who were exalted and ennobled by far-from-impartial memoirists. It was not unusual for a wide variety of shady individuals, adventurers, opportunists, as well as common criminals, hooligans, and the riffraff of Russian society, frequently referred to as "petty rabble" (*shpanka*), to join the ranks of the "selfless freedom-fighters," and to use lofty slogans to justify what in reality was pure banditry. This clearly criminal activity is evident in the analysis of the terrorist practices of the various parties, and is emphasized in the chapter subsections that deal with the combatants (*boeviki*) and their respective approaches to the practice of expropriation, which assumed various forms, including robbery, extortion, and blackmail.

Differentiating between revolutionaries and criminals in this period can be difficult, especially in cases involving individuals with lengthy histories of contact with the police authorities. Such a person might be arrested as a common criminal initially, then return to the court system several years later to be sentenced to a lengthy term of imprisonment for participation in a political assassination attempt, and finally end up in court again on rape charges.[14] Contemporaries of the 1905 revolution themselves often found it impossible to separate the many acts of common criminality from the politically motivated acts. It was not unusual, for example, for a young revolutionary planning an expropriation to count on using half of the loot to help the downtrodden proletarians, and the other half to buy himself a small estate abroad, reasoning that, "as much as he sympathizes with the socialists . . . he considers their hope for a just social order totally unrealizable, [and] as much as he hates the bourgeoisie . . . he cannot help but envy it."[15] In this regard, on the basis of new evidence, this study asserts that many robberies traditionally considered revolutionary expropriations must be recognized instead as ordinary criminal undertakings in which the profits were used for personal gratification by representatives of the new type of radical in the post-1905 period, when, as Struve observed, "a flood of fast-living and pleasure-seeking burst into the revolution."[16]

In contrast to the nineteenth century, when revolutionary robberies of any type were extremely rare,[17] and a dissolute life-style was not prevalent among extremists, the phenomenon of the revolutionary bandit became so widespread as to warrant a separate examination in the chapter entitled, in accordance with a popular cliché of the period, "The 'Seamy Side' of the Revolution." As part of this discussion, it will be demonstrated that in addition to the criminal element attracted to the radical camp, an unusually large number of individuals with clearly pathological disturbances also joined the revolutionary ranks. This is particularly evident not only from the stream of mental breakdowns and the acknowledged suicidal urge[18] widespread among the Russian terrorists, but also from the fact that many of them exhibited unquestionably sadistic behavior, committing acts of striking cruelty. An equally important fact neglected in the scholarly literature is that the new type of terrorist did not hesitate to employ the assistance of juveniles, who participated widely in combat activities following the outbreak of revolution in 1905.

In the nineteenth century, or at least during the active period of the People's Will, terrorism was most commonly the tool of a tightly knit conspiracy of conscious, theory-oriented revolutionaries, for whom the intricate details of socialist dogma were essential both in forming their radical outlook and in guiding their activities. In contrast, many terrorists of the new type not only preferred to act on their own, often spontaneously and without sanction from the organizations they claimed to represent, but also demonstrated complete indifference to ideological issues, considering debate over theory to be idle talk and an excuse for not fighting.[19] In the years of revolutionary crisis, action thus gained in importance for the extremists of all political persuasions involved in terrorist operations inside of Russia, who proved by deed their preparedness to depart from the general ideological principles advocated by their respective emigré theorists abroad in order to achieve immediate results.

Specifically, more than ever before the extremists were willing to put aside ideological and programmatic disputes for the sake of a united effort among terrorists of various party affiliations. Based on new research, the chapter entitled "The United Front" emphasizes the fact that to date historians have assigned disproportionately large significance to the boundaries between the revolutionary organizations. Despite the squabbles in Paris, Geneva, and other centers of emigré politics, these boundaries were not absolute for the practitioners operating inside of Russia. From their perspective, they and their fellow revolutionaries all fought a common enemy—the autocracy—and party differ-

ences, especially on a theoretical level, often appeared artificial. This perception led to a situation in which terrorists of competing organizations frequently
joined together in preparations for political assassinations and expropriations.
This was particularly true of Russian revolutionaries operating abroad, who
were known for their consorted actions with foreign extremists, an important
issue in the analysis of Russian terrorism within the larger context of Western
radicalism.

The discussion of revolutionary terrorism in Russia would not be complete
without an examination of another political formation in the antigovernment
camp, the Constitutional Democratic Party, whose members were known simply as the Kadets. Contrary to the general assumption in the historical literature
that they were the stronghold and embodiment of Russian liberalism, this
study demonstrates that while the Kadets themselves never participated in violence, they welcomed and often even indirectly encouraged terrorist activities
in the party press and in their State Duma speeches, perceiving that these acts
served to weaken the tsarist regime and thus benefited the entire Russian opposition movement, liberals as well as radicals.

The final chapter of this book, which takes a look at "The End of Terrorism
in Russia," first examines the circumstances that contributed to the decline of
terrorist activity in Russia after 1908, evaluating the general question of the
extent to which the collapse of the 1905–1907 revolution predetermined the
end of terrorism. A goal here is to assess the effectiveness of the courts martial,
introduced in 1906 by Prime Minister Petr Stolypin to combat the violence in
the empire. The chapter then discusses the sensational discovery of a police
agent at the head of the SR Combat Organization, the so-called Azef affair, and
its significance in discrediting political assassination as a radical tactic. The
rest of the chapter, however, illustrates the fact that despite the marked decline
in terrorist activity in the decade preceding 1917, the idea of revolutionary
terror remained very much alive. This is illustrated not only by the final major
strike against the government by the new type of terrorism, the assassination
of Stolypin in 1911, but also by various minor combat ventures and, significantly, great plans on the part of the extremists to revive terrorism.

In attempting to illuminate various obscure and often controversial issues,
this book, especially in its first and final chapters, relies in part on memoirs,
journal and newspaper articles, monographs, and other sources published in
the Russian Empire, in the USSR, and in the West. Although the secondary
literature on Russian terrorism is relatively limited, the extensive research
dealing with contemporary terrorist theory—the result of significant efforts by
political scientists—contributed to the formulation and analysis of several
problems central to this study, and also helped place Russian terrorism in the
proper context of modern political violence.[20] In the main, however, this work
is founded on documents from the three richest archival collections of Russian
revolutionary source materials in the West. Some of the statistical data and

most of the descriptions of terrorist acts and the actions taken by the authorities against them are drawn from the large collection of newspaper clippings on political violence in the Archive of the Socialist-Revolutionary Party, held by the International Institute of Social History in Amsterdam. These and many other materials from this depository were also a natural base for the chapter dealing with the Party of Socialists-Revolutionaries. The chapters on the Social Democrats and the anarchists, as well as "The 'Seamy Side' of the Revolution" and "The United Front," owe much to two invaluable collections located at the Hoover Institution on War, Revolution and Peace at Stanford University: the enormous private archive of Boris I. Nicolaevsky, and the files of the Foreign Agency of the Okhrana (tsarist secret police), known as the Okhrana Collection. The materials found in the Okhrana files for the most part proved very reliable, despite the tendency of the police to denigrate the radicals. The chapter on the Kadet Party draws heavily from two important primary sources, the stenographic records of the first and second Duma sessions, and issues of the Kadet daily organ, *Rech'* (Speech). Due to the overwhelming volume of information available in the West, and also the analytical structure of this book, extensive research in Soviet archives was not required, but the unpublished materials held in the State Archive of the Russian Federation (Gosudarstvennyi Arkhiv Rossiiskoi Federatsii, or GARF), formerly known as the Central State Archive of the October Revolution (Tsentral'nyi Gosudarstvennyi Arkhiv Oktiabr'skoi Revoliutsii, or TsGAOR) complement and support the conclusions of this study.

Chapter One

REVOLUTIONARY TERRORISM IN THE EMPIRE

BACKGROUND, EXTENT, AND IMPACT

> Revolution was becoming the fashion.
> —*Victor Chernov*[1]

BACKGROUND

IN DETERMINING the preconditions for the intensification of extremist activity in Russia around the year 1905, scholars note the peculiar coexistence within one country of social and economic modernization and political backwardness. This circumstance created irreconcilable tensions among and within newly emerging social groups, whose members suddenly found themselves out of place in the traditionally static structure of the autocratic system. It was among these superfluous people, who quickly became alienated and frustrated, that most potential terrorists originated. They then joined various revolutionary organizations struggling against the contemporary order by means of a relentless stream of violent acts.

In the 1860s and 1870s radical circles consisted predominantly of individuals who belonged to the privileged groups of Russian society, either by birth, or by virtue of an education that raised them socially and intellectually above their origins.[2] In the early twentieth century, in contrast, the overwhelming majority of terrorists emerged from the first generation of artisans or unskilled laborers forced to move from the countryside to nearby cities or towns in the hope of finding employment in small workshops and developing industrial enterprises. Most of these young men from impoverished peasant families found life in the city arduous, and adaptation to it difficult. In addition to the fact that they often lived in miserable economic conditions, psychological adjustment was exceedingly slow. It was these people, then, who were most susceptible to radical agitation and propaganda following the outbreak of revolutionary events in 1905, and it is not surprising that at least 50 percent of all political assassinations committed by the SRs were performed by workers.[3] Although no reliable figures are available, numerous sources indicate even greater participation of artisans and unskilled (and frequently unemployed) workers in the terrorist acts perpetrated by other radical groups, especially the anarchists.

Simultaneously, women were proving increasingly willing to become involved in extremism. This was particularly true of women from upper- and middle-class backgrounds, for "though by 1900 the Russian revolutionary movement was attracting to its ranks increasing numbers from the lower classes, this process was much more marked among the men."[4] As a result of rapidly changing family relations and the spread of literacy, self-assertive girls and young women could no longer be confined to the home; at the same time, however, they were denied higher education, along with any role in the political process, and in general were offered little opportunity to realize their intellectual ambitions. This drove a number of them into the ranks of the radical outcasts, where their male comrades were willing to give them greater recognition than they could reasonably have expected within the traditional establishment.[5] Moreover, these women found ample opportunity to assert themselves among the radicals by taking part in underground and occasionally very dangerous operations. To a large extent, this accounts for the fact that women comprised nearly one-third of the SR Combat Organization, and approximately one-fourth of all Russian terrorists at the beginning of the twentieth century.[6]

Their participation in the revolution was marked by selfless devotion, as well as by extreme fanaticism, and to a certain extent their readiness to sacrifice themselves for their beliefs was a projection of the Russian Orthodox concept of the woman-martyr into the entirely secular realm of radical politics.[7] At the same time, this mode of behavior was equally common among Jewish women, who were even more restricted in their homes and within their traditional social milieu than their Russian counterparts, and in one estimate, came to compose some 30 percent of the SR female terrorists. Their readiness to embrace terrorism had to do in part with the fact that "in becoming revolutionaries, they severed links with their families and past traditions at a deeper level than men did. By joining the movement, a Jewish girl was not only opposing her parents' political beliefs, but was also flouting one of the very foundations of Jewish society—her role as a woman in the family."[8]

In general, the individuals—men as well as women—who belonged to the new breed of terrorist were drawn from the various minorities within the empire, including the traditional Jewish community, the nationalities of the Caucasus, Poland, and the Baltics, much more frequently than in the nineteenth century. This category of extremists consisted largely of people of lower social origins and minimal education. In recruiting them for combat activities, radical leaders usually appealed to their nationalist sentiments, enlisting them not so much for sociopolitical causes as for the national liberation movements.

This is not to suggest that terrorism no longer inspired or attracted members of the more privileged social strata (occasionally even among descendants of aristocratic families), and the rapidly growing *raznochintsy*, including university students, professionals, and other representatives of the educated and intellectual milieu. Many who considered themselves part of the Russian intelligentsia had emerged from the nineteenth century deeply angered by Alexander III's counterreforms, which had curtailed, or de facto revoked, the major political concessions of the 1860s. They were also frustrated by the apparent failure of their own efforts to introduce gradual improvements in Russia's socioeconomic situation during the so-called epoch of small deeds (*epokha malykh del*), from the mid-1880s to the 1890s. Increasing numbers of these educated individuals moved rapidly in the direction of extremism, no longer considering it possible to conduct peaceful and effective work within the framework of the existing political system.[9]

Many of them returned to the idea of terrorism partly as an indirect result of a severe famine following a crop failure in 1891, coupled with devastating cholera and typhus epidemics that ravaged European Russia in 1891–1892. While the immediate cause of the mass starvation was meteorologic, the general poverty in the countryside intensified the effects of the natural disaster.[10] The government's efforts to ease the situation were supplemented by the work of many volunteers—primarily students and liberal professionals among the intelligentsia—who went to the villages to participate in relief operations.[11] While many of these liberals sincerely desired to help the peasants, a significant number of radicals seized the opportunity and sought to set in motion a new wave of revolutionary activity by turning the hungry masses against the tsarist regime.[12] Revolutionary circles emerged everywhere in the provinces affected by the famine; their members energetically printed and distributed antigovernment literature and openly agitated for violence against state officials, the police, and the wealthy, blaming them for the misfortunes of the peasants and the poor townsfolk.[13]

Both the authorities and the revolutionaries recognized the famine and epidemics of 1891–1892 as the impetus for an increase in radical thinking and activity in the central Russian regions.[14] There was, however, a major obstacle to the spread of radicalism, for even the most idealistic believers in the progressive nature of the Russian peasantry had to admit that the villagers were extremely hostile toward strangers. They distrusted doctors and nurses, and thought that educated people would bring them nothing but harm. Some peasants even believed that the government had sent the medical personnel with orders to poison them, and in several areas physicians were badly beaten and driven away. Moreover, when the radicals attempted to turn the violent crowds against the authorities, they found the villagers no more willing to listen to fiery speeches than they were to accept medical aid. The peasants saw no connection between their misfortunes and the central administration, and in fact were grateful for the material assistance from the government, calling it the "tsar's ration."[15] The peasantry thus proved to be the complete opposite of a "conscious revolutionary force," causing many opponents of the tsarist regime to question their ability to mobilize the still sleepy Russian masses. Some of the people active in the countryside in the early 1890s therefore began to seek other means of fighting the government, and at this point returned to the idea that in order to ensure mass participation, it would be necessary to ignite the revolution for the people by means of individual terrorist acts.[16]

While not all the opponents of the autocracy were willing to dedicate their lives to the work of professional revolutionaries or terrorists, by the final years of the nineteenth century greater tolerance and even cooperation between a large part of educated Russian society and the extremists was a fact. Liberal circles demonstrated sympathy toward terrorists as early as 1878, during the sensational trial and acquittal of political vigilante Vera Zasulich. Subsequently, while the moderates condoned violence immediately after the 1 March 1881 assassination of Alexander II, their tendency to side with the revolutionaries against the government became even more evident during and after the era of his son's counterreforms. According to the memoirs of Vera Figner, in her youth one of the most active members of the People's Will's Executive Committee:

> Society saw no escape from the existing condition; one group sympathized with the violence . . . while others regarded it only as a necessary evil—but even they applauded the valour and skill of the champion. . . . Outsiders became reconciled to terrorism because of the disinterestedness of its motives; it redeemed itself through renunciation of material benefits, through the fact that the revolutionist was not satisfied with personal well-being . . . it redeemed itself by prison, exile, penal servitude and death.

Liberal society thus came to behold in the late nineteenth-century terrorists "examples of self-sacrifice and heroism, persons of rare civic virtues," who were "motivated by a deep humanism . . . and for this reason even their outrages were forgiven."[17] This attitude could only nourish extremism, for "as a rule, it has been argued convincingly, terrorists tend to be particularly successful if, in an already unstable society, they are able to muster a small degree of actual, and a large degree of potential support."[18]

Moreover, in the subsequent decades even some adherents of more conservative principles, frustrated by the defensive and excessively cautious policies inherited and reaffirmed by the administration of Nicholas II, became resistant to joining the authorities' efforts against the extremists, preferring to remain aloof from the political process (or at least the government structure), and finding consolation in berating both sides.[19] Furthermore, despite their disdain for revolutionary dogma, many moderates and even conservatives largely ceased to accept the official view that all radicals and terrorists were common criminals or "half-wit boys."[20] To them, this was a narrow-minded and indeed dangerous approach to the dilemma of extremism in Russia, for it failed to spur the autocracy to find solutions to at least some of the country's urgent socioeconomic and political problems.

This attitude on the part of the progovernment forces clearly did not strengthen the official cause, and the tolerance, understanding, and even absolution of revolutionary tactics prevalent among the liberals, coupled with their tendency to condemn the authorities for implementing countermeasures, impaired the administration's position further. Additionally, by the mid-1890s the liberals had already begun to demonstrate their willingness to join in the struggle against the existing political regime alongside the radicals. This tendency became especially evident when representatives of the antigovernment camp sought, after more than ten years of disorganization following the dissolution of the People's Will, to unite their forces into coherent and formidable political formations, to develop modern ideological principles, and to define appropriate tactics for combatting the autocratic regime. Their initial fleeting success was in organizing the Party of People's Rights (Partiia narodnogo prava) in September of 1893. This short-lived and heterogeneous entity included revolutionaries as well as liberals, a combination that to a large extent predetermined the group's inability to formulate a policy on the tactic of revolutionary terror.[21] Although the Party of People's Rights was disbanded by the police in April of 1894, it established a precedent for the creation of modern political parties in the Russian Empire. A new phase of political activity began, during which all of the major radical antigovernment organizations active in the early twentieth century originated, including finally in 1901 the Party of Socialists-Revolutionaries.

The formation of the PSR, with its undisguisedly proterrorist stand, revised theoretical justification for terror as a form of antigovernment struggle, and improved organizational structure, greatly contributed to the spread of political assassination in Russia. In part this was a consequence of an increase in the number of terrorists and their supporters so dramatic that "there was never a shortage of people" willing to participate in SR-sponsored terror.[22] Equally important, however, was the fact that this newly created party was gradually able to establish a stronger "technical base" (tekhnicheskaia baza) for successful terrorist operations.

First of all, the SRs could now count on much greater financial support, and devoted particular effort to fund-raising campaigns at home and especially abroad, developing significant expertise in this area.[23] Benefactors willing to contribute to the Russian revolutionary cause preferred to donate large sums to an organized political party rather than to petty extremist groups or individual radicals.[24] A steadily expanding treasury allowed the PSR to provide not only for the maintenance of its combatants, but also for the extensive purchase of the weapons and explosives essential for terrorist undertakings. Finally, the establishment of a substantial party network visibly facilitated the smuggling of arms and dynamite into Russia from abroad. As other radical groupings developed into full-fledged political organizations, these considerations became applicable to them as well.[25]

Another factor contributing significantly to the intensification of violence in the empire was the fact that scientific progress and technical innovations had greatly simplified the production of terrorist weapons and basic explosive devices. According to one contemporary, "The manufacturing of bombs assumed enormous proportions, and there were such successes in this technology that now any child could make an explosive device from an empty sardine can and drugstore supplies. . . . Bomb shops were opening in every city."[26] Not surprisingly, people soon began to "talk about bombs as if about an ordinary thing, as if about literature," and the nickname for a small bomb, or "orange," passed into the general vocabulary of the times.[27] "Beware of oranges!" was a joke of the day, and there were many satirical poems in circulation:

People have started getting wary,
They consider fruit quite scary.
A friend of mine as tough as granite
Is frightened of the pomegranate.
Policemen, ready to bark and grumble,
At the sight of an orange now tremble.[28]

Contemporary aphorisms on the subject of explosives appeared, including one that stated, "Luck is like a bomb—it can strike one man today, another tomorrow."[29] Although meant to be entertaining, some of this dark humor also reflected the general dissatisfaction with broader problems in the Russian socioeconomic and political reality. One popular anecdote ridiculed Minister of Finance Count Sergei Witte, who had "decided to replace gold currency with dynamite, since dynamite is streaming into [Russia] while gold is streaming out."[30]

This revival of the terrorist mood around the turn of the century followed an interlude of superficial tranquility that began after the successful regicide carried out against Alexander II by the People's Will in 1881. Despite continuing underground agitation for violence within isolated revolutionary circles, not a single major terrorist act took place in Russia in this period, with the exception of the abortive attempt to assassinate Alexander III made on 1 March 1887 by the Ul'ianov conspiracy (a group that included Lenin's older brother, Aleksandr Ul'ianov). The years between this strike and the mid-1890s were thus a time of deceptive calm before the storm. Until the emperor's demise from natural causes in the fall of 1894, the descendents of the People's Will remained intent upon settling accounts with the man they blamed for what they regarded as the unbridled tyranny rampant in the country. Indeed, in 1893 police informers reported that preparations for another terrorist attack "of primary significance" were well underway.[31] The death of Alexander III did not deter some proponents of terrorism, especially abroad, who continued to develop plans for major assassinations immediately after his son, Nicholas II, assumed the throne, and before the new tsar had had a chance to reveal his political intentions; the most essential of their plans still involved regicide. Other conspirators, while proceeding with work on such new explosive devices as bombs filled with nails, resolved not to undertake direct terrorist action before the coronation ceremonies, allowing Nicholas an opportunity to announce political reforms and concessions.[32] When he assured the anxiously awaiting public that he had no intention of promoting such changes, and would do everything in his power to continue the policies of Alexander III, regicide again became the primary objective for most advocates of terrorist tactics.[33] The goal was impractical, however, and strictly theoretical, but remained for this generation of radicals a sacred and cherished dream. Their fantasies on the subject frequently involved farfetched schemes, including the construction of a flying apparatus to drop explosives on the Winter Palace.[34]

Simultaneously, by the turn of the century a growing number of Russian revolutionaries, the most ardent and outspoken of whom was the soon-to-be-famous Vladimir Burtsev, then residing in London, openly asserted that it was time for a new wave of political terror, "at least as [powerful] as in the years 1879–1880 and even more so." Although they never abandoned the assassination of the tsar as an ultimate goal, they now considered less important state officials suitable targets for their acts.[35] In Russia, an obscure extremist group formed early in 1901, whose members professed themselves socialists-terrorists and placed primary emphasis on political murder, proclaimed as its initial objective the assassination of Minister of the Interior Dmitrii Sipiagin. Their resolution reveals the importance they attached to public opinion, for they justified their choice of target in part by asserting that the killing of this powerful reactionary official would "elicit complete approval not only from the oppositional elements, but from Russian society as a whole." Following the act against Sipiagin, the group planned to direct its forces against the procurator of the Holy Synod, Konstantin Pobedonostsev, and only then, having gained sufficient experience at combat work, would they proceed with an attempt on the life of Nicholas II.[36]

Prior to the formation of the PSR, the anarchists, along with representatives of the neo-Populist circles adhering to the principles of the defunct People's Will, were particularly active in developing plans for political assassinations.[37] Terrorist practices also spread gradually throughout the border regions of the empire, such as Poland, where members of the Polish Socialist Party (PPS), already active at the end of the nineteenth century, occasionally eliminated "enemies of the revolution," including police informers and strikebreakers. Among the Jewish opponents of the regime, several groups also began to express the need to form combat detachments and commence terrorist action.[38] For the most part, however, the few terrorist acts that occurred in the empire in this period were carried out by terrorists of the new type: obscure individuals, extremists in spirit with unclear ideological preferences, who did not belong to any particular organization and committed violent acts on their own initiative.[39] Already by 1897 some of these individuals were resorting to indiscriminate violence for strictly personal reasons. In one case, a worker named Andreev who had lost his job expressed his frustration by attacking a representative of the establishment, a uniformed army general attending a concert in Pavlovsk.[40] Some early instances of individual terror carried with them a more direct political message, the most notable being the first assassination committed in Russia in the twentieth century—the murder of conservative Minister of Education N. P. Bogolepov on 14 February 1901 by a recently expelled university student, Petr Karpovich.[41]

Perhaps the primary significance of this act lay in the fact that it seemed to validate a prediction made earlier by a number of proponents of terrorist tactics: "The first successful bomb will gather thousands of supporters under the banner of terror [and] the financial means will flow in."[42] The radicals in Russia were evidently tired of the eternal disputes about theoretical issues and programs, considering these idle discussions a waste of energy that produced no results. Increasingly, the opinion prevailed that "as long as a despot reigns, as long as everything in the country is determined by an autocratic government, no debates, programs, manifestos will help. Action is needed, real action . . . and such action under present conditions is only: the most widespread, versatile terror.[43]

It is highly significant that through their terrorist attacks some radicals sought to provoke the authorities to further repressions, which they assumed would increase public dissatisfaction and lead to a general uprising.[44] Thus, in a situation in which "more and more frequently voices were heard in Russia in favor of terror," it was hardly surprising that as early as the summer of 1901, even before the creation of the PSR evoked immediate strong sympathy for its proterrorist stand, concerned representatives of the tsarist administration feared that revolutionary activity in the empire would take the form of a series of sudden terrorist acts in the immediate future.[45] At the same time, while the radicals were already prepared to take up firearms and dynamite, and the "hearts and souls of the revolutionaries in Russia were strained to the limit," everyone in the antigovernment camp seemed to be awaiting the signal for a major extremist campaign to begin, for the "first strike of some sort of *veche* bell calling for the most intense revolutionary struggle."[46] Their patience was not tested for long, as the anxiously anticipated signal for direct terrorist action promptly came on a Sunday early in 1905.

The events of Bloody Sunday, 9 (22) January 1905, when government troops killed and wounded hundreds of workers and their families marching to the Winter Palace to present a petition to the tsar, are traditionally considered the beginning of the revolutionary crisis.[47] The episode has appropriately been treated in recent scholarship within the context of the complex socioeconomic, political, and diplomatic factors that contributed to the gradual radicalization of Russian politics. Throughout the empire the actions of the revolutionaries validated a general tendency noted by students of political violence: "When an unpopular authoritarian regime . . . experiences setbacks and exhibits signs of decomposition, certain underground or exile parties may seek to hasten its collapse by waging a terrorist campaign." These parties are especially eager to turn to terror during periods of a regime's transformation.[48] Yet, while emphasizing the intensifying agrarian and urban problems, the general process of modernization, and the altering of political consciousness, along with the unexpected and devastating domestic effects of the Russo-Japanese War of 1904–1905, all leading up to the outbreak of the revolution, it is equally essential to stress, as some scholars do, that "objective circumstances *per se* are not a sufficient, perhaps not even a necessary condition of terrorism."[49]

Russian terrorism became particularly widespread at a time when, in the words of William Bruce Lincoln, "Suicide, murder, sexual perversion, opium, alcohol—all were part of Russia's Silver Age."[50] This was a period of intense cultural and intellectual turmoil and decadence when many of the era's highly individualistic and turbulent minds sought, in their artistic ecstasy, the "poetry in death."[51] For increasing numbers of educated Russians, who had rejected not only the official Orthodox church but also the very fundamentals of faith and Christian spirituality, experimentation with various substitutes became a way of life. In the course of this search for a new ideology, many came to embrace the idea of revolution as a suitable guiding formula for shaping their outlook and actions. Thus around 1905, when the most perceptive members of Russian society, particularly in the literary elite, began to predict the imminent collapse of the entire traditional order, their pessimism reflected not only a sense of approaching political crisis, but, more broadly, an awareness of a spiritual catastrophe befalling the country. To a few, most notably the greatest contemporary poet, Aleksandr Blok, it was evident that behind all the politics, revolutionary bloodletting had become commonplace because "some different higher principle is needed. Since there is none, rebellion and violence of all sorts take its place."[52] A simple political solution could thus do little to settle the inner conflicts of Russian society.

It is no wonder, then, that contrary to the prevailing conviction that "the weapon of political violence would be snatched out of [the extremists'] hands" by the establishment of a constitutional order,[53] the terrorist acts did not end with the issuing of the Imperial Manifesto on 17 October 1905, guaranteeing basic personal liberties to all Russian citizens and granting legislative powers to the State Duma. In fact, the revolutionaries took this concession for what it indeed was—a sign of weakness—and only intensified their efforts to bring down the existing political order. On the whole, "the worst forms of violence began only . . . after the promulgation of the October Manifesto,"[54] when the premeditated tactic of the radicals to weaken the government to the point of collapse plunged the country into a bloodbath. Few could remain impartial witnesses to the events:

> There were days when several major terrorist acts went hand-in-hand with dozens of smaller attempts and assassinations of low-ranking administrative officials, not counting the threatening letters received by almost any police official; . . . bombs were thrown on any pretext or without one; bombs could be found in baskets of wild strawberries, in postal packages, in coat pockets, . . . on church altars. . . . Everything that could be blown up exploded, from liquor stores to gendarme offices . . . and statues of Russian generals . . . to churches.[55]

A list of the more sensational terrorist acts perpetrated by the radicals against leading political figures in the early years of the century, while impressive, does not convey the magnitude of the phenomenon. Although several prominent members of the government were assassinated, including Sipiagin in April of 1902, his successor as minister of the interior, Viacheslav von Plehve, in July of 1904, and even the tsar's uncle, the governor-general of Moscow, Grand Duke Sergei Aleksandrovich, in February of 1905, these were only isolated instances of terror, the majority of which were executed by a single terrorist group, the PSR Combat Organization. When all varieties of violence assumed mass proportions following the outbreak of the revolution, political assassinations and expropriations also began to be perpetrated en masse.

The government found itself fighting to preserve the existing order against numerous adversaries: peasants who were killing landowners and burning their estates; striking workers fighting on the barricades; soldiers and sailors firing on their officers and throwing them overboard; the non-Russian nationalities taking up arms against the imperial authorities in the borderlands; cohorts of the radicals, ready for violence, assuming control of entire towns; and the intelligentsia cheering the revolt all the while. Under these conditions widespread terrorism became both the catalyst for and the result of Russia's internal crisis. On the one hand, individual assassination attacks and expropriations played a primary role in undermining the political and economic stability of the tsarist regime, inhibiting its efforts to wage an effective antirevolutionary war on multiple fronts. On the other, terrorism was allowed to assume enormous proportions only as a consequence of a whole complex of revolutionary events in Russia—events that many contemporaries characterized as "bloody anarchy," or simply, "one vast madhouse."[56]

THE EXTENT OF TERROR

The magnitude of the revolutionary terrorism is evident even from the incomplete statistics available, which clearly indicate that in Russia in the first decade of the century political assassinations and revolutionary robberies were indeed a mass phenomenon. During a one-year period beginning in October

1905, a total of 3,611 government officials of all ranks were killed and wounded throughout the empire.[57] Nor did the convocation of the First State Duma in April 1906 put an end to the terrorist practices, which, along with various mass forms of revolutionary upheaval, continued to plague Russia throughout 1906 and 1907. By the end of 1907 the total number of state officials who had been killed or injured came to nearly 4,500.[58] The picture becomes a particularly terrifying one in consideration of the fact that an additional 2,180 private individuals were killed and 2,530 wounded in terrorist attacks between 1905 and 1907, for a grand total of more than 9,000 casualties in the period.[59]

Detailed police statistics indicate that despite the general weakening of the revolutionary storm by the end of 1907, a year in which, in one estimate, terrorists were responsible for an average of approximately 18 casualties each day,[60] assassinations continued with almost the same intensity they had manifested at the height of the revolutionary anarchy in 1905. From the beginning of January 1908 through mid-May of 1910, the authorities recorded 19,957 terrorist acts and revolutionary robberies, as a result of which 732 government officials and 3,051 private persons were killed, while 1,022 officials and 2,829 private persons were wounded. Altogether during this period, terrorists were responsible for 7,634 casualties throughout the empire.[61]

In estimating total casualties for this era of revolution, it is necessary to take into account not only the very earliest incidents in the wave of political assassinations, that is, those before 1905, but also those that took place in 1910, and 1911, climaxing with the final major act of antigovernment terror—the fatal wounding of Prime Minister Stolypin on 1 September 1911—and ending with the last recorded terrorist plots in 1916. Moreover, it is also very probable that, in the general chaos of the revolutionary situation, a significant number of local acts went unregistered and did not become part of either the official statistics or the records of the radicals. It therefore seems justifiable to conclude that in the period under consideration, close to 17,000 individuals became victims of revolutionary terrorism.

These casualty figures do not reflect the frequency of politically motivated robberies, or the economic damage resulting from expropriations, which after 1905 became a source of constant concern for the authorities. Yet, in the words of a liberal journalist, robberies took place daily "in the capitals, in provincial cities, and in district towns, in villages, on highways, on trains, on steamboats. . . . [expropriators] take sums in the tens of thousands, but also do not shy away from single rubles."[62] In the month of October 1906, 362 politically motivated robberies took place in the empire, and on a single day, 30 October, the Police Department received some 15 reports of expropriations at various state institutions. According to Ministry of Finance calculations, from the beginning of 1905 to mid-1906 alone, revolutionary banditry cost the imperial banks more than 1,000,000 rubles.[63] Over the course of a single year beginning in October 1905, there were 1,951 robberies, of which 940 were directed against state and private monetary institutions. In 1,691 of these cases the revolutionaries escaped detention, which contributed to their increasingly bold attempts to stage large-scale expropriations; it is estimated that in this period expropriators confiscated 7,000,000 rubles.[64] As was also the case with political assassinations, even after the government's efforts against the practice of revolutionary robbery began to show definite results, expropriations continued to rage throughout the country, ultimately losing any close connection with political developments and with the faltering mass movements. In a span of only two weeks, from 15 February to 1 March 1908, a total of nearly 448,000 rubles fell into the hands of the radicals.[65] Over time the extremists gained experience and skill, enabling them on a number of occasions to acquire hundreds of thousands of rubles in a single act.[66]

State and private finances also suffered as a result of the psychological damage inflicted by the expropriations on the population at large. Many people considered it unsafe to invest their funds in any financial institution, a fear reflected in a popular joke published as the definition of "bank" in the imaginary *Newest Encyclopedic Dictionary*: "In the old days, this was a place to safeguard your money."[67] As expropriation activity intensified, it soon became equally dangerous for the ordinary citizen to keep his money at home. After 1905, the enormous figure of expropriated state funds must be increased by the hundreds of thousands of rubles confiscated by radicals from private individuals, allegedly for political purposes.

Whereas in the nineteenth century every act of revolutionary violence was a sensation, after 1905 terror became so widespread that many of the country's newspapers no longer bothered to publish detailed reports on every attack. Instead, they introduced special new sections dedicated exclusively to chronicling violent acts, in which they printed daily lists of political assassinations and expropriations throughout the empire.[68] After 1905 these terrorist enterprises indeed became part of everyday life in Russia, and, as some radicals admitted, a mass psychosis developed, a true "epidemic of combat activity" (*epidemiia boevizma*).[69]

This epidemic was even more in evidence in the border areas of the empire than in the central Russian provinces, and of all the borderlands the Caucasus region was especially affected by the intensified wave of bloodshed and anarchy that followed the promulgation of the October Manifesto. Local representatives of the tsarist administration proved incapable of controlling the deteriorating situation in various cities and towns of the region, where extremist leaflets and publications were distributed openly, mass antigovernment meetings were held daily, and the radicals collected enormous donations for revolutionary purposes with complete impunity. It was unusual to encounter an unarmed man on the streets, and the tsarist security forces were helpless against the combat organizations, whose members did not even bother to conceal their identities or occupations; robbery, extortion, and murder became more common than traffic accidents.[70]

Available statistics permit only a very rough estimate of the extent of violence in these provinces. Information of this type was reported sporadically in the peripheral areas of the empire, and the central authorities in St. Petersburg often included cases of political assassination and revolutionary robbery in the same reporting categories as ordinary criminal acts. This was especially true after 1907, when the Ministry of Internal Affairs tallied 3,060 terrorist attacks throughout the Caucasus, of which 1,732 were classified as robberies that left 1,239 people dead and 1,253 injured. While these numbers are obviously inflated, in part because they include casualty figures resulting from the ongoing struggle between the Armenians and the local Muslims, figures compiled by the local authorities are no more reliable. Seeking to justify his policies and diminish any impression of inactivity and incompetence that he might leave on his superiors, the Russian viceroy (*namestnik*) in the Caucasus, Count I. I. Vorontsov-Dashkov, offered a clearly understated total count of 689 terrorist attacks in 1907, which allegedly left 183 officials and 212 private individuals dead, and 90 officials and 213 private citizens injured. Claiming that it was impossible under the prevailing circumstances to differentiate between politically motivated expropriations and common robberies, Vorontsov-Dashkov provided composite figures for acts of banditry in the region: 3,219 in 1905, 4,138 in 1906, and 3,305 in 1907. Despite the fact that these statistics must be treated cautiously, even the most conservative estimate of the extent of violence in the area speaks for itself, as does the fact that terrorists in the industrial center of Armavir, claiming to represent various revolutionary organizations, assassinated some 50 local businessmen in the single month of April 1907, often in broad daylight. By then the radicals' total gain from extortion was nearly 500,000 rubles in that city alone.[71]

While in the Russian capitals and large provincial centers the PSR was the party most actively involved in terrorist practices, in the Caucasus the Armenian Revolutionary Party "Dashnaktsutiun" (Union), was responsible for the overwhelming majority of terrorist attacks. This organization, founded in the region in 1890, and operating under the motto "Freedom or death," had acquired significant strength and sympathy among the local population by 1903, largely because of its nationalist orientation. Initially, its primary efforts were directed toward liberation of the Armenians living under Turkish rule. The party enjoyed the support of the central Russian administration in this goal, which was fully in accord with tsarist foreign policy directed against Turkey. But following St. Petersburg's 12 June 1903 edict bringing Armenian church property under imperial control, and thus undermining the economic foundation of the Armenian nationalist forces led by the Dashnaktsutiun, the party leadership assumed a militantly anti-Russian stand.[72]

The party's position as a unifying force for the oppressed and divided nation was responsible for its enormous popularity among various patriotic elements across the entire territory of Russian Armenia. The Dashnaktsutiun was able to organize numerous well-armed combat forces composed primarily of thousands of Armenian refugees from Turkey—young, homeless, propertyless vagabonds with no family ties—who had been permitted in 1901 to settle in various cities of Russian Transcaucasia. Most of them were not trained in any trade and knew only how to use their knives. At the same time, the organization acquired enormous funds as a result of voluntary and forced donations from the Armenian population for its war against the Muslims—contributions that became particularly generous after the beginning of virtual civil war between the Armenians and the Tatars in the Caucasus in 1905.[73]

The outbreak of the revolutionary upheaval in the same year led to a split in the Dashnkatsutiun movement. While many rightist elements in the party still emphasized the old goals of combating the Turks and unifying the Armenians under the protection of the Russian government, the leftists, influenced by Russian Socialist-Revolutionary ideology and tactics, joined other radical forces in their war against the autocracy. Their primary socioeconomic and political demands included self-determination for the entire Armenian nation. It was these Dashnaki revolutionaries, hardened by their bloody struggles with the Turks and the Tatars, who for the time being dominated the decision-making process in the party, simultaneously using relentless violence to establish control over various localities in the Caucasus.

In addition to physically eliminating those who opposed their political objectives, the Dashnaki forced wealthy citizens to pay predetermined taxes (occasionally as much as eighty thousand rubles annually) for the benefit of the Dashnaktsutiun. They purchased weapons, set up bomb laboratories, and also assumed community administrative and judicial functions, punishing anyone who appealed for help to the legal civil and police authorities instead of the local revolutionary committee. In some instances, police officials had no choice but to acknowledge the omnipotent position of the party, negotiate with its representatives, and cooperate in solving some of the immediate problems of the day.[74]

By early 1907 the Dashnaki practice of indiscriminate violence, which persisted despite the return of property confiscated by the tsarist government to the Armenian church, had caused the party to lose much of its former popularity and support, but the Dashnaktsutiun continued to play a primary role in maintaining the reign of terror in Transcaucasia until at least 1909.[75] At the same time, after 1905 the revolutionary situation in Armenia, Georgia, and other areas of the region gave rise to various smaller and less organized extremist formations and isolated combat detachments, some adopting such revealing names as Horror (Uzhas), or the anarchist-communist Death to the Capital (Smert' Kapitalu), both of which operated in a fashion similar to the Dashnaki.[76] In the Georgian town of Telavi, a militant organization of unclear radical orientation calling itself the Red Hundreds (Krasnaia sotnia) followed the Dashnaktsutiun example, sentencing its opponents to death, extorting dues from nearby villages, and forcing the local population to terminate payment of all legal taxes. For many of these terrorist groups, nationalist objectives clearly superseded any socioeconomic goals. The Caucasian All-Muslim Union "Dfai" (Kavkazskii Vsemusul'manskii Soiuz "Dfai"), for example, formed in August–September 1906, used assassination as a means of fighting both the "Armenian influence and the russification" policies of the imperial authorities.[77]

Simultaneously, the number of Caucasian terrorists of the new type—affiliated with no party and demonstrating no preference for any particular trend of revolutionary thought—dramatically multiplied. Some of these individuals quickly became leaders of small but ferocious semicriminal gangs calling themselves simply freedom fighters, or occasionally anarchists, and effectively terrorized entire provinces for months. Indeed, what largely contributed to the success of the Dashnaktsutiun, other radical groupings, and individual extremists in the Caucasus (a number of whom, incidentally, were scions of local aristocratic families), was the fact that their terrorist methods usually encompassed many of the traditional forms of violence and banditry endemic to the region, including the burning of crops and prohibition of harvest operations, abduction of women, enormous ransom demands for kidnapped children, and, of course, vendetta.[78]

Even more than in the Caucasus, revolutionary terror in the Kingdom of Poland was colored by nationalist tones. The entire history of the region, in contrast with most of the Caucasian territories, was marked by staunch refusal to accept Russian domination. By the turn of the twentieth century, the Poles' struggle for national liberation was already a long-standing tradition and a primary preoccupation of nearly all participants in Polish political life, moderate as well as radical. For most revolutionaries, it outweighed any allegiance to socialism, and whereas the Russian imperial government benefited to some degree from the disunity and frequent hostility among the various nationalities in Transcaucasia, it faced a greater danger from Poland, unified in its quest for independence.

The statistics summarizing terrorist casualties in Poland, although incomplete, are as revealing as they are in the Caucasus. In 1905–1906, terrorists reportedly killed 790 military, gendarme, and police officers, and wounded 864. In the course of combat operations, extremists detonated 120 bombs and other explosive devices, injuring or killing 142 persons. According to more detailed figures, in the city of Warsaw alone, 83 police and military officers were killed, and 96 wounded in 1906, rendering 15 officials each month victims of revolutionary terror. These numbers do not include casualties among private citizens, and do not take into account the devastating effects of political assassinations and expropriations in the years after 1906.[79] A government source claims 327 officials and 631 private individuals were killed or wounded in terrorist attacks throughout the province of Warsaw between October 1905 and the end of February 1908. In the same period an additional 1,009 civil servants and private persons fell victim to revolutionary terrorism in other Polish provinces.[80]

As in the Caucasus, a powerful organization operated in Poland that adopted political assassination and expropriation as its primary tactics after 1904; in subsequent years this group, the Polish Socialist Party, became the primary source of violence in the region. On 31 October 1904 members of the PPS had their debut in mass combat in the form of simultaneous terrorist attacks on Warsaw police officers, and a few months later, during the party's Seventh Congress in 1905, it officially approved the use of terror against enemies of the Polish nation. In spite of its socialist principles, the party did not at this time recommend that terror be employed against the bourgeoisie, except in instances when individuals contributed directly to the counterrevolutionary cause by appealing to the police or the military. Rather, the PPS originally conceived of political assassination not only as an instrument of revenge and a means of eliminating prominent proponents of repression, but also as an exceptionally effective tool for destabilizing Russian imperial authority in Poland. Correspondingly, the Seventh Congress sanctioned the formation of a special combat section of party conspirators, whose abbreviated Polish name, Bojowka, soon came to be identified with the wave of political violence.[81]

As in other regions in the empire, the local Polish revolutionaries considered the concessions granted by the October Manifesto unsatisfactory, and only intensified their terrorist practices following its promulgation, with the violence spreading from Warsaw to outlying localities. Their activities soon encompassed assaults on the lives and property of capitalists and wealthy landowners, as well as expropriations targeting banks, stores, post offices, and trains.[82] In order to accommodate the PPS's growing demand for combatants to implement its terrorist policies, the party invested major effort in recruiting potential terrorists among the peasants, encouraging them to form village detachments modeled after the Bojowka. Moreover, in 1906, an underground combat school opened in Krakow, where special instructors trained new terrorist cadres for the party.[83]

Despite the party's formal structure, the PPS leadership could do little to curb the strong tendency of the terrorists formally under its command to become self-sufficient. More often than not the combatants' actions were independent of Central Committee control, with the terrorists' understanding of who their immediate enemies were overriding that of the Central Committee. Relatively few of the *boeviki* were driven by long-term political objectives: while they occasionally selected a leading representative of the Russian administration in Poland for a carefully planned and sensational act, such as the attempt on the life of the governor-general of Warsaw, G. A. Skalon, in the summer of 1906, in the overwhelming majority of cases the combatants were motivated by personal hatred and desire for revenge, with their efforts aimed against suspected police agents, local street cops, Cossacks, guards, prison officials, and soldiers. They also targeted low-ranking civil officials—the faceless servants of the establishment with whom the extremists came into frequent direct contact and conflict, and who were exterminated en masse.[84]

Many of these undertakings, including acts of purely symbolic significance, such as the bombing of churches and of statues commemorating the Russian soldiers who died during the Polish insurrection of 1863,[85] were in complete accord with the general policies of the party. This was also true of the notorious Bloody Wednesday incident on 2 (15) August 1906, when PPS terrorists attacked scores of police and military patrols simultaneously in various sections of Warsaw, killing nearly fifty soldiers and policemen, and wounding twice that number.[86] However, although throughout 1905 and 1906 the combat accomplishments of the Polish Socialists greatly contributed to the weakening of Russian control over the region, the terrorists increasingly came under attack from the more moderate members of the party, who protested the lack of discrimination in the extremists' practices and personal behavior. These protests intensified the party's internal conflicts, and hastened the approaching schism in the PPS forces.[87]

The formal break came at the Ninth Party Congress early in 1907, when the PPS split into two factions. The larger of the two groups, and the more moderate, was the Lewica (Left), which shifted its emphasis away from Polish national self-determination to the establishment of a socialist order, thus moving closer to the Polish Social Democrats. The second, and more radical group, paradoxically called the Prawica (Right), was also known as the Revolutionary Faction. Although this group never renounced its socialist principles, it relegated them to the background for the sake of the original prime objective of the PPS: Polish independence. Differences in tactical matters also came to the fore at the congress, and whereas the moderates resolved not to implement terrorist methods in any form, the radical nationalists, who included in their ranks most members of the Bojowka, headed by Joseph Pilsudski (future head of the Polish state), advocated the extensive use of terror and expropriation for the purpose of disorganizing and weakening Russian imperial authority in Poland. Considering themselves the only legitimate heirs of the original PPS, this extremist minority set out to begin a new phase of the terrorist campaign immediately.[88]

The "bacchanalia of murders" and expropriations continued to rage across Poland.[89] Although the largest and most active terrorist party operating in the region, the PPS was not the only group that had incorporated political assassination and expropriation into its program. The Polish Workers' Socialist Party, whose participants seceded from the Revolutionary Faction of the PPS in November 1907 in protest against the despotic control exerted by the party's educated leadership over the activities of its workers' cadres, was one such group. Insisting that the proletarians must take the task of liberation into their own hands, this small group, whose program did not differ substantially from that of the PPS, allowed its combatants to practice terror on their own initiative.

A larger offshoot of the PPS was the Polish Socialist Party "Proletariat," which split away from the mother organization as early as 1900, primarily as a result of adopting the tactic of systematic terror, which the PPS at that time renounced. Members of Proletariat further insisted that the Polish revolt was doomed if it did not become an integral part of the all-Russian revolution, with the immediate objective of forming a federal state, in which Poland would be a separate republic. Ultimately, the party expected to unify all territories of partitioned Poland in a single republic within an envisioned United States of Europe. In tribute to its vaguely socialist goals, Proletariat advocated not only the assassination of imperial officials, but also economic terror, which was to protect the toilers from the capitalists, factory directors, managers, and other exploiters. In 1905–1906, the party used terror to support strikes, and occasionally staged political assassinations. Despite its violent rhetoric, however, it proved unable to match the intensity of the PPS terrorist campaign, to which Proletariat lost many of its active members by 1907.[90]

Various nonsocialist groupings also contributed to the continuing violence in Poland. Of these, the most radical nationalist organization was the People's Worker's Union (Zwiazek robotniczy narodowy), whose militantly anti-Russian stand led to a resolution to "spill the blood not only of traitors, but also of anyone who becomes an obstacle to the motherland's happiness." Although prompt police action prevented the Union from carrying out its death sentences on a number of tsarist officials in the region, the group did conduct several successful terrorist acts against Russian school inspectors as a means of fighting the imperial policy of forced russification of Polish youth.[91] Other groups actively practicing terrorism in Poland in these years included various anarchist and semianarchist organizations, such as the Warsaw Group of Anarchists-Communists-International. Their efforts, like those of their comrades in Russia and the Caucasus, consisted primarily of staging holdups and throwing bombs through the windows of wealthy citizens in extortion attempts, activities that continued well after the weakening of the revolutionary storm in 1907.[92]

Although no other border region of the empire produced formidable terrorist formations to match the Dashnaktsutiun or the PPS, the intensity of violence in the Baltic provinces in these years was unexpectedly great, especially in consideration of the fact that in contrast to the native Caucasian and Polish populations, the inhabitants of Latvia, Lithuania, and Estonia had little prior history of open rebellion against the imperial order. Yet startlingly, over a two-year period ending in January of 1906, the city police force in Riga alone lost 110 people—more than one-fourth of its members—to extremist attacks.[93] Once again the statistics demonstrate a tremendous increase in terrorist activity after the issuance of the October Manifesto: whereas in September and October of 1905 there were 69 and 64 acts of political terror in Riga, respectively, including expropriations, the following month the number more than doubled to 143 attacks.[94] In 1907, the director of the imperial Police Department informed the State Duma that in two Baltic provinces, Livonia and Courland, there had been 1,148 terrorist acts, as a result of which 324 persons, mostly policemen and soldiers, lost their lives.[95] And according to the official figures of the governor-general's office, in the Baltic region in 1905–1906 there were 1,700 terrorist attacks and assassinations, and another 3,076 armed assaults.[96]

The sudden escalation of terrorist activity in the Baltics was to a large extent the result of a vicious cycle. Even opponents of the government did not deny that in response to the numerous strikes, demonstrations, and intensifying acts of violence, all instigated by the revolutionaries, the authorities were forced to implement particularly severe repressive measures, such as declaring martial law in a number of Baltic areas and resorting widely to the use of military force.[97] In retaliation, the radicals attacked government officials with increasing zeal and cruelty. This in turn led to further sanctions from St. Petersburg and local officials, many of whom were members of the German nobility, which traditionally played a dominant role in the region. Mutual hostilities in the Baltics thus escalated, and as the bloody struggle between revolutionary and counterrevolutionary forces continued, inflicting hardship and devastation on the local population, many began to perceive and treat representatives of the tsarist regime as foreign invaders, against whom all means, including terror, were justified. The severity of the internal crisis is reflected in a fictitious anecdotal newspaper announcement: "Opening soon will be an exhibition of the revolutionary movement in the Baltic provinces. Among the exhibits are reported to be: a real live Latvian, a German castle that has not been destroyed, and a policeman who has not been shot."[98]

Within the Baltic region, revolutionary violence was most widespread in Latvia, where radical socialists and anarchists carried out terrorist acts and expropriations daily in Riga and other urban centers,[99] with local extremists gaining nearly complete control in some areas. Like their Dashnaki counterparts in the Caucasus, members of various radical organizations, united in the Latvian capital in the Federal Committee of Riga (Federativnyi Rizhskii Komitet), not only supervised strikes by factory, railroad, telegraph, and postal workers, but virtually took over the administrative machinery of the city, which had nearly ceased to function in the revolutionary chaos. The Committee arbitrarily levied its own taxes, prohibited all trade, and conducted hastily prepared but tightly controlled trials in which defense attorneys were assigned without the consent of the accused. The revolutionaries handed out death sentences and implemented them immediately, in some instances in advance of a decision by the revolutionary tribunal. Furthermore, agents of the Committee assumed the right to assault private residences, conduct searches, confiscate money and personal possessions, and decide which representatives or supporters of the old administration were to be executed, frequently taking advantage of the situation to settle accounts with personal enemies. Significantly, the Committee not only established its own police patrols to control the streets, but also its own secret police, or spies, whose task was to reveal disloyalty to the new authorities. Offenders were arrested and occasionally executed for such crimes as "insulting the revolutionary regime."[100]

The extremists engaged in assassinations and expropriations of state and private property with equal frequency in smaller Baltic towns and the surrounding areas.[101] In the countryside the most active perpetrators of terrorism were the forest brothers, members of militant bands particularly numerous in late 1905 and 1906. Most of the forest brothers were inveterate rebels and *boeviki* forced by the repressive measures implemented by the government in 1905 to flee into the Latvian countryside and live in the woods.[102] These revolutionary guerrillas, usually operating in gangs of ten to fifteen, were primarily of peasant origin, and often included semicriminal elements. They became notorious for their swift and bloody looting raids targeting not only castles and country estates occupied by local barons and wealthy landowners, but also farms and villages, where the resident peasants were forced to provide them with food, money, and shelter.[103] Anyone offering resistance was mercilessly executed, and according to a government source, in rural districts terror began to be implemented against "landowners and stewards of estates, and then against Russian Orthodox priests and pastors, *volost'* foremen, their assistants, clerks and teachers who did not comply with the agitators' demands to support the revolt. Such individuals were labeled 'spies,' sentenced to death," and killed.[104]

Because the local nobility, and particularly the German barons, with their strong military traditions, resisted intimidation by the forest brothers and quickly organized their own self-defense units, they became primary targets for the partisans' attacks, along with the police, gendarmes, and the Cossacks, all of whom made desperate and initially unsuccessful attempts to halt the widespread violence and anarchy in the countryside.[105] The partisans not only robbed and murdered wealthy landlords and nobles, activities that became agreeable diversions for the forest brothers, but also plundered and torched estates—acts that even some local revolutionaries considered vandalism, for in the process large libraries, priceless paintings, and numerous other works of art were destroyed.[106] According to central government figures issued in the winter of 1906–1907, of 130 estates in the Riga district alone, 69 were devastated and burned, with the total damages running as high as 1.5 million rubles.[107] Still, in many left liberal and neorevolutionary circles, the forest brothers enjoyed the popularity and glory of local Robin Hoods. One memoirist tells of a young woman who belonged to a club made up of the offspring of wealthy families, whose members pretended to be Jacobins. The young lady declared her desire to marry a forest brother acquaintance, but asked him first to kill her reactionary father.[108]

Revolutionaries in other Baltic provinces exerted major efforts not to be surpassed by the Latvian radicals in the intensity of their terrorist campaigns; by the spring of 1905 combat detachments had formed in nearly every sizable town in the northwestern regions of the empire.[109] These groups executed individual terrorist acts and assaults on small shops, liquor stores, taverns, private homes, and churches. In Estonia, representatives of formal socialist organizations, including the PSR, did not even claim to direct their attacks primarily against high-ranking government officials and prominent exploiters among the bourgeoisie. Instead, like the local forest brothers and the numerous obscure terrorist groups, they were involved in mostly small-scale expropriations, as well as cases of vendetta against petty officials, clerks, conservative teachers, clergy, and indeed anyone suspected of not condoning their activities, or of refusing to make financial donations to the cause. Motivated only by their immediate objectives, these terrorists of the new type for the most part did not bother to reflect on long-term goals, and were always alert for any "capitalist who could be killed and robbed." Before widespread arrests throughout Estonia and the other Baltic regions in early 1908 put an end to the mass terror, many of these raiders were involved in dozens of violent acts and had difficulty remembering how many times they had taken part in terrorist attacks, or what exactly had happened during a given operation.[110]

The Duchy of Finland was the border area least affected by revolutionary terror, largely due to its special semiautonomous constitutional status within the Russian Empire. Nevertheless, because of strong separatist tendencies in all spheres of Finnish society, extremists found that they could operate within the imperial borders, only a short train ride from the capital, with little fear of reprisal. Most representatives of the Finnish regional administration, even at the highest levels, sympathized with the revolutionary cause; many police officials were Social Democrats, and some belonged to the Finnish Party of Active Resistance (Finska Aktiva Motstandsparti), similar in tactics to the PSR. They were not about to assist the central government against the terrorists, who, in their own words, found in Finland a safe refuge where they felt at home, "like fish in water."[111] Local law enforcement officers were strikingly considerate of the radicals' needs, and the "attitude of the policemen toward the combatants was very comradely." The Finnish authorities readily extended the extremists various favors, such as arresting Okhrana surveillance agents (filery) as suspicious characters, creating obstacles to the extradition of revolutionaries to Russian custody, aiding the extremists in prison escape attempts, and even assisting in the transportation of bombs and dynamite.[112] Finnish educated society and the progressive bourgeoisie were also nearly unanimous in their support of the Russian underground, and as a result, after 1905 Finland became an arsenal of explosive devices that the extremists had smuggled from abroad in large quantities, or manufactured in special laboratories, occasionally even testing them on Finnish soil.[113]

While there was no mass terrorist campaign in Finland, isolated political assassinations did take place. Almost all of them occurred in Helsinki, where the revolutionaries staged attempts on the lives of government officials ranging from Governor-general N. I. Bobrikov on 3 June 1904, and Procurator of the Finnish Senate M. Johnson (Ionson) on 6 February 1905, to gendarme officers, common policemen, and soldiers.[114] Although rare, expropriations also occurred, including a notable incident in Vyborg on 31 August 1906, when radicals confiscated twenty thousand Finnish marks from a railroad employee.[115]

The discussion of the extent of terror in the empire would not be complete without mentioning specifically the unprecedented bloodshed in the areas of the Jewish Pale. By 1900, almost 30 percent of the individuals arrested for political crimes were Jews, and while in 1903 only 7,000,000 of the total 136,000,000 inhabitants of imperial Russia were Jewish, the membership of the revolutionary parties was approximately 50 percent Jewish, in sharp contrast to the more balanced situation in the radical camp in the 1870s.[116] Although the disproportionately high percentage of Jews among the Russian extremists is a complex and controversial phenomenon, it appears appropriate to suggest here that the traditional explanation requires certain modifications.

Scholars have emphasized that "in order to explain the large numbers of Jewish terrorists it is not enough to note that Jews were oppressed in the Russian Empire." There is no doubt that at a time when many young Jews were breaking away from their predominantly religious and traditional milieu, most of them were forbidden entry into Russian society, deprived economically, and thus forced into the ranks of the opposition to the restrictive establishment. At the same time, however, the overwhelming majority of leading Jewish revolutionaries and terrorists "had been fully assimilated into Russian society, and were beneficiaries of its educational and economic institutions." Dozens of less prominent Jewish extremists could hardly claim to be in a less advantageous socioeconomic position than most members of their predominantly conservative communities, where in the 1870s families sometimes observed the ceremonial week of mourning (*shivah*) when a son or daughter joined the radicals, and where, after the turn of the century, many were appalled by the revolution, wishing that "the ministers . . . would hang all these rotten guys" who only knew how to throw bombs.[117] It thus appears superficial to cite direct government oppression as the sole factor accounting for the situation that Zionist Chaim Weizman reported to Theodore Herzl in June 1903: "It is a fearful spectacle . . . to observe the major part of our youth—and no one would describe them as the worst part—offering themselves for sacrifice as though seized by a fever."[118]

In their writings on Jewish involvement in the Russian revolutionary movement, several thinkers, foremost among them Nikolai Berdiaev, noted that the Jewish radicals had emerged from an environment dominated by the profound, centuries-old pride and spiritual burden of being the chosen people. These writers sought to trace the roots of Jewish radicalism to a concept that lies at the heart of the Jewish national and religious identity—the messianic ideal. Connected with the dream of a Jewish homeland and the quest to overcome the tremendous catastrophe of the diaspora and the associated misfortunes and injustices that have befallen the Jews throughout history, the messianic tradition encompasses the belief that salvation and glory will ultimately be attained by the entire Jewish nation on earth, rather than by selected individuals following death. That Judaic thought is consistently directed to the future realization of these goals can be seen as the key to understanding the Jewish mentality and its inner drives, even in individuals who have renounced their religious faith and turned to atheism.[119]

Indeed, having on the surface broken all ties with religion, Jewish radicals merely reshaped and restated the traditional messianic outlook to conform to the new historical situation and intellectual concepts. The old beliefs verbalized in a new and slightly altered form are particularly notable in the teachings of Karl Marx, whom Berdiaev called "a very typical Jew." A materialist who denied any higher principles, Marx transformed the idea of a messiah leading the Israeli people to an ultimate paradise on earth into a theory envisioning the eventual redemption of the world from oppression and injustice by the new chosen people—the proletariat.[120] This adaptation of familiar assumptions to the atheist perception of reality (which included Marx's emphasis on class, rather than individuals, as the only active agent in the historical process) proved extremely attractive to many Russian Jews, who began to participate in radical politics in large numbers directly proportionate with the degree of dissemination of Marxism in the empire late in the nineteenth century.[121]

This explanation of Jewish radicalism in no way relieves the imperial government of its share of responsibility for the radicalization of Jewish youth. The pogroms in the 1880s, followed by a wave of anti-Semitic violence in Kishinev in 1903, and in Odessa, Minsk, and Kiev in 1905, greatly contributed to the process. Furthermore, the lack of opportunity for the economic growth, career, and social advancement that would undoubtedly have provided many assimilated Jews new long-term interests and objectives, literally forced them to join the revolution, in which they then invested all their hopes.[122]

The internationalist doctrine of Marxism, with its working-class orientation, had more appeal for Jews than the peasant-oriented *narodnik* philosophy of the SRs, which for many rank-and-file Jewish radicals was tied to the "traditional Russian ethos with its undertones of pogroms, reaction, obscurantism, and Slav chauvinism." Marxism did not force them to break ties with their Jewish past as radically as populism did, and this largely accounts for the fact that Jews composed no more than 15 percent of the PSR forces, although their number probably ran higher among the PSR leadership.[123] At the same time, many revolutionaries, Jews and non-Jews alike, while intellectually impressed with the scientific approach of Marx's orthodox followers (particularly among the Mensheviks and Bundists), seemed unable to reconcile their emotions with the Marxists' strictly rational worldview, where there was no room for anything beyond materialistic calculation and practical analysis. Wishing to suffer and sacrifice themselves for their newly acquired quasi-religious convictions, many young Jewish extremist neophytes, who chose not to join the less-than-scientific and more violent SRs, devoted themselves wholeheartedly to the Maximalist and especially the anarchist causes, which "provided the strong attraction which ruthlessness of method holds out to the impatient." In part this was also because of all the revolutionary trends, these two, aiming as they did for the total destruction of the traditional establishment as a prerequisite to the restructuring of society, were the least abstract or theoretical, and required no sophisticated intellectual preparation from their followers; this was convenient for some of the less educated Jewish recruits, who were often half-literate in Yiddish and barely able to read Russian. Thus, although many revolutionary leaders preferred not to use Jews as executors of terrorist acts for fear of raising anti-Semitic sentiments, some Maximalist and anarchist groups did not have a choice: in their composition, they were almost entirely Jewish.[124] The phenomenon did not escape the attention of contemporary liberal press satirists who mockingly reported: "Eleven anarchists were executed at the city jail; fifteen of them were Jews."[125]

A large percentage of the terrorist acts perpetrated by Jews occurred in the areas of the Pale, where the revolutionaries, primarily the anarchists, assaulted representatives of the local administration, most of whom were low-ranking police officers, Cossacks, and soldiers.[126] They also staged small-scale expropriations and attacked local businessmen, especially those who showed resistance. In one incident in the tiny industrial town of Krinki, factory owners sought to protect themselves from the anarchists in January 1906 by forming a union, but during their initial meeting the revolutionaries set off a bomb in the synagogue where the gathering was taking place.[127]

In the Pale more than in other areas in the empire, the radicals directed their efforts against private citizens of monarchist leanings and other conservative opponents of the revolution. Anyone who espoused patriotic, nationalist, or progovernment views could be labeled a member of the Black Hundreds (Chernosotenets), against whom violent acts were justified if only because subscribing to such views implied direct or implicit support of the anti-Jewish pogroms. While it was no secret that members of monarchist and right-wing groups did participate enthusiastically in the anti-Semitic violence, on many occasions revolutionary extremists in the Pale clearly elicited reprisals from the conservatives—reprisals initially directed not against the Jewish population as a whole, but exclusively against the Jewish revolutionaries. This was especially true when the radicals threw bombs or fired shots at participants in patriotic or religious meetings and demonstrations, as well as at individual

Christians, occasionally inflicting casualties on innocent bystanders, including children and the elderly, and thus inflaming anti-Semitic sentiments and provoking confrontations and retaliation. The result was often bitter fighting and substantial bloodshed on both sides, and—escalating the tragedy—mob violence against the peaceful Jewish populace.[128]

Despite the bloody consequences of revolutionary terrorism for the predominantly apolitical Jewish settlements, certain Jewish nationalist groups, such as the Zionist-Socialist Worker's Party, regarded terror as an appropriate method of struggle against the establishment.[129] Jewish revolutionary tribunals issued sentences against local enemies, while isolated radicals staged armed raids on private property.[130] Moreover, it was not uncommon for Jewish revolutionary extremists to offend the traditionalists in their communities with acts bordering on sacrilege, such as using temples as strategic sites for gun battles and bombings—acts that invited Cossack assaults on these houses of prayer.[131] It is not surprising then that many ordinary Jews, especially the elderly, were critical of the young Jewish extremists whose terrorist activity led to pogroms: "They were shooting but we are being beaten."[132]

The activities of the Russian revolutionaries were not limited by the borders of the Russian Empire; when forced to live in emigration, many extremists, despite their foreign status in various Western countries, continued their terrorist enterprises. The overwhelming majority of radicals involved in combat activities abroad were anarchists or members of obscure extremist groups operating for the most part in Western and Central European capitals and industrial centers, where terrorism, perpetrated primarily by local anarchists, was not an unknown phenomenon by the turn of the twentieth century, although it never reached the intensity of the revolutionary violence in tsarist Russia.[133] At the same time, some Russian SRs and SDs in Europe made use of their freedom from constant Okhrana surveillance to engage in activities usually more common among the anarchists, such as the manufacture of explosive devices. These devices, while intended primarily to be smuggled into Russia, were occasionally used against adversaries abroad.[134] This practice began as early as the 1890s and continued well after the suppression of the first Russian revolution.[135] Like their comrades at home, a number of Russian terrorists abroad were wounded and lost their lives in accidental explosions resulting from the unskilled or careless handling of homemade bombs.[136]

On a number of occasions, emigré party leaders, particularly in the PSR Central Committee, expressed their disapproval of terrorist projects undertaken in foreign countries, especially those providing safe havens for political emigrants from the Russian underground.[137] This notwithstanding, many radical Russian expatriates, lacking opportunities to direct their attacks against the tsarist administration and the wealthy in their native country, relentlessly planned, and occasionally proceeded with, assassination attempts against Rus-

sian statesmen and officials stationed abroad, as well as members of the Romanov dynasty residing and traveling in Europe, most notably Nicholas II and his
mother, the Empress Dowager Marie.[138] At the same time, the extremists readily used violence against anyone they suspected of having police connections,
including former radicals seeking to escape revolutionary vengeance by fleeing abroad.[139]

For most of these revolutionaries, hatred for the ruling circles and aristocratic elite in Russia extended to the counterparts of these groups in foreign
states. They concentrated their efforts with increasing frequency on individuals they held responsible for oppressive sociopolitical conditions under other
monarchies, particularly in Germany and the Hapsburg Empire, Bulgaria, and
Turkey. This international orientation toward the liberation of the enslaved
masses led a number of Russian anarchist units and isolated anarchists abroad
to contemplate the assassination of Emperor Wilhelm II of Germany in 1903,
1906, and 1907.[140]

Russian extremists residing in conservative European states took advantage
of their comparative security to prepare for future expropriations. In Austria
the SRs and anarchists trained special cadres for expropriation raids into Russia.[141] Russian radicals freely executed political robberies in their host countries: the notorious Bolshevik *boevik* Kamo (Semen Ter-Petrosian) made preparations for using bombs to rob the Mendelssohn Bank in Berlin;[142] a group of
anarchists residing in Turkey in 1907 planned a "grandiose expropriation" of
several million rubles, probably from the wealthy Greek Orthodox monastery
at Mt. Athos, an attractive target for the extremists;[143] finally, a number of
isolated extremists took their chances at quick profits by means of blackmail
and extortion, often on behalf of fictitious organizations such as the Nonparty
Emigrés of the City of Vienna.[144]

Characteristically, the Russian radicals did not limit the scope of their activity to countries with conservative political systems, and committed acts of
violence in liberal democratic and republican states such as England, France,
and Switzerland. In this, they contrasted sharply with their predecessors in the
People's Will, who rejected the practice of terrorism in a democracy on principle, as they proclaimed in their celebrated letter of condolence in September
1881 on the occasion of the assassination of the American president, James
Garfield.[145] This suggests that at least for some of the extremists of the new
type, and for virtually all the anarchists and revolutionaries of obscure ideology, the claim that they were struggling against despotic regimes in Russia and
abroad was a dubious one, or, at the very least, not the primary reason for their
terrorist practices.

The anarchists were especially open about their true stand: "Would it make
any difference for me which [nation's] bourgeoisie to throw a bomb at?" asked
Vladimir Lapidus (Striga) in a letter written to his comrades just before he died

in a May 1906 bomb explosion in the Bois de Vincennes on the outskirts of Paris. "Take revenge on the base bourgeoisie wherever it may be."[146] Accordingly, he entertained plans to toss a bomb into a restaurant frequented by wealthy aristocrats.[147] There are also indications that anarchists in Brussels sought to avenge the deportation of several of their comrades from Belgium by assassinating that country's minister of justice, while in France several revolutionaries, probably also anarchists, took preliminary steps toward a terrorist act against French Prime Minister Georges Clemenceau by renting an apartment in his building and making inquiries about his habits and schedule, as well as by trying to raise the funds necessary for the operation.[148] In addition, the head of the Okhrana agency in Paris had gathered enough evidence by the spring of 1906 to suspect a group of Russian anarchists of planning an attack on one of three possible targets: the Paris Stock Exchange (to punish the capitalists for contributing to a recent French loan to Russia), the police (who had arrested sixty Russians in May Day demonstrations), or the Russian Imperial Embassy and Consulate in the French capital.[149]

The French government was understandably concerned about the violence that frequently erupted following emigré revolutionary meetings in Paris, where on at least one occasion a bomb explosion wounded several people, including two policemen.[150] Like their counterparts at home, the Russian anarchists abroad put up armed resistance to local authorities during house searches and arrests, and in one such incident the well-known terrorist Zeliger-(Zeilinger-) Sokolov was responsible for mortally wounding a police commissar and an officer while resisting arrest in Ghent.[151] Finally, isolated Russian radicals of uncertain ideology and party affiliation also engaged in terrorist acts, as when a revolutionary by the name of Iakov Lev started shooting at French troops in Paris on May Day in 1907.[152]

On a number of occasions anarchists, in complete disregard for the hospitality of their liberal hosts, carried out expropriations that claimed the lives of innocent citizens. The anarchist Rostovtsev, after escaping to the West from a Russian prison, made an abortive attempt to hold up a bank in Montreux; he succeeded only in killing several bystanders and was barely rescued from a lynch mob by the Swiss police.[153] Anarchists in Geneva, Lausanne, and other Swiss cities were equally eager to benefit from the bourgeois financial establishment by means of expropriations, as were their comrades residing in Great Britain and France; they also occasionally directed extortion attempts against wealthy Russian citizens living abroad, including some who were known supporters of the revolutionary cause.[154]

In their efforts to find new sources of revenue, the Russian extremists proved enterprising and less than scrupulous. On at least one occasion in 1906 or 1907, an unidentified group of Russian radicals sent a death threat letter to the operators of a casino in Monte Carlo demanding the sum of twenty thousand rubles;[155] anarchists in Brussels confiscated three thousand francs from a fellow revolutionary among their Belgian comrades.[156] Finally, one anarchist admitted to having robbed the world-famous Russian singer Fedor Shaliapin in Nice, even though the celebrity was well known for his support of the revolution, and was cheered in antigovernment circles for his daring performances of radical and antimonarchist hymns from the stage of the Russian imperial theater.[157]

Like the anarchists, isolated extremists and obscure radicals outside of Russia were responsible not only for extortion letters, the so-called mandates sent from abroad to wealthy individuals throughout the Russian Empire,[158] but also for bloody expropriations in London (including the Tottenham outrages on 23 January 1909) and other European cities that resulted in multiple casualties among the local police forces as well as the private citizenry. Their victims included children, and it is hardly surprising that the reaction of the European public and even many Russian political emigrés was frequently one of shocked indignation at such indiscriminate use of violence.[159] According to Lenin's wife, Nadezhda Krupskaia, writing in her memoirs about their life in Switzerland, probably the most tolerant and hospitable of the European countries hosting Russian political emigrés, "The only talk was about the Russian expropriators" among the horrified citizens of Geneva in 1907. Since a large percentage of the individuals involved in political robberies were of Caucasian origin, the mere sight of one of Lenin's Georgian guests was sufficient to provoke a cry of horror from Krupskaia's landlady, as she slammed the door in the face of this live expropriator on her doorstep.[160]

Taking advantage of such reactions, the Russian imperial government sought official international cooperation against the revolutionaries. Because the authorities faced the threat of terrorism even in democratic countries, primarily from the anarchists, these efforts were fairly successful. As early as 1904, several European governments entered into formal agreements for joint efforts against the anarchists, and occasionally cooperated as well against smugglers of weapons and explosives.[161] At the same time, however, to a large extent in response to pressure from influential socialist and liberal circles abroad, government officials even in conservative Germany and Austria-Hungary (not to mention the more progressive regimes) were often unwilling to collaborate with official tsarist policies, especially when it came to the extradition of escaped prisoners and known assassins affiliated with extremist socialist organizations.[162] European popular opinion, and also many individual members of Western official circles, tended to regard the Russian comrades as freedom fighters, justified in principle (if misguided in tactics) in their struggle against the despotic and semibarbaric regime in their motherland. In the words of British statesman J. Ramsay MacDonald, they wished the Russian revolutionaries "God speed."[163] Clearly, these attitudes did not strengthen the position of a Russian government already shaken by bloody revolution at home.

THE IMPACT OF TERRORISM ON GOVERNMENT AND SOCIETY

The enormous wave of terror achieved its primary purpose as early as 1905: the authorities were confused and exhausted, with all their "strength and means for struggle completely paralyzed."[164] Government officials experienced a sense of helplessness bordering on despair: "Every day there are several assassinations, either by bomb or revolver or knife, or various other instruments; they strike and strike anyhow and at anybody . . . and one is surprised that they have not yet killed all of us."[165] A sarcastic anecdote from the period conveys the mood: "Last evening His Excellency the Governor-general held a small reception at his residence, at which he accepted congratulations from his subordinates on the three-week anniversary of his successful command of the area."[166]

Such sentiments were in no way groundless or exaggerated, and by the summer of 1907 top police officials in St. Petersburg were ready to set aside all other matters, including investigations of revolutionary agitation, illegal printing operations, labor strikes, and other noncombat manifestations of revolutionary activity, in order to concentrate on their most urgent problem, the extremists' plans for political assassinations and expropriations.[167] To a large extent this change of focus came about because the new type of terrorism differed from nineteenth-century revolutionary violence not only in the numbers of its victims, but also in their identities. Prior to 1905 the extremists took great care in the choice of their targets, directing their efforts only against representatives of the administration whom they considered particularly outstanding as oppressors of the people, responsible for unusually cruel repressive or punitive measures. At that time, radical terrorists did not attack and kill state servants and private individuals randomly and en masse.[168]

After the outbreak of the revolution, on the other hand, in the midst of the widespread violence and chaos, "human life was cheapened" and soon "was not worth a penny" to the assassins.[169] Whereas in 1879 adherents of the People's Will, emphatically denying any intention of punishing their enemies by kidnapping members of their families, argued in print that each individual was "personally responsible for his own actions," by 1903 Burtsev advocated taking government officials and members of the bourgeoisie hostage for the sole purpose of using them as bargaining chips in later negotiations with the authorities; and in 1905 Baltic revolutionaries readily seized hostages from among the peaceful population.[170] A perfect illustration of the striking difference between the old and new types of terrorism is an incident in which PPS members murdered a police informer's father in order to use the funeral as an opportunity to assassinate the son, their real target.[171]

As far as victims among government employees were concerned, terror was carried out indiscriminately against police and military authorities, state officials of all ranks, street policemen, soldiers, guards, and all others who fell into the extremely broad category labeled by the revolutionaries, "watchdogs of the old order." Of the 671 employees of the Ministry of the Interior killed or injured by terrorists between October of 1905 and the end of April 1906, only 13 held high administrative positions, while the other 658 were city police-men, coachmen, and security personnel.[172] It became especially common for the new breed of professional terrorist to shoot or toss bombs into passing military and Cossack units, or their barracks, without provocation.[173] In gene-ral, the wearing of any uniform was sufficient to qualify an individual as a potential candidate for a terrorist bullet or for other methods of attack widely adopted after 1905. Combatants out on the streets for an evening's excursion would toss sulfuric acid in the face of the first uniformed street policeman or guard they encountered.[174] There are numerous examples of indiscriminate violence indicating that terrorism not only became an end in itself, but also in a very real sense evolved into a sport in which the participants regarded their victims as nothing more than moving targets.[175] In 1906–1907, many of these "woodchoppers" (drovokoly), as one revolutionary labeled them, particularly among the anarchists and the Maximalists, competed against each other to see who had committed the greatest number of robberies and murders, and often exhibited jealousy over others' successes.[176]

In Naimark's view, "Against this background, the government's reaction to the mounting terrorist campaign can only be characterized as vacillating and irresolute."[177] In particularly unstable border areas and the Jewish Pale the authorities did not even dare to show themselves in the streets, for all defend-ers of the old order were targets for gunfire on sight. According to one official report, the incidence of nervous ailments in the gendarme corps escalated dra-matically.[178] Although individual members of the police and military forces revealed outstanding personal courage and selfless dedication to the govern-ment cause,[179] many thought only of saving themselves, and either applied for immediate retirement and fled their posts, or simply refused to appear for duty to replace their assassinated predecessors.[180] Street policemen were also said to have demonstrated cowardice occasionally, allowing combatants to disarm them without any resistance and begging the extremists to spare their lives.[181] In one particularly striking example, after personal guards of a well-known Latvian terrorist by the name of Epis repeatedly fired at policemen who had made several unsuccessful attempts to arrest the radicals' chief, the officers refused to obey orders and instead began saluting the revolutionary hero every time they encountered him on the street.[182]

In their reports to the central administration, local officials, living in con-stant "terrible panic," admitted being completely powerless to control events, and described their authority as "only nominal."[183] The situation was no better in larger Russian cities and towns, including the capitals; in 1905 members of the imperial family and the court, as well as a number of top officials of the tsarist administration, all prime potential targets for terrorist attacks, voluntarily submitted themselves to virtual house arrest. The head of the St. Petersburg Okhrana faced constant insubordination from his agents, who threatened to go on strike out of fear of the revolutionaries.[184] Prevailing wisdom held that any high-ranking defender of the regime was doomed to fall victim to the omnipotent terrorists, and sooner rather than later. This sentiment was the subject of a darkly humorous dialogue allegedly set in an editor's office: "Secretary: 'The biography of the new governor-general has been on my desk for three days now. Shall I go through it?' Editor: 'No, don't bother. We'll send it directly to the obituary department.'"[185]

The impact of terrorism on the lives of common citizens of the Russian Empire was perhaps even greater, swept as they were into a "revolutionary tornado" in which daily "murders flooded the periphery and the center with blood,"[186] and the concept of private property seemed to have lost all value for the new type of Russian terrorist. While the late nineteenth-century revolutionaries almost without exception rejected the practice of expropriation with an "unconcealed feeling of disgust," few of their post-1905 descendents had any scruples about the violent assaults perpetrated daily throughout the country.[187] Moreover, regarding prosperous individuals as symbols of reaction or exploitation, the radicals frequently terrorized such people without bothering to seize any property, sometimes using verbal threats and sometimes physical attack, for the purpose of punishing them solely for belonging to the privileged strata of society. In addition, revolutionary vengeance often fell upon citizens who failed to prove themselves friends of the antigovernment movement, including members of monarchist clubs, associates of patriotic or conservative publications, and the clergy, as well as technical professionals and industrialists who refused to ingratiate themselves with local union leaders and agitators. Uncooperative merchants, especially those who organized their employees into self-defense groups in order to protect their property, also paid with their lives, as did coachmen who hesitated to provide their services to extremists fleeing the scene of an attack. Judges and official court investigators were also victims of terrorist acts, as were witnesses who testified against the revolutionaries. These people often received threatening letters calling them informers, and some were subsequently murdered. In one such case in the Baltics in 1905, witnesses who had testified at the trial of an extremist were murdered by the convicted radical's comrades, who left handwritten notes intended to intimidate others: "A dog's death to the spy."[188]

Despite the bloody impact of revolutionary terror on everyday life throughout the country, the custom of exonerating the extremists continued in many liberal and intellectual circles, and a number of widely read literary works, notably stories by Leonid Andreev, reflect the sympathy felt in educated society for the rough and daring *boeviki*.[189] Partly under the influence of these and many other prorevolutionary publications, some bearing the signatures of such celebrities as Maxim Gorky and Vladimir Korolenko, scores of liberals, who themselves had little taste for violence, came to acknowledge both an ethical and a social obligation to provide the combatants with shelter, money, and proper documents, and even went so far as to offer their apartments for the concealment of weapons and explosive devices.[190] Indeed, in liberal circles, which included university professors, teachers, engineers, journalists, lawyers, and doctors, as well as industrialists, bank directors, and even government officials, assistance to the extremists came to be considered a "sign of good manners."[191] This attitude inevitably contributed to the spread of violence by stroking the radicals' egos and indirectly encouraging them to further action, since the extremists were fully aware of the numerous "fans of terror" among the educated Russian elite who "privately applauded every terrorist act" even as they publicly advocated (and personally preferred) more "cultured methods of struggle" against the autocracy.[192]

Similarly, some individuals among the lower strata of society, especially workers who had accepted the radicals' interpretation of the terrorist struggle as an effort to liberate the toilers, were willing to assist the terrorists in a variety of ways. Many donated money specifically for the purchase of weapons, while others helped with the manufacture of explosives. The proprietor of one small tin shop was offered payment by revolutionaries for his services, but refused to take the money: "I am soldering the bombs free of charge."[193] Occasionally, common people were prepared to use violence to help the extremists; in widespread locations there were incidents of crowds of ordinary citizens attacking police convoys and liberating arrested terrorists. In the early stages of the revolution, notably in the border regions, the local populations were especially antagonistic toward the Russian administration and openly refused to provide aid to wounded officials.[194]

At the same time, potential victims of revolutionary violence sometimes attempted to defend themselves. An archpriest in Kazan' employed two personal bodyguards, and monks in a local monastery applied for permission to carry revolvers.[195] In communities in the remote regions of Siberia, the Far East, and the borderlands, where revolutionary committees had taken over the administrative machinery, the inhabitants sought organized means of establishing minimal security. Thus in Riga, when citizens found it useless to appeal to the legal authorities for protection of their lives and property in 1905, they united in formal groups such as Self Defense (Selbstschutze) and the Society for Neighborly Help (Nachbarhilfe), which together consisted of some fifteen hundred members, and to some extent were able to ward off the revolutionaries' assaults by armed retaliation.[196] There were instances, however, when such unions altered their priorities, moving from self-protection to offensive violence; this was the case with the Green Hundreds (Zelenaia sotnia), an organization formed in August 1907 in Baku by Armenian property owners who eventually themselves became involved in quasi-anarchist activities.[197] In the same city, well-to-do industrialists employed the services of formidable armed bodyguards recruited from the local underworld of thugs and daredevils. These bodyguards, known as *kochi*, were ready to risk their lives protecting their employers against the extremists, but also commonly took part in various forms of crime and violence.[198] Finally, some enterprising individuals also sought to extract personal benefit from the general chaos. Former convicts and other semicriminal elements in the Baltics occasionally approached people on the streets and offered their services as paid assassins; over time the cost of murdering an enemy dropped precipitously, with such services available for less than three rubles per victim.[199]

Still, the overwhelming majority of the peaceful populace was fearful and passive, simply hoping to survive the terrible times. In localities particularly affected by the revolutionary anarchy, such as Riga, where gunfire was regularly heard on the streets, a man leaving his house did not know whether he would return, and could not be sure that upon his return he would find his family alive.[200] As the violence escalated, the victims of terror increasingly were innocent bystanders, including many women and children, who happened to be present at the scene of a bomb explosion or indiscriminate shooting at the police or military.[201] The population was terrorized and intimidated to such an extent that in some areas undertakers and priests were afraid to provide their services for the victims of revolutionary terror, and close relatives were too frightened to show up at their funerals.[202]

Fear came to dominate the behavior of many individuals. When several doctors in a Baku hospital received threatening letters in the spring of 1907 demanding large contributions to a local anarchist organization, they abandoned their patients, going into hiding or fleeing abroad.[203] After 1905, when increasing numbers of expropriators redirected their attention from state property and large enterprises to petty targets such as small shops, private apartments, and even passersby, in Ekaterinoslav and other active centers of revolutionary violence not only the bourgeoisie, but also civil servants, artisans, and intellectuals "installed double and triple bolts on their doors, made secret peepholes to check every visitor, and even in the daytime let strangers in only after hesitation and substantial interrogation. Everyone was seized by panic; everyone expected raids."[204]

At the same time, since in the eyes of many witnessing the indiscriminate violence, and especially the expropriations, the revolution was "covered with a thin coating of dirt and abomination," it was not unusual for some individuals who had previously sympathized with the radicals to collaborate with the authorities by turning in extremists or by assisting police officers arresting radicals at the scene of a crime, often expressing their anger by themselves physically assaulting the terrorists.[205] In Baku property owners contributed to the government cause financially, covering at one point more than two-thirds of the total expenses for maintenance of the police forces.[206] These people were driven by practical, rather than ideological, considerations, for as the terror and anarchy reached an apogee in the country, many common citizens "began to confound revolutionaries with ordinary bandits."[207]

Chapter Two

THE PARTY OF SOCIALISTS-REVOLUTIONARIES

AND TERROR

> An SR without a bomb is not an SR.
> —*Ivan Kaliaev*[1]

THE ONLY consolidated leftist party in Russia proper that formally incorporated terrorist tactics into its program was the Party of Socialists-Revolutionaries, which came into existence when a number of autonomous neo-Populist groups in Russia and abroad united into a single organization in late 1901. Although not unique in proclaiming political assassination an expedient revolutionary method, the PSR came to be perceived as the party of terror,[2] since it was particularly notorious for its highly planned and frequently successful assassination attempts aimed at representatives of the central government in St. Petersburg and Moscow. No other Russian terrorist group could claim similar credit.

Because of the party's obvious significance, several scholars have analyzed its activities in general and specifically its terrorist practices.[3] Since the political assassinations carried out by the PSR had tremendous impact on the country's political life in the first decade of the twentieth century, they have also been mentioned in various works examining the general state of affairs in Russia in this period. There are, however, certain aspects of SR terrorist activity that have either gone unnoticed or have been largely misinterpreted by both contemporary observers and present-day scholarship. Additionally, the abundance of previously unavailable or neglected primary and archival materials dealing with SR-perpetrated terror suggests that a new look at the SR combatants is warranted, along with a fresh approach to several issues within the general topic.

THEORY

On the pages of the newly established SR central organ, *Revolutionary Russia* (*Revoliutsionnnaia Rossiia*), the party leadership initially affirmed in January of 1902 its intention to begin "unavoidable and expedient" terrorist activity "when it finds [such action] appropriate."[4] In formally adopting political assassination as an instrument in their antigovernment struggle, the SR leaders were prepared to contradict at least in part the contemporary cliché: "One does not talk about terror, one does it,"[5] and from the outset sought to develop a coherent theoretical foundation to justify terrorist methods. A major factor that spurred and facilitated these efforts to give a scientific base to the party's practical policies was the advent of Marxism.

The SRs regarded the terrorism practiced early in the party's existence as a continuation of the terrorist tradition of the People's Will, whose members the SRs perceived as their "direct predecessors and spiritual fathers."[6] The spread of Marxist ideas required all revolutionaries of the neo-Populist trend to modify their opinions, however, including their stands on radical tactics. Indeed, as early as the 1890s a strict adherent to the tactical principles of the People's Will who had not taken into account the newest postulates of socialist theory was rare. By the time the PSR emerged as a formal organization, Marxism was such an integral part of the Russian revolutionary movement that party leaders could not afford to ignore it if they wished to attract supporters to their cause.

According to the standard interpretation of orthodox Marxist doctrine, an isolated individual act fails to influence historical development in any significant way. Only mass movements can be considered agents of history, with alterations in political systems ("superstructures," in Marxist phraseology) solely dependent on class relationships. Since the individual's role in history is so limited, his physical elimination can produce only an equally minimal change in the overall historical process, no matter how seemingly important his position is. It follows then that one-man terrorist acts are nothing more than futile attempts by courageous and selfless idealists to change the iron laws of history.

Unable to ignore this logic, the SRs, who from the beginning formulated their ideology not only on the principles emphasized by Populist writers such as P. L. Lavrov and N. K. Mikhailovskii, but also on the works of Marx, sought to adapt their proterrorist stand to what they perceived as scientific theory. They therefore insisted that their tactic of political assassination was inseparable from the general struggle of the toiling masses. Chief party theoretician Viktor Chernov proclaimed:

> We argue for the implementation of terror in a whole series of situations. But for us, terrorist means are not some self-sufficing system of struggle, which by its own inner strength alone inevitably must break the enemy's resistance and force it to capitulate. . . . Conversely, for us terrorist acts can only be part of this struggle, a part that is inseparably linked to the other parts . . . [and] interwoven into a single complete system along with all other methods of partisan and mass . . . assault on the government. Terror is just one of many kinds of weapons, . . . just one of many technical methods . . . that only together with the other methods can be [effective].[7]

In accordance with the Marxist viewpoint, SR theoreticians constantly reiterated that the party's primary objective was not individual terror, but "the revolutionarization of the masses."[8] Terrorist acts were therefore to be "based on the needs of [the workers' and peasants'] movement and to complement it, but at the same time to give impetus to manifestations of the mass struggle by inciting a revolutionary mood among the masses."[9]

In addition to the agitational and propaganda value of the terrorist acts, which were to radicalize the toilers, popularize the revolutionary cause, and "awaken even the sleepiest philistines . . . and force them, even against their will, to think politically," terrorism as envisaged by the SRs was to perform two other important functions: to protect the revolutionary movement and to bring fear and disorganization into the ranks of the government.[10] The party leadership thus expected that the threat of immediate terrorist retaliation would force the government to curtail its repressive measures against the revolutionaries, and that the terrorist acts would justify themselves "as a means of self-defense, as a necessary weapon of protection, without which the completely unchecked violence of autocratic arbitrariness would transgress all bounds."[11] At the same time, assassination of the most prominent representatives of the tsarist regime was bound to have a disorganizing effect instilling fear in their successors and thereby rendering them more conciliatory: "Guns and bombs were, if not to destroy the State, at least to force it to make concessions to 'society.' "[12]

Especially on this last point the SR theoreticians had already departed from a strictly Marxist conceptualization of historical change. After all, the assassination of one oppressor, even of the highest rank, and his replacement by another, even a more benevolent one, would at best amount to only a superficial political improvement, and would not eliminate what for all socialists was the true evil—the capitalist substructure of the Russian state. Equally heretical from the orthodox Marxist point of view was the SR argument defining appropriate targets for the party's terrorist tactics. According to one proclamation, typical in its portrayal of the SR stand on terror, attacks were to be directed primarily against high-level administrative officials, rather than the tsar, because it was easier: "No minister can settle firmly in a palace as if in a fortress."[13] Absorbed in their own enthusiasm for terrorist action, the SRs sometimes abandoned all efforts to remain within the Marxist framework, arguing, for instance: "As in the past, when leaders decided the outcomes of battles by one-to-one fighting (*edinoborstvo*), so too the terrorists, in their one-to-one struggle with autocracy, will win freedom for Russia."[14]

The SRs' most frequent acts of terror, including some for which they became best known, characteristically belonged to none of the three categories of terrorism defined by their party theoreticians, having more to do with revenge for what the revolutionaries considered past crimes against the people. And more often than not, in meting out bloody punishment to "oppressors" and "executioners," the SR *boeviki* had little interest in their leadership's primary justification of terror as part of the all-out class struggle of the toiling masses. To carry out terrorist acts against state leaders and officials of the highest ranks, primarily in St. Petersburg, Moscow, and the larger provincial cities, by direct order of the party's headquarters abroad—activities referred to as "cen-

tral terror" (*tsentral'nyi terror*)—the PSR Central Committee established a separate terrorist unit late in 1901 that assumed the title of "Combat Organization."

THE COMBAT ORGANIZATION

The most characteristic feature of the Combat Organization's activities was
their conspiratorial nature. In contrast to the structure of the People's Will,
whose theoreticians, organizers, and terrorists were essentially the same people,
involved in all the various spheres of the party's activities, the PSR leadership
was guided by prevailing opinion in the revolutionary milieu regarding the
necessity of adopting a strictly professional approach to revolutionary and especially combat work. Accordingly, the PSR Central Committee introduced for
the first time a division of responsibilities, and organized a small contingent of
revolutionaries inside Russia "whose sole function was to prepare and carry
out assassinations" in maximum separation from all other party activities.[15]
Thus behind the creation of the SR terrorist organization lay the conviction
that the key to success in its activities was the use of specialized cadres dedicated exclusively to combat work and operating in the strictest secrecy. As a
result, the terrorist group's isolation from the rest of the party became so complete that most prominent members of the PSR "had absolutely no idea of what
was going on in the Combat Organization," and at times doubted its very
existence.[16] Even the Central Committee had no right to interfere in its internal
affairs, and at least in the initial stages most civilian PSR leaders, who like
Chernov were personally reluctant to participate in violence, made no attempt
to change this practice, as long as the respected and nearly revered combatants,
surrounded by an aura of danger and mystery, continued to bring glory to the
party through their sensational feats of terrorism.[17] This situation could not
exist without consequences, for according to Laqueur's observation of terrorist
practices in general,

> There was always resentment against the "politicians" who risked so little and had
> therefore no moral right to dictate a course of action to the terrorists—unless it
> coincided with the wishes and the convictions of the "fighters." In short, there was
> almost always dissension and competition between the political and the terrorist
> wing of the movement, and a tendency toward full autonomy among the terrorists.[18]

This generalization may certainly be applied to the SR combatants, who, as
a result of their conspiratorial work and secluded life-style in Russia, "developed their own values and their own elitist *esprit de corps*. . . . Solidarity
among themselves ranked higher than their obligation of loyalty to the party."
The Combat Organization thus gradually turned into a sect whose members
conceived of themselves as the "true bearers of Russia's revolutionary
cross,"[19] and not only committed terrorist acts, but also revered terror as a

sacred thing. Significantly, the SR Central Committee fell under the same spell and, contrary to all theoretical principles describing terrorism as only a supporting tool for the party's activity among the masses, came to treat the practice of central terror as the most important aspect of the party's work.[20] This is particularly evident from the fact that in allocating party funds, the SR leaders admitted not to have denied the Combat Organization anything; "in case there were no funds, they cut down on . . . [any other] activities, but never on combat affairs."[21] As a result, the combatants very quickly "adopted the arrogant view that it was they who accomplished the truly revolutionary deeds," and in the spirit of the new type of terrorist, they "showed a marked skepticism toward any kind of theory and hardly bothered about the party's internal political debates," or, for that matter, politics in general.[22]

Of the three leaders of the Combat Organization—Grigorii Gershuni, Boris Savinkov, and Evno Azef—none ever expressed any interest in theoretical controversies. Gershuni's role in the party was strictly that of an organizer and a recruiter; Savinkov simply had no time for theory, for he was involved personally in assassinations, to which he attributed primary significance; Azef, an enigmatic figure exposed in 1908 as a police agent, never concealed his skepticism about socialist dogma, and openly proclaimed that he would remain in the party only until constitutional order was established in Russia. He thereby acquired the mocking title of "Kadet with terror" (*kadet s terrorom*).[23]

Among the rank-and-file terrorists many were even less inclined to adhere to Socialist-Revolutionary ideology. Convinced anarchist Fedor Nazarov, for example, was a onetime member of the SR Combat Organization who "in his views stood far from the PSR programme," as did bomb-maker Dora Brilliant, who "was not interested in programmatic questions . . . [with] terror personifying the revolution for her, and with her entire world confined to the Combat Organization." Similarly, Boris Moiseenko was "a man of independent and original opinions [and] from the party's point of view . . . a heretic on many issues. He did not attribute much significance to peaceful work, and regarded conferences, meetings, and congresses with badly concealed disdain. He believed in terror alone." Abram Gots declared himself a follower of Emmanuel Kant, and Mariia Benevskaia was an ardent Christian who never parted with the Gospels.[24] Similarly, Ivan Kaliaev, known as "the poet" among his comrades, composed prayers in verse exalting the glory of Almighty God, and assassin Egor Sazonov explained in a letter written to his parents from prison:

> My Socialist-Revolutionary beliefs merged with my religion. . . . I think that we, the socialists, continue the work of Christ, who preached brotherly love among the people . . . and died for the people as a political criminal. . . . Christ's demands are clear. Who follows them? We, the socialists, want to carry them out, we want the kingdom of Christ to come to earth. . . . When I heard my teacher saying: take up your cross and follow me . . . I could not abandon my cross.[25]

The congenial atmosphere and solidarity within the Combat Organization was thus based not on any commonly held set of ideological precepts, but rather on what appears to have been the deep need shared by nonconformists who had rebelled against the norms of their environment to consolidate within a small circle their "psychological identity at a time of great societal instability and flux." The resulting group cohesion was magnified by external danger that tended to "reduce internal divisiveness in unity against the outside enemy" in an illegal situation "fashioned into a common destiny . . . under the pressure of pursuit." The consequence was that members of the Combat Organization tended to submerge their own identities in the group to form a "group mind."[26]

It is thus clear why the terrorists' inclination to follow orders from civilian party leaders was minimal, and why even in the earliest stages the SR leadership's control over the *boeviki* was slight. In addition, the Combat Organization had full control over its own independent treasury, which accumulated substantial funds earmarked exclusively for terrorist undertakings, and this also served to increase the combatants' autonomy from the Central Committee.[27] The Combat Organization planned and carried out the technical details of its terrorist acts without consulting the Central Committee, allegedly in order to maintain the conspiracy for the protection of the terrorists, and also because they considered such matters beyond the competence of anyone not directly involved with terror. It also constantly sought to establish timing and choice of targets as its own prerogatives, despite a party statute dictating that such matters were to be determined solely by the central leadership.[28]

Even the Combat Organization's initial terrorist attack, the 2 April 1902 assassination of Minister of the Interior Sipiagin in St. Petersburg, demonstrates not only the perpetrators' disregard for the theoretical principle that terror was to be auxiliary to the PSR's efforts to revolutionize the masses, but also their alienation from the party itself. SR Stepan Balmashev, dressed in the uniform of an aide-de-camp, entered the Mariinskii Palace and while handing the minister an envelope containing the official's death sentence, took two point-blank shots at him.[29] It is noteworthy that the SR Central Committee adopted this independent action as a party deed *post factum*, and formally declared the Combat Organization to be part of the PSR only after its success.[30]

This initial victory opened the SR terrorist campaign, and on 29 July of the same year Foma Kachura (Kachurenko), a woodworker using bullets doused in strychnine, took a shot at Prince I. M. Obolenskii, governor of Khar'kov, as the prince was leaving the theater. The terrorist missed his target, but wounded the city's chief of police, who happened to be nearby.[31] In the following months, the police succeeded in arresting a number of people close to the Combat Organization, including Gershuni's main associate, Mikhail Mel'nikov, but on 6 May 1903, an SR named Egor Dulebov fired at the governor of the Ufa province, N. M. Bogdanovich, and this time the Combat Organization had better luck: the assassins managed to escape, and one more alleged hangman was eliminated. The SR leadership did not choose to tie these acts to the struggle of the toiling masses, and in their proclamations spoke merely of revenge for government repressions and of instilling fear and confusion into the ranks of the oppressors.[32] As for the masses, the SRs expressed the hope that heroic deeds committed in the existing "atmosphere of official repression" would soon awaken the toilers and unite them into a powerful movement.

The chief initiator of all these acts was a former pharmacist and one of the PSR organizers, Grigorii Gershuni, whom the police considered "an artist in terror," and the radicals pronounced the "tiger of the Revolution."[33] Gershuni never resorted to arms personally, but according to A. I. Spiridovich, a former Okhrana official who had come to know him well, he was

> a convinced terrorist, clever, cunning, with an iron will, . . . [who] possessed an incredible gift to take hold of . . . the inexperienced, easily carried-away youth. . . . His hypnotizing eyes and especially persuasive speech subjugated those he spoke to and made them his ardent admirers. A person on whom Gershuni began working would soon totally submit to his will and become an unquestioning executor of his orders. . . . There is something satanic in this pressure and influence of Gershuni on his victims.[34]

Leonid Rataev, another leading police official who at one time headed the Foreign Agency of the Okhrana, was of the opinion that Gershuni "possessed the power of influencing people almost to the point of hypnotism."[35] His fellow revolutionaries also considered Gershuni a "soul hunter," and compared him to an awe-inspiring Mephistopheles, with "eyes that penetrated one's soul and . . . an ironical smile on his face."[36]

Gershuni was indeed able to attract a number of young idealists into the Combat Organization. Sipiagin's assassin, Balmashev, an impressionable and rather naive student who had been drawn to the revolution by his Populist father, was one of these, as were a young army lieutenant, Grigor'ev, and his wife, Iurkovskaia, with whom Gershuni worked for months until he obtained their agreement to participate in a terrorist act. He then improvised an immediate attempt on the life of the procurator of the Holy Synod, Pobedonostsev, which was to take place during Sipiagin's funeral. According to the plan, Grigor'ev's shots at Pobedonostsev were to create panic, during which Iurkovskaia, dressed as a male gymnasium student, would try to kill the governor of St. Petersburg, General Kleigels, as well. Notwithstanding Gershuni's "hypnotic powers of persuasion," however, Grigor'ev took pity on the elderly Pobedonostsev at the last minute and could not force himself to pull the trigger, thus precluding both attempts.[37]

Similarly, Foma Kachura, chosen by Gershuni for the attack on Obolenskii solely because his status as a worker would lend the assassination attempt greater ideological significance, later revealed the enormous influence that the leader of the Combat Organization exerted upon him. "Kachura trembled before him," Spiridovich recalled; "In prison, he began to testify against Gershuni only when he saw a picture [of his chief] . . . in a prisoner's robe and handcuffs."[38] During the investigation, Kachura repented his crime and asserted that if Gershuni had not stayed with him until the moment of the act, constantly urging him on, he would not have dared to fire. For their part, the SR leaders merely wished to extract additional prestige for the party from Kachura's action. Passing over his renegade behavior at the trial in silence, they exalted him in their publications as a hero of the people, neglecting to mention that it was Gershuni who dictated to the simple-minded worker, word for word, the letter that was supposed to have been a personal explanation to the public of his idealistic revolutionary venture.[39]

The heroic, almost mythological picture of Gershuni provided by the SRs, especially after his death in 1908, thus requires revision. Contrary to his reputation as a superb judge of character, Gershuni was often less than successful in choosing supporters, who were seemingly relieved to be out from under his spell as soon as he left their immediate vicinity and was no longer able to control them. Even Mel'nikov, his deputy in the Combat Organization, proved unprepared for selfless sacrifice.[40] Moreover, when Gershuni himself was finally arrested in Kiev in May of 1903 and facing a death sentence, he too was willing to sacrifice his revolutionary idealism when his life was at stake, despite his much-glorified courage and will power. Whereas previous generations of Russian revolutionaries had used their trials as opportunities to hail the revolution, frowning upon pleas for mercy addressed to the tsar, Gershuni, like many other terrorists of the new type, desperately denied involvement with any political assassination, and then appealed to Nicholas II for pardon. He succeeded in exchanging his death sentence for a life term at hard labor, but, according to police sources, many of his fellow party members considered his behavior unworthy and fainthearted, and experienced great difficulty countering the claims of their Social Democrat critics that Gershuni's stature was exaggerated, his reputation undeserved.[41]

Gershuni's apprehension ended the initial active period of the Combat Organization, which then had to replace its arrested cadres and adapt its activities to new technical methods and new leadership. In the technical sphere, the group undertook a change in its weaponry, exchanging revolvers for dynamite. Since initially it was difficult to smuggle explosives into the country from abroad (their bulk transportation from Western and Southeastern Europe did not become established prior to the outbreak of the revolution in 1905), the terrorists were forced to construct most of their bombs inside Russia. This difficult and dangerous work, carried out by dilettantes, claimed two lives in one year: Aleksei Pokotilov died on 31 March 1904 while assembling bombs in the Northern Hotel in St. Petersburg, and Maximilian Shveitser met the same fate on 26 February 1905 in the Hotel Bristol. In both cases the destructive power of the explosions was enormous: the suites where the laboratories were located and the rooms immediately adjacent were demolished, and the corpses of the terrorists were mangled: Pokotilov was recognizable only by his unusually small hands, and parts of Shveitser's body were found in the nearby public gardens.[42]

After May 1903 Boris Savinkov succeeded Gershuni as the organizer and commander of the SR *boeviki* in Russia, personally recruiting many new members and playing a primary role in detailed preparations for terrorist acts. In reading Savinkov's memoirs, it is difficult to determine precisely what motivated his involvement in revolutionary activities, but his example clearly confirms that combatants "often join an organization for reasons other than ideological commitment . . . [and that the] popular image of the terrorist as an individual motivated exclusively by deep and intransigent political commitment obscures a more complex reality."[43]

The son of a judge in Warsaw, Savinkov enjoyed many advantages as a young man: education, adequate means to live comfortably, extensive connections (his wife was the daughter of well-known Populist writer Gleb Uspenskii), and a handsome appearance, which contributed to his reputation as a womanizer. Many people of similar biography joined the revolution, but few demonstrated such profound indifference to socialist dogma, indeed to all theoretical issues and even to the alleged purpose of his struggle, the liberation of the workers and peasants. In his early youth in the 1890s he paid the mandatory tribute to Marxism and its required agitation among the workers, but his reminiscences, which deal with his subsequent activities as a terrorist—clearly the most successful part of Savinkov's revolutionary career—convey a shift in his interests exclusively to immediate goals, that is, how to succeed in killing one state leader or another; underlying motives are left unclear. In the words of one of Savinkov's SR acquaintances who later left the party, "Deep social indifference and increasing egocentrism gradually became his distinguishing traits." Contrary to what would be expected of a revolutionary, it was not the people or the masses, but the inflated ego of this "thrill-seeking adventurer" that was most critical in shaping his behavior.[44]

While it is only possible to speculate about Savinkov's inner motives for terrorist activity, his first novel, *The Pale Horse* (*Kon' blednyi*), published in 1909, and to some extent his second, *That Which Never Happened* (*To, chego ne bylo*), published in 1912, both under the pseudonym "V. Ropshin," may serve as personal statements, revealing certain aspects of his complex personality.[45] Savinkov's psychological analysis of the terrorists depicted in the two works created a scandal among the SRs, with a number of prominent party members considering the works "counterrevolutionary in . . . essence," and slanderous of the terrorists and indeed the very idea of terror. A number of them insisted that he suspend publication and be expelled from the PSR, notwithstanding all his former achievements.[46]

Savinkov's first novel is particularly revealing. Written in the first person with the goal of analyzing the mentality of a revolutionary assassin, the book is highly imitative of works by two popular contemporary decadent writers, Dmitrii Merezhkovskii and Zinaida Gippius, who strongly influenced the style of the novel and even suggested its title. The author as narrator describes a group of terrorists, prototypes of Combat Organization members, revealing the range of motives that drove them as individuals to bloodshed. Strikingly, in Savinkov's depiction, whatever meagre idealism and self-sacrifice might once have existed among these revolutionaries has drowned in a sea of cynicism, stupidity, moral corruption, and pure criminality. In the words of historian Aileen Kelly, "*Pale Horse* was a savage demystification of the monolithic hero."[47]

The central character and leader of the terrorist band, who bears many of the author's traits, is portrayed as a lonely and crippled soul, with an invariably skeptical approach to all ideas and ideals. On several occasions he admits that he himself does not know why and for what goals he participates in terror.[48] In complete alienation not only from the rhetorical "people," but indeed from his own comrades, he is totally involved and entrapped in his own inner conflicts, and "spits on the whole world."[49] His egoism, contempt, and profound indifference to the fates of others, victims and fellow terrorists alike, are boundless and, prepared to shed blood, he finally puts himself above its value by committing a murder for strictly personal reasons. In short, Savinkov's novel, in which, incidentally, the author demonstrates a typical Silver Age inclination to flirt with religion, or, rather, a quasi-spirituality and apocalyptic mentality, can be seen as a poor version of Dostoevsky's *The Devils*. Considering the novel's autobiographical element, it is significant that even in his own eyes, Savinkov, a renowned terrorist and onetime member of the SR Central Committee, appears to be none other than the embodiment of a certain Nikolai Stavrogin.[50] As Kelly perceptively notes, echoing Struve, "The novel also charts the emergence of a new type in whom moral certainty has become moral indifference— the highly specialized technician of revolution."[51]

At the same time, it cannot be denied that as a combatant Savinkov possessed personal courage and was a gifted organizer, for it was under his leadership that the Combat Organization carried out two of its most spectacular acts. After lengthy surveillance, the terrorists were able to establish the habitual movements of Minister of the Interior Plehve, who was regarded with particular hatred by the revolutionaries. On 15 July 1904, as the minister made his way to a regular appointment with the tsar, Egor Sazonov (also known as Abel, or in Russian—Avel') ran up to his carriage and tossed in a bomb that killed Plehve instantly, seriously injuring the terrorist.[52] This accomplishment which many SRs had long regarded as a "question of honor for the party," tremendously enhanced the prestige of the Combat Organization within the PSR and among the other revolutionaries and their sympathizers.[53] The terrorists then began to prepare for an equally sensational assassination attempt against Grand Duke Sergei Aleksandrovich, governor-general of Moscow.

In the meantime, however, they were diverted by two unexpected opportunities in the capital. While carrying out surveillance of Governor-general D. F. Trepov in St. Petersburg, members of the Combat Organization branch working in that city learned by chance the schedule of Minister of Justice Murav'ev. Although the terrorists did not have the sanction of the Central Committee, and its only member in St. Petersburg, Nikolai Tiutchev, argued firmly against the act, considering the victim too insignificant, Savinkov held true to his own logic: "If there was a chance to kill Murav'ev, it was impossible not to take it if only because the assassinations of Trepov and Grand Duke Sergei were not guaranteed to be successful."[54] The attempt on Murav'ev took place on 19 January 1905 but failed.

The second opportunity was even more appealing to the terrorists. A member of the Combat Organization, Tat'iana Leont'eva, daughter of the vice-governor of Iakutsk and an aristocratic mother, was granted the honor of selling flowers at a ball to be attended by Nicholas II in December of 1904. Leont'eva, a dedicated terrorist of questionable emotional stability, immediately proposed that she assassinate the tsar, and again, without waiting for the party leaders to consent, the terrorists enthusiastically approved her decision. In fact, Savinkov characteristically declared, "It would be necessary to kill the tsar even if it were to be formally prohibited by the Central Committee."[55] Leont'eva, however, did not get a chance to participate in this act of open insubordination to central party leadership on the part of the terrorists: the ball was abruptly cancelled.

By then, the Moscow contingent of the Combat Organization was ready to strike against the imperial family. The assassination of Grand Duke Sergei Aleksandrovich took place on 4 February 1905, when a large homemade bomb hurled by Savinkov's close friend Ivan Kaliaev exploded with a thunder heard even in remote corners of Moscow, causing many to think it was an earthquake. At the site of the explosion, "there lay a shapeless heap . . . of small parts of the carriage, of clothes, and of a mutilated body . . . [with] no head. Of the other parts, it was only possible to distinguish an arm and part of a leg." The bomb also severely injured the coachman, as well as the terrorist himself, who was arrested, tried, and hanged.[56]

On the practical level, these two major victories—the assassinations of Plehve and the Grand Duke—brought "plenty of money and no shortage of candidates to the Combat Organization."[57] Even among the conservatives Plehve had been known for his resistance to any steps toward reform, and was considered a bureaucrat to the core of his brain, who stifled and "compromised the government like no other minister." His assassination brought widespread recognition for the PSR and its terrorists, especially since "not a word of remorse was spoken" about the victim's demise from any quarter.[58] The Grand Duke was also generally regarded as a reactionary, and his title as well as his close relations with the tsar had additional symbolic value, since he was the first member of the royal family to have been assassinated since 1881. Moreover, his assassination confirmed for the party's supporters that the initial victory against Plehve had not been an accident. These two acts, however, were the Combat Organization's final successful undertakings as it came to the end of what was later to be referred to as its heroic period. In March 1905 the police, acting on information provided by a secret agent, SR Nikolai Tatarov, arrested seventeen members of the Combat Organization, and according to Savinkov, "never again did it achieve such strength and such significance."[59]

Of the old *boeviki*, there remained only Dora Brilliant and several candidates to the Combat Organization who had not yet been tried in action. Savinkov, unshaken by the unexpected arrests, proceeded with preparations for the assassination of Trepov in St. Petersburg, who by this time was the most hated man in Russia. However, constant police surveillance of the terrorists, aided by Tatarov's information, forced him to abandon the act for the moment.[60] The terrorists then made plans to kill Grand Duke Vladimir Aleksandrovich, commander-in-chief of the St. Petersburg military district, whom they held responsible for opening fire on the crowds in the capital on Bloody Sunday. They also took steps toward the assassinations of Kleigels, now governor-general of Kiev, and Baron Unterberger, governor of Nizhnii Novgorod. These efforts also produced no results, and the Combat Organization thus proved totally impotent between February and October 1905. When Nicholas II issued the October Manifesto, the PSR Central Committee, despite the loud protests of all members of the Combat Organization and the *boeviki* in the periphery, ordered a stop to the party's terrorist activity, considering it inappropriate under the new constitutional order. No longer required to remain in the capitals, most SR terrorists dispersed to the provinces, and, in Savinkov's words, "The Combat Organization disintegrated."[61]

Savinkov and other dedicated advocates of terror were not ready to comply with the Central Committee's decision, however. In this period he nurtured a number of fantastic plans for terrorist acts, including the arrest of Count Witte—chairman of the Council of Ministers, the bombing of the St. Petersburg section of the Okhrana, and the destruction of all electrical and telephone lines in the capital.[62] None of Savinkov's personal schemes ever materialized, but following the government's suppression of the December uprising in Moscow, the new Central Committee elected at the First Congress of the PSR, held in Finland from 29 December 1905 to 4 January 1906, declared its intention to resume terrorist activities.[63] The Combat Organization was to be rebuilt and strengthened with new members. They numbered about thirty and their future course was determined for them: the Central Committee resolved that the next two primary targets of central terror would be Petr Durnovo, minister of the interior, and Vice Adm. F. V. Dubasov, governor-general of Moscow. For obvious political reasons, both acts were to be consumated before the opening of the First Duma session.[64] The governor-general was chosen as the first to be killed, and at approximately the same time the following joke circulated in Moscow: " 'Good for Dubasov, such a difficult moment and he did not lose his head.' 'Don't worry, he will lose it yet.' "[65]

Except for an act of revenge against the police informer Tatarov, who was killed in Warsaw in front of his parents on 4 April,[66] the attack against Dubasov was the final success of the Combat Organization, but its success was only partial. After several failed attempts to get close to the target, on 23 April 1906, four days before the Central Committee's deadline, Boris Vnorovskii, dressed as a naval officer, threw what looked like a box of candies, wrapped in gift paper and tied with a ribbon, under Dubasov's carriage, producing a powerful explosion. As a result, the terrorist and Dubasov's aide-de-camp, Count Konovnitsyn, were killed instantly, and the coachman and several bystanders were slightly wounded; the governor-general was thrown out of his carriage and escaped with minor injuries.[67] Then, on 26 April a new issue of the satirical journal *Sprut* (*Octopus*) came out with a timely riddle:

Question: What is the difference between the European ministers and ours?
Answer: The European ministers get thrown out of office, and ours get blown out![68]

On 27 April the Duma session opened, and the PSR Central Committee, although it had boycotted the elections, reaffirmed its intention to end its terrorist activity.[69] Indirectly, the SR leadership thus saved the life of the minister of the interior, against whom the Combat Organization proved unable to execute an attack in the time available; it was similarly unable to carry out a terrorist act against Minister of Justice M. G. Akimov. These setbacks, as well as several abortive attempts to assassinate two military figures who had played leading roles in the suppression of the December uprising in Moscow—Maj. Gen. Georgii Min, commander of the famous Semenovskii Regiment, and Colonel Riman—were additional reminders of the repeated failures that had haunted the Combat Organization since the March 1905 arrests. The wounding of Dubasov was the only exception to this pattern, and many party members had already begun to question the way central terror was conducted, arguing that the series of failed attempts could not be accidental.[70]

Following the dissolution of the First Duma in July 1906, however, the Central Committee once again altered its policy on terrorist acts, and officially resumed terror, determined to implement all possible means against the "proponents of reaction," foremost among them Minister of the Interior Stolypin, who had recently been named to the additional post of prime minister. Considered by the revolutionaries to bear major responsibility for the dissolution of the Duma, Stolypin became the primary target of the Combat Organization, which persistently plotted his assassination, but to no avail. To protect his family, Stolypin accepted the tsar's invitation to move into the Winter Palace, from which he traveled by water to his daily appointments with Nicholas II in Peterhof. It was virtually impossible for the terrorists to use bombs against the minister, since they were unable to get close enough to him, and so in the late fall of 1906 they were forced to abandon their efforts and acknowledge yet another failure.[71]

Almost desperate, Savinkov attempted to compensate by assassinating V. F. von der Launits, governor of St. Petersburg, but after even this less significant act proved impossible because of constant police surveillance, he resigned as head of the combatants, along with Azef, who at the time served as the PSR Central Committee representative in the Combat Organization. The Central Committee appointed two prominent SRs, Sletov and Grozdov, as replacements, but the *boeviki*, consistent with their closed-circle mentality, refused to recognize the outsiders as leaders and chose instead to disperse. By the beginning of 1907, the Combat Organization had thus fallen apart once again, this time never to be reassembled in its former membership and capacity.[72]

LOCAL TERRORIST ACTIVITY

This did not mean, however, that the PSR was ready to abandon the tactic of political assassination, for the Combat Organization was not the only terrorist body at the disposal of the party, whose many activists continued their terrorist practices throughout the empire. The SR leadership frequently relied on smaller terrorist or combat units (*boevye druzhiny*), on the flying combat detachments (*letuchie boevye otriady*), and on isolated individuals to carry out assassinations.[73] This was in addition to the multitude of SR terrorists who, with the outbreak of revolutionary disturbances in 1905, began to operate in the provinces on the orders of their local committees or even on their own initiative, with no direction whatsoever from the center. As was also true of the participants in centrally planned assassination attempts, a lack of adherence to SR dogma was evident among the perpetrators of terror in the local combat bands. All of these groups differed from the Combat Organization, however, in their size, material status, and a third important factor: while the central terrorist body of the party resembled the Executive Committee of the People's Will in its choice of targets and its operational methods, the smaller combat units came to represent the new type of terrorist in their largely indiscriminate behavior and increasing callousness toward bloodshed, as well as in the composition of their ranks, which included many individuals who could not be considered conscious revolutionaries and socialists.

One of the most active of the several SR terrorist groups operating in St. Petersburg was the PSR Northern Flying Combat Detachment (Severnyi Boevoi letuchii otriad), which came into being in the second half of 1906. Unlike the Combat Organization, this terrorist unit was not directly subordinate to the PSR Central Committee, and although it did occasionally act on its orders, more frequently it functioned under the direction of the St. Petersburg party committee. What is significant, however, is that 80 percent of the *boeviki* in the Northern Flying Combat Detachment were not official members of the PSR, and "had joined the group for a motley of reasons, ranging from an excess of youthful revolutionary ardour to a desire for personal revenge."[74] One of the most notorious of the group's terrorist undertakings claimed by the SR Party took place on 13 August 1906, when Zinaida Konopliannikova succeeded in assassinating General Min.[75]

At the head of the Northern Flying Combat Detachment was the Latvian Al'bert Trauberg, more commonly known simply as Karl. He was a terrorist of such courage and determination that Azef warned his police superiors, "as long as he is free, you cannot be in peace."[76] It was Trauberg who assigned another female terrorist, Evstiliia Rogozinnikova, to kill the head of the St. Petersburg Prison Department, A. M. Maksimovskii, on 15 (28) October 1907. It was also Trauberg who, in the typically indiscriminate manner of the new type of terrorist, devised a plan according to which state leaders were to be eliminated en masse not for any particular offense, but merely because of their positions. His idea was to throw a bomb into the right-hand section of the State Council (Gosudarstvennyi sovet) assembly hall, where the conservative members were seated, including the ministers. Since future ministers were often selected from the conservative appointees to the State Council, this strike was directed not only against current members of the cabinet, but also against potential state leaders who had not yet had a chance to prove themselves enemies of the people. The act was to have been carried out by a terrorist posing as a journalist, but the scheme never materialized because of police efficiency in establishing Trauberg's whereabouts and apprehending him.[77]

The planned attack against the State Council was not an isolated case of indiscriminate violence; in fact, the terrorists of Trauberg's Northern Flying Combat Detachment seemed to specialize in mass killings. In the summer of 1907, seeking to assassinate War Minister A. F. Rediger, they planned to set off a bomb during a session of the Military Council. The authorities discovered this plot, and during the investigation that followed the terrorists' arrests one revolutionary revealed, "The organization had decided to kill all the ministers and their deputies, beginning with those who were least guarded."[78]

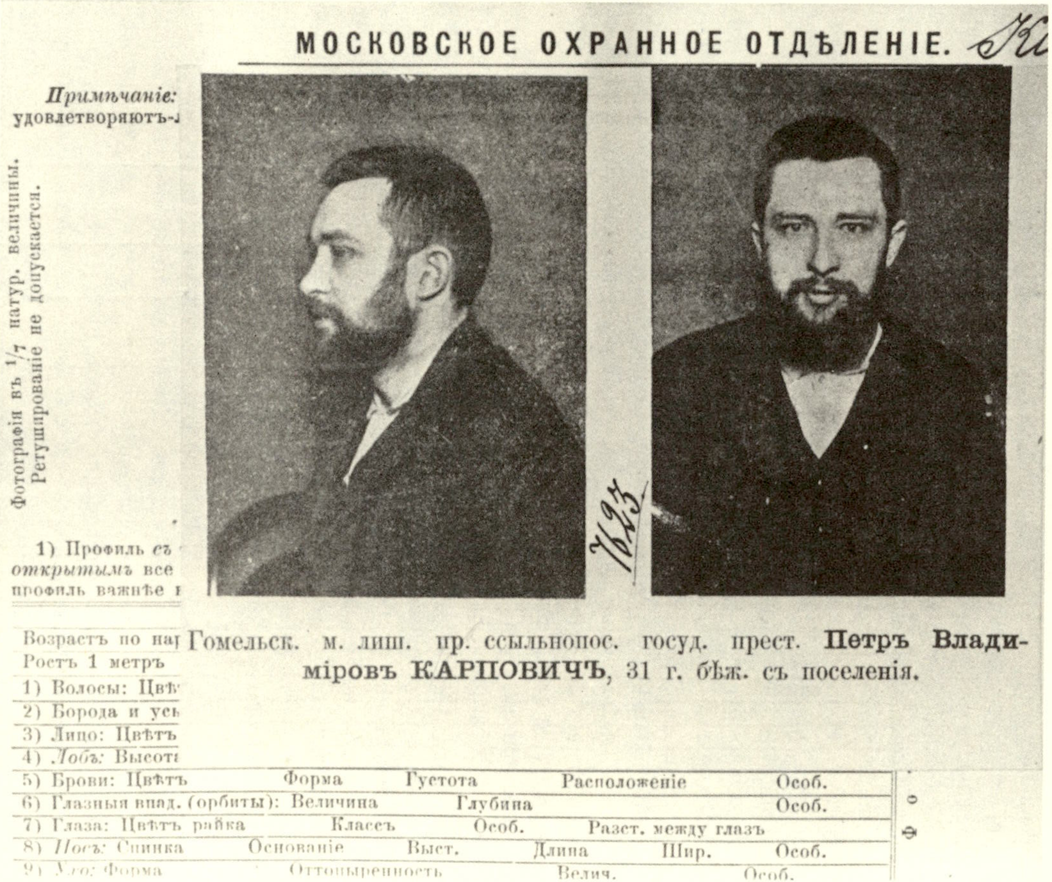

1. Petr Karpovich

2. Grigorii Gershuni

3. Mariia Seliuk

4. Egor Sazonov

5. Ivan Kaliaev

6. Boris Savinkov

7. Al'bert Trauberg (Karl)

Trauberg's arrest, although a serious blow to the Northern Flying Combat Detachment, did not cause the terrorists to abort their preparations for other sensational acts, and at the end of 1907 they redirected their efforts toward attempts on the lives of Grand Duke Nikolai Nikolaevich, uncle of the tsar, and Minister of Justice I. G. Shcheglovitov.[79] A. V. Gerasimov, head of the St. Petersburg Okhrana, could not trace the remaining members of the group until his agent provided him with the name of Anna Rasputina. Surveillance of Rasputina immediately established that she and her comrades had set up a regular meeting place in the Kazanskii Cathedral, where, posing as supplicants deep in prayer, they exchanged information and explosives. The police were thereby able to establish the network of connections among the terrorists, and by 7 February 1908 were ready to proceed. Nine members of the Northern Flying Combat Detachment were arrested, among them Mario Kal'vino (Vsevolod Lebedintsev), who had been outfitted as a living bomb and was prepared to throw himself under Shcheglovitov's carriage. At the time of his arrest he shouted to the policemen: "Be careful. I am wrapped around with dynamite. If I blow up, the entire street will be destroyed."[80] The police succeeded in taking him safely into custody, and a week later the terrorists were tried. Seven of them, including Rasputina and Lebedintsev, were sentenced to death and hanged.[81] The courage of the revolutionaries at the scaffold impressed even the official procurator witnessing the hanging: "How these people died. . . . no sighs, no remorse, no pleas, no signs of weakness. . . . They came to the place of their execution with a smile on their faces. These were real heroes."[82] The public was also moved by this execution; angry voices expressed protest, and Leonid Andreev was inspired to write his popular story, "Seven Who Were Hanged" (Rasskaz o semi poveshennykh).

There were other SR terrorist groups operating in the capital at the time, including Lev Zil'berberg's combat unit, known as the Combat Detachment of the Central Committee (Boevoi otriad pri Tsentral'nom Komitete), originally intended to serve as a replacement for the Combat Organization. The group had its first success on 3 January 1907 when one of its members, Evgenii Kudriavtsev ("the Admiral"), shot and killed von der Launits, long a prime target for assassination attempts. On the eve of the attack von der Launits had ignored an Okhrana warning to take proper precautions.

The police were able to capture Zil'berberg on 9 February 1907, but his group continued and even intensified its efforts. On 13 February a lucky coincidence saved the life of Grand Duke Nikolai Nikolaevich, when an explosive device planted near his train was discovered by a soldier minutes before detonation. In the same month Gerasimov received information that the terrorists were planning an act against Nicholas II himself. An investigation revealed that as early as the summer of 1906 the revolutionaries had attempted to recruit Nikolai Ratimov, a Cossack in the imperial convoy, to assist in the attack on the tsar, and perhaps even to act as its primary perpetrator. Ratimov, while pretending to go along with the terrorists' plan, continuously reported on his radical contacts to the Okhrana, allowing the authorities to gather enough evidence for a trial.[83]

On 31 March 1907 twenty-eight people connected with the conspiracy were arrested, and during the trial of eighteen terrorists that followed in the summer of 1907, the PSR Central Committee issued an official denial of any party connection with this plot and its perpetrators, asserting that the SR leadership had not ordered any of the accused to act against the tsar.[84] At the same time, the defense attorneys, among them the most prominent liberal lawyers in Russia—V. A. Maklakov, N. K. Murav'ev, N. Sokolov, and A. S. Zarudnyi—sought to demonstrate that the St. Petersburg Okhrana had exaggerated the case out of all proportion by attempting to portray several young revolutionary enthusiasts as full-fledged members of the formidable PSR and hardened terrorists.[85] Gerasimov, however, was able to present enough evidence to convince the judges that the plot against the tsar had indeed been initiated by the SR Central Committee. As a result, the three leaders of the conspiracy, B. I. Nikitenko, V. A. Naumov, and B. S. Siniavskii, were sentenced to death, and the fifteen other, less important members of the group, received various sentences of hard labor and exile.[86]

The PSR Central Committee's false denial of responsibility for terrorist activities in this instance was not unique. The party's high command adopted a similar stance, for example, following the SR execution of the hero of the Bloody Sunday events in St. Petersburg, the priest and charismatic proletarian leader Father Georgii Gapon, who had turned police informer soon after the fateful day of 9 January 1905. For the SR high command, which had established ties with Gapon despite its subsequent public denial of the fact, he became a prime target for assassination. In contrast to most earlier cases in which SR-perpetrated terrorist acts were planned and executed by groups of combatants, the Central Committee assigned a single man to carry out its death sentence on Gapon, Gapon's friend and revolutionary colleague, Petr Rutenberg (Martyn), who had marched beside him to the Winter Palace, and saved his life by leading him to safety when the troops began shooting at the crowd. To make Gapon's police ties evident to his supporters, the Central Committee decided that Rutenberg must kill both Gapon and his primary police contact, P. I. Rachkovskii—head of the political section of the Police Department—during one of their secret meetings.[87]

In February 1906, Gapon visited Rutenberg in Moscow and confided his secret police work to his friend. He asked Rutenberg to help him obtain information on the Combat Organization, for which the police officials allegedly had promised to pay one hundred thousand rubles. Acting with Central Committee sanction, Rutenberg pretended to consider Gapon's proposition, and in bargaining with the priest about division of the payment insisted on a meeting with Rachkovskii—a meeting that would provide Rutenberg an opportunity to

kill both intended victims.[88] As time passed and Rachkovskii proved too prudent to meet the revolutionary on his terms, Rutenberg grew increasingly impatient and finally decided to get rid of Gapon alone, thus violating the orders
of the Central Committee.[89]

On 28 March 1906, Rutenberg lured Gapon to a deserted house near the
Finnish border, supposedly to conclude their negotiations. Several workers
were hidden in a room adjacent to the one where Gapon was urging Rutenberg
to betray his comrades. Convinced of Gapon's treachery, the workers, who
had formerly been his ardent admirers, rushed out of their hiding places and,
ignoring Gapon's pleas, placed a rope around his neck and hanged him on a
hallstand.[90]

At the time of this murder the SR leaders had recently agreed to participate
in a public trial of Gapon to be held abroad. Following the act, therefore, they
had no desire to admit that the traitor had been executed with their sanction
prior to the hearing. To get themselves out of this awkward situation, the Central Committee used the fact that against its orders Gapon had been murdered
without Rachkovskii as a pretext not to recognize the assassination as a party
act.[91] The PSR leaders were also concerned about the anticipated negative
reaction of the masses, with whom they believed Gapon was still extremely
popular as a hero who had nearly lost his life presenting the petitions of the
poor to the tsar on Bloody Sunday; they feared that the workers would suspect
that he had been killed as a result of party rivalry and petty intrigues.[92]

The person who paid for the evasiveness of the SR leadership was Rutenberg, who found himself transformed from a revolutionary vigilante in the
eyes of the public to a common criminal suspected of murdering Gapon on his
own initiative for private motives. The Central Committee had clearly betrayed Rutenberg's trust; perhaps wishing simultaneously to compromise the
government, it even failed to deny the widely circulating rumors that Rutenberg was a police agent, who had killed the revolutionary priest on orders from
the authorities.[93] For many years Rutenberg persistently demanded an official
party statement confirming that he had been ordered to kill Gapon by its Central Committee, but the SR leaders were equally persistent in dismissing his
claims.[94]

An analysis of the numerous political assassinations planned and executed
in or near the capital, either by the central Combat Organization or the smaller
terrorist units, leaves little doubt that the repeated assertions of party ideologists that SR terror was always integrated into the mass movement of workers,
peasants, and soldiers largely remained lip service to theoretical principles.
Most of these acts were intended as revenge, although some were planned
primarily to advance the antigovernment struggle. In 1907, for example, the
authorities in St. Petersburg succeeded in disrupting SR preparations for "a
number of terrorist acts against the highest military commanders . . . in order
to promote a revolutionary mood in the army."[95]

As one student of early SR activities, Maureen Perrie, correctly observes, "SR terrorism was more effective in the years 1902–4, when the mass movement was only in its early stages, than in the revolutionary years 1905–7."[96] In the first place, the high-level victims of the initial years of SR-perpetrated terror were well chosen to symbolize the struggle against state repressions. Secondly, the sensational murders, with such prominent victims as Plehve and Grand Duke Sergei Aleksandrovich, not only produced tremendous agitational effects, but also led directly to substantial compromises by the tsarist government. Plehve's successor as minister of internal affairs was the liberal Prince P. D. Sviatopolk-Mirskii, and an announcement of political reforms in February 1905 followed immediately upon the Grand Duke's assassination.[97] On the other hand, although the number of SR terrorist acts increased sharply in this period, contributing immensely to the destabilization of the Russian provinces, after 1905 the SRs largely failed to achieve significant success at the central level in any of their three main objectives for terror: to retaliate, to propagandize the revolution, and to weaken the central authorities enough to force concessions.

According to statistics compiled by the SRs, 205 terrorist attempts took place against government officials of various ranks throughout the empire between 1902 and 1911, and there is ample evidence to suggest that the actual number was even greater.[98] In the revolutionary chaos of 1905–1907 the numerous SR groups, operating in small towns and villages as well as in the provincial and district (*uezd*) centers, were so isolated from the party headquarters abroad, and so autonomous in their actions, that many cases of SR-perpetrated violence never made it into the official annals of the PSR. In addition, it was not uncommon for individual SRs to engage in terrorist activities, including political assassinations, entirely on personal initiative, without the formal consent of their local groups. Clearly, the PSR did not assume responsibility for many of these acts, which were executed against petty officials and other figures of relative unimportance.[99] In 1905–1907 people lost their lives daily in unrecorded terrorist attacks, and the sources are also far from consistent in accounting for the numerous casualties among bystanders at the scenes of explosions.

In the atmosphere of anarchy reigning in Russia in the revolutionary years, it was often difficult to establish responsibility for an individual terrorist act. This task was rendered even more difficult by competition among terrorist groups seeking credit for successful assassinations, associated in their eyes with political prestige for the parties, and personal glory for the perpetrators. Among the many examples of such behavior, one particularly telling episode occurred in Kiev in the early spring of 1905, when an SR revolutionary misrepresented himself as the terrorist who had escaped after taking several shots at Okhrana chief Spiridovich, severely wounding him. Friends of the alleged hero attempted to save him from police apprehension by smuggling him abroad, and appealed for help to the Kiev SR committee, which, however, refused to assist, arguing that it had not sanctioned the act. It soon became clear that the real perpetrator was not a member of the PSR; he was in fact Okhrana informer torn by guilt for his betrayal of the revolutionary cause, and seeking revenge. This did not prevent the Kiev SRs from subsequently printing thousands of leaflets claiming credit for the "heroic execution of the committee's sentence against . . . Spiridovich by one of its members."[100]

Just as the terrorists of the new type in the central Combat Organization sought to secure their independence from the civilian party organs, it was not unusual for their comrades in the provinces to disregard Central Committee resolutions, and even violate them on occasion. This insubordination was especially evident in the reactions of various provincial groups to the Central Committee's resolution to discontinue terrorist activity following promulgation of the October Manifesto. Many local SRs were outraged at what they felt was opportunism and compromise with the dying autocracy. Ekaterina Izmailovich, who on 22 January 1906 would shoot and seriously wound Vice Admiral P. G. Chukhnin, the commander of the Black Sea Fleet in Sevastopol' responsible for suppression of a mutiny on the cruiser *Ochakov* in 1905, called the decision of the party's leadership "a betrayal of the people's cause." Numerous other SRs resolved to disobey the Central Committee and continue their local terrorist practices.[101] Accordingly, after October 1905, despite the PSR's formal declaration of a halt to all terrorist activity, with the exception of acts against individual government agents implicated in particularly harsh repressive measures, SRs throughout Russia continued to kill state officials, members of the police and the military forces, informers and spies.[102] This was also true immediately following the opening of the First Duma, when the party leadership again proved powerless to control its terrorists.[103]

A growing number of SR *boeviki* differed substantially from members of the Combat Organization in the ease and seeming indifference with which they proceeded with their plans, even when they entailed extensive bloodletting. The Combat Organization conducted its activities in a fairly cautious manner, and in its initial period Gershuni employed methods intended to minimize the unnecessary deaths of innocent bystanders, preferring revolvers to bombs, and favoring, in the words of Vladimir Zenzinov, a onetime combatant, "direct and heroic strokes to the face of the enemy."[104] Later, during Savinkov's tenure as the terrorists' leader, Ivan Kaliaev is known to have hesitated to throw a bomb under Grand Duke Sergei Alexandrovich's carriage when he finally encountered the tsar's uncle after weeks of surveillance, because the Grand Duke's wife and the children of a relative were also in the carriage.[105]

On the other hand, it is hardly possible to accept without modification Zenzinov's assertion that "these principles . . . became characteristic of the entire terrorist activity of the party even after G. A. Gershuni," and "turned into

traditions of SR terror for all later times and for the whole period of its existence."[106] An assassination attempt against Lieutenant-general Nepliuev, commander of the Sevastopol' fortress, illustrates that ordinary Russian citizens
were not safe from the bloody consequences of SR terror. During a parade
celebrating the Emperor's coronation day on 14 May 1906, two terrorists acting with the knowledge and assistance of the Sevastopol' SR committee, but
without its direct order, attempted to kill Nepliuev with homemade bombs.
Armed with the deadly, unstable explosives, they mingled with the large
crowd of spectators, waiting for the general to pass, but when one of them,
sixteen-year-old Nikolai Makarov, darted out and threw his bomb under Nepliuev's feet, it failed to explode. At that moment there was a thunderous blast
from another direction: the bomb of the second terrorist, a sailor named Ivan
Frolov, had detonated prematurely, instantly killing the assassin and six bystanders, and leaving thirty-seven wounded.[107]

This attempt on Nepliuev's life was not an isolated episode of indiscriminate SR violence. Since public appearances presented the best opportunities
for the assassins to approach high-ranking officials, the SR terrorists used
occasions such as church services and public prayers for their strikes.[108] Significantly, by 1905 it was no longer necessary for a prominent government
official to bear personal responsibility for harsh repressive measures in order
to elicit the wrath of local PSR groups. For example, after shooting Adjutant
General Count Ignat'ev, a member of the State Council, with poisoned bullets
in the city of Tver' on 9 December 1906, terrorist Sergei Il'inskii explained
that he had acted because the count served a government that "went against
the people and hanged [them]," and also because Ignat'ev "was close to the
court."[109]

Local SR groups and individual party members, as opposed to the Combat
Organization and other terrorist units in the capital, directed their efforts
against less prominent enemies than Nepliuev and Ignat'ev, often because
there were not many high officials in their areas to serve as targets. They also
showed little compassion for police agents and traitors in their own ranks,
proclaiming, "Spies must be eliminated at all times simply because they are
spies."[110] In this attitude the SRs differed little from their revolutionary predecessors, but it was only in the bloodstained years beginning in 1905 that they
began to direct their efforts against large numbers of such low-ranking targets
as local street policemen, gendarmes, prison officials and military personnel,
as well as private individuals, including factory managers, guards, and dvorniks, all considered "active forces of reaction."[111]

The rationale behind these assassinations, as stated by the revolutionaries
themselves, reveals a great deal about their new perception of the way the
antigovernment struggle was to be conducted. During a meeting of a special
combat committee (*boevoi komitet*) under the St. Petersburg PSR Committee
that took place on 14 September 1906 in Finland, the revolutionaries resolved

"to begin partisan warfare immediately not only to acquire [financial] means or to inflict some damage on the government by killing a specific police official, but mainly to keep the militant spirit up in the [combat] detachments by constant partisan attacks [and] to accustom them to danger, thereby keeping them in practice."[112]

Only one person present at the meeting, a representative of the Central Committee, argued strongly against the random murder of street policemen, considering it "senseless to kill a person only because he wears a uniform." After some debate, the revolutionaries reached a compromise, adopting a resolution in keeping with the general spirit of the gathering: "not to assassinate individual street policemen, but to distribute leaflets [demanding] that everyone leave police service. Those who do not quit will be proclaimed enemies of the people and . . . killed while on duty."[113]

As if to qualify themselves as terrorists of the new type, the SRs were prepared by 1905 to kill representatives of the hated regime en masse. On many occasions this intention did not remain on paper only: SR terrorists tossed bombs at passing military detachments in Ekaterinoslav and Odessa, and at Cossack squadrons in Gomel'.[114] In one incident a member of a local SR committee planted a homemade bomb under a railroad car carrying low-ranking gendarmes, slightly wounding several of them.[115] The SRs also planned train wrecks, and in December 1905 made unsuccessful preparations to destroy a train carrying government troops to Moscow to suppress the uprising.[116]

In their composition, membership, and ideological sophistication, the local terrorist groups also differed significantly from the revolutionary idealists of previous generations. Indeed, Combat Organization members who deviated from or disregarded orthodox PSR thought were truly representative of the entire new breed of terrorists, for more often than not local combatants were equally uninterested in dogmatic questions and theoretical controversies in the socialist world. Many intrepid *boeviki*, while fully prepared to spill blood and die in the fight for freedom, discarded theoretical issues with disdain and did not possess enough rudimentary knowledge of class theory to be called socialists. SR N. D. Shishmarev, for example, who killed Mogilev, head of the Tobol'sk hard labor prison, in August 1909, openly stated that activists who became too preoccupied with dogmatic issues lost much of their revolutionary zeal, resolve, and determination. Shishmarev's comrades were well aware that he was hardly a strict adherent to the party program, but since "in those times militant temperament [and revolutionary] enthusiasm were valued more than anything else," they considered him a true SR, notwithstanding his flaws in the sphere of theory.[117]

Similarly, more than a few revolutionaries joined SR terrorist groups without familiarizing themselves with the general goals and principles of the party. Grigorii Frolov, a former woodworker responsible for the assassination of

Governor Blok of Samara, admitted that he was "completely inexperienced in the revolutionary sense," having met true revolutionaries only twice in his life while serving short prison terms for minor political offenses. Initially Frolov had been attracted to the Bolsheviks, but soon turned to the more militant SRs, and involved himself in PSR combat activities not because he had become a convinced Socialist-Revolutionary or terrorist, but for no better reason than "to find out what kind of party it was."[118] Many years after the end of his terrorist career, describing the head of the Samara *boeviki* in his memoirs, Frolov still wondered "why it so happened that the process of choosing members for such extremely important organizations as the combat groups was assigned to a very young and absolutely inexperienced nineteen-year-old comrade, totally incapable of selecting the right people."[119] So limited was the political awareness of some revolutionaries that one such liberator of the people, while fully prepared to help a terrorist organization, in his zeal made no effort to determine its exact title and party affiliation.[120]

Given the limited theoretical preparation of its combatants, the party could not expect them to demonstrate any awareness of its principle requirement of integrating terrorist operations with the various manifestations of the mass movement in the country. The overwhelming majority of local political assassinations were carried out in complete isolation from the revolutionary activities of the toilers, a fact the SR leaders occasionally implicitly admitted by stating that the much-desired armed uprising was impossible in the near future, while at the same time urging the combatants to proceed with the killing of petty officials and low-ranking policemen.[121]

This is not to say that terrorism was never associated with the economic struggle. In 1905, for example, the SRs in Riga killed dozens of factory managers and directors they held responsible for harsh working conditions or knew as opponents of labor strikes and other forms of worker protest.[122] In the same period there were special PSR combat units in the Urals that used terrorism to advance the workers' movement in this industrial region.[123] In the Caucasus the SRs played an active role in the Caspian sailors' strike in Baku, where terrorists operating under the direction of the SR party committee in the spring of 1907 issued letters threatening employers who refused to rehire strikers. They also blew up a large ship, causing approximately sixty thousand rubles in damage, and murdered a ship captain who tried to stop the disturbances.[124]

Reluctant to conform blindly to the official party principles, many SR activists felt compelled to reevaluate their personal positions vis-à-vis individual and economic terror. Their new views often deviated significantly from orthodox Socialist-Revolutionary thinking, and attempts by the PSR leadership to bring the heretics under stricter central control caused many of them to break away from the parent organization to join a separate faction, the Maximalists.

THE MAXIMALISTS

From the very formation of the PSR, the party defined and promoted political terror as "attacks on government officials, including spies and informers." Beginning approximately in 1904, however, groups emerged within the SR forces that advocated the use of economic terror "as a means of integrating terrorist activity more closely into the mass movement." Economic terrorism, incorporated in 1905–1906 into the broader Maximalist trend, assumed various forms, including agrarian and factory terror (*agrarnyi i fabrichnyi terror*), and revolutionary expropriations.[125]

From the outset, the attitude of the PSR toward agrarian terror was ambivalent. On the one hand, as early as 1902 the SR Peasant Union recommended peaceful means of economic struggle, such as wage strikes and rent boycotts, but added that if these were unsuccessful the peasants should resort to "destructive violence against the landowner—illegal pasturing of animals and chopping of wood," arson (in peasant jargon, the "red rooster"—*krasnyi petukh*), the seizure of crops and foodstuffs, raids on estate buildings, and violence against landowners and their agents.[126] On the other hand, the SR leaders often renounced agrarian terror since it was difficult for the party to control the traditional peasant violence against landowners and their property and to guide it in accordance with the party's general goals in the countryside.[127] At the same time, the SR leadership feared that the PSR "might become isolated from the 'spontaneous' peasant movement if it condemned all forms of economic struggle other than peaceful and organized ones."[128]

This last consideration forced a number of SRs to form a group of agrarian terrorists in Geneva, under the leadership of a veteran Populist, Ekaterina Breshko-Breshkovskaia (Babushka or the Grandmother of the Russian revolution), and M. I. Sokolov (Cain, or "the bear"), who by 1904 began to insist that the party play an active role in all peasant activities, including the militant ones, initiating and coordinating violent acts in the countryside. In November of the same year the Geneva group issued a resolution on special combat detachments to carry out "local agrarian and political terror with the goal of eliminating and disorganizing all direct representatives and agents of the contemporary ruling classes."[129]

The followers of Breshkovskaia and Sokolov were on the whole the younger and more radical SR practitioners, who came to be opposed by the older generation of emigré revolutionaries. In general, those who sought to prevent the party's involvement in agrarian terror were more at ease with theory than with fieldwork among the peasantry. And they demonstrated genuine fear of the spreading anarchy in the countryside, arguing that the party should stay away from it since it was nearly impossible to control peasant violence.

The Central Committee was prepared to compromise with the advocates of agrarian terror, and allow acts against the Cossacks and guards on the landowners' estates, proclaiming such attacks part of the political, rather than the economic, struggle.[130] In certain cases the SR leadership also explicitly advocated violence against landowners and their property.[131] Moreover, the Central Committee permitted the agrarian terrorists, a minority within the PSR, to remain in the party and promote their views, provided they did not preach them to the peasants. Sokolov, however, upon his return to Russia, immediately violated this condition and in fact began to agitate for other forms of economic terror as well, urging the workers and peasants to "beat up tsarist officials, capitalists and landowners."[132] His attempts to convert the SRs throughout the empire to agrarian terrorism were quite successful, particularly in the western provinces, the Ukraine, and Belorussia, but in April 1905 Sokolov and his followers were arrested in the town of Kursk, an event that "virtually destroyed the agrarian terrorists as an organized faction within the party."[133]

Still, in the words of Perrie, "Agrarian terrorism was a plank in the Maximalist programmes of 1906, . . . [although] SR-Maximalism was in practice more concerned with economic terror in an urban rather than a rural context."[134] For the Maximalists economic terror in the urban areas meant primarily factory terror, that is, the use of coercion against the lives or property of factory owners to promote the workers' cause in the economic struggle. Factory terror came to be especially widespread in industrial regions such as the Urals, as well as in the Caucasus and the northwestern provinces, notably in the town of Belostok. Maximalist policies were based on an underlying conviction that "only with bombs can . . . we make the bourgeois grant concessions."[135] And the official SR position was as ambiguous on the issue of factory terror as it was on agrarian terrorism: while criticizing and often condemning it in theory, party leaders allowed and even encouraged terrorist acts against capitalists.[136]

Predictably, the attitude of the Maximalists toward political assassination was also more radical than that of the orthodox SRs. Repelled by what they regarded as excessive central control of the SR terrorists and lack of autonomy in the PSR combat policies, especially following the October 1905 PSR decision to halt terrorist activities, the Maximalists broke all formal ties with the party early in 1906, and united into the Union of SR-Maximalists (Soiuz eserov-maksimalistov).[137] Throughout the single year of the Maximalist Union's existence as a separate political entity, its members, headed by Sokolov (himself a onetime member of the SR Combat Organization), were involved in a number of sensationally bloody terrorist attacks, and were responsible for much indiscriminate violence before the arrests of more than one hundred revolutionaries in the summer and fall of 1906 split the organization into disconnected groups of a semianarchist character.[138]

Chernov had good reason to describe the terrorist practices of the Maximalists as pogrom-like mass killings, for they acknowledged that the history of their movement was marked by a "criminally light-minded attitude toward their own and other people's lives."[139] This was the result not of occasional misbehavior by individual terrorists, but of officially sanctioned policy; at the First Conference of the SR-Maximalists, held in October 1906, the group's leaders resolved to turn away from separate terrorist attacks to mass terror. Those present at the conference voted to undertake combat actions not only against the most hated representatives of the administration, but also against entire institutions, arguing, "Where it is not enough to remove one person, it is necessary to eliminate them by the dozen; where dozens are not enough, they must be gotten rid of in hundreds."[140]

Perhaps the most shocking example of this lack of concern for human life was an attempt on the life of Stolypin on 12 August 1906. Three Maximalists, two dressed in the uniforms of gendarme officers, and one in civilian clothes, tried to enter Stolypin's villa on Aptekar'skii Island in St. Petersburg, but were stopped by the guards, and with the cry, "Long live freedom, long live anarchy!" blew themselves up in the anteroom with sixteen-pound bombs.[141] Gerasimov, who arrived soon after the explosion, described the scene: "The whole house was shrouded in heavy smoke. The entire facade was destroyed. All around lay fragments of the balcony and the roof. Under the debris—the broken carriage and writhing wounded horses. Moans were heard all around. There were pieces of human flesh and blood everywhere."[142] By chance the explosion caused relatively little harm to one room—Stolypin's office. He thus survived another terrorist attempt on his life, and the only damage he suffered was the staining of his face and clothing when his ink well was thrown from his desk by the force of the explosion.[143] The location and timing of this assassination attempt provide a perfect example of Maximalist indifference to the value of human life, for these radicals chose to carry out the act when it was easiest to approach the Prime Minister—during his visiting hour. They thus became responsible not only for injuring Stolypin's fourteen-year-old daughter and four-year-old son, but also for a total of approximately sixty other casualties, of whom, according to official statistics, twenty-seven were killed, including women and several elderly people.[144]

The attempt on Stolypin's life also demonstrates the Maximalist tendency to plan major operations in the capital, where they could kill large numbers of people in each operation, maximizing impact. One of their proposed actions was an attack against the St. Petersburg Okhrana. The plan entailed sending a carriage full of dynamite into the courtyard in front of the police building where it was to explode with tremendous force. The Maximalists prepared enough explosives to destroy the massive structure entirely, with the intention of killing all Okhrana personnel present, either by fire or by burying them under the debris.[145] According to police sources, the Maximalist dissidents, like their counterparts in the SR Northern Flying Combat Detachment, also made plans for a terrorist act against the State Council, and for a major explosion in the tsar's residence at the Winter Palace.[146]

In Moscow, the Maximalists demonstrated a similar lack of discrimination in designating targets and an equal carelessness in execution of their plans. After the defeat of the December uprising, many who had survived the fight on the barricades began to specialize in individual terrorist acts, and launched a campaign to hunt down rank-and-file members of the police force. In one case, a Maximalist, with typical disregard for his own life, rang the doorbell of a police-occupied apartment, and then fired randomly at anyone who showed up in the corridor. He escaped, leaving at least three people dead.[147]

In the outlying areas the Maximalists seemed even more anxious to fire at anyone who wore a police or military uniform,[148] and in addition were commonly involved in acts of violence with criminal undertones. Having evaded control by the SR leadership, members of at least sixty-eight Maximalist organizations operating throughout the empire by 1907[149] gradually ceased to see any obstacles to a campaign of what came to be, along with agrarian and factory terror, the third aspect of their policy of unrestrained economic terror—revolutionary expropriations, to which both the SRs and the Maximalists resorted in practice far more frequently than to agrarian and factory violence.

EXPROPRIATIONS

While the SR Combat Organization directed its efforts exclusively to assassination, never claiming responsibility for assaults on private property or the state's economic institutions, SR groups in the periphery engaged in such forms of revolutionary violence as robberies, financial confiscations, forced donations, and other means of expropriation. The local SRs began confiscating private and state property primarily in the western provinces as early as 1904, and by mid-1906 these acts reached epidemic proportions, inflicting losses totaling millions of rubles on the state and on private individuals throughout the empire. Many local SR organizations operated mainly on expropriated funds,[150] thus forcing the party leadership to begin paying particular attention to the issue of politically motivated robberies.

The SR leaders quickly became aware that in practice actions theoretically considered revolutionary expropriations often turned into purely criminal undertakings that attracted a variety of shady individuals and even undisguised bandits into the socialist ranks. It was not at all unusual for a small combat unit that had originated and initially operated under the direction of a local SR organization to separate from the parent group over time, with the *boeviki* "acting independently, procuring means for their party, as well as for their own upkeep, through assaults and threats. . . . Their activity more and more amounted to acquiring means exclusively for themselves. Soon, they formulated an appropriate ideology . . . and became anarchists," terrorizing the peaceful population.[151] As cases of extortion, blackmail, arbitrary illegal taxes and dues, violent attacks, and other forms of expropriation multiplied, becoming particularly common after the revolution began to suffer serious defeats in the second half of 1906, these activities served to lower the party's prestige and increase the general demoralization among the local activists.[152] In response the PSR leadership sought to develop a formal policy vis-à-vis expropriations, and found it necessary to alter its views several times, always in the direction of limiting the conditions under which expropriations were permissible.

During the debates at the First Party Congress in late December 1905 and early January 1906, the SRs initiated discussion on the issue of expropriation, for although by the time this gathering took place, SR-perpetrated robberies were not yet common, they did occasionally occur. They became so frequent and violent over the course of the next year, however, that a number of SR leaders began to express alarm. One person determined to fight the expropriations, which he considered common criminal acts and an immeasurable evil, was Gershuni. For this terrorist leader the issue was not a matter of "bourgeois ethics": the party had to "fight this evil . . . not because of the 'sanctity of private property,' but because these [acts] destroy and corrupt . . . [the SR] organizations, debase the revolution, and sap its strength."[153] He attempted to convince his fellow party members of the "incredible demoralization that the expropriations bring into the ranks of the revolutionary activists," and also argued in his usual pragmatic style that the amount of money already lost by the party because potential donors were outraged by the practice of expropriation and "shied away from helping the revolution," was greater than the total amount acquired in all revolutionary robberies combined.[154] Gershuni then urged the SRs to put a stop not only to the expropriation of private property, but also, with rare exceptions, to revolutionary robberies of any kind, imploring party organizations not to accept or use stolen money.[155]

The majority of the SR leadership, however, did not share Gershuni's concern for the purity of the party's reputation and its revolutionary ideals, and in the fall of 1906 the Second Party Council approved the expropriation of money and weapons belonging to the state. There were two qualifications to this decree: revolutionary robberies were permitted exclusively under the control of the SR regional committees, and during these acts arms could be used only against policemen and gendarmes. Anyone who participated in expropriations of private property was to be expelled from the PSR.[156] This decision, as well as many similar resolutions issued by local organizations aiming to stop the spread of this semianarchist behavior among the SRs in the periphery,[157] produced little effect, and after passionate debate at the Second Congress in February of 1907, the party leadership agreed that the expropriation of state property was to be sanctioned only under the close direction of the Central Committee, and that in all such acts the participants must strive to keep their attacks bloodless.[158]

Still, the SR leaders could not ignore the fact that, in the words of Perrie, "once the principle of terrorist violence against life and property was conceded, it was impossible to place limits on its application."[159] In fact, none of the criteria established by the party leadership for "legitimate" robberies were ever observed by rank-and-file party members. The expropriation of private property continued, despite all efforts of the SRs to disguise this fact.[160] Outraged comrades occasionally took action against the offenders, and a number of SRs were expelled from the party for assaulting grocery stores and small businesses; some were killed for "banditry" and for staging "revolting expropriations."[161] This did little to curtail the practice, however, and provincial and district committees then chose between two options: they either accepted and justified limited private expropriations as permissible "because of the critical [historical] moment," or asserted categorically in their leaflets that perpetrators of local expropriations who undertook robberies in the name of the PSR in reality had nothing to do with the party.[162] This was probably true in some cases, but in many others the SRs obviously tried to evade responsibility for acts illegal even from the party's standpoint. Notably, one SR apprehended after a private expropriation planned to proclaim himself a Maximalist or an independent revolutionary during his trial, "in order not to compromise the honor of the SR Party."[163]

Equally frequently the SRs were responsible for acts of extortion, in which a person of means would receive a carelessly handwritten note bearing the local party seal with a statement similar to the following: "The Worker's Organization of the Party of Socialists-Revolutionaries in Belostok requires you to contribute immediately . . . seventy-five rubles. . . . The Organization warns you that if you fail to give the above-stated sum, it will resort to severe measures against you, transferring your case to the Combat Detachment."[164]

SRs also commonly disregarded the second qualification established by party leaders in connection with revolutionary robberies, that is, that expropriations were to be conducted under the strict control of the Central Committee. Local SR groups rarely informed the central leadership about assaults planned against state and private property, and also failed to report acts that had already taken place. Moreover, individual SRs frequently perpetrated expropriations on their own initiative and at their own risk, without first seeking the sanction of even their local organizations.[165] It is therefore virtually impossible to establish exactly how many of the hundreds of expropriations that occurred in banks, post offices, state liquor stores, private shops, churches, clinics, and all other imaginable institutions and businesses throughout the empire after 1905 were carried out by Socialists-Revolutionaries.

Many expropriations were far from bloodless, for numerous SRs in the periphery failed to make serious efforts to spare the lives of innocent bystanders.[166] Individuals they considered exploiters were particularly vulnerable, and the extremists included in this category not only landowners, store proprietors, and other capitalists, but also those who, though far from wealthy, happened to be in the way of the revolutionaries by virtue of their employment as police or in the private service of the wealthy. Some SR expropriators victimized the poor, occasionally even robbing and murdering peasants.[167] Moreover, the worst fears of some SR leaders did materialize: corrupted by frequent and indiscriminate violence and easy profits, many SR combatants distanced themselves from the party's objectives and goals, and began to lead lives of debauchery financed by money allegedly confiscated for revolutionary purposes.[168]

These tendencies were evident to an even greater extent among the Maximalists, who were more extreme than their former SR comrades both in the use of assassination as a revolutionary tool and in their approach to expropriation. The Union of SR-Maximalists in fact did not place any restrictions on the way expropriations of money and property were to be conducted, thus allowing its adherents in the periphery complete freedom in determination of targets and methods. As a result, Maximalist enterprises were often more reminiscent of common crimes than of the idealistic exploits of revolutionary socialists. With equal frequency, the practices of local Maximalists, operating under no authority strong enough to prevent them from abusing what they saw as their revolutionary right to confiscate superfluous funds, were indistinguishable from those of the anarchists who on principle refused to recognize any authority whatsoever.

By the spring of 1906 the opposition faction of the Moscow SR Committee, soon to be incorporated into the Union of SR-Maximalists, became independent from the PSR not only in tactical policies (resorting to terrorist practices after the Central Committee explicitly stated its intention to cease militant activities), but also in financial matters. On 7 March of that year its combat group, headed by former Moscow University student Vladimir Mazurin, expropriated approximately eight hundred thousand rubles from the Merchant Bank of Moscow.[169] This abundance of funds enabled the oppositionists to attract a number of local SR organizations into the dissident camp at the expense of the PSR, literally bribing and buying committees in Ekaterinoslav, Riazan', and Stavropol', along with several groups in the Caucasus and the capitals. Leaders of the opposition and Maximalist factions were thus able to gather substantial forces under their command, although the new movement was significantly weakened by petty squabbles among individual revolutionaries and entire groups over the use of the expropriated funds, and by mutual accusations of waste and embezzlement.[170]

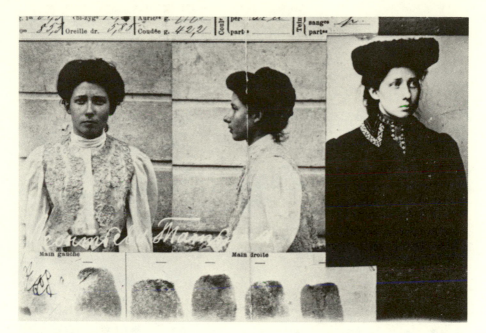

8. Tat'iana Leont'eva

9. Mikhail Sokolov

10. Stolypin's office after the 12 August 1906 Maximalist attack

11. Vladimir Mazurin

In the meantime the armed robberies continued, and on 14 October 1906 several combatants from Sokolov's group, acting under the leadership of one Comrade Sergei, carried out the most spectacular robbery of state funds ever executed by the Maximalists, the Fonarnyi Lane (Fonarnyi pereulok) expropriation, which took place on the street of that name in St. Petersburg. Armed with browning pistols, the revolutionaries attacked a heavily guarded carriage transporting more than six hundred thousand rubles in bank notes and currency from the St. Petersburg harbor customs office to the Treasury and the State Bank. The Maximalists counted on the element of surprise and staged their assault at noon on a crowded street in the very heart of the capital. Several combatants began to shoot at the convoy and throw bombs, while the rest of the expropriators managed to snatch sacks containing nearly four hundred thousand rubles. They swiftly transferred the money to a waiting carriage occupied by a lady whose face was hidden under a veil, and then sped away, leaving their comrades to cover their escape with rapid fire at the police.[171]

While few local Maximalist groups could aspire to prizes of this magnitude, throughout the country Maximalist radicals, daring to the point of fanaticism and often willing to risk lives for the most insignificant rewards, were responsible for a large number of smaller robberies that in their sheer quantity contributed greatly to the enormous damages suffered by the state and by private citizens. In St. Petersburg an independent Maximalist unit headed by Nikolai Liubomudrov carried out a series of minor expropriations, robbing grocery stores, street vendors, bars, post offices, and churches. In contrast to the SRs, they made no attempt to differentiate between state and private property in their expropriation efforts, and their simple logic had much more in common with primitive anarchism than with scientific socialism: "If there is no work, no salary, nothing to live on, then one has to expropriate money, food, and clothing"; the struggle with the exploiters was to be conducted by one means only—economic terrorism.[172] Similar attitudes guided many Maximalist groups in the periphery, who also frequently engaged in extortion, dispatching letters to local wealthy citizens threatening execution if money were not delivered expeditiously.[173]

THE PURIFICATION OF MANKIND

Few documents shed better light on some of the shadier aspects of the Russian Socialist Revolutionary movement than *The Purification of Mankind* (*Ochistka chelovechestva*), a booklet written by Ivan Pavlov, one of the chief theoreticians of Maximalism, that came out in Moscow in 1907. Ignored in the scholarly literature, the essay presents an illuminating discussion of the theory and methodology exemplary of the new type of terrorism. It was written in the period when the Maximalist trend had already begun its steady decline and was suffering systematic defeats under the particularly effective measures of the authorities, who by that time were arresting one revolutionary circle after another. Although this treatise did not become an official part of the Maximalist platform, it does incorporate a number of fundamental Maximalist ideas, and may thus be regarded as true to the direction taken by an extremist branch of Socialist-Revolutionary thought.

According to Pavlov, mankind is divided not only into ethnic, but also into ethical races. From his perspective, those who control political authority (representatives of the government, bureaucracy, and the police), as well as economic power (the capitalists and all other exploiters) acquire so many negative traits that they must be isolated into a separate race, based on their moral worthlessness. This race of predators was, in Pavlov's words, "morally inferior to our animal predecessors: the vile characteristics of the gorilla and the orangutan progressed and developed in it to proportions unprecedented in the animal world. There is no beast in comparison with which these types do not appear to be monsters."[174]

Perhaps the most threatening aspect of this situation for the camp opposite the predator race, that is, for the morally superior race (among whom Pavlov counted "the best altruists" in the revolutionary movement, and especially the terrorists), was that negative qualities were inevitably transmitted by the villains to succeeding generations. Most children of oppressors and exploiters were, according to the author, bound to "exhibit the same malice, cruelty, meanness, rapacity, and greed" as their parents.[175] It followed then that in order to save, or purify, mankind from the menace of the rapidly multiplying forces of these morally corrupt and bestial degenerates, their entire race must be exterminated before they took over the world. Developing his thesis in very broad terms, Pavlov left unanswered the question of the exact methods whereby the worst part of the human species was to be destroyed; the practical details could be worked out later.[176]

Pavlov's brochure thus advocated organized mass terror on the largest possible scale, namely, true civil war, with one section of the population aiming to eliminate the other completely. In its sweeping cruelty and advocation of endless violence to justify a theoretical principle, this essay was unprecedented not only in the Russian revolutionary tradition, but also in modern radical thought in general. What was especially significant, however, was that it aroused no negative feelings, indignation, or protests, and even failed to provoke controversy within the ranks of the Maximalists or, for that matter, among socialists of any other ideological trend. Amid the anarchy and bloodshed reigning in Russia at the time the booklet was written, the new type of revolutionary did not seem at all repulsed by Pavlov's theory of races, perhaps regarding it as an original analysis of the contemporary socioeconomic and political climate. Nor was Pavlov alone in advocating mass terror for the purpose of creating a superior social order. Another former Populist-turned-

Maximalist, M. A. Engel'gardt, also argued in favor of red terror en masse, and even calculated that in order for socialism to take strong root in Russia, it would be necessary to eliminate no fewer than twelve million counterrevolutionaries, including land and factory owners, bankers, and priests.[177]

Although the Maximalists did not accept Pavlov's treatise as an outline of the formal program for their movement, he continued to be considered "the brightest ideologist of Maximalism."[178] It is worth speculating whether it is simply a historical coincidence that in the twentieth century, which has been dominated by totalitarian ideology and persecutions—first in accordance with Marxist class principles and then as a result of Nazi preoccupation with race and ethnicity—the initial traits of totalitarianism were in evidence among the revolutionary extremists in Russia, and in particular among the Maximalists, who were directly descended from the Party of Socialists-Revolutionaries and regarded by the SRs as flesh of their flesh.[179] There is no doubt, in any case, that in their practical implementation of terrorist tactics many SRs and Maximalists clearly demonstrated behavior characteristic of the new type of revolutionary. Their unorthodox disregard of both ideology and the disciplinary obligations imposed by their central organizations, as well as their unrestricted indulgence in bloodshed and the confiscation of private property, classify these combatants as representatives of the new generation of extremists commonly found after the turn of the century not only within the Socialist-Revolutionary ranks, but also in other trends inside the Russian radical camp.

Chapter Three

THE SOCIAL DEMOCRATS AND TERROR

> All our combat and terrorist work is now a matter of history.
> If twenty-five years ago we did not make a show of this aspect of
> our activity for tactical reasons, at present those considerations
> are no longer sound. The Social Democrats committed
> many acts of partisan warfare.
> —*N. M. Rostov*[1]

IN THEIR CREDO and tactics the Russian Social Democrats consistently declared their opposition to participation in the widespread terrorist activity that plagued Russia in the early years of the twentieth century. Prominent members of the Russian Social Democratic Labor Party (RSDRP) typically asserted that "using bombs for individual terrorist acts was out of the question since the party rejected individual terror as a means of struggle" with the government.[2] Frequent references to the theoretical incompatibility of the scientific laws of Marxist doctrine with political assassination have led historians studying the period to assume that the various SD factions rejected terrorism in practice as well.[3] The facts, however, suggest the contrary, namely, that token Marxist declarations opposing the terrorist struggle did not prevent any of the Social Democratic organizations operating in the Russian Empire at the time from supporting and often participating in individual acts of political violence. While in terms of sheer numbers the impact of SD-perpetrated terror on Russian daily life was limited in comparison with that of the SRs or the anarchists, the terrorist and expropriation activities of the SDs cannot be ignored.

BACKGROUND AND ANTITERRORIST THEORY

The debate among revolutionaries over the appropriateness of individual political assassination as a means of attaining revolutionary ends did not originate with the formation of Social Democratic organizations at the end of the nineteenth century. It can be traced as far back as the period of the first major revolutionary organization in Russia, Land and Freedom (Zemlia i volia), in the late 1870s. By the beginning of the twentieth century the controversy was thus well established.

One of the most critical issues leading to the schism in the Land and Freedom organization in the summer of 1879 was the debate over terrorism. The textbook assumption that one faction of the party, the People's Will, established itself as a relentless practitioner of political assassination, while the other group, Black Partition (Chernyi peredel), became an ardent opponent of individual terrorist acts, is not entirely accurate. In the first place, even before the schism Land and Freedom had been responsible for a number of bloody attacks on government officials, many of them successful.[4] Moreover, Black Partition leaders Georgii Plekhanov, Vera Zasulich, and Lev Deich, who in Geneva in 1883 formed the first Russian Social Democratic organization, Liberation of Labor (Osvobozhdenie truda), initially did not oppose terrorism on any practical or moral grounds. In fact, two members of this trio were personally implicated in terrorist attacks: Zasulich wounded Trepov, governor-general of St. Petersburg, in January 1878, setting a wave of revolutionary terror in motion in Russia; Deich instigated and took part in an 1876 act intended to punish an alleged traitor, his former comrade N. E. Gorinovich, personally beating him with a club and torturing him by pouring sulfuric acid over his face.[5]

In the first program issued by the Liberation of Labor group in 1884, Plekhanov and his colleagues recognized "the necessity of the terrorist struggle against the absolutist government," claiming to "disagree with the Party of the People's Will only in questions of the so-called seizure of power and . . . the immediate activity of socialists in the working class milieu."[6] They did not reject terror, but felt that the People's Will put too much emphasis on unrealistic plans for a coup d'état, and dedicated excessive energy and resources to individual acts at the expense of other crucial aspects of the revolutionary struggle, particularly propaganda among the masses. Indeed, far from suggesting that terrorist tactics be eliminated, Plekhanov seemed to assign them a primary role in future revolutionary developments: "There is no other strata besides the workers that in the decisive moment can bring down and finish off the political monster wounded by the terrorists. Propaganda among the workers will not eliminate the necessity for the terrorist struggle, but will create for it new and unprecedented opportunities."[7]

At the birth of the Russian Social Democratic movement, the revolutionaries thus disagreed only on the scope of terrorism relative to other modes of antigovernment activity. Over the decades of political effort and theoretical debate terrorism came to be regarded as a crucial point of disagreement among the revolutionaries, for the advocates of individual acts of violence as effective tools to overthrow the government did not consider them the only appropriate methods of struggle. And since all radical socialists recognized the importance of mobilizing the masses (whether peasant or proletarian), and disagreed only on the effectiveness of one-man action, the latter became a key point in establishing party differences.

As the controversy gained importance in the eyes of the radicals, despite the relative inactivity of the terrorists in the late 1880s and early 1890s, opponents of terrorist tactics felt an increasing need to justify their viewpoint by means

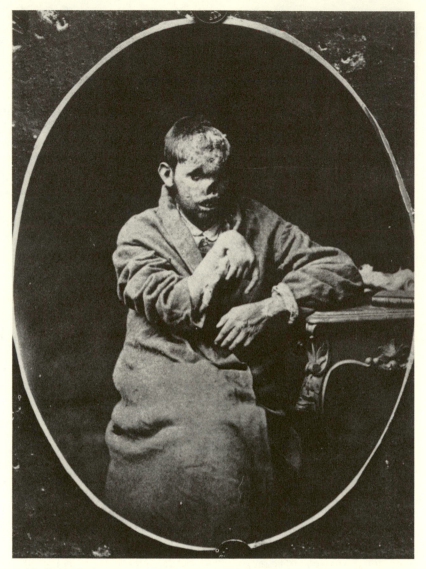

12. N. E. Gorinovich, victim of 1876 terrorist attack

of a scientific principle. They took initial steps in this direction in the last years of the century, at a time when advocates of terrorism were attempting to resurrect the practice. Subsequently, after the formation of what came to be the major rival for the Social Democrats—the Party of Socialists-Revolutionaries, which openly incorporated terrorism into its program—it was even more expedient for the Social Democrats (by 1903 also united into a single party)

13. Lev Deich, one of Gorinovich's attackers

to strengthen their antiterrorist stand by giving it a theoretical foundation. They settled on Marxist principles as the basis for a campaign of criticism launched on the pages of their periodicals against all proponents of political terror.

In this they proved more orthodox than Marx himself, who had paid tribute to revolutionary terrorism as an appropriate method of struggle under certain historical circumstances.[8] Still, the dogmatic adoption of class doctrine compelled the SDs to insist that rather than sacrificing their young lives for a tactic that was doomed to failure, a more effective course of action for the combatants would be to direct their efforts toward agitation among the true forces of progress, the proletarian masses, against the oppressive socioeconomic and political order.

In addition to their historical public opposition to terrorism, a tradition fortified by a new Marxist theoretical foundation, the SDs had another reason to resist compromising their official stand on political assassinations: the issue provided a useful tool in their efforts to recruit followers at the expense of the

PSR. Regardless of all other considerations, theoretical or tactical, the SD leaders felt the need to separate themselves from the leadership of the SR organization, with whom the SDs were unable to agree not only on how to bring about revolution, but even on how to organize and lead their cadres in this prerevolutionary stage.

Reluctant to relinquish control over their respective parties' central organs and, more significantly, their financial resources, the leaders of the RSDRP and the PSR stubbornly preferred to be generals of smaller armies, without having to share power with outsiders, even if united they would have commanded a significantly larger force. Having chosen to pursue their common revolutionary goals on their own, separate from the PSR, the Social Democrats, who already faced problems competing with the Socialists-Revolutionaries for support for their respective agrarian programs, sought to compensate by criticizing the SRs, along with all other proponents of terrorist action, for their inability to comprehend and adhere to the iron laws of Marxist doctrine.[9] The issue of terrorism thus became a pawn in interparty political intrigues.[10]

By the fall of 1902 every issue of the official SD organ *Iskra* (Spark) addressed the growing threat of terrorism. The SD newspaper campaign was part of their "resolute and systematic struggle against the terrorist tactics proclaimed and implemented by the SRs."[11] Particularly noteworthy were the reactions of the SD publications to the February 1901 attempt on the life of Minister of Education Bogolepov by Petr Karpovich, and to the April 1902 assassination of Minister of the Interior Sipiagin by Stepan Balmashev. Whereas most independent socialists and revolutionaries who adhered to the People's Will ideology (many of whom subsequently entered the ranks of the PSR) glorified the heroic deeds of Karpovich and Balmashev as the beginning of a new era of terrorism, leaders of the Russian Social Democratic movement such as Zasulich came out strongly against terrorist methods: "The transfer of control over the struggle for liberation to a handful of heroes . . . will not harm autocracy," for it would leave the toiling masses and broad general public in the position of passive observers.[12] Plekhanov was no less critical in his comments on the Karpovich affair on the pages of the SD publication *Zaria* (Dawn):

> Terrorist activity and political agitation among the masses . . . can go hand in hand, supporting and complementing each other only under the most infrequent and absolutely exceptional conditions. Today we do not have a single one of these conditions, which will not appear for a long time yet. At present, terror is not expedient, and therefore it is *harmful.*[13]

Lenin also came out solidly against the PSR terrorist tactic, arguing that "by incorporating terrorism into its program and by preaching it as a means of political struggle . . . the Socialists-Revolutionaries are causing the most serious harm to the movement, destroying the inseparable link between socialist work and the masses of the revolutionary class."[14] In his view, terrorist activity distracted the potential organizers of the proletariat from this truly essential task and since, as he put it, "without the working people, all bombs are . . . powerless *a priori*," terror disrupted "not the government, but the revolutionary forces."[15]

Along with the *Iskra* group, other Social Democrats joined in these antiterrorist outbursts. Contributors to the newspaper *Iuzhnyi rabochii* (Southern Worker) emphasized that terror was "not a new means of struggle; this method was already tried once and turned out to be worthless. . . . This is why terror was unanimously rejected when the revolutionary movement was reborn in Russia under the banner of Social Democracy. . . . There was no more talk about terror: the revolutionaries had learned by bitter experience."[16] *Arbeiter Stimme* (Workers' Voice), official organ of the Jewish Bund, proclaimed, "The struggle should not be of individual people against individual oppressors; we will achieve our goals only by means of the organized struggle of the entire working class against the political and economic regime as a whole."[17] Finally, in the summer of 1901 at a conference held abroad and attended by representatives of all Russian Social Democratic organizations, the revolutionaries adopted the following resolution: "We consider it necessary to oppose decisively the view that terror must be a required concomitant to the political struggle in Russia."[18]

Although Social Democrats of various affiliations approached the issue of terrorism in this manner on a theoretical level, and this was what they chose to proclaim publicly when it came to defining their general outlook, differentiating between those who developed and popularized official party goals and slogans, and those who implemented them in practice is crucial.[19] The latter were seldom concerned with any historical tradition of rivalry between the advocates and opponents of terrorist tactics, particularly since many of them had sympathized in their youth with the terrorists; some changed sides frequently in the debate over terror.[20] Nor were many of them preoccupied with adhering to the strict orthodoxy of Marxist doctrine; conversely, relatively few of the professional revolutionaries operating in the empire possessed a thorough knowledge of theory, or, for that matter, much interest in it.[21] Finally, a large percentage of the SD rank and file were indifferent to interparty rivalries in Geneva and Paris, and in fact regarded the SRs and other supporters of terror as *comrades d'armes* in their everyday conspiratorial work.[22] For all these reasons, their attitudes toward terrorism differed substantially from the picture portrayed by their party leaders on the pages of their official publications.

Moreover, some party functionaries concerned themselves exclusively at times with theoretical questions, but at other stages of their revolutionary careers found themselves required to become practitioners and formulate their views vis-à-vis terrorism from an entirely different standpoint. Lenin was one such revolutionary. His pre-1905 theoretical statements opposing terrorism, directed first and foremost against the SRs, are in obvious contradiction of his practical policies with regard to terrorist methods implemented after the outbreak of revolutionary activities in 1905, under the altered circumstances and new concerns of the day.

Terrorism in Practice: The Bolsheviks

For Lenin, as leader of the Bolshevik faction of the RSDRP, the proper stand on the issue of terrorism was never a question that could be settled once and for all; his position varied with changes in his political objectives and priorities.[23] Accordingly, in 1902 he castigated his SR rivals for their defense of terrorism, "the uselessness of which was so clearly proven by the experience of the Russian revolutionary movement,"[24] while only the previous year he had declared that his party "never rejected terror on principle, nor can . . . [it] do so."[25] Prior to the outbreak of revolution in 1905 Lenin adhered to his earlier theoretical formulations, and labeled any terrorist activity "an inexpedient means of struggle," for it clearly was not "one of the operations of the fighting army [of the proletariat], closely related and adapted to the entire system of struggle."[26] He thus rejected terror conditionally, "pending a change in circumstances."[27] With the outbreak of antigovernment violence in 1905, he faced a compelling need to formulate for his faction a set of practical policies with regard to political terror.

A number of considerations forced him to seek a definite stand. First of all, he could not avoid recognizing the fact that SR and anarchist terrorist tactics were clearly succeeding in destabilizing the regime by spreading fear and confusion among the authorities. Lenin also had to concede the longstanding SR claim that terrorist activity could be extremely effective in radicalizing both the peasantry and the proletariat.[28] Furthermore, under the conditions prevailing in 1905, with anarchy swiftly replacing order and with neither the government nor the revolutionary leaders, particularly those in emigration, exercising much control over the local activities of their supporters, Lenin realized the necessity of turning the acts of "inevitable guerrilla warfare" throughout the empire to the advantage of his party and the revolution as he saw it.[29] Even on the theoretical level terrorist activity seemed to be better justified at that point: at a time when terrorism had assumed enormous proportions and involved virtually every stratum of the population, terror could no longer be regarded as a means of individual protest and instead had to be considered a component of the mass rebellion against the entire sociopolitical order. For Lenin it was also significant that whereas "traditional Russian terrorism was the work of plotting intellectuals," after 1905 workers or unemployed persons were usually its primary perpetrators.[30]

With these considerations in mind, Lenin finally synthesized his views. At that particular historical moment, terror was appropriate for revolutionary purposes as long as it was "actually able to merge with the mass movement."[31] This position was essentially no different from the formula the SRs espoused in their rhetoric: "We call for terror not instead of work among the masses, but indeed for this very work and simultaneously with it."[32] Now that he felt the time was ripe, Lenin called for "the most radical means and measures as the only expedient ones," not excluding decentralized terrorist activity, for which he advocated the creation of armed units of a revolutionary army, "varying in size, starting with two or three people . . . self-armed with whatever means are available," units that were in reality identical to the combat groups and flying detachments of the Socialists-Revolutionaries.[33]

In fact, he was now willing to go even further than the SRs, and at times neglect all attempts to reconcile terrorist activity with the scientific principles of Marxism, arguing, "Combat detachments can and must take every opportunity for active work, without delaying their attacks until the time of the general uprising." They must "at once begin combat training in immediate operations, at once."[34] In essence, Lenin was all but ordering a series of the terrorist acts he had previously condemned, calling for attacks against policemen and government spies, whose extermination was now, in his view, "the duty of every decent person."[35] He was little troubled by the obvious anarchic nature of such acts, urging his followers not to fear these "experimental attacks": "They may, of course, degenerate into extremes, but this is tomorrow's problem . . . dozens of sacrifices will be compensated for."[36]

Having formulated his new tactics, Lenin immediately called for their practical implementation, and according to one of his closest associates, Elena Stasova, he became at this time an "extremist partisan of terror."[37] As early as October 1905 he openly urged his followers to kill spies, policemen, gendarmes, Cossacks, and members of the Black Hundreds; to blow up their headquarters, along with police stations; and to throw boiling water on soldiers or fling acid at the police.[38] Then, not satisfied by the scope of the party's involvement in terrorist activity, in a letter to the St. Petersburg Committee Lenin complained: "With horror, with real horror I see that [the revolutionaries] have been talking about bombs for half a year now, without having made a single one!"[39]

Eager for immediate action, Lenin even defended strictly anarchist methods against the arguments of his fellow SDs: "When I see Social Democrats proudly and smugly proclaiming: 'We are not anarchists, or thieves, or robbers, we are above this; we reject guerrilla warfare,' I ask myself: 'Do these people understand what they are talking about?' "[40] Finally, in August 1906, the official stand of the Bolshevik faction of the RSDRP was stated publicly when its organ, *Proletarii* (Proletarian), advised the combat groups "to end their inactivity and undertake a series of guerrilla actions . . . with the minimal 'destruction of the personal safety' of peaceful citizens and with the maximum destruction of the personal safety of spies, active members of the Black Hundreds, high-ranking officers of the police, the military, the navy and so on and so forth."[41]

In reality, however, Lenin's concern over a lack of Bolshevik terrorist activity was groundless; his followers throughout the empire were involved in numerous individual acts of violence. These terrorist outbursts were for the most part not controlled by the party leadership, which was isolated from the real action, and the acts thus had little connection with the party's larger political objectives, or its immediate strategy. In addition, the actions were rarely reported either to party headquarters abroad, or to other central SD organizations, such as those in St. Petersburg and Moscow, or even to local leaders in the provincial centers. In fact, since the Bolsheviks had no official body responsible exclusively for political assassinations, along the lines of the SR Combat Organization, their terrorist activity, like that of local terrorists of the SR and Maximalist trends, assumed a predominantly anarchistic character.

Bolshevik terror struck a variety of targets, but the most common victims were individuals suspected as police informers, provocateurs, and traitors. There was little effort to assure a fair trial, and in fact any revolutionary regarded with suspicion by his comrades was likely to become a victim of violent reprisals, usually leading to his death.[42] Even the most respected party members were vulnerable to this assumption of guilty until proven innocent. One Bolshevik recalled that several of his comrades, considering him a possible traitor, accosted him and pointed revolvers in his face, while he, naively suspecting nothing, took it all as a friendly joke.[43] In many other cases the terrorists dispatched suspected enemies of the people quickly, frequently performing the execution with extreme brutality.[44]

While the physical elimination of police spies was regarded by the revolutionaries as a necessary means of cleansing their ranks of individuals who endangered the group or interfered with its activities, other terrorist acts vividly demonstrated vengeance as a key motive. This was true, for example, of the assassination of a prison executioner responsible for implementing death sentences against a number of revolutionaries.[45] The Bolshevik perpetrators of this attack could not reasonably have expected it to prevent future death sentences from being carried out; in this case they did not even attempt to come up with a more theoretically sound justification than vengeance. Bolsheviks were responsible for many similar acts of revenge directed in particular against policemen and Cossacks who came into bloody confrontation with revolutionaries involved in agitational work.[46] Vengeance and efforts to intimidate their enemies into inactivity also led to Bolshevik violence against various conservative elements of the population, all of whom the revolutionaries labeled members of the Black Hundreds. This was their motive when on 27 January 1906, in accordance with a decision of the Petersburg Committee of the RSDRP, a Bolshevik combat detachment attacked the tavern Tver', a meeting place for factory workers in the shipbuilding industry who were also members of the monarchist Union of the Russian People. Some thirty patrons were present when the terrorists threw three bombs into the tavern, and as the workers attempted to flee the building, the Bolsheviks waiting outside fired revolvers at them at close range. As a result of this attack two persons were killed and approximately twenty wounded; the terrorists escaped unharmed.[47] Similarly, in the Ural city of Ekaterinburg, members of the Bolshevik combat detachment headed by Iakov Sverdlov persistently terrorized local supporters of the Black Hundreds, killing as many suspected tsarist loyalists as they could.[48]

Along with their use of assassination to intimidate supporters of the tsarist regime, the Bolsheviks also sought to unleash confusion and panic among the authorities themselves and thus diminish their ability to resist the spreading violence. The extremists dealt mercilessly with their targets, who were primarily local government workers ranging from factory police inspectors to city policemen and police officials of various ranks.[49] Commenting on these terrorist attacks, some Bolsheviks could not but acknowledge the destructive nature of violence for violence's sake: "In the fall of 1907 . . . militant youth lost control and began to deviate toward anarchism, . . . killing guards, city policemen and gendarmes. . . . They were feverishly aroused (*zarazheny*) and believed it was merely necessary to act."[50] Two Bolshevik terrorists, for want of anything better to do at the time, "chased Cossacks, just waiting for a convenient moment to 'entertain' them with bombs." The Cossacks, however, always rode in single file, making their ranks less vulnerable to attack, so the two combatants threw their bombs into the police barracks instead, enjoying the resulting show: "When the burning fuses hiss, the policemen jump out the windows."[51]

The Bolsheviks carried out many terrorist assaults on government officials not only without any formal resolution by central party organizations, but also without the consent of local cell leaders. A decision to commit a murder often originated spontaneously with an individual party member who immediately implemented it in a reckless fashion. One such murder was the assassination of Police Sergeant (*uriadnik*) Nikita Perlov on 21 February 1907 near the village of Dmitrievki. It was carried out by two Bolsheviks, Pavel Gusev (Severnyi) and Mikhail Frunze (Arsenii):

The attempt on Perlov's life was not an organized plot, a premeditated decision of the party organization, but was a result of a minute's impulse of Mikhail Vasil'evich [Frunze]. . . . During a meeting of propagandists . . . someone looked out the window and noticed that Perlov had just arrived. . . . Frunze jumped up, . . . called for Gusev to follow him, and despite the protests of all present, ran outside. In a few minutes shots were fired. . . . It seemed like a good opportunity to Frunze, circumstances were right for an attack, and so the decision was made immediately.[52]

Some Bolsheviks apparently did not regard the elimination of low-ranking officials and police personnel as an adequate contribution to the revolutionary cause, and considered competing with SR central terror in the assassination of state leaders. According to one former terrorist, members of his combat group decided to kill Dubasov, governor-general of Moscow. As in other cases, they "began this affair, too, without the permission of the party organization . . . [and had already] established surveillance, but the SRs found out about it, and decided that this was their monopoly," forcing the Bolsheviks to abandon their preparations.[53] Like the SRs, the Bolsheviks in St. Petersburg developed plans to assassinate Colonel Riman.[54] A. M. Ignat'ev, a leading Bolshevik close to Lenin in the post-1905 period, and a man of active imagination never intimidated by adventure, suggested an elaborate scheme for kidnapping none other than Nicholas II from his Peterhof residence.[55]

While in most cases the party's involvement in terrorism had little to do with the mass movement, there were instances that justified the theoretical claims of the Bolshevik leaders, at least in part, that terror was an integral part of the class struggle. According to prominent Bolshevik Vladimir Bonch-Bruevich, when the Semenovskii regiment entered Moscow in 1905 with orders to suppress the December uprising in that city, he proposed to the St. Petersburg Party Committee to immediately seize "a couple or so grand dukes" as hostages, "put them in a secluded place and keep them under constant threat of certain and immediate execution if one drop of proletarian blood was spilled on the streets of Moscow."[56] Prior to this, a Bolshevik combat unit in the capital, in an attempt to support the December uprising, had made unsuccessful preparations to blow up a train carrying government troops from St. Petersburg to Moscow.[57] The Bolsheviks also made plans to shell the Winter Palace, in case of major disturbances, using a cannon confiscated from a naval guard station.[58]

Certain other aspects of Bolshevik terrorist activity may be regarded as part of the economic struggle of the masses as well, particularly when the struggle expressed itself in the strike movement. The revolutionaries directed attacks not only against factory owners, managers, and police who attempted to defend the capitalists,[59] but even against workers who failed to support the strikes, boycotts, and other forms of proletarian protest. The beating of strike-

breakers was not uncommon, and opponents of strikes were mercilessly executed. On occasion the Bolsheviks also used special stink bombs, which were
quite effective in driving people from their work places.[60]

The Bolsheviks made a number of attempts to sabotage the military mobili-
zation efforts of the government by planting explosives on railways.[61] They
also used individual acts of violence to interfere with preparations for elections
to the First Duma, which the Social Democrats had resolved to boycott. Regarding the introduction of parliamentary order in Russia as a palliative, and
thus a threat to the revolution, the Bolsheviks, in addition to conducting widespread agitation against the Duma, adopted a policy of active resistance to the
elections, organizing armed attacks on polling centers to confiscate and destroy the official tabulations of local election results.[62] These actions, and perhaps also the armed seizure of publishing houses and presses for the purpose
of printing revolutionary leaflets and newspapers,[63] may be considered part of
the mass struggle. Other outbursts of violence, including firing at police during
house searches, arrests, or escape attempts,[64] should be regarded as individual
acts, with little connection to any theoretical principles adopted by the Social
Democratic leadership.

Some Bolshevik activities that may have begun as part of the revolutionary
struggle of the proletariat were in practice quickly transformed into terrorist
ventures. The weapons obtained by means of arms smuggling and explosives
manufacturing, activities that party leaders claimed were undertaken solely in
preparation for mass uprisings,[65] in fact frequently proved useful in isolated
boevik attacks. This occurred even in the central party organizations: in St.
Petersburg, Leonid Krasin (Nikitich), a member of the Central Committee and
head of its Combat Technical Group (Boevaia tekhnicheskaia gruppa pri TsK
RSDRP), chief organizer of all primary Bolshevik combat affairs in this period
and one of Lenin's closest associates ("the only Bolshevik whose opinions
Lenin took into account"),[66] personally participated in the assembly of bombs
for terrorist acts.[67] Abroad, Maksim Litvinov (Meer Vallakh), one of the most
active functionaries in Lenin's faction, was busy smuggling weapons to comrades in the Caucasus where, as he was fully aware, they were used almost
exclusively for terrorist purposes.[68]

At this time the Bolsheviks rarely concealed their terrorist activities from
the public. They were, however, responsible for a number of political assassinations that for various reasons were carried out under such secrecy that it is
now difficult to reestablish the facts, or even to prove definite Bolshevik involvement. A striking example was the 1907 assassination of celebrated poet
and social reformer Count Il'ia Chavchavadze, perhaps the most popular national figure in early twentieth-century Georgia, and in many eyes, "the father
of Georgia and its prophet."[69] According to one author, in this region "the
vicious struggle was between two camps: the Social Democrats, headed by

[Bolshevik] Filip Makharadze, and the national democrats, under the leadership of 'the great Il'ia' Chavchavadze."[70] Chavchavadze did much to undermine the Bolsheviks' position in his public criticism of the SD program, but more important, his enormous personal popularity drew the people, and particularly the peasants, to the nationalist cause and away from radical socialism. When a vilifying campaign against Chavchavadze on the pages of the local Bolshevik journal, *Mogzauri* (Traveller), produced little effect, the SD committee issued a death sentence against him.[71]

Several shady individuals attacked and brutally murdered Chavchavadze near the village of Tsitsamuri on 30 August 1907. While it was generally suspected at the time that the Social Democrats were responsible for the act, the local Bolshevik leaders, fearing the outrage of the mourning nation, and wishing simultaneously to divert blame to "the hirelings of the tsarist secret police," alleged to have killed Chavchavadze for his anti-Russian stand, continuously denied any connection to the assassination.[72] At the same time, several individuals implicated in the murder made no attempts to conceal their roles, with one SD boasting publicly: "I . . . a militant revolutionary and a party member, killed Il'ia Chavchavadze . . . like a dog, with my right hand."[73] An analysis of local sources leaves little doubt that the Bolsheviks were behind the murder of the great poet; there are in addition persuasive reasons to believe that one of the assassins might have been Sergo Ordzhonikidze, who later became a leading Soviet communist official.[74]

Terrorist practices thus became the norm not only for Bolshevik party underlings, but also for its most prominent leaders, who did not hesitate to order assassinations when they deemed such action appropriate. In at least one instance, the Bolsheviks killed a traitor solely on the basis of a direct command from Krasin.[75] Moreover, the Bolshevik leaders seemed to consider murder an option in solving problems within their own exclusive circle. When V. K. Taratuta (Viktor), a onetime member of the Bolshevik Central Committee, was thought to have compromised the faction by his unethical conduct, Krasin is said to have openly declared that if Taratuta's scandalous behavior were to become public knowledge, he would assign somebody to kill him.[76]

For the Bolsheviks, then, terrorism became an effective and frequently used tool, employed on various levels of the revolutionary hierarchy. As was also true of many SRs, whose terrorist activities Lenin justifiably interpreted as a series of one-man acts,[77] the acts of terrorism perpetrated by the Bolsheviks for the most part had little to do with the party's ideological principles and objectives. Bolshevik terror became but one more effective weapon in the arsenal that individual radicals and even entire groups chose to employ, since in the revolutionary struggle all means were appropriate. The Bolsheviks were audacious enough in this matter to "consciously declare that . . . [they] shall not stop at any means."[78]

TERRORISM IN PRACTICE: THE MENSHEVIKS

From the outset the Mensheviks were consistent in rejecting terrorism as a method of political struggle, at least on the central party level. Unlike Lenin, who sought to compensate for far-from-scientific practices by means of solid theoretical justifications, such prominent Mensheviks as Pavel Aksel'rod, Fedor Dan, and Iulii Martov never allowed pragmatic considerations to alter their principal assumption of the harmful long-term effects of individual acts of violence. Of the Menshevik leaders, Martov was especially determined to keep the Social Democrats away from political assassinations and expropriations, on many occasions declaring his unambiguous opposition to guerrilla actions.[79]

This did not mean that the Mensheviks ignored the significance of major terrorist attacks as a means of enhancing the political prestige of a revolutionary organization. Realizing how much the PSR benefited from the assassination of Sipiagin, *Iskra* devoted many pages to demonstrating that Balmashev had acted independently from the Combat Organization, which had thus falsely assumed for itself the honor associated with this act.[80] The Mensheviks also recognized the benefits to be derived from political murders for general revolutionary purposes. Many faction activists celebrated the successful assassinations of Sipiagin, and especially the hated Plehve, along with the rest of the radical community, acknowledging the favorable impact of these terrorist acts on their common efforts to overthrow the forces of reaction.[81]

While considering the terrorists misguided in their belief that individual action was compatible with Marxist theory, the Menshevik leaders did not regard the *boeviki* as enemies of the revolution, and on many occasions declared their admiration for such dedicated proponents of terrorism as the "heroic Grigorii Andreevich Gershuni."[82] Furthermore, in response to the numerous assassinations of state and military officials after 1905, the orthodox Marxists exonerated the terrorists and publicly held the government entirely responsible for the bloodshed in Russia.[83]

In addition, some Menshevik leaders were clearly less confident in their antiterrorist policy than others. Although the conventional view holds that in contrast to Lenin, Plekhanov rejected terror as "a matter of principle,"[84] he in fact did waver at times. Perhaps in tribute to the ideals of his early youth, he was apparently tempted to concede the effectiveness of terrorist methods, but was confronted with Martov's unyielding opposition.[85] When forced to renounce terrorist practices for the time being, Plekhanov argued: "Each Social Democrat must be a terrorist à la Robespierre. We will not shoot at the tsar and his servants now as the Socialists-Revolutionaries do, but after the victory we will erect a guillotine in Kazanskii Square for them and many others."[86] Even such persistent opponents of terrorism as Zasulich and Martov took the view that on certain extraordinary occasions, "terror as an act of revenge was unavoidable."[87] In describing the "individual revolutionaries [who] enter the government's camp in order to strike down one of the enemy's leaders there with a well-aimed blow," Martov also argued that unlike the "armed bands of tsarist servants," who did not stop at any cruelty or immorality to crush the revolutionary movement, "the people's fighters honestly obey the rules of war."[88] Another well-known Menshevik, Vladimir Kopel'nitskii, openly endorsed partisan activity, thus giving his comrades cause to suspect him of being a closet Bolshevik.[89]

Menshevik involvement with individual acts of violence, however, was not limited to wagging a finger at the mischievous deeds of the terrorists, while providing them moral support. Here again it is essential to differentiate between what the top party leadership claimed in its rhetoric and what ordinary party members did in practice, for members of the Menshevik faction were often willing to aid the terrorists and expropriators despite obvious theoretical and programmatic disagreements.[90] Moreover, on a number of occasions the Menshevik attitude toward terrorism was essentially no different from that of the SRs and the anarchists. This was particularly true inside the prisons, where the Mensheviks voted with the hardened terrorists to eliminate especially oppressive prison officials.[91]

Furthermore, in obvious violation of their faction s policies, the Mensheviks took active part in assembling bombs and other explosive devices used in terrorist acts. Indeed, all members of the Southern Combat Technical Bureau of the RSDRP Central Committee (Iuzhnoe Voenno-Tekhnicheskoe Biuro pri TsK RSDRP), established in late 1905 in Kiev primarily for bomb production, were Mensheviks.[92] In their *post factum* attempts to justify this activity, these revolutionaries persistently asserted the urgent need to prepare weapons for the impending general armed uprising of the proletariat.[93] In fact, however, most of the bombs ended up at the immediate disposal of SD combat units.[94] Although these units did use some of the weapons in mass protests, they no less frequently employed the explosives in individual acts, including an incident in which a Menshevik bomb killed a Cossack and a policeman in the town of Sormovo, a rebellious bastion of Social Democracy.[95] Like all the other extremist organizations, the Mensheviks attacked the police with bombs and revolvers during house searches.[96]

The Mensheviks, generally regarded as the least extremist of the SDs, also engaged in economic terrorism, and indeed, according to one party activist, sometimes were "surprisingly close to the anarchists, the supporters of direct action" in this sphere.[97] One revolutionary recalls that when the director of an oil company in Baku received an order from a Menshevik group to leave the city in twenty-four hours under threat of death, he complied immediately, apparently aware of the group's past practices in similar situations.[98]

Although this Menshevik organization did not officially sanction arson as a tool of revolution, it did set fire to oil rigs as a means of applying pressure to the proprietors.

In another case a Baku industrialist, familiar with the tactics of the various revolutionary parties, declared his confidence in the favorable outcome of a Menshevik-controlled strike in his factory, basing his optimism on the idea that the Mensheviks, as Social Democrats, would be reluctant to resort to violence. In reaction, an irritated young Menshevik in charge of the negotiations felt compelled to prove his group's revolutionary enthusiasm. He posted armed guards at the office doors, and announced that the factory owner would receive neither food nor water until the end of the strike, and that any attempt to call for help would result in the dynamiting of the factory. It then took only one hour for the differences between the industrialist and the strikers to be settled, but as the Menshevik terrorist-negotiator himself admitted, his "behavior could hardly be called entirely Social Democratic."[99]

The Caucasus, most notably Georgia, was the region where central Menshevik control was least effective. Largely as a result of the ancient tradition of vendetta in the region, violence was a normal part of life, and the local Georgian Menshevik forces differed substantially from their relatively peaceful counterparts in Russia proper.[100] If local Mensheviks in the Russian provinces frequently resorted to bloodshed and, for example, in the city of Voronezh reproached their Bolshevik colleagues for their inactivity, insisting on partisan guerrilla actions,[101] their comrades in Georgia ignored theory with even greater regularity for the sake of achieving immediate results. Indeed, Menshevik involvement in assassination was greater in the Caucasus than in any other region of the empire.

The Mensheviks in Georgia did not deny that although they considered "one good demonstration more beneficial for . . . [their] goal than the assassination of several ministers," all of their organizations resorted to political murder "in case of need."[102] Similarly, a leader of the Georgian Menshevik movement, Noi Zhordaniia, admitted that the Social Democrats employed terror as a weapon for "the creation of panic among the police."[103] Another prominent Menshevik, Noi (Naum) Ramishvili, led a combat organization, and was personally involved in the acquisition of bombs.[104] The Georgian Mensheviks did not spare petty officials in local districts;[105] nor did they refrain from pursuing revenge, directing it against high-ranking advocates of repressive counterrevolutionary measures, including the chief of staff of the Caucasian military district, General Griaznov, whom they killed in Tiflis in January of 1906.[106]

In the turbulent Caucasus, as in most other regions of the empire, the Social Democrats still largely constituted a single force, despite the official split into Bolshevik and Menshevik factions in 1903. Many local RSDRP organizations ignored the dissension in the SD headquarters abroad until at least 1905, and in some cases even later, and continued to act as a single party. Despite the fact that, as the Bolsheviks bitterly admitted, "the directing organs of the Party passed entirely into Menshevik hands," making the "rally of the masses to the Menshevik position inevitable,"[107] many rank-and-file SDs in the Caucasus still referred to themselves simply as Social Democrats, without specifying a faction.

It is thus only possible to speculate about the precise factional loyalties of many RSDRP terrorists in the Caucasus, although they do seem to have been predominantly Menshevik.[108] It is also impossible to list all of their successful acts, let alone the abortive attempts, to eliminate enemies of the revolution. Aleksandr Rozhdestvenskii, who early in his career served as a liberal assistant prosecutor in Tiflis, remembered "countless assassinations of government officials," a situation that quickly turned into a "bloody nightmare in the Caucasus," especially in Georgia, where the Social Democratic Workers' Party was "most influential and numerous at the time" of the first Russian revolution.[109] There, in spite of the fact that many SD committees discouraged terrorist tactics in their rhetoric, and at formal meetings and congresses made speeches forbidding them, a particularly bloody confrontation with Cossacks would cause the rank and file to alter their views about individual acts of violence: "Revenge, revenge, revenge . . . these were the words that came from the hearts of our comrades. . . . Social Democrats who reject terror in principle now must turn to it as the only means of struggle."[110]

Consequently, RSDRP activists in the Caucasus proceeded to stage terrorist attacks against government officials, police employees, military personnel of various ranks, prison authorities, wealthy industrialists and factory managers, as well as members of the aristocracy.[111] While many terrorists answered to local party committees, and some even received special remuneration for their services, a significant number of these acts were undertaken entirely on personal initiative, with minimal regard for the theoretical principles and tactical policies of the RSDRP as a whole. One Baku SD combat unit activist known as Little Vladimir took it upon himself to terrorize local police, killing them "like gamebirds."[112] Little consideration was shown for the value of human life, and another SD terrorist enthusiastically reported to his comrades that although a bomb thrown into a store had missed the owner of the establishment, it had nevertheless killed and injured several other people present at the time of the attack.[113]

In describing the widespread terrorist activity underway at the time in other regions of the Russian empire, sources confirm the unity of the SD forces.[114] Police and revolutionary documents also show that while the SD terrorists did not spare a single category of government servant, most of their wrath seemed to target spies and renegades within their own organizations, along with individuals considered members of the Black Hundreds.[115] In their zeal to punish government and police collaborators, the SDs sometimes proved rather careless, acting without having made a thorough investigation. They beat an innocent person to death on one occasion, and on another nearly killed a fellow revolutionary and his wife, realizing only at the last moment that he was the victim of slander.[116]

In the common efforts of all revolutionaries to paralyze the will of the authorities, the Social Democratic groups staged terrorist attacks not only against individual representatives of the government and the police who were particularly effective in opposing the revolutionary movement,[117] but also against defenders of the tsarist regime en masse. In Samara, a "group of *bombisti*" under the direction of the RSDRP committee tried unsuccessfully to throw bombs down on the soldiers of a local army unit from a balcony.[118] It then did not take long for many Social Democrats to realize that "such actions, which presented an opportunity for ample initiative to young and hotheaded fighters, contributed to the breakdown of overall party discipline," and, no less significantly, that "by taking up arms . . . the organization unwittingly and against its will had to deviate from a clear Social Democratic line of action, moving closer to . . . the tactics of the SRs."[119]

Unwilling to tolerate this state of affairs, and also realizing that the revolution was in decline by the end of 1906, some local Bolshevik-Menshevik organizations implemented urgent measures against their deviating members. Frequently referred to internally as "terrorists" or "*boeviki*," many of these cadres had ceased to follow orders from their group leaders, their units degenerating into semianarchic forces.[120] Without waiting for directives from the central party headquarters abroad, which formalized its drastic resolutions against all partisan activity only at the Fifth Party Congress in London in May of 1907, many regional SD committees began to reduce membership in the combat units on their own initiative, to discharge some *boeviki* and disarm others. These measures usually amounted to halfhearted attempts to control the terrorists, as when a Menshevik committee in the Caucasus suggested to one combat detachment leader, whose group resembled a criminal gang and was to be dissolved, that he choose and keep at hand the "strongest and most courageous fighters, who could be used to carry out terror."[121] Although party organizations were often powerless to restrain the combatants and quick to deny responsibility for their actions, the SD committees did occasionally accept services from these same terrorists.[122] In general, however, these purges created widespread dissatisfaction among the SD *boeviki*, causing many of them to break their ties with the Russian Social Democratic Labor Party and seek new comrades, primarily among the anarchists.[123]

TERRORISM IN PRACTICE: NATIONAL SD ORGANIZATIONS

When Vladimir Burtsev asserted in 1902 that the "Social Democrats are not such genuine opponents of political terror as they portray themselves to be,"[124] the statement was equally applicable to the Bund, the All-Jewish Workers' Union in Lithuania, Poland, and Russia. Formed in 1897, it was the first formal

Social Democratic organization in the Russian Empire, and in April 1906 at the Fourth SD Congress in Stockholm it joined the RSDRP on an autonomous basis. The Bund leadership persistently declared that political and economic terror, as a system, was entirely contradictory to the party's tactics, and that terrorist acts therefore "should under no circumstances be incorporated into . . . its program."[125] Like the Bolsheviks, the members of the Bund seemed to reject the use of assassination not on principle, but only under particular historical conditions, proclaiming: "At the present time, we consider the terrorist struggle to be inexpedient."[126] Like the Mensheviks, however, the Bundists never formally acknowledged terror as a suitable tactic, which nevertheless did not prevent the Bundist leadership from offering moral support to terrorists of various party affiliations, and did not stop local Bundists from occasional participation in terrorist acts.[127]

In accordance with their resolution that "spontaneous or contemplated terrorist acts should serve as agitation points in enhancing [revolutionary] consciousness in the workers' milieu and in society,"[128] the Bundist leaders rarely missed an opportunity to use political assassinations perpetrated by other groups for the benefit of the revolution as a whole by lauding the heroic deeds of the terrorists against the hated tsarist regime. In February of 1902, for example, they issued a special leaflet entitled "1 March" in which they glorified the assassination of Alexander II by the People's Will: "Let us remember today our great revolutionary predecessors who demonstrated so much heroism in the struggle with the tsarist government. Let the memory of these selfless heroes and fighters . . . give us new strength for the struggle against the accursed autocracy."[129]

Many Bundists applauded terrorist methods openly at official party congresses, with fourteen local committees publicly advocating terrorism.[130] Their arguments were persuasive enough to force most participants at the August 1902 Fifth Conference of the Bund held in Berdichev to vote in favor of adopting a resolution on the expediency of "organized revenge."[131] Less than a year later, "in considering that individual murders—whether undertaken with a goal to avenge, to threaten, or to punish—are nothing but a form of terror," a majority at the Zurich party congress in June 1903 declared its "decisive disagreement with the resolution on organized revenge adopted at the Fifth Conference of the Bund." Even here, however, an active minority insisted on recording its independent view: "Feeling negatively about terror as a means of struggle against autocracy, we find that if organized mass protests . . . are impossible, then an organized terrorist act may be allowed."[132]

If leaders of the Bund felt justified in providing such unambiguous recognition of the terrorists' methods, local Bundist functionaries, typically more radical and less theoretically inclined than the party generals, were prepared to go even further and actually participate in terrorism. This was especially true after the outbreak of general violence in 1905, when in a number of centers of Jewish radicalism, such as Odessa, Bundist combat activities were more successful than those of the local SRs.[133] A police source thus justifiably saw no contradiction in describing one Jewish revolutionary as both a "serious Bundist" and "a terrorist by conviction."[134] As was true of other revolutionary groups, revenge was among the primary motives for assassinations perpetrated by Bundists, especially against police employees and collaborators. There were many instances when, in clear contradiction of conventional Marxist thinking, members of the Bund resorted to bloody retaliation, as in the small Jewish settlement of Zhagory, where at the end of 1905 all "authority came to be in the hands of the Bundists. . . . The revolutionary administration sentenced two provocateurs to death [and] the verdict was carried out." The Bundist organization in control of this tiny town "also planned the execution of the old district police officer and others."[135]

Perhaps the most notorious and widely discussed act of Bundist revenge took place in Vil'na on 5 (18) May 1902, when Girsh Lekert shot and superficially wounded Governor Viktor von Val', who was responsible for ordering the flogging of twenty young Jewish workers following a May Day street demonstration.[136] The governor's use of corporal punishment had produced an immediate wave of indignation among the Bundists, and the party's Central Committee issued a proclamation passionately condemning the repressive measures of the authorities. This proclamation, in clear contradiction of the party's official stand, was direct in inciting revenge:

> We cannot think and talk calmly about what happened in Vil'na. From thousands of hearts emerges one common cry: vengeance! . . . We are convinced that an avenger will arise from among the Jewish proletariat, who will take revenge for the outrage upon his brothers; and if human blood is to be spilled, the entire responsibility will be on the tsar and his wild servants.[137]

Lekert answered this unambiguous call for action, and the Central Committee exalted his act of martyrdom: "Honor and glory to the avenger, who sacrificed himself for his brothers!" Even the Foreign Committee of the Bund, usually uncompromising in its antiterrorist position, "in an atmosphere that approached hysteria," asserted, "In cases such as the . . . [May] execution in Vil'na, the revolver is the only means to ease the intolerable sufferings of the stricken social conscience, so that people will not suffocate with stifling indignation."[138]

Although they usually resorted to terrorist attacks for revenge, to punish, and occasionally to avoid being arrested,[139] members of local Bundist organizations also employed violence for another purpose—to threaten or terrorize their enemies to the point of complete paralysis. This was particularly evident during the crisis of 1905–1907, when amid the constant struggle between the government forces and the forces of the revolution many radicals set aside their scientific principles for the sake of action. The Bundists were certainly no exception. Local Bund activists, such as those in Gomel', carried out swift attacks against anyone they considered a defender of the tsarist regime, "terrorizing the police, the military and all 'loyal' Russian inhabitants."[140]

Not all of the Bund's victims were notable opponents of the revolution: a police constable in the small rural town of Suvalki was seriously wounded with a dagger while making his rounds;[141] Bundist bombs killed a number of Cossacks on duty in Gomel', and in a separate incident cut down several members of a mounted dragoon patrol in the provincial town of Borisov.[142] Indeed, the least protected rank-and-file members of the police forces presented especially attractive targets for the Bundist terrorists,[143] and even the Bund leaders felt compelled to acknowledge that the numerous "attacks upon soldiers . . . provoked the irritation of the military against the revolutionary movement."[144]

Like other Social Democrats, the Bundists employed physical force during strikes and in other situations in which economic interests were involved: "This [was] the so-called 'economic terror,' which the organization denounced, but to which it nevertheless quite frequently resorted."[145] For instance, along with his Bundist comrades, Lekert, before his attempted assassination of von Val', used physical coercion to force strikebreakers to leave their work places.[146] Bundists also made it their responsibility to insure that shops and businesses remained closed during strikes, and police orders that they be kept open often had no effect, for according to one Bundist *boevik*, the "owners feared us more than they did the police."[147] In October 1905, during workers' disturbances in Gomel', and in December of the same year, during a general strike against industrial and trade enterprises in Kovno, members of the Bund's special combat units used violence to put a stop to all work in these towns, shooting at government troops in the process.[148] The Bundists also settled private conflicts between supporters of the revolution and their employers by violent means.[149]

Bundist terror was used to interfere with the elections to the First State Duma. Like the Bolsheviks, the Bundists not only agitated for its boycott, but also attacked polling centers, and by force of arms confiscated and destroyed election lists. In their zeal to sabotage peaceful parliamentary work, they often went even further than other Social Democrats. In Bobruisk, for example, they broke up preelection meetings with petards and similar small explosive devices, and by shooting into the air.[150] These outbursts of violence in connection with the Bund's official policy of active boycott occurred so frequently that even in the earliest stages of the election campaign, in January 1906, revolutionary leaders warned their fellow party members on the pages of their newspapers against overly fervent acts that could lead to armed excesses.[151]

The Bund's choice of targets thus resembled the practices of all other terrorists, except in two respects: first, that most of the party's activity took place in or near Jewish settlements and almost never in the capitals; and second, that some terrorist activity was perpetrated by the organization under the aegis of self-defense against the Jewish pogroms. With this latter goal in mind, the Bundist revolutionaries joined (and organized) "Jewish self-defense units" (*otriady evreiskoi samooborony*), allegedly always formed to protect the local population in the Pale against anti-Jewish violence.[152] Frequently, however, self-defense activities became political acts of offensive terror against the government and its supporters.

There is much evidence illustrating this alteration of intentions. According to a report from the security police in Rostov-on-Don, in the synagogues of this city and in the town of Nakhichevan' there were frequent gatherings of Jewish and Christian extremists armed with weapons provided by the local Jewish community for the purpose of forming self-defense units. During these meetings speakers incited members of the units to "merciless violent action" against the local authorities. As a result of this radical agitation, self-defense activists began to shoot in the streets, wounding, among others, a number of children.[153] In addition, the authorities received information from various sources that the revolutionary leaders had recruited a special combat group from among the members of the self-defense unit, and issued orders to hurl explosive shells at certain local officials, including the governor of Rostov-on-Don.[154] Leaders of the Jewish community in the little town of Amdure asked the authorities for help against the radicals, and informed the police of the location of a storehouse of weapons belonging to the self-defense organization. These elderly Jews clearly felt that the local self-defense activists were more concerned with committing antigovernment violence and increasing the general anarchy than with protecting Jewish interests.[155]

Indeed, with its intimidation tactics, the Bund managed to terrorize and antagonize not only representatives of the tsarist regime, but also the poor and generally apolitical Jewish population within the Pale. Using threats and violence the party took upon itself the role of arbitrator in economic disagreements between laborers and employers and even in private conflicts. Equally important, the young Bundists insulted community religious sentiment by breaking into synagogues during holiday services and using the threat of arms to disperse the congregations so that they could hold their own revolutionary meetings there.[156] Often, when the authorities intervened and cleared the synagogue of radicals, Bund leaders in their subsequent proclamations tried to present the incidents as government assaults on Jewish national values and the traditional Jewish way of life, neglecting to mention that revolutionaries had fired shots at the police inside the temple. This was the case in the city of Minsk in October 1905, and also in Lepel' in January 1906, where Bundists beat policemen unconscious as soon as they realized that the officers had come to the synagogue alone, without the support of additional troops.[157] Not surprisingly, some Bundists were aware that their terrorist methods were a "heavy burden for wide sections of the population, calling forth their animosity toward the revolutionaries."[158]

A similar situation developed in the Baltic region, where "the events of 1905 and the subsequent years took place with an intensity not to be found in other regions of Russia"; partly for this reason the Latvian Social Democrats were significantly more inclined toward terrorist action than the rest of the RSDRP, with the possible exception of their Caucasian counterparts.[159] The Latvian Social Democratic Workers' Party, formed in the summer of 1904, and known after 1906 as Social Democracy of the Latvian Land (Sotsial Demokratiia Latyshskogo kraia), carried out its revolutionary work under circumstances that tended to promote spontaneous terrorist action.

First of all, the SD organizations in Latvia were quite autonomous from the central leadership of the RSDRP, partly by virtue of their geographical isolation from the capitals, but more particularly because they joined the Russian Social Democratic Labor Party only nominally, and relatively tardily, in May 1906 at the Fourth Congress.[160] Especially in tactical questions, the Latvian SDs were thus under little practical RSDRP control, and adopted their own methods without concerning themselves too much with the norms established by central party theoreticians abroad for the party as a whole.

In general, the Latvian SDs demonstrated minimal interest in the subtle nuances of Marxist theory, because like the Georgian SDs, they recruited new members primarily from the lower social strata, most notably among young unskilled workers and the poorest peasants. Understandably, these uneducated and often illiterate novices in the revolutionary ranks had little patience for theoretical debate over whether the assassination of individual political figures was an expedient form of struggle from the Marxist point of view.[161] They chose their methods in accordance with circumstances and used terror when it seemed suitable, at best leaving it to their leaders to justify their actions by whatever principles seemed appropriate. The most notable examples of such revolutionaries are to be found among the forest brothers. A significant number of these guerrillas chose to label themselves Social Democrats, although their knowledge of Marxist doctrine and accountability to the RSDRP were virtually nonexistent. This helps to explain why many of the Latvian SDs more closely resembled common bandits than the idealistic freedom fighters that subsequent memoirists persistently attempted to portray. Autonomous in their actions and ideologically ignorant, many of them used revolutionary slogans to justify strictly criminal activities.[162] This was so evident at the time that when some of these radicals, or even entire bands, proclaimed themselves to be part of Social Democracy of the Latvian Land, as was the case with one SD combat unit in Riga that called itself the Red Guard (Krasnaia gvardiia), the formal position of the Social Democratic organization toward such a group was "to ignore [it] as a simple gang of bandits."[163] While recognizing the lack of socialist sophistication among these small bands, however, it would be unfair to disregard the sincerity of the nationalist sentiment that motivated many of their acts, which clearly aimed at liberating the motherland from foreign invaders. Their attacks on Russian bureaucrats and German barons were at least in part a result of frustrated nationalism and hatred for powerful outsiders.

A certain degree of nationalism was characteristic of all the national Social Democratic parties. In clear contradiction of Marxist principles, which allow little place for national consciousness and loyalty to a homeland, many Latvian Social Democrats, like their comrades in the Caucasus and the western provinces of the Russian Empire, perceived the Russian administrators in their region as foreign conquerors.[164] Social Democrats with greater ideological awareness frequently found it convenient to make use of the patriotic feelings of the local populace, inciting them to political terror with nationalist overtones.

On numerous occasions, Latvian SDs stated that before the 1905 revolution and in its earliest phase their party, concerned solely with the organized activities of the masses, "did not admit to terrorist tactics," and at the very most engaged only in "armed self-defense."[165] One SD even claimed that initially there were no terrorist acts in Latvia at all, if (he continued rather inconsistently) "one does not treat the assassination of low-ranking police officials as terrorism."[166] For the Latvian SDs, however, armed self-defense often signified "rendering harmless the most dangerous enemies [such as] police spies, traitors, and the most vicious among the landlords and the government hangmen."[167]

It was the combat organization of the Latvian SD Party, organized in 1905 and operating in Riga and its suburbs, and the combat detachment of the SD Party committee in Libau (Libava) that were largely responsible for these assassinations. From February to June of 1905, the latter group alone carried out twenty armed assaults on "flunkeys of the counterrevolution."[168] At the same time, according to a former terrorist, "Each party member immediately became a *boevik* if only he had a revolver in his pocket."[169] In fact, few of the Latvian guerrillas waited for party sanction before proceeding with a terrorist act. It was far from uncommon for an SD terrorist to make a spontaneous decision to throw homemade explosives at a passing Cossack patrol.[170] Little wonder then that even the sympathizers admitted that many such attacks had "nothing in common with the revolutionary struggle of the proletariat."[171]

There may be reasonable doubt as to whether the Latvian SDs practiced terror prior to the end of 1905, but it is evident that in the upheaval that followed, "the Latvian Social Democratic Party came close to the Party of Socialists-Revolutionaries in the nature of its terrorist activity."[172] In 1906–1907, "under the influence of the events," certain SD combatants "changed their opinions about terror, [and] planning began for relatively large-scale acts, such as those against Governor-general A. N. Meller-Zakomel'skii, Chairman of the Military Tribunal V. F. Osten-Saken, the heads of the investigative and security police."[173]

In practice, "largely due to the lack of discipline and self-control among the comrade *boeviki*," none of the large-scale acts planned against the highest administrative officials in Latvia materialized. It was easier to attack the city policemen, poorly protected against partisan action, or even the military. Such terrorist acts did not involve sophisticated and detailed preparations, exact execution of a plan, or precision in taking orders from activist superiors—all skills vitally important for an organized political assassination, and seemingly lacking among the Latvian SDs. According to a fellow revolutionary, "As much as a Latvian *boevik* was courageous and daring, and as much as he scorned death, he was still extremely reckless and undisciplined."[174] And so, like all other representatives of Social Democracy in the empire, the Latvian SDs directed their attacks primarily against low-ranking administrative officials and the police, with perhaps the only unique characteristic in the borderlands being the relatively large number of acts perpetrated against Russian military units, which played a particularly active role in pacifying these areas.[175]

In the rural districts and the Baltic countryside, along with economic disturbances and mass peasant uprisings, there were many incidents of violence that can only be considered acts of political and economic terrorism. Most of these acts are attributable to the forest brothers, many of whom were former members of SD combat units still active in the area, along with the Latvian SD combat organization. The forest brothers primarily responsible for the ongoing bloodletting and anarchy in the rural areas thus became an auxiliary force for the Riga combat organization and other guerrilla detachments of the Latvian SD Party, whose leaders turned to the partisans for aid in terrorist acts and expropriations outside the larger urban centers, and especially against the barons and wealthy landowners or the Cossacks and military units stationed near their estates.[176]

These vagrant radicals terrorized the Latvian countryside throughout 1906, but by the end of the year, with significant assistance from the outraged barons and the increasingly cold weather, the government was able to organize effective roundups and arrest many of them. The rest were forced to flee the area, since the rural population was less inclined to cooperate with the extremists as a result of a special penalty in an amount ranging from 50 to 250 rubles imposed by district officials on any farmer known to sympathize with the revolutionaries.[177] While some Latvian SDs escaped abroad, others continued their terrorist activities elsewhere in the empire, notably St. Petersburg and Finland.[178] One of their undertakings, described by a Latvian revolutionary in a terrorist anecdote, was especially daring: after making the acquaintance of a housemaid who worked in Stolypin's villa, two renegade Latvian SDs made plans to assassinate the prime minister in his own quarters, but were unable to do so when their inside contact was fired.[179]

The Latvian *boeviki* also faced problems originating in their own camp, specifically in the headquarters of the Latvian Social Democratic Workers' Party. The SD leadership realized that their combat activities could not advance the mass workers' movement, for, as one author put it, "their struggle, despite all courage and sacrifices, was carried out under the sign of the ebb, not the flow of the revolutionary wave."[180] The Latvian SD leaders were also undoubtedly aware of the ideological negligence and seemingly criminal character of the forest brothers, whose terrorist activities more often than not were under little control of the party. This was why in August 1906, at the unifying congress of the SD organizations in Riga, the Social Democracy of the Latvian Land's Central Committee resolved to liquidate the forest brothers, who had "discredited the party by their banditry," and were therefore to be expelled from its ranks.[181] Several of the more moderate Latvian SD leaders proclaimed their determination to put an end to all terrorist activity and to disband the combat detachments—a decision that did not prevent a number of the brigand groups from continuing to carry on their terrorist activities throughout the next year.[182]

In concluding this analysis of the involvement of various national Social Democratic parties in political terror, a brief mention of several other peripheral SD organizations that engaged in terrorist acts, albeit with less frequency than the rest of the Social Democrats, is in order. The group known as Social Democracy of the Kingdom of Poland and Lithuania (the Polish Social Democrats), which joined the RSDRP at the same time as the Bundists and the Latvian SDs, was the least involved with terrorist activities of all the SD factions. Before the latter half of 1905 the Polish SDs seemed to take a passive, and sometimes even negative stand, on this tactical issue, especially in comparison with the PPS, which spilled more blood in Poland than any other local revolutionary organization. Indeed, when terrorists began shooting randomly at the police in the middle of a crowded Warsaw square in October 1904, the Polish Social Democrats denounced this first major terrorist attack by the PPS as a criminal action.[183]

At the same time, however, along with other SD organizations, the Polish Social Democrats unambiguously called for revenge following the repressive measures by Governor von Val' of Vil'na:

> This barbarity caused even greater hatred and contempt for the tsarist government, inciting a thirst for sacred vengeance. . . . Patience has its limits. It is not our fault if the revenge, hatred, and indignation of the people turned into violence. Von Val' himself asked for it. All responsibility will be on the tsarist servants—von Val' and his assistants. . . . vengeance will befall each of you.[184]

The crisis of 1905 led the Polish SDs to reconsider their position with regard to terror. In order to clarify their new stand it is perhaps best to compare it with that of the PPS, noting that while the latter advocated terrorism in principle as an effective method of antigovernment struggle, the former concentrated their primary efforts on organization and political education of the proletarian masses, "without rejecting the application of mass terror in a revolutionary situation."[185] In theory, the implementation of mass terror was to become part of the general class struggle, with terrorist activities serving to enhance the revolutionary consciousness of the proletariat.

As was true of other SD groups, reality was far removed from theory. Late in 1905, in order to promote terror, the Polish Social Democrats established their own Warsaw Combat Organization (Organisacia Bojowa), whose debut in terrorism took place 11 November 1905 when the party *boeviki* assassinated a retired colonel and his tenant as alleged leaders of the local Black Hundreds.[186] The Warsaw Combat Organization then divided its cadres into combat groups assigned to different sections of the city, and additional isolated acts followed that had little connection with any mass movement; the Polish Social Democrats dedicated particular effort to exposing and murdering police informers, often choosing cemeteries as secluded locations for executions.[187]

It was Feliks Dzerzhinsky, future chairman of the Soviet Cheka (Vserossiiskaia Chrezvychainaia kommissiia po bor'be s kontrrevoliutsiei i sabotazhem, or All-Russian Extraordinary Commission for the Struggle against Counterrevolution and Sabotage), who along with other Polish Social Democrats sought to organize the terrorists and subject them to strict discipline under SD leadership.[188] And yet, as was also true in other rebellious border areas, disregard for human life was extreme, and radical activity steadily degenerated into banditry. Corrupted by constant bloodletting carried out with near impunity after 1905, a number of Polish SD terrorist groups began to kill and rob indiscriminately until local party committees felt the need to disarm them and expel the most stubborn "hooligan *boeviki*" from the party.[189] Their readiness to resort to violence of an arguably criminal nature and often to shed innocent blood as part of their terrorist practices could in no way be compared in scale with the combat activities of the PPS, but this did not prevent the police officials from including Social Democracy of Poland and Lithuania "among the organizations which recommended terror against the government."[190]

On the whole, then, individual members of every faction of the Russian Social Democratic Workers' Party found it useful under various circumstances to make use of terrorist methods. In addition, among the independent national SD forces that were not officially part of the RSDRP, although professing to adhere to Marxist principles and dogma, the largest and most intimately involved with political terror were the Lithuanian Social Democratic Party and the Armenian Social Democratic Organization (Gnchak). Members of these two groups, unrestrained by control from any central party organization, tended to be involved in violence of a criminal nature more extensively than the other Social Democrats.

Many members of the Lithuanian Social Democratic Party were totally ignorant or negligent of the philosophical differences among the various trends of revolutionary ideology. One member of the Lithuanian SD Party, Iosif Kunitskii, who, in the opinion of the Russian secret police, was "the chief and most harmful enemy of security and order in the northwestern region" of the empire, organized a group of Lithuanian terrorists who proudly called themselves anarchists.[191]

In at least one case, the use of violence by Lithuanian SDs was so extreme that the party's leaders became alarmed, and felt compelled to investigate the conduct of a terrorist by the name of Ivan Lidzhus, a member of a regional committee, eventually expelling him from the party for hooliganism and banditry.[192] By his own admission, Lidzhus personally murdered approximately thirty people, and was found guilty of a number of crimes between 1907 and 1908: he took part in the assassination of an alleged police informer who was a personal enemy; he robbed a chapel; on a number of occasions he forcibly seized money from local foresters, wounding at least one of them; he misappropriated money for his own needs in the name of the party; and along with several comrades he took upon himself the right to administer justice and mete out punishment in a number of villages. In addition, he refused to comply with the statutes of the party, simply because he did not like its tactics.[193]

Members of the Armenian Socialist Democratic organization, the Gnchakisty, openly adopted terrorist methods "as a means of self-defense, for revolutionary agitation, and as a weapon against harmful actions of the authorities." On 14 October 1903 they staged an attempt on the life of the commander-in-chief of the Caucasus, Prince Golitsyn, whom the revolutionaries held responsible for the policy of state confiscation of church property in the region. Golitsyn anticipated the attack, however, wore chain mail, and was only slightly wounded.[194] Interestingly, for this assassination attempt the leaders of the Gnchak organization had recruited the so-called *feda*, that is, individuals who had resolved to sacrifice themselves for the good of the nation.[195] The reputation of this party was not unspoiled, and, according to a police source, by 1908 the Gnchak organization, "due to abuse of their positions by its bosses" in Paris, had "lost its former influence" and begun to suffer from internal dissension.[196] As control from central headquarters diminished and the party began to split, criminal behavior became increasingly common among its members. An independent group that called itself the Reorganized Gnchakisty and operated primarily abroad limited its practices "exclusively to robberies and murders even among the cadres of their own party with an aim to obtain means of subsistence." In New York they murdered a wealthy Armenian by the name of Tarshandzhian, who had refused to make a donation to the group; in Egypt they killed an Armenian writer, Arpiarian, who had published evidence of the criminal activity of his fellow countrymen.[197] Former members of the Gnchak party, along with various other small and obscure SD groups—dissenters from formal Social Democratic organizations—thus gradually turned away from politically motivated terror to revolutionary robbery.[198]

THE EXPROPRIATIONS

Along with individuals who performed assassinations in the name of the revolution, every Russian Social Democratic organization included members who participated in violent robberies and forcible confiscations of government and private property. The ambiguity demonstrated by many SD leaders toward political assassination, renouncing it in theory while allowing and even sanctioning its practice, was also evident in their treatment of expropriations. Most of the SD generals at least initially unequivocally refused to disapprove of politically motivated robberies. At the 1906 RSDRP Stockholm congress the delegates explicitly rejected "the expropriation of money from private banks as well as all forms of compulsory contributions for revolutionary purposes."[199] At the same time, however, the SD *boeviki* were urged to confiscate weapons and explosives, and to carry out expropriations of state funds and public possessions with the permission of their local organs of revolutionary authority and under the condition of complete accountability.[200] Members of combat detachments were thus led to believe that it was legitimate under certain circumstances to expropriate state and public property.[201]

Formal sanction was never openly pronounced, however, and the only SD faction leader who blatantly declared robbery an acceptable means of revolutionary struggle was Lenin. Thus, although other representatives of the SD forces in the Russian Empire resorted to expropriation without the formal approval of their leadership, the Bolsheviks were the only Social Democratic organization that undertook these fund-raising activities systematically, in a planned fashion.

Lenin did not confine himself to slogans or the mere awareness of Bolshevik participation in combat activities. As early as October 1905 he proclaimed the necessity of confiscating government funds,[202] and soon became personally involved in the partisan tactics of the party. Along with two of his closest associates at the time, Krasin and Aleksandr Bogdanov (Malinovskii), he secretly organized a small group within the predominantly Menshevik Central Committee of the RSDRP that came to be known as the Bolshevik Center, primarily with the purpose of raising money for his faction. The existence of the group "was concealed not only from the eyes of the tsarist police, but also from [other] party members."[203] In practice, this meant that the Bolshevik Center was set up clandestinely to supervise expropriations and various forms of extortion.[204]

A former leading Bolshevik, Grigorii Aleksinskii, stated that from 1906 to 1910 the Board of Three, or Small Trinity, as the leaders of the Bolshevik Center were subsequently nicknamed, directed many expropriations. Perpetrators of these acts "were recruited from among the uncultured but zealous revolutionary youth, ready for everything." Throughout the empire they "robbed post offices, train station ticket offices, sometimes trains, even staging their crashes beforehand."[205] Because of the region's volatility, the Caucasus proved particularly suitable for their exploits.

The Bolshevik Center received a steady flow of desperately needed funds from the Caucasus, thanks to one of Lenin's most loyal lifetime followers, Semen Ter-Petrosian (Petrosiants), a man of questionable mental stability better known as Kamo the Caucasus brigand, as Lenin half-mockingly labeled him.[206] Beginning in 1905, Kamo, with the support of Krasin (who provided general supervision and bombs assembled in his St. Petersburg laboratory), organized a series of expropriations in Baku, Kutais, and Tiflis. His first robbery on the Kodzhorskaia road near Tiflis took place in February of 1906, netting between 7,000 and 8,000 rubles. In early March of the same year Kamo's group assaulted a bank coach on a busy street in Kutais, killed the driver, wounded a cashier, and escaped with 15,000 rubles, which they immediately shipped to the Bolsheviks in the capital in wine bottles.[207] Fortune always seemed to smile on Kamo, but his most notorious robbery was the "Tiflis ex," which took place on 12 June 1907: in a central square of the Georgian capital, the Bolsheviks threw bombs into two stagecoaches loaded with notes, coins, and currency from the Tiflis State Bank. Leaving dozens of bystanders dead or wounded, Kamo and his gang escaped the scene of the crime shooting revolvers and carrying with them 250,000 rubles in bank notes destined for the Bolshevik Center abroad.[208]

Kamo was the heart of the Bolshevik Caucasian combat or "technical" group organized exclusively to carry out expropriations.[209] However, according to Tat'iana Vulikh, a revolutionary with close ties to the Georgian terrorists: "the chief leader of the combat organization was Stalin. He did not take part in its undertakings personally, but nothing went on without his knowledge."[210] Kamo was thus left with all the practical tasks and, in addition, was the main link between the Bolshevik faction leadership and its *boeviki*, who, although they remained members of the RSDRP in principle and were recognized as such by their comrades, had to resign formally from their local organization in order not to compromise it by their acts, for many of their deeds clearly violated the party's policies on terror and expropriations.[211]

Kamo recruited his cadres primarily among the local outlaws, who "had no principles and were a menace on the roads," but whom he brought under discipline and inspired with revolutionary spirit.[212] The *boeviki*, including Kamo, possessed only a rudimentary knowledge of socialist theory and expressed little concern about the programmatic disagreements within the RSDRP. Once

14. Leonid Krasin

15. Kamo (Semen Ter-Petrosian)

when present at a heated debate over the agrarian issue between a Menshevik and a Bolshevik, Kamo evidently misunderstood the nature of their disagreement: "What are you arguing with him for? Let me cut his throat," he calmly told his Bolshevik friend.[213] Indifference to theory aside, the "idealistic gangsters" in Kamo's group literally worshiped Lenin, the incarnation of the party in their eyes, whose every word was unbreakable law. According to Vulikh, "They would have followed Lenin even against the entire party, despite all their loyalty to it."[214] One of the combatants, Eliso Lomidze, who had not met Lenin in person and had never been seen with a book in his hands, claimed that the goal of his life was to acquire "200,000–300,000 rubles and give them to Lenin, saying 'Do anything you want with them.' This was generally the attitude of all the other members of the group."[215]

The combat organization, while constantly preparing for "a major affair," was aware that the party needed money regularly, and engaged in many minor expropriations. Still, the expropriators were frustrated when their efforts yielded results as trifling as the several thousand rubles stolen from a pawnshop in Tiflis.[216] They also used extortion against local industrialists, with armed *boeviki*, on Stalin's orders, distributing specially printed forms specifying the contribution payable to the Baku Bolshevik Committee.[217]

One of their carefully planned major affairs is particularly interesting. In addition to Kamo, who had acquired such a glorious reputation as a result of the Tiflis expropriation that all members of the Bolshevik faction, including Lenin, flattered and "courted him in the most incredible manner," Krasin and Litvinov were the only Bolsheviks aware of the preparations for the robbery.[218] The plan developed by Kamo and Krasin, the Bolshevik Center's minister of finance,[219] envisaged an unprecedented expropriation totaling 15 million rubles in gold and notes held in a certain government money depot. Because of the physical weight of the proposed haul, the Bolsheviks planned to take only 2–4 million rubles and destroy the rest. This act, in their estimate, would provide the faction with financial support for five or six years. After the expropriation the Bolsheviks intended to renounce the practice publicly with the hope of saving the party's image, although Kamo declared unambiguously that if their plans were to materialize, "There will be as many people killed during this 'ex' as in all the 'ex's' that have taken place up 'til now combined, at least 200 people."[220] The scheme proved to be a total fiasco, however: in late 1907 and early 1908, as a result of timely information received by the Okhrana from Iakov Zhitomirskii, one of its best agents abroad, the police in Germany and other Western European countries were able to make a number of swift arrests, including those of Kamo and Litvinov.[221]

Kamo's organization in the Caucasus was not the only group used by the Bolshevik Center for expropriations, for Bogdanov was also able to establish close contacts with several combat detachments in the Urals. In this region, at a conference in Ufa in February of 1906, Bolshevik activists passed an affirmative resolution on future expropriations. Subsequently, in June and July of that year, the Bolshevik Regional Committee of the Urals, disregarding the decisions of the Stockholm Congress of the RSDRP, confirmed this unpublished resolution.[222]

In some estimates, beginning with the outbreak of the 1905 revolution, the Bolshevik *boeviki* carried out more than one hundred expropriations in the Urals.[223] The local leader of the combat groups responsible for much of this activity was Ivan Kadomtsev, who was assisted by his brothers Erazm and Mikhail.[224] Under their direction the Ural Bolsheviks not only confiscated weapons and explosives from government and private depots, but also attacked and disarmed individual soldiers and gendarmes.[225] Further, in violation of the Stockholm Party Congress resolution forbidding assaults on private property, the Ufa Bolshevik committee, experiencing difficulty publishing their leaflets and proclamations, confiscated supplies and equipment from private publishing houses, along with entire printing presses.[226]

The *boeviki* in the Urals also expropriated public and private funds, attacking post offices and factory administration buildings, liquor stores, and artels.[227] One of the most significant of their robberies was the 26 August 1909 assault on a mail train at the Miass station. In a sudden attack on the depot, a group of Bolsheviks killed seven guards and policemen and stole bags containing approximately sixty thousand rubles in paper money, and twenty-four kilograms of gold, large portions of which the expropriators subsequently shipped abroad.[228] The police succeeded in arresting a number of participants, who were then put on trial. Notably, it was Aleksandr Kerensky, future prime minister of the Russian Provisional Government, who conducted their defense for the enormous honorarium of ten thousand rubles—money, as he was undoubtedly aware, drawn from the expropriated funds.[229] When one of the *boeviki*, disguised as a prosperous merchant, approached Kerensky to offer him payment in exchange for his legal services, he referred to his comrades in the Urals as bandits, and spoke in a base street jargon that betrayed his criminal origins.[230]

Bolshevik assaults on government, public, and private property also occurred in other areas,[231] but in the Caucasus and Urals their activities "degenerated into shady enterprises of the worst kind."[232] Indeed, many of the Bolshevik *boeviki* began to stage robberies simply "to stay in practice," usually without notifying their party organizations, and their actions quickly came to bear a strong resemblance to those of common criminals.[233] In one such case, a combat detachment that had initially operated under the directives of the Bolshevik Center gradually began to stray toward autonomy during the second half of 1906, and when the band of expropriators offered the party only a portion of the money stolen in a factory robbery during which they had killed a cashier, the SD leadership refused it flatly and reprimanded the combatants. But "it was already too late; they were disintegrating rapidly and soon descended to 'bandit attacks of the most ordinary criminal type.' Always having large sums of money, the fighters began to preoccupy themselves with carousing, in the course of which they often fell into the hands of the police."[234]

Thus the wishful resolution of the First Conference of the RSDRP Military and Combat Organization convoked by the Bolsheviks in November 1906 in Tammerfors, which proclaimed expropriations to be "nothing but the confiscation of means . . . from the government and their transmission into the hands of the people," preferably without bloodshed, was rendered useless.[235] And the brutal reality did not escape general attention within the RSDRP. Martov openly proposed expelling the Bolsheviks from the party for what he considered illegal expropriations; Plekhanov stressed the need to fight "Bolshevik Bakuninism"; Fedor Dan called the Bolshevik members of the Central Committee a company of common criminals, and other Mensheviks considered "Lenin and Co." swindlers.[236] The Bolshevik Center (B. C.) was the object of an epigram composed by Menshevik wisecrackers:

"How do you like those 'ex's'?" B. C. was questioned once.
"I love them," B. C. answered. "They're lucrative for us."[237]

Thus, even before a major scandal erupted over the Bolsheviks' attempts to exchange money stolen in the Tiflis expropriation—an extremely embarrassing episode for the entire RSDRP that in the eyes of many European sympathizers transformed it into a criminal gang[238]—the Menshevik leadership of the party was ready to strike against the Bolshevik Center.

For the most part, the never-ending discord between the Bolshevik and Menshevik leaders in emigration had little to do with differences on theory; according to Boris Nicolaevsky, a participant in the revolutionary events and lifelong student of Bolshevism, "Behind the raging debates on the philosophies of Marxist materialism and empirical criticism lay the politics of another kind of material: money."[239] The Mensheviks were particularly irritated by the fact that Lenin and other Bolshevik leaders used the expropriated funds first and foremost to defeat their intraparty rivals in the emigré squabbles or, as Nicolaevsky put it, "for acquiring power over the party."[240]

Lenin's primary objective was indeed to strengthen the position of his own supporters within the RSDRP with money, and, according to Bogdanov, to make certain people and even entire organizations financially dependent on the Bolshevik Center.[241] Leaders of the Menshevik faction were painfully aware that Lenin was operating with enormous expropriated sums,[242] subsidizing the Bolshevik-controlled St. Petersburg Committee at the rate of at least one thousand rubles monthly, and the Moscow Committee at half that rate. At the same time, relatively little of the proceeds from the Bolshevik robberies ended up as general party funds, and the Mensheviks were outraged not so much by the fact that expropriations took place as by their own largely unsuccessful attempts to force the Bolshevik Center to place the proceeds at the disposal of the predominantly Menshevik RSDRP Central Committee, whose revenues in bad times did not exceed one hundred rubles a month.[243] Relations between the two factions were not improved by incidents such as the occasion when prominent Bolshevik Litvinov sent two Georgian terrorists to the RSDRP headquarters to demand forty thousand rubles, which had been obtained by expropriations and had already been spent by the Central Committee, threatening that if the money were not returned to the Bolsheviks, the Georgians would "bump off" (*ukokoshat'*) one of the Central Committee members.[244]

Lenin's followers also used the proceeds to fortify their ranks in advance of party congresses. Their enhanced position just before the opening of the Fifth Party Congress in London, for example, was, according to Boris Souvarine, "largely due to the enormous resources obtained by the 'ex's,' which made it possible for them to maintain a legion of militants, to send emissaries to all quarters, to found journals, to distribute pamphlets, and to create more or less representative committees," all with the goal of obtaining additional mandates for delegates to the congress.[245] Moreover, in 1906–1907 the Bolsheviks utilized the expropriated funds to subsidize exclusively Bolshevik-controlled schools for combat instructors in Kiev, and for *bombisti* in L'vov.[246]

In 1910 they also used expropriated funds to establish an SD school in Bologna, Italy, which quickly became a stronghold of the Bolshevik group Vpered (Forward).[247]

The Fifth Party Congress came as a fortunate opportunity for the Mensheviks to attack the Bolsheviks for their "banditlike practices," particularly because, despite all their efforts, on a number of issues the Bolsheviks were outnumbered by a coalition comprised of the Mensheviks, the Bundists, and certain Latvian SDs. Even the Poles, the Bolsheviks' loyal allies at the congress, did not support Lenin's position on guerrilla warfare. Realizing that the revolution was lost for the time being, the Social Democratic leaders felt the need to resolve the fundamental tactical question of whether to terminate the party's conspiratorial operations and concentrate on legal parliamentary activities, or to maintain its underground forces in a constant state of alert. Although sincere in their belief that "in the present moment of relative slackening, partisan assaults inevitably degenerate into purely anarchist methods of struggle" that demoralized the party,[248] the Mensheviks seemed to be aiming first and foremost at the embarrassing combat activities of their Bolshevik colleagues, especially since no one in the party except the Bolshevik Center extracted much profit from them. Consequently, on 19 May 1907 the congress passed an essentially anti-Bolshevik resolution stating that "party organizations must conduct an energetic struggle against partisan activities and expropriations" of any nature, and that "all specialized fighting squads . . . are to be disbanded."[249]

In theory, this decision was to put an end to all involvement on the part of the Social Democrats in terrorist activities and expropriations. In practice, however, such resolutions had no effect on the Bolsheviks, as evidenced by the Tiflis expropriation, the Miass robbery, and a number of other local attacks on government and private property carried out by groups of terrorists and expropriators who simply proclaimed themselves to be nonparty (*bespartiinye*) while acquiring money for Lenin's faction.[250] This continuation of expropriation activity could probably have been predicted at the congress, for Lenin was not moved by Martov's calls to revive the purity of revolutionary consciousness. He listened to these appeals with undisguised irony, and if a widely circulated anecdote is credible, during the reading of a financial report, when a speaker mentioned a large donation from an anonymous benefactor, "X," Lenin quipped, "Not from a certain Mr. X but from an ex" (*Ne ot iksa, a ot eksa*).[251] While continuing the expropriations, he and his associates in the Bolshevik Center also received funds from such shady sources as fictitious marriages and forced donations.[252] Finally, Lenin's habit of defaulting on his faction's debts angered even his own supporters.[253]

Despite Menshevik efforts to portray the Bolsheviks as black sheep, and, in Dan's words, the disgrace of the RSDRP family,[254] Lenin can hardly be considered the sole culprit. While no other SD organization had a secret body paralleling the Bolshevik Center that existed primarily for the purpose of raising funds by more than questionable means, the Mensheviks and the national SD groups were themselves involved in expropriations on numerous occasions. In addition, the situation as it was described at the London congress, with combat units under various party committees said to have turned into "isolated conspiratorial cells," separated from the masses and demoralized by banditry,[255] encompassed not only the Bolshevik expropriators but those of all other Social Democratic organizations as well.

The Mensheviks resorted to expropriation less frequently and in a less systematic, organized, and effective manner than the Bolsheviks, but a revolutionary from Georgia nevertheless reported that the local Menshevik combat detachments "do whatever they feel like." In addition, the Okhrana was aware in 1907 that the Mensheviks had at their disposal fifty thousand rubles acquired not long before as a result of an expropriation in Tiflis; ironically, one of the *boeviki* killed in the action was a former Menshevik delegate to the Stockholm congress.[256] Menshevik activities were also not limited to the Caucasus. Several Mensheviks expropriated between 7,000 and 8,000 rubles from a Kiev post office in February of 1906.[257] Despite Regional Committee reprimands for "Bolshevik-like" practices, Mensheviks made an abortive attempt to expropriate one hundred thousand rubles on the Moscow-Warsaw railroad line.[258] A more lucrative affair, on the other hand, was their robbery of a mail train from Sevastopol', an action that, along with a number of other expropriations, was directed by Al'bin (Artem), a prominent Menshevik well known among the *boeviki* for his experiments with explosives.[259] And it was common knowledge within the party that the Menshevik-controlled RSDRP Central Committee elected at the Fourth Congress "regularly used money acquired by expropriations."[260]

Similarly, members of united (Bolshevik-Menshevik) SD groups widely engaged in expropriations of state and private funds.[261] Like revolutionary assassination, these activities were particularly common in the Caucasus, where in 1906 the central SD organization acquired two hundred thousand rubles from an expropriation targeting the Kviril'skii Treasury.[262] In addition, in such regions as Guriia, local RSDRP committees extensively employed coercion to collect twenty kopeks a month from each inhabitant; they also imposed special taxes on the population to be used to purchase arms and finance the operating expenses of the SD groups.[263] In Baku the bourgeoisie was so intimidated by the SD combatants that the sums demanded were always delivered promptly.[264] In localities outside the Caucasus, such as the towns of Kostroma and Ivanovo-Voznesensk, the SDs staged armed assaults on liquor stores and practiced extortion. Unable to maintain control over the expropriators, the SD leaders in the periphery complained, "Certain members of combat detachments, in cooperation with outsiders, behave like true hooligans and steal everything they can get their hands on."[265] In some areas these activities became an impossible burden on the peaceful population. In the Georgian region of Akhalgori a gang of sixteen Red Guerrillas robbed the inhabitants of an entire valley and forced peasant families to leave their homes and seek refuge away from their land.[266] Many members of local SD groups could not reconcile themselves with the antipartisan resolutions of the RSDRP leadership in London,[267] and continued to engage in terrorist acts and expropriations long after May of 1907.

State and private property alike were targets for expropriations by national SD groups. Bundists operating in the Jewish Pale openly violated official party policy by taking direct action against the bourgeoisie and assaulting banks, post offices, factories, stores, and private homes.[268] Their once staunch revolutionary idealism deteriorated into cynicism after 1905, paralleling the shrinking disregard for the sanctity of life and property. A Bundist in the town of Nizhnii-Seversk, for example, participated in an expropriation led by a local anarchist gang leader, after the anarchist promised the young freedom fighter a new coat valued at one hundred rubles.[269] Other Bund activists extorted donations for revolutionary purposes from wealthy citizens, with the amount of individual forced contributions dependent upon the victim's social standing.[270] Thus when the Grodno Bund Committee distributed leaflets claiming that their organization had "nothing to do with . . . the hooligans who storm into people's homes, revolvers in hand," demanding money in the name of the Bund[271] the Bundists probably convinced few of the local citizens of their sincerity.

In Latvia the SDs carried out expropriations not only in the countryside, relying upon assistance from the forest brothers, who frequently supported themselves by attacking post offices and liquor stores,[272] but also in the larger towns and urban centers. Their fund-raising activities were often marked by the characteristic peculiarity of offering their victims receipts for the proceeds.[273] After having been defeated and forced to flee from their motherland, many Latvian SDs practiced expropriation in other parts of the empire, raiding, for example, a post office in St. Petersburg and the estate of Prince Golitsyn in the province of Novgorod. In the fall of 1906 several Latvian SDs, "for fun," tried unsuccessfully to seize money at the State Senate, and planned an assault on the St. Petersburg palace of Grand Duke Aleksei Aleksandrovich.[274] Perhaps the most sensational of their acts was a robbery in Finland at the Helsinki branch of the State Bank, where the combatants hoped to procure funds to finance their escape abroad. On 13 February 1906, in broad daylight, a group of Latvian SDs, including several Central Committee members, killed a guard, locked all bank employees and customers in a back room, and escaped with at least 150,000 rubles, leaving behind an empty can that triggered a bomb scare.[275]

Although representatives of Polish-Lithuanian Social Democracy at the London congress acknowledged the necessity of fighting banditry within their ranks,[276] they did not protest the "lucrative proceedings" employed by their eminent leader, Leo Tyshko, "on mutual account with Lenin."[277] And if the assaults on state and private property committed by members of independent Social Democratic groups such as the Lithuanian SDs and the Armenian Gnchakisty are taken into consideration,[278] it is possible to conclude that representatives of all factions of the RSDRP and the national organizations in the Russian Empire, as part of their overall terrorist practices, were as actively engaged in expropriations as they were in political assassinations, theory notwithstanding.

Within the Russian SD movement, it would thus be inappropriate to attribute equal responsibility for terrorist activities to the trend's various factions and subgroups. The Russian Mensheviks and the Bundists, as well as the Polish and Lithuanian SDs, resorted to combat operations with much less enthusiasm than the Bolsheviks and their comrades in Latvia and the Caucasus. And in these border regions, national sentiments blended with socialist principles to drive the *boeviki* to direct action. In the broader perspective of the Russian revolutionary movement as a whole, terror played a much smaller role in the strategy of the SDs than it did for the SRs: while central to the SR and anarchist programs, political assassination and revolutionary robbery served as secondary weapons in the arsenal of the SD extremists. Whereas the SRs regarded terrorism as a method for attaining the general long-term goals of the revolution, the SD combatants had much in common with the anarchists in using individual violence to accomplish more immediate and local objectives.

Chapter Four

TERRORISTS OF A NEW TYPE

THE ANARCHISTS AND THE OBSCURE EXTREMIST GROUPS

> Only enemies of the people can be enemies of terror!
> —*Khleb i volia, 1905*[1]

"TO DEMOLISH the contemporary order" absolutely, to do away with all laws and courts, all religion and churches, all property and property owners, all traditions and customs and their adherents, were the immediate objectives of every anarchist in the Russian Empire. They sought as their ultimate goal the complete liberation of man from all artificial restraints in order to render him totally independent from both God and the devil. Their means to these ends would be the social revolution, defined by the anarchists as any direct action, particularly terror, expropriation, and the destruction of state institutions, that would shake the foundations of the contemporary order. These direct actions would be taken "without entering into any compromises with the bourgeoisie and . . . without putting forth any concrete demands," and would lead to the final destruction of both capitalism and the state, followed by their replacement with an egalitarian communal society, free from oppression and even the minimal control necessarily exerted by any form of government.[2]

According to Paul Avrich, the leading authority on Russian anarchism, "The very nature of the anarchist creed, with its bitter hostility toward hierarchical organizations of any sort, impeded the growth of a formal movement."[3] Indeed, Russian anarchism can barely be regarded as a movement at all, for no united anarchist organization existed, and there were no strictly defined or centrally coordinated policies on any programmatic or tactical issue, including the tactic of terrorism. It is possible, however, to establish at least some patterns of behavior characteristic of the various independent anarchist groups dispersed throughout the Russian Empire.

There were few anarchists in Russia prior to the twentieth century, with the first groups beginning to operate under the black banner of anarchism toward the end of 1903 in Belostok, Odessa, Nezhin, and other areas. They did not arise spontaneously, but rather as a result of defections from other political organizations, primarily the Party of Socialists-Revolutionaries and the various factions of the Social Democratic Workers' Party. With the outbreak of revolutionary disturbances in 1905, and throughout the next two violent years, anarchist groups, in the words of Belostok anarchist committee leader Iuda Grossman, "sprang up like mushrooms after a rain," in cities, small towns, and villages.[4] According to Avrich, the pattern was the same throughout the empire. In the Ukraine, in the Caucasus, and especially in the western provinces, where anarchism became widespread in Riga, Vil'na, and Warsaw, as well as in smaller towns such as Gomel', Grodno, and Kovno, a handful of disaffected SDs or SRs united into small anarchist cells that then formed loose federations and plunged into radical activity of every sort, most notably terrorism.[5]

SDs and SRs chose to leave their organizations for a variety of reasons. Many from the lower strata of society, especially workers, had become alienated from party leaders whom they considered theorizing intellectuals, feeling that they preferred ideological debate, which did nothing but divide the revolutionaries, to any radical action. Even party members who were slightly more theoretically inclined became disillusioned by the SRs' preoccupation with the agrarian question, and objected to the Marxist insistence upon the necessity of establishing the parliamentary democracy that, according to socialist dogma, would mark the stage preceding the withering of the state. Indeed, as the anarchists argued in one of their proclamations, since democracy protected capitalist oppression it was as much an enemy as autocracy. Therefore with both political systems: "only one language was possible—violence." The working class was not to make any distinction among the various forms of government, for a revolutionary worker could "enter the democratic parliament, the Winter Palace, or any police-state establishment only . . . with a bomb!"[6]

Tactically, the dissenters from the SR camp, while in complete agreement with their party's practice of political terror, wished to extend those methods to the economic sphere, and use them against capitalists and other exploiters.[7] Dissident SDs left the RSDRP in protest of its official antiterrorist stand and the consequent shortage of practical combat work.[8] Still, Avrich justifiably asserts that the "socialist parties of Russia, in contrast to those of Western Europe, with their strong reformist taint, were sufficiently militant to accommodate all but the most passionate and idealistic young students and craftsmen and the rootless drifters of the city underworld."[9] It was these restless, and primarily youthful, individuals, unable to control their rebellious spirits and conform to the rules and discipline of any structured political organization, who tended to leave the formal political parties to become anarchists, all questions of ideology and tactics aside.[10]

Despite the fact that even after 1905 the anarchists were relatively few in number compared to the SRs and the SDs,[11] they were responsible for many more political assassinations than any of the larger political organizations or parties. It is impossible to estimate with any degree of precision exactly what percentage of the total number of terrorist acts were carried out by the anarchists, for the local authorities seldom specified an individual terrorist's political sympathies in their reports. The anarchist groups themselves, isolated from one another and with no central organizational structure, did not maintain accurate statistical records. There is little doubt, however, that the majority of the estimated seventeen thousand casualties of terrorist acts between 1901 and 1916 were victims of anarchist attacks. Some of the individuals represented by these statistics had been carefully selected as assassination targets, but many were accidental casualties killed and wounded as bystanders at the scenes of bomb explosions, revolutionary robberies, or shoot-outs between anarchists and the police. The influence of anarchism on Russian life in the opening decade of the twentieth century thus appears to have been "quite out of proportion to the number of its adherents."[12] Many of these adherents represented the generation of the new type of terrorist, at least in terms of the theoretical justification of their policies.

Anarchist Theory

Walter Laqueur is entirely correct in asserting that the anarchist movement "made no theoretical contribution to the cause of the armed struggle" in Russia. Unlike the PSR, which provided its supporters a new ideological justification for terrorist activities, the Russian anarchists did little to develop a scientific foundation for their policy of individual violence, and instead confined themselves to a few appeals in the style of the semi-Futurist manifesto issued in 1909, which complained of the "poisonous breath of civilization," and urged, "Take the picks and hammers! Undermine the foundations of venerable towns! Everything is ours, outside us is only death. . . . All to the street! Forward! Destroy! Kill!"[13] Within this unsophisticated philosophy, however, the various anarchist circles in Russia and abroad offered a variety of reasons for adopting terrorism as their primary tactic.

Among the most notable anarchist groups, one of the least radical was a circle of followers of Petr Kropotkin, the leading theoretician of Russian anarchism, then residing in London. The group was headquartered in Geneva, and led by Georgian anarchist G. Gogeliia (K. Orgeiani) and his wife Lidiia. It published the monthly journal *Khleb i volia* (*Bread and Liberty*), and its members therefore came to be known as Khlebovol'tsy. They considered themselves Anarchists-Communists, that is, adherents of Kropotkin's doctrine promoting a free communal society in which each person was to "give according to his abilities and be provided according to his needs." Like the SRs, and especially the SDs, they attributed the primary role in the revolutionary movement to the masses, and although Kropotkin stated that he was "not afraid to proclaim: do whatever you like, act entirely in accordance with your own discretion," he warned his followers against acts of violence isolated from the mass of the people.[14]

In his opinion, individual terrorist acts could produce no significant change in the existing sociopolitical order. As for revolutionary expropriations, while the practice justifiably transferred funds from the bourgeoisie to those who represented the cause of the oppressed, it did nothing to contribute to the total elimination of private property—the ultimate goal of all anarchists.[15] Moreover, the Khlebovol'tsy could not deny that frequently individuals who called themselves anarchists merely used the elevated rhetoric of freedom fighters to conceal the criminal nature of their activities. The anarchist leaders conceded, for example, that many local organizations "allowed various dregs of society, thieves, and hooligans to . . . operate under the banner of the anarchists-communists," that often "the bomb-thrower-expropriators . . . were no better than the bandits of southern Italy," and that their behavior demoralized the true adherents of anarchism and discredited the movement in the eyes of the public.[16] And yet, while insisting on preserving the purity of radical traditions and their own moral image, Kropotkin's disciples were clearly unprepared to renounce terror as a revolutionary tactic.[17]

After reviewing existing philosophies on the question of political assassination, the Khlebovol'tsy came to the conclusion that it was artificial to distinguish, as all revolutionary parties did, between political and economic terror, for it was the duty of all anarchists to struggle not only against the state, but also against capitalist oppression. They argued further that centralized terror as practiced by the SRs was unjustified in its very essence, for the final decision to proceed with a particular act should be made by the terrorist himself, with no influence or pressure from any other individuals or organizations.[18] Although both these principles were bound to promote a terrorist mood among the anarchists by eliminating restrictions on the use of violence, especially against targets considered capitalist oppressors, and although they left much room for uncontrolled individual initiative, leaders of the Khlebovol'tsy also emphasized that the use of indiscriminate violence against petty servants of the state or the bourgeoisie was incompatible with the revolutionary conscience.[19]

Instead, the Khlebovol'tsy openly sanctioned only defensive terror, which encompassed retaliation against particularly odious members of the police force and the Black Hundreds. Likewise, the Khlebovol'tsy expressly permitted "acts of violence impelled by outraged conscience or compassion for the oppressed."[20] They proclaimed that formal sentences, trials, executions, and similar "bourgeois remnants" practiced by various revolutionary parties violated their creed. In the atmosphere of general oppression, the anarchists were not to judge or execute; they were to defend themselves and implement vengeance.[21] At the same time, like the SRs, they hoped and expected that their terrorist enterprises would contribute to the revolutionary "propaganda by deed," awakening the masses and inciting them to further struggle.

The public renunciation of indiscriminate terror by Kropotkin and his followers was echoed by certain other anarchists, the most ardent of whom were the Anarchists-Syndicalists (Anarkhisty-Sindikalisty), whose leader in Russia was D. Novomirskii (Iakov Kirillovskii), and who formed a large association in Odessa known as the Southern Russian Group of Anarchists-Syndicalists (Iuzhno-russkaia gruppa anarkhistov-sindikalistov). According to Novomirskii, under the circumstances prevailing at the time, the struggle for the liberation of the poor was to be economic, and therefore the immediate goal of the anarchists was to disseminate propaganda in the factories and organize labor unions as agents of the class struggle against the bourgeoisie. In his opinion, random expropriations and other isolated terrorist acts against representatives of the hated political regime did nothing to educate the proletariat, and merely nourished "coarse and bloodthirsty instincts." On the other hand, the effective uses of violence, according to Novomirskii, included not only strikes and boycotts, but also such methods of economic terror as assaults on factory managers, sabotage, and the expropriation of government funds and property.[22]

In their theoretical outlook on terrorist activity, a number of anarchist groups thus appeared relatively restrained. Indeed, their views sometimes seemed more moderate than those of the SRs and especially the Maximalists, and at least in the case of Novomirskii, the anarchist stand on terror approached the general principles of the Social Democrats. These anarchist groups, whose leaders took the time to expound upon their policies toward political assassinations, represented, however, a minority among the anarchist forces; the great majority of the anarchists cheered indiscriminate, reckless, and boundless violence, considering "the existing state oppressions and economic enslavement to be sufficient motives . . . for direct attack, collective or individual, on the oppressors and exploiters, requiring no justification."[23]

Bezmotivniki

The largest and most active anarchist organization in Russia was a federation of groups dispersed primarily through the frontier provinces of the west and south, and known as Chernoe Znamia (Black Banner). Like the Khlebovol'tsy, the Chernoznamentsy considered themselves Anarchists-Communists. In their tactics, however, they were prepared to go beyond Kropotkin's idea of individual action merely as a supplement for the mass struggle against political and economic oppression, and adhere more closely to the principles of conspiracy and uninterrupted violence advocated by the late father of Russian anarchism, Prince Mikhail Bakunin. Suspicious of large-scale organizations, they did not support the Anarchists-Syndicalists' claims regarding the leading role of the trade unions in the liberation of the proletariat, clearly preferring immediate sanguinary action to patient propaganda against the capitalists. Thus, soon after the appearance of the Chernoe Znamia organizations in 1903, their leaders, particularly in Belostok, came up with their own unique outlook on terrorist activity.

For the Chernoznamentsy, every act of violence against political oppression in Russia, however random and senseless it might appear to the general public, was justified in a situation that by 1905 approached civil war. In the atmosphere of universal conflict and mutual hatred between the rebellious slaves and their former masters, the liberators of the people, as the anarchists saw themselves, did not need special provocation to direct their vengeance against any agent of the autocracy. Political assassination was no longer to be used simply as a clearly motivated punishment for specific harsh or repressive measures on the part of a certain proponent of reaction; indeed, the anarchists recognized the arbitrary nature of the terrorism they promoted, and even assigned it a special label: "motiveless terror" (*bezmotivnyi terror*). In accordance with this entirely new concept, which originated and became widespread around 1905, violence no longer required immediate and direct justification; anyone wearing a uniform was considered a representative of the government camp and was therefore subject to execution at any moment as an enemy of the people. According to the advocates of motiveless terror, all defenders of the tsarist regime, including those who served the government only as a result of forced conscription or to make a living, deserved the death penalty.[24] The principles hailed by the *bezmotivniki* thus provided justification for any extremist who decided to toss a bomb into the middle of a military unit, a Cossack patrol, or a police squad.

Moreover, in accordance with the rules of motiveless terror, it was the duty of every anarchist to fight against the representatives of economic oppression, which, in the eyes of the Chernoznamentsy and similar groups, such as the Anarchists-Individualists (Anarkhisty-Individualisty), was no less enslaving than the political conditions of the autocracy. In the struggle against private property, the anarchist creed justified the death of each and every industrialist, estate and factory owner, and even their managers—representatives of the capitalist world who were exploiters by the very nature of their position.[25] In fact, these radicals perceived as guilty of economic oppression "not some social order, but everyone who supported that order and used it for his own benefit."[26] With this in mind, the anarchist leaders urged their followers to cast aside their scruples when throwing bombs into theaters or restaurants, since it would be unusual for anyone who did not belong to the class of exploiters to frequent such places of entertainment, created especially for the amusement of the bourgeoisie.[27] This policy seemed particularly appropriate also because, as the Anarchists-Communists stated in one proclamation, in comparison with political terrorism, "economic (antibourgeois) terror was a better means of propaganda for ... the [anarchist] ideas among the proletariat."[28] The Anarchists-Individualists went even further and proclaimed themselves free to attack and kill anyone, even if the only aim behind the murder was personal gratification, for, in their perception, any terrorist act, without distinction, contributed to the destruction of the bourgeois world in its own way.[29]

The anarchists strove both to bring down what they considered an oppressive political and economic order, and to destroy the spiritual foundations of contemporary state and society. Representatives of the Anarchist-Communist branch of the movement sanctioned unprovoked or motiveless terror against reactionary intellectuals and thinkers, and, even more frequently, against the clergy.[30] In the eyes of these anarchists, even the physical symbols of state and spiritual enslavement, such as triumphal arches and statues of civil and military leaders, as well as church buildings, were appropriate targets for explosives.[31]

The Black Banner organizations recruited most of their members from the lower strata of the population in the border regions, and especially in the areas of the Jewish Pale.[32] Although the anarchists had relatively few supporters in the central Russian provinces and the capitals, a number of smaller groups operated in these areas that in their radicalism and fanaticism yielded nothing to the extremist Chernoznamentsy. Perhaps the most prominent of these organizations was a militant sect based in St. Petersburg in 1905, with smaller circles operating in Kiev, Minsk, and Warsaw, that called itself *Beznachalie* (Without Authority). Like the Chernoznamentsy, the Beznachal'tsy claimed to be Anarchists-Communists and were equally passionate exponents of motiveless terror.

The leader of the Beznachalie radicals, a man in his early twenties, was a namesake of the emperor, Nikolai Romanov, and therefore assumed the alias "Bidbei" (Bidbeev). Bidbei urged his followers to strike merciless blows against each and every government official and policeman; any such attack, he argued, was a step toward the liberation of the people. Moreover, in Bidbei's view, it was essential to direct terrorist operations against all property holders, with any such act considered progressive, for it sowed class discord and incited the oppressed masses to the struggle with their masters. In the true spirit of motiveless terror the Beznachal'tsy adopted the battle cry, "Death to the bourgeoisie!" as their slogan and their fundamental policy, considering it sufficient, in the words of one anarchist, "to see a man in white gloves . . . to recognize in him an enemy who deserves death."[33]

After 1907, when much of the organized antigovernment activity and mass violence had been suppressed, the majority of Bidbei's followers preoccupied themselves exclusively with the economic aspects of terror. At a time when many former radicals, particularly among the workers, had become disillusioned with revolutionary ideals and returned to their work places, many Beznachal'tsy insisted that a true anarchist must not participate in production. He "must not, by his work in a factory or in a shop, strengthen and enhance the position of the same bourgeoisie that is subject to merciless extermination. A 'true' anarchist ought to satisfy his material needs by means of robberies and the theft of possessions from the wealthy to be utilized for his personal needs."[34]

In essence, Bidbei and his disciples declared total war on contemporary society as a whole, which they considered corrupt to the core, and which they sought to destroy by terror of every sort. A number of smaller anarchist groups, such as the Anarchists-Individualists, followed their call for direct action justified by the very claim that it required no justification.[35]

Anarchist Terror in Practice

Regardless of the theoretical disagreements among the anarchists as to how extensively terrorist methods were to be implemented, all anarchist organizations were to one degree or another proponents of political assassination. None of these groups questioned the principle of terrorist action, and so their discord concerned only the finer points of theory supporting individual violence, and the details determining the selection of targets.

While paying lip service to agitation and propaganda among the proletariat, in practice many anarchist groups were preoccupied entirely with terror and rarely concerned themselves with the more gradual aspects of the antigovernment and anticapitalist struggle. According to a former extremist, "There was almost no anarchist who, upon joining the ranks of the movement, did not become 100 per cent *boevik*, ready for one act or another every minute. The revolutionary situation . . . created an atmosphere of total militancy [*boevizm*]," especially during the years of 1905–1906.[36] All in all, anarchists were the best representatives of the new type of terrorist, not only in their choice of victims, but also in the very process by which they elected to proceed with terrorist acts.

As far as choice of targets was concerned, all anarchists except the Khlebovol'tsy, who resided primarily abroad and thus confined themselves largely to theoretical statements, were prepared to prove in practice their readiness to kill randomly and in large numbers. Even the more moderate Anarchists-Syndicalists, who did not believe that political assassination could liberate the people from domination by capital, supported any murder associated with their policy of all-out economic terror. Following the outbreak of the first Russian revolution, therefore, the anarchists became engaged in terrorist enterprises that would have been unthinkable to the nineteenth-century revolutionaries, and indeed were repugnant to many nonanarchist radicals operating after 1905.

Like members of all other revolutionary organizations, the anarchists seized every opportunity to settle scores with the countless police spies within their ranks,[37] or to attack individuals who assisted the authorities in arresting revolutionaries or testified against them in court.[38] Along with representatives of the radical socialist groups, the anarchists shot and threw bombs at policemen conducting house searches or making arrests. On these occasions the anarchists often chose to end their own lives with their last bullets rather than fall into the hands of the authorities.[39] They also killed while attempting to liberate imprisoned comrades, sometimes undertaking extremely risky schemes. In one such episode, a group of them broke into a church where prisoners were attending an Easter service, freed all the prisoners present, and killed their guards.[40] Anarchists occasionally assaulted publishing houses and forced the workers, under threat of immediate execution, to print their leaflets and proclamations.[41] Finally, while individual anarchists and isolated groups made elaborate plans to assassinate governors-general and other leading state figures, including members of the imperial family[42]—plans that for one reason or another invariably failed—these extremists, like many SRs and some SDs, always welcomed an opportunity for revenge against local military commanders, heads of peripheral Okhrana and gendarme departments, civilian and prison authorities, as well as priests and rabbis who castigated the radicals in their sermons.[43] And yet, in one respect their violent practices contrasted sharply with those of other revolutionary organizations, including most Maximalists: the anarchists frequently focused their terrorist attacks, both individual and collective, against government employees of all categories and ranks for the sole reason that they considered all servants of the autocracy guilty by virtue of their uniforms. The conflict between the authorities and the radicals was so deep, and the mutual hatred so profound, that, as one revolutionary recalled, some anarchists could not tolerate even the sight of a police officer passing by in the street.[44] It is hardly surprising then that perhaps the most common targets for random attacks were street policemen, who were visible enough to attract the attention of anyone seeking an opportunity to express anger. Following the outbreak of revolutionary activities in 1905 street policemen became victims of anarchist terror in broad daylight in great numbers.[45]

In many situations the anarchists sought to produce the maximum propaganda effect among the proletarians by their terrorist acts, and on occasion this entailed the provocation of what they labeled "counterrevolutionary violence." On 24 April 1905, for example, a number of anarchists in Odessa assembled near the city Duma, "for the purpose of initiating disturbances, and [then] showing resistance to the police who would [show up to] suppress the disorders, by throwing a bomb into their ranks."[46]

Many policemen spared from the terrorists' bullets were forcefully disarmed by the anarchists,[47] and the authorities were aware of the fact that individual members of the police force in major centers of radical activity such as Odessa and Ekaterinoslav, as well as the border areas, were especially vulnerable to the extremists' attacks while on patrol. The only solution found was a desperate one—the use of the military, with three soldiers sometimes posted to protect a single policeman guarding a bank, post office, zemstvo or treasury building. Military units were also assigned to guard police stations.[48]

The anarchists frequently demonstrated great personal courage in their willingness to sacrifice their lives for the revolutionary cause. They were especially eager to do so for the sake of a sensational mass assassination of government employees, since, as was stated in the leading Anarchist-Communist publication, *Buntar'* (*Rebel*), "individual terror is incapable of solving the problems facing the anarchists."[49] In a typical incident, on 27 May 1906 two anarchists took advantage of an opportunity to settle their accounts with the local authorities in Belostok by attacking an entire detachment of police officers and murdering their leader.[50] Similarly, so frequently did anarchists stage assaults on mounted Cossacks assigned to maintain order that the troops stopped appearing on the streets for fear of being ambushed. In some instances, terrorists seeking revenge against one policeman or another devised ingenious maneuvers to entice their intended victims from their relatively protected headquarters.[51] The police were not safe even there, however, for the anarchists repeatedly managed to get close enough to the heavily guarded Okhrana and gendarme administration buildings to toss bombs or other explosives inside. With the heedless determination of true fanatics, anarchists made their way into police headquarters in various parts of the country and blew themselves up with dynamite, along with everyone present. Nisan (Nisel') Farber, one of the most active members of a Belostok anarchist group, was responsible for such an exploit in October 1904.[52]

Occasionally, anarchists also set off explosives in churches[53] and threw bombs into synagogues where local Jewish community leaders held their meetings,[54] but perhaps most characteristic of the indiscriminate terror were the frequent terrorist attacks against the military, usually common soldiers stationed in areas plagued by terrorist activities. One such center of anarchist violence was Ekaterinoslav, where in the stormy days of October 1905, the authorities reported numerous incidents of revolutionaries firing revolvers at rank-and-file troops, and throwing bombs at military units. The soldiers and officers were subject to danger on literally every corner; there were no safe streets in the city, for bombs fell on the defenders of order from balconies,[55] and explosive devices were even planted in the Cossack barracks.[56]

Unlike their fellow revolutionaries in the socialist camp, whose immediate goal was a political revolution, the anarchists considered the capitalist order as formidable an enemy as the state, and therefore attacked anyone who represented the oppressive economic order, namely factory owners and directors, managers, merchants, land and store owners, and all other exploiters. Significantly, attacks on the worst individual capitalist offenders went hand in hand with uninterrupted mass terrorist acts against the bourgeoisie in general. In accordance with the slogan of several Anarchist-Communist groups in Moscow and Odessa, "The death of the bourgeoisie is life for the workers," anyone who was not an unpropertied proletarian deserved to be killed.[57]

It is impossible to account for every one of the terrorist acts perpetrated by the anarchists against property owners, but clearly the range of these targets was very wide, from wealthy bankers and factory directors to the owners of small estates and petty shoemakers' shops who might have refused concessions to striking employees, called for police or soldiers during workers' disturbances, supported harsh fines and firing policies, or possessed reputations for being unsympathetic to the toilers' needs. The anarchists often directed their attacks not only against the owners and administrators of a particular industrial or business enterprise, but also against its managers, technicians, engineers, and other specialists who, in the eyes of the frequently less than sophisticated radical workers, belonged to the oppressors' camp by virtue of their education, position, or even physical appearance.[58] In one case, *bezmotivniki* killed the three sons of a factory owner,[59] and occasionally the Anarchists-Communists tossed bombs into small shops simply as a "protest against private property."[60]

At the same time, the anarchists constantly planned and implemented terrorist acts against the bourgeoisie en masse. In January 1906 at a conference called by the advocates of motiveless terror, the extremists resolved to set off a massive explosion during the next All-Russian Congress of Mining Industrialists. Local anarchist groups made similar decisions. In Belostok, for example, they worked out a plan to place explosives, or "infernal machines," along the largest street in the town, so that "all the main bourgeois would be blown up into the air."[61]

The anarchists' deeds often conformed with their plans, and unlike terrorists from other revolutionary organizations, these radicals extended their motiveless attacks to individuals who simply appeared more fortunate in their economic status than the proletarians, even when they could not be charged with direct exploitation of the unpropertied classes. There were many incidents in which anarchists used violence against the bourgeois for the sole reason that these people were relatively well dressed. This was the case when an anarchist from Ekaterinoslav seeking class revenge tossed a bomb into a first-class railway compartment full of apparently prosperous passengers.[62] One of the best-known similar cases was the 17 December 1905 bombing of the Libman Cafe in the terror-ravaged city of Odessa. If the anarchists intended this attack as a sensational statement against representatives of the hated socioeconomic order, they succeeded only in part: the explosion claimed a dozen victims, caused a great deal of damage to the building, and indeed became a front-page newspaper story. It turned out, however, that the cafe was not an exclusive restaurant for the wealthy, but rather a second-class establishment and a gathering place of the intelligentsia.[63]

Along with its characteristic choice of targets, the new type of terrorism perpetrated by the anarchists was distinguished by the motives behind the acts. By virtue of the anarchists' contempt for organized political formations, and conversely, because of their primary interest in the unrestricted "development of the individual," more frequently than the representatives of any other radical organization, they staged terrorist attacks on personal initiative, quite suddenly and on a whim, their actions autonomous even from any local anarchist leadership. There are numerous examples to justify this assertion. In one incident late in 1906, Anarchist-Communist Beniamin Fridman, while waiting in hiding to ambush and kill the head of a Grodno prison, noticed a jail warden approaching. Knowing that this man was extremely unpopular, Fridman immediately "decided that this dog well deserved a bullet too," and took several shots at him.[64] Another episode illustrates that in setting targets for their acts, anarchists often relied on hearsay and readily assumed the worst regarding atrocities perpetrated by agents of the government. Aleksandr Kolosov, a member of an anarchist group in Tambov, heard a rumor that a young woman revolutionary had been raped in a local prison, apparently by prison personnel. His immediate reaction was to grab his revolver and set off to kill the head of the prison. Fortunately for the prison official, however, Kolosov happened to meet the young woman's fiancé on the way, who told him that the rumor was nonsense.[65]

In contrast to the radicals of the late nineteenth century, with their common inclination for abstract thinking and theorizing, the anarchists were largely indifferent to intellectual matters. Moreover, the educational level of these terrorists of the new type was on the whole extremely low, partly because many active anarchists came from impoverished Jewish families in the Pale, and, as in the case of Nisan Farber, did not know a word of Russian.[66] The majority of anarchists of strictly Russian origin also came from a working-class background and had received minimal schooling. They refused to see this as an obstacle to their revolutionary activities, however, and one of these combatants reportedly liked to repeat with pride, "I have not read a single book, but in my heart I am an anarchist."[67]

What the radicals referred to as "revolutionary consciousness" was also very low in many of these terrorists, who tended to disregard all theoretical issues, whether questions of socialist ideology or anarchist creed. It was entirely typical that a member of an Anarchist-Communist group in Odessa, engaged in casual conversation with a comrade, could not defend his revolutionary views, was unaware of the differences among the programs of the existing political parties, and—even more significant—considered it unnecessary to familiarize himself with the various philosophies, because, in his opinion, during a revolution it would simply be more important to act.[68] Fully conscious of the fact that many of their comrades were underdeveloped in their theoretical outlook, the anarchists indicated that for them the primary characteristic of a good revolutionary was to have "combat in his blood" (*boevaia zhilka*).[69]

Some of the terrorist acts perpetrated by various anarchist groups and their isolated members after 1905 can be considered part of the ongoing economic struggle of the proletarians against their capitalist employers. Farber, for example, attacked Avraam Kogan, the director of a large textile mill, with a knife, seriously wounding him. The attack took place on the Jewish Day of Atonement, Yom Kippur, on the steps of the synagogue, and was committed in retaliation for the hiring of strikebreakers during a work stoppage.[70] This terrorist act was a far from isolated instance of individual violence used as a tool to advance the mass movement of the workers: anarchist groups, particularly those of Anarchist-Syndicalist orientation, were responsible for numerous bloody incidents of economic terror, such as seizures of bakeries and state-owned liquor stores, bombings of trams and railways that continued to operate during strikes, and the murder of a printing press director who rejected the demands of striking employees.[71] The port of Odessa became the center of constant terrorist activity in 1906–1907, when the Anarchists-Syndicalists were responsible for blowing up several commercial steamships and killing two captains unpopular among the seamen.[72] In the great majority of their terrorist undertakings, however, the anarchists, like the SDs and the SRs, admittedly failed to make serious efforts to connect their individual acts of violence with the general antigovernment movement of the toiling masses.[73]

Indeed, for many of these extremists, who unlike most of their predecessors were not dedicated to preserving the purity of either the revolutionary tradition or their own ethical images, the decision to employ violence was not at all based on a conviction that terror was an expedient means in the struggle for liberation. Although they usually justified their acts by lofty talk of emancipating the oppressed, their underlying motives were often less elevated, for, as Avrich notes, reckless and frustrated youths, among whom were certain "self-styled Nietzschean supermen," often "satisfied their desire for excitement and self-affirmation by hurling bombs into public buildings, factory offices, theaters, and restaurants."[74] Many anarchists, foremost among them the notorious Bidbei, admired Sergei Nechaev, the black sheep of the nineteenth-century Russian revolutionary movement, because of his promotion of the unscrupulous use of violence for personal aims and his insistence that the radicals enter into cooperation with "bandits—the only true revolutionaries in Russia."[75]

Common banditry was in fact particularly widespread in the anarchist ranks, much more so than among any other proponents of the revolution. Former vagabonds, professional thieves, and other denizens of the criminal world joined the anarchists in relatively large numbers. This was at least in part because the movement provided a convenient justification for their behavior, not only by suggesting that contemporary society was responsible for all criminal activity on the part of its impoverished, alienated, and frustrated members, but also by offering an elevated explanation for their conduct by classifying their crimes, whether murder or robbery, as progressive steps contributing to the destabilization of the sociopolitical order.[76] Any criminal action thus became part of the general revolutionary struggle, and so, as Laqueur points out, the "dividing line between politics and crime was by no means always obvious and clear-cut."[77]

Following Bakunin's example, the anarchists welcomed all the base rabble, all the outcast elements and renegades of society, into their ranks as brothers and comrades, emphasizing the great revolutionary potential of thieves, tramps, the *lumpenproletariat*, and other shadowy individuals.[78] As early as 1903, for example, with the goal of converting bandits into true fighters for the radical cause, members of the first anarchist organization in Belostok, which called itself the International Group, "Struggle" (*Internatsional'naia Gruppa "Bor'ba"*), began revolutionary agitation among common thieves, some of whom subsequently became very effective revolutionaries. Many anarchists serving prison terms also agitated among the criminals, believing that the antigovernment cause would be greatly enhanced if the criminal prisoners who had formerly murdered and robbed for selfish motives were to proclaim themselves revolutionaries and engage in the same activities for the sake of liberating the proletariat.[79] These transformations notwithstanding, members of other political parties began to reproach the anarchists for falling under the influence of criminals to the extent that the anarchists themselves turned into thieves.[80]

In places of exile, where political convicts comprised tiny colonies among the frequently hostile local inhabitants, the anarchists joined together in their own small bands, often referred to as "the hooligan component of the exiles." These radicals insisted on their anarchist title and progressive beliefs, but this did not prevent disorderly excesses. In a revealing episode that took place in the Vologda region after the defeat of the revolution in 1907, a celebration was held honoring the anniversary of a bomb explosion in the French parliament. During the festivities, members of a local anarchist group became drunk, began to fight among themselves, and broke windows in their apartment. When a Social Democrat later reproached the anarchist leader, the anarchist attacked and beat his fellow revolutionary with a stick. Debauchery, brawls, and casualties were the order of the day among these revolutionaries.[81]

The mutual sympathy between the anarchists and common bandits proved beneficial for the revolutionaries, at least in terms of attracting new supporters from the criminal world to the antigovernment movement.[82] The same, however, cannot be said about the long-term moral implications of this relationship, for the presence of criminals in the anarchist ranks "caused friction, corruption and eventually demoralization."[83] Under the influence of this dark element, many anarchist groups deteriorated into semicriminal gangs occupied primarily with robbery and looting for personal profit.[84] In 1906–1907, according to St. Petersburg Okhrana chief Gerasimov, these organizations, operating under the anarchist flag, were not at all revolutionary in their ideological outlook; they merely used anarchist rhetoric to justify pure banditry.[85]

This was also true of the anarchists operating in and around Moscow during approximately the same period. A relatively large anarchist group led by a convinced proponent of motiveless terror, Savel'ev, was to a large extent composed of hard-core thieves and murderers who had fled from the police in the Vladivostok region to central Russia, where they joined forces with the anarchists and continued their criminal activities. One of them, a deserter from the navy named Filippov, admittedly had no interest in the anarchist program, failing to grasp its meaning until his arrest, and was only eager for action and its material results. This man claimed responsibility for eleven murders, and his comrades had similar backgrounds: his girlfriend was a registered prostitute, a second fugitive sailor had been sentenced to hard labor for taking part in killing a priest and robbing a church, and that convict's lover was a thief with a police record.[86]

The situation was little different in the provinces, where by early 1906 the "decay of the anarchist organizations reached its highest point, when throughout all of Russia . . . groups of the so-called 'Black Ravens' (Chernye vorony) began to appear . . . gangs of green young bandits, whose adventures were occasionally colored by red romanticism."[87] Along with the Black Ravens, there were other banditlike anarchist groups active under names such as Black Terror (Chernyi terror),[88] or without any name, such as the relatively large formation of anarchists operating in Kiev and Vil'na, led by a certain Ustinov, which quickly degenerated into a criminal gang engaged in looting and other profit-oriented violence. Their behavior led local revolutionaries to dissociate themselves entirely from them, and to spread rumors that participants in this organization were "not real anarchists by conviction," but rather hooligans purposely "let loose by the government."[89]

Criminals or freedom fighters, the anarchists contributed immensely to both the escalation of bloodletting in Russia, and the devaluation of human life in the prevailing atmosphere of rampant violence. Typically, Ekaterinoslav anarchist Fedosei Zubar' attacked and nearly killed a worker, who turned out to be a member of a local SD group, solely for trying to remove an anarchist proclamation from a wall.[90] Another terrorist, accused in the course of his trial of having accidently killed a schoolgirl during a 1907 anarchist attack on Moscow street policemen, responded, "I am very sorry about this, but it is impossible not to have innocent victims in a time of war."[91] In several cases, the anarchists proved only too willing to use their skills as political assassins in strictly criminal acts of murder for personal motives, including jealousy.[92] Many of these extremists themselves recognized the existence of a phenomenon that Iuda Grossman labeled "a mechanical militancy," claiming that under its influence an individual "automatically 'makes attempts,' as if infatuated with the terrorist 'art for art's sake.' "[93]

Violence committed habitually to the point of complete loss of any significance is apparent in the brief biography of an anarchist from Belostok, as it was presented in an obituary written by fellow revolutionaries. According to his comrades, the activities of Movsha Shpindler (Moishe Grodner) were "marked by incredible diversity." In addition to distributing leaflets and illegal literature among factory workers, and helping with the underground printing press, he procured weapons, took part in at least one expropriation, and numerous other terrorist attacks. Along with two friends, he made plans to kill the head of a prison in the town of Grodno; he also liberated a comrade, wounding several soldiers in the prison convoy in the process. He threw a bomb into the carriage of the governor-general of Belostok, Bogaevskii, and even after he was forced to flee from Belostok, "killed a spy there . . . on his every return." Death came when he shot himself with his last bullet after a bloody confrontation with the police during a house search. The early years of Shpindler's life are also not without interest, for before he joined the anarchists, "he was a professional thief, much respected in his milieu for his dexterity, and nicknamed 'golden hand.'" He knew no other trade and lived from hand to mouth. Shpindler, the anarchists conceded, "was not too familiar with the fine points" of their program, but they nevertheless characterized him as "one of the most devoted [and] perfectly honest comrades . . . in the entire Russian movement."[94] His comrades' tribute portrays Shpindler as a true terrorist of the new type.[95]

No doubt there were numerous anarchists very different in background, intellectual sophistication, and ethical awareness from Filippov, Shpindler, and their kin. Left-wing sources, including the memoirs of revolutionaries, frequently insist that there were many principled people with firm ideological convictions among the anarchists, but that they "stayed somewhat aside from the organization of the Anarchists-Communists," and preferred to associate with the Syndicalists, who were less apt to take part in motiveless terror.[96] Even police officials, who tended to view and classify most extremists as hardcore criminals, remarked upon the great faith in a revolutionary utopia evinced by individual anarchists, and their total dedication to the cause, which led to displays of outstanding personal courage and selfless determination to live in accordance with the anarchist ideal. A leading Okhrana officer, Police Captain (*rotmistr*) Petr Zavarzin, a man who could not be accused of radical sympathies, admitted that during his service he came into contact with many such "anarchist-fanatics and ascetics," who dressed in rags, ate only enough to avoid starvation, and forbade themselves any pleasure or entertainment bearing even a trace of luxury.[97] The same author asserted, however, that along with the bandits, idealists, and zealots, a whole range of people found their places in the ranks of the anarchist movement, including:

> weak-willed people, simply drawn into predatory activity, depraved half-educated persons . . . and immature youths, corrupt to the core. Of course, the membership of the groups was also partly made up of the scum of various revolutionary parties, who in their agitation followed an always popular and easily apprehended ideology: alienation of wealth, negation of [private] property, stealing what has been stolen (*grab' nagrablennoe*), and so on.[98]

Plekhanov's words, written some fifteen years prior to the outbreak of mass violence in 1905, thus proved truly accurate: "It is impossible to guess where a comrade anarchist ends and where a bandit begins."[99]

Obscure Extremist Groups

This label can be applied to the numerous groups operating apart from the mainstream antigovernment movement throughout the Russian Empire after 1903, and especially following the outbreak of revolutionary events in 1905. Having for diverse reasons isolated themselves or broken away from the major revolutionary organizations and even the anarchists, various alienated individuals, too rebellious to remain within the framework of any political formation, banded together in small, loosely organized gangs of revolutionary extremists, prepared for the moment to cooperate in practical matters. Most of these radicals either deviated from the ideological principles advocated by the established radical parties, or, more commonly, could not confine themselves to specific tactical programs, usually wishing to go beyond the limits of what these organizations considered legitimate and justified revolutionary means. The primary point of disagreement as far as tactics were concerned was the issue of terror and expropriations, and the dissenters' attitude vis-à-vis these methods clearly betrayed them as terrorists of the new type. These independent radicals had failed to develop any firm ideological principles differing from those advocated by the established political parties, and practiced uninterrupted violence without making any serious attempts to justify it with dogma, readily engaging in a range of criminal enterprises that had little to do with revolutionary goals and were perpetrated instead for personal material profit.

The various groups classified here as "obscure" included former representatives of all the revolutionary organizations, but the overwhelming majority of independent extremists were dissidents from the Socialist-Revolutionary cells operating in the provinces after 1905. As was true of most defectors to the anarchists, many former SRs objected first of all to the control of terrorist activity by a party leadership empowered to regulate these activities in accordance with the overall political goals of the organization, initiating and halting them at will. Secondly, these nonconformists denounced the restrictions officially imposed by the party on economic terror, and specifically the prohibitions against the expropriation of private property. Even though these acts never ceased in practice, isolated individuals within the PSR still resented the obligation to adhere to its discipline, pay lip service to its tactical policies, and refrain from attractive ventures proscribed because they might stain the party's reputation.

Numerous SRs thus left the PSR to escape its central civilian control of terrorist activities. In the town of Aleksandrovsk in 1905, one Socialist Revolutionary, outraged by what he considered a senseless decision on the part of the local committee, left the organization and set up an independent terrorist unit, continuing to call himself an SR for a while.[100] In the city of Gomel', a number of defectors from the PSR united in 1905 into a group whose members called themselves Independent Socialists-Revolutionaries, and formed terror-ist detachments that were autonomous from all the local SR combat forces. Along with terrorist attacks against police and civil authorities—acts that were quite within the SR tradition—these extremists indulged in uncontrolled eco-nomic violence, often directing their wrath against estate managers, with their actions acquiring Maximalist and even anarchist overtones. These independent revolutionaries were apparently disinterested in any aspect of socialist ideol-ogy, and this tendency, in combination with their use of coercion to secure funds from private individuals for terrorist operations, caused the local Social-ists-Revolutionaries to dissociate themselves entirely from these obscure figures, and to deny any previous links with them.[101]

In their attitude toward violence, many former SRs among the independent radicals drifted gradually toward anarchism. A group known as the Uncom-promising Ones (Neprimirimye), formed in Odessa in November of 1903, hav-ing formally broken from the local SR Committee over tactical matters, re-nounced or ignored all aspects of SR thinking, but retained their fascination with political murder. In addition, they embraced such anarchist goals as the systematic destruction of factories and plants as a necessary part of the anti-bourgeois struggle.[102] Dissatisfied and frustrated members of the PSR also united initially into small radical units with no firm ideological views or pro-gram for practical actions before eventually joining the organized opposition of the Maximalists. This was the case with one terrorist group in Belostok that adopted the self-explanatory title of the Young Ones (Molodye), and later merged with the general Maximalist movement. In the interim their political outlook came close to anarchism, for they wholeheartedly accepted the anar-chist views on terror and violence, and disagreed only with their negative stand on the question of organization. This, however, was of minor importance; as one former member of this circle confessed, they "were not much concerned with ideology."[103]

In part for this reason, and also because of the widespread desire of many former SRs to escape the control of any authority, they not only ruptured ties with their organization, but also chose not to join its formal Maximalist oppo-sition. Instead, many who considered themselves Maximalists in spirit pre-ferred to preserve their independence even from this loose confederation of SR oppositionists, and, like the notorious hero of the small town of Klintsy, Com-rade Savitskii (a born gang leader, nicknamed for his adventures "the new Nat Pinkerton and Rinaldo-Rinaldini" by the local press), formed their own tiny autonomous bands, oriented exclusively toward combat activities.[104]

Similarly, following the outbreak of violence in 1905 many members of the Russian Social Democratic Workers' Party declined to wait patiently for the full development of capitalist relations, which, according to an underlying principle of Marxism, would create a truly revolutionary situation, with the proletariat finally ready to take over the means of production, the most fundamental feature of industrial society. Many Social Democrats sought immediate action, and therefore chose to disregard the incompatibility of their behavior with the theoretical principles of the SD organization. For the most part, however, members of local SD groups possessed only a limited notion of and interest in even the most basic Marxist postulates, and thus it was not difficult for people such as Vasilii Podvysotskii, a young SD worker from Odessa, to conclude under the influence of government repressions in 1907: "Our eyes will pop out before we live to see the concentration of capital. No, brothers, let's turn to terror instead!" Podvysotskii's comrades agreed: "What is the use of padding out empty theory? Our brothers are being hanged, and we are supposed to wait patiently. . . . How long are we to wait, until everyone is hanged?"[105] In complete agreement, Podvysotskii and his followers joined together in an independent combat group entirely anarchist both in spirit and in its practical actions, devoted primarily to robbing the wealthy.

The most familiar example of renegade SDs active in obscure terrorist guerrilla groups involves a relatively large contingent of *boeviki* operating in the Ural region under the leadership of the almost legendary Aleksandr Lbov. Originally a worker from the town of Perm', in 1905 and early 1906 Lbov sympathized with the Social Democrats, took part in the organized movement among the workers at local cannon factories, and commanded a combat detachment. When the police began to make arrests in 1906, Lbov went underground and lived in the forest with a growing retinue that organized itself into a guerrilla band. By the end of the year, the unit was reinforced by new blood when a group of St. Petersburg Maximalists, fleeing from the authorities following the Fonarnyi Lane expropriation, joined Lbov's combatants. The guerrilla detachment then began to implement Lbov's version of the most efficient way to liberate the proletariat,[106] rejecting what they referred to as the "well-known Social Democratic nonsense" that professional or party organizations served as agents directing the workers in their struggle against the capitalist exploiters and their government protectors. To these extremists, all complicated schemes of action were superfluous. Their own program was simple and to the point: "If there is worker dissatisfaction, there is a need for reprisals against the individual objects of this dissatisfaction."[107] With this in mind, the combatants launched assassination attempts against factory directors, shop managers, and other prominent figures in the local industrial community perceived as hard-liners in economic and political matters. They also engaged in expropriations against factory offices and liquor stores, and caused general panic among the population. The inhabitants of this region nicknamed the gang leader "Terror of the Urals" (Groza Urala).[108]

Members of the various national factions of the RSDRP also commonly broke away from the control of their central organizations to form obscure and usually short-lived SD combat groups. As an example, a radical minority of the Latvian Social Democratic Workers' Party became dissatisfied with the

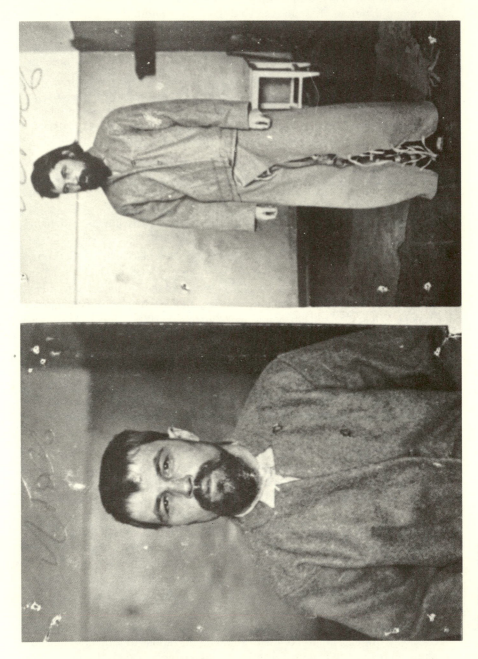

16. Aleksandr Lbov

17. A bomb laboratory

18. Disassembled homemade Anarchist-Communist explosive device

organization's apparent lack of progress in consolidating the Riga workers into a powerful proletarian force. When the leaders of this tiny faction demanded decisive and immediate action, a schism developed, with the dissenters breaking away from the mainstream of Latvian Social Democracy and establishing themselves as a separate organization called Forward (in Latvian, "Uspeekschu"), which soon changed its name to the Latvian Social Democratic Union and formed combat units that participated actively in numerous political assassinations throughout Latvia.[109]

The same tendency to break formal ties with Social Democratic organizations to pursue independent and often violent action was evident in the Caucasus. The extremist group known as Terror of the City of Tiflis and Its Districts (Terror g. Tiflisa i ego uezdov) was originally part of the local SD organization, but had broken ties with it for the sake of unrestrained violence. Ultimately, however, as a result of continuous clashes with the nationalist forces in Tiflis, they chose to return to the control and protection of the Social Democrats.[110] In the same city, a number of Georgian SDs united in opposition to the formal SD Committee because it refused to sanction expropriations. This radical minority was expelled from the Caucasian organization and formed its own autonomous group, the Union of Revolutionary Social Democrats (Soiuz Revoliutsionnykh Sotsial Demokratov), which staged revolutionary robberies in Tiflis and Kutais during the winter of 1906–1907.[111]

In addition to the many obscure combat groups loosely associated with the SR and SD movements, numerous other terrorist bands operated throughout the Russian Empire that chose not to ally themselves with either the socialist or the anarchist camp, despite their persistent vague claims in support of the revolutionary nature of their activities. The claims were often justified by practical policies, as in the case of a St. Petersburg group that by its very name, Death for Death (Smert' za smert'), aimed to strike terror in the hearts of the enemy. Its immediate plan of action called for the assassinations of a number of prominent statesmen in the capital, including Stolypin, Trepov, and Durnovo.[112] Another such group was a band of some twenty revolutionaries, also operating in St. Petersburg, calling themselves the Group of Terrorists-Expropriators (Gruppa terroristov-ekspropriatorov). At their October 1907 trial, members of this band were convicted of attempting "to bring down the existing political regime in Russia by force and to replace it with a democratic republic," starting with an attack on a monastery near the town of Grodno. One of the radicals was sentenced to ten years of hard labor for his participation in an attack on another monastery, where the terrorists had planted explosives to destroy the revered Icon of the Virgin of Kursk.[113]

Obscure revolutionary groups like these were even more active in the periphery. An underground circle of about a dozen independent extremists operating in the town of Voronezh united themselves in 1907–1908 into the League of the Red Fuse (Liga krasnogo shnura), with the ambitious objective of ending the contemporary sociopolitical order in Russia. The fact that they did not even pretend to know what new order was to replace the old oppressive one did not deter the League from developing an immediate plan of action involving a series of political assassinations of public and private figures. All members of the League of the Red Fuse were arrested before they could implement their farfetched schemes, although they had managed to carry out several armed robberies in Voronezh.[114] In other cities and towns throughout Russia numerous bloody acts of violence were perpetrated by equally obscure groups, such as, for instance, the Black Cloud (Chernaia Tucha) revolutionary cell in the province of Chernigov, and the Storm (Groza), a combat detachment in the town of Rogachev whose members called themselves Terrorists-Individualists.[115] Finally, various small terrorist units emerged in the border areas of the empire in this period, including the Socialist Union (Sotsialisticheskii soiuz), formed in 1899 in the Baltics. By 1905 the Union was actively perpetrating political assassinations and assaults on estates, proving in practice that its "tactics were much further to the left than those of the Social Democracy of the Latvian region."[116]

There were many terrorist groups in the first decade of the twentieth century with such ambiguous ideological foundations that it is frequently impossible to establish with any degree of certainty the raison d'être or political orientation of a particular clandestine circle. Universal rampant violence apparently needed no justification for a group made up of four young men and a girl who plotted the murder of Kropotkin in London, feeling that the leading Russian anarchist exerted too moderate an influence over his followers, holding back the forces of revolution.[117] Another group, the party of the Independent Ones (Neza-visimye), worked out a charter stating that this secret society had been

> organized for the struggle against all sorts of violence, regardless of its source, whether initiated by social organs, political parties, or state institutions. . . . Whatever forms violence . . . reveals itself in, whether as terror on the part of extremist parties, or in the form of coercion by bureaucratic organs of the state mechanism . . . any victim will always find most energetic protection from the party against oppression of the individual. The party admits into its ranks people of all ages, without discriminating against any sex, religion, nationality and profession. A priest, a socialist, and a state official enjoy equal votes in the party.[118]

Judging from the opening section of this charter, the Independent Ones appear to have been a variety of vigilante police force, determined to protect all victims of organized violence, right- or left-wing, indiscriminately. The statement on tactics that follows the discussion of the general goals of the organization vividly demonstrates, however, that the elevated language about defending the innocent and the oppressed was directed against the authorities only, for the party resolved to implement terror "in all cases of aggressive behavior by the government, the police, the inspirators of the bureaucracy and its spiritual ideologists." The Independent Ones also proclaimed their right to administer justice and implement death sentences four days after a verdict. Because this group included "confiscation of the enemy's material means" in its "punitive measures against persons and institutions that oppress individual freedom," it is evident that, despite the obvious contradiction, the Independent Ones, who claimed to struggle against all sources of violence, promoted their cause primarily by resorting to the very same tactics.[119]

In addition to the obscure extremist organizations that exerted at least minimal efforts to portray themselves as true revolutionaries with the semblance of an ideological profile, there were other terrorist bands unwilling even to go this far. The sources give no indication that members of these groups considered themselves anything but common outlaws. In prisons, for example, they did not demand the special treatment usually accorded political convicts, and normally passed their terms among the thieves and murderers.[120] One such group of about a dozen fugitive hard labor convicts proved obedient tools in the hands of their chief, Grigorii Kotovskii, a legendary figure in Bessarabia prior to the 1917 revolution. Kotovskii came from a noble family, and from his childhood found himself in frequent conflict with his superiors in school and employment (having been fired for embezzlement), and "fanatically fascinated by the criminal world." A tireless adventurer, Kotovskii became infatuated with brigand life, and as early as 1903 began to take vengeance on the milieu in which he grew up.[121] Although he was said to have occasionally made contributions to the local SR Committee, probably to promote its work among the peasantry, Kotovskii was not formally affiliated with any party. He demonstrated no ideological preferences, directing his activities against the wealthy in general, and expropriating anything he could get his hands on, from currency held by city banks to Persian carpets in private homes. Kotovskii liked to think of himself as a Russian Robin Hood, or "an ideological thief," and although he fully indulged his love of wine, women, and entertainment, he also claimed to have distributed a share of his loot among the poor.[122]

These claims notwithstanding, both the authorities and his criminal acquaintances regarded him as a daring gang leader (*ataman*), and his followers as a band of burglars and vagabonds. In the winter of 1906, after one of his men betrayed him to the police for the handsome reward of ten thousand rubles, Kotovskii was tried not as a political prisoner, but as a common criminal.[123] His life-style, manners, and even language (his lexicon was rich in street and prison jargon) suggest that this treatment was not inappropriate, a conclusion reinforced by Kotovskii's imprisonment as a common bandit and the chief of a smash-and-grab gang for a while even after the 1917 February revolution, when all political prisoners of the late tsarist regime were granted liberty, regardless of their offenses.[124]

With the escalation of the revolutionary upheaval after 1905, many *boeviki*, even among those formerly determined to prove themselves dedicated freedom fighters rather than raiders and profiteers, abandoned all efforts to defend their actions with theoretical principles. Their only justification for participating in revolutionary banditry was an alleged desire to help their comrades implement vague ideals involving a revolutionary utopia. They openly confessed, "We are weak in theories and incapable of carrying out party work. We are of no use, except for obtaining money by means of 'ex's.'"[125]

EXPROPRIATIONS

There were, however, some anarchist and obscure revolutionary organizations that made genuine efforts to develop a convincing theoretical justification for their policy of expropriations, although none of these explanations involved particularly deep or sophisticated reasoning. The dominant rationale among these extremists held that instead of humiliating themselves by begging for financial donations from the liberals, or relying upon contributions from the economically deprived proletarians, the revolutionaries must live off the capitalists—the rich merchants, the land and store owners—and other bourgeois exploiters. By expropriating their money and possessions, the radicals were to sustain themselves as full-time professional revolutionaries, and purchase the weapons and explosives required to overthrow the state and the bourgeoisie.[126]

Within the anarchist camp the radicals could not agree as to how persistent they ought to be in carrying out their program of economic terror. Whereas members of the Black Banner organization argued that the workers must continue to labor in the factories and shops despite exploitation and injustice, adherents of the Beznachalie trend declared that a true anarchist must not participate in capitalist production, because in so doing he enhanced the strength of the very bourgeoisie that was liable to most ruthless extermination. Furthermore, the Beznachal'tsy insisted that a consistent revolutionary would not support the existing economic system by buying any consumer products; instead, he should satisfy all his needs through the expropriation of private property from the exploiters and oppressors.[127] Other adherents of the Anarchist-Communist trend, as well as some obscure extremist groups, such as the Uncompromising Ones in Odessa, echoed these themes. Arguing for the necessity of raiding commercial warehouses and stores, they proclaimed that "thievery was . . . merely a product of the existing political order [and therefore] was not a crime."[128]

It is impossible to estimate with precision the total funds expropriated by the anarchists throughout Russia in the first decade of the twentieth century, because few of the many autonomous groups engaged in these activities considered it necessary to keep records of incoming resources or expenditures. Still, the amount of damage caused by anarchist expropriations can be appreciated from the large number of newspaper reports describing major robberies such as a foray that took place in the Bessarabian provincial town of Khotin on 17 October 1908, when Anarchists-Syndicalists made a swift attack on a mail coach and escaped with nearly eighty thousand rubles. In a similar incident, a group of Anarchists-Communists seized sixty thousand rubles in state funds at the Verkhnedneprovsk railway station.[129] The serious losses suffered by the government as a result of assaults on state-owned liquor stores must also be considered, along with the arms and explosives stolen in repeated anarchist raids on weapons depots and military arsenals.[130]

Losses suffered in anarchist attacks on public property were especially considerable in the border regions, where amid the pervading anarchy after 1905, the radicals proceeded with their expropriations without discriminating among the various institutions and societies that appeared to be potential sources of profit. Indeed, to many of these extremists, any educational, cultural, or even charitable establishment represented the hated socioeconomic order. In a letter to his comrades, a proud anarchist in Georgia wrote that "robberies take place as they did before. On the twentieth of September lots of institutions were robbed in Tiflis, including . . . a secondary school (*gimnaziia*)."[131]

The overwhelming majority of anarchist expropriations, however, were assaults against private individuals and enterprises, largely because these targets tended to be less heavily guarded than financial institutions, and the risk of apprehension was proportionately smaller. At the same time, the profits obtained as a result of acts directed against the personal property of the bourgeoisie were usually also comparatively smaller than the profits from attacks aimed at state banks and other monetary depots. This is not to suggest that the anarchists did not pursue substantial sums of easy money by raiding large private enterprises, such as a sugar factory in the province of Kiev from which they stole ten thousand rubles in cash.[132] Attempts to expropriate funds from various cooperative associations of workers and artisans were equally common. These artels, formed to facilitate temporary work, often accumulated several thousand rubles by the end of a project, and thus were particularly attractive.[133] For the most part, however, the anarchists and members of obscure revolutionary groups chose more modest targets for their expropriations, preferring small stores, petty businesses, and private homes, where their chances of escaping safely with at least some reward for their efforts were greater. Since they ran out of funds quickly, these radicals constantly sought new sources of immediate profits, and thus by the sheer frequency of their assaults compensated for the relatively small size of the take.

The anarchists directed their primary efforts against members of the bourgeois establishment considered guilty of direct exploitation. On 21 March 1908, for example, an Anarchist-Communist group calling itself the Internationale set off an explosion at the door of a Warsaw apartment belonging to a merchant, Liuzer Tsarkes, and then stole 2,800 rubles from him.[134] In the same city anarchists carried out a similar raid on the office of a banker named Bern-shtein, who was forced at gunpoint, with two browning pistols held at his temples, to hand over 1,200 rubles.[135] The anarchists operating in the central Russian provinces were equally unscrupulous. Among the numerous achievements of the fugitive sailor Filippov was a break-in at the home of a wealthy elderly widow near Kaluga. After strangling her and her gardener to death, he and his band escaped with a large sum of cash and many valuables.[136]

The list of expropriations of money and private possessions from individuals the anarchists considered bourgeois oppressors, the most common of whom were small store owners, continues almost indefinitely.[137] This does not mean, however, that these extremists were satisfied merely to "steal what has been stolen," for along with confiscation of property from the rich and the middle-class, the anarchists expropriated from petty officials, priests, and virtually anyone who had any possessions. Although such victims usually bore no direct responsibility for the alleged economic exploitation of the proletariat, they were mortal enemies of the extremists by virtue of their positions in society.[138]

The poor were also vulnerable to the extremists' attacks. An old woman selling lemons on the streets of Odessa was murdered by anarchists.[139] They stole payroll funds from a St. Petersburg factory cashier—money that was to have been paid out to the workers the next day.[140] In the Turukhansk region a group made up of exiled Anarchists-Communists and other radicals killed and robbed a police official who, as the expropriators knew in advance, was carrying state stipend money to be delivered to their fellow convicts.[141] This particular group of banished extremists deserves special attention, for after an initial robbery in exile late in August of 1908, about a dozen of them began to travel from village to village, and over the next six months they maintained a reign of terror over the general population. The record of their activities is astonishing in the mere repetition of indiscriminate acts of killing and looting. In the month of December they managed first to liberate two of their imprisoned comrades in the village of Sumarokova, killing or wounding two guards and three bystanders in the process, and then embarked on an extended crime spree that included robbing a number of villagers, murdering a policeman, liberating several other political prisoners, and wounding a Cossack. They then raided a post office in the village of Chulkova, acquiring 198 rubles in cash, seized arms and warm clothing in neighboring small settlements, and robbed another dozen people. When the group reached its final destination late in the month, the town of Turukhansk, they released a political convict from prison, killed a policeman, two Cossacks, a merchant, and a suspected traitor among the local exiles, and robbed another post office. They then stole six pounds of gunpowder, and disarmed all the inhabitants of Turukhansk before moving on. On the road, the group robbed seven more people and set fire to the home of a man who refused to provide them with reindeer for transportation. A few days before they were arrested by a military unit dispatched by local authorities to restore order in the area, these extremists, who referred to themselves as freedom fighters, committed their final act: after kidnapping a merchant, from whom they had already extorted 1,500 rubles, the radicals demanded more. When he refused, they tortured him by cutting off an ear, flaying him, and throwing boiling water on him. Since he still refused to cooperate, the revolutionaries killed him.[142]

Although such physical cruelty was exceptional,[143] extortion was a common method of fund-raising for the anarchists and members of obscure extremist groups. In fact, it was they who most widely practiced blackmail by written mandates, notifying individual victims that they were to contribute a specified sum of money to the revolutionary cause by a certain date, or be killed. The demands ranged from as little as twenty-five to as much as twenty-five thousand rubles.[144] The extremists also employed other forms of extortion: a group calling itself the "Black Falcon anarchists-blackmailers" (anarkhisty-shantazhisty-Chernyi Sokol) was formed in Odessa in 1906 with the primary objective of gathering, or inventing, compromising information about selected individuals who were then informed that unless extortion money was paid, the incriminating evidence would be made public.[145] On other occasions, the radicals did not even bother with formal extortion letters, merely showing up in person at the door of a victim, waving their revolvers and yelling, "Your money or your life!"[146] Not surprisingly, citizens who considered themselves potential extortion targets quickly realized that it was safer to take large sums of money to the bank, keeping only what was needed for daily expenditures in their homes. The anarchists thus were rarely able to obtain much on the first visit, but having presented their demands, they usually arranged a return appointment.[147] Most victims of extortion chose to comply with the radicals, and most refusals resulted in immediate reprisals, frequently in the form of a bomb tossed into the home or office of an obstinate merchant or store owner, as a punishment to him and a warning to others.[148]

The anarchists employed extortion not only against exploiters of the poor, but also against intellectuals and professionals, including doctors, medical attendants (fel'dshery), and dentists,[149] despite the fact that many of these people held liberal views and were quite willing to assist the revolutionaries in various ways. One dentist in Ekaterinoslav made his apartment available as a gathering place for the local Bundists, but his residence turned out to be less than secure: during a Bund Committee meeting members of an obscure extremist group tossed a bomb through a window as a response to the dentist's previous refusal to comply with their demands for money.[150]

Amid the general bloodletting and cruelty were occasional humorous incidents associated with the anarchist practice of unrestricted economic violence, including robberies committed for minimal personal profits. In Kiev, on 14 June 1908, a man and a woman walked into a shoe store, pointed a pistol at the owner, and presented him with a demand letter from local anarchists. The store owner was most relieved to discover that the total demand amounted to three pairs of boots, which he promptly provided.[151]

The majority of extremists engaged in expropriation for personal gain did not limit themselves to such insignificant booty. Indeed, the anarchists acknowledged that many of their comrades came to consider expropriation a lucrative, if risky, profession, and "turned to the practice . . . as a trade."[152] These quasi-revolutionaries even began to make mutually profitable deals with members of the bourgeoisie who were sometimes seeking revenge against enemies and therefore willing to provide the expropriators with addresses and precise financial information about potential targets for extortion.[153]

For many anarchist groups, revolutionary robbery became a priority, if not their sole objective; other radical activities, such as propaganda and agitation among the proletarian masses, were largely abandoned and only occasionally conducted between expropriations if time permitted. Of all anarchists convicted by the tsarist courts, more than 60 percent were sentenced for armed assaults.[154] The extremists often had so much expropriated money at their personal disposal that their leaders became alarmed by the epidemic of petty robbery and tried to limit the practice. Some organizations operating under the banner of anarchism warned their members in special proclamations that the revolutionaries were being demoralized and corrupted by criminal elements in their ranks, and that the general public had become unable to perceive the difference between common theft and expropriation.[155] Several prominent anarchists, most notably the Anarchist-Syndicalist leader Novomirskii, sought to purge their organizations of professional bandits and purify the revolutionary camp by such measures as prohibiting small-scale expropriations and the extortion of money by means of mandates. These orders were almost universally ignored, however, and in some areas banditry among the revolutionaries became so widespread that the local leadership threatened abusers with death.[156]

Even this produced no results, and by 1907 the large criminal and borderline components of the anarchist and obscure extremist organizations, many of whom "did not have the slightest conception of anarchism," were generally referred to as "the scum of the revolution," and were submerged in a bacchanalia of debauchery and dissipation.[157] Expropriators often quarrelled over loot, and after dividing the take, broke up the revolutionary cell, with each going his own way. Ironically, some of these alleged enemies of capitalist exploitation used the stolen cash to buy a small store or other business of their own. Others, accustomed to a situation in which large sums of money were readily available, developed an extremely careless attitude toward spending, and squandered large sums, often tens of thousands of rubles, on luxuries, prostitutes, and alcohol.[158] By 1908 many anarchists therefore admitted that all the lofty ideals of their movement had drowned in a sea of banditry, and that after all the crimes perpetrated by the extremists, nothing remained of the fundamental anarchist slogan that proclaimed expropriation "a great gift from anarchy to the people."[159]

Although the Russian anarchists and radicals of obscure political orientation presented a "varied assortment of independent groups, without a party program or a measure of effective coordination,"[160] their role in promoting violence during the revolutionary decade was greater than that of any organized political formation in the country. Moreover, their lack of ideological discrimination, their careless approach to bloodshed, and their inclination for unethical and undisguisedly criminal behavior place a substantial percentage of these extremists in the category of the new type of terrorist. Their impact on the Russian revolution was enormous, gradually stripping it of its idealism and exposing its darker aspects.

Chapter Five

THE "SEAMY SIDE" OF THE REVOLUTION

THE CRIMINAL ELEMENT,

THE PSYCHOLOGICALLY UNBALANCED, AND JUVENILES

> They scream, "Down with the expropriators, the robbers, the criminals. . . . But the time of rebellion will come, and they will be with us. On the barricades, a hardened burglar will be more useful than Plekhanov."
>
> —A. Bogdanov[1]

CRIMINALITY AND ETHICS AMONG THE TERRORISTS

ALONGSIDE the new type of terrorists affiliated with the various formal antigovernment organizations or the numerous groups of more obscure ideological origin were many individuals actively engaged in the full range of radical activities whose motives had little to do with revolutionary objectives. Particularly in the period following the outbreak of the political crisis in 1905, and continuing nearly through the collapse of the imperial regime in 1917, increasing numbers of the revolutionaries engaged in terrorism carried out assassinations and expropriations for personal gain, criminal purposes, or for irrational reasons. Although scholars of prerevolutionary Russia have paid minimal attention to this phenomenon, which was referred to by its contemporaries as the "seamy side" of the revolution (*iznanka*, or *nakip' revoliutsii*),[2] examination of the issue provides a new perspective on the traditional image of the Russian antigovernment movement.

The strikingly low level of ideological awareness evident in the new generation of Russian extremists involved in mass terror in these years cut across the entire revolutionary camp, affecting all the radical parties to some extent.[3] While some terrorists did possess at least a vague perception of what the diverse extremist groups in Russia represented, overall they tended to demonstrate a substantial lack of political consciousness. One haphazardly formed gang of expropriators in the village of Khutora raided the home of a local priest and left with a total of twenty-five rubles. Although acting on the orders of an anarchist organization, they naively declared themselves to be "from the party of revolutionaries."[4]

Since a growing number of these radicals, particularly in the periphery of the empire, were illiterate (including such renowned revolutionaries as Bundist terrorist Girsh Lekert), they could hardly be expected to exhibit a profound understanding of the finer points of revolutionary doctrine, or to impress their party leaders with their political sophistication.[5] Among the revolutionaries who could read and write, many expressed themselves with great difficulty and confusion, and when questioned were able to justify their terrorist activities only with half-literate and clumsy street language made up primarily of clichés. Typical slogans called for revenge against the "scoundrels," or exclaimed, "Long live the revolution! . . . To hell with everything else!"[6] The revolutionary leaders were fully aware of this situation, and one prominent Social Democrat, Grigorii Aleksinskii, even insisted that the "semiliterate boys and girls" implicated in terrorist acts and expropriations should be expelled from their organizations. He did so, however, "with great sadness," noting that among these youngsters were individuals "sincerely convinced that by killing street cops and zemstvo guards, and by carrying out armed robberies of post offices, risking in these undertakings their own lives and the lives of others, they were 'struggling for socialism.'"[7]

A wide range of stimuli proved critical in driving young men and women to terrorist acts—stimuli that were frequently personal and arose from deepseated emotional problems and conflicts, rather than from radical zeal or a solid grounding in revolutionary theory. One of the most common motives for participating in violent crimes with political overtones seems to have been the inability to accept personal failure or control anger, accompanied by a primitive desire for immediate revenge. Terrorist acts arising from such motives were frequently interpreted by the liberal and left-wing press as a form of revolutionary struggle, justified by oppressive political or economic circumstances. Examples of this phenomenon include a May 1905 attempt by a postal worker, a labor activist about to be fired, on the life of his superior, and an unsuccessful attack in August of the same year by a porcelain factory worker, dismissed for poor job performance, against his shop manager.[8] Terrorists also used violence to protect their own interests or to punish individuals they believed had victimized them. This was true in the case of PSR member Vasilii Troitskii, a military conscript who sought revenge against an army general who had attempted to discipline him for participation in revolutionary activities.[9] In addition, some radicals who had not been formally implicated in serious political crimes but nevertheless found themselves under police surveillance, or were victims of other forms of official harassment, sometimes "became more and more exasperated," experienced bitter feelings toward the authorities, and, "having suffered enough, . . . decided to avenge" themselves and others in similar situations.[10] As one of them put it: "I am thirsty for revenge. I am ready for terror out of personal vengeance. I want to kill those insects to show them their nothingness and cowardice. If you only knew how they sneered at me and how my self-esteem suffered. I am against terror, but there's one jerk I've decided to kill, and kill him I will."[11] Occasionally, individuals angered by the arrest or execution of extremist relatives contemplated retaliation against the authorities.[12] Thus a certain number of the attacks described by the anti-tsarist Russian or foreign presses as acts of revolutionary terrorism were acts of revenge that probably had nothing to do with the political goals and convictions of their perpetrators, and would be more accurately categorized as common crimes.[13]

Another strong personal motive for participation in terrorist activities was the desire for publicity, which some terrorists hoped to attain by planning and executing a major political assassination that "by its boldness must amaze the entire world."[14] Vladimir Burtsev, whose quest for fame was apparent even to his comrades, may be counted among these radicals. Other revolutionaries, such as Lidiia Ezerskaia, the SR who assassinated Governor Klingenberg of Mogilev, dedicated themselves to terrorism either from boredom, or a need for self-assertion. Ezerskaia apparently realized, at the age of thirty-eight, that with no talents as an organizer, literary propagandist, or agitator among the workers or peasants, she had nothing better to do, and "time was slipping away." She felt that she could not apply herself to peaceful work, and since "these thoughts of her uselessness to the revolution were ruining her life," Ezerskaia chose Klingenberg as a sufficiently reactionary figure to serve as the target for the terrorist act that was to justify her existence.[15] Similarly, according to Amy Knight, for notorious SR *boevik* Fruma Frumkina, "terrorist motives stemmed from a deep feeling of inadequacy and a desire to confirm her own importance as an individual."[16]

After violence became a way of life for the entire country in 1905, an increasing number of terrorists viewed their activities, in the words of one revolutionary, "as a very interesting game," with some of them operating under a "delusion of a position of pseudogreatness."[17] Conversely, the depreciation in the value of human life in this period led many terrorists to feel that their own lives were worth very little. As a result, a significant number of them were prepared not only to dispose freely of the lives of the oppressors, but also to risk their own. One terrorist attempting to explain his motives for joining a group stated: "I am terribly fed up with my life. More than anything, I am sick of the way I lived before."[18] Other terrorists and expropriators planned various acts simply because they suffered from an obsession with "enterprises and adventures"; one professed, "I cannot live peacefully. I like danger, so as to feel the thrill."[19]

Many of the extremists who turned to terrorism for various personal reasons in the initial decade of the twentieth century joined the revolutionary ranks because of the opportunity the situation in the Russian Empire presented for material gain through criminal behavior. Some individuals falsely represented themselves as affiliated with well-known radical organizations, such as the Party of Socialists-Revolutionaries, which went to great lengths through its official local organs to assure the public that "thugs" claiming to represent PSR committees had no connection with the party whatsoever. This did not prevent the pseudo-SRs from seeking to profit by robbing private citizens in the name of the party; they went so far as to present their victims credentials, sometimes printed on official SR stationery, and sometimes of their own counterfeit manufacture.[20]

The behavior of legitimate members of various local radical organizations frequently demonstrated that their underlying motives for joining the revolution were either questionable, or coexisted with darker elements of their personalities. Embezzlement of party funds, for example, was so widespread among the rank-and-file extremists that party leaders, much to their embarrassment, were forced to acknowledge the problem publicly and introduce special measures to combat it.[21] Despite the fact that radicals suspected of embezzlement were often tried in revolutionary courts of honor or tribunals, which expelled them from the ranks of their organizations and occasionally even sentenced them to death, the party generals were unable to halt the practice, which intensified and assumed critical proportions by 1907.

All parties within the Russian revolutionary movement shared this problem to one degree or another, but reactions of the various groups differed according to their own traditions. The central PSR leadership endeavored to conceal the problem wherever it cropped up, to prevent damage to the reputation of the party as a whole. When it became evident, for example, that Boris Savinkov could not explain how he had spent thirty thousand of the two hundred thousand rubles allocated to him in 1910 to finance a terrorist act, the SR leaders chose not to proceed with a potentially embarrassing investigation, despite the fact that the situation had a depressing impact on them; they limited themselves to expressing official displeasure with Savinkov's behavior.[22] This incident was not unique, for other prominent members of the PSR, including Nikolai Rusanov, one of its founders, were also suspected on several occasions of misappropriating party funds. In all such cases the party leaders seemed to adopt a silent policy of closing their eyes to the problem.[23]

Since PSR members in the provinces were frequently implicated in behavior that suggested they were less than altruistic freedom fighters, it became increasingly difficult for the SR central leadership to conceal the problem from their fellow party members and the public. The editors of a leading SR publication, *Banner of Labor* (*Znamia Truda*), received many reports to the effect that following a revolutionary robbery the SR participants had failed to deliver the proceeds to the local party treasury, dividing the money among themselves instead. More often than not these reports did not appear in the official SR publications, and remained unnoticed among the dusty papers filed in the party archives.[24]

At the same time, however, some SRs were prepared to take steps to retrieve funds they believed had been stolen from the organization by corrupt members. In one case, an unidentified revolutionary took part in a 1908 SR expropriation in Moscow and then disappeared with twenty thousand rubles. His comrades tracked him to Paris, where he and his wife had settled and opened a private shop, and paid a surprise visit to his home. Under the threat of death they demanded that he return the stolen money to the PSR treasury. Realizing that his life was indeed in danger, the former radical yielded to pressure and repaid half of the sum he owed the SRs.[25]

In the periphery the Socialists-Revolutionaries tended to employ their own methods to halt the widespread embezzlement, differing little in this regard from the renegade SRs who left the party to join the Maximalist movement, since they frequently implemented extreme measures against the embezzlers, including death sentences. Among the Maximalists themselves embezzlement flourished. Partly because of their predilection for random robberies, and also because they did not consider it necessary to account for expropriated funds to any central authority, large sums of money stolen by Maximalists ended up in private hands. It was thus not uncommon for them to accuse one another of misappropriating tens of thousands of rubles and spending large sums on personal expenses.[26]

These accusations were often justified. According to Gerasimov, the central Maximalist organization in the capital "lived in such a grand style, and the stealing of money by certain elements close to it was so significant," that within six months of a major expropriation from the Merchant Bank of Moscow, the Maximalists were nearly out of funds.[27] Similarly, several months after the Fonarnyi Lane expropriation, only sixty thousand of the four hundred thousand rubles could be accounted for. In the words of one Maximalist leader, G. A. Nestroev, rank-and-file members of the Maximalist combat organization who were responsible for transferring the money from one safe place to another, and therefore had access to the funds, "used them without any control . . . for whatever purposes." Two of these revolutionaries were suspected of escaping with twenty-five thousand rubles each.[28] Equally suspicious was the fact that well-known Maximalist Solomon Ryss (Mortimer) offered the police official who arrested him in April 1907 a bribe of fifty thousand rubles, allegedly provided by the organization for his release.[29] Like the SRs, the Maximalists rarely chose to conduct thorough investigations of embezzlement incidents. In contrast to the SR leadership, however, they displayed contempt for anything resembling the traditional bourgeois legal process, and typically, according to one Maximalist, even the suspicion that funds had "stuck to the hands" of an expropriator was enough to provoke a death sentence. This was especially true of Maximalists in the periphery.[30]

Unauthorized use of party funds also occurred within the SD factions, including particularly the Bolsheviks, who participated in expropriations throughout the empire. These activities provided not only substantial sums for local SD treasuries, but also an abundance of easy money for the combatants' pockets.[31] One Bolshevik extremist by the name of Aleksandr Kalganov, so inclined toward unruliness and violence that his comrades considered him an anarcho-Bolshevik, organized a special detachment of young radicals whose sole goal was to stage revolutionary robberies. Although in theory the funds they expropriated were to be used exclusively for Bolshevik party expenses, there are indications that at least part of the stolen money may have ended up in the hands of the combatants, and particularly of Kalganov himself. Originally an impoverished proletarian, he was subsequently able to purchase a house for himself and his family.[32] In numerous other cases, particularly in the Caucasus, members of the SD movement known to have executed successful revolutionary robberies were later able to live luxurious lives, and "spent money without restraint."[33]

The special resolutions designed to halt the embezzlement of party funds passed by the Social Democrats at their party congresses reveal their alarm regarding the spread of this practice.[34] Although they were occasionally willing to expel offenders from their organizations,[35] there is no evidence that the SDs resorted to the extreme physical means employed by other groups, such as the Maximalists, and particularly the anarchists.

The anarchists, on the whole, were even less scrupulous than the Maximalists about stealing from state financial institutions and private citizens. Indeed, some radicals openly acknowledged that by 1907 many anarchists had degenerated from ideological extremists into simple expropriators.[36] It was among these revolutionaries of the new type that the largest number of embezzlers were to be found, who were difficult to "distinguish from . . . the real thieves," as their own comrades asserted.[37] Members of anarchist groups throughout the Russian Empire and abroad were accused not only of misappropriating funds from their organizations' treasuries for personal expenses, but also of stealing directly from their fellow radicals.[38] Much to the indignation of the extremist leaders and the idealists in the revolutionary ranks, instances of anarchists pilfering jewelry and small sums of cash from the homes of their comrades were not at all uncommon. While some insisted that the only appropriate punishment for these antirevolutionary deeds was death, occasionally the erratic and violent behavior of a thief upon exposure, as well as the insignificance of his gain, led others to suggest that "he was afflicted with some mania."[39]

The national revolutionary organizations in the border areas were also not exempt from these problems. While their members may have favored the elevated language of national liberation, in their actions many of them differed little from ordinary bandits. One representative of the Dashnaktsutiun movement had direct dealings with a local criminal gang, to whom he sold, without party authorization, weapons belonging to the Armenian nationalists.[40] Following a successful expropriation of 315,000 rubles from the Dushet Treasury in April of 1906—one of the few sensational revolutionary robberies in the Caucasus carried out by the Revolutionary Party of Georgian Socialists-Federalists—a large portion of the expropriated money remained in the personal possession of a certain Kereselidze, one of the robbery's organizers. After fleeing to Geneva, Kereselidze openly enjoyed an opulent lifestyle, with extravagantly expensive lodgings and the rare luxury of a private automobile, freely admitting to fellow emigrés that he was able to satisfy his expensive tastes because of his good fortune in Georgia.[41] Among the Polish Socialists, even PPS Central Committee members were reportedly involved in fraudulent mismanagement of party funds.[42]

As a result of the successful infiltration of left-wing ranks by undercover agents, and the persistent interception of revolutionary mail by the tsarist political police, the officials were well informed about the extent of the embezzlement problem among the radicals, which was especially widespread among extremists involved in expropriations. In Perrie's view, the popularity of these activities derived to a large extent from the "apparent legitimization of theft in the eyes of criminal elements who kept the stolen money for their own purposes rather than handing it over to party funds."[43] Many of these self-professed liberators of mankind openly expressed cynicism regarding the most fundamental ethical norms. One revolutionary asked a comrade, "Tell me, why can one not lie? Why can one not steal? . . . What does 'dishonest' mean? Why is it dishonest to lie? What is morality? What is [moral] filth? These are but conventions."[44] Some of the new terrorists declared that as far as they were concerned it was plainly foolish to sacrifice their lives today for life in the future,[45] a statement that would have appeared heretical to earlier generations of Russian revolutionaries. Realizing that such relativity in basic human values, as well as revolutionary ethics, was widespread among the terrorists, the police sought to exploit their moral degeneration, frequently attempting to recruit embezzlers as informers, along with other combatants known for their shaky revolutionary convictions.[46]

These efforts often proved successful. Sources reveal that many of the revolutionaries who were caught misusing party funds also accepted money from the Russian government for their services as spies. This was particularly true of individual Maximalists and anarchists, and even if it is not always possible to determine definitively whether a combatant guilty of embezzlement had also betrayed his fellow radicals to the authorities, grounds for reasonable suspicion are frequently present.[47] Thus, as soon as one SR expropriator, Fetisov (Pavlov), realized that his comrades intended physical retaliation for misbehavior on his part with regard to the profits from a robbery, they were all arrested, and Fetisov alone had the good fortune to escape. His luck continued when he and several other revolutionaries attempted to cross the Russian border, and once again all but Fetisov were captured by the authorities.[48]

In recruiting informers among the radicals, the authorities realized that they were dealing with unreliable individuals requiring control. The police justifiably suspected that because of their unscrupulous behavior and their tendency to disregard all ethical considerations when presented with an opportunity for personal profit, the informers were likely under appropriate circumstances to betray the government's cause as they had betrayed the cause of the revolution.[49] Indeed, on numerous occasions the authorities received information from their own undercover agents about close ties between the radicals and representatives of foreign powers hostile to the Russian Empire, including Japan and Turkey. There were reports of extremists accepting financial or other assistance from foreign adversaries willing to support any radical actions targeting the establishment in Russia, and specifically terrorism, which more than any other activity was likely to destabilize and weaken the tsarist regime.[50]

There is evidence that this practice began as early as the Russo-Japanese war of 1904–1905, and that it revived on the eve of the First World War, when the PSR, the PPS, and other radical organizations received substantial funds and shipments of weapons directly from Japan and Austria.[51] The idea that foreign enemies of the tsarist government were to be regarded by the radicals as temporary allies became particularly widespread after the outbreak of war in Europe in 1914. At that time, for example, two Caucasian expropriators were hired by Turkish military authorities to serve as guides across Georgia, and also to incite the native population against the Russian administration.[52] Two other radicals, the SD Ivan Klochko (Zhuk), and the Dashnak Marko Tarasov, who had both escaped from the Caucasus to Turkey during the post-1907 "era of reaction," were busy in 1914–1915 organizing the transportation of dynamite into the Russian Empire with the help of smugglers. They received money and explosives from officials in Constantinople and, according to police information, "did not attempt to conceal the fact that they were acting as agents of the Turkish Government."[53]

The tsarist authorities were not alone in their conviction, especially after the revolutionary storm began to subside late in 1906, that the still numerous combat groups throughout the country were recruiting new members largely "from the lowest dregs of society";[54] the revolutionaries sometimes could not disguise their own contempt for the new variety of terrorist, referring to some of them as "common bandits."[55] Furthermore, instead of investing major effort in the education of candidates for their ranks in the spirit of rebellion, or even tempting them with fame and eternal glory as revolutionary heroes, the parties often preferred simply to hire new troops.

A potential terrorist did not always know whether the individuals recruiting him for an assassination attempt represented any particular antigovernment organization or were merely using him as an instrument of personal vengeance. Some newcomers agreed to become political assassins after receiving advances as insignificant as fifteen rubles, along with a handful of bullets and a promise of larger sums to be paid upon successful execution of the act. At other times, even small cash payments were unnecessary, and a few drinks were sufficient to ensure successful recruitment.[56] Although even in the late nineteenth century extremists occasionally agreed to take part in terrorist acts only after advance payment of sums sometimes as small as eight rubles,[57] the phenomenon of terrorist mercenaries became much more widespread in the early years of the twentieth century.

Party officials also motivated rank-and-file terrorists with small amounts of cash, supplemented by promises of future rewards. In one incident, a Polish *boevik* who reported that he had personally killed seven policemen and taken part in three robberies received the sum of eighteen rubles from a visiting PPS representative, "for now." The combatant openly admired the man's large and expensive gold watch, and later described how the PPS functionary used the avarice for further encouragement, playing on both material and patriotic incentives: "He patted me on the shoulder, saying 'Proceed with your work, comrade, and you will have watches and money, and Poland will be grateful to you forever.'"[58] There is also reason to believe that certain individuals not formally affiliated with any revolutionary organization were compensated for their assistance to the extremists during expropriations.[59] Out of fairness it must be noted, however, that occasionally an individual offered employment as a political assassin had no alternative but to cooperate or risk becoming a victim of terrorism himself.[60] One revolutionary from Warsaw, with no apparent previous history of involvement in violence, was labeled a provocateur by a fellow radical, and ordered to settle accounts with his own brother, who had been accused of treachery. If he dared to refuse, he was strongly recommended to "avoid further encounters with his comrades."[61]

Finally, by 1907 few contemporaries could ignore the fact that in cooperation with common criminals, an increasing number of the "freedom fighters" was involved in "banditry and robberies in most cases not for any political motives, but exclusively for the satisfaction of their base instincts." The authorities were convinced that in this situation the "criminal activity of this category of malefactors has lately been directed not so much against the existing state order in Russia as against those principles upon which any social order is founded, regardless of the form of government." Some liberal periodicals shared this opinion, asserting that "revolutionary terror . . . was mixed with the mere dissoluteness [*raznuzdannost'*] of general criminality. The SRs were overrun with petty SRs (*eseriki*), and the petty SRs—with hooligans."[62] Far from attempting to contradict these assertions, SR terrorist leader Gershuni was even more explicit in lamenting that as many as nine-tenths of all expropriations were acts of common banditry.[63]

Extremists were often linked by friendship with criminals such as professional burglars,[64] and were themselves found guilty of crimes that they did not even try to represent as revolutionary.[65] Iakov Gol'dshtein, who enjoyed a reputation among his comrades in exile in London as a serious anarchist, was arrested by the British authorities and sentenced to twenty-five days in prison for petty theft.[66] In another case two former Baltic forest brothers living in exile in Boston committed a mass murder in 1908 for strictly personal reasons. Unemployed and in need of money, they walked into a liquor store, stole fifteen dollars, and in making their escape applied their past combat experience so effectively that they killed and wounded dozens of policemen.[67] Anarchist Iankel' Litvak, living in France in 1909 under the alias "Ianche," was involved in a counterfeiting operation there.[68] Finally, Andrei Kolegaev, a well-known member of the PSR residing in Europe in 1910, and future Commisar for Agriculture under the Bolsheviks, accepted a commission from the former wife of fellow SR Nikolai Tiutchev to kidnap Tiutchev's children. Kolegaev abducted the children without undue concern about possible consequences; he assumed (in this case, incorrectly) that any dedicated radical would consider it beneath his revolutionary dignity to appeal for help to the bourgeois police.[69]

In addition, many criminal fugitives from tsarist justice who escaped abroad elected to portray themselves as political emigrés, especially when facing possible extradition to the Russian authorities.[70] Since it was simplest for them to master the uncomplicated theoretical principles of anarchism, most of them chose to proclaim themselves supporters of this particular revolutionary trend. Although it is often difficult to differentiate between the sincere revolutionaries and the outlaws using the title to escape prosecution, certain cases leave no doubt that genuine criminals became radicals of convenience. The Georgian bandit Makharashvili was among a gang of thieves who robbed a wealthy Armenian in Kutais in the fall of 1913. He escaped to Paris but was imprisoned by French authorities, and exerted all efforts to be treated as one of the political emigrés for fear of extradition.[71] In many instances, the outlaws continued their criminal activities while posing as revolutionaries: they involved themselves in robberies, forged the seals of various organizations and unions, extorted money, and carried out other mischief.[72] In few localities were these activities as open as in Lithuania, where many self-styled "anarchists had long since turned into hooligans," and extremists would approach local peasants with offers to settle accounts with their landlords for small monetary compensation: "For twenty rubles one landowner could be killed."[73]

An examination of how these pseudorevolutionaries spent their easily acquired funds reveals much about the new generation of Russian extremists. A striking number of them exhibited a penchant for a generally dissolute and corrupt life-style, marked by alcoholism and drunken debauchery. Some radicals complained in their private correspondence about the severity of problem drinking among their comrades, and the formal party organization also attempted to deal with it at their conferences and congresses, incorporating clauses condemning the practice into their official resolutions.[74] As was frequently the case with official decisions made at the central level, these resolutions had little impact on the revolutionary activists throughout the country, who either ignored or were unaware of the opinions of their leaders on the subject of alcohol. Some party generals, while clearly realizing that heavy drinking affected the performance of the rank and file, and especially of the combatants, closed their eyes to the problem, partly because of their knowledge that some of the most prominent activists in the central party organizations were not blameless. Certain PPS Central Committee members used party funds for their alcoholic binges, and SR Combat Organization member Aleksei Pokotilov was known for his heavy drinking and wild carousing; his constantly trembling hands may have caused the accidental bomb explosion in the Northern Hotel in St. Petersburg that killed him. Another combatant, Boris Bartol'd, at one time a close associate of Savinkov, was an open alcoholic prone to bouts of heavy drinking. When his carousing became so blatant and scandalous for the reputation of the PSR that he caused extensive and visible damage to his face during a drunken binge, many SRs came to consider him unreliable and certainly an inappropriate person to charge with combat responsibilities. Finally, Savinkov himself, exhausted by the stresses of his underground work, found distraction in gambling and "tried to alleviate his tension by increasing his consumption of alcohol and opiates. When opium failed to provide him with sufficient sedation, he began injecting morphine."[75]

Where the extremists were under less direct control from the party high command, as in the periphery and the smaller combat groups in the capitals, unlimited alcohol consumption was even more in evidence than in the central, more disciplined groups. Some combatants previously regarded by their comrades as the foremost fighters indulged their habits with almost no fear of punitive sanctions from the party leaders.[76] The heavy drinking, debauchery, and generally corrupt life-style of many of the radicals required substantial amounts of money, which in many cases came from expropriations.[77] One revolutionary summed up the situation in a letter to a friend: "Universal dullness [and] triteness are growing greater and greater. Plain cretinism . . . a pile of dung."[78]

In much the same way, extremists living abroad complained about the "disgusting behavior" of radical activists in emigration, who "started brawls and fights in the streets almost every night," partly as a result of the heavy drinking, which, according to one disappointed and indignant revolutionary, reached its apogee in 1908.[79] Some Russian radicals abroad engaged in criminal behavior in order to finance their appetites for alcohol and dissipation. Thus, two expropriators living in Brussels paid a surprise visit to a wealthy merchant on 4 February 1909, threatened him with revolvers, and stole three thousand francs from him, which they "successfully wasted on carousing."[80]

The problem of alcoholism among the Russian extremists was predictably exacerbated under conditions in the prisons, hard labor colonies, and places of exile, where, according to one revolutionary, life was marked by "nonstop drunkenness." His reminiscences describe a vivid scene in Iakutsk, where a group of fifteen radicals drank all day, with one man dying, apparently of alcohol poisoning. When the doctor arrived, he found one person lying unconscious next to the corpse, with a third drunkard still trying to force his dead companion to drink another round, while the others continued with their orgy.[81]

The situation in the penal institutions can only be partly explained by the physical and psychological hardships prevalent there. Many former revolutionaries note in their reminiscences that while serving time in various punitive institutions in the empire after 1905, they were shocked to find that "in a political sense, the membership of the hard labor convict and exile population had significantly deteriorated," compared with previous generations of imprisoned radicals. Their realization resulted from encounters with typical representatives of the seamy side of the revolution, some of whom had previously served terms for various common crimes; others had been sentenced by the tsarist government for the first time for acts of political terror and expropriations, but in reality were genuinely criminal elements guilty of straightforward banditry.[82] This perhaps should not have been a shocking revelation, for as many memoirists acknowledged, within their own combat detachments individuals who could be considered street thugs, drunken riffraff, hooligans or bandits, worked alongside the most committed revolutionaries.[83]

Once in prison, these extremists of the new type indulged in the same activities as the criminal prisoners: heavy drinking, wild games, total idleness "on principle," crude jokes and tricks, as well as gambling, all accompanied by constant cursing.[84] Unlike previous generations of revolutionaries, who despised their captors and refused to have anything to do with them, many convicted *boeviki* were

> "buddies" with their guards . . . [and] begged the jailers for . . . cigarette butts. . . . This touching idyl, however, was broken now and again: occasionally, for one reason or another, a combatant would start a fight with a guard he had embraced only moments before. A quarrel would begin, during which the combatant, pouring out filthy and abusive language, swore to tell his comrades outside the prison that this particular guard is a "b . . . h" and ought to be "blown away."[85]

While insisting that they were dedicated defenders of the oppressed, suffering at the hands of the tsarist authorities for their revolutionary convictions, the combatants in fact despised many of their fellow political prisoners as intellectuals who wasted their time reading, studying, or participating in theoretical debates. Preferring to associate instead with the criminal detainees, the *boeviki* shifted continually between fleeting friendships and carousal with their new comrades, and petty disputes and brawls with them. At the same time, in the frequent conflicts between the political prisoners and the common criminals, it was not unusual for anarchists and other politicals to side with the criminals, even if it meant taking physical action against their socialist comrades.[86]

Descriptions of prison life in Russia at the time reveal that the inmates frequently "feared their own comrades more than the jailers; they were afraid to enter the hall without a knife in their pocket," in part because every prisoner was constantly forced to defend his life and property from other convicts, regardless of whether they were common thieves, unaffiliated revolutionaries and expropriators, or formal members of the SD, SR, anarchist, or other organizations.[87] Even within prison walls the anarchists "staged expropriations according to all the rules of the art," targeting their own comrades among the political prisoners.[88] While the criminal convicts, the anarchists, and those who simply called themselves expropriators were prime agressors in these clashes, which frequently turned into knife fights with lethal outcomes, the behavior of the victims often differed little from the primitive violence exhibited by the attackers. As one prison veteran recalled, "Every day conflicts flared up between us and the riffraff. Both sides frequently reached for their knives, ready to lunge at one another in a bloody fight."[89] Another former convict described a prison acquaintance, an SR terrorist frequently involved in such clashes, who "evinced a special passion that turned into rage. In such a moment, it meant nothing to him to kill a person."[90]

Many extremists evinced similar behavior outside prison walls. Violent incidents are described in which an SR combatant and expropriator beat a fellow party member senseless on the street following a disagreement, and a Lithuanian SD terrorist punished an enemy with a rod or whip.[91] In general, the murders carried out by formal members of antigovernment organizations or by individuals only loosely associated with the revolutionary movement vividly demonstrate not only that the decision to take a life was often made lightly and the act itself bore little significance for the perpetrator, but also that in implementing such a decision, the extremists frequently exhibited unnecessary cruelty bordering on sadism. This is evident, for example, in a murder that took place in Ufa on 31 March 1904. Several revolutionaries of unknown party affiliation, suspecting a comrade of dealing with the police, decided to do away with him. They lured him to the outskirts of town, and without giving him an opportunity to explain himself, attacked him with a knife, stabbing him in turns as one attacker wore out and passed the unresisting victim on. They reportedly enjoyed cutting his throat, and then attempted to decapitate him.[92]

An even more revealing manifestation of cruelty was the cold-blooded program proposed in 1911 by the notorious *boevik* Kamo as a means of cleansing the Bolshevik party of all real and potential police informers. Kamo, residing abroad at the time, suggested that he and several other combatants dressed in gendarme uniforms stage a fake arrest of leading party activists in Russia: "We will come, arrest you, torture you, run a stake through you. If you start talking, it'll be clear what you're worth. That way, we'll catch all the provocateurs, all the cowards."[93] Unaccustomed to confining himself to idle talk, Kamo, entirely serious about the feasibility of his proposal, set out for Russia to implement it. Both his plan and his judgment regarding its practicality suggest a degree of psychological abnormality in this prominent extremist.

Psychologically Unbalanced Terrorists

The tendency for mentally unstable individuals to be attracted to violence was noted even in the nineteenth century, and it must indeed be recognized that for many combatants the decision to participate in terrorist activity was the result of an obvious mental imbalance. Laqueur is entirely justified in cautioning against sweeping definitions that claim, for example, that all "terrorists are criminals, moral imbeciles, mentally deranged people or sadists (or sado-masochists),"[94] but as Vera Figner observed, speaking of the young idealists, "The weaker their nervous system, and the more oppressive the life around them, the greater was their exaltation at the thought of revolutionary terror."[95] The disharmony of their inner selves and the inability to overcome it, in many cases resulting in outright insanity, often led frustrated and emotionally damaged individuals to seek radical solutions to resolve their deeper conflicts. They justified these solutions by resorting to sometimes elegantly stated ideological arguments and theories, and by claiming unconditional allegiance to the revolution, the party, or their comrades.[96] In Jerrold Post's words, terrorists are "driven to commit acts of violence as a consequence of psychological forces, and . . . their special psycho-logic is constructed to rationalize acts they are psychologically compelled to commit."[97] Some extremist leaders, undoubtedly aware of the connection between mental illness and violence, recruited emotionally vulnerable individuals for terrorist work, a number of whom were recognized by contemporary medical experts as "unconditional degenerates." The parties often invested considerable effort in equipping these new combatants with an appropriate ideology, although their ideological training usually excluded theoretical issues beyond the fundamentals of revolutionary dogma.[98]

The personality of Kamo presents a striking example of an individual whose derangement became a catalyst for violent behavior that in the prevailing circumstances of the era happened to take revolutionary form. Partly as a result of a traumatic childhood marked by repeated beatings inflicted by a domineering stepfather, among other difficulties, Kamo suffered from unresolved passions, anxieties, and drives, and experienced difficulty functioning under normal conditions. Even in the early years of his revolutionary career, prior to his arrest in Berlin in the fall of 1907, Kamo's behavior frequently revealed signs of an unstable and turbulent personality.[99] While confined to a German prison following his apprehension he was subjected to a thorough psychiatric examination, and was found by experienced physicians to be deranged. Despite all subsequent assertions by the Bolsheviks that he was feigning insanity to avoid extradition, there is little doubt that Kamo succeeded in convincing the doctors of his sickness precisely because he was seriously ill.[100] At that time even his party comrades (including Lenin himself, whom Kamo revered) recognized that he was suffering from a psychiatric disorder and required clinical treatment.[101]

Understandably, the emotional problems experienced by the terrorists covered the entire range of mental illness, but consistent with standard psychiatric research, both Russian and Western, which has long noted that "social disturbance leads to an increase in the quantity of mental illness and suicide,"[102] the incidence of suicide in Russia increased following the outbreak of revolution in 1905. Individuals seeking escape from unbearable situations found varied means of killing themselves. For some, terrorism was a means of flirting with "the mysticism of death,"[103] or an indirect way of disposing of lives torn apart by emotional complexes, weaknesses, and conflicts. As Knight observes, "Suicidal tendencies were part of the terrorist mentality, for a terrorist act was often a suicidal mission."[104] The Russian extremists thus differed little from their counterparts operating throughout the world, both at that time and later in the century, who, according to Ariel Merari, were not only prepared to be killed, but in fact desired it.[105] This was the case, for example, when twenty-one-year-old Evstiliia Rogozinnikova, a member of the PSR Northern Flying Combat Detachment, made her way to the offices of the St. Petersburg Prison Department on 15 (28) October 1907 with the intention of assassinating its head, Maksimovskii. She wore thirteen pounds of nitroglycerin strapped to her body, along with a detonating device, and was prepared to blow up the entire building. She shot and killed Maksimovskii, missing her chance to make use of the explosives. At her trial, obviously deranged, Rogozinnikova reportedly "broke her silence only by periodic gales of laughter."[106]

A significant percentage of active Russian terrorists had already made one or more attempts on their own lives prior to 1905.[107] Despite inner torments that caused them to desire death as a release, many of them rejected the idea of senseless self-extermination. They turned instead to revolutionary terrorist acts likely to end their lives abruptly in a manner that would lend their suicides the aura of a heroic deed.[108] Others who contemplated death, but for various reasons were unwilling to act, found that they could rid themselves temporarily of their deep sense of dissatisfaction, confusion, frustration, and anxiety by projecting their self-loathing toward others, and killed government employees, police officers or agents, or anyone else who qualified as an oppressor or exploiter. Oliver Radkey is correct in noting that in some terrorists "the spirit of destruction was combined with moral sensibilities of a very high order" that compelled these revolutionaries to atone for their assassinations—in their eyes justifiable from the sociopolitical standpoint, but nevertheless grievous—through the sacrifice of their own lives.[109] To a greater extent, however, this deficiency of the psychological strength required to meet the pressures of living, sometimes accompanied by an underlying desire to escape through death, explains why a substantial number of extremists elected to end their own lives when faced with the possibility of arrest, even in situations in which the fear of captivity was completely irrational. They killed themselves rather than risk falling into the hands of the authorities and being forced to continue to live throughout the long process of an official investigation, trial, and imprisonment.[110] Some clearly welcomed the death sentences handed down by tsarist authorities. The SR terrorist who assassinated General Min in 1906, Zinaida Konopliannikova, was so eager to die that according to an observer at her execution, she "went to her death as one would go to a holiday festivity."[111]

As criminal behavior spread among the new type of terrorists, and revolutionary violence became a mass phenomenon, psychological instability as well became increasingly common after 1905. The fact that death was a permanent and accepted component of daily existence had a profound psychological impact, especially upon those who confronted it directly. For the terrorists, whose reality encompassed the necessity of adjusting to both inflicting death and acknowledging it as part of their life-style, the pressure was enormous, and could be tolerated only by exceptionally strong personalities.[112] It is hardly surprising then that a large number of assassins and expropriators experienced (and were frequently treated for) emotional breakdowns of varying severity. It was not unusual for combatants to become extremely nervous and even hysterical in the course of planning their attacks. For example, immediately prior to attempting to assassinate Plehve, SR Mariia Seliuk proved unable to tolerate the pressure of underground life, became completely unbalanced, and lost the ability to function as a terrorist. Her fear of constant police surveillance grew into true paranoia, and she perceived spies and agents in everyone, including the children on the streets. She locked herself inside her apartment, but found the self-imposed solitary confinement unbearable. Seeking escape from her escalating panic, she broke down and turned herself in to the police.[113]

In the majority of cases, once the would-be assassins crossed a psychological barrier and embarked on terror, there was no turning back. In Knight's words, "Terror became the focal point, their *raison d'être*. The ultimate political and social goals were overshadowed by the immediacy of the terrorist campaign and their participation in it."[114] Due to the nature of their conspiratorial work, the terrorists were forced to live in nearly complete isolation from all life outside their own tightly knit clandestine group. As one terrorist, a young Jewish girl known as Mariia Shkol'nik, expressed it, "The world did not exist for me."[115] Inevitably for most of these terrorists, a consequence of this isolation and tension was "the progressive loss of the faculty to evaluate the political effect of their own deeds with any degree of realism";[116] having lost all perspective, they thus came to concentrate totally on the terrorist act in planning at any given moment, so that the act became for them an idée fixe.

Obsessed with visions of committing political murders, combatants frequently exhibited erratic behavior, at times even acknowledging their own irrationality. The female terrorists "seemed to view their roles as revolutionaries in an intensely personal way," and among them the urge to give themselves totally to one idea, in this case the idea of terror, was particularly evident. SR Frumkina confessed, "I have always been strongly enticed by the idea of carrying out a terrorist act. I have thought, and still think, only of that, have longed and still long, only for that. I cannot control myself."[117] This overwhelming drive dominated Frumkina's thoughts, desires, and indeed her entire existence, causing her to undertake repeated terrorist attacks, which she tried to implement in reality as spontaneously and irrationally as she envisaged them in her troubled fantasies. After her offer to stage an assassination was rejected by PSR leaders, she decided to act on her own, and contemplated a number of armed assaults, including several she attempted in prison, rationalizing them as "revenge for the hard labor convicts."[118]

Largely because of their mental instability, many terrorists tended to act impulsively in carrying out assassination attempts, and their inability to exercise patience and caution frequently resulted in grave miscalculations affecting the terrorists themselves, their comrades in the combat groups, and their victims. Tat'iana Leont'eva, the young woman who had been involved in an SR Combat Organization plot to assassinate the tsar at a ball in 1904, was arrested in 1905 for participation in an SR conspiracy against Trepov, but was soon released to her parents because she exhibited "strong signs of mental illness." Her parents sent her abroad hoping that she would recover in one of the psychiatric clinics in Europe, but her mental health visibly deteriorated. As she stated in a letter to her comrades, "I am in deep torment. . . . Being so far away from my country at a time when the most intense work is beginning, I cannot remain calm. It is beyond my strength and understanding." Consumed by the thought of involvement in a terrorist act, frustrated and depressed by what seemed to her the unresponsiveness of her fellow SRs, Leont'eva joined a Maximalist group in Switzerland. In August 1906 she shot and killed a seventy-year-old businessman from Paris who was staying in her hotel; because of her confused state, he appeared to her to resemble former Russian Minister of the Interior Durnovo, whom the revolutionaries were at that time plotting to assassinate.[119]

Many terrorists were described by their fellow radicals as "turbulent and unbalanced," "hysterical," or "suicidal," and some were openly recognized as "completely abnormal." For these individuals prison time and hard labor terms, which understandably had a tremendous impact even on emotionally stable individuals, were particularly difficult. Many proved unable to tolerate their confinement and suffered breakdowns, ending their days in asylums and hospitals.[120] Their fellow inmates were often reluctant to fall asleep for fear that one of their deranged comrades would turn violent in the night and use a knife against a sleeping neighbor.[121] Many, such as Sofiia Khrenkova, a mother of three and onetime member of the SR Combat Organization, committed suicide. Three years after her arrest in 1905, Khrenkova became psychotic and immolated herself in prison.[122] Even Gershuni, self-control and iron will notwithstanding, reportedly made an attempt on his life during his imprisonment.[123] Perversely, for many combatants emigration proved an equally trying experience, in part because of its routine and inactivity, which drove a number of them to psychosis and suicide.[124]

Nothing more vividly illustrates the extent of emotional disturbance among the terrorists than the numerous cases of revolutionary violence involving behavior classifiable only as sadistic. The internal tendency toward emotional pathology among the extremists was undoubtedly exacerbated after 1905 by the turbulence in their external social environment, in which constant violence and bloodshed inevitably conditioned the citizenry in general and the assassins in particular to accept that individual lives had little value and were not indispensable. It is hardly surprising then that many of those who caused the bloodshed became increasingly indifferent to the physical suffering of others. This tendency toward cruelty was in turn reinforced by the idea of revolutionary necessity—the dominant and much-propagandized notion that all means were permissible as long as they served the final end of the antigovernment struggle. For terrorists already inclined toward sadistic behavior this provided a justified outlet for inner tensions. The need to inflict pain was transformed from an abnormal irrational compulsion experienced only by unbalanced personalities into a formally verbalized obligation for all committed revolutionaries. In one instance of particularly severe flogging and torture, administered impulsively by a member of Kamo's Caucasian terrorist group, the perpetrator, when challenged by a horrified comrade, explained that his actions were justified by the need to determine whether the victim, a fellow revolutionary, was guilty of embezzling party funds.[125]

The same tendency is evident in the way many terrorists punished political enemies. Revolutionaries hanged petty government officials,[126] and radical Kiev railroad workers looking for vengeance threw traitors into vats of boiling water.[127] In 1905 Baltic revolutionaries mutilated the bodies of their victims, and inscribed profanity on the corpses of murdered Russian military personnel.[128] Physical torment was not uncommon, with some radicals admittedly being "cruel to the point of inhumanity";[129] they tortured police agents to death and excised their tongues as a "symbolic gesture."[130] In one particularly gruesome episode, several members of the Polish Socialist Party lured a former comrade to a Rome hotel room in March 1909, and apparently acting according to a premeditated plan, mutilated him by slashing off his nose and ears.

The victim died, apparently as the result of torture; his corpse was chopped into pieces and the remains were hidden in a large chest and left to be found by the local authorities.[131]

In some cases terrorists did not bother to conceal that their motives differed strikingly from any concept of revolutionary necessity. After participating in numerous violent killings, some individuals began to enjoy the act of spilling blood for its own sake. One member of the PPS known by the alias "Gypsy" admitted after his arrest that he had murdered nineteen police officers and gendarmes without any help from his fellow radicals. Gypsy always attended the funerals of his victims:

> He felt an uncontrollable urge to see the body of the man he had murdered; he was interested in whether or not the bullet had hit the spot at which he aimed, something that he found out from conversations with relatives saying farewell to the deceased. He confessed that in the beginning it was difficult for him to kill, but by the third or fourth time the act of taking a life was already making an unusually pleasant impression on him. Seeing the blood of his victim gave him a special feeling, and therefore he felt an increasing urge to experience this sweet sensation again. This is why he has committed so many murders of which he does not repent in the least.[132]

Admittedly, information available in the sources regarding the mental state of these terrorists is usually indirect and thus rarely allows for persuasive generalization about this particular category of extremists—those with apparent sadistic tendencies. Nevertheless, although it is frequently impossible to determine and analyze the roots of pathological behavior in individual combatants, there is evidence to support the contention that female as well as male terrorists exhibited remarkable cruelty, and that this perhaps unexpected behavior on the part of the women in the movement was highly valued by their fellow extremists, who found the female terrorists very useful in executing violence.[133] Sometimes physical illnesses or disfigurements produced an escalating self-loathing projected by the afflicted individual onto others, resulting in increasing frustration ultimately expressed in violent acts that were later rationalized as political actions. Sexual abnormalities undoubtedly played a role in driving certain individuals to bloodshed as well. This was probably the case in an incident involving a young hermaphrodite whose gender ambiguity was discovered following his arrest for the political murder of a police official.[134] Age was also a significant factor in shaping the terrorists' actions. The younger assassins, much more commonly than the adults, seemed to demonstrate instability in both their psyches and their value systems. This tendency, a result of their youthfulness, was frequently accompanied by adolescent faith in their own immortality. This combination produced a significant degree of irresponsibility in their attitudes toward their own lives and the lives of others, and together with their boundless energy, rendered them particularly suitable for recruitment as terrorists of the new type.[135]

JUVENILES

The participation of juveniles in terrorist activities was a significant problem that came to the surface of Russian public life following the outbreak of general violence in the country in 1905. The image of a schoolboy waving his revolver and shouting revolutionary slogans left a striking impression on contemporaries, regardless of their political persuasions. It also entered into popular humor: in one of the morbid anecdotes circulating at the time, a teacher asked his pupils to name the greatest inventor of the century, and one student immediately volunteered, "Browning!"[136]

Although it is difficult to estimate with accuracy what percentage of the terrorist acts in Russia at the time were performed by individuals who were under twenty-one years of age and therefore legally considered minors (*nesovershennoletnie*), there was, according to one member of the SD terrorist detachment, "one invaluable quality which all of us [combatants] possessed in abundance and which was of the greatest assistance to us: our youth. The oldest of us was twenty-two at the time";[137] the younger members were fourteen or fifteen years of age.[138] Similarly, nearly 22 percent of all SR terrorists were between the ages of fifteen and nineteen, and another 45 percent were between twenty and twenty-four.[139] In Belostok one combat unit formed in 1905 was composed entirely of school children who belonged to the PSR.[140] Sixteen-year-olds also joined the Maximalists,[141] and among the anarchists the number of minors, some as young as fourteen,[142] was even greater, with one participant noting that a primary characteristic of this movement after the turn of the century was the extreme youth of the majority of its members.[143] According to Avrich, some of the most active members of the Black Banner organizations were only fifteen or sixteen years of age, and "the history of these youths was marked by reckless fanaticism and uninterrupted violence."[144] The participation of teenagers in radical politics in the borderlands was also widespread,[145] and this led Lev Trotsky to assert that the growing percentage of Russian terrorism's victims who had merely been wounded, as opposed to killed, indicated that the shooting was increasingly carried out "by untrained amateurs, mostly by callow youngsters."[146]

As party leaders "created a cult of dynamite and the revolver, and crowned the terrorist with a halo . . . murder and the scaffold acquired a magnetic charm and attraction for the youth."[147] At the same time, however, the fact that "terrorism was particularly attractive to the young," was only partly due to "the opportunities it offered for heroic self-sacrifice,"[148] and is perhaps primarily attributable to the notable tendency among juveniles, and particularly teenagers, to be dominated and largely conditioned by the collective psychology of their milieu. Since few citizens of the empire remained untouched by the unprecedented upheaval, it was only natural for adolescents, and even younger children, to wish to take active part in the events that affected the lives of the adults around them to such an enormous degree.[149] In this sense, a prediction made by an oppositionist in 1904 proved perceptive: "I think that soon children will play revolution. . . . The gymnasium girls, who had not the slightest idea about it, are now involved in it in one way or another."[150] Children indeed began to play at being terrorists, in one instance placing a bomb made from a watermelon painted black and stuffed with garbage at the front door of a police officer.[151]

The influence of the collective mentality was profound even on adolescents who did not participate actively in the sociopolitical life of the country, occasionally leading to tragic results. Sixteen-year-old Leibish Rapoport, outraged by his mother's rudeness to his girlfriend, ran away from his home in Ekaterinoslav in the spring of 1906. He took a small amount of his parents' money with him, and considered suicide, but then wrote the following letter:

> Mother.
> With your idiotic questions and investigations you are tormenting the poor and innocent girl Liuba. . . . You ought to know that your provocateur-like actions . . . will not do you any good. . . . Keep in mind that I am presently a member of a combat organization of revolutionary terrorists, and in accordance with the committee's sanctions, must go . . . to various Russian cities to stage terrorist acts. But I will not hesitate to stay here and take pleasure in shooting a bullet through the head of an old biddy like you. I will report you at the committee meeting, and I am quite certain that my comrades will not begrudge the bullets for your murder.

After his arrest, "wishing to die to show that his mother was guilty of his death," the boy claimed responsibility for the recent assassination of Governor-general Zheltonovskii, and expected to be executed in two or three days. Instead, he spent many months under investigation and strict psychiatric observation before a military court sentenced him to a twelve-year prison term in 1909. Because of his mother's tireless efforts to prove her son's innocence, and a public campaign on his behalf, he was released in 1912.[152]

In an even more tragic case, another sixteen-year-old schoolboy, in Kiev this time, followed closely the lurid press campaign in defense of SR assassin Mariia Spiridonova, in custody for murdering Tambov official Gavrila Luzhenovskii, allegedly in retaliation for his harsh treatment of the peasants. The boy was deeply moved by the vivid, often naturalistic descriptions of the sufferings of this nineteen-year-old terrorist at the hands of the authorities, and came to believe that he "madly, endlessly loved" her. When she was sentenced to prison, the boy, unable to continue living without the hope of seeing her, drowned himself, explaining in a suicide note to his best friend:

> I prayed at her portrait, breathed the idea of her always, and thought that when they would pardon her, I would fall at her knees and tell her everything. But there is no

amnesty and it seems there will never be any for my dear Mariia who is dying out there in Pugachev's tower and will not survive her sentence. Therefore I leave this world earlier to go where there is no Pugachev's tower—I will soon see her there.[153]

In considering motives for the widespread participation of minors in extremist activities, another factor of primary importance in the natural course of maturation should not be neglected, namely, the need to assert oneself as an individual with a unique identity, a developed set of values, and a well-defined world outlook. This process usually involves borrowing the values of others, thereby validating them. In the chaos and instability that reigned in 1905, in politics as well as in individual lives, many juveniles seemed to sense that the moment was extraordinarily propitious for youthful rebellion; traditional values were subject to doubt, and could easily be replaced with the radical ideas prevalent among adults involved in revolutionary politics. The youngsters' impulses to assert themselves in the rapidly changing world by joining the revolution was further reinforced by the glorification of the most extreme forms of struggle, including terror and politically motivated robberies, in the left-wing press. The romanticized image of the heroic freedom fighter presented in these publications was particularly appealing to the young. Given the evident desire of so many juveniles to prove themselves heroes, as well as their tendency toward spontaneous and often irresponsible decision-making, their willingness to take part in the most risky extremist undertakings against the establishment is easily understandable. As one former radical, who in his youth had belonged to an SR terrorist detachment, later admitted, "It was easy for me to become a combatant, and it was even easier to become a revolutionary."[154]

A fair percentage of the teenage terrorists and expropriators were led to involvement in violence by economic hardship, which in many cases amounted to destitution. This was especially true of the Jewish youth, who made up the largest component of the anarchist cadres. Frustrated by their inability to escape poverty, they readily joined the adults in their struggle against the socioeconomic conditions imposed by the tsarist regime, which seemed to offer no opportunities for them. To a great extent, this situation accounts for the fearlessness of these teenagers: they simply had nothing to lose by becoming terrorists.[155] In part, this also accounts for their participation in extortion and expropriation, which provided quick and therefore tempting methods of obtaining large sums of money.[156]

Not all and probably not even the majority of the adolescent extremists were destitute, however. A factor that clearly facilitated the transformation of boys (and occasionally girls) from more prosperous circumstances into terrorists was that some of the youngsters going through a period of typical teenage rebellion against the authority of their families and other adult mentors during the years of revolutionary ferment were particularly susceptible to the attractions of radicalism. They sought, on the one hand, to liberate themselves personally from the control of authoritarian parents and teachers, and, on the other, to legitimize this natural desire for independence by adopting an intellectually or morally justifiable public cause for rebellion. The revolutionary situation in Russia, marked by the constant sounds of terrorists' bullets and bomb explosions, and colored by the blood of the country's leading statesmen, provided the youngsters a seemingly lofty outlet for their mundane drives.

Other rebellious teenagers who plunged into radical activities closely resembled the adult extremists who belonged to the seamy side of the revolution. Some of these juveniles were criminal delinquents, but in most cases they were petty troublemakers and dropouts—streetwise, neglected minors with crude language and manners to match, already possessed of a semicriminal mentality and value system. Even when formally affiliated with a school they tended to be indifferent to their studies, preferring to devote their time to gambling, heavy drinking, and sexual promiscuity, all conducted in an atmosphere tinged with vague political radicalism. Significantly, there appears to have been some correlation between the level of revolutionary enthusiasm and the extent of ethical corruption among the underage extremists. According to the naive memoirs of one radical seminary student, Vasilii Kniazev, who was entirely absorbed in the revolution, "It turned out that I myself was a fairly big cheese. . . . It was I who introduced cardplaying in school in Homeric proportions. When people did not have change, they played for matches. . . . The male seminary [students] drank more and more. Drinking also spread to the girls' boarding school . . . love raged like some kind of smallpox." Petty theft also ceased to be taboo.[157]

In many cases, juveniles who had alienated themselves from their peers through unacceptable conduct, and had generally cut themselves off from all normal walks of life, found release for their frustrations in revenge against anyone they felt had treated them unfairly. Frequently, these adolescents did not blame the political regime or even the educational system for their problems, tending instead to take action against personal enemies, such as gymnasium and seminary principals and teachers who may have limited their opportunities for a successful and respectable future within the framework of the existing traditional social order by giving them failing marks or expelling them for misbehavior.[158] Affected by the continuing violence in the adult world, juveniles seeking personal revenge occasionally resorted to brutal attacks against these authority figures, using homemade explosive devices, revolvers, daggers, and in several instances, sulfuric acid.[159] In some cases, students even formed their own terrorist groups, such as the Combat Organization of the Classical Gymnasium of Tula.[160] Some of these youngsters were shaken by their crimes, and became desperate to find idealistic explanations for them. Under the influence of the left-wing terminology of the day they occasionally justified their assaults after the fact as acts of terror against oppressors and proponents of the despotic regime in the empire. A number of these teenagers subsequently joined professional terrorists in revolutionary organizations in Russia and abroad.[161]

A considerable number of adolescents used weapons not only against schoolmates who belonged to Russian patriotic groups, cooperated with school officials, or otherwise exhibited conservative leanings, but also against peers who simply chose not to participate in student protests.[162] In one incident in the town of Bel, a gymnasium pupil named Rygel', who had left school after participating in a student strike in 1904, decided to continue his studies and was readmitted. He received several threatening letters from radicals ordering him to quit, and when he refused even after they repeatedly tossed stones into his apartment, two members of a local revolutionary organization attacked him on the street on 9 September 1905 and threw sulfuric acid in his face.[163]

Like many of the adults engaged in combat activities, some juvenile terrorists suffered from a degree of psychological imbalance, exhibiting an inclination toward hysteria and an inability to reconcile inner urges and conflicts with external reality. A significant number of adolescents had contemplated killing themselves before becoming involved in revolutionary violence and assassinations. Sixteen-year-old Venedikt Chaikovskii, a student at a high school (*real'-noe uchileshche*) who was about to be expelled for academic failure, stole his father's revolver in desperation, thinking initially of taking his own life. By chance, however, he ran into a math teacher who had given him an unsatisfactory evaluation, and "the thought of suicide momentarily gave way to the urge for revenge." But whereas Chaikovskii, who only wounded his victim, was merely a "hysterical personality . . . subject to nervous fits,"[164] other youthful extremists exhibited more serious pathological behavior and some received formal treatment for mental disorders. The seminary student Kniazev was one such radical youth. A simpleminded young man of extreme energy, hyperactive and unable to control his impulses on any level, he left written descriptions of his nervous attacks and breakdowns that reveal the emotional instability for which he was placed under psychiatric observation.[165] A contemporary liberal psychologist commented that among such youths there were many "mad ones who choose the means of political assassination in order to end their lives."[166]

Perceiving distinct advantages in selecting youths for combat duties, adult terrorists readily recruited minors for terrorist operations, motivated by psychological as much as practical considerations. They recognized how easy it was to exploit both the desire of the youngsters to assert themselves as heroes, and the fearlessness in the face of death typical of many adolescents, who "talked with enthusiasm about dying 'in action,' and not even for the sake of the revolutionary 'cause.'"[167] Any psychological instability in a potential juvenile activist only made the youngster more desirable as a terrorist. Clearly, the adult radicals also appreciated the fact that in many combat situations the teenagers were more likely to succeed than the older, more experienced combatants, if only because the police were less likely to suspect them of participating in clandestine activities, dealing with weapons and explosives, or harboring murderous intentions. It is also probable that some revolutionaries who enlisted the assistance of children took into consideration the fact that if apprehended, juvenile terrorists would rarely be treated with the same severity in the tsarist courts as more mature extremists.

The radicals found a wide variety of ways to employ adolescents in terrorist operations. Teenagers were used to surveil the movements of potential targets among police officers, or keep watch near buildings housing Okhrana offices slated for bombing. When combatants en route to locations where terrorist attacks or expropriations were to take place considered carrying arms and explosives too risky, minors were used to transport the weapons. Teenagers assisted in the manufacture and concealment of explosives, and also participated in a wide range of actual terrorist attacks and expropriations.[168] Some combat detachments, particularly under the PSR and the Bolsheviks, organized and trained future replacements by enlisting the youngsters in specially formed youth cells (*iacheiki*). Terrorists who were themselves minors systematically schooled their fourteen-year-old brothers and other teenagers, primarily from among first-generation factory workers, by assigning them various underground and occasionally hazardous tasks.[169] Sometimes they were charged with the execution of terrorist acts despite the fact that, according to one SR combatant, these youngsters were intellectually "underdeveloped and without any revolutionary education, just recently assigned as apprentices to a party cell."[170] The adult combatants also encouraged the youngsters to engage in malicious vandalism, such as plugging oven (*pech'*) chimneys before the Russian Shrovetide celebration in order to cause panic and disrupt the traditional preparation of pancakes for the holiday. On the one hand, such "mischief was . . . a form of protest against the petty bourgeoisie," but on the other, "it was originally used for educational purposes,"[171] to prepare the youths for staging more dangerous acts.[172]

For most juvenile participants in terrorist activities, their new life as underground freedom fighters was an intoxicating game, full of secrecy, mystery, danger, and idealistic rhetoric. Some of these adolescents claimed to perceive the true beauty of life in "death for death's sake, in the heroic deed for the sake of the heroic deed."[173] The general atmosphere of conspiracy in the name of lofty ideals reinforced their enthusiasm for combat work and was therefore continuously encouraged by the older and more experienced terrorists, who in the eyes of the youngsters were "surrounded by the aura" of heroes.[174] Under their influence, the youthful recruits undertook terrorist acts on their own initiative and enthusiastically sought opportunities to prove themselves. In this spirit, Levka Bilenkin, a seventeen-year-old anarchist, made an independent decision to blow up a police station on 1 May 1906, "to celebrate the proletarian holiday."[175]

Whereas some adolescent terrorists imitated the adults in directing their efforts against Okhrana agents, shop managers, police and prison authorities, and even high officials of the tsarist administration,[176] others admitted that in choosing targets for their acts, they were guided by a cliché that quickly became a slogan: "If there's no one better, you'll do!"[177] On occasion the juveniles executed attacks indiscriminately, killing at random and for no apparent reason other than the fact that their victims wore the uniforms of police officers, soldiers, and Cossacks; they also fired guns and planted bombs in stores, cafes, and other public places.[178] Despite the rapid dissemination of radical ideas after 1905, the ability of these youngsters to justify their actions consciously with revolutionary rhetoric was limited, and their logic usually resembled the unsophisticated reasoning at work in certain earlier instances of terrorist activity. This is exemplified by an incident on 8 March 1898, when an underage extremist named Ufimtsev, influenced by illegal publications romanticizing the exploits of the extremists of the 1880s, incited his friends to set off an explosion in the Znamenskii monastery in Kursk, "hoping to do something outstanding, having to do with danger . . . something that might draw general attention," and by destroying the Icon of the Blessed Virgin, "shake the faith in this revered relic."[179] In a number of instances teenagers attempted to blow up portraits of Nicholas II in their schools, risking casualties among their fellow students.[180] Underage radicals experimenting with homemade bombs and other explosive devices also caused accidental detonations in schools and seminaries.[181] Some juveniles, paralleling the more sadistic adult terrorists, exhibited extreme cruelty, with one Jewish boy in Gomel' throwing sulfuric acid in the face of a policeman at his post in June of 1904.[182]

At times, the force drawing the youngsters into terrorist action had nothing to do with revolutionary convictions. One thirteen-year-old Warsaw girl, the daughter of a woman who fell in love with and became "literally the slave" of a Polish terrorist, was enlisted by the extremists in spite of protests and pleas from her mother, who claimed to have no sympathy for the revolution and to be "revolted by terror." Other involuntary young recruits were forced to transport dynamite, prepare explosives, conceal weapons, and even to participate in actual terrorist operations. The youngest Russian associated with terrorist activity was Lisa, the three- or four-year-old daughter of "Comrade Natasha" (F. I. Drabkina), a Bolshevik *boevik* who required her daughter's company for conspiratorial cover when she carried explosive mercury fulminate.[183] A number of juvenile combatants, such as a pair of drunken youths who staged an unsuccessful assault on a small store, acted with little regard for ideological justification.[184] Some youngsters pretended to acquit their behavior by radical slogans, as did one seventh grader who tried to prove theoretically that the only true revolutionary act was to "expropriate the expropriators;" other participants in revolutionary robberies were "children who loved money, simple as that."[185] There is evidence that radical organizations in the periphery, particularly the Baltics, sometimes simply hired fifteen- and sixteen-year-olds for terrorist activities, occasionally paying them as little as fifty kopeks.[186] These people, both the employers and their young hirelings, were among the terrorists of the new type who so clearly represented the seamy side of the revolution.

Chapter Six

THE UNITED FRONT

INTERPARTY CONNECTIONS AND COOPERATION

> Political terror has such decisive importance for the life of our
> motherland, its influence is so profound [and] all-encompassing,
> that all disagreements among terrorists *must disappear* before it.
> Political terror . . . must become the dominating factor in estab-
> lishing relations among the groups that recognize its great
> significance. All supporters of political terror should feel like mem-
> bers of a single family, by merging one way or another into one
> league of *political terror*.
> —*Vladimir Burtsev*[1]

MOST REVOLUTIONARY PARTIES in Russia deviated in practice
from their theoretical statements regarding terrorism, which either
condemned political assassination and expropriation altogether, as
was the case with the Social Democrats, or, like the Socialists-Revolutionaries
and some anarchists, established restrictions for their use. Here, the traditional
scholarly emphasis on the ideological differences among the various antigovernment groups is thus inappropriate. Moreover, although historians have
often stressed the individuality of the left-wing organizations, and pointed to
defensive tendencies to account for a supposed disunity within the Russian
revolutionary movement, there were nevertheless solid grounds for interparty
connections and cooperation, all ideological conflicts and rivalry among party
elites notwithstanding. In contradiction of the usual assumption that the "revolutionaries hated the bourgeoisie as much as they hated one another,"[2] some
scholars have recently suggested that the Russian antigovernment camp was
not as divided as it has traditionally been depicted. In his study of the 1880s,
Naimark suggests that "unity among radicals, ideological flexibility, and
mutual help and tolerance" were part of the "heritage of the revolutionary
movement."[3] Michael Melancon emphasizes that the same mutual cooperation
was characteristic of the left bloc in the twentieth century, when at all levels
various parties and factions "informally coordinated activities and, at key
times, resorted to official inter-party arrangements."[4] This becomes apparent
from an examination of the practical policies of the various left-wing groups
toward terrorism—probably the most radical feature in the activity of any subversive organization, and the most extreme manifestation of revolutionary
psychology.

SOCIALIST-REVOLUTIONARY COLLABORATION WITH OTHER RADICALS

Partly because of their constant efforts to prove the Marxist foundation of their theoretical program and practical policies, the SR leadership was cautious about entering into joint ventures with groups whose ideology or actions raised questions about their adherence to the scientific socialist creed. At the same time, some PSR leaders, particularly Il'ia Rubanovich, its representative to the Communist International, who had long cherished the dream of a single united party of socialists, did take steps toward closer relations with the various Marxist organizations,[5] and several PSR congresses and conferences passed formal resolutions allowing temporary combat and tactical alliances between SR party members and the Social Democrats. The SRs were to maintain even more permanent contacts with various national revolutionary organizations that shared fundamental ideological principles, including the Polish Socialist Party, the Latvian Social Democrats, the Revolutionary Party of Georgian Socialists-Federalists, the Jewish Socialist Party (Serp), and the Armenian Dashnaktsutiun.[6] On the other hand, the SR leadership was guided by a general policy of avoiding joint action or even negotiation with the bourgeois opposition parties, or with anarchist and similar extremist groups, including the renegade SRs of the Maximalists. This, however, was but a general direction publicly advocated by the leadership; as in other fields of party activity, reality often differed significantly from the established party line.

Following the arrest of Gershuni in May 1903, the Combat Organization terrorists, absorbed in the conspiratorial work, severed their spiritual connections with the SR organization as a whole. They became so autonomous and scornful of the activities of the party's emigré leaders, living in safety away from the center of revolutionary activity and theorizing about PSR programs and policies, that they felt no obligation to adhere to the principles provided by these civilian generals. Given their lack of interest in dogma, their tendency to depart from SR orthodoxy, and their freedom from effective control by the central party leadership abroad, there were no obstacles preventing the Combat Organization terrorists from cooperating with terrorists of other radical trends.

Boris Savinkov, who succeeded Gershuni as head of the Combat Organization but did not share his devotion to the fundamentals of PSR ideology, was open to joint efforts with groups whose political outlooks differed from those of the SR majority, provided that terrorist activity was sufficiently high on their list of revolutionary priorities and outweighed party differences on theory. As a result, he not only tolerated ideological dissidents inside the Combat Organization, but also attempted to establish contacts with the Maximalist defectors from the PSR. In a revealing dialogue with Maximalist leader Mikhail Sokolov, Savinkov tried to convince him of the benefits of collaboration between the SR and Maximalist forces, and obtain his consent for consorted action, independent of party politics: "Why can't we work together? As far as I'm concerned, there are no obstacles. It makes no difference to me whether you are a Maximalist, an anarchist, or a Socialist-Revolutionary. We are both terrorists. Let us combine our organizations in the interest of terror." Savinkov further argued that programmatic disagreements should not stand in the way of combat work, and that it was impermissible for terrorists to fight among themselves over such secondary issues as the socialization of factories. For his part, Sokolov conceded in principle that the terrorist work would be much more successful if the SRs and the Maximalists worked together, lamenting the fact that his comrades would never agree to this arrangement because the SRs were enemies of the Maximalist opposition: "You have declared war on us." To this Savinkov gave a characteristic reply: "Not we, but the Party of Socialists-Revolutionaries," thus drawing a sharp distinction between the interests of the Combat Organization and the official line of the PSR.[7]

Still, in Moscow and other cities cooperation between the SR terrorists and the Maximalists never ceased, and despite the persistent efforts of the central PSR leadership to isolate its members from the harmful influence of the dissidents, individual SRs were usually prepared to support their former party comrades in various undertakings. The Maximalists readily reciprocated, and it was therefore not unusual for sums as large as fifty thousand rubles to be transferred to official SR organizations by sympathetic Maximalists, often to the indignation of Maximalist leadership.[8]

SR terrorists were also willing to coordinate their efforts with the work of other, more ideologically distant groups than the Maximalists. Even at the central level of the party, certain leaders were eager to join forces with other combat groups. Nikolai Chaikovskii, one of the oldest and most prominent of the SR leaders, became an ardent proponent of partisan warfare during the 1905 revolution, advocating the formation of guerrilla bands composed of *boeviki* from various parties, and even extremists with no definite political preferences, united merely by their willingness to oppose the contemporary regime with arms.[9] Prepared to implement his plan, Chaikovskii traveled to the Urals to negotiate with Alexander Lbov, with whom the SRs maintained rather close ties, for coordination of efforts with his combat organization.[10] Rubanovich, not wishing to limit himself to agitation for the benefits of greater cooperation between the SRs and the SDs, established private, secret contacts with several anarchists abroad. There is evidence that he was aware of anarchist preparations for an attempt on the life of the Grand Duke Vladimir Aleksandrovich, in which, incidentally, several members of the PSR were also involved.[11]

On the local level revolutionaries were not completely free from interparty squabbles and competition, and this was evident from the constant migration of individual members among the various radical groups.[12] Sometimes inter-

party rivalry resulted in mutual verbal abuse, threats, fights, and the expropriation of party funds and weapons.[13] It occasionally took even more extreme
forms, resulting in physical violence. This was the case, for example, in the
town of Vainly, where local anarchists murdered the owner of a sugar factory
named Braunson or Bramson, a convinced SR who had served a term in
exile.[14] Revolutionary activists often expressed antagonism toward former
party members who had left to engage in independent activity, especially expropriations, and had thus stopped contributing to party treasuries. Loyal
members of the formal organizations tended to regard these defectors as bandits, and occasionally became involved in bloody confrontations with them
over loot.[15]

These incidents of hostility, however, were rare in comparison with the
widespread cooperation among local SRs with other revolutionary groups
throughout the empire. This cooperation was not limited to nonviolent activities such as joint publication of underground literature, convocation of frequent interparty meetings, demonstrations, conferences, and occasionally even
the formation of mixed organizations, such as, for example, the Leftist Club
(Klub levykh), formed in Paris at the beginning of November 1910 by representatives of the SR, Maximalist, and anarchist movements.[16] Not allowing
dogmatic differences to interfere with combat activities, the SRs also became
involved in terrorist enterprises with other radicals without first obtaining official sanction from the central PSR governing bodies, or even informing them
of their plans.[17]

Given their lack of discrimination in combat methods, it is not surprising
that many Maximalists joined their anarchist comrades not only in assassination efforts, such as planning for the murder of Grand Duke Nikolai Nikolaevich,[18] but also in expropriations. One of these armed assaults was an unsuccessful attempt to confiscate two hundred thousand rubles from the office
of the Moscow-Kazan' railroad; one anarchist was killed and several other
extremists arrested, with two subsequently tried and sentenced to death.[19]
More important, joint revolutionary robberies involving SRs and anarchists
were also common. In one such incident, members of an SR cell in Odessa
collaborated with a local group of Anarchists-Syndicalists in a bank holdup,
acquiring thousands of rubles in profits.[20] Odessa SRs also joined forces with
the Anarchists-Communists for the purpose of organizing terrorist acts and
expropriations.[21]

Cooperation between SRs and other extremists in the periphery was particularly widespread in the chaotic days of 1905, when, for example, "in May the
SRs of Belostok joined the anarchists to form a significant segment of the
revolutionary movement there. Their violence reached a peak of sorts in their
'expropriations,' a nice term for outright robbery and extortion," which even
the local Bundists considered little better than hooliganism.[22] In 1906, the SRs
and the anarchists in Ekaterinburg organized the Union of Active Struggle

against Autocracy (Soiuz aktivnoi bor'by s samoderzhaviem). Its members "in their goals and actions were common thieves (*naletchiki*)," preoccupied with assaults on local churches to requisition gold, silver, and other valuables.[23]

On occasion the SRs joined forces with extremist groups of obscure or unspecified ideology, but very definite orientation toward political violence and especially revolutionary robberies. One of several bands whose members called themselves Terrorists-Expropriators (*terroristy-eksropriatory*), primarily assaulted private apartments, but also undertook larger expropriations, including an attempted robbery at a monastery near Grodno in December 1906. There were several SRs in the group, including Evstiliia Rogozinnikova, the notorious terrorist heroine extolled in the official party press for her role in the assassination of Maksimovskii.[24]

In the border areas, where the SRs had traditionally been outnumbered by nationalist revolutionaries and the Social Democrats, they were fully prepared to ally themselves temporarily with local extremists, who typically possessed a better grasp of the current political situation in the outlying regions, and also enjoyed the support of a larger constituency—a factor that ultimately signified a fuller treasury. In various areas of the Caucasus, for example, SR groups approached the Maximalists to establish coordinated terrorist activity.[25] In the Georgian cities of Tiflis and Kutais the practical policies of the SRs were essentially no different from those of the most extreme proponents of anarchism, who acknowledged that many SRs were with the anarchists in their hearts, and that they often went into action together.[26]

While the local SRs in Georgia acted on their own initiative, in Baku SR cooperation with the nationalist revolutionary terrorist organization Dashnaktsutiun assumed an official character. When the Dashnaki issued a formal declaration that any representative of the tsarist administration who attempted to confiscate weapons, conduct house searches, or make arrests among the local population would be mercilessly eliminated, the Baku PSR Committee immediately issued a special proclamation formally announcing its intention to assist the Armenian comrades actively in punishing gendarmes, policemen, and other tsarist officials.[27] In addition, in their persistent efforts to smuggle arms and explosives into the Russian Empire by way of the Black Sea and the Caucasus, the SRs often joined forces temporarily with local nationalist rebels that had little or no interest in socialist ideals, and nothing in common with the SRs other than hatred of the Russian administration.[28]

Ties between the SRs and local extremists were similarly close in Poland. Jan Tychinsky, for example, a member of the PPS combat brigade responsible for a number of terrorist attacks in the town of Radom, personally led an assault on a prison to liberate notorious SR activist Michurin.[29] In L'vov representatives of the PSR, the PPS, and several other radical organizations formed a group in 1909 to uncover and eliminate police agents in the revolutionary ranks.[30] Following the 1909 decision of PPS leaders to halt terrorist operations temporarily, party dissidents outraged by the action occasionally offered their combat services to the PSR.[31]

In the Baltics, as well as the Duchy of Finland, the SRs were also willing to join forces with various national revolutionary organizations in their common struggle against the Russian government. Upon his arrival in Zurich, Moisei (Mikhail) Kobylinskii, a Riga representative of the SR newspaper *Syn Oteche-stva* (*Son of the Fatherland*), went to work assisting in the manufacture of explosives for Latvian national revolutionary forces.[32] Additionally, according to police information, secret negotiations took place in Tammerfors in May 1909 between the remnants of the PSR Northern Flying Combat Detachment and representatives of the Finnish revolutionary party Voima for the purpose of cooperating in an assassination attempt against the tsar.[33] In 1904–1907 the SRs also maintained very close ties with the Finnish Party of Active Resistance, whose primary aim was the liberation of the Duchy of Finland from Russian rule. Given the Finnish group's strictly nationalist tendencies, and their limited concern with social issues, the only basis for cooperation between the two organizations was that both considered political assassination one of the most effective means of struggle against the tsarist government.[34]

Beyond the borders of the Russian Empire, SRs participated in political robberies alongside other extremists, and these episodes included a well-publicized 1908 expropriation in Lausanne, Switzerland staged by SRs in concert with anarchists.[35] SR collaboration with other radicals continued well into the years following suppression of the intense 1905–1907 antigovernment activity. As late as 1913 members of a combined SR-anarchist group in Belgium entertained schemes for a joint combat detachment to travel to Russia for the express purpose of carrying out expropriations.[36] Various extremist organizations were thus confident of SR assistance in terrorist ventures, and one incident appears especially significant in this regard. In planning an assassination attempt against Stolypin, in the fall of 1907 members of a joint anarchist-Maximalist group in Geneva proposed to smuggle a bomb into a State Duma session with the help of one of the deputies—a member of the Socialist-Revolutionary Party.[37]

Cooperation within the RSDRP

Like the SRs, revolutionaries in the various branches of the RSDRP found that in the crucial days of the 1905–1907 crisis they could no longer afford to allow theoretical disputes, which had dominated their outlook in the less hectic pre-revolutionary period, to remain an obstacle in the common struggle against the tsarist administration. Bolsheviks and Mensheviks, along with representatives of the Bundist, Latvian, and other national SD organizations, thus began to demonstrate in practice that dogma could be subordinated to the more immediate concerns of the day, and even renounced altogether at the peak of revolutionary activity. This is especially evident in the collaboration on terrorist operations among various groups within the RSDRP.

On the central level the most active SD factional cooperation occurred in the acquisition of weapons and explosives, with Bolshevik associates of Leonid Krasin playing a primary role in 1905–1907. Using their established connections with arms dealers abroad, particularly in Belgium and England, they assisted other SD organizations, including the Mensheviks, the Bundists, the Latvians, and the Poles, in the complicated process of purchasing and transporting arms and explosives materials into Russia,[38] where they were used for eliminating police agents and strikebreakers, liberating imprisoned comrades, attacking state-owned liquor stores, and other terrorist activities.[39] Cooperation among SD forces in the capitals also included the January 1906 bombing of the tavern Tver' in St. Petersburg, an action in which several Latvian SDs played primary roles.[40]

In Moscow, Bolshevik and Menshevik *boeviki* worked together, discarding their differences as theoretical disputes meaningless in battle; and predictably, such cooperation was even more common in the periphery.[41] In Dvinsk Russian Social Democratic combatants (who apparently chose not to specify their programmatic preferences and collaborated successfully on a combined Bolshevik-Menshevik committee), "during the restless days [in 1905] usually acted in contact with the '*boeviki*' of other revolutionary organizations, among which the Bund's combat detachment was particularly strong."[42] The SD combat detachment in Vil'na, which consisted primarily of "professional *boeviki*," was formally joined after October 1905 with a similar combat unit of the local Bund committee under a single leadership, and during the next two years its Russian and Jewish members were responsible for numerous acts of terror and expropriation.[43]

In border localities such as Latvia, cooperation among SD combatants, regardless of their party affiliations, was even more evident. The omnipotent and omnipresent Federal Committee of Riga, consisting of Bolsheviks, Mensheviks, Bundists, and Latvian SDs, sanctioned numerous terrorist acts, including executions of street policemen and low-ranking officials designated members of the monarchist Black Hundreds by the radicals.[44] One of the most significant of the Committee's achievements was a daring attack on the central city prison on 7 September 1905, during which they liberated Martyn Latsis (Kriuger), a prominent activist in the Latvian Social Democracy organization.[45] Members of the Federal Committee, many of whom had previously been implicated in assaults on state liquor stores, turned quickly to expropriations, the most common form of which was the confiscation of guns from private weapon shops.[46] After October 1905 divisions of the Federal Committee were formed in a number of cities throughout the Baltic region, including

Libau and Mitau. Following the example of the central organization in Riga, local SDs turned to terrorist activities as members of these interfactional combat brigades.[47]

Finally, even beyond the borders of the Russian Empire a tendency toward practical cooperation was evident among all SDs with terrorist inclinations. As early as 1905, a number of Social Democrats of unspecified programmatic preferences residing in Western Europe entertained plans for joint terrorist ventures that, according to police sources, included the formation of a small combat organization to be headed by Mark Broido and his wife Eva, both close friends of Savinkov.[48] Representatives of the various RSDRP organizations were thus clearly prepared to disregard faction boundaries for the sake of cooperation in combat activities. They were also willing to join forces for similar purposes with revolutionaries from other groups and parties, some of which stood very far from the fundamental principles of Russian Social Democracy.

Russian SD Collaboration with Outsiders

In their public statements and party periodicals, the RSDRP leaders rarely missed an opportunity to define the borders distinguishing them from all revolutionaries outside the SD camp, and to condemn their rivals' unorthodox ideologies and unworkable programs. The PSR, which presented the most significant challenge to Social Democratic thinking, therefore received an avalanche of criticism and verbal abuse, and was labeled everything from counterrevolutionary to anarchistic. The SRs responded with similar statements, publicly charging the SDs with behavior unworthy of revolutionaries, including squandering expropriated funds on liquor.[49] At times the SD-SR rivalry expressed itself in threats and intimidation, and there are indications that these threats were occasionally carried into practice, as was the case when an SR group in Baku sanctioned the murder of a local Menshevik as an alleged police spy.[50] And yet, although mutual accusations never ceased, and covered all imaginable sins, from political demagoguery to betrayal of revolutionary ideals, leading members of both parties recognized the expediency of setting aside disagreements for the sake of cooperation.

According to police sources, as early as February 1905 negotiations for a possible formal unification of SD and SR forces specifically for joint terrorist ventures were moving along rapidly, with such prominent SRs as Rubanovich, Mark Natanson, and Mikhail Gots discussing the prospects for terrorist acts with a number of leading representatives of the RSDRP abroad.[51] In the meantime, SR and SD organizations inside Russia were already demonstrating resolve to fight the government together in joint terrorist operations, which continued throughout 1905–1907.[52]

Although collaboration among Russian socialists predated the outbreak of revolutionary activity, the expedience of consorted action became particularly evident after 1905, when radicals in various parts of the country not only rendered each other occasional assistance in daily tasks, and enjoyed cordial relations, but also combined into semiformal SR-SD groups and committees for long-term cooperation over the entire range of revolutionary enterprises, from propaganda to individual acts of terror to mass uprisings.[53] Because of the SR influence, these organizations frequently took a very active stance on the issue of terrorism. *Boeviki* from the United Ural SD-SR Group (Ob"edinennaia ural'skaia gruppa s.-d. i s.-r.), which came into existence before the revolution, took part in various 1905 combat operations, including throwing bombs at policemen and Cossacks trying to break up an illegal gathering of workers.[54]

The SRs and SDs also collaborated in extortion and the expropriation of private property, which were particularly widespread in the Caucasus, despite all official rejections of these methods by party leaders on both sides. In Kutais, for example, the Social Democrats imposed a special revolutionary tax on prosperous local citizens, targeting merchants in particular. Under threat of confiscation of all property, the merchants were required to collect specific sums among themselves and submit a minimum total of five hundred rubles each month to the SD organizations. Observing how lucrative these methods were for their fellow socialists, the local SRs sought a share of future profits and managed to secure the consent of the SDs (who largely controlled the market) to collect three hundred rubles monthly for their own needs.[55]

Given the less than dogmatic attitude toward political violence demonstrated by Lenin's followers, it is hardly surprising that among the various factions of the RSDRP it was the Bolsheviks who contributed the most to the terrorist practices of non-SD parties. Even before the 1905 revolutionary activity reached its zenith, the majority of the Bolshevik leaders favored close cooperation with the SRs in combat matters. During the deliberations of the Third Congress of the RSDRP in the spring of 1905, Bolshevik M. G. Tskhakaia, while assuring his comrades that the SRs were not strong enough anywhere in the country to be a serious consideration, gave credit to their combat detachments and advocated "in time of revolution . . . using even their assistance and entering into alliance with them."[56] Tskhakaia's viewpoint was evidently shared by the majority of the SDs present at the party's Third Congress, which passed a resolution instructing party members to oppose the SRs in ideological and programmatic matters, while at the same time expressly permitting occasional joint SD-SR combat operations. To use Lenin's expression, the Bolsheviks and the Socialists-Revolutionaries were to "march apart, but strike together."[57]

Under the circumstances, the Bolsheviks operating inside of Russia, and facing the practical difficulties of revolutionary tasks, tended to neglect the first part of the congressional resolution regarding points of theoretical disagreement between the SDs and the SRs, and concentrate on the second part dealing with consorted action. There were still tensions and open conflicts among the revolutionaries, but it appears that most disagreements were petty squabbles resulting from rivalry over practical matters, such as control of party treasuries and manpower, rather than irreconcilable issues of dogma. And any rivalry was outweighed by the fact that both in the capitals and the periphery more often than not each side could count on the other for assistance and cooperation in a wide range of joint ventures.

Motivated by this comradery, many SDs readily provided the SR *boeviki* with money, shelter, and other aid. The Bolshevik wife of a well-known left Menshevik, Nikolai Sukhanov, helped Petr Romanov, an SR combatant wanted for the 1907 murder of the head of the gendarmes in Samara, to hide from the police.[58] Individual members of Bolshevik combat units who had been implicated in political robberies joined representatives of the PSR in minor terrorist operations without seeking official sanction from the party's central organs.[59] Significantly, in some areas the Bolsheviks reported that they got along better with the SRs than with their brother Mensheviks.[60]

Bolsheviks in the capitals were as prepared as their fellow party members in the periphery to render assistance to the SRs in terrorist enterprises. This was strikingly true of Krasin, who was apparently prepared to extend his help to any representative of the radical camp. Thus in 1907, during a trial of SRs arrested in connection with the terrorist activities of the SR Northern Flying Combat Detachment, Krasin and a number of his associates in the Combat Technical Group entertained plans to liberate the imprisoned SRs, among whom were personal friends and acquaintances; because of prompt action by the police, the plans did not materialize.[61] Having organized a special combat technical bureau (*voenno-tekhnicheskoe biuro*), a laboratory in St. Petersburg that produced bombs, hand grenades, and various devices classified as infernal machines, Krasin impressed his SR contacts with the quality of the Bolshevik explosives.[62] In addition, *boeviki* under Krasin's command occasionally operated alongside SR terrorists in combat activities in the capital.[63]

Krasin also proved of substantial assistance to the Maximalists. The enormous sixteen-pound bombs used in the Maximalist assault on Stolypin's house on Aptekar'skii Island, as well as the explosives utilized in the Fonarnyi Lane expropriation, were produced in the Bolshevik laboratory under Krasin's immediate supervision.[64] In general, despite all efforts on the part of the Bolshevik leadership to maintain strict secrecy around their combat operations, individual terrorists could not be prevented from making private contacts with their counterparts among the Maximalists. Many Bolshevik combatants, apparently envious of the terrorist exploits of the Maximalists, continually reproached their party leaders for the restrictions that prevented them from perpetrating acts of equal significance.[65]

Krasin and his associates established mutually beneficial contacts among the anarchists as well. Wishing to learn from the rich anarchist experience in the field of bomb construction, revolutionaries in Krasin's entourage who had established a laboratory for manufacturing explosives near the Russo-Finnish border in the summer of 1907 shared their facilities with a group of anarchists who probably lacked the means to establish their own bomb production shop and were happy to combine efforts with the Bolsheviks.[66] Of incidental interest is the fact that one of the texts on the preparation of explosives that the Bolsheviks consulted while working in this and other underground bomb shops was *Laboratory Techniques* (Laboratornaia tekhnika) by E. A. Goppius, an Anarchist-Individualist who worked closely with the Bolsheviks in the Moscow branch of the combat technical bureau, and in 1917 formally joined the Bolshevik party.[67]

In much the same way, Bolsheviks involved in combat practices in the more remote areas of the empire often found it convenient to cooperate with local anarchists.[68] Additionally, Bolsheviks abroad granted favors to the anarchists, and Viktor Taratuta, the unsavory confidant of Lenin, was implicated not only in attempts to exchange the money appropriated by the Bolsheviks in the Tiflis expropriation in June 1907, but also in providing assistance to anarchist comrades in similar operations involving their own expropriated funds.[69]

In the border areas, the Bolsheviks successfully cooperated not only with local SDs, but also with other radical organizations. Lenin's followers from St. Petersburg entered into negotiations with the Dashnaktsutiun party in the Caucasus in the spring of 1907, and subsequently forwarded a large shipment of rifles to these revolutionaries from the capital.[70] It was apparently more essential for Krasin and his associates to establish friendly relations with the Finnish activists, although the Bolsheviks understood that this cooperation could only be of temporary duration. In 1906–1907 both sides found it beneficial to share their experience in the transportation of weapons from abroad and the manufacture of bombs. Krasin, accompanied by Professor Mikhail Tikhvinskii, a chemist and the leading Bolshevik explosives expert, traveled to Helsinki in the summer of 1906 to display the newest bombs to the Finnish revolutionaries, carrying a demonstration model in a camera case.[71] While in Helsinki, Krasin also established contact with Dr. A. Terngren, a leading member of the Finnish national movement for passive resistance to the russification policies of the tsarist government, who at one point after the 1917 revolution held the post of Finnish ambassador to Paris. Despite their moderate tendencies, Terngren and other advocates of passive resistance were willing to assist the Bolsheviks in arms smuggling and the manufacture of explosives.[72]

In their terrorist operations, Bolsheviks also joined forces with various obscure gangs of a half-revolutionary, half-criminal nature—notably the partisans operating under the leadership of Lbov throughout the Perm' region in the Urals. Trying to keep their activities as secret as possible even from members of their own party, a number of Lenin's followers sought to establish a mutually profitable relationship with the Lbovtsy, who, during the summer and fall of 1907, "went on the warpath, robbing a number of banks, factories, post offices, and wealthy citizens." There were many subsequent complaints from Lbov's band about the Bolsheviks in this frequently uneasy alliance. In July 1907, for example, Lbov's Perm' Partisan Revolutionary Detachment paid the Bolshevik Center six thousand rubles in advance for weapons from abroad, but despite a duly executed contract, the Bolsheviks failed to deliver the promised weapons and refused to refund the money.[73] Similarly, there are indications that when the time came for division of the proceeds from several joint expropriations, the Bolsheviks benefited at the expense of the Ural bandits.[74]

Perhaps still more significant was the readiness of Lenin's associates to cooperate with common criminals, who had even less interest in socialist ideals than the shady followers of Lbov, but who could nevertheless be very useful partners in operations involving weapons smuggling and arms sales. Despite all subsequent claims of Bolshevik memoirists that some of their criminal supporters were so proud of their participation in the antigovernment struggle that they refused payment for their services,[75] in the majority of cases the bandits were clearly less than altruistic. Usually they demanded money for their assistance, and there appears to have been a tendency for the Bolsheviks in possession of the largest sums of expropriated funds to be the most willing to do business with contrabandists, common crooks, and arms dealers. Not surprisingly, in these temporary alliances there were ample grounds for conflict and mutual grievances. In one dispute, Bolsheviks in the Ural region sent a representative to Kiev to find out why they had not received a shipment of weapons for which they had already paid the arms smugglers. What the Bolshevik envoy was able to discover was characteristic of the nature of these unstable revolutionary-bandit alliances: the contrabandist, who had indeed already received payment from the SDs, had no intention of handing over the weapons, for he had apparently promised the entire shipment of Bolshevik arms to other clients, who in this case happened to be anarchists. The arms dealer finally agreed to comply with Bolshevik demands only under the extreme pressure of a pistol at his temple.[76]

Although renouncing isolated terrorist acts as ineffective in theory, the Bolsheviks, including Krasin's Combat Technical Group, were usually eager to assist in preparing for assassination attempts, even when such an attempt was contemplated by private individuals unaffiliated with any revolutionary party or organization. One member of the Bolshevik Combat Technical Group in St. Petersburg, N. K. Chetverikov (Mikhail L'vovich), received information that a sailor on Nicholas II's yacht, *Shtandart*, had decided on his own to set off an explosion on board the ship during one of the imperial family cruises in the Baltics, but did not know where to obtain a bomb. Seizing the opportunity, Chetverikov encouraged the sailor to proceed with his preparations, and promised to provide him with the necessary explosives as soon as he was ready to act against the tsar.[77]

National SD Collaboration with Outsiders

The Bolsheviks were not the only representatives of the Social Democratic movement willing to join other extremists in common terrorist operations. The Bundists, who frequently migrated in and out of other radical formations,[78] also demonstrated readiness for interparty cooperation. Relationships between Bundists and revolutionary organizations outside the SD camp were at times uneasy, as is evident from the barrage of leaflets issued by Jewish SDs to discredit rival extremists, particularly anarchists. The anarchists often reciprocated, with the resulting hostility rising to verbal abuse and threats.[79] And yet, "a common readiness to face fire" usually drew the Bundists closer to other radicals,[80] as exemplified by their attempts to enlist other revolutionary parties in the Bund-organized joint committees for self-defense, initially formed as a countermeasure against anti-Semitic violence, but often evolving into semi-terrorist combat units.[81] With equal frequency, despite warnings and direct prohibitions from the central party leadership, the Bundists joined the SRs in terrorist acts. Examples of this collaboration are numerous: after Veinreikh the Rich, a prominent citizen in Belostok, insisted that local authorities maintain Cossack units in town as a deterrent to revolutionary activity, several SRs and Bundists, in strict secrecy from their respective organizations, formed a small terrorist band and staged an unsuccessful attempt on his life, taking several shots at him during services at his synagogue before a large congregation.[82] In Kreslavka, a tiny town in the Jewish Pale, a local police official was seriously injured in a bomb blast set off by Bundist and SR terrorists working together.[83] Finally, in the town of Zhitomir, the Bundists offered assistance to SR combatants in an attack they were planning against the local governor and police chief, hoping to provide the SRs a volunteer assassin who would become another Girsh Lekert.[84]

Interparty cooperation also flourished in the Baltic provinces, and especially in Latvia. According to one Riga revolutionary, terrorists facing police or military opposition tended to "forget about quarrels among parties," and join forces in such enterprises as attempts to liberate prisoners, risking their lives and freedom regardless of the ideological loyalties of the detainees.[85] An SD-SR band that formed in Riga late in 1908 chose not to define its long-term theoretical or political objectives, and only identified its immediate aims, which were strictly terroristic. Among other violent acts, it planned the assassinations of Koshelev—chairman of the Riga Military Court, the chief of the central city prison, and the head of the local police, as well as an explosion inside police headquarters. There seem to have been no internal ideological conflicts or even mild disputes in this interparty group, which, however, did not have a chance to implement much of its ambitious program, with the exception of the wounding of Koshelev on 31 January 1909, before it was broken up by the police.[86] Similarly, there is evidence that in Lithuania local *boeviki* joined the SRs in acts of violence against suspected police informers.[87]

The SDs in the Baltic provinces also formed temporary alliances with the anarchists, and occasionally even joined forces with them on a permanent basis. Franz Glott, an active member of a Latvian Social Democratic Workers' Party combat detachment in Libau, decided at one point in his revolutionary career to throw his lot in with the local anarchists.[88] Conversely, in Estonia a number of anarchists joined a local SD combat unit, which then staged a series of violent terrorist acts and expropriations marked by gruesome violence and tortures, the most notorious of these being the 17 February 1907 murder of State Council member Baron Budberg, from whom the extremists stole seventeen thousand rubles and other valuables, partially for personal use, ignoring all appeals to revolutionary consciousness by the central RSDRP leadership.[89]

ANARCHIST COLLABORATION WITH OTHER RADICALS

The nature of the anarchist creed allowed its followers freedom to enter into contracts among themselves as necessary for practical operations, but with the proviso that these contracts could be broken at will. At times individual groups questioned the tactics of other anarchist units (such as small-scale expropriations of private property), or used coercion against one another when they failed to settle their differences peacefully in financial matters or in defining spheres of influence and territorial monopolies.[90] Still, the majority of the anarchist groups considered mutual assistance obligatory in all revolutionary activities, including terrorism. Additionally, since fundamental anarchist doctrine required no justification for most forms of violence on either political or ethical grounds, given the existing conditions of enslavement by the tsarist establishment, the anarchists rarely missed an opportunity to accept a proposition from anywhere within the revolutionary camp for common terrorist efforts.

This is evident both in the attitude of the anarchist leadership abroad regarding other antigovernment organizations, and in the personal position on this issue assumed by the movement's most celebrated theoretician, Petr Kropotkin. In a letter to a friend in 1904, Kropotkin stated that the PSR was a "halfway" revolutionary formation, whose members were little different in their dogmatic preferences from the Social Democrats, despite their public advocation of individual violence. Nevertheless, in Kropotkin's view, it "would simply be criminal to oppose the only combat group in Russia; . . . it is even necessary to help it as much as possible."[91] Additionally, on at least one occasion, Kropotkin acted as a mediator between his followers in Lausanne and the Bundists, who had complained to him about the local anarchists' intentions to expropriate Bundist funds.[92]

In accordance with the recommendations of their leader, the anarchists abroad frequently cooperated with other radicals in solving the immediate problems of emigré life, such as the necessity of investigating suspected police informers within their ranks.[93] More significantly, anarchists living in Western Europe occasionally offered assistance to other revolutionary groups judged sufficiently radical to adopt terrorist methods against the Russian authorities. S. I. Bukhalo, an anarchist engineer who lived in Munich and was known for his innovations in explosives and artillery, worked for ten years on a powerful new flying machine, and indicated his willingness to share his invention with any terrorist organization whose primary objective was regicide. A shortage of funds was partly responsible for his inability to establish his own production shop, and so in January of 1907 he entered into negotiations with Evno Azef, who, on behalf of the PSR, was able to offer him as much as twenty thousand rubles from private sources. This allowed the inventor to hire workers and begin assembly, with the understanding that upon completion the device would be delivered to the PSR Combat Organization, which planned to use it to drop bombs on the imperial residences in Tsarskoe Selo and Peterhof.[94]

In Russia, hostilities between the anarchists and the socialists were common. In their typically heedless fashion, the anarchists used force to break up the meetings of other revolutionaries, made assassination threats against their opponents, particularly the SDs, imposed fines on their fellow radicals, and expropriated other parties' funds. The socialists frequently expressed animosity toward the anarchists, at times retaliating with counterthreats and even acts of violence.[95] At the same time, in addition to accommodating the constant migration of the most radical (and usually least disciplined) defectors from other parties to their ranks,[96] the anarchists actively provided the revolutionary community whatever assistance they could, freely distributing, for example, leaflets giving detailed instructions for the production of bombs.[97] Other radical groups repaid them in kind, and the interparty alliances between the anarchists and socialist extremists extended even to carrying out terrorist acts for each other. One example of this occurred in 1906, when members of the Polish Socialist Party made preparations for an attempt on the life of Major General Seletskii, head of the Warsaw Military Court, in response to his issuance of guilty verdicts against two local Anarchists-Communists.[98]

MULTIPARTY ORGANIZATIONS

As it was common for representatives of two independent revolutionary groups to undertake joint terrorist ventures, so too members of several organizations agreed to participate in coordinated combat activities. This collaboration often took the form of joint consultations and conferences, with cooperative combat acts the primary feature on the agenda. At a conspiratorial meeting in Finland in the summer of 1906, participants included such prominent figures of the revolutionary movement as SRs Natanson and Azef, Dzerzhinsky—leader of the Polish SDs, and Lenin.[99] Even more frequently, representatives of several groups combined forces for immediate practical action, such as the acquisition of weapons and explosives. Cooperation in the purchase of arms and their transportation to Russia from abroad took place among groups of diverse ideologies,[100] and throughout Russia, loosely organized federations of all the socialist parties established and maintained large arsenals.[101]

Interest in consorted terrorist efforts was also demonstrated by the revolutionaries who joined the numerous and diverse unions (*soiuzy*). These inter-party organizations, widespread after 1905, coordinated the political and economic efforts of various mainstream professional groups and societies, at times evincing genuine radicalism. One of these revolutionary organizations was the St. Petersburg Railroad Union, or VIKZhel (Vserossiiskii ispolnitel'-nyi komitet soiuza zheleznodorozhnikov—the All-Russian Executive Committee of the Union of Railroad Workers), that included the whole spectrum of activists from all factions of the antigovernment movement, from liberals to anarchists. In December 1905 the Railroad Union leaders, as part of their effort to promote the ongoing Moscow uprising by initiating large-scale revolutionary disturbances in the capital, resolved to blow up a key bridge on the Nikolaevskii railroad in the hope of, on the one hand, preventing the efficient transportation of government troops and, on the other, instigating a major railroad strike, which would in theory lead to a general strike involving the entire working population of St. Petersburg.[102]

Another similar organization in the capital was the Soviet of the Unemployed (Sovet bezrabotnykh),[103] with the militant group known as the Combat Workers' Union (Boevoi rabochii soiuz) operating under its auspices. This group welcomed into its ranks any and all supporters of radical tactics, regardless of whether they belonged to any particular revolutionary organization; however, exhibiting a prejudice common among radical proletarians, they strictly excluded representatives of the intelligentsia. To a large extent this union was made up of industrial laborers who had been fired from their factories and plants for political unreliability. It was convenient for the Union's organizers to choose volunteers for combat enterprises from these cadres, who, in the words of one of the group's leaders, "could hope to restore their position in life only by means of the victory of the revolution."[104] It thus did not take long for the combatants to embark upon the terrorist path, choosing suspected members of the monarchist Black Hundreds as their primary targets. On 3 April 1906, a number of intoxicated Combat Workers' Union members encircled the home of an allegedly reactionary shop manager, Vasilii Snesarev, and set it on fire with all of its inhabitants inside.[105]

The organization and structure of the Combat Workers' Union were marked by anarchist tendencies. Its detachments in the various sections of the city were almost entirely autonomous and possessed independent treasuries in constant need of replenishment, with the leaders of these combat units consequently entertaining plans for revolutionary robberies in addition to their other terrorist activities. For a while members of the union's Central Committee discussed in detail the possibility of staging an expropriation against the wealthy Valaam Monastery, a favorite destination of religious pilgrims located on Lake Ladoga. The revolutionaries failed to carry through with this robbery, in part because of its predicted negative impact on the general public, and in part out of fear of the resulting moral disintegration of the participants—a consideration that did not, however, deter the combatants from taking part in various smaller-scale expropriations of weapons and private property from other targets.[106]

The Railroad Union and the Combat Workers' Union were not unique in manifesting this tendency toward interparty cooperation, and indeed many other *boeviki* from revolutionary organizations in the capitals joined together for terrorist operations. In one instance, Krasin ordered an associate, Iurii Grozhan, to manufacture two large hand grenades and deliver them to Lev Trotsky, then a supporter of the Mensheviks and one of the leaders of the St. Petersburg Council of Workers' Deputies (Sovet rabochikh deputatov), a multiparty assemblage of revolutionaries joined for the purpose of coordinating antigovernment activities. On another occasion, in October 1905, the Council of Workers' Deputies commissioned experts in the Bolshevik combat technical bureau to produce two unusually powerful explosive devices to be used for disrupting telegraph communications in the capital.[107] Similarly, hoping that a series of terrorist acts would contribute to the uprising in Moscow, in December of 1905 representatives of numerous combat groups called a general meeting to work out the details for several major projects, including the takeover of a government arsenal in that city, the arrest of Governor-General Dubasov, and an attempt to blow up the same bridge on the Nikolaevskii railroad targeted unsuccessfully by the Railroad Union radicals in St. Petersburg at about the same time.[108]

A similar situation developed in the provinces, where in over fifty cities radical socialists united into Councils of Workers' Deputies,[109] based largely on the examples of similar organizations in the capitals. These multiparty formations were to organize and coordinate strikes, lockouts, and other forms of labor protest, activities frequently promoted by purely terrorist means. Sometimes the revolutionaries did not bother to conceal their intended methods, as was true in an incident in the Dmitrov district near Moscow, where representatives of the regional Council of Workers' Deputies resolved that it was inappropriate for the socialists to appeal to the bourgeoisie for financial support for striking factory workers; instead, local landowners were to be obliged to provide assistance under threat of the forced confiscation of their property, and violence against their persons. Several radicals chosen to implement this unanimous decision of the Council traveled from one small town or village to another harassing selected landlords, who did not dare to resist the demands of these armed extortionists.[110]

Multiparty terrorist operations were equally widespread in the more remote regions of the empire, such as the Urals and along the Volga River, where various combinations of SRs, Bolsheviks, and anarchists joined together in guerrilla detachments. The tendency to form a united front of all revolutionary forces was especially strong in the Jewish Pale and the border regions, particularly Georgia, Poland, and Latvia, where militant nationalists easily disregarded dogmatic differences for the sake of immediate tasks.[111] A striking manifestation of this phenomenon was the well-publicized January 1906 assassination of General Griaznov in Tiflis, carried out by local Mensheviks, and sanctioned by a unanimous resolution of several antigovernment organizations, including the SRs, the SDs, the Armenian Droshakist group, and the Georgian Socialist Federalists, united "for the purpose of a few common ventures."[112]

The multiparty groups in outlying areas also engaged in revolutionary robberies. In 1908 one hastily assembled gang in Belostok included five Maximalists, a few SDs, some anarchists, a number of people of dubious party affiliation, and finally several individuals who turned out to be police agents. The initial enterprise of this combat detachment was an assault on a train carrying nearly two million rubles, but because of poor organization, inexperience, and the presence of police informers among the radicals, it proved a complete fiasco, with most of the participants falling into the hands of the authorities.[113]

Practical cooperation among Russian terrorists in exile abroad was conducted along the same lines as collaboration inside the empire. Wealthy immigrants from various parts of the Russian Empire frequently extended a friendly hand to less fortunate revolutionaries with ideological outlooks entirely different from their own. In Paris, for example, Prince Abashidze, a convinced supporter of the Georgian Socialists-Federalists, provided financial assistance to various political emigrés, including a number of anarchists who frequently abused his generosity.[114] An interesting case involved Vladimir Burtsev, who, consistent with his long-standing objective of using a series of sensational terrorist acts to shake the Russian autocracy, set out in 1907 to form his own combat union with the help of an associate named Krakov. They recruited terrorists not only from Burtsev's small collection of *narodovol'tsy* supporters, but also among the anarchists and the Maximalists, with the stipulation that all agree to proceed with the group's political assassination plans.[115]

Perhaps the most far-reaching attempt to unite representatives of all revolutionary groups and organizations, as well as extremists outside formal party structures, was the formation late in 1908 of the Union of the People's Vengeance (Soiuz narodnoi mesti) in St. Petersburg. This organization was specifically "founded upon recognition of the need for a terrorist struggle against the existing order and . . . the broadest possible cooperation among all oppositional elements." Except for these two criteria, members of the Union were free to profess any ideological creed and to follow any political program, from anarchism to the principles of the Kadet Party.[116] Although the ultimate objective of the Union was regicide, to be carried out simultaneously with widespread mass terror directed against high-ranking officials and prominent representatives of the bourgeoisie throughout the country, its leaders initially limited themselves to two immediate goals: the assassinations of Prime Minister Stolypin and the chairman of the Third State Duma, N. A. Khomiakov. Police records indicate that individuals suspected of affiliation with this group included people with such diverse backgrounds as the Social Democrat Grigorii Aleksinskii, who was director of an agricultural college in Moscow, and Vasilii Struve, brother of the famous liberal publicist. The authorities, however, apparently did not regard the Union of the People's Vengeance as a serious threat, correctly assuming that a lack of material means would prevent it from proceeding with its terrorist plans, since the Union's bylaws prohibited the expropriation of private property and allowed the confiscation of state funds only under extreme circumstances.[117]

INTERNATIONAL COOPERATION

A sense of the solidarity of all oppressed toilers, regardless of national origin, pervaded the revolutionary movement, necessitating a multinational approach to the problem of their emancipation that paralleled the active interparty cooperation among terrorists within the borders of the Russian Empire. This awareness was evident not only among the internationally oriented Marxists and the anarchists, but also among the SRs and even in the majority of the nationalist revolutionary groups. Partly as a result of this outlook, Russian terrorists of various ideological orientations readily extended their contacts beyond the extremist compatriots, who shared their specific goals regarding the end of the tsarist autocracy, to foreign revolutionaries active outside of Russia. Russian terrorists thus came to operate within the general European and worldwide radical context.

Attempts to establish mutually beneficial working relationships with terrorists abroad had further appeal for the Russian extremists because of common beliefs in the international solidarity of all left-wing antiestablishment forces. Western revolutionaries considered their Russian comrades legitimate members of the worldwide revolutionary brotherhood. Indeed, from the 1880s European and American socialists and anarchists felt a moral obligation to provide all possible psychological and practical support to the radicals in Russia, particularly because they fought against the hated tsarist autocracy that was, in the words of prominent French socialist Jean Jaurès, "the most powerful obstacle preventing implementation of the socialist order everywhere."[118]

The international revolutionary community demonstrated this attitude on numerous occasions. It was expressed not only by radicals who shared the views of their Russian comrades on the expediency of terrorist practices, but also by activists opposed to the use of extremist methods in a Western European setting. The British Social Democrats fell into the latter category, but nevertheless openly asserted that in the struggle with "the butcher Nicholas and the hangman Stolypin, along with all of their beastly camarilla of grand dukes and other gangster Black Hundreds," violence was the only solution.[119] The German SDs unconditionally supported this view, feeling that while the PSR was not really as close to the German Social Democratic Party as Russian Social Democracy, it too was a member of the Socialist International, and:

> Its use of terror cannot be a reason for its expulsion from the International. Terrorism, which is renounced in principle by Socialist parties in countries where at least some degree of lawful order exists (for instance, in Germany), is quite acceptable as a means of self-defense in countries such as Russia, where the government is an organized gang of bandits.[120]

Radical German SD leader Karl Liebknecht persistently argued that the only methods of struggle in Russia were those of the People's Will, echoing Marx's familiar assertion that terrorist activities were a "specifically Russian, historically inevitable means of action."[121] Even the supporters of renowned Marxist writer Eduard Bernstein, a prominent member of the moderate faction of German Social Democracy, publicly expressed regret that Russian Minister of the Interior Plehve was killed instantly by an SR bomb, and did not suffer.[122]

Along with the theoretical solidarity between the Russian revolutionaries and their Western counterparts against the traditional order everywhere, pragmatic considerations were of no less importance in the international cooperation of terrorists. Radicals in Russia, and particularly the anarchists, regularly distributed terrorist literature produced in the West, usually translating it into Russian to accommodate the majority of their cadres.[123] Numerous other practical benefits for the Russian revolutionaries resulted from their cooperation with extremists in various countries on the European continent, in England, and America, not the least of which was assistance in the production, procurement, and smuggling of weapons.

Although activists from many organizations within the Russian revolutionary camp were actively involved in arms trafficking in Russia and abroad, the only one that approached the task systematically was Krasin's Combat Technical Group, which from the time of its formation early in 1905 continuously extended its connections abroad precisely for the purpose of obtaining assistance in weapons and explosives production. Leading activists of the group established contact with a number of foreign radicals, concentrating their attention primarily on the Bulgarian revolutionaries, partly due to the fact that over the years they had indicated their willingness to cooperate with the Russian extremists,[124] but also because they were known for their successes in bomb manufacturing. One of the Combat Technical Group's leading technicians, the chemist Skosarevskii (Omega), was commissioned in 1905 to make a trip abroad, where he established contact with Bulgarian anarchist Naum Tiufekchiev, a talented innovator in combat technology who taught Skosarevskii "the secret of the Macedonian bomb." The relationship between the Bolshevik and the Bulgarian terrorists proved durable, and several of Krasin's associates, including Nikolai Burenin, a prominent member of the Combat Technical Group, repeatedly consulted Tiufekchiev on similar technical matters.[125] Simultaneously, representatives of the SR party residing in Bulgaria actively cooperated with local Macedonian and Armenian radicals, some of whom had terrorist records and considerable combat experience against the Turks, and were especially willing to help the SRs procure explosive devices.[126] A number of times Macedonian specialists even traveled to Russia to assist in establishing laboratories and shops for producing explosives.[127] The Caucasus became the primary destination for foreign-made weapons, although the revolutionaries were quite adroit at smuggling explosives into the Baltic provinces as well. Their successes are reflected in a satirical telegram allegedly dispatched from Riga: "The first shipment of oranges has arrived from abroad. Because several deaths have resulted from their use, the governor has ordered a ban on future imports of these fruits. Citizens have decided to grow oranges in their own homes."[128]

The tsarist authorities were well informed about the active involvement of European radicals in the Russian terrorists' efforts to obtain arms and ammunition from abroad.[129] The German Social Democrats, along with comrades from England, France, and Belgium, although anxious to conceal their activities from their respective governments, were particularly eager to help, largely by raising money for the Russian extremists.[130] The Bolsheviks seemed to have been the primary beneficiaries of these policies on the part of the German SDs, although the Mensheviks were also able to obtain their share, and the Latvian SDs acknowledged in their financial reports occasional subsidies from German SD sources, including substantial sums from the Central Committee of the German Social Democratic Party.[131]

The German SDs proved useful to the Russian terrorists in a variety of other matters, including legal assistance on several occasions when Russian radicals were tried in German courts for subversive and criminal activities. When Kamo was arrested in Berlin for illegal arms dealing and possession of explosives, and faced probable extradition to Russia, Martin Liadov, a Bolshevik with extensive connections among the German SDs, acting on Lenin's orders, appealed for help to Karl Liebknecht, who commissioned his friend and comrade, Oscar Kon, an SD representative to the German Parliament, to act as Kamo's defense attorney. At the same time, Liadov was able to organize a major press campaign in Kamo's support.[132]

American socialists also offered the Russian extremists considerable assistance, particularly in their efforts to obtain refuge in the United States. The Society of Friends of Russian Freedom and similar left-wing organizations staged public protests against the American immigration laws, which in their view discriminated against the revolutionaries. Their efforts became particularly fierce after the United States Congress voted in March 1914 to deny entry visas to socialists, syndicalists, and terrorists from other nations. In their joint agitation campaign, Russian radicals residing in the U.S. and their American supporters did all they could, albeit unsuccessfully, to demonstrate to the public that the new law was the direct result of the tsarist government's interference in internal American policymaking, allegedly by its appeal to Congress requesting formal expulsion of the Russian extremists from the country.[133] Furthermore, Russian police authorities were aware that on numerous occasions large financial donations were transferred from obscure American sources to the Jewish Bund, specifically for the purpose of purchasing arms.[134]

Predictably, the international anarchists were more willing than other segments of the European radical community to join forces with the Russian revolutionary camp. European and American anarchists chose not to differentiate among the various branches of the Russian left-wing movement, and so it was natural, for example, for the Italian anarchists to help a former terrorist from Riga secure a job abroad, or to offer the Russian SRs newly developed bombs of enormous destructive capability, designed specifically for use against government troops.[135] In accordance with decisions adopted at several of their congresses, anarchists from many countries united in direct action against the establishment, and during one secret gathering in Amsterdam in September 1907 resolved to organize a worldwide Anarchist International with headquarters in London. At this congress, a motion was passed in support of mutual assistance among anarchists of various nations in matters that could not be settled locally. The Russian revolutionaries, for example, needed help in acquiring weapons to be smuggled into the empire; in return, several Bohemian anarchists suggested that a few Russian expropriation specialists be sent to them as instructors.[136]

Similar attempts to establish cooperation among anarchists from different European nations occurred in subsequent years. In 1910 a Polish anarchist named Shiuts established contact with Spanish anarchists in Paris, from whom he received financial aid and an assignment to carry out a terrorist act in Catalonia.[137] In 1911, Russian, Rumanian, Austrian, and other anarchists residing in Vienna established a new periodical of international anarchist and terrorist orientation. This journal, to be published simultaneously in Russian, French, and German, and entitled *Rasstroistvo!—Bouleversement!—Der Umsturz!*, would be primarily concerned with agitation for direct terrorist action and practical guidelines for the manufacture of explosives. Its contributors would include such prominent representatives of the European anarchist movement as Petr Kropotkin.[138]

During the 1905–1907 revolution, Russian anarchists abroad maintained particularly close ties with French and Italian anarchists;[139] in the subsequent period, when the situation in several European states became less favorable for radical political emigrés, a significant number of them were forced to seek refuge in the United States and join forces with anarchists there, many of whom were also foreign nationals from various European countries. Their primary focus therefore remained on Europe, and when two extremists, an Italian, Giovanni Kuneo, and a Russian Jew, Beki Edel'son, came to New York in April 1916 to form a new international anarchist group, their plan was to commission members to travel to Germany, Italy, and Russia to assassinate the monarchs of these countries. The undertaking was to be financed with the assistance of another anarchist group in Chicago, as well as comrades in Europe.[140]

Russian extremists sometimes participated in undisguisedly criminal enterprises initiated by foreign anarchists. A Russian revolutionary by the name of Nikolai Sofronskii fled to France and like many political emigrés in Europe found himself in financial difficulty. This led him to make contact with a group of French anarchists, whose primary occupation was counterfeiting and distributing ten-franc gold coins. Sofronskii organized a dozen associates of obscure political persuasion to help him market the base coins provided by the French anarchists.[141]

Representatives of various national revolutionary groups from the Russian Empire, including members of the PPS as early as 1901, also readily cooperated with foreign anarchists.[142] From the mid-1890s, however, radical nationalist subjects of tsarist Russia usually preferred to deal with extremist European nationalists. This was true for a number of Armenian revolutionaries, including an individual mentioned in police reports as "Khan," who portrayed himself as a moderate agitator for Armenian national liberation to ease the collection of substantial financial donations from his fellow countrymen, most of whom had little sympathy for violence. According to his revolutionary comrades, however, Khan was a convinced international terrorist who donated portions of the money collected from the Armenians to Russian extremists, and was also known to have cooperated actively with various radical nationalist groups in the Balkans.[143] Mutual assistance between the Armenian revolutionaries and radical nationalists abroad continued into the initial years of the twentieth century, and in 1905 Russian imperial police authorities were aware that the members of the Armenian Droshakist group not only cooperated actively with Russian extremists, but also had extended their contacts to the Macedonian revolutionaries, greatly facilitating their efforts to smuggle weapons and explosives into the Caucasus via the Black Sea.[144]

In the overwhelming majority of cases, Russian terrorists willingly accepted any combat assistance offered by foreign comrades, with the anarchists frequently assuming the task of coordinating the activities of the internationalist cadres. In 1907 the International Combat Group (Boevaia internatsional'naia gruppa), operating under the leadership of Russian anarchists abroad, selected from its members a special International Combat Detachment (Boevoi internatsional'nyi otriad) to conduct a series of acts of political and economic terror in Russia.[145] It is unclear whether this group indeed included any foreign extremists, but soon after the outbreak of violence in Russia in 1905, European and specifically Italian anarchists expressed their desire to be in the avant-garde, to form "volunteer detachments for the Russian Revolution," and to go to Russia to take part in terrorist activities there. They wrote passionate appeals to prominent figures in the Russian anarchist community in immigration, seeking advice on how best to put their plans into practice, offering explosive devices, and even demonstrating their determination and devotion by studying the Russian language.[146] In 1906, Russian police authorities received information that Italian anarchists were planning attempts on the lives of Nicholas II and the Sultan of the Ottoman Empire.[147]

A number of foreign extremists did manage to make their way into Russia. A French anarchist who identified himself as "Robert" and claimed to have taken part in an unsuccessful attempt in Paris to blow up a carriage in which the president of France and the King of Spain were riding, subsequently traveled to Odessa with the intention of continuing his terrorist practices in Russia.[148] For the most part, however, foreign radicals preferred the border regions of the empire for their terrorist operations. Franz Glott, a Prussian subject, retained extensive revolutionary connections in Berlin while operating as a terrorist in Latvia.[149] Similarly, revolutionaries in the Caucasus frequently enjoyed the assistance provided by comrades from various parts of Turkish Armenia and Transcaucasia, who, for example, played a primary role in a 1903 terrorist attempt on the life of Count Golitsyn in Tiflis.[150]

By 1907, as the political situation in the empire became increasingly desperate for the revolutionaries, they welcomed foreign supporters into their ranks even more readily, with several European anarchists, dedicated to combatting establishment forces regardless of their national origin, assuming leadership positions among their Russian comrades. Avgust Vaterlos (Johannes Goltsman), a Belgian Jew who for several years had played a prominent role among the German anarchists, operating under the alias Sen-Goi, traveled to Russia early in 1907 to persuade anarchist groups there to participate in the international anarchist congress to be held in Amsterdam later that year. Devoted to

the liberation of Western Europe, Vaterlos succeeded in establishing cooperation with an anarchist conspiracy in Warsaw planning to assassinate Kaiser
Wilhelm II of Germany. The radicals held the kaiser responsible for exerting
pressure on the Russian government to oppress the Poles, but more important,
Vaterlos and other extremists hoped that a sensational terrorist act would raise
the spirits of anarchists throughout the world. Upon his arrival in Warsaw in
March of 1907, Vaterlos realized that anarchist efforts there suffered from a
severe shortage of funds, which he set out to remedy. Vaterlos collaborated
with members of the PPS in Kovno and Lodz, and in June of the same year led
an unsuccessful expropriation attempt against a wealthy Jew in the town of
Ozorkov, in the course of which he fell into the hands of the Polish authorities.[151]

Foreign revolutionaries thus proved loyal comrades in the struggle against
the tsarist autocracy, and the Russian expatriates in Europe tried to repay them
in kind at every opportunity, assisting Western extremists in subversive operations in their countries. This was especially true prior to the outbreak of revolutionary events in 1905, when many radical emigrés rushed back to Russia. Lev
Aleshker (A. Dal'), a well-known Anarchist-Communist, was one such re-
turnee, who in the years leading up to 1905 demonstrated his internationalist
stand by associating with French extremists and working exclusively toward
promoting the anarchist cause abroad.[152] In addition, members of the antigovernment nationalist organization known as the Finnish Liberation Union made
substantial financial donations to the European revolutionary community, especially when the money was intended for terrorist operations. In October of
1909, for example, the Finns transferred one hundred thousand francs from
their account in the Ofre Norrlands Bank in Stockholm to the radical Tribunal
of the International Liberation Union in Paris, specifically for the purpose of
staging sensational political assassinations.[153]

In the years preceding the First World War, foreign radicals frequently appealed to the Russian revolutionaries for assistance in resolving political and
diplomatic issues by terrorist methods. Early in 1914, for example, several
Bulgarian anarchists sought Russian aid in preparations for an assassination
attempt against the imperial foreign minister, Sergei Sazonov, who they
claimed was considered by the entire Bulgarian nation the primary source of
the country's diplomatic troubles the preceding year.[154] Russian involvement
with the Serbian Black Hand organization is an established fact, although the
extent of their knowledge about preparations for the murder of Archduke Fer-
dinand at Sarajevo in July of 1914 remains unclear.[155]

Radicals in the Russian Empire also demonstrated their allegiance to the
international revolutionary cause by supporting the struggle against the establishment in such turbulent regions as Persia, and at times foreign extremists
chose Russian territory as their battlefield. The radical Persian nationalist organization Mudzhakhidy staged terrorist acts in the Caucasus in 1907 exclu-

sively targeting Persian officials.[156] In 1908 the Russian authorities became aware that revolutionaries in the Caucasus were actively involved in secret attempts to transport arms and explosives into Persia, and that weapons used in an unsuccessful assassination attempt against Shah Muhamed Ali in Teheran that year were of Russian origin, having probably come from Baku or Lenkoran. Some Armenian and Georgian extremists personally smuggled weapons across the border to Persia, and also participated in revolutionary activities in that country.[157]

Russian terrorist practices also gave impetus to the revolutionary movement in other non-European countries such as India, where in 1906 the extremists proclaimed: "The days of prayer have gone. . . . Look to the examples of Ireland, Japan and Russia and follow their methods."[158] According to Laqueur, a British committee investigating terrorism in India noted that nationalist propaganda dwelt heavily upon the "Russian rules" of revolutionary violence, but there were cases of direct active collaboration as well, for example, when Indian terrorists received instruction in the practice of terrorism from the SRs. Assistance was provided in 1908 when a Russian chemical engineer gave Indian nationalists in England a manual for the manufacture of bombs. A Russian student translated it into English for the revolutionary Free India Society in London; the manual was then cyclostyled and sent to India.[159]

Proponents of terrorist action thus supported extremism regardless of its specific ideology, as long as it was directed against the contemporary establishment. Disagreements on theory among the political groupings seem to have been of secondary significance to the practical policies of the Russian radicals. Moreover, the favorable response of most Russian extremist organizations to the question of whether to unite their forces for the sake of successful terrorist acts led to a certain "plasticity of the boundary lines between the various groups," suggesting that "Russian political parties had not yet achieved a high degree of definition; they were movements, operating in daunting circumstances, rather than parties." Honoring "separatism more in the breach than in the practice,"[160] rank-and-file radicals and their leaders in the Russian left bloc rarely regarded dogmatic, organizational, or even national barriers as obstacles to immediate pragmatic cooperation. Considering all revolutionaries in Russia and throughout the world their comrades in spirit, they were not afraid to act together, as a united front.

Chapter Seven

THE KADETS AND TERROR

> It is no accident . . . that many Russian liberals . . . wholeheartedly
> support terror and presently try to bolster the rise of
> a terrorist mood.
> —*V. I. Lenin*[1]

THE UNPRECEDENTED ESCALATION of terrorist activity in 1905–1907 required all political groups and organizations to define their positions toward revolutionary violence. The Constitutional Democratic Party (Kadets), also known as the liberal Party of People's Freedom, which came into being as a coherent organization in October of 1905, was no exception. In contrast to all other political groups, both to its left and right, whose practical policies toward terrorism vividly demonstrated their true stand on this issue, the Kadet position vis-à-vis terrorist tactics was far more ambiguous. Driven by their overwhelming desire to witness the end of the tsarist regime, even the most peaceful-minded representatives of the leftist camp were generally sympathetic to terrorist tactics and, along with the radicals of all socialist trends, and every extremist in the anarchist movement, hailed political assassinations. Such moderates as the People's Socialists (Narodnye sotsialisty) and members of the Trudovik group, who stood closely to the right of the PSR and largely shared its ideology and program, although advocating less conspiratorial activity and objecting to the SR boycott of the first State Duma, were clearly unwilling to denounce the effective terrorist tactics.[2] In fact, while these groups never became responsible for acts of violence themselves, deputies of the Trudovik faction in the Duma such as L. V. Kartashev and Teslia publicly proclaimed the terrorists, "the glorious, famous martyrs . . . the exalted people, the most honest and selfless representatives of our country." The moderate socialists openly justified the extremists' actions against "the enemies of the people," with whom "the struggle may only be to the end."[3] Not only the anarchists, the Maximalists, the SRs, and the SDs, but the entire left flank of the opposition was thus primarily concerned with the effectiveness of the struggle against the authorities; no organization in that camp was prepared to reject terrorism on ethical grounds.

While it is true that formulation of the various stands on terrorism was not "a matter of abstract morality . . . [and] all parties approached the problem of assassination not from the point of view of the Biblical commandment but from the vantage point of the historical interests represented,"[4] morality was, at least in their rhetoric, the main argument that the right-center (the Union of 17 October, or Octobrists) and the conservatives used against any political assassination, whether from the left or right. Realizing the devastating effect of daily assassinations, which undermined the very principle of law and order, both the Octobrists and the conservatives came out against "any murder, so revolting no matter where it comes from," that "duty and honor demand immediate denunciation of terror."[5] Similarly, Professor V. D. Kuz'min-Karavaev, a representative of the small Party of Democratic Reforms, positioned just to the left of the Octobrists, did not hesitate to "condemn murders from the left camp decisively."[6]

It thus appears that the only major political organization that failed to clarify publicly its formal position with regard to terrorism was the Kadet Party. While claiming not to support the principle of political assassination, its leadership nevertheless repeatedly refused to "proclaim the moral condemnation of political murderers."[7] This ambiguity in the Kadet stand has largely escaped scholarly attention,[8] although the party's attitude toward political assassinations is of critical significance: it may be regarded as a key issue in determining how far along the revolutionary path the Kadets, who are generally considered to have been the embodiment of Russian liberalism, were prepared to go to achieve their political objectives. An attempt to establish the position of the Party of People's Freedom on terrorist activity, focusing on the period of the first two State Dumas, and to underline the reasons for and ultimate consequences of the Kadet policy toward radical tactics, also indicates a great deal about the characteristics of Russian liberalism as a distinct political trend.

KADET POLITICAL OBJECTIVES AND TACTICS

The Constitutional Democratic Party, proud to have as its members "the flower of the Russian intelligentsia," indeed included an exceptionally large number of "brilliant talents and prominent public figures."[9] Its many writers, journalists, zemstvo intellectuals, lawyers, and other educated professionals could hardly be considered bloodthirsty villains who welcomed violence for its own sake. There were dissidents within the party who clearly disagreed with the group's ambiguity vis-à-vis terror, although determining their numbers is difficult, for they were usually reluctant to break party discipline, and at the most went only so far as to declare in general terms their personal opposition to violence.[10] It is questionable, furthermore, whether in determining the official position of the party as a whole on political murder, it is appropriate to rely exclusively on the statements of individual members rejecting bloodshed and anarchy. By themselves, vague outbursts against violence from various Kadets meant little, for even the extremists (except perhaps a small number of anarchists and a few psychologically unbalanced individuals characterized by one revolutionary as "cannibals") never openly declared themselves fond of killing as an end in itself.[11] The SRs, for example, exerted considerable effort to convince their audience in the Duma that they were "opponents of any bloodspilling . . . valuing human life above all else."[12] The public stand of the Constitutional Democrats on the issue of political assassination was a tactical question that the party leadership had to resolve for the party as a whole, regardless of the private views of individual members.

Historians trace the gulf between the politically conscious Russian intelligentsia and the conservative tsarist state at least as far back as the abortive Decembrist uprising and its brutal suppression in 1825, with the westernized intellectual elite persistently regarding the autocratic government as its deadly enemy. Throughout the nineteenth century the gap continued to widen, with little chance for a bridge, especially after the epoch of counterreforms late in the century; by 1905 this estrangement had already become an integral part of the liberal mentality in Russia. At the same time, the intelligentsia's failure to overcome its sociocultural alienation from the largely unorganized masses of peasants and workers, as well as from the predominantly apolitical bourgeoisie, created a permanent problem for the liberal opposition—the absence of broad social support.[13] As a consequence the small and isolated liberal movement was virtually required to ally itself with the revolutionary camp. In order to realize at least some of their political goals the liberals relied on the revolution, sharing with the radicals their immediate aim of overthrowing the autocratic regime or compelling it to change drastically. To sustain this policy of "no enemies on the left," the Russian liberals, and particularly the Kadets, were prepared to make conciliatory gestures to the radicals, adopting an apologetic stand with regard to the extremists' methods, and thus indirectly sacrificing their own moderate position. This tendency is especially evident in the liberals' attitude toward political violence. Considering their aversion to bloodshed on the one hand, and the fact that terror was a primary revolutionary tactic implemented by their extremist allies on the other, the appropriate stand on terrorism was a constant dilemma and, in the words of Thomas Riha, always "a painful matter for the Kadets."[14]

Kadet policy on terrorism was not a new problem at the time of the official formation of the party. Before October 1905 the Kadet forerunners, as part of a semiformal organization of Russian constitutionalists known as the Union of Liberation (Soiuz Osvobozhdeniia), while calling themselves moderates and refusing to take part in violent acts, came to share the fundamental objective of the radicals "to make every effort immediately to eliminate the brigand gang which has usurped state power."[15] With this in mind, as early as September and October of 1904 at a conference in Paris, the left-wing Osvobozhdentsy joined the SRs and other socialist organizations for concerted action against the government, with the terms of their agreement allowing each group to choose and pursue its own tactics, not excluding terrorism.[16] At this stage, there was no question that most leaders of the Union of Liberation had reconciled themselves to terrorist tactics, for in the opinion of future Kadet Party leader Pavel Miliukov, the political situation was too serious to permit moral scruples.[17] Petr Struve, then a prominent member of the Union and editor-in-chief of its main organ, *Osvobozhdenie* (*Liberation*), agreed, arguing, "As long as the stronghold of autocracy has not been destroyed, anyone who is fighting against it represents not 'a grave danger' but a great blessing."[18] The spread of radicalism in Russia was certainly not to be feared, according to one article in *Osvobozhdenie*, for the "revolutionary movement could not create any chaos or any anarchy," and therefore "liberalism must recognize its solidarity with . . . the revolutionary trend."[19]

In accordance with this recommendation, rank-and-file members of the Union of Liberation joined the united front with the radicals.[20] They turned their homes into refuges for terrorists,[21] and provided the SRs with monetary support, evidently considering terror an effective political tool.[22] In the words of Count Petr Dolgorukov, later a member of the Kadet Central Committee, "the 'political spring'" of the new liberal Minister of the Interior, Sviatopolk-Mirskii, "owed everything to the bomb that killed Plehve" in July of 1904.[23] Another active member of the Union of Liberation in St. Petersburg, S. P. Miklashevskii (Nevedomskii), openly exonerated and praised Egor Sazonov, calling him an example worthy of followers.[24] Miliukov made statements in the same spirit, arguing, for example, that Ivan Kaliaev, the SR assassin of the Grand Duke Sergei, "had been sacrificed for the good of the people."[25] As time went on and the probability of a successful revolution increased, the Union of Liberation as a whole proved increasingly inclined to follow the tactics suggested by Miliukov in June 1905: "All means are now legitimate against the terrible threat which exists by the very fact of the continued existence of the present government. And all means should be tried."[26]

The issuance of the October Manifesto did not cause the Kadets to adopt more moderate behavior since the government still refused to meet a number of their demands, such as the abolition of all extraordinary decrees (*iskliuchitel'nye zakony*), the expulsion from the administration of officials the Kadets considered responsible for public outrage, the promulgation of a law regulating the forthcoming elections to the Constituent Assembly, and the formation of a new liberal Council of Ministers composed of representatives of educated Russian society.[27] Inspired by the apparent demoralization of the government, and by what the liberation movement had already managed to achieve, thanks in part to radical tactics, Miliukov asserted on behalf of the newly formed party that "nothing was changed and the war still was going on."[28] At their First Congress, which took place in October of 1905 during the "days of freedom," the Kadets confirmed their solidarity with their "allies on the left," placing themselves alongside the revolutionaries, "on the same left wing of the Russian opposition movement."[29] At their Third Congress, held just before the opening of the First Duma in April 1906, when an announcement was made regarding a terrorist attempt on the life of Dubasov, governor-general of Moscow, a number of Kadet leaders expressed their approval by applauding.[30]

At this time the Constitutional Democrats proved extremely helpful in assisting the radicals procure funds for their combat enterprises. At the Kadet club in St. Petersburg representatives of various extremist organizations were allowed the use of a traditional Russian method of fund-raising: they passed around a hat with small notes inside explaining various ways donations would be used. Prince D. I. Bebutov, one of the club's founders and a leading member of the Kadet Party, admitted that he "was not upset by the inscription 'for a combat organization' in the hat; on the contrary, that is what [he was] especially sympathetic to." Worried, however, about the security of the revolutionaries present at the club, Bebutov suggested that it would be less risky and more lucrative for them if they permitted him to collect the donations for them personally once a week, and the radicals accepted this generous offer.[31]

The Constitutional Democrats continued their financial assistance to the revolutionaries, and about two weeks after the opening of the Duma session in early May of 1906, took part in a fund-raising session for the SRs in Paris. At that meeting a prominent Moscow lawyer and member of the Kadet Central Committee, M. L. Mandel'shtam, predicted a new phase in the struggle against the autocracy, and glorified such heroes as Gershuni, Sazonov, and Kaliaev.[32] The following month at a secret meeting in St. Petersburg, the Kadets reportedly agreed to contribute money to the SRs' revolutionary activities, "until the downfall of autocracy."[33]

In evaluating the Kadets' political orientation after October 1905, it is therefore difficult to exclude them from the revolutionary camp and consider them true guardians of moderate policy merely because they refused to participate in actual bloodshed and were not socialists.[34] In fact, some members of the party's Central Committee were prepared to declare that they had always been and would always remain revolutionaries, that "to disavow the revolution would be tantamount to disavowing" themselves, and that "anyone who wishes to fight against the revolution must leave the party."[35]

The radicalization of Russian politics was undoubtedly to the Kadets' advantage, for as one party leader subsequently explained, the threat of the expanding "revolution could force the authorities to make concessions."[36] Many outside observers also noted that for years "political terror had been taken into account by the liberals," for they "used the life and even the death of terror in their own interests."[37] Primarily, the Kadets hoped to obtain what seemed to be their most immediate goal: the establishment of parliamentary order through the formation of a new responsible ministry (*otvetstvennoe ministerstvo*) accountable to the Duma and composed of representatives holding seats in that legislative body.[38] If this concession could have been extracted from the weakened authorities, the Constitutional Democrats would certainly have been its primary beneficiaries. There was little chance that Nicholas II would include members of any left-wing revolutionary parties in his new cabinet.[39] Similarly, controlling positions in the ministry would probably not have been assigned to the Octobrists, since such an action would hardly have satisfied or pacified the Duma majority. Their very desire to obtain the tsar's approval of the establishment of a Kadet-dominated cabinet therefore forced the Constitutional Democrats to retain their ability to present themselves as respectable moderates opposed to violent tactics.[40] Reflecting the image that the leadership of the newly formed party was trying to build for itself, a 1905 newspaper caricature depicts a liberal bowing low before Nicholas II and pleading, "Your Majesty, grant the constitution, or the SRs will shoot."[41] The Kadet leaders, in pursuing this seemingly advantageous political game, thus had to be extremely cautious in maneuvering between the authorities and the extremists, wishing to persuade the former that the Party of People's Freedom was the only group capable of stopping the widespread anarchy, and hoping to use and control the latter, with whom they undoubtedly wished to break as soon as parliamentary order was established.[42]

Until that time, however, though not daring to admit openly their temporary solidarity with the terrorists, for whose methods the liberals personally had no regard, but who were nevertheless to do the dirty work necessary to undermine the government, the Kadet leadership was afraid to be politically compromised in the eyes of the public as loyal collaborators with the regime. According to the memoirs of A. V. Tyrkova-Vil'iams, long a member of the Kadet Central Committee, "Relations between the authorities and public opinion were too strained. Just the appearance of Stolypin on the [Duma] tribune immediately called forth a seething of hostile feelings, sweeping away any possibility for an agreement."[43] It thus becomes clear that "for all its professions of adherence to the law, [the Kadet Party] could not bring itself publicly to renounce political violence, in part because it needed the threat of violence to hold over the government, and in part because it feared offending its radical constituency."[44] Manifestations of their solidarity with the revolutionaries are most evident in the Kadets' position on the issues of political amnesty and capital punishment, in the rhetoric they used to describe terrorist acts and their perpetrators, and in their persistent and systematic resistance to all pressure to denounce revolutionary terrorism formally.

POLITICAL AMNESTY AND CAPITAL PUNISHMENT

The Kadets considered "total amnesty for so-called political . . . crimes" to be "an absolutely indispensable and particularly urgent measure." It was therefore the first issue that the party raised at the opening session of the Duma on 27 April 1906.[45] Indeed, the amnesty question was so crucial for the Kadets that they were prepared to warn Nicholas II on 30 April that the Constitutional Democratic Party "is not afraid of conflict . . . and will not try to avoid" it, threatening that "conflict will be inevitable if the amnesty is not granted."[46] It is unlikely that the Kadets' appeals to liberate "those people who sacrifice their lives for the sake of their goals"[47] were purely humanitarian gestures; to please their radical constituents, the Kadets' primary objective was to obtain political amnesty for the terrorists.

This aim was clearly evident behind the Kadet rhetoric of the period, for Nicholas II had already granted a partial political amnesty on 21 October of the previous year.[48] Still, representatives of both the State Council and the Duma asked the tsar to pardon a larger number of political criminals, although the two chambers could not agree on who was to be included in the new amnesty. Whereas the overwhelming majority of the State Council adopted a resolution begging the tsar to extend amnesty to nearly all political criminals except the terrorists,[49] the Kadet-dominated Duma refused to support the appeal from the State Council. For the Kadets, the key word was "total,"[50] which was in effect but another way to insist upon political amnesty for the terrorists. Yet it was not until much later that Miliukov finally admitted that the Kadets "certainly could not have refused amnesty to the terrorists."[51]

For the Constitutional Democrats, the issue of political amnesty was closely connected with persistent demands for the abolition of capital punishment. Denouncing the government, which drowned Russia in blood and "covered the country with the shame of lawless executions and imprisonments," the party Duma spokesmen, such as V. D. Nabokov, vice-chairman of the Kadet Central Committee, not only declared, "The country awaits total political amnesty," but also insisted that "the death penalty can never and under no conditions be indicated [for it is] impermissible even as a court sentence."[52] Just as their support of political amnesty arose largely from tactical considerations, their fiery speeches against the repressive measures of the regime were probably not motivated solely by sincere opposition to capital punishment on moral grounds; if this had been the case, the party would not have refused to support the Octobrist Party Duma platform, which was in complete accord with the Kadet position on both amnesty and capital punishment, but also called for "an appeal with the same request [to the terrorists], asking them not to use the death penalty, which is as shameful for the country as capital punishment from above."[53] It is also noteworthy that in responding to Stolypin's argument that the proposed Kadet ministry would have no administrative experience and would drive the country into anarchy, Miliukov is said to have declared: "We are not afraid of this. . . . If necessary, we would put guillotines in the squares and would deal mercilessly with all who would fight" the government.[54]

Although often suggesting that the escalating terrorist activity would cease once the government's repressions and executions were halted,[55] the Kadets had little reason to assume that such a cause and effect relationship really existed. The country's experience following the granting of the October Manifesto, which not only did not stop but in fact increased the level of violence in Russia, probably showed the Kadets, as it did the authorities, that they could not expect the radicals to put down their arms in response to a new concession, such as the abolition of capital punishment. Rather, for the Kadet Party capital punishment became a tactical issue, since they found it politically profitable to embarrass the authorities by insisting upon the abolition of the death penalty, something that, as the Kadet leadership was fully aware, the government regarded as a premature action, which, in the midst of the bloody revolution in the empire, would weaken the existing regime still further by eliminating its main weapon against terrorist activity.[56] It is not surprising then to find a contemporary concluding, "It is for the terrorists that the Kadets demanded total amnesty at the first opportunity; it is for the sake of the terrorists that they strive for the abolition of capital punishment, for *without* the terrorists the Kadets are powerless in their struggle against the Autocracy and the authorities."[57]

KADET RHETORIC AND THE TERRORISTS

Along with their attempts to abolish capital punishment and obtain amnesty for the terrorists, Constitutional Democrats such as N. N. Shchepkin, a member of the party's Central Committee, professed their "moral solidarity" with all freedom fighters, arguing that everyone in the opposition movement, including the Kadets themselves, "in accordance with his own abilities, tried to shake" the autocratic regime, which indeed ended with the October Manifesto.[58] In a speech on 4 May 1906 one member of the Kadet Duma faction, I. L. Shrag, acknowledged the oppositionists' common debt to the terrorists, who "did not spare their lives . . . in order to achieve that freedom . . . in obtaining which they played such an enormous, outstanding role."[59] The Constitutional Democrats thus exonerated the radicals, with Shchepkin declaring that the party "no longer considers the so-called political criminals to be criminals," since the hated regime, "the last vestiges of which are yet to be done away with in the Duma . . . is in effect overthrown."[60] The Kadets, however, remained unprepared to condemn the terrorist activity that continued even under the new constitutional order. Instead, on a number of occasions they claimed that they understood the political assassinations and even considered them to have "a certain social advisability," since these acts were directed against proponents of reaction and "enemies of the people."[61]

   Sharing a common enemy with the radicals, the Constitutional Democrats were clearly determined to shift the emphasis away from the terrorists and turn the government into the guilty party. Thus Nabokov, speaking before the Duma on 26 May 1906, portrayed the authorities as murderers.[62] Miliukov continuously stressed that terrorist activity was logical in the current political situation, in which the terrorists were innocent victims of tyranny and lawlessness from above.[63] Claiming that the government had been the first to resort to severe measures, provoking the terrorists to respond with their attacks, such outspoken Duma representatives as Shrag denounced the authorities, "who did not stop at anything . . . to retain their power," and defended the terrorists, exclaiming, "How then can you even expect them . . . not to answer with the same?"[64] The Kadets thus suggested that all politically motivated murders were committed in response to the atrocities of government functionaries, and justified the terrorists by arguing (as did party Duma deputy N. V. Ognev on 19 July 1906) that they "are filled with indignation at the impunity of various administrative oppressors; they are afraid of the prospect of further horrors from some Luzhenovskii or his like; and, having no means of peaceful influence on these monsters, they decide to commit a crime."[65]

This statement, however, was hardly an accurate representation of reality, and there is little doubt that the Kadets were aware of its fallacy. It was common knowledge that the new type of terrorist considered any government official a satisfactory target for an assassination attempt. The newspapers were full of evidence to support what Grigorii Frolov revealed many years later with reference to his July 1906 assassination of Blok, head of the tsarist administration in Samara: "I did not know what kind of person the Samara governor was and what sort of official career he had, but at that time this was unimportant. He would probably have been killed even if he were the best governor."[66] After Tat'iana Leont'eva murdered an elderly man, mistaking him in her confused mental state for Minister of the Interior Durnovo, the Kadets reported in their daily newspaper, *Rech'*, that she expressed her regrets but added: "In these difficult times it does not matter if there is one person more or less in the world."[67] Similarly, in the Duma the Kadets were often informed of savage random attacks on innocent civilians, including incidents of revolutionaries tossing bombs into streetcars in Riga,[68] and one particularly bloody episode that occurred in Warsaw on 14 November 1905 when the Anarchists-Communists in one of their numerous acts of motiveless terror threw two bombs, packed for additional effect with nails and bullets, into a large family cafe in the Hotel Bristol with over two hundred customers present. They did it not to seek revenge for real or imagined "horrors from some Luzhenovskii or his like," but rather, "to see how the foul bourgeois will squirm in death agony."[69] The Kadets were also aware that a number of terrorist attacks were carried out by paid assassins who were themselves completely indifferent to the political motives of the various revolutionary committees that had hired them, and that often what had previously been regarded as the idealism of terror gradually degenerated into the pure banditry of the seamy side of the revolution.[70] Thus, only their wish to dissociate themselves from the government and to support the revolutionary cause drove the Kadets to proclaim all terrorists reluctant heroes who were greatly "troubled by the injustice reigning in society," unable to "separate their words and emotions from their deeds."[71]

As part of their propaganda campaign, the Kadets were prepared to use every available journalistic and propagandistic device. Nabokov, for instance, compared the revolutionary anarchists to that ardent opponent of all bloodshed, "the greatest anarchist—Count Lev Nikolaevich Tolstoi."[72] In Kadet rhetoric, the terrorists were not only justified in their actions by the very existence of the hated government, they often emerged as the most honest and principled of Russian citizens, unwilling to tolerate what others, with more servile natures, were ready to accept. Ognev argued, for example, that if one were to consider the terrorists' "individual qualities, as they were drawn by their biographers and their prison comrades, then it would turn out that these political criminals are not at all villains by nature. In their personality, these are people of a special moral delicacy, of a sensitivity greater than that of ordinary people," who overlook or merely talk about obvious social evils.[73]

The Kadets encouraged the public to regard the terrorists as innocent victims of the regime, even portraying them as martyrs and near saints. It certainly was not accidental that the Constitutional Democrats reminded their audiences of a familiar prose poem by Ivan Turgenev, "The Threshold" (Porog), in which a young woman revolutionary is portrayed as both a fool and a saint, with the author clearly leaning toward the latter image.[74] Having stressed how difficult it was for the heroine of the poem to decide to commit a crime, Ognev (who happened to be a priest) declared in his Duma speech on 19 June 1906, "Gentlemen, I see familiar traits . . . in this young woman. I recognize in the face of this girl the traits of Zasulich, Volkenshtein, Izmailovich, Spiridonova and others," clearly suggesting that all these terrorist women ought to be treated more as martyrs than as fools or criminals.[75] Equally suggestive is an article in *Rech'* in which V. Azov, giving a compassionate description of "Marusia" Spiridonova following her murder of Luzhenovskii, stated: her "life (*zhizn'*) ended. And then began her *zhitie*," employing a term used in Russian exclusively to indicate the life of a saint.[76] Another Kadet, I. Pustoshkin, went even further, comparing the extremists to Christ: "Remember that Christ, too, was declared to be a criminal and was subjected to a shameful execution on the cross. The years passed, and this criminal—Christ—has conquered the whole world and become a model of virtue. The attitude toward political criminals is a similar act of violence on the part of the authorities."[77]

The Constitutional Democrats also found it useful to concentrate particular attention on such questions as the government's actions against juvenile terrorists. The Kadets chose not to refer to this particular group of extremists as "terrorists," and attacked the government for persecuting "minors."[78] Such Kadet Duma spokesmen as M. Bobin and N. Katsenel'son cited cases in which, for example, a "poor unfortunate" girl, just one year out of school, was sentenced to death, or a fifteen-year-old boy, who had attempted to kill a police officer, was said to have been brutalized by the local authorities.[79] The Kadets were undoubtedly aware of the severe problem of teenage terrorism,[80] but they used the sensitive issue to appeal to the emotions of their audience. By describing the suffering of the young terrorists in bloody, grossly exaggerated, and often unsubstantiated detail, they clearly sought to compromise the government.[81]

REFUSAL TO DENOUNCE REVOLUTIONARY TERROR

Kadet policy on violence, consistent with the party's previous tactics, revealed what Tyrkova-Vil'iams and other former leaders later admitted was the unambivalent "solidarity with which the entire opposition movement, socialists as well as liberals, refused to denounce terrorism."[82] Immediately prior to convocation of the First Duma, and during its initial meetings, when the government seemed greatly weakened and the Kadets were at the height of their political prestige, the party did not find it necessary to conceal its true position, unequivocally refusing to condemn assassination as a political tactic.[83] Subsequently, whenever confronted with instances of terrorist activity, which they promptly reported in their publications,[84] the Kadets did everything they could to avoid expressing their position on leftist political murders. When reporting an assassination, Kadet publicists preferred merely to state what had happened, and at the very most (usually in extreme circumstances when many innocent civilians were killed), they would go so far as to reaffirm their general aversion to violence.[85] In such cases, however, they always remembered to hold the government primarily responsible for the anarchy in Russia.[86] Still, neither in *Rech'*, which supposedly followed a path of "frank liberalism,"[87] nor in the official Kadet weekly, *Vestnik Partii Narodnoi Svobody* (*Herald of the Party of People's Freedom*), was there ever a single article directly condemning political assassination from the left during the revolutionary years.

The Kadet stand on violence varied from case to case and appeared to be determined largely by the political persuasions of both the victim and his assassin. This becomes clear in comparing the Kadets' position on revolutionary terrorism with their attitude toward terror from the right. Along with their persistent denunciations of the government for its repressive measures against the left-wing extremists, the Kadets strongly emphasized a particular danger from the right, attacking such groups as the monarchist Union of the Russian People. In their campaign against this group the Kadets frequently accused its members of trying to fight against the revolution by revolutionary means, such as staging assassinations of prominent public figures who ardently opposed the government. It was these assassinations, and not political murders from the left, that the Kadet Party was most eager to condemn.

In comparison with the widespread revolutionary violence, terrorist acts from the right were rare,[88] but this did not prevent the Constitutional Democratic press from insisting that "the Black Hundreds have spilled so much human blood in Russia . . . that the terrorist revolutionaries and the anarchists could never catch up with them."[89] Similarly, while the Kadets usually dedicated only a few "impartial" lines to assassinations of governors, ministers, and lower-ranking officials, they filled numerous pages of their publications with information about the murder of former Kadet Duma deputy Mikhail Gertsenshtein, passionately condemning "such insane . . . [and] shameful means of struggle" as "wild and barbarous violence . . . treacherous . . . infamous . . . villainous murder."[90] Clearly, the Kadets could hardly have been expected to be as deeply troubled by the death of a "reactionary bureaucrat" as they were by the murder of a prominent member of their own party, but when three civilian engineers were assassinated in the course of three days, *Rech'* harshly condemned "the senseless, blind, useless" murder of the two liberal engineers, and only briefly and rather indifferently reported the death of the third, whose previous unpopularity among local workers was well known.[91] After receiving a threatening letter from an obscure terrorist organization, one of several groups calling themselves the Uncompromising Ones, the editors of the Kadet newspaper immediately announced that the authors of the note must surely have been right-wing extremists, despite the fact that they had expressed unambiguous revolutionary allegiances.[92]

For a while, the Kadets seemed able to maintain this rather evasive stand, but controversy in the new Duma in the spring of 1907 finally forced them to demonstrate in a more direct way that they were indeed unwilling to denounce revolutionary terrorism. Upon convocation of the Second Duma following elections largely boycotted by the socialists, the Kadets, no longer enjoying a position of unchallenged dominance, found themselves under fierce attack. Both the conservatives and the Octobrists, in pursuit of their own political goals and wishing to embarrass their rivals on the immediate left, publicly accused the Constitutional Democrats of "indulging and instigating" political assassinations for the sake of promoting revolution, which they claimed was the Kadets' "roots" and "nourishment."[93] The Kadets' opponents on the right had a strong case against them: such moderate Constitutional Democrats as A. I. Shingarev, and even V. A. Maklakov, one of the more conservative members of the Central Committee, criticized the government for its actions against "the poor terrorists and expropriators," and denounced the regime for allowing people "to be led to the gallows as cattle to the slaughterhouse."[94] Since they claimed to oppose violence and bloodshed, the Kadet spokesmen should, their opponents argued, also be expected to condemn bloodshed in the form of political assassination.[95] Instead, as Conservative Duma deputy V. V. Shul'gin observed on 12 March 1907, "In the newspapers of this party we will never find a single line denouncing these murders. . . . We are always told that these . . . [terrorists] are all heroes, all fighters for freedom."[96] In fact, the Kadets themselves admitted that their party "never allowed itself to berate terrorists."[97]

The Kadet position was even further complicated and weakened by the fact that both the moderates and the conservatives in the Duma were willing to express their opposition to political violence from all sources, whether left or right.[98] At the same time they urged the Kadets to "denounce . . . the terrorist acts," and to express their "wish to put an end to these murders," demanding, as did Octobrist representative P. V. Sinadino on 13 March 1907, "Is it possible that you do not wish to add these words only out of stubbornness?"[99]

Clearly it was not stubbornness, but a carefully formulated policy, so essential that such Kadet leaders as I. I. Petrunkevich considered it better for the party to perish than suffer "moral destruction" as a result of denouncing revolutionary tactics and rallying behind the government or cooperating with its supporters on the right.[100] While objecting strenuously in the party press to their opponents' accusations that they were sympathetic to murder, the Constitutional Democrats persisted in their policy of refusing to condemn terrorist acts.[101] Since, however, an open declaration of their solidarity with the radicals would immediately have placed them in the revolutionary camp in the eyes of the government, the Kadets did everything in their power to avoid a direct statement in any form on the terrorist issue. Caught in a dilemma, they therefore desperately sought excuses in the Duma to suspend, or at least postpone, all discussions of the question that would inevitably have exposed their true stand. For this reason the Kadet faction, in the speeches of Shingarev and A. A. Kizevetter on 13 March 1907, insisted that the Duma was no place for condemning anything or anybody: "We are not convened here to draft a resolution or to voice worthless words and complaints. No matter how much we are begged, we will not follow a path that is completely inappropriate for the Duma."[102] On previous occasions, however, the Kadets had not objected when rightist terror was denounced in the Duma, and during the debates on capital punishment in May of 1906 they argued, in the words of representative A. G. Sipiagin, that it was wrong "to talk about a parliamentary form before men's lives . . . [when] people were dying."[103] In their attempts to avoid all public discussion of this sensitive issue, the Kadets received considerable assistance from the chairman of the Duma, Kadet F. A. Golovin, who was, contrary to the requirements of his position, clearly far from impartial in supervising the debates.[104]

The Kadet avoidance tactic did not go unchallenged, and in early April of 1907 thirty-two members of the Duma formally demanded that the question of condemning terrorist activity be placed on the Duma's agenda.[105] The conservatives and moderates in the Duma particularly stressed the need to raise the issue of political violence, although the representatives of the left stated that they too had nothing against discussing the question, and indeed seemed to welcome the opportunity to condemn the government and express openly their sympathy for the terrorists.[106] The Kadet faction, caught in the middle, reaffirmed its policy not to denounce terrorist activity, and over the course of a six-week period repeatedly voted to postpone all discussion of the issue.[107] In the end these efforts were successful, and soon those who dared to bring up the question were derided and informed that they would never be able to force the Duma to condemn political assassinations.[108] The controversy dragged on until 15 May 1907, when the Kadets formally and finally stated their refusal to consider the declaration "denouncing murder, terrorism, and violence."[109] They thus succeeded in removing the question from the agenda of the Second Duma, but in the process failed to meet the challenge from their Octobrist opponents "to prove that . . . [the Party of People's Freedom was] a constitutional party and not a revolutionary one."[110]

CONSEQUENCES

The policy of half-concealed and cautious support for the revolution, particularly as manifested with regard to the issue of terrorism, ultimately seems to have caused more harm than good to the Constitutional Democratic Party. For one thing, the Kadets' tactics did not remain secret, exposing the party to criticism from all sides. The radicals were clearly aware of the ambiguity of the Kadet position, and scourged the Constitutional Democrats as the party that "called on others for actions that the party itself rejects," and relied on outside forces to bring its program into being.[111] The conservatives also claimed to understand the true politics of the Kadets, considering the party "the head and tail of the revolution."[112] Nor did the government conceal its views concerning the Party of People's Freedom, and Prime Minister Stolypin, while persistently attempting to establish cooperation with the moderate forces against the revolutionaries, was obviously outraged by Kadet behavior, to the point of denouncing the Kadets as "a gang . . . the members of which claim to be peaceful [and] harmless . . . but in their criminal activity do not stop at either widely organized deceit or murderous villainy [*dushegubstvo*] when required by circumstances."[113]

Kadet support for the terrorists also caused a split in the party itself, which lost a large number of individuals who might have been loyal supporters of its program had the Kadet means of implementing it been less radical. Many potential Kadets could not subordinate their genuine aversion to violence to the party's tactics. They chose instead to remain outside the Kadet organization, from where they could openly express their opposition to political assassination and even criticize the Party of People's Freedom for not being "decisive enough in condemning terrorist acts."[114] Such prominent figures as Dmitrii Shipov, who initially had a great deal of sympathy for the Kadets, chose not to join the party, believing that the Constitutional Democrats "had undoubtedly begun to proceed along the revolutionary path."[115] Similarly, Prince Evgenii Trubetskoi, a well-known constitutionalist, formally broke his ties with the party because he was disillusioned by its support for such tactics as terrorist activity.[116] The left-wing faction prevailed within the Kadet organization, attracting more radical elements to the party in the process, perhaps even at the expense of the socialists. Yet among those who chose to remain in the Kadet ranks, such prominent Central Committee members as Struve and Maklakov, as well as Duma deputy S. N. Bulgakov, were reluctant to go along with the organization's policies concerning terrorist activity, even breaking party discipline on rare occasions for the sake of their personal convictions.[117]

There was another serious negative ramification of the Kadet tactics with regard to terrorism. As a result of Miliukov's refusal to denounce political assassination publicly, or at least to issue an unsigned denunciation in *Rech'*, even after Stolypin made it a condition for legalization of the Party of People's Freedom, the Constitutional Democrats remained "illegal" or "unregistered."[118] This allowed the authorities to close their congresses and meetings and to invoke the law against them under various pretexts.[119] But even these continuous problems with the party's legal status seem insignificant in comparison with the truly unfortunate and indeed tragic long-term losses that were the apparent consequence of the Kadets' unwillingness to dissociate themselves from the extremists.

In the spring and summer of 1906 the government, greatly threatened by the ongoing revolution and anarchy, was already sufficiently weakened to take steps toward bridging the gap between itself and society by entering into semi-official negotiations with the Kadet leaders, who were invited into the cabinet along with representatives of the Octobrists and other moderates. In the new coalition ministry, which would enjoy the confidence of the people and therefore be capable of leading the country toward peaceful restoration and reform, the Kadets were to hold leading posts, including Minister of Internal Affairs, Minister of Foreign Affairs, and possibly even Chairman of the Council of Ministers. Hoping that "the revolutionary pathos" which, in Maklakov's words, many Kadet leaders "did not wish to extinguish" for the time being,[120] would force the government to grant further concessions, Miliukov insisted that the new ministry be made up exclusively of members of the majority party in the Duma—that is, representatives of the Party of People's Freedom. Believing the authorities to be increasingly paralyzed by the widespread violence, Miliukov, who did most of the negotiating for the Kadets and "already felt himself a premier," was unwilling to accept compromise.[121] He declared that the Kadets would fill all ministerial posts or would accept none at all, but at the same time demonstrated no intention of softening the party's program to make it more palatable for the government,[122] or of departing from the policy of supporting the extremists in Duma speeches and the press. Such tactics proved miscalculated: although at the time it appeared quite likely that the tsar might yield to their demands,[123] the Kadets' "moderate radicalism" ultimately backfired, contrary to all their expectations of imminent political victory. Their aggressive behavior in the Duma with regard to the agrarian question, and, of equal importance, their support for the extremists, finally decided the issue against the Kadet cabinet. In the words of Tyrkova-Vil'iams, "The terrible question of terror was one of the underwater rocks against which the first [Duma] broke"—an event that undermined the dominant position of the Constitutional Democrats.[124]

Not everything was lost at that point, and although Kadet influence was much less significant in the Second Duma than it had been in the first, the party was still a major political force.[125] Had it revised its tactics of treating the government as a traditional enemy and all revolutionaries as its temporary allies, it would perhaps have been able to work productively within the established constitutional framework. To be sure, in the new political situation the Kadets could no longer hope to win concessions by taking the more confident authorities by siege, or to pursue a policy that a member of the party's Central Committee, Prince Shakhovskoi, defined as "a need to uproot (*skovyrnut'*) the government."[126] Indeed, increasingly afraid that the authorities would dissolve the Second Duma, the Kadets were even prepared to make some conciliatory gestures.[127] Nevertheless, the words of Octobrist deputy Mikhail Stakhovich proved prophetic: "Remember, Gentlemen, that if the State Duma does not denounce political assassinations, it will commit one against itself."[128]

Reluctant to break away from the united antigovernment front, and perhaps still hoping that the central administration would back down in the face of mass political violence, the Kadets refused to take this step, which, in effect, "doomed the Second Duma, for it took out of Stolypin's hands the one weapon he had to stave off mounting Court pressure for another dissolution."[129] When the Duma was finally disbanded in early June 1907, the Constitutional Democratic Party emerged tremendously weakened, no longer enjoying its former dominant position on the Russian political scene.

If in the course of Russian history, as Astrid von Borcke correctly points out, "the autocracy screened the intelligentsia from the experiences and disappointments of practical politics and thus nourished their maximalism,"[130] the year 1905 altered the situation drastically. Yet, having obtained an opportunity to become a leading liberal political force working successfully within the new constitutional system in Russia, the Kadets tragically lost it in 1905–1907, largely through their reluctance to step into the gap between the intelligentsia and the state, dissociate themselves from the revolutionary camp, and declare unambiguously their opposition to radical tactics such as terrorism.[131]

Chapter Eight

THE END OF REVOLUTIONARY TERRORISM IN RUSSIA

Where bombs are used as an argument, ruthless retribution is
certainly a natural response!
—*P. A. Stolypin*[1]

THE GOVERNMENT RESPONSE: FROM HESITATION TO REPRESSION

CONFRONTED by the dramatic escalation of revolutionary violence after 1905, the government of Nicholas II faced the necessity of adopting urgent measures to end the ongoing crisis. While trying to repress various forms of mass protest in the cities and the countryside, the authorities were simultaneously required to find new ways to combat terrorist activity. Initially, however, the Russian imperial administration proved inadequate in meeting this challenge. The shock of the swiftly spreading anarchy and daily bloodletting was partly responsible for the failure of the tsarist administration to implement immediate radical measures against the extremists. Additionally, this failure can be attributed to the mild, apathetic, and indecisive personality of Nicholas II himself, and also to the evident concern in the highest spheres of the government and court that overtly repressive actions would convey to Russia's Western European allies an image of the country's rulers as semi-Asiatic barbarians, and of the country itself as an uncivilized backwater.[2] Perhaps even more important to the highest state authorities was the threat of further alienating liberal circles in their own country.

Liberal society persisted in its traditional unequivocally apologetic stance vis-à-vis the extremists, and the pressure it exerted on official circles was indeed a major factor accounting for the initial hesitation of the government in the face of revolution. Even during the escalation of violence, many government functionaries, influenced by the liberals, continued to view the radicals as selfless if misguided martyrs, mercilessly persecuted by the omnipotent state, despite the fact that the motives and practices of the new variety of terrorist had obviously changed drastically compared to the majority of their nineteenth-century predecessors. As a result, many civil and military officials, including some among the highest ranks, not only resisted implementing severe measures against the terrorists, but also could not conceal their personal admiration and sympathy for the "unfortunate politicals."[3] Moreover, individual members of the tsarist administration were occasionally willing, at the risk of their own careers, to extend favors to extremists fighting against the very establishment that these state servants represented.[4]

At least in the period surrounding the outbreak of full-scale revolutionary war with the government in 1905, the radicals seemed to consider the consequences of extremist activity to be outweighed by its advantages for the revolutionary struggle. They undertook their acts relatively confident that if caught and tried they would in all likelihood be rescued from the most severe punitive measures by the interference of their liberal lawyers, and by pressure from the sympathetic public opinion of society at large.

At first glance, conviction statistics give no indication of leniency toward the extremists on the part of the state in these years. According to an antigovernment source, in a six-month period beginning in October 1905 the authorities imprisoned and exiled nearly 3,300 people for political crimes ranging from possession of illegal publications to armed assault.[5] The important factor here, however, is the actual duration of time served, for although lengthy terms were an option, in practice they were seldom used. Police Department official Rataev describes the discouraging and paralyzing effects of the judicial system's leniency on the tsarist regime's primary defenders, the law enforcement personnel:

> The latest verdicts in political trials are truly horrifying, for after several months, all those convicted, having spent their terms in confinement, return to the path of revolutionary activity with redoubled energy. In reading such verdicts one really loses heart and all energy. . . . What is the use of wasting money on the investigation and detainment of people who will be locked in prison for several months at best and then let loose with an opportunity to go back to their previous work.[6]

Many radicals, and especially the young idealists, did not fear imprisonment and hard labor, and even welcomed the experience, for in their minds penal servitude was the true test of a revolutionary's convictions and fortitude. At the same time, their anticipation of the opportunity to breathe the air of prison, "saturated with the indomitable spirit of the best fighters" and revolutionary heroes of the past,[7] was accompanied by an awareness that at least until early 1907, when conditions in most penal institutions noticeably worsened, "discipline and supervision were often shockingly lax."[8] In this period, political prisoners rarely complained of cruel and abusive treatment. On the contrary, according to Mariia Spiridonova, who spent nearly ten years in tsarist penal servitude for the murder of Luzhenovskii, "In 1906, life was free in prisons. . . . The regime in hard labor was . . . very liberal." She describes life in the Akatui prison for political convicts:

> There was complete freedom. The prisoners . . . were allowed to take walks deep into the forest for the whole day. And in the village, about two miles from the prison, lived several dozen of the convicts' families. . . . Fathers and husbands were allowed to stay with them overnight. They simply lived with their [families] and showed up at the prison just to make themselves seen.

All in all, Spiridonova asserts, the prisons closely resembled clubs where intense social interaction prevailed, marked by feelings of comradery and intellectual fulfillment.[9] Indeed, since "opportunities for reading and conversation were usually plentiful," according to historian Hugh Phillips, prison turned into "an informal, but effective, school of higher learning for revolutionaries."[10] Frequently the radicals were able to continue their antigovernment activities during their confinement, as was the case in Kiev when a revolutionary committee directed a strike from prison after all of its members had been arrested, and continued to issue proclamations during their time in custody.[11]

These circumstances led an official government newspaper to declare that it was "about time to reform . . . places of confinement by turning them from places of entertainment and tranquil life into real prisons, the way they are, for example, in England."[12] Significantly, in their memoirs many former convicts confirm this positive depiction of prison life prior to 1907, stating that they carried with them to freedom rather pleasant memories of their terms in tsarist penal institutions, where life had been "merrier than any wedding."[13] The same was true to an even greater degree of life in places of internal political exile.

Contributing to the lack of fear of punishment on the part of the revolutionaries was the fact that understaffing in the prisons, together with the incompetence of the personnel and the inadequacies of many antiquated prison facilities, created a situation in which many, if not most, escape attempts succeeded.[14] At the same time, the majority of those who remained in custody did so almost by choice—they "'consented' to stay in confinement . . . voluntarily and temporarily . . . so that they would surely soon become free" legally, and avoid the life of a wandering fugitive.[15] As far as internal exile was concerned, according to Rataev, it "existed solely on paper. The only people who did not run away from [places of exile] were the ones who did not want to do so, who for personal reasons had no need to escape."[16]

This view is supported by evidence that a large percentage of the terrorists imprisoned or exiled before 1907 did manage to liberate themselves and emigrate or go into hiding; some of them did so more than once during their revolutionary careers.[17] Radicals who chose emigration usually did not bother to obtain foreign passports; in fact, many received permission from sympathetic local officials to go abroad in lieu of serving out their sentences of Siberian exile.[18] When extremists were forced to leave Russia as fugitives they frequently crossed the poorly guarded imperial border with the financially motivated collaboration of professional contrabandists.

The inability of the tsarist administration to adapt quickly to the new requirements created by the crisis also contributed to the relative freedom of action enjoyed by the extremists in the initial stage of the revolution. This problem was especially serious in the border regions, where government officials complained about the impotence of the understaffed and underpaid police force in the face of rapidly multiplying enemies in the antigovernment camp. The largely outdated weapons, and especially the cumbersome rifles and sabres used by the police against the radicals, many of whom were equipped with the most advanced firearms smuggled from abroad, proved an equal disadvantage.[19] Perhaps even more unfortunate for the government's cause was its failure to provide any psychological or ideological incentive for its poorly educated and often barely literate rank-and-file defenders, forced to risk their lives in a struggle with fellow countrymen who professed themselves in the most elevated language to be sincerely motivated by their revolutionary creed.

The authorities' incompetence in the fight against the daring and increasingly adroit revolutionaries quickly became evident enough to serve as the subject of popular satire. In one joke, police officers were allegedly given the following "new energetic directives" after a bank robbery:

1. Guard thoroughly those sites that have [already] been robbed by the malefactors;
2. Report all robbery cases no later than an hour before their occurrence;
3. Take photographs of criminals who have disappeared without a trace;
4. Send the entirety of stolen sums to police headquarters without delay as material evidence;
5. Travel around the city and ask each individual inhabitant whether it was he who stole the money from the bank.[20]

This is not to suggest that the tsarist government remained entirely passive. Beginning in 1905 many regions across the empire were placed under martial law, and by August 1906 eighty-two of the country's eighty-seven provinces were under intensified security (*usilennaia okhrana*).[21] That year, having succumbed to panic, the government abandoned its respect for the legal niceties that prevailed after October 1905, and allowed civilians to be tried in the military courts "on the flimsy basis of police inquest alone," without an official preliminary investigation.[22] These measures, however, proved insufficient to diminish the anarchy, especially since the initial indecisiveness of the tsarist authorities in combating extremism had contributed so much to its intensity. It was not until July 1906, when Petr Stolypin assumed his post as the chairman of the Council of Ministers while retaining his position as minister of the interior, that the government began to take harsh and largely effective steps to stop the raging violence.

Stolypin's immediate motive for launching a campaign of countermeasures was the nearly successful attempt on his life at his villa on Aptekarskii Island in August 1906: "the most sensational manifestation of terrorism which continued to hold the country in its bloody grip."[23] Under the circumstances, as Richard Pipes justifiably asserts, "no government in the world could have remained passive";[24] after all, it was the revolutionaries who in their rhetoric constantly referred to their activities as warfare against the establishment, and having declared war, they had to expect retaliation. Since the Second Duma had not yet been elected, Stolypin, pressured by the court to use drastic measures to restore order quickly, resorted to Article 87 of the Fundamental Laws, which authorized the government to issue emergency decrees when the legislature was not in session. Regretting this deplorable necessity, on 19 August 1906 the prime minister introduced a system of field courts-martial for civilians.[25]

In areas under either martial law or extraordinary security (*chrezvychainaia okhrana*), the governors and commandants of the military districts were authorized to turn over to the military courts individuals whose involvement in such extremist practices as terrorist attacks and assassinations, political robberies and banditry, armed assaults on and resistance to authorities, as well as manufacturing, concealing, or utilizing explosive devices, was so obvious as to require no investigation. Each of these courts was to consist of five officer-judges appointed by local military commanders. Although defendants could call on witnesses, they were not allowed access to legal advice during the hearings, which were also closed to the public. But perhaps the most severe aspect of field court justice was the swiftness of its action: the courts convened within twenty-four hours of the crime and reached a verdict in forty-eight hours; the sentences could not be appealed and were to be carried out no later than twenty-four hours after pronouncement.[26]

The introduction of the field courts system immediately elicited an angry outcry from left-wing and liberal circles. Even the majority of the regime's conservative supporters, including Chief Military Procurator V. P. Pavlov, "a man not noted for the quality of his mercy," recognized that this system of jurisprudence only vaguely resembled legality.[27] It was equally obvious that it offered no safeguards against errors and abuses of the judicial process.[28] Its inhumanity was demonstrated by the fact that in practice the most typical sentences handed down by the field courts were death and hard labor.[29] Most prisoners sentenced to death were promptly executed, and by the time this law expired in April 1907, eight months after its issuance, more than one thousand revolutionaries, predominantly terrorists and expropriators, had been shot or hanged by the military execution squads.[30]

Field court justice was not the only new burden imposed on the military by the central administration; because the regular police and gendarme forces had proven powerless to preserve internal order and security, the army, which from the early days of the revolution was widely used to suppress worker unrest and agrarian disorders, was also charged with many other functions aiming to deter terrorist attacks and expropriations. Soldiers guarded banks, post and telegraph offices, liquor stores, hospitals, trains and railroad stations, as well as other potential targets of terrorism. Similarly, prisons and even police stations were considered too vulnerable without the protection of military patrols, especially in the most anarchic centers of revolutionary violence, such as Warsaw, where soldiers were assigned to assist street policemen and even to replace them. In other border regions, particularly the Caucasus and the Baltics, the army was used in punitive expeditions against extremist enemies of the regime.[31] Despite the protests of the high military command that these practices demoralized the troops and allowed for no regular national defense training, Stolypin's Council of Ministers insisted on the involvement of the army in the implementation of urgent measures to defeat the most formidable of Russia's foes at the moment—her internal enemies.[32]

The regular military and civil courts continued to operate alongside the system of courts-martial; although considerably more lenient with accused extremists than the extraordinary field courts, especially where women and juveniles were concerned,[33] they, too, toughened as part of Stolypin's repressive program. Whereas in 1905 only ten of the death sentences issued by military courts to civilian defendants were carried out, according to the statistics of the Police Department, this number increased to 144 by the end of 1906. In the following year the figures rose dramatically again, to 1,139, and as the revolutionary upheaval declined, dropped to 825 by 1 January 1909, and to 717 by the end of that year.[34] Still, "the revolution never ended for the military judicial network," for although the number of civilian defendants abated sharply after 1908, it "never subsided to the normal level (less than fifty defendants) which had characterized the period before 1905." Nicholas II repeatedly expressed dissatisfaction at delays in cases tried in military district courts, insisting that the procedure be hastened and simplified. Some judges who disregarded the law and issued sentences lighter than those prescribed by the code were reprimanded. And if the government could not legally return to the field courts-martial, the desire to prevent new outbreaks of revolutionary violence caused it to take steps toward the "closest possible approximation of them." One example is an amendment of the military judicial code enacted on 27 June 1907 that "slashed the period statutorily prescribed for preliminary investigation from three days to one."[35]

With the revolution on the defensive, judicial repressions continued. A contemporary source estimates that in 1908 and 1909, 16,440 civilian and military defendants were convicted for political crimes, including armed assault; of these, 3,682 were sentenced to death, and 4,517 to hard labor.[36] Although these judicial statistics are clear indicators of the ferocity of the government's struggle against the revolution, it still must be emphasized that many of the executions ordered were never carried out, having been replaced with terms of hard labor and imprisonment. Thus, from 1 January 1905 to 20 April 1907, fewer than one-third of the civilians sentenced to death by military district courts were in fact hanged or shot. As in the case of the field courts-martial, the overwhelming majority of crimes punished by execution were terrorist acts and expropriations.[37]

Gerasimov and other officials lamented that as late as 1905 internal security was "a caricature of the secret political police."[38] The incompetence of the police and their futile efforts to prove themselves useful also served as sources for numerous anecdotes, including an imaginary journalist's report from Tambov: "Last night a powerful blizzard stormed the city, but was turned back by the efficient action of police personnel. Three Social Democrats were arrested in the process, 'due to a regrettable error.' "[39] Therefore, along with the drastic judicial measures implemented against the extremists, the government took urgent steps to introduce innovations in internal security. The immediate objective was to enhance the power of the police forces, especially by improving investigative methods used in cases of state crimes, and by recruiting new cadres to be equipped with weapons more suitable for antiterrorist warfare. The authorities implemented these measures simultaneously with the issuance of administrative orders affecting the lives of common citizens, such as curfews and restrictions on movement and assemblies. Local officials conducted frequent searches and imposed fines on owners of apartments and houses used by revolutionaries as warehouses for bombs and explosives, as hideouts, or as sniper posts from which to shoot at police officers on the streets. Some administrators even tried, albeit with little apparent effect, to introduce the quasi-legal practice of arresting citizens who failed to assist the police with arrests.[40]

In addition, the authorities in both the capitals and the periphery sought to toughen the detention system by appointing more competent and loyal personnel, and by increasing their compensation. These efforts contributed to major changes in prison conditions for revolutionaries, although guards and wardens still often hesitated to implement harsh measures against convicted combatants, due to a "somewhat exaggerated assumption about the omnipotence" of their fellow terrorists outside the prison walls.[41] As the courts meted out longer prison terms to growing numbers of radicals, places of detention became so crowded that, as the minister of justice admitted to the Duma on 1 March 1908, "there will soon be nowhere to put the people serving their punishment terms."[42] At the same time, constant searches and limitations on movements of inmates within prisons, as well as strict discipline, resulted in fewer escapes. Furthermore, after 1907 many extremists, and especially the anarchists no longer received special treatment as political convicts and in most prisons were equal in status with common criminals. This measure not only interfered with their receiving material aid from such organizations as the Red Cross, but also stripped them of their previous privileged status as ideological dissidents, and their consequent immunity to the various punitive and occasionally arbitrary and abusive disciplinary measures imposed by prison administrators, including rudeness, the use of irons, confinement to special dungeon cells, corporal punishment, and recourse to arms in cases of minor insubordination by inmates.[43]

Prisons were not the only places where the government's eagerness to restore order resulted in excesses. Unable to escape the conditioning effects of the prevailing violence and cruelty, by now accepted as almost normal in Russian political life, supporters of strong measures in local administrations, particularly in the periphery, at times misused their authority and were guilty of both arbitrariness and outright illegalities. In his eagerness to fight the revolutionary menace, General Dumbadze, commandant of Yalta, mercilessly harassed the peaceful Jewish population, which he endeavored to drive out of the area under his command. Dumbadze also became notorious throughout Europe for his striking overreaction in an episode that took place on 26 February 1907: having been attacked by a terrorist who fired at him from a neighboring house and then shot himself, the commandant called for troops. On his order they surrounded the private residence, arrested everyone inside, and then burned the building to the ground, along with the adjacent house and a cypress garden.[44]

Similar incidents were particularly extreme in the border areas and remote corners of the empire. In the Baltics, the military's punitive measures against the terrorists reportedly included killing their hostages and intimidating the local populace.[45] The situation inspired a humorist to pen a fictitious telegram from Minister of the Interior Durnovo to General Rennenkampf, who was in charge of an army expedition in Siberia: "I sincerely request that no one higher in rank than governor-general be arrested."[46] Baron A. V. Kaul'bars, commander of the Odessa military district, an area overrun with anarchy and terror, acquired sufficient notoriety for his repressive measures to be made the subject of a popular satirical poem entitled, "Two Beasts":

The panther was the jungle's plague.
Kaul'bars was Odessa's rogue.
The panther ate men, one by one.
Kaul'bars shot men with a gun.
The panther ate men to feel good.
Kaul'bars did not need such food.
The panther's destiny is a cage,
Kaul'bars'—medals, speeches, a stage.
One shot men, the other ate:
Why should they have a different fate?
Let the panther speak from the stage,
Let's put Kaul'bars in the cage.
You mean the panther is a beast,
And Kaul'bars is a man, at least?
Nowadays, it is my stand,
A general cannot be a man.
Nowadays, if you insist,
A general is just a beast.
Let's send Kaul'bars to the jungle,

With the panther let him tangle.
In the jungle, let those beasts
Have themselves a merry feast.[47]

Excesses associated with attempts to suppress terrorist activity and the revolution in general caused public outrage and undermined the government's and specifically the army's reputation not only with critics at home and abroad, but also among loyal supporters of the regime. Simultaneously, a marked decline in morale was noted among army personnel accused by the antigovernment press of using civilians as "moving targets for conducting experiments with weapons."[48] Many military officers, as well as rank-and-file soldiers, "were frankly miserable about fulfilling their state-imposed repressive tasks";[49] this was especially true of military officials responsible for implementing such quasi-legal measures as the field court-martial sentences. Their resistance to duty was particularly strong in cases involving juvenile extremists sentenced to hard labor and prison terms and, in a few exceptional cases, death. During the execution of three teenage Anarchist-Communist expropriators from Riga on 23 October 1906—an event that prompted cries of protest in the liberal press—soldiers on the firing squad reportedly were scandalized and deliberately missed their targets, with one official suffering an attack of nerves.[50]

Although the antagonism of liberal society toward the authorities was genuine, it would be inaccurate to accept its assertions that the harsh measures against the extremists had no impact on the restoration of public order.[51] And while Lev Tolstoy, outraged by the draconian military justice, denounced the cold-blooded antirevolutionary violence perpetrated by the state in his famous essay, "I Cannot Keep Silent!" (Ne mogu molchat'!), Octobrist leader Aleksandr Guchkov defended it as a cruel necessity[52] that did put an end to the relative impunity with which the terrorists had carried out their acts prior to the summer of 1906.

The radicals began to attribute their failures to the ferocity of the government's repressive policies as early as 1906, referring to the authorities as butchers,[53] and in 1907 blamed the end of the revolution on Stolypin's extraordinary measures, citing the field courts-martial in particular.[54] Government representatives throughout the empire reported significant decreases in incidents of revolutionary violence, especially after mid-October 1906. In the Baltics the decline in extremist activities continued in the first four months of 1907; according to official figures, by January murder and arson cases had already decreased to a third of the December 1906 level. And it is hardly coincidental that within a month after the abolition of the field courts-martial in April 1907, cases of these revolutionary outbursts in the Baltics multiplied again, nearly doubling.[55]

Although the field courts-martial gallows, labeled by Kadet Duma spokesman Fedor Rodichev "Stolypin's neckties,"[56] did deter some extremists, they

failed to eliminate the outbursts of terrorist activity, and especially expropriations, altogether. The statistics summarizing political assassinations and robberies demonstrated this fact to Prime Minister Stolypin quite clearly.[57] Individual violence began to decline steadily only as part of the general weakening
of the revolutionary storm and all its mass manifestations late in 1907.[58] This
process was attributable not only to the repressive measures of the government, implemented simultaneously with a series of socioeconomic and agrarian reforms authored by Stolypin, but also to the growing exhaustion and disappointment of the intelligentsia and the common people. There was a gradual
realization that with the authorities now resolved to prevail, concessions could
no longer be obtained by violent actions, which would only lead to further
misery, fruitless bloodshed, and devastation.[59] One Iaroslavl' revolutionary
described the impact of this realization in a letter to a comrade abroad:

> Life here proceeds listlessly, and this is a general phenomenon. In activist circles the
> mood is depressing. The activists ran away like mice, and everyone is busy curing
> the wounds inflicted during the exciting times on his material situation, his family,
> his nerves, and occasionally his neck. Run for dear life. Incidentally, our technicians
> and [literature and weapons] carriers . . . turned out to be good businessmen. . . . The
> workers also want to live in grand style, without fear, intelligently and interestingly.
> It is impossible to lure them into the [antigovernment] discussion groups, but they
> go to the public lectures in droves. . . . No one wants [revolutionary] books; . . . in
> the libraries our authors are covered with dust. . . . Everyone knows that there is
> nothing to do and that all doors and wallets are closed to us.[60]

THE AZEF AFFAIR

The low spirits and gloom prevalent in liberal and revolutionary circles after
early 1907 were reinforced by a stunning revelation that largely discredited
terrorist tactics in the eyes of many former advocates, who as a consequence
entirely "lost their faith in themselves, in people, and in their cause."[61] This
dramatic episode was subsequently labeled the "Azef affair," after its central
personage, Evno Filipovich Azef (1869–1918), who was also known as
"Azev," "Nikolai Ivanovich," "Valentin Kuz'mich," "Tolstyi," and by a number of other aliases. "Unexampled in the annals of the Russian revolutionary
movement,"[62] the story of Azef is inseparable not only from the history of SR
terrorism, but also from the history of radicalism in general; certainly no other
controversy surrounding a single person elicited such heated debate and incan-
descence of passion in the antigovernment camp.

The son of a poor Jewish tailor, Azef first offered his services to the Police
Department in 1892, while studying engineering in Germany and enduring the
hardships of hunger and cold. His initial monthly police salary was fifty rubles,

and it steadily increased as he expanded his contacts in revolutionary circles abroad and his information became more valuable to his police superiors. After receiving his diploma in electrical engineering at Darmstadt in 1899 he returned to Russia, where he put himself at the disposal of the famous chief of the Moscow section of the Okhrana, Sergei Zubatov.[63]

Azef quickly established himself in revolutionary circles inside Russia, aiming especially to form ties with neo-Populist and terrorist groups, such as the Northern Union of Social Revolutionaries in Moscow. He became particularly close to the Union's leader, A. A. Argunov, and when in the fall of 1901 the police, acting exclusively on Azef's information, made arrests among the revolutionaries, Argunov entrusted all the affairs of the Union to Azef, giving him full credentials to represent the group abroad. In accordance with the police plan to insinuate an agent into the very heart of the empirewide organization, at the end of November 1901 Azef again left Russia to participate in negotiations for unification of the numerous socialist-revolutionary groups scattered throughout the country.[64]

These negotiations led to the formation of the Party of Socialists-Revolutionaries, in which from its earliest days Azef played a prominent role, gradually becoming intimate with such PSR leaders as Chernov, Mikhail Gots, and eventually also the foremost SR terrorist leader, Gershuni. By July of 1902 his position in the newly formed party was already so notable that his police superiors were forced to bring him to the attention of Plehve. Contrary to the Police Department's general regulations for secret agents, which limited their involvement in party activity, the minister of the interior ordered that Azef "try to penetrate into the party center and the Combat Organization."[65]

This he did with much skill. By the end of 1904 he had entered the SR Committee Abroad (Zagranichnyi Komitet), and in 1906 became a fully empowered member of the party's Central Committee. He also served as the primary link between the Central Committee and the Combat Organization, and at one point, in the autumn of 1907, its temporary head. Simultaneously, until his formal retirement from the police in the spring of 1908, Azef maintained contact with several high-level Okhrana officers, providing them firsthand information on the activities of the Central Committee and other leading organs of the PSR, as well as the plans and operations of the Combat Organization.[66] At several points his ties with the secret police weakened, and during one period, from the end of 1905 to mid-April 1906, they were temporarily disrupted altogether.[67] In general, however, it is accurate to state that his nearly fifteen-year tenure as a police agent was at that time unprecedented in length and significance. That the authorities were fully appreciative was reflected in his salary, unusually large for a police agent: at the end of Azef's service, he was receiving as much as one thousand rubles monthly.[68]

On several occasions in the course of Azef's career the revolutionaries suspected him of police connections,[69] but for a variety of reasons he always managed to escape exposure. In Germany in 1893 the radical students simply did not get around to serious investigation of local rumors regarding his police contacts, and by 1906, when leaders of the PSR received warnings from a number of sources accusing Azef of being an informer, his reputation as a revolutionary was so well established, and his position within the organization so prominent, that the SRs dismissed the warnings as attempts to slander the entire party through him.[70]

This made the position of another accuser, Vladimir Burtsev, that much more difficult. The editor of a historical journal, *The Past* (*Byloe*), and a long-standing proponent of terrorist action, Burtsev always remained an independent revolutionary and was not a formal member of the SR Party, although he stood close to it through his acquaintance with many of its leaders.[71] In May of 1908 he formally notified the PSR Central Committee that he had reason to believe Azef to be a police spy. Initially, few of the SR leaders were prepared to listen to Burtsev, but he persisted, presenting one piece of evidence after another, and eventually disclosed the testimony of a retired director of the Police Department, A. A. Lopukhin, revealing the identity of the spy within the SR Central Committee. This led the dumbfounded SRs to initiate a formal investigation, the results of which proved devastating for the party's prestige. On 26 December 1908 the PSR Central Committee was forced to go public with the case and reveal Azef's police connections. On 7 (20) January 1909 the SR leaders issued another official statement listing the terrorist acts in which Azef had allegedly played an initiating role, thereby declaring him an agent provocateur.[72]

This announcement produced a sensation, with Burtsev acquiring the title of the "Sherlock Holmes of the Russian revolution," and Azef "immediately becoming one of the most famous people in the world."[73] Members of the Combat Organization, refusing to believe in Azef's involvement with the police, perceived the press campaign against him as yet another attempt by the civilian SRs to interfere in the affairs of the fighters, with a leading *boevik*, Petr Karpovich, threatening to shoot the entire Central Committee if it dared to prosecute the terrorists' chief.[74] So scandalous was the discovery that even members of the PSR high command who heard the evidence of Azef's police connections could not fully comprehend it, and left him an opportunity to acquit himself—an opportunity that Azef promptly employed in the midst of the general confusion to save himself by changing his identity and going into hiding, spending years abroad as a fugitive from SR vengeance.[75]

The story of Evno Azef is unique not merely because the presence of this police agent at the heart of a major political party made it possible for the authorities to prevent a number of terrorist attacks, some of which, particularly those aimed at the tsar and Prime Minister Stolypin, could have radically altered the course of Russian history; it is of equal significance that the shock of his exposure was so tremendous that the PSR was unable to recover or heal the moral wound that the scandal inflicted upon it, at least until the countershock of the First World War diverted the revolutionaries' attention.[76] The "Azef affair caused the party incalculable harm,"[77] primarily because the reputation of this foremost terrorist organization in Russia was hopelessly discredited. The revolutionaries were compelled to recognize this fact even on the pages of their official organs, going so far as to say that the "SR Party does not exist as an organization . . . it is defeated and has disintegrated."[78] Despite the effort the SR leadership devoted to redirecting the attention of its membership and the general public from its own blunders by blaming the government for using illegal and criminal methods of investigation, the party leaders no longer enjoyed their former respect and prestige even among their own followers. Some of those who "suffered the most terrible moral shock of their entire life"[79] joined the so-called new Opposition consisting of members of the Paris Group of Socialists-Revolutionaries and former activists who had abandoned the PSR in large numbers in protest against the Azef affair. The findings of the specially elected SR Judicial Commission of Inquiry into the Azef Case (Sudebno-sledstvennaia Kommissiia po delu Azefa) that began its investigation in November of 1909 were hardly in favor of the SR Central Committee, whose "moral authority [had] received an irreparable blow"; its members were accused of negligence and incompetence to the point of malfeasance, and were declared responsible for "all kinds of rubbish: hierarchical arrogance [general'stvo], bureaucratism, nepotism, chasms in the PSR between leadership and rank and file, periphery and center, etc." To a certain degree, these charges were legitimate, contributing to the lack of mutual trust and the new tendency in the party no longer to exempt anyone from suspicions of corruption and even treason.[80]

Moreover, in a situation in which, in the words of one revolutionary after Azef's unmasking, "all the idols were thrown down, all values awaited their reevaluation,"[81] many party members began to question the appropriateness of terrorist tactics in general. While the initial reaction of the Central Committee was to halt all organized combat operations for an unspecified period, in part for lack of money, with individual leaders such as Rubanovich and Natanson emerging as "ardent opponents of terror at the present moment," other well-known SRs adhered to "the second type of argument [which] was marked by opposition in principle to this party method, and implied its total cessation."[82]

In contradiction of its claims that Azef was an agent provocateur,[83] the SR leadership did everything to demonstrate that "terrorism remained as pure as it had always been," since the party's combat activities were initiated not by Azef personally but by the Central Committee, while the Combat Organization, in executing death sentences, heard only the voice of the people represented by the PSR. Such arguments did little to dissuade many rank-and-file revolutionaries from the belief that they owed all their past successes to a government agent, a conviction that rendered the very principle of centralized terrorism meaningless and discredited it beyond redemption.[84] It was at this time that a growing number of leftists in the party began to resemble the Maximalists in promoting decentralization of the party's forces and greater autonomy for individual groups (including terrorist squads) within the PSR.[85] And if the SR veterans, trying to hide their panic, despair, and even tears, sought to bolster optimism among their followers by assuring them of the quick revival of the party, the younger activists were skeptical about its ability to survive the deep crisis at all. These feelings were reinforced by the apparent inability of the Central Committee to mobilize manpower and any significant material resources, or to formulate a meaningful plan of action for the future. The general mood of demoralization, depression, and extreme pessimism was particularly evident among the SR terrorist cadres.[86]

The scandal also had a profound effect on revolutionary circles outside the PSR. The party's numerous critics in the leftist camp secretly enjoyed the SR humiliation and sought to benefit by promoting their own programs and attracting would-be SR supporters to the Maximalist, anarchist, or SD organizations; many former proponents of combat methods were strengthened in their present renunciation of terrorism and centralized conspiratorial tactics in general.[87] Partly because organized political murder had lost its romantic aura in the eyes of liberal public opinion, the number of assassinations decreased dramatically after the Azef affair.

The prestige of the SR party was further damaged by the subsequent unmasking of several other government agents in leading SR circles.[88] Particularly embarrassing for the party was the case of Aleksandr Petrov (Voskresenskii), who, like the infamous Maximalist Solomon Ryss, violated the fundamental revolutionary code of ethics by offering his services to the secret police early in 1909 when he was in custody and facing hard labor for his role in operating a dynamite laboratory in Saratov. He later claimed to have done so in order to be useful to the revolution by familiarizing himself with the Okhrana's methods of investigation, but the stigma of his police connections remained troublesome for the party. In the end, realizing that all attempts to outwit his Okhrana superiors were futile, he staged a bomb explosion on 8 December 1909 that killed the head of the St. Petersburg security police, Colonel Karpov.[89]

Yet, amid the general disappointment and chaos, some steadfast advocates of extremist tactics did not give up, proclaiming that the time had come "not to 'shame and compromise,' but to 'fight and terrorize.'"[90] These radicals argued that for the revival of terrorism as a revolutionary tool it was essential to stage at least a few successful assassinations. In the upper circles of the PSR, especially abroad, along with much discussion of the need to place limitations on local terrorist attacks and expropriations, and the eventual decision at the Fifth Party Council in May 1909 to end agrarian and factory terror, there was general agreement about the need to open a new page in the history of centralized terrorism with the primary objective of assassinating the tsar.[91] It was Boris Savinkov who in 1909, acting with the sanction of the Central Committee, set out to accomplish this goal by resurrecting the Combat Organization and purifying its honor with a new terrorist campaign.[92] In the course of the following year, however, his efforts produced no results, primarily because his reputed ability to select suitable cadres seemed to have failed him: of the ten or twelve members of his group, three turned out to be police agents.[93]

Simultaneously, independent SR terrorist groups began to form abroad and in the peripheral areas throughout the empire, sometimes acting in cooperation with Maximalists. A number of leading emigré party members supported the idea of a new phase of local terror against government officials and private citizens from the bourgeois establishment, and sought to promote SR combat efforts in Russia by raising funds specifically for the purpose of terrorist enterprises, including acts of vengeance against authorities inside tsarist prisons.[94] Two such assaults took place in 1911—a 15 April attempt on the life of Vologda Prison Inspector Efimov, followed by an 18 August attack on the head of the Zerentui hard labor prison, Vysotskii, in Siberia.[95]

Revolutionaries from other parties also sought to prove that terrorist tactics were still viable. Although it was primarily the anarchists who claimed responsibility for these occasional violent acts, in 1911 PPS combatants demonstrated that they too had not renounced the practices of eliminating police informers or expropriating state property: in that year assaults on street policemen in Poland became frequent enough to cause separate discussion in the Duma.[96]

The Last Major Attack

These isolated acts could not be compared to the terrorist operations of the 1905 revolutionary era in their number, intensity, or significance. After 1908 the relatively infrequent combat ventures conducted primarily in the periphery by extremists demoralized by the implications of the Azef affair, and executed outside of any mass movement context in the now peaceful internal situation in the empire, had little impact on the country's political life. There was, however, one major exception to this trend: the assassination of Prime Minister Stolypin in Kiev on 1 September 1911 by revolutionary Dmitrii Bogrov.

In 1905–1907 the radicals made several abortive attempts on Stolypin's life, and in the postrevolutionary period many of them still considered the elimination of the hated statesman at any cost their prime objective. Stolypin's efforts to strengthen the traditional order through a series of socioeconomic reforms made him a foe of the revolutionaries, and his famous challenge to the extremists and their sympathizers from the Duma floor in 1906, "You will not intimidate us" (*ne zapugaete*), accompanied by his implementation of severe measures intended to crush the revolution, elevated him to the status of an archenemy.[97] Yet the significance of the final sensational terrorist act executed under the old regime lies not only in the choice of the target—probably the most talented Russian minister since the death of the outstanding nineteenth-century reformer Alexander Speransky—but also in the fact that its perpetrator can legitimately be included in the category of terrorists of the new type.

Bogrov, a twenty-four-year-old attorney's assistant, came from a wealthy and largely assimilated Jewish family. His father, although not a formal member of the Kadet Party, stood close to its left wing in his political convictions. By the age of fifteen the younger Bogrov had established contacts among radical gymnasium students, and after flirting for a while with socialist ideas, in 1906 became a member of an anarchist-communist group in Kiev, even though he occasionally called himself an anarchist-individualist. Anarchism was the logical choice of ideological affiliation for this man, who had always resented control by any formal organization, allowing no outside restrictions on his thinking and behavior. "I am my own party" (*ia sam sebe partiia*), the teenage Bogrov once stated, and to his last days he professed the belief that a revolutionary could successfully operate alone, without any interference and guidance from a party leadership.[98]

This stand conveniently corresponded to his ethical position, described by a sympathetic friend: "He always laughed at 'good' and 'bad.' Despising conventional morals, he developed his own, whimsical and not always comprehensible."[99] Perhaps a more objective observer would classify his outlook as cynical, a judgment supported by the fact that, ideological inclinations notwithstanding, in 1907 he offered his services to the Kiev Okhrana, which he supplied with information leading to the apprehension of his SR and Maximalist friends until late 1910. Although Bogrov attributed his behavior to disappointment in his comrades, who, he argued, "for the most part pursued strictly criminal goals," it was in part financial need that drove him to become an agent. While Dmitrii, according to his brother, had been coddled by their parents to the point that he "did not know the meaning of refusal in any of his more or less reasonable wishes," he frequently ran out of money and needed his police salary of 100–150 rubles each month to support his one irresistible passion: gambling.[100] Apparently this did not seem to Bogrov to run counter to his past revolutionary activities; after all, he did claim to have his own logic, perhaps justifying his behavior by the need to know the enemy from the inside. Moreover, "Why not introduce yourself to the lion and tickle his whiskers? Another exciting game, a gamble for higher stakes."[101]

Bogrov's comrades, who had initially suspected him of embezzling party funds, were convinced of his police connections by the summer of 1911. On 16 August a revolutionary paid Bogrov a visit and informed him that the radicals intended to make a public announcement of his treason and kill him soon thereafter. The messenger then made a proposition not uncommon among terrorists after the era of the People's Will: Bogrov could salvage his life and reputation by committing a terrorist act against one of his official superiors. The radicals gave him until 5 September to plan his attack, and suggested Col. N. N. Kuliabko, chief of the Kiev Okhrana, as an appropriate target. Bogrov rejected this suggestion, however, apparently regarding Kuliabko as too insignificant. He considered assassinating Nicholas II, who was expected to pay a ceremonial visit to Kiev in the near future, but changed his mind for fear of precipitating anti-Jewish violence. Eventually, Bogrov made up his mind to kill Stolypin, whom he had always claimed to hate passionately as the "most intelligent and talented . . . the most threatening enemy" and, in his opinion, the source of all evil in Russia.[102]

To facilitate his task, Bogrov made use of his police connections, and notified Kuliabko of a fictional terrorist plot against Stolypin and Minister of Education L. A. Kasso, both due in Kiev at the same time as the tsar. Kuliabko, concerned primarily with the safety of the monarch and having no reason to suspect his apparently reliable agent of disinformation or criminal intent, did nothing to prevent Bogrov from following Stolypin's every movement; on two occasions he was able to come very near to the prime minister, although not close enough for a clear shot. Finally, anxious to exploit what seemed to him his final opportunity to approach Stolypin, on 1 September Bogrov threw caution aside and demanded from Kuliabko a ticket for that evening's opera performance at the Municipal Theater—a ticket otherwise impossible to obtain because of the elaborate security arrangements surrounding the tsar and his ministers. Kuliabko complied, and Bogrov, exhausted by nervous anticipation, arrived at the theater an hour before the start of Rimskii-Korsakov's *Tale of Tsar Saltan.*

During the second intermission two shots, barely audible in the crowded theater, were followed by the piercing screams of spectators seated near Stolypin, plunging everyone present into stupefied silence. All eyes were fixed on the mortally wounded prime minister, who, after the initial shock,

> with slow and sure motions put his service hat and gloves on the barrier, unbuttoned the tunic, and seeing the waistcoat thick with blood, waved his hand as if saying, "It is finished!" He then sank into a chair and clearly and distinctly . . . said, "I am happy to die for the Tsar." Seeing the tsar enter the loge and stand in front, he lifted his hands, making signs for him to withdraw. But the tsar did not move . . . [and Stolypin], viewed by all, blessed him with a broad sign of the cross.

Bogrov had been quite close to Stolypin when he fired his pistol, partly because of the limitations of his weapon, and partly because of his own weak eyesight. In the crowded theater, surrounded by witnesses and a panicked crowd, and with many military officers present, as well as fifteen state officials and ninety-two security agents, he had no real hope of escaping and was apprehended almost immediately. Stolypin died in the hospital on 5 September. Four days later a military court sentenced Bogrov to death, and during the night of 10–11 September he was hanged.[103]

Regardless of his professed political principles, this terrorist of the new type planned and performed Stolypin's assassination alone and for entirely personal reasons. After the ultimatum from his former comrades, he faced the choice of a shameful death at the hands of the revolutionaries as an unscrupulous traitor, or capital punishment at the hands of the tsarist government for a deed that would clear his stained reputation, as well as leave his name in the annals of history as a martyr and hero who dared to take up arms against the embodiment of the traditional order in Russia. It was not difficult for Bogrov to resolve this dilemma. However, his decision does not explain his unwillingness to pursue a third alternative, that is, to try to stay alive, perhaps by following Azef's example and escaping into hiding.

Choosing and planning for escape and the subsequent life of a fugitive requires a strong will to live and substantial energy, along with adequate material resources. Although the resources were probably available in Bogrov's case through his family, there is reason to suspect that he lacked the desire to continue living. Still a young man, he left an impression on those close to him of a bitterly disillusioned and cynical old person whose life was meaningless and empty; he seemed to anticipate nothing but long years of empty existence approaching an equally meaningless death. His friends were struck by the fact that "he deliberately lived a dissipated life" that "was not worth dragging out," and also by his "complete dissatisfaction with his bourgeois life-style, with his legal work, with the way he passed his time." A man characterized by his radical comrades as "internally dismal and autumnal," and who assessed his future, as Bogrov did, as "nothing but an endless number of [meat] cutlets,"[104] admitting feeling "depressed, bored and . . . lonely," would seem unlikely to exert a great deal of energy to preserve such an existence. One acquaintance indeed sensed suicidal tendencies in his personality, and the well-known publicist A. A. Izgoev wrote in retrospect, "It is quite understandable that the thought could occur to a compromised 'revolutionary-Okhrana agent' to end his life by some outstanding terrorist act. Such was the psychology of . . . Bogrov."[105]

It is possible to go even further and suggest that for Bogrov, as for a number of other extremists, committing a major terrorist act under circumstances that guaranteed apprehension and execution, was a subliminal form of suicide. Admittedly disinterested in his senseless life,[106] but perhaps wishing to avoid an equally senseless self-inflicted death, Bogrov was predisposed to seize the opportunity offered by his dilemma to lend a rational justification to the suicidal tendencies in his personality. He clearly planned and executed the act knowing that he would die as a result.[107] With the "passionate personality of a gambler, he could not live by routine and quietly; he always sought intense sensations . . . and striking experiences in everything," including this last sensational political murder that led directly and inevitably to his own death.[108]

19. Mariia Spiridonova in prison

20. Dmitrii Bogrov

The Final Years

Stolypin's assassination was the last major strike of the new type of terrorist into the very heart of the contemporary political order. Amid the general jubilation in leftist circles in Russia and abroad over the death of "the official murderer," "the hangman," "the despot," and "the vile creature,"[109] Bogrov's police connections and questionable character quickly became public knowledge, provoking a long-standing controversy debating whether leading Okhrana officials were behind the plot to assassinate Stolypin, a contention not supported by the available sources. While the primary impact of the act was to discredit conspiratorial tactics further,[110] minor incidents of terror continued in the years preceding the outbreak of the First World War. According to Police Department figures, the year 1912 witnessed 82 acts of revolutionary terrorism in the empire, including 22 in the Caucasus, 13 in Poland, and 9 in Siberia.[111] These incidents were unrelated to any mass sociopolitical unrest in the country, which manifested itself primarily in the form of labor disturbances prior to 1914.

Although lacking the means to revive widespread intensive terror, most proponents of revolutionary extremism never renounced political assassination on principle, and on the contrary continuously developed plans for future combat operations. This was true especially of the PSR, whose activists in Russia, according to a somewhat exaggerated police report, were in their hearts all fervid terrorists.[112] Abroad, the PSR leadership managed to raise considerable funds for future political assassinations, and just a few days after Stolypin's murder, police officials in St. Petersburg received information that a group of rank-and-file SRs in Paris was demanding that the Central Committee "immediately organize terror in Russia," having drawn up a list of suitable targets among the highest officials in the civil and military administration.[113]

By the summer of 1912 many SRs, especially among the rightists in the so-called Liquidators group, had renounced the old theoretical justifications of terrorism as anachronistic and utopian. They reached this conclusion, heretical to SR ideology, partly as a result of the Azef affair, and partly because of Savinkov's failures, both as an organizer of central terror in 1909–1910, and in his relations with the Central Committee thereafter. Despite this opposition, however, certain SR leaders reportedly made plans to initiate a new phase of terrorist activity for the purpose of sabotaging the elections to the Fourth Duma. Simultaneously, the Central Committee initiated a systematic proterrorist campaign on the pages of *Znamia Truda* designed to recruit new *boevik* cadres among the young party activists. In 1913, in accordance with a decision made at their Vyborg conference in May reaffirming the old tactical terrorist methods of the party, the SRs attempted to organize a small combat detachment for the purpose of finally realizing their long-standing goal of regicide.

At the same time, they contemplated political assassinations of several high-ranking Russian officials.[114]

As before, the SRs did not wish to confine themselves to extremist violence within the empire's borders, and so a group of SRs in Paris advocated terrorist acts outside of Russia, calling for particularly merciless treatment of government informers. Suspects were to be interrogated with pistols held to their heads, and shot at the moment their police connections were confirmed.[115] Chernov also urged his followers to take full advantage of scientific progress in military technology, and according to police evidence a number of SR leaders secretly discussed the possibility of using aircraft in terrorist operations. Their most sensational proposal was an aerial attack to be staged during festivities honoring the three hundredth anniversary of the Romanov dynasty.[116]

Despite these preparations, the party remained demoralized and splintered, and could claim no practical combat successes. It proved difficult for the central leadership to recruit either trustworthy *boeviki* or capable combat commanders, and so most of the party's central terrorist efforts were de facto left to such shady and unstable individuals as Savinkov's unreliable, alcoholic associate, Boris Bartol'd, but his attempts to resurrect the Combat Organization era proved of no avail.[117] Local SR groups in Russia and isolated individuals abroad still refused to acknowledge the stalemate in combat practices, and eagerly seized any opportunity to demonstrate the viability of terror as a political tactic. Relentless *boevik* Petr Rukhlovskii urged his party superiors to increase the organizations's revenues by allowing him to use his old contacts in the Urals and resume his former occupation: the expropriation of state funds.[118] A group of SRs in Penza, intent on developing an agenda to bring them closer to the anarchists, attempted to organize large-scale expropriations in their city, and in 1914 dispatched a dozen activists to St. Petersburg for the same purpose.[119]

Representatives of other Russian political organizations also discussed and occasionally implemented plans for combat operations. After escaping from prison, the Bolshevik Kamo returned to Russia in 1912 "to procure money for the Party, which was at that time in considerable straits." After consulting with Krasin in Moscow, Kamo and the survivors of his old Caucasian terrorist squad attempted on 24 September to repeat the 1907 success of the Tiflis expropriation by staging a major robbery on the Kodzhorskii road near that city. The robbery failed because of successful defense efforts by the police.[120] After 1911, other less well-known SDs also became involved in combat enterprises, as did members of a few obscure extremist societies. One such group based in France whose members called themselves free socialists (*vol'nye sotsialisty*) appealed to the SR leaders abroad for financial assistance in organizing terrorist acts against several Russian ministers.[121] In addition, ordinary citizens living in the Russian Empire still periodically received threatening letters from individuals claiming to represent obscure revolutionary groups abroad involved in various shady enterprises.

The anarchists in Russia and beyond its borders never gave up the practice of executing anyone accused of police connections. Moreover, some anarchists and obscure extremists occasionally offered their services to the PSR as assassins, although the party usually rejected these offers for fear of being compromised.[122] In 1912, however, a number of anarchists joined with SRs in St. Petersburg for consorted terrorist operations against representatives of the central administration, including Minister of Education Kasso and the tsar himself.[123] And in the following year, members of at least one isolated anarchist group in Paris departed for Russia with the intention of carrying out terrorist acts.[124] In remote areas such as central and eastern Siberia, Zabaikal'e and the Far East, anarchists and other political exiles continued to associate with criminal fugitives. They formed gangs for the purpose of plundering villages and small towns, an activity that intensified in these areas in 1912–1913, and operated under such straightforward names as the Party of Robbers (partiia Grabitelei).[125]

Certain radical nationalist organizations also sought to resurrect terrorist practices, with the Polish Socialists claiming that their efforts were "for the sake of prestige," and "to demonstrate to the proletariat the strength and might of the party." These claims encouraged individual acts of vengeance and the expropriation of state property, including assaults on mail trains, with some degree of success. In addition, the PPS maintained a combat school in L'vov, where in collaboration with militant nationalists cadres were prepared for the future struggle against Russian domination; in May of 1912 the school graduated 25 skilled new *boeviki*.[126] In the same month a joint conference was held in L'vov of the RSDRP, Prawica, Lewica, and two obscure Polish organizations—the Revolutionaries-Avengers Group (Gruppa revoliutsionerov-mstitelei), and the Union of Active Struggle (Soiuz aktivnoi bor'by—a joint SR-anarchist group). A secret resolution was adopted to initiate a series of large-scale expropriations, with the proceeds to be divided among the parties present. The Revolutionaries-Avengers Group took this resolution especially seriously, targeting both state and private assets.[127]

Similarly, in the years leading up to the First World War Latvian revolutionaries reportedly entertained plans for terrorist operations targeting in particular participants in earlier punitive tsarist military expeditions in the region, in one instance planning an attack on the life of the Empress during her travels in England in 1913. In Finland, representatives of the Party of Active Resistance resolved in 1912 to remove high-ranking pro-Russian officials by any means possible, including direct violence. Finally, as late as 1914 the Armenian Dashnaktsutiun, by that time directing its primary efforts against the Turkish authorities, continued to regard terror and extortion in Russia as appropriate fund-raising methods.[128]

Although the outbreak of the First World War evoked a rise in patriotic sentiments even among the Russian revolutionaries, some of whom went so far as to support the imperial government's cause for the duration of the international conflict, the war came to be perceived by the leftists in the radical camp as a beneficial development bound to weaken the autocracy; they therefore did not abandon their belief in the expediency of extremist tactics even during the hostilities. A number of SR extremists proceeded with their experiments in new bombs and explosives, and actively sought opportunities to incorporate recent developments in aviation into terrorist acts.[129] The SRs planned ahead as well, and organized *boeviki* for individual and mass terrorist attacks, "in order to be prepared for the moment the war ended."[130]

The anarchists also continued practical preparations for violent acts in the midst of the European calamity, quickly adapting to the altered political and international circumstances that presented new opportunities for the radical cause.[131] According to police sources, late in 1915 Russian Anarchists-Communists in America secretly received the sum of ten thousand dollars from German officials and accepted a commission to blow up the headquarters of Russia's chief military emissaries in the United States. While some Russian anarchists opposed the undertaking, others were able to recruit American and Italian comrades to form an international terrorist unit. The activities of this particular group, however, never resulted in anything beyond the initial planning of various acts directed against Russia's military establishment and its representatives abroad.[132]

At the same time, occasional obscure semicriminal extremist groups, including one led by Bessarabian *ataman* Grigorii Kotovskii, reemerged in the periphery to terrorize landlords and other wealthy citizens.[133] In the Caucasus, where juvenile participation in violence was a well-established tradition, a band known as the Revolutionary Union of Kutais Students (Revoliutsionnyi Soiuz uchashchikhsia goroda Kutaisa) operated in 1912, and one of its members, Iona Lorkipanidze, was responsible for shooting and wounding the principals of the city's classical gymnasium and a high school.[134] Terrorism was very much alive in Armenia as well, where on 8 July 1916 individuals claiming to represent the nonexistent Erevan Terrorist Organ (Erevanskii terroristicheskii organ) posted handwritten announcements in various parts of the city containing threats against store owners who raised the prices of basic consumer goods.[135] Even in Finland several local terrorists were arrested in September 1916 in the town of Iuviaskiula and accused of conspiring to assassinate the governor of Uleaborg.[136] That same year, Russian Army Chief of Staff General M. V. Alekseev received an anonymous letter threatening Nicholas II with the fate of his late uncle, the Grand Duke Sergei Aleksandrovich, and also promising to "do away with his son, Aleksei [the twelve-year-old tsarevich], separately."[137]

With terrorism in Russia thus far from Trotsky's description of it as the "property of history" at this point,[138] preparations for violence continued until the new revolution in February 1917, along with occasional, if infrequent, terrorist acts, such as assassinations of prison officials,[139] and the murder of a

21. (*Top*) Burned remains of a Revolutionaries-Avengers hideout in Lodz raided by police on 3 April 1911. The fire was set by the revolutionaries. (*Bottom*) Burned bodies of several Revolutionaries-Avengers.

provocateur in the town of Zlatoust in the spring of 1916, an incident involving Bolsheviks.[140] The participation of radical SDs in this isolated act was not altogether an accident, for, ironically, it was by then the Bolshevik faction of the RSDRP that was particularly concerned with the question of terror. Reasserting his long-standing position on revolutionary terrorism, Lenin affirmed in a 25 October 1916 letter to a fellow socialist: "We are *not at all against* political murder," but "individual terrorist activities can and must be beneficial only in direct immediate connection with the mass movement."[141]

Lenin was prepared to modify his theoretical principles once again, however, when he deemed it necessary for practical results and did so in December 1916, two months prior to the outbreak of the mass disturbances that were destined to end Russian imperial history. In response to an inquiry from the Bolsheviks in Petrograd regarding the official party viewpoint vis-à-vis the implementation of terror, Lenin related his personal opinion: at that historical moment terrorist activities were permissible. The only condition was that in

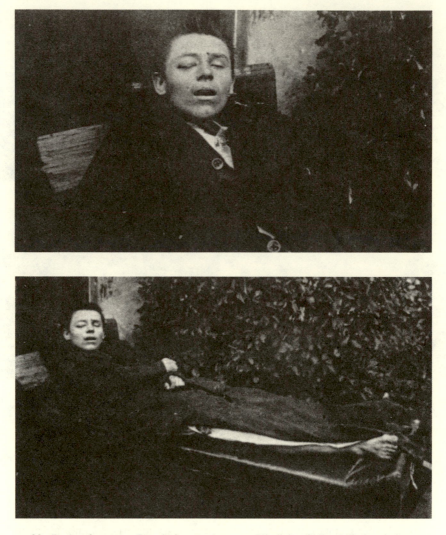

22. Body of a young Revolutionary-Avenger, Vladislav Skiba, killed resisting arrest

the eyes of the public, the initiative for the acts was to come from individual party members and smaller Bolshevik groups in Russia, with no major organizations taking responsibility for the deeds. To this recommendation Lenin added that he hoped to be able to convince the entire Central Committee abroad of the expediency of his stand.[142] Time itself, however, removed the issue of terrorism from the immediate agendas of the Bolshevik and the other political parties, as the tempestuous developments of February 1917 dictated new objectives and concerns for all Russian revolutionaries.

EPILOGUE

ANALYSIS OF TERRORIST ACTIVITY in the last two decades of the Russian imperial regime produces a number of revealing conclusions about the antigovernment movement, the crisis of 1905–1907, the ability of the tsarist administration to defend itself against internal enemies seeking its immediate demise, and the political culture in prerevolutionary Russia. Examination of the new type of terrorism allows a reevaluation of the conventional view of this generation of Russian extremists, who have not traditionally been presented in historiography as fundamentally different from their nineteenth-century predecessors. One of the key objectives of this study has been to demonstrate that there was indeed a new breed of radical on the Russian political scene at the beginning of the twentieth century, and that these "terrorists of a new type," despite their distinctive national and local characteristics, were the forerunners of the modern extremists in Europe and the rest of the world who in recent decades have caused political violence to assume "the proportions of a global epidemic."[1] The perspective gained from placing early twentieth-century Russian terrorism into its proper historical and global context, taking the uniqueness of the Russian situation into account but not overstating it, is essential for a complete understanding of the phenomenon.

The existing statistics on terrorism in Russia illustrate that contrary to the characteristic assertions of Marxist and neo-Marxist scholars, the mass violence committed by workers, peasants, soldiers, sailors, and students was not the only, or indeed even the most prominent feature, of the Russian revolutionary upheaval. While it is essential to study and understand these movements, it would be misleading to neglect the sudden intensification of individual terrorist activity, since the latter phenomenon did as much as the former, if not more, to destabilize the tsarist regime politically and psychologically, particularly in the post-1905 period.

The terrorists hastened the downfall of the tsarist regime not only by assassinating prominent state leaders, but also by killing thousands of capable lower-level civil and military officials. The officials who did not themselves become targets of terrorist attacks continuously lived in fear for their lives and the lives of their families—a fear that undoubtedly had an adverse effect on both their attitudes and the way they performed their official duties. To a large extent, the revolutionaries succeeded in breaking the spine of Russian bureaucracy, wounding it both physically and in spirit, and in this way contributed to its general paralysis during the final crisis of the imperial regime in March of 1917. The power of the extremist or tiny radical minority to influence politics, often underrated but very much in evidence in subsequent events of the twentieth century, thus was already at work in Russia at the time.

In post-1905 Russia, terror was no longer restricted to a particular conspiratorial society or even an entire ideological movement. No matter what the rhetorical statements of the different parties might have been, in practice this tactic became a tool used to some degree by all socialist and anarchist organizations in the Russian revolutionary camp. Similarly, the new terrorists exhibited a tendency to slacken their ties with their mother organizations for the sake of the autonomy and uncontrolled activities of a close-knit militant group dominated by a sense of conspiracy and alienation not only from bourgeois society, but also from their civilian fellow party members. Many of them also exhibited a clear lack of interest in even the most fundamental aspects of revolutionary dogma, and were inclined to sacrifice ideology to immediate practical objectives. This indifference to theory is further illustrated by the willingness of representatives of the leftist parties to take part in combat operations as a united front, setting aside ideological or programmatic disputes. Similar interparty connections and cooperation have been noted throughout the twentieth century among terrorists of diverse ideological causes worldwide, united in pragmatic solidarity like their Russian predecessors by their common reliance upon violence to achieve their goals.

In many cases members of a single terrorist group, including the most cohesive of them, the Combat Organization of the PSR, were not united by even an approximately similar set of ideological principles. Their philosophical outlooks ranged from Christian ethics to anarchist fascination with destruction, with a strong component of cynicism common. Not a few of these new radicals seemed to doubt the very legitimacy and appropriateness of their final goal in the struggle—the liberation of the toilers from political and economic oppression—betraying at times total indifference to the masses. A consequence of their complete absorption in clandestine preparations for terrorist operations, and their isolation from the mainstream of their parties' cadres and ideological and nonmilitant activities, was that the combatants lost all perspective and any general sense of higher purpose, neglecting the question of an ultimate justification for their deeds. In short, for the new type of *boevik*, who concentrated his entire attention on an immediate combat task, a successful terrorist act was transformed from a means into a final and self-evident end, with his victims completely depersonalized as mere symbols of a hated reality. Significantly, these features of the new Russian terrorism not only rendered its participants different from most of their forerunners in the Russian revolutionary movement, but also placed them in the avant-garde of the twentieth-century terrorism practiced by their successors of various nationalities throughout the world. The indiscriminate use of violence, so ubiquitous in the prerevolutionary period in Russia, spread in the following decades far beyond the empire's borders to create a situation in which "victims are unable to do anything to avoid their injury or destruction, because the terrorist has his own code of values by which he judges whom to hurt. The conventions of war—the rights of neutrals, noncombatants, hostages, prisoners of war—have no standing in the eyes of the terrorist. Anyone is fair game."[2]

This observation is directly linked to the study's attempt to fill a critical gap in the history of the Russian radical movement, that is, the failure of most scholarly works to question the claims of the radicals about the purity of their ranks, and to recognize that the "seamy side" of the revolution was as much in evidence in early twentieth-century Russia as it has subsequently become in other countries. Without denigrating the selfless idealism and sincere revolutionary convictions of many extremists, this book seeks to provide illustrations for the findings of other scholars who have stressed the nonpolitical incentives of combatants joining terrorist organizations: "to belong to a group, to acquire social status and reputation, to find comradeship or excitement, or to gain material benefits."[3] An awareness of such aspects of the new type of terror as the involvement of common criminals and psychologically unstable individuals in the liberation struggle, and the recruitment of adolescents and children for combat purposes, contributes to a more balanced picture of the antiestablishment movements in Russia and elsewhere.

The violence so notable in the tsarist empire early in the twentieth century was not an exclusively Russian phenomenon, for episodes of politically motivated bloodshed also occurred in other countries in those years, as is demonstrated by the international cooperation among terrorists. It is quite true, however, that while isolated individuals committed occasional political assassinations in Western and Central Europe, India, and the United States, nowhere between the turn of the century and the outbreak of World War I were terrorist practices so widespread as in tsarist Russia.

Placing this phenomenon of extensive violence in the broader temporal perspective of Russian history, it appears appropriate to attribute it at least in part to the social underdevelopment of a country that until the turn of the century "lacked the basic preconditions for organized collective social protest on any scale." Neither the peasants, despite their spontaneous and short-lived unrest (motivated nearly exclusively by the narrow agenda of land ownership), nor the numerically insignificant and psychologically uprooted urban proletariat, nor the weak and largely indifferent middle class could serve as a cohesive social stratum capable of promoting such a protest.[4] The intelligentsia, alienated from the autocratic state and deprived of support from any broad segment of society, was sufficiently frustrated to turn to radicalism, rendering itself incapable of contributing to the orderly development of the country's political culture by helping to correct one of tsarist Russia's fundamental flaws—the absence of a strong liberal tradition.

This deficiency becomes particularly evident in consideration of the benevolent attitude toward and indirect encouragement of revolutionary terrorism by the Kadet Party, which was part of the united antigovernment front in spirit, if not in action. Until 1917, Russian liberalism tended not to recognize the existence of any enemies in the radical camp, and therefore must be placed much further to the left than what came to be perceived as its proper place in the political center in Western Europe;[5] the Kadets, contributing to the radicalization of the political process, must then be regarded as revolutionaries rather than liberals in the traditional sense of the word. The tragedy of Russian politics was that there was no substantial true liberal movement to take the place of the Kadet Party at the center of the political spectrum, to soften the revolutionary passions and stand firmly behind a legal order based on modern judicial and legislative norms.

Unable to bring the moderates to its side or to provide a nonviolent political outlet for those who took the terrorist path, the imperial government found itself compelled to use sheer force to eliminate a problem that by 1905 was clearly out of control. However, even direct military action against the revolutionaries was only partially successful, and the traditional assumption that the government was able to restore tranquility and order by the end of 1907 does not correspond fully with the facts. Although subsiding, the enormous wave of terrorism continued to sweep over Russia well into 1910. Indeed, even in the following years, including the years of the First World War when homemade bombs no longer exploded in the streets of Russian cities and government employees no longer fell victim to extremists' bullets, the authorities could hardly claim victory over the terrorists, for representatives of the various radical left-wing organizations, far from renouncing terror, never ceased to develop plans to revive this tactic, right up to the outbreak of revolution in February of 1917.

The analysis of terrorism in Russia allows an assessment of the relative stability of the tsarist regime in the face of the extremists' efforts to shake the establishment. The Russian example confirms that terrorist practices occur with increasing frequency and intensity in societies where peaceful change is an option. "Regimes willing to use unlimited coercion and which dominate access to the mass media are ones which rarely suffer terrorist episodes," and this helps explain the passivity of the experienced Russian terrorists reluctant after October 1917 to fight Bolshevik rule. In the democracies, weak authoritarian or relatively open societies, on the other hand, terrorism apparently takes root and thrives.[6]

For years scholars have debated whether it was the willingness of the tsarist authorities to introduce political reforms that drove the alienated and frustrated opponents of autocratic rule to terror, or, conversely, the terrorists who diverted a government already heading for change to political stagnation and repression. While both approaches are only partially defensible by themselves, they are mutually complementary, and if history were to seek a guilty party in 1905 Russia, it would have to convict both sides. For although there is no doubt that the assassinations and expropriations did provoke the official repressions, it is also true that the very first terrorist gunshots in the initial years of the twentieth century were clear indicators of the generally unhealthy state of Russian political life. And despite the fact that during the entire decade the government treated revolutionary terrorism as one of its most pressing problems, the autocracy failed to grasp the essence of what these indicators were really suggesting. That fatal error contributed to the revolution that ultimately swept the traditional order away, even as it struggled against the symptoms of the deadly disease rather than striving to eliminate its deeper causes.

Radicalism in the last decade of the Russian imperial order, although temporarily forced underground, was not defeated in principle; it survived as an ultimate solution to the country's problems to a large extent because the "autocracy, with its policy of hesitant ruthlessness—either too harsh or not harsh enough," merely angered society without being capable of liquidating the opposition.[7] In spite of a brief period of temporary reconciliation during the earliest phase of the First World War, the deep rift between government and society—a rift that had already evolved into a long-standing tradition in Russia—never disappeared. Permanently dissatisfied with the government's socioeconomic, educational, and military reforms, and always resentful of its stubborn reluctance to grant political concessions, the Russian revolutionary opposition still awaited an opportunity for open expression. As would also be true in other countries, this could only help to prepare the extremists for the resumption of violence.

In evaluating the long-term consequences of terror in the early years of the twentieth century, it is critical to recognize that the phenomenon produced an entire generation of new revolutionary cadres, radicals of an entirely new type, who knew how to shed blood and did so much more easily than their predecessors. In the fateful year 1917 this readiness for violence proved most useful in eliminating all real and potential opposition to the revolution. Just prior to the outbreak of the revolutionary disturbances in Petrograd, from the floor of the Fourth State Duma on 27 February, Aleksandr Kerensky publicly advocated the removal of the tsar by terrorist methods—a measure he had reportedly proposed during the 1905 crisis as well.[8] More significantly, following the Bolshevik takeover in October, numerous practitioners of terror found themselves employing their skills in political murder and coercion, their actions demonstrating a certain continuity in the Russian extremist tradition.

Many former terrorists in the years after 1917 found themselves engaged in nonpolitical and strictly bourgeois occupations. A notable example is SR Petr Rutenberg, who engineered the assassination of Father Gapon in 1906, and later emigrated to Palestine and became a distinguished industrialist there, founding an electric company.[9] Others, however, such as Viacheslav Malyshev, a veteran of the PSR Northern Flying Combat Detachment, although involved in peaceable professions, remained terrorists in their hearts. After fighting in the civil war against the Bolsheviks, Malyshev emigrated to Jerusalem and became a monk. In 1949, as an archimandrite and dean of St. Nicholas Russian Orthodox Church in Teheran, he wrote a letter to Chernov, his former party chief (then residing in New York), in which he compared himself to "an old army horse that has heard the sound of a military trumpet," and proposed to resume, "with God's help," direct political action against the Bolsheviks, perhaps via the Soviet-Iranian border.[10] Still, with the exception of a few scattered attempts on the lives of prominent Soviet leaders, including the wounding of Lenin in August of 1918, the terrorists who had fought against the tsarist government by means of political assassination were reluctant to use this tactic against their former comrades in the extremist faction of the RSDRP, partly because they were still not entirely free of the feeling of solidarity in the revolutionary ranks. The most notable exception to this was Boris Savinkov, who proved as willing to risk his life in combat against the Bolsheviks during the Civil War as he had been during the struggle against the autocracy in 1905.

On the other hand, a surprisingly large number of the participants in terrorist practices under the tsarist regime remained in Russia after the Bolshevik takeover and involved themselves in consolidating the Soviet state by promoting Lenin's policy of "red terror." For many professional extremists whose primary occupation before 1917 was bloodletting, the revolution presented an opportunity to return from their places of imprisonment or foreign exile and apply themselves once again to what they did best. After the Bolshevik takeover they joined and often led such organs of state-perpetrated terrorism as the provincial and district sections of the infamous Cheka, headed in the early days of Soviet rule by "Iron Feliks" Dzerzhinsky, who had reportedly been treated a decade before for a mental illness referred to as "circular psychosis," and his deputies Martyn Latsis and Mikhail Kedrov, all previously involved in extremist practices.[11] Former terrorists also worked in the revolutionary tribunals, and after 1922 in the repressive organs of the GPU (Gosudarstvennoe politicheskoe upravlenie or State Political Administration). Significantly, Bolsheviks were not the only former terrorists contributing to Soviet red terror. Other Social Democrats, as well as former Maximalists, Left Socialists-Revolutionaries, and anarchists, still considering all revolutionaries to be part of one united front, also offered their services to the repressive machinery of the Bolshevik-controlled state.[12]

The Soviet regime, as it revealed itself in the months after the Bolshevik takeover, was indeed founded on and owed a great deal to terrorist pathology. It was in the Urals, where in 1905 Bolshevik terrorist activities had been especially widespread, that Lenin's followers were most successful in reassembling their old combat cadres after 1917.[13] Several combatants who had proven their loyalty and zeal in Bolshevik expropriations in the area during the first Russian revolution were charged with tasks regarded as crucial by the new Soviet leaders. A. Miasnikov, who had become mentally unbalanced while serving a term at hard labor for his combat activities in 1905–1907, was a member of the Cheka in 1918, and in June of that year was personally responsible for the murder of Grand Duke Mikhail Aleksandrovich Romanov.[14] Former *boevik* Konstantin Miachin (V. V. Iakovlev) escorted the family of Nicholas II from Tobol'sk to Ekaterinburg in 1918, where they were subsequently executed on orders from Moscow.[15] Petr Ermakov, another combatant active in 1905–1907, was a member of the three-man firing squad that massacred Nicholas II, his wife Alexandra, their five children, a valet, cook, parlormaid, and Eugene Botkin—the family doctor, on 16 July 1918. A fanatical revolutionary, Ermakov later claimed to have shot and killed the tsarina, Doctor Botkin, and the cook, using his mauser.[16] It is now established that the secret directive to murder the imperial family in Ekaterinburg was issued by Lenin, head of the Sovnarkom (Sovet narodnykh Kommissarov, or Council of People's Commissars), and Sverdlov, chairman of the Central Executive Committee. Under the tsarist regime, the former had been an ardent proponent of the Bolsheviks' combat enterprises, and the latter had taken active part in these violent practices.

In various regions of Soviet Russia, Communists implementing the policy of red terror showed themselves to be true representatives of the seamy side of the revolution, echoing the behavior of the 1905–1907 activists. Unrestricted violence was used by these underlings to intimidate real and alleged counterrevolutionaries, as well as the peaceful populations of remote areas. Mass murder, robbery, rape, beatings, and torture were common; heavy drinking, drug use, and startling sadism were rampant within the Cheka, the tribunals, the people's militia, the Red Army, and among local Soviet government appointees, leading Bolshevik party leaders frequently to classify their subordinates as bandits. "Red banditry," whose practitioners included individual Bolsheviks, peripheral party cells, and even entire organizations operating beyond the control of the central leadership, and sometimes in direct confrontation with it, swept across entire districts in the initial years of Soviet rule.[17]

There were times when the survival of the Soviet state depended upon the terrorist measures previously mastered by its founders. On 17 November 1917, immediately following the Bolshevik takeover, the State Bank in Petrograd refused to recognize the Sovnarkom as a legitimate authority or to allow it access to government funds. With the new administration facing a desperate financial situation, V. R. Menzhinskii, Commissar of Finance, appeared at the bank in person and with the help of his guards forced the employees to open the vaults, from which he removed five million rubles. Menzhinskii slipped the money into a velvet bag, which he "triumphantly deposited on Lenin's desk. The whole operation resembled a bank holdup,"[18] carried out in the style of prerevolutionary Bolshevik expropriations.

A number of the founders and leading figures of the Soviet state previously involved in extremist practices continued them in modified forms after 1917. Kotovskii, who had terrorized Bessarabia earlier in the century, became an equally legendary commander of a Bolshevik cavalry division during the Russian civil war, while Mikhail Frunze, who had served time in a tsarist prison for a terrorist act in 1907, found himself Commissar of War in the Soviet republic. Kamo, that "artist of the revolution," as Gor'ky once called him, returned to the Caucasus in the fall of 1918 to take part in Cheka activities in Baku, and in the summer of 1919 was charged by the Bolshevik Central Committee with the formation of a terrorist group to be sent into the territory occupied by the forces of General A. I. Denikin. While preparing for this operation, Kamo finally had a chance to implement one of his most cherished ideas, the 1911 scheme of testing the loyalty of his cadres by fear and torture. During a training exercise, the prospective members of his terrorist group were attacked, taken captive, and brutally interrogated by a group they assumed to be a band of White soldiers, but who in reality were Kamo's assistants in disguise wearing enemy epaulets. The captors flogged their prisoners and staged fake hangings, and a number of the Bolsheviks broke under the torture, thus justifying in Kamo's eyes his method of separating the "real Communists" from the cowards.[19]

Other prominent Bolsheviks made the transition from prerevolutionary terrorism to positions of authority under the Soviet regime. Leonid Krasin, who bore major responsibility for the party's combat activities prior to 1917, later became the official Soviet diplomatic representative in London. Nikolai Burenin, Krasin's right-hand man in the Combat Technical Group, became involved in various financial machinations of the Bolshevik leaders after the revolution, including a scheme to hide large quantities of secretly printed currency to be used by Lenin and his associates in case a successful coup forced them underground again.[20] Maksim Litvinov, a former expert in procuring weapons for the Bolshevik combatants, moved up through the ranks to become the Soviet Foreign Minister in Stalin's government.

Perhaps no one symbolizes the terrorist foundation of the Soviet regime better than Stalin himself. His early career as a professional revolutionary, including his years of involvement in shady enterprises in the Caucasus, left a distinctive mark on his style as a state leader. In spite of his persistent efforts to conceal his past, it revealed itself in his pathological personality and actions, causing President Franklin D. Roosevelt to remark that although he had expected the head of the Soviet government to be a gentleman, he found in the Kremlin a former Caucasian bandit.[21] In implementing his fantastic schemes for reshaping the lives and minds of the people through a "revolution from above," Stalin relied heavily upon his many subordinates, whose experience, ideology, and psychology were marked by red banditry. These representatives of the seamy side of the revolution lived to realize their full potential under Stalinism, a system that demanded their brutal assistance from below.[22] Yet it was Stalin—a typical revolutionary of the new type who came to be invested with power more absolute than any modern state leader ever achieved—who was able to complete the unprecedented experiment of building an elaborate system of repression founded on state-sponsored terrorism.

NOTES

Archives

ACh	Arkhiv V. Chernova, International Institute of Social History, Amsterdam
AK	Arkhiv L. B. Krasina, International Institute of Social History, Amsterdam
AM	Arkhiv L. P. Menshchikova, International Institute of Social History, Amsterdam
AR	Alexander Rozhdestvenskii Collection, International Institute of Social History, Amsterdam
AS	Arkhiv samizdata, Radio Liberty, Munich
GARF	Gosudarstvennyi Arkhiv Rossiiskoi Federatsii, Moscow
Nic.	Boris I. Nicolaevsky Collection, Hoover Institution Archives, Stanford, California
Okhrana	Arkhiv Zagranichnoi Agentury Departamenta, Politsii (Okhrana Collection), Hoover Institution Archives, Stanford, California
PSR	Arkhiv Partii Sotsialistov-Revoliutsionerov, International Institute of Social History, Amsterdam

An effort has been made to streamline the archival reference process without sacrificing essential information. In references to Western archival materials, box and folder numbers, as appropriate, are indicated in a shortened form adequate to allow the reader to locate individual archival documents. "Okhrana XXIVh-4C" thus refers to the Okhrana Collection, box XXIVh, folder 4C. Similarly, "Nic. 435–27" means Nicolaevsky Collection, box 435, folder 27. GARF citations are more complex, and may include reference numbers for a document's collection (*fond*, or f.), inventory list (*opis'*, or op.), case file (*delo*, or d.), and section (*chast'*, or ch.); "ob." (*oborotnyi*, or reverse) following a page number directs the reader to the back side of the page.

Journals

KA	*Krasnyi arkhiv*
KL	*Krasnaia letopis'*
KS	*Katorga i ssylka*
PR	*Proletarskaia revoliutsiia*
VE	*Vestnik Evropy*

Articles from these journals, and other Russian and Soviet periodicals dealing almost exclusively with historical documents and memoirs, are cited in full the first time they occur in the notes, and in an only slightly shortened form thereafter. Publication information to allow the interested reader to locate an article is provided with each reference. These articles therefore do not appear in the bibliography as separate entries, although the periodicals themselves are listed there.

Memoirs, documents, and newspaper articles that are part of archival collections are treated similarly, with full initial references slightly shortened in subsequent citations. Again, the reader will have no difficulty determining the locations of these materials from individual notes, and so they are not listed separately in the bibliography, although the archival collections themselves do receive mention.

All other sources in the notes are published documents and secondary works cited in shortened form throughout the notes and listed in full with place and date of publication in the bibliography.

Other Important Abbreviations

GD 1906	*Gosudarstvennaia Duma. Stenograficheskie otchety.*
	Sessiia pervaia, 1906, zasedaniia 1–38
GD 1907	Sessiia vtoraia, 1907, zasedaniia 1–53
PSS	*Polnoe sobranie sochinenii*
Report to DPD	Report to the Director of the Police Department

A reference to the stenographic records of the State Duma sessions (*GD*) will thus include the year, session (*zasedaniia*), volume, and page number as follows: *GD* 1906, 15–1:643.

INTRODUCTION

1. Despite their ideological tendentiousness, interesting Soviet works on the People's Will include S. S. Volk, *Narodnaia volia, 1879–1982* (Moscow-Leningrad, 1966); and N. A. Troitskii, *"Narodnaia volia" pered tsarskim sudom* (Saratov, 1971).

2. See, for example, Adam B. Ulam, *In the Name of the People, Prophets and Conspirators in Prerevolutionary Russia* (New York, 1977); appropriate sections in the classic by Franco Venturi, *Roots of Revolution: A History of the Populist and Socialist Movement in Nineteenth-Century Russia* (New York, 1970); and a more recent article by Astrid von Borcke, "Violence and Terror in Russian Revolutionary Populism: *The Narodnaya Volya*, 1879–83," in Wolfgang J. Mommsen and Gerhard Hirschfeld, eds., *Social Protest, Violence and Terror in Nineteenth- and Twentieth-Century Europe* (New York, 1982), 48–62.

3. Norman M. Naimark, *Terrorists and Social Democrats. The Russian Revolutionary Movement under Alexander III* (Cambridge, Mass., 1983).

4. According to Naimark's statistics, there were two failed assassination attempts in the 1860s, and approximately thirty-five successful terrorist acts between 1877 and 1881 (Naimark, "Terrorism and the Fall of Imperial Russia," lecture [Boston University, 14 April 1986], 4).

5. Although A. I. Spiridovitch's *Histoire du terrorisme Russe* (Paris, 1930) was written by a former tsarist police official, and is far from analytical and definitive, it should be noted as a valuable compilation and the only general account.

6. For the most part, existing works about these parties were authored by prominent Bolshevik functionaries and are entirely didactic and polemical. Typical examples include A. V. Lunacharskii, *Byvshie liudi. Ocherki partii es-erov* (Moscow, 1922); Iu. Steklov, *Partiia sotsialistov-revoliutsionerov* (Moscow, 1922); A. Platonov, *Stranichka iz istorii eserovskoi kontrrevoliutsii* (Moscow, 1923); Ia. Iakovlev, *Russkii anarkhizm v velikoi russkoi revoliutsii* (Moscow, 1921); and V. Zalezhskii, *Anarkhisty v Rossii* (Moscow, 1930).

7. The most important examples of secondary literature on the PSR are noted in the corresponding chapter. On the 1905 revolution, see: Sidney Harcave, *First Blood: The*

Russian Revolution of 1905 (New York, 1964); John Bushnell, *Mutineers and Revolutionaries: Military Revolution in Russia, 1905–1907* (Bloomington, Indiana, 1985); Walter Sablinsky, *The Road to Bloody Sunday* (Princeton, New Jersey, 1976); Shmuel Galai, *The Liberation Movement in Russia 1900–1905* (Cambridge, England, 1973); and especially a new study by Abraham Ascher, *The Revolution of 1905: Russia in Disarray* (Stanford, 1988), among others.

8. This author concurs with Walter Laqueur, a leading authority on revolutionary terror, that "any definition of political terrorism venturing beyond noting the systematic use of murder, injury and destruction or the threats of such acts toward achieving political ends is bound to lead to endless controversies," and that "it can be predicted with confidence that the disputes about a comprehensive, detailed definition of terrorism will continue for a long time, that they will not result in a consensus and that they will make no notable contribution toward the understanding of terrorism." Still, it seems useful to offer one such definition, that of the *Encyclopaedia of the Social Sciences*, published in the 1930s, which characterizes terrorism as the "method (or the theory behind the method) whereby an organized group or party sought to achieve its avowed aims chiefly through the systematic use of violence." This definition suggests that terrorism differs in substance not only from state terror but also from mob violence and mass insurrection (Walter Laqueur, *Terrorism* [Boston-Toronto, 1977], 81n, 135). It is also appropriate to bear in mind that terrorism is a tactic of intimidation, and the extremists' aim is thus "to use terror to weaken the will of the community or government and to undermine morale. It is a form of secret . . . psychological warfare" (Milton Meltzer, *The Terrorists* [New York, 1983], 6–7).

9. Cited in A. Serebrennikov, ed., *Ubiistvo Stolypina. Svidetel'stva i dokumenty* (New York, 1986), 319. Some former radicals entirely agreed, and offered similar definitions of "the new breed of combatants and expropriators" (A. Lokerman, "Po tsarskim tiur'mam. V Ekaterinoslave," *KS* 25 [1926]: 186).

10. *Sekira* 12 (1906): 7, Nic. 436–2.

11. For an excellent discussion of Nechaev's personality and activities, see Philip Pomper, *Sergei Nechaev* (New Brunswick, New Jersey, 1979).

12. Naimark, "Terrorism and the Fall of Imperial Russia," 21.

13. Kropotkin, *Russkaia revoliutsiia i anarkhizm, Doklady chitannye na s'ezde Kommunistov-Anarkhistov v oktiabre 1906 goda* (London, 1907), 40; Gershuni, "Ob ekspropriatsiiakh," undated letter to comrades, pp. 2, 1, Nic. 12–1.

14. E. Koval'skaia, "Po povedu stat'i M. P. Orlova 'Ob Akatui vremen Mel'shina,'" *KS* 52 (1929): 164.

15. V. I. Sukhomlin, "Iz tiuremnykh skitanii," *KS* 55 (1929): 104. P. Murashev cites similar examples in "Stolitsa Urala v 1905–1908 gg.," *KS* 4 (65) (1930): 49, 51.

16. Cited in Serebrennikov, *Ubiistvo Stolypina*, 319.

17. For some isolated examples, see *Spisok lits razyskivaemykh po delam departamenta politsii* (St. Petersburg, 1899): 38, 64, Okhrana XIIId(1)-4.

18. Laqueur, *Terrorism*, 130.

19. For an illuminating discussion of the lack of interest in any abstract principles on the part of this new generation of radicals, see Lokerman, "Po tsarskim tiur'mam," *KS* 25 (1926): 186, 189.

20. This book concurs with the many studies emphasizing that although there is no "particular psychological type, a particular personality constellation, a uniform terrorist mind . . . people with particular personality traits and tendencies are drawn dispropor-

tionately to terrorist careers. . . . Several authors have characterized terrorists as action-oriented, aggressive people who are stimulus-hungry and seek excitement." They are "frequently driven by thirst for action rather than rational consideration of consequences." Among the Russian terrorists "individuals with narcissistic and borderline personality disturbances" were strikingly common. Such individuals typically suffer from "a damaged self-concept," idealizing their inflated egos while projecting onto others "all the hated and devalued weakness within. . . . Unable to face his own inadequacies, the individual with this personality style needs a target to blame and attack for his own inner weakness," which leads him to "find especially attractive a group of like-minded individuals whose credo is, 'It's not us—it's them; they are the cause of our problems'" (Jerrold M. Post, "Terrorist Psycho-Logic: Terrorist Behavior As a Product of Psychological Forces," *Origins of Terrorism*, Walter Reich, ed. [Cambridge, 1990], 27–28, 31; Laqueur, *Terrorism*, 119). Observers of modern terrorist practices throughout the world also note the phenomenon referred to in this study as the "new type of terror," pointing out that whereas "the early terrorist groups abstained from acts of deliberate cruelty . . . with the change in the character of terrorism, 'left-wing' and 'right-wing' alike, humane behavior is no longer the norm. . . . The political terrorist of recent vintage . . . has liberated himself from moral scruples" (Laqueur, *Terrorism*, 222). Furthermore, experts cite "occasions on which the groups have developed links to or simply deteriorated into criminal gangs" (Leonard Weinberg and William Eubank, "Political Parties and the Formation of Terrorist Groups," *Terrorism and Political Violence* 2 [2] [Summer, 1990], 129).

CHAPTER ONE
REVOLUTIONARY TERRORISM IN THE EMPIRE

1. V. M. Chernov, *Pered burei* (New York, 1953), 169.

2. Von Borcke, "Violence and Terror in Russian Revolutionary Populism," 59–60.

3. Maureen Perrie, "Political and Economic Terror in the Tactics of the Russian Socialist Revolutionary Party before 1914, in Mommsen and Hirschfeld, *Social Protest, Violence and Terror*, 68, Table 6.2. Naimark's figure is even higher: in his estimate, workers carried out some 70 percent of SR terrorist acts (Naimark, "Terrorism and the Fall of Imperial Russia," 5).

4. Proletarian and peasant women were little affected by the ideas of feminism, which usually went hand in hand with political radicalism; in comparison with men, they were considerably more restricted in mobility and had a much lower literacy rate (Amy Knight, "Female Terrorists in the Russian Socialist Revolutionary Party," *The Russian Review* 38 [2] [April 1979]: 144).

5. Knight analyzes the social backgrounds of women terrorists in ibid., 144–45.

6. Naimark, "Terrorism and the Fall of Imperial Russia," 5; Laqueur, *Terrorism*, 121.

7. A number of female Russian terrorists were perceived by their comrades as "monastic" types (Boris Savinkov, *Vospominaniia terrorista* [Khar'kov, 1926], 117).

8. Knight, "Female Terrorists," 145–46.

9. See, for example, a police agent's report from 1901, Okhrana VIj-11.

10. Richard G. Robbins, Jr., *Famine in Russia 1891–1892* (New York, 1975), 1–8.

11. The administration proved to be competent and effective in organizing one of the largest relief campaigns in Russian history. According to Robbins, "The range of gov-

ernment activity was remarkable, exceeding by far official efforts in previous famines" (ibid., 168). The volunteers were organized primarily by the zemstvos, local institutions officially established in 1864 with a broad range of responsibilities in the areas of education and general welfare (for details on the zemstvos see T. Emmons and W. S. Vucinich, eds., *The Zemstvo in Russia* [Cambridge, Mass., 1982]).

12. Some radicals claimed that liberal aid to the peasants indirectly helped the government overcome the crisis and thus only strengthened the "sickly regime" in Russia (O. V. Aptekman, "Partiia 'Narodnogo Prava,'" *Byloe* 7 [19] [1907]: 189; see also G. Ul'ianov, "Vospominaniia o M. A. Natansone," *KS* 4 [89] [1932]: 71). From this time on, this attitude was not atypical among the government's opponents, one of whom was particularly explicit in a private letter: "If, God willing, we have a bad harvest this year, you'll see what a game will begin" ("Iz otcheta o perliustratsii dep. politsii za 1908 g.," *KA* 2 [27] [1928]: 156).

13. Ul'ianov, "Vospominaniia o M. A. Natansone," *KS* 4 (89) (1932): 73; Chernov, *Zapiski*, 95.

14. See, for example, Spiridovich, *Partiia Sotsialistov-Revoliutsionerov*, 25; and S. Nechetnyi (S. N. Sletov), "Ocherki po istorii P. S.-R.," *Sotsialist-Revoliutsioner* 4 (1912): 19.

15. Victor M. Chernov, *Zapiski Sotsialista-Revoliutsionera* (Berlin, 1922), 95; V. V. Shirokova, *Partiia "Narodnogo Prava"* (Saratov, 1972), 26; G. S., "Muzhitskii dobrokhot," *KS* 5 (78) (1931): 131.

16. This process was very similar to the evolution of the Populist propagandists of the 1870s into practitioners of terror. According to Sof'ia Perovskaia, one of the leaders of the People's Will, she and her comrades were forced to resort to terrorism as the only means to awaken the masses after vain attempts to do so by means of agitation (Viacheslav Venozhinskii, *Smertnaia kazn' i terror* [St. Petersburg, 1908], 25; see also Venturi, *Roots of Revolution*, 505, 577). In general, observers have noted that the "inability of those who identify with the plight of the poor or the victims of discrimination to mobilize the support of those segments of society most adversely affected by these circumstances . . . has led radicals in various parts of the world to constitute themselves as terrorists" (Weinberg and Eubank, "Political Parties and the Formation of Terrorist Groups," 126).

17. Cited in James Frank McDaniel, "Political Assassination and Mass Execution: Terrorism in Revolutionary Russia, 1878–1938," Ph.D. dissertation (University of Michigan, 1976), 97–98; Laqueur, *Terrorism*, 111.

18. Manfred Hildermeier, "The Terrorist Strategies of the Socialist-Revolutionary Party in Russia," in Mommsen and Hirschfeld, *Social Protest, Violence and Terror*, 84.

19. See, for example, "Iz obshchestvennoi khroniki," *VE* 10 (1906): 873.

20. S. E. Kryzhanovskii, *Vospominaniia* (Petropolis, n.d.), 208.

21. The new organization was officially called the Social-Revolutionary Party of the People's Rights, but it inherited its abbreviated name from the People's Will, replacing the word "will" with the seemingly more legitimate "rights" (Chernov, *Pered burei*, 77–78). At the same time, its members tried to dissociate themselves from the tactical concepts preached by the People's Will, arguing that neither a few bombs nor a circle of conspirators could destroy the autocracy; only a "political party in the real sense of this word can do the job" (Naimark, *Terrorists and Social Democrats*, 237; see also Chernov, *Zapiski*, 143).

22. M. Vishniak, "Tragediia terrora," *Novoe russkoe slovo*, 24 March 1957, Nic.

267–6. The tremendous increase in terrorist cadres over the fifty-year period between 1860 and 1910 is best demonstrated by comparison: whereas there were no more than 100 extremists in the early 1860s, and some 500 adherents of the People's Will in 1879, by 1907 the avowedly terrorist PSR counted 45,000 members. These numbers do not include sympathizers: approximately 1,000 for the radicals of the 1860s, 4,000–5,000 for the People's Will, and roughly 300,000 for the SRs (Naimark, "Terrorism and the Fall of Imperial Russia," 4). To these figures must be added the thousands of members and supporters of other terrorist organizations formed early in the twentieth century.

23. On SR efforts to raise money, see: an undated letter from Emma Goldman to E. Breshkovskaia, PSR 1-1; June 1905 police report, Okhrana XVIb(6)-2; copy of a letter signed "S. R. Shakmeister" in New York to Rubanovich in Paris, 1 February 1907, Okhrana XVIIn-5A(the same document is also found in PSR 3-286); an unaddressed letter from Gershuni to L. S., 15 January 1907, p. 1, and a letter from Gershuni to his brother Pavel, 16 February 1907, p. 1, both in Nic. 12–1; agent's report from New York, 12 June 1907, Okhrana XXVa-2B; agent's report from Paris, 2 December 1906, Okhrana VIj-15C.

24. See: "Iz Obzora vazhneishikh doznanii o gosudarstvennykh prestupleniiakh za 1901 god," 252, Nic. 197–7; and 26 April (9 May) 1905 police report, Okhrana XXIVi-1A.

25. "Svedeniia o vvoze oruzhiia v Rossiiu, snosheniia s komitetami v Rossii i svedeniia o deiatel'nosti revoliutsionnykh organizatsii," undated, Okhrana XXIVh-5N; 13 (26) December 1905 police report, Okhrana XXIVh-4C. Russian revolutionaries developed extensive contacts with European arms dealers and manufacturers, and as a result of the 1905–1906 events in Russia one German armaments factory in Herstal more than doubled its production of browning pistols (S. M. Pozner, ed., *Boevaia gruppa pri TsK RSDRP[b] [1905–1907 gg.]. Stat'l i vospominaniia* [Moscow-Leningrad, 1925], 64).

26. Cited in A. I. Spiridovich, *Istoriia bol'shevizma v Rossii* (Paris, 1922, reprinted New York, 1986), 120.

27. "Doneseniia Evno Azefa," *Byloe* 1 (23) (1917): 221.

28. *Strely* 9 (7 January 1906): 7, Nic. 436–7; *Iskry* 8, PSR 2-132.

29. "Aforizmy," *Zabiiaka* 3 (26 January 1906): 7, Nic. 436–13.

30. *Nagaechka* 4:9, Nic. 435–27.

31. Two undated police telegrams, Okhrana XXIVi-1A; see also unaddressed police note from Paris dated 7 (19) May 1890, Okhrana XVIb(4)-1; report from the Imperial Russian Embassy in London dated 26 March (7 April) 1894, Okhrana XIX-13. The sentiments of Vera Figner demonstrate the importance of the single act of regicide for the People's Will. She felt that everything was "atoned for by this blood of the Tsar, shed by our hands"; as a result of his death, "reaction must come to an end and give place to a new Russia" (cited in McDaniel, "Political Assassination and Mass Execution," 89).

32. See, for example, "Prilozhenie k #21–22 'Znameni Truda,'" PSR 3-236; June 1895 police report, Okhrana XXIVi-1A.

33. Especially infuriating for the revolutionaries and liberals alike was a speech on 17 January 1895 in which the tsar proclaimed to a delegation from various zemstvo and gentry assemblies that dreams of representation in internal affairs were senseless because he intended to "defend the basis of the autocracy as firmly and as steadfastly as did [his] unforgettable late father" (V. Burtsev, ed., *Za sto let, 1800–1896* [London,

1897], 264; also see Richard Pipes, *Struve: Liberal on the Right, 1905–1944* [Cambridge, Mass., 1980], 154).

34. 22 November (4 December) 1896 police report, Okhrana XXVb-1; Stepan N. Sletov, *K istorii vozniknoveniia partii sotsialistov-revoliutsionerov* (Petrograd, 1917), 61–62; see also 27 May 1895 police report, Okhrana XXIVi-1A.

35. V. L. Burtsev, *Doloi tsaria!* (London, n.d.), 16–17, PSR 1-19; undated letter from Burtsev to Shishakin et al., PSR 8-710; 22 April (4 May) 1894 police report, Okhrana XXIVi-1A. On Burtsev's arrest, trial, and eighteen-month imprisonment in London in 1898 for preaching regicide, see Burtsev, *Doloi tsaria!*, 44–56, PSR 1-19; and 4 December 1903 police report, Okhrana XIIIc(2)-2C.

36. 22 December 1901 report to DPD, Okhrana XIIIb(1)-1, Outgoing Dispatches (1901), doc. 11.

37. See, for example, June 1895 police report, Okhrana XXIVi-1A.

38. See, for example, *Obzor vazhneishikh doznanii, proizvodivshikhsia v Zhandarmskikh Upravleniiakh za 1897 god* (St. Petersburg, 1902), 111–14; Burtsev, *Doloi tsaria!*, 1, 20, PSR 1-19.

39. See, for example, "Vzryv v Znamenskom monastyre v Kurske," a clipping from an unidentified and undated newspaper, PSR 3-293; "Aprel' 27 1899 g.," Nic. 71–7.

40. Kropotkin, *Russkaia revoliutsiia i anarkhizm*, 51; see also GARF f. 102, DPOO, op. 1902, d. 500: 86; and Police Department materials, protocol dated 17 September 1901, St. Petersburg, PSR 8-675.

41. Burtsev, *Doloi tsaria!*, 17, PSR 1-19.

42. 22 December 1901 report to DPD, Okhrana XIIIb(1)-1, Outgoing Dispatches (1901), doc. 11.

43. Ibid.

44. 16 October 1901 police report, Okhrana XIX-12A.

45. 4 June 1902 police report, Okhrana XVIa-2; 20 July (2 August) 1901 report to DPD, Okhrana XVIa-2; see also "Iz Obzora vazhneishikh doznanii," 250, Nic. 197–7; and a 1901 agent's report, Okhrana VIj-11.

46. 22 December 1901 report to DPD, Okhrana XIIIb(1)-1, Outgoing Dispatches (1901), doc. 11. The *veche* was a medieval popular assembly called to meeting by the ringing of a bell.

47. The reaction of the Russian political emigrés to the news of Bloody Sunday is revealing. One SD recounted, "Surprisingly, no one among the Russians was depressed. . . . On the contrary, [they] were in a lively, uplifted mood. It was clear that 22 (9) January would be the signal for a victorious struggle" (O. Piatnitskii, *Zapiski bol'shevika* [Moscow, 1956], 65).

48. Weinberg & Eubank, "Political Parties and the Formation of Terrorist Groups," 141.

49. Laqueur, *Terrorism*, 145.

50. William Bruce Lincoln, *In War's Dark Shadow: The Russians before the Great War* (New York, 1983), 351.

51. Cited in Venozhinskii, *Smertnaia kazn' i terror*, 28.

52. Alexander Blok, "The People and the Intelligentsia," in Marc Raeff, ed., *Russian Intellectual History: An Anthology* (New Jersey, 1978), 362.

53. This opinion was particularly promoted by the Russian liberals (see, for example, P. Struve, "Nashi neprimirimye terroristy i ikh glavnyi shtab," *Osvobozhdenie* 55 [2 September 1904]: 83).

54. Jacob Walkin, *The Rise of Democracy in Pre-Revolutionary Russia* (New York, 1962), 207; P. Kropotkin, *The Terror in Russia. An Appeal to the British Nation* (London, 1909), 36; A. Tyrkova-Vil'iams, *Na putiakh k svobode* (New York, 1952), 57–58; S. Arkomed, "Krasnyi terror na Kavkaze i okhrannoe otdelenie," *KS* 13 (1924): 73; and *Rech'* 81 (6 June 1906): 1.

55. Cited in Spiridovich, *Istoriia bol'shevizma*, 120–21.

56. "25 let nazad. Iz dnevnika L. Tikhomirova," *KA* 4–5 (41–42) (1930): 114; words of Count Sergei Witte cited by Naimark in "Terrorism and the Fall of Imperial Russia," 19.

57. Alfred Levin, *The Second Duma; A Study of the Social-Democratic Party and the Russian Constitutional Experiment* (New Haven, Conn., 1940), 21 n. Partial figures for the period from October 1905 through March 1906 are given by Viktor P. Obninskii in *Polgoda russkoi revoliutsii* (Moscow, 1906), 152.

58. N. S. Tagantsev, *Smertnaia kazn'* (St. Petersburg, 1913), 92.

59. Ibid. The figures presented by Strakhovsky are somewhat different: "738 officials and 645 private persons were killed during 1906, while 948 officials and 777 private persons were wounded. In 1907 no fewer than 1,231 officials and 1,768 private persons were killed and 1,284 officials and 1,734 private persons were wounded" (Leonid I. Strakhovsky, "The Statesmanship of Stolypin: A Reappraisal," *Slavonic and Eastern European Review* 37 [1958–1959]: 357). This total of 9,125 casualties for the years 1906–1907 is very close to Levin's and Tagantsev's rounded figure of 9,200. Since Tagantsev's numbers probably include murder cases with no connection to political causes, and since, on the other hand, Strakhovsky's numbers would be larger if casualties for 1905, and especially its final months, were included, the figure of approximately 9,000 people killed and injured by terrorists in 1905–1907 can probably be accepted as accurate. Compare these statistics with those, almost certainly underestimated, given by Petr Kropotkin, who claimed that from October 1905 to the end of 1907 casualties totaled 7,148 (Kropotkin, *Terror in Russia*, 36).

60. "Smertnaia kazn' v Rossii ostaetsia?" *Novoe vremia*, 22 January 1910? [*sic*], PSR 4-346.

61. 16 May 1910 police report, Okhrana XXIVi-2m. Very similar numbers, with only four more government officials recorded as killed, are presented in an undated police typescript in French entitled, "Hors la Loi," p. 9, Okhrana XIIc(1)-2E. For somewhat lower figures for 1908, see "Smertnaia kazn' v Rossii ostaetsia?" PSR 4-346. Alternate figures of approximately 6,000 killed and wounded victims of terrorism from 1905 through mid-1909, which, however, do not seem to be complete, may be found in "Gody reaktsii," *KA* 1 (8) (1925): 242; and in Martin McCauley's *Octobrists to Bolsheviks. Imperial Russia 1905–1917* (London, 1984), 46.

62. "Iz obshchestvennoi khroniki," *VE* 8 (1907): 842.

63. Laqueur, *Terrorism*, 105; Boris Souvarine, *Stalin (A Critical Study of Bolshevism)* (New York, 1939), 93; *Volia* 89 (10 [23] December 1906): 26, PSR 7-592; William C. Fuller, Jr., *Civil-Military Conflict in Imperial Russia 1881–1914* (Princeton, New Jersey, 1985), 150.

64. Clipping from an unidentified newspaper, 17 October 1906, PSR 4-346. Many combatants attempted to conceal their faces during expropriations, giving rise to the following anecdote: "Due to an increase in the incidence of bank robberies, mask and costume businesses are showing large profits. A domino mask goes for sixty rubles

(rental), a harlequin for more than eighty. The administration intends to institute price controls in order to curb the merchants' greed" (*Zarnitsy* 6 [1906]: 2, Nic. 436–17).

65. This figure may include the proceeds of ordinary armed robberies as well as political expropriations (clipping from *Russkoe slovo* 8 [March 1908], PSR 4-346).

66. See, for example, 17 March 1909 police report, Okhrana XXVc-1; and 16 May 1910 police report, Okhrana XXIVi-2m. After a daring assault on a mail train at the little station of Bezdany on the St. Petersburg–Warsaw line on 14 (27) September 1908, Polish terrorists escaped with more than two million rubles (Souvarine, *Stalin*, 105; Laqueur, *Terrorism*, 105).

67. *Vodovorot* 6 (1906): 12, Nic. 436–11.

68. Some liberal publicists spoke out against such indifference toward the daily bloodshed (see, for example, "Iz obshchestvennoi khroniki," *VE* 12 [1906]: 886).

69. Lokerman, "Po tsarskim tiur'mam," *KS* 25 (1926): 179; G. Nestroev, *Iz dnevnika maksimalista* (Paris, 1910), 74.

70. "Bor'ba s revoliutsionnym dvizheniem na Kavkaze v epokhu stolypinshchiny," *KA* 3 (34) (1929): 188, 191.

71. Ibid., 187, 191, 201, 204, 218–19. According to one memoirist, "Terrorist activity . . . assumed gigantic proportions, [and] in 1904–1905, in the various corners of the Caucasus, attacks and political assassinations of representatives of the old regime occurred almost daily" (Baron [Bibineishvili], *Za chetvert' veka*, 85). Other sources indicate that more than one thousand terrorist acts were committed between 1904 and 1908 in the Caucasus (Souvarine, *Stalin*, 90; Leon Trotsky, *Stalin* [New York, 1967], 96).

72. "Obzor Kavkazskikh revoliutsionnykh partii" (1 September 1909): 3, 5, 7, Okhrana XXa-1B. Imperial policy in Armenia turned many patriots into enemies of Russia "thirsty for blood" (excerpt from an unsigned letter written in Kiev to Charlotte Abramson in Geneva, 22 October 1903, Okhrana XXa-1A; 18 December 1903 police report, Okhrana XIIIc[2]-2C; "Dashnaktsutiun. Obvinitel'nyi akt" [28 May 1911]: 4, Nic. 256–5). A number of secret Armenian nationalist organizations included representatives of the clergy among their members, and readily employed terror in their struggle against the confiscation decree (see, for example, 4 December 1903 police report, pp. 2–3, Okhrana XIIIc[2]-2C). Liberal jurist Aleksandr Rozhdestvenskii discusses terrorist attacks against the Russian clergy in "Desiat' let sluzhby v Prokurorskom Nadzore na Kavkaze" (Santiago, Chile, 1961), p. 21b, AR.

73. "Bor'ba s revoliutsionnym dvizheniem na Kavkaze," *KA* 3 (34) (1929): 205, 209–10, 219; "Obzor Kavkazskikh revoliutsionnykh partii," 10, Okhrana XXa-1B.

74. The assertions of Vorontsov-Dashkov that government officials had no dealings with the Dashnaki do not bear serious scrutiny ("Bor'ba s revoliutsionnym dvizheniem na Kavkaze," *KA* 3 [34] [1929]: 205, 208–10, 219, 189, 192–93, 200; "Dashnaktsutiun. Obvinitel'nyi akt," 6–7, 10–11, 239, 243, 247–49, Nic. 256–5). In an unprecedented move during the bloody Armenian-Tatar confrontations in 1905, the viceroy elected to rely on the revolutionaries to end the ethnic violence, and issued two thousand Berdan rifles to the local SDs (Rozhdestvenskii, "Desiat' let sluzhby," p. 49, AR).

75. "Dashnaktsutiun. Obvinitel'nyi akt," 11–12, Nic. 256–5; and "Kavkazskii terror," *Moskovskie vedomosti* 75 (5 April 1909), PSR 4-346. As late as 1910, the party leadership issued resolutions to "strengthen combat capabilities and reply with terror" to any hostile actions on the part of the Russian authorities in Armenia (copy of a 26

January 1910 police report, Okhrana XXa-1A). Although the April 1907 Fourth Congress of the Dashnaktsutiun in Vienna passed a resolution acknowledging various excesses on the part of the Dashnaki in the Caucasus, prohibiting them from collecting forced donations, and imposing the death penalty for extortion, the party leadership revoked this resolution at its Seventh Congress in August 1913 on the grounds that the party was "threatened by a financial crisis" (4 [17] April 1914 report to DPD, Okhrana XXa-1A).

76. For a list of other groups, see Arkomed, "Krasnyi terror na Kavkaze," *KS* 13 (1924): 77; see also P. P. Zavarzin, *Zhandarmy i revoliutsionery* (Paris, 1930), 113; 18 February 1914 police report, Okhrana XIIIa-16B; 9 March 1914 police report, Okhrana XIIIa-17A; 10 (23) November 1914 report to DPD, Okhrana XXIVa-1B; "Revoliutsionnaia Partiia Sotsialistov-Federalistov Gruzii," 23 October 1909, 8–9, 18, 35, Nic. 80–7 (for the same document, see Okhrana XXa-2; and Nic. 11–22).

77. "Bor'ba s revoliutsionnym dvizheniem na Kavkaze," *KA* 3 (34) (1929): 189; "Obzor Kavkazskikh revoliutsionnykh partii," 35, Okhrana XXa-1B; see also 17 March 1905 police report, p. 1, Okhrana XIIIc(2)-6A.

78. Rozhdestvenskii, "Desiat' let sluzhby," 55, AR; "Bor'ba s revoliutsionnym dvizheniem na Kavkaze," *KA* 3 (34) (1929): 193–194; "Dashnaktsutiun. Obvinitel'nyi akt," 241, Nic. 256–5; 1 April 1904 police report, Okhrana XIIIc(2)-4A; 4 (17) August 1907 report to DPD, Okhrana XXVc-2m.

79. "Krovavye itogi," clipping from an unidentified newspaper, PSR 2-137. According to police records for the province of Warsaw, which includes the Polish capital city, between 1 September and 17 November 1906, there were 170 assassination attempts against state officials and private individuals, and 161 assaults on property (GARF f. 102, DPOO, op. 1906 [II], d. 9, ch. 20: 31–32).

80. GARF f. 102, DPOO, op. 1909, d. 201: 7, 9, 10 ob., 11, 13, 16 ob., 17 ob., 19 ob., 21 ob.

81. "Pol'skie revoliutsionnye i natsionalisticheskie organizatsii," September 1909, pp. 14–15, Okhrana XIX-12A. For descriptions of some of the party's terrorist enterprises, see: 12 May 1905 police report, pp. 7–9, Okhrana XIIIc(2)-6B; 13 (26) July 1906 report to DPD, Okhrana XVIb(4)-1; 7 (20) August 1906 police report, Okhrana XIIc(2)-2D; 28 September (11 October) 1906 report to DPD, Okhrana XVIIr(2)-1E; and 26 August (8 September) 1906 report to DPD, Okhrana XIX-13.

82. For examples, see: 26 August (8 September) 1906 report to DPD, Okhrana XIX-13; P. P. Zavarzin, *Rabota tainoi politsii* (Paris, 1924), 108–9, 137–39; I. Zhukovskii-Zhuk, "Krovavoe udostoverenie," *KS* 13 (1924): 149; clippings from an unidentified newspaper dated 12 February 1909, and from *Sibir'*, 18 March 1909, PSR 7-602.

83. "Pol'skie revoliutsionnye i natsionalisticheskie organizatsii," 16–17, Okhrana XIX-12A; copy of a report from the head of the Warsaw Okhrana to the Police Department, 31 October 1906, Okhrana XIX-13; 13 June 1906 police report, Okhrana XXIVi-2D.

84. See, for example, Zavarzin, *Rabota tainoi politsii*, 27–28, 115–19, 128–30; 15 September 1905 police report, pp. 1–2, Okhrana XIIIc(2)-6C; 16 (29) July 1907 report to DPD, Okhrana XIX-13.

85. 11 March 1904 police report, p. 5, Okhrana XIIIc(2)-4A.

86. I. N. Moshinskii (Iuz. Konarskii), "F. E. Dzerzhinskii i varshavskoe podpol'e 1906 g.," *KS* 50 (1928): 17; see also Souvarine, *Stalin*, 93.

87. As a typical example, the combatants were so indiscriminate in their policy as to treat anyone wearing a Russian uniform as an enemy, and so indifferent to the nonterrorist activities of the PPS that radical soldiers who were active members of the party's own military organization occasionally became victims of PPS terror (S. Pestkovskii, "Bor'ba partii v rabochem dvizhenii v Pol'she v 1905–1907 gg.," *PR* 11 [1922]: 43).

88. "Pol'skie revoliutsionnye i natsionalisticheskie organizatsii," 19–20, 24–28, Okhrana XIX-12A; "Doklad o Pol'skoi Sotsialisticheskoi Partii /P.P.S./ /byvshei revoliutsionnoi fraktsii 'pravitsa'/," (2) (15) March 1911 (Paris), Okhrana XIX-12A. In 1909 the Revolutionary Faction usurped the original name of the party, and began referring to itself as the PPS ("Obzor deiatel'nosti i nastoiashchego polozheniia Pol'skoi Sotsialisticheskoi Partii /P.P.S./ i Sotsial-Demokratii Pol'shi i Litvy /P.S.-D./," 17 [30] January 1911, [Paris], Okhrana XIX-12A).

89. Zavarzin, *Rabota tainoi politsii*, 137; see also GARF f. 102, OO, op. 1908, d. 143:2.

90. "Pol'skie revoliutsionnye i natsionalisticheskie organizatsii," pp. 31–33, 35, Okhrana XIX-12A. For descriptions of terrorist acts perpetrated by Proletariat, see a 28 September (11 October) 1906 report to DPD, Okhrana XVIIr(2)-1E; "Obzor deiatel'nosti i nastoiashchego polozheniia Pol'skoi Sotsialisticheskoi Partii," Okhrana XIX-12A.

91. "Pol'skie revoliutsionnye i natsionalisticheskie organizatsii," 41–42, Okhrana XIX-12A; Zavarzin, *Rabota tainoi politsii*, 141–42.

92. 15 September 1905 police report, p. 6, Okhrana XIIIc(2)-6C; see also Zavarzin, *Rabota tainoi politsii*, 14–15. Some former members of the PPS, united in anarchist groups, also participated in the planning of assassinations and large-scale expropriations (copy of a note from the head of the Warsaw Okhrana to the director of the Police Department dated 5 February 1908, Okhrana XIIIc[1]-1A, Incoming Dispatches [1908], doc. 175).

93. Tagantsev, *Smertnaia kazn'*, 160–61. P. Grauzdin discusses some of these assassinations in "K istorii revoliutsionnogo dvizheniia v Latvii v 1905 godu," *KS* 7 (92) (1932): 108; see also "Pribaltiiskii krai v 1905 g.," *KA* 4–5 (11–12) (1925): 269.

94. "Pribaltiiskii krai," *KA* 4–5 (11–12) (1925): 279.

95. Richard Pipes, *The Russian Revolution* (New York, 1990), 165.

96. Ia. K. Pal'vadre, *Revoliutsiia 1905–7 gg. v Estonii* (Leningrad, 1932), 69. For additional police figures on terrorist acts and their victims, see GARF f. 102, DPOO, op. 1905, d. 2605:145–47.

97. I. Ianson [Braun], "Latviia v pervoi polovine 1905 goda," *PR* 12 (1922): 49.

98. *Satiricheskoe obozrenie* 1 (1906): 2, Nic. 436–1.

99. See, for example, "Doklady S. Iu. Vitte Nikolaiu II," *KA* 4–5 (11–12) (1925): 151; *Volia*, issues 89 (10 [23] December 1906): 26, and 90–91 (24 December 1906 [6 January 1907]): 42–43, in PSR 7-592; "Sovremennaia letopis' " in three 1906 issues of *Byloe*: 7:321, 326; 10:342, 350–51; and 11:332, 335, 337; 3 March 1905 police report, pp. 18–19, Okhrana XIIIc(2)-6A; police reports dated 12 May 1905, pp. 10–11, and 28 July 1905, p. 16, Okhrana XIIIc(2)-6B; police reports dated 11 August 1905, p. 12, 1 September 1905, pp. 4, 7, 8 September 1905, pp. 11, 14–15, and 15 September 1905, p. 8, Okhrana XIIIc(2)-6C; Paul Avrich, *The Russian Anarchists* (Princeton, New Jersey, 1967), 54; Obninskii, *Polgoda russkoi revoliutsii*, 48–51, 121, 154–55, 160, 163, 165, 167; "Pribaltiiskii krai," *KA* 4–5 (11–12) (1925): 269, 286.

100. "Pribaltiiskii krai," *KA* 4–5 (11–12) (1925): 271–72n.

101. Ibid., 269, 273–74; Obninskii, *Polgoda russkoi revoliutsii*, 50, 156, 163; police reports dated 10 November 1905, p. 29, and 29 September 1905, pp. 1, 8, 11, Okhrana XIIIc(2)-6C; Pal'vadre, *Revoliutsiia 1905–7 gg. v Estonii*, 72–73.

102. "Obzor partii, primykaiushchikh k RSDRP," 1910, 30–31, Okhrana XVIb(6)-1C; see also Grauzdin, "K istorii revoliutsionnogo dvizheniia v Latvii," *KS* 7 (92) (1932): 108–9; Ia. Peters, "1905 god v Libave i ee okrestnostiakh," *PR* 11 (46) (1925): 201; Ernest O. F. Ames, ed., *The Revolution in the Baltic Provinces of Russia* (London, 1907), 95–96.

103. For the bourgeoisie, i.e., the relatively well-to-do farmers, the forest brothers also occasionally introduced taxes ranging from fifty to one hundred rubles ("Review of D. Beika's *God lesnykh brat'ev*" [in Latvian, undated], 11–12, Nic. 121–5; see also "Obzor partii primykaiushchikh k RSDRP," 31, Okhrana XVIb[6]-1C).

104. "Pribaltiiskii krai," *KA* 4–5 (11–12) (1925): 269. A former revolutionary described how one of these guerrillas "literally terrorized police informers and traitors," sometimes shooting through their pillows at night from behind the windows, "as a joke" (*Ianis Luter Bobis. Stranitsy zhizni revoliutsionera-podpol'shchika. Sbornik statei i vospominanii* [Riga, 1962], 132).

105. See "Review of Beika's *God lesnykh brat'ev*," 5–6, Nic. 121–5; Ianson (Braun), "Latviia v pervoi polovine 1905 goda," *PR* 12 (1922): 35; 8 September 1905 police report, p. 6, Okhrana XIIIc(2)-6C; Obninskii, *Polgoda russkoi revoliutsii*, 159; clipping from newspaper *Reforma*, 2 June 1906, PSR 4-346.

106. *Ianis Luter Bobis*, 131. For an account of the July 1906 destruction of the castle of Count Medem, see "Review of Beika's *God lesnykh brat'ev*," 6, Nic. 121–5.

107. Altogether, 230 estates were destroyed in the province, with damages totaling 4,239,000 rubles. In addition, 343 estates and castles suffered major damage totaling 7,818,614 rubles in other Baltic territories (GARF f. 102, DPOO, op. 1905, d. 2605:144–44 ob.; "Pribaltiiskii krai," *KA* 4–5 [11–12] [1925]: 279n). In 1905–1906, the governor-general's office tallied 1,274 cases of arson in the Baltic region (Pal'vadre, *Revoliutsiia 1905–7 gg. v Estonii*, 69).

108. "Review of Beika's *God lesnykh brat'ev*," 4, Nic. 121–5.

109. I. Iurenev, "Rabota R.S.-D.R.P. v Severo-Zapadnom krae (1903–1913 gg.)," *PR* 8–9 (31–32) (1924): 188.

110. Pal'vadre, *Revoliutsiia 1905–7 gg. v Estonii*, 69–70, 72–73, 84–85, 118–25, 155, 159, 161–65. N. Rostov describes a mass terrorist campaign in the Estonian city of Revel in "S pervoi volnoi. Vospominaniia o piatom gode," *KS* 20 (1925): 48–49; see also Obninskii, *Polgoda russkoi revoliutsii*, 50–51, 154.

111. Excerpt from an unsigned letter from Terioki, dated 24 December 1906, to Roginskii in Paris, Okhrana XIIIc(1)-1A, Incoming Dispatches (1907), doc. 9; see also "Zapiska o politicheskom polozhenii Finliandii," 21 August 1909, p. 23, Okhrana XXI-2; "Pervaia konferentsiia voennykh i boevykh organizatsii R. S.-D. R. P.," *PR* 4 (27) (1924): 81; Liadov, *Iz zhizni partii v 1903–1907 godakh* (Moscow, 1956), 174–75.

112. Liadov, *Iz zhizni partii*, 190; Pozner, *Boevaia gruppa pri TsK RSDRP(b)*, 52, 81, 169, 192–93; "Pervaia konferentsiia voennykh i boevykh organizatsii R. S.-D. R. P.," *PR* 4 (27) (1924): 80–81; Savinkov, *Vospominaniia terrorista*, 193; 29 September 1905 police report, pp. 8–9, Okhrana XIIIc(2)-6C; A. B. Gerasimov, *Na lezvii s ter-*

roristami (Paris, 1985), 98; N. Burenin, "Memoirs of an Old Revolutionist," pt. 1: "1901–1906 in Finland," (undated typescript), p. 17, AK; see also V. M. Smirnov, "Finliandiia—krasnyi tyl revoliutsii 1905 goda," *KL* 5–6 (44–45) (1931): 15–16; 16 (29) May 1908 report to DPD, Okhrana XVIIm-5. Evidence that local officials occasionally accepted bribes from Russian revolutionaries suggests that Finnish aid was not always altruistic (see, for example, 22 September [5 October] 1907 report to DPD, Okhrana XXI-1).

113. Burenin, "Memoirs of an Old Revolutionist," pt. 1: "1901–1906 in Finland," 74–75, AK; N. E. Burenin, *Pamiatnye gody. Vospominaniia* (Leningrad, 1967), 89, 99–100, 260; Pozner, *Boevaia gruppa pri TsK RSDRP(b)*, 33, 81, 168–69, 184–89; *Leonid Borisovich Krasin ("Nikitich") Gody podpol'ia* (Moscow-Leningrad, 1928), 238, 260; "Doklady S. Iu. Vitte Nikolaiu II," *KA* 4–5 (11–12) (1925): 146; Smirnov, "Finliandiia," *KL* 5–6 (44–45): 23.

114. Smirnov, "Finliandiia," *KL* 5–6 (44–45) (1931): 10; police reports dated 29 September 1905, p. 9, 25 August 1905, pp. 10, 17, and 11 August 1905, p. 20, Okhrana XIIIc(2)-6C; Savinkov, *Vospominaniia terrorista*, 193; telegram from Paris dated 3 (17) [*sic*] June 1904, Okhrana XIIIc(3)-16A; "Iz pisem gen. N. N. Levashova A. N. Kuropatkinu," *KA* 2 (15) (1926): 221; *Revoliutsionnaia Rossiia* 72 (1907), PSR 4-346; clippings from unidentified French newspapers, "Attentat en Finlande" and "Meurtre d'un officier de gendarmerie," Okhrana 86 (1905), pp. 110, 135; "Zapiska o politicheskom polozhenii Finliandii," 5, Okhrana XXI-2; 16 May 1910 police report, Okhrana XXIVi-2m.

115. 28 September (11 October) 1906 report to DPD, Okhrana XVIIr(2)-1E; "Ob ekspropriatsiiakh," *Nastuplenie* 12 (25 September [8 October] 1907): 1–2; see also GARF f. 102, DPOO, op. 1910, d. 1910: 60 and op. 1905, d. 2605; "Iupiter serditsia," *Anarkhist* 1 (10 October 1907): 17.

116. Naimark, "Terrorism and the Fall of Imperial Russia," 4; Leonard Schapiro, *Russian Studies* (New York, 1988), 266.

117. Schapiro, *Russian Studies*, 273; V. Shul'gin, *Dni* (N.p., 1925), 53–54.

118. Cited in Naimark, "Terrorism and the Fall of Imperial Russia," 16.

119. Nikolai Berdiaev, *Smysl istorii* (Paris, 1969) 108–9, 113–19.

120. Ibid., 109.

121. Needless to say, Berdiaev's claim that the Jew is easily attracted to revolution and socialism had nothing to do with the vulgar anti-Semitism common among his conservative contemporaries. He was primarily concerned with the general tendency, and conceded that the messianic consciousness and the striving for realization of paradise on earth essential in the Jewish tradition do not necessarily shape the mentality of every biological Jew, and may also be inherent in non-Jews (ibid., 119, 128).

122. While many tsarist bureaucrats considered the Jews a "sinister race bent on subverting and destroying Christian society," more enlightened police officials acknowledged that it was the numerous restrictions that turned many Jewish people against the regime (Pipes, *Russian Revolution*, 178).

123. Schapiro, *Russian Studies*, 274–85, 283; Knight, "Female Terrorists," 146; Naimark, "Terrorism and the Fall of Imperial Russia," 4.

124. Schapiro, *Russian Studies*, 284; Naimark, "Terrorism and the Fall of Imperial Russia," 4–5; see also Knight, "Female Terrorists," 144; and 11 (24) December 1910

police report, Okhrana XVIb(4)-1. To cite only one example, of eleven Anarchist-Communist terrorists executed in Warsaw in January 1906, ten were Jews and one was Polish (Obninskii, *Polgoda russkoi revoliutsii*, 48).

125. *Vampir* 2 (1906): 2, Nic. 436–10.

126. See, for example, 17 March 1905 police report, p. 9, Okhrana XIIIc(2)-6A; police reports dated 28 April 1905, pp. 8–9; 12 May 1905, p. 3; 21 July 1905, p. 27; and 4 August 1905, pp. 19, 25, all in Okhrana XIIIc(2)-6B; 29 September 1905 police report, p. 10, Okhrana XIIIc(2)-6C; GARF f. 102, DPOO, op. 1902, d. 500: 87–88; Obninskii, *Polgoda russkoi revoliutsii*, 118; A. D. Kirzhnits, *Evreiskoe rabochee dvizhenie* (Moscow, 1928), 128.

127. Kirzhnits, *Evreiskoe rabochee dvizhenie*, 369, 258.

128. Robert Weinberg, "Workers, Pogroms, and the 1905 Revolution in Odessa," *Russian Review* 46 (1987): 63. Instances of radicals using bombs and firearms to provoke violent reactions from conservatives, with commentators sympathetic to the revolutionaries reporting inaccurately that the monarchists had fired on unarmed crowds, are described in Kirzhnits, *Evreiskoe rabochee dvizhenie*, 213, 317–18; and in a 10 November 1905 police report, p. 13, Okhrana XIIIc(2)-6C.

129. Kirzhnits, *Evreiskoe rabochee dvizhenie*, 184, 371; see also 21 July 1905 police report, p. 14, Okhrana XIIIc(2)-6B.

130. See, for example, Obninskii, *Polgoda russkoi revoliutsii*, 108, 118.

131. 28 April 1905 police report, p. 9, Okhrana XIIIc(2)-6B.

132. Shul'gin, *Dni*, 53–54.

133. See, for example, Kropotkin, *Russkaia revoliutsiia i anarkhizm*, 51. According to one estimate, between 1851 and 1900, which the author calls "quite a busy period for European assassins," there were attacks, "either actually or potentially fatal, on a total of about forty prominent Europeans, including Russians, and also including as a single case Vaillant's bombing of the French Chamber of Deputies in 1893" (Franklin L. Ford, "Reflections on Political Murder: Europe in the Nineteenth and Twentieth Centuries," in Mommsen and Hirschfeld, *Social Protest, Violence and Terror*, 6).

134. See, for example, copy of a report from agent Krauso, 1907, Okhrana XXIVh-4K; 4 (17) January 1908 report to DPD, Okhrana XXIVi-1B; copy of a letter from Deputy Minister of the Interior P. Kurlov to Foreign Minister A. P. Izvol'skii, 30 January 1909, Okhrana Va-3; 29 October 1910 police report, Okhrana XXa-1A; 7 August 1906 police report, Okhrana VIj-15C; excerpt from a letter signed "P." in Brussels to V. I. Smol'ianinov in Moscow dated 30 January 1909, Okhrana XIIc(1)-1B; 11 June 1906 police report, Okhrana XXIVi-1A; 8 (21) June 1906 report to DPD, Okhrana Vf-2; copy of a letter, signature illegible, sent from the town of Liege to A. I. Eramasov in St. Petersburg, 26 February 1909, Okhrana XVIIo-1; 11 (24) December 1910 police report, Okhrana XVIb(4)-1; Savinkov, *Vospominaniia terrorista*, 73, 119.

135. See, for example, an unaddressed police note from Paris dated 7 (19) May 1890, Okhrana XVIb(4)-1; *Spisok lits*, 506–8, Okhrana XIIId(1)-4; 3 (15) August 1894 police report, Okhrana XXIVi-1A. In Austria, Russian revolutionaries organized a special school for the production of bombs (2 September 1910 police report, Okhrana XVIb[5]-5A).

136. See, for example, Avrich, *Russian Anarchists*, 65; police reports dated 25 November (8 December) and 30 November (13 December) 1905, Okhrana XXIVi-1A;

"Russkii revoliutsioner v Vene," translation of an article from the Polish newspaper *Kurjer Warszawski* 74 (2 [15] March 1906), Okhrana XXIVi-1A; "Essai de Bombes," clipping from an unidentified French newspaper, Okhrana 84 (1905), p. 24.

137. See, for example, agent's report from Paris dated 16 October 1909, Okhrana XVIb(3)-1A; 22 November (5 December) 1913 report to DPD, Okhrana XVIIi-3D(w).

138. See, for example, "Un Attentat" and "L'Attentat de Berne," clippings from unidentified French newspapers, Okhrana 73 (1904), p. 193; *Volia* 45 (4 August 1906): 2, PSR 7-569; 13 (26) November 1908 police report, Okhrana XXVIIb-1; 28 January (10 February) 1909 report to DPD, Okhrana XXVIId-3; police report translated from German, 1910, Okhrana XVIb(4)-2; 18 October 1910 police report, Okhrana XVIb(3)-1A; 8 May 1907 police report, Okhrana XXIVi-2F; 11 June 1906 police report, Okhrana XXIVi-1A.

139. See, for example, 20 May (2 June) 1908 report to DPD, Okhrana XXVIId-1; Zavarzin, *Rabota tainoi politsii*, 135–36; 2 April 1909 police report, Okhrana XIX-6; "Vengeance de Terroristes," *Le Journal*, 22 July 1908, Okhrana XXIVi-2H.

140. 11 June 1906 police report, Okhrana XXIVi-1A; 8 (21) April 1903 police report, Okhrana XIIIb(1)-1B, Outgoing Dispatches (1903), doc. 39; 27 July (9 August) 1906 report to DPD, Okhrana XVIb(4)-1; I. I. Genkin, "Sredi preemnikov Bakunina," *KL* 1 (22) (1927): 180; see also decoded police telegram 445 from Orlov in St. Petersburg dated 28 February (13 March) 1907, Okhrana XIIIc(3)-23; decoded police telegram 1844 from Orlov in St. Petersburg dated 28 August (10 September) 1907, Okhrana XIIIc(3)-25.

141. 2 September 1910 police report, Okhrana XVIb(5)-5A.

142. Souvarine, *Stalin*, 99.

143. 3 (16) January 1907 report to DPD, Okhrana XIIIb(1)-1A, Outgoing Dispatches (1907), doc. 2; see also 4 (17) June 1912 report to DPD, Okhrana XVIb(5)-4; and 22 December 1908 police report, Okhrana XIIIc(1)-1F, Incoming Dispatches (1908), doc. 1112.

144. "Russische Banditen in Wien," *Zeit*, 2 November 1908, Okhrana XVIIt-1.

145. Von Borcke, "Violence and Terror in Russian Revolutionary Populism," 56.

146. *Pis'mo Vladimira Lapidusa* (n.p., 1907), 1, 7; see also Avrich, *Russian Anarchists*, 65.

147. "Compte rendu du proces du nomme Sokoloff, Alexandre (Chambre des Appeals Correctionnels—4 Decembre 1906)," p. 5, Okhrana VIj-15C.

148. Copy of a letter to Eramasov with signature illegible, Okhrana XVIIo-1; 2 (15) April 1909 letter to Foreign Minister Izvol'skii signed "Nelidov," Okhrana Va-4; 2 (15) February 1909 and 30 April (13 May) 1909 reports to DPD, Okhrana XXIVi-1B.

149. 22 April (5 May) 1906 report to DPD, Okhrana XIIIb(1)-1B, Outgoing Dispatches (1906), doc. 127.

150. "Otrazhenie sobytii 1905 g. za granitsei," *KA* 2 (9) (1925): 40.

151. 30 April (13 May) 1909 report to DPD, Okhrana XXIVi-1B; newspaper clipping from *Russkoe slovo*, 10 February 1909, PSR 2-132; see also "Srazhenie v Londone," clipping from *Russkie vedomosti*, PSR 2-150.

152. "Sobytiia dnia," clipping from an unidentified newspaper, 21 April 1907? [*sic*], PSR 2-150; see also clipping from *Parus*, 20 May 1907, PSR 8-650.

153. Avrich, *Russian Anarchists*, 70; see also "Vesti iz zagranitsy," *Izvestiia Oblastnogo Komiteta Zagranich. Organizatsii*, 8 (1 July 1908): 5, PSR 1-88.

154. See, for example, "Vesti iz zagranitsy," 5, PSR 1-88; 16 (29) January 1908, 22 April (5 May) 1908, and 20 November 1908 reports to DPD, Okhrana XXVc-1; copy of a letter from Kurlov to Izvol'skii, Okhrana Va-3; 4 (17) June 1912 report to DPD, Okhrana XVIb(5)-4; 29 December 1907 (11 January 1908) report to DPD, Okhrana XXVd-1; "Ubiistvo polismenov," clipping from *Russkie vedomosti*, PSR 2-150; 15 August 1907 report from agent Dmitriev in Switzerland, Okhrana IIb (Switzerland)-2; 29 February (13 March) 1908 report to DPD, Okhrana XIIIb(1)-1A, Outgoing Dispatches (1908), doc. 81; 23 January (5 February) 1909 report to DPD, Okhrana XIIIb(1)-1A, Outgoing Dispatches (1909), doc. 67; "Pis'ma iz-za granitsy," *Nasha gazeta*, 1 February 1909, PSR 2-132.

155. 7 (20) July 1907 report to DPD, Okhrana XXVd-1.

156. Excerpt from a letter to Smol'ianinov from "P.," Okhrana XIIc(1)-1B; excerpt from a 18 February 1909 letter to L. B. Levitman in Moscow from "Vladimir" in Brussels, Okhrana XXVc-1.

157. 4 (17) June 1912 report to DPD, Okhrana XVIb(5)-4; Gerasimov, *Na lezvii s terroristami*, 55.

158. See, for example, March 1906 police report, Okhrana XVIb(5)-5A; 18 April (1 May) 1906 police report, Okhrana XXIVi-1A; copy of a 16 October 1906 report to DPD, Okhrana XXII-1A.

159. See: copy of a letter from Kurlov to Izvol'skii, Okhrana Va-3; William J. Fishman, *East End Jewish Radicals 1875–1914* (London, 1975), 272, 287–88; 15 January 1911 police report, Okhrana XVIb(3)-4; copy of an open letter from the Central Foreign Bureau of the RSDRP dated 26 April 1907, PSR 3-235; copy of a letter to Eramasov, signature illegible, Okhrana XVIIo-1; excerpt from a 22 March 1909 letter to F. Ia. Zimovskii in St. Petersburg from "Maksim" in Nancy, France, Okhrana XIIIc(1)-1B, Incoming Dispatches (1909), doc. 346. According to police sources, Russian SDs in Switzerland financed an anarchist trip to Russia "in order to get rid of them and their various enterprises, such as expropriations and the like which could bring nothing but harm to all Russians" in Switzerland, by turning the local people against them (30 August 1907 report from agent Dmitriev, Okhrana IIb-2[Switzerland]). Sometimes the Russian socialists were able to persuade Maximalists and anarchists to refrain from expropriations abroad (see an excerpt from a letter to Smol'ianinov from "P.," Okhrana XIIc[1]-1B; 18 [31] January 1913 report to DPD, Okhrana XVIb[5]-1; see also a 15 August 1907 report from agent Dmitriev in Switzerland, Okhrana IIb-2[Switzerland]).

160. Cited in I. Dubinskii-Mukhadze, *Kamo* (Moscow, 1974), 102–3; see also excerpt from a 4 April 1909 letter from "Liudvig" in Liege to E. Rainer in Kiev, Okhrana XIX-7. Along with the Caucasian extremists, representatives of other national groups, including Finns residing in Stockholm, also took part in terrorist enterprises abroad (see, for example, 14 [27] September 1906 report to DPD, Okhrana XIIIb[1]-1C, Outgoing Dispatches [1906], doc. 290).

161. 17 March 1904 police report, Okhrana XIIId(1)-9; "Protokol," Okhrana Va-3; see also an excerpt from an intercepted unsigned letter dated 18 November 1903 written from Geneva to N. P. Litova in St. Petersburg, Okhrana XVIId-1A; 16 (29) November 1906 report to DPD, Okhrana XXIVh-4I; "Otrazhenie sobytii 1905 g." *KA* 2 (9) (1925): 44, 48–49. European governments also took steps against Russian extremists affiliated with radical socialist organizations (see, for example, *Pervaia russkaia revoliutsiia 1905–1907 gg. i mezhdunarodnoe revoliutsionnoe dvizhenie*, pt. 1. [Moscow, 1955],

216–17; excerpt from an intercepted letter dated 6 January 1908 to Shapiro in Odessa from "Shura" in Lausanne, Switzerland, Okhrana XXVd-1; 22 April [5 May] 1908 report to DPD, Okhrana XXVc-1; "Vesti iz zagranitsy," 6, PSR 1-88).

162. Letter from P. A. Stolypin to A. P. Izvol'skii dated 19 February 1909, Okhrana Va-4; letter from Nelidov to Izvol'skii dated 2 (15) April 1909, Okhrana Va-4; 25 November (8 December) 1905 police report, Okhrana XXIVi-1A; 11 (24) May 1906 report to DPD, Okhrana XIc(5)-1; 8 (21) October 1907 report to DPD, Okhrana XXIVh-1; May 1907 police report, Okhrana XXVc-2C; 9 (22) and 14 (27) January 1908 reports to DPD, Okhrana XVIIl-2; 10 (23) May 1907 report to DPD, Okhrana Vf-2; 12 October 1907 police report, Okhrana VIj-16B; 15 January 1914 police report, Okhrana XVIIs-1; 19 April (2 May) 1916 report to DPD, Okhrana XXVc-2M. According to Okhrana sources, on at least two occasions the French police even warned Russian extremists about ongoing surveillance (2 July 1909 report to DPD, Okhrana XVIb[5]-5B).

163. Ames, *Revolution in the Baltic Provinces*, x–xi; see also Dubinskii-Mukhadze, *Kamo*, 125, 133–134, 151.

164. "Pis'mo V. V. Ratko," 43.

165. "Pis'ma E. P. Mednikova," 111; see also "Dopros Gerasimova," 3.

166. "Telegrammy," *Ezh* 1 (n.d.): 13, Nic. 435–12.

167. Decoded telegram no. 1294 from St. Petersburg dated 12 (25) June 1907, Okhrana XIIIc(3)-24.

168. This is not to suggest that instances of indiscriminate violence were not occasionally evident during the active period of the People's Will. To cite one example, members of the People's Will intent on assassinating Alexander II set off a huge explosion on 5 February 1880 that tore through the center of the Winter Palace, killing and injuring sixty-seven people (Naimark, "Terrorism and the Fall of Imperial Russia," 13).

169. Kropotkin, *Russkaia revoliutsiia i anarkhizm*, 40; "Iz obshchestvennoi khroniki," *VE* 8 (1907): 848.

170. Cited in Zhordaniia, *Bol'shevizm*, 80; Zeev Ivianski, "The Terrorist Revolution: Roots of Modern Terrorism," in David C. Rapoport, ed., *Inside Terrorist Organizations* (London, 1988), 133; "Khronika vooruzhennoi bor'by," *KA* 4–5 (11–12) (1925): 170.

171. Zavarzin, *Rabota tainoi politsii*, 128. In another incident involving the PPS, revolutionaries afraid that the son of an elderly Warsaw furniture store owner would report PPS members among his employees to the police, beat up the shopkeeper and severely injured him by shooting him in the head, as a warning to the son (26 May [8 June] 1906 report to DPD, Okhrana XIX-13).

172. *GD* 1906, 23–2:1128, and 4–1:232.

173. See, for example, Dubinskii-Mukhadze, *Kamo*, 49; "Pribaltiiskii krai," *KA* 4–5 (11–12) (1925): 273; "Khronika vooruzhennoi bor'by," *KA* 4–5 (11–12) (1925): 167, 175; 17 March 1905 police report, p. 9, Okhrana XIIIc(2)-6A; 29 September 1905 police report, pp. 7–8, Okhrana XIIIc(2)-6C.

174. See, for example, 3 March 1905 police report, pp. 5–6, 18, Okhrana XIIIc(2)-6A.

175. "Pribaltiiskii krai," *KA* 4–5 (11–12) (1925): 272.

176. M. Rakovskii, "Neskol'ko slov o Sikorskom," *KS* 41 (1928): 147.

177. Naimark, "Terrorism and the Fall of Imperial Russia," 19.

178. "Iz materialov Departamenta Politsii," PSR 1-26.

179. See, for example, Rozhdestvenskii, "Desiat' let sluzhby," 50, 55, AR; 27 January 1905 police report, p. 15, Okhrana XIIIc(2)-6A; 4 January (6 February) 1909 report to DPD, Okhrana XXVIIb-1.

180. See, for example, P. Arshinov, *Dva pobega. Iz vospominanii anarkhista 1906–9 gg.* (Paris, 1929), 9; "Dekabr'skie dni v Donbasse," *KA* 6 (73) (1935): 107, 118; Kirzhnits, *Evreiskoe rabochee dvizhenie*, 176; *Volia* 33 (7 July 1906): 3, PSR 7-569; I. Grossman-Roshchin, "Dumy o bylom," *Byloe* 27–28 (1924): 176; "Krest'ianskoe dvizhenie v Zapadnom Zakavkaz'e v 1902–1905 gg.," *KA* 2 (99) (1940): 111, 115; Ivan Myzgin, *So vzvedennym kurkom* (Moscow, 1964), 23; Grauzdin, "K istorii revoliutsionnogo dvizheniia v Latvii," *KS* 7 (92) (1932): 109.

181. Fuller, *Civil-Military Conflict*, 165; E. N. Andrikanis, *Khoziain "chertova gnezda"* (Moscow, 1960), 101. One government official admitted having a revolver in his pocket when he was assaulted by radicals, but complained, "I know what a browning is like: just one nudge and it starts shooting all of a sudden" (K. Basalygo, "Revoliutsionnoe dvizhenie v Khar'kove v 1905–6 gg.," *Letopis' revoliutsii* 1 [6] [Gos. Izdaltel'stvo Ukrainy, 1924], 134).

182. I. Riabkov-"Pchela," "Kak ia popal na rabotu pri nashem podpol'nom pravitel'stve i chto imenno vypolnial," *PR* 3 (1921): 221.

183. Individual representatives of local administrations in the border areas occasionally decided that the only way to combat the revolution was to adopt its tactics. They organized small terrorist bands for the purpose of assassinating radical activists—a practice that brought minimal results and contributed to the general anarchy (see, for example, "Krest'ianskoe dvizhenie v Zapadnom Zakavkaz'e," *KA* 2 [99]: 111, 115; and Grauzdin, "K istorii revoliutsionnogo dvizheniia v Latvii," *KS* 7 [92] [1932]: 109).

184. "Pis'ma E. P. Mednikova," in B. P. Koz'min, ed., *Zubatov i ego korrespondenty* (Moscow-Leningrad, 1928), 112–13; "25 let nazad. Iz dnevnika L. Tikhomirova," *KA* 2 (39) (1930): 63; "Iz dnevnika Konstantina Romanova," *KA* 6 (43) (1930): 113–15, and 1 (44) (1931): 126, 128; Gerasimov, *Na lezvii s terroristami*, 9, 35.

185. Supplement to the journal *Signaly*, vyp. 1 (St. Petersburg, 8 January 1906), Nic. 436–3.

186. Tagantsev, *Smertnaia kazn'*, 141.

187. "Iz obshchestvennoi khroniki," *VE* 9 (1906): 422–23.

188. "Pribaltiiskii krai," *KA* 4–5 (11–12) (1925): 273, 281; Ermakovskii, "Trukhanskie sobytiia, 1907–1908 gg. (Vospominaniia uchastnika)," *KS* 39 (1928): 120; materials of the Amur PSR Committee, PSR 3-171; Pal'vadre, *Revoliutsiia 1905–7 gg. v Estonii*, 137; "Krest'ianskoe dvizhenie v Zapadnom Zakavkaz'e," *KA* 2 (99) (1940): 111.

189. Souvarine, *Stalin*, 104; Laqueur, *Terrorism*, 41; see also Naimark, "Terrorism and the Fall of Imperial Russia," 16.

190. Gorky gave large monetary contributions to the SR and Bolshevik combatants, and also made his Moscow apartment available as a hiding place for the terrorists and a bomb laboratory (A. A. Bitsenko. "Dve vstrechi s M. Gor'kim," *KS* 41 [1928]: 64–65; Burenin, *Pamiatnye gody*, 114; 28 February [13 March] 1906 report to DPD, Okhrana XVIb[6]-1A; 24 January 1905 report to DPD, Okhrana XVIIa-2K). Andreev also turned his summer house into a place of refuge for combatants (20 March [2 April] 1914 report to DPD, Okhrana XXVc-1). After the issuance of the October Manifesto, the Ekateri-

noslav bourgeoisie bought all available weapons and distributed them among the local SRs and Bundists (Nestroev, *Iz dnevnika Maksimalista*, 42–43). For other examples of society's assistance to the extremists, see Murashev, "Stolitsa Urala," *KS* 4 (65) (1930): 52–53; Iosif Genkin, "Anarkhisty," *Byloe* 3 (31) (1918): 174; Pozner, *Boevaia gruppa pri TsK RSDRP(b)*, 39–40, 128; A. Zonin, "Tovarishch Kamo," *PR* 8–9 (31–32) (1924): 128; 3 (16) March 1911 report to DPD, Okhrana XXVb-2N.

191. *Leonid Borisovich Krasin ("Nikitich")*, 142.

192. V. Dal'nii, "Terror i delo Azeva," *Izvestiia Oblastnogo Zagranichnogo Komiteta* 9 (1909): 10, PSR 1-88. Some radicals readily acknowledged the liberals' silent approval of terror as a contribution to the revolutionary cause (leaflet issued by the Nizhnii Novgorod SR Committee, May 1905, PSR 4-320).

193. Iurenev, "Rabota R.S.-D.R.P. v Severo-Zapadnom krae," *PR* 8–9 (31–32) (1924): 188; Pozner, *Boevaia gruppa pri TsK RSDRP(b)*, 122.

194. See, for example, 29 January 1904 police report, pp. 1–2, Okhrana XIIIc(2)-4A; 4 August 1905 police report, p. 23, Okhrana XIIIc(2)-6B; police reports dated 25 August 1905, p. 10; 1 September 1905, p. 7; and 8 September 1905, p. 15, Okhrana XIIIc(2)-6C.

195. *Volia* 69 (29 September 1906): 3, PSR 7-569.

196. "Pribaltiiskii krai v 1905 g.," *KA* 4–5 (11–12) (1925): 273; Grauzdin, "K istorii revoliutsionnogo dvizheniia v Latvii," *KS* 7 (92) (1932): 108–109; see also Rozhdestvenskii, "Desiat' let sluzhby," p. 48(b), AR; "Bor'ba s revoliutsionnym dvizheniem na Kavkaze," *KA* 3 (34) (1929): 193–94.

197. GARF f. 102, DPOO, op. 1912, d. 80, ch. 3:54–54 ob.; "Bor'ba s revoliutsionnym dvizheniem na Kavkaze," *KA* 3 (34): 195.

198. K. Zakharova-Tsederbaum, "V gody reaktsii," *KS* 60 (1929): 77–78.

199. "Pribaltiiskii krai," *KA* 4–5 (11–12) (1925): 272.

200. Ibid.

201. See, for example, AM 10-CC, p. 552; clipping from newspaper *Reforma*, 4 July 1906, PSR 4-346; Kirzhnits, *Evreiskoe rabochee dvizhenie*, 174, 262; N. I. Faleev, "Shest' mesiatsev voenno-polevoi iustitsii," *Byloe* 2 (14) (1907): 66; clippings from newspaper *Tovarishch* dated 12 and 15 May 1907, PSR 4-346; "Sudebnaia khronika," *Tovarishch* 375 (19 September 1907), PSR 8-650; clipping from newspaper *Stolichnaia pochta*, 8 February 1908, PSR 3-293; 17 March 1905 police report, pp. 10–11, Okhrana XIIIc(2)-6A; 19 May 1905 police report, p. 4, Okhrana XIIIc(2)-6B; police reports dated 11 August 1905, p. 12, 1 September 1905, pp. 7, 13, and 29 September 1905, p. 7, Okhrana XIIIc(2)-6C; *Al'manakh. Sbornik po istorii anarkhicheskogo dvizheniia v Rossii* (Paris, 1909), 16, 30, 59; "Khronika vooruzhennoi bor'by," *KA* 4–5 (11–12) (1925): 175, 179; Obninskii, *Polgoda russkoi revoliutsii*, 154, 156, 159–60, 162–63, 166.

202. "Krest'ianskoe dvizhenie v Zapadnom Zakavkaz'e," *KA* 2 (99) (1940): 114; see also Kirzhnits, *Evreiskoe rabochee dvizhenie*, 274.

203. Clipping from *Novoe vremia*, 16 May 1907, PSR 4-346; see also "Dashnaktsutiun. Obvinitel'nyi akt," 11, Nic. 256–5.

204. Lokerman, "Po tsarskim tiur'mam," *KS* 25 (1926): 180; see also "Khronika vooruzhennoi bor'by," *KA* 4–5 (11–12) (1925): 173.

205. Gershuni, "Ob ekspropriatsiiakh," [undated letter to comrades], pp. 1–2, Nic. 12–1; Obninskii, *Polgoda russkoi revoliutsii*, 155–56; 17 March 1905 police report,

p. 9, Okhrana XIIIc(2)-6A; 28 July 1905 police report, p. 7, Okhrana XIIIc(2)-6B; 11 August 1905 police report, p. 17, Okhrana XIIIc(2)-6C; see also Lokerman, "Po tsarskim tiur'mam," *KS* 25 (1926): 180–81; 14 (27) February 1912 report to DPD, Okhrana XIX-12B.

206. "Bor'ba s revoliutsionnym dvizheniem na Kavkaze," *KA* 3 (34) (1929): 216.

207. Trotsky, *Stalin*, 99.

CHAPTER TWO
THE PARTY OF SOCIALISTS-REVOLUTIONARIES AND TERROR

Portions of this chapter are included in the author's article, "Aspects of Early Twentieth-Century Russian Terrorism: The Socialist-Revolutionary Combat Organization," *Terrorism and Political Violence* 4 (2) (1992): 23–46.

1. Savinkov, *Vospominaniia terrorista*, 37.

2. Francis Ballard Randall, "The Major Prophets of Russian Peasant Socialism: A Study in the Social Thought of N. K. Mikhailovskii and V. M. Chernov" (Ph.D. dissertation, Columbia University, 1961), 148.

3. The historiography of the PSR prior to the 1917 revolution is not voluminous. Among the mass of literature dealing with the Russian revolutionary movement in the twentieth century, only a few published works are dedicated directly to the SRs, touching on their terrorist policies, including: Manfred Hildermeier, *Die Sozialrevolutionäre Partei Russlands: Agrarsozialismus und Modernisierung in Zarenreich (1900–1914)* (Cologne, 1978); A. I. Spiridovich, *Partiia sotsialistov-revoliutsionerov i ee predshestvenniki (1886–1916)* (Petrograd, 1918); Sletov, *K istorii vozniknoveniia Partii Sotsialistov-Revoliutsionerov*; three initial chapters in Oliver H. Radkey's study, *The Agrarian Foes of Bolshevism: Promise and Default of the Russian Socialist-Revolutionaries, February-October 1917* (New York, 1958); several sections in Maureen Perrie's book, *The Agrarian Policy of the Russian Socialist Revolutionary Party: From Its Origins through the Revolution of 1905–1907* (Cambridge, England, 1976); references in Michael Melancon's *The Socialist Revolutionaries and the Russian Anti-War Movement, 1914–1917* (Columbus, Ohio, 1990); and in C. Rice's *Russian Workers and the Socialist-Revolutionary Party through the Revolution of 1905–1907* (New York, 1988). There are also several Soviet monographs on the SRs, such as K. V. Gusev's *Partiia eserov: Ot melkoburzhuaznogo revoliutsionarizma k kontrrevoliutsii* (Moscow, 1975); and B. V. Levanov's *Iz istorii bor'by bol'shevistskoi partii protiv eserov v gody pervoi russkoi revoliutsii* (Leningrad, 1974). A number of articles, both Western and Soviet, have concerned themselves in part with SR terrorist tactics, including Manfred Hildermeier's "Neopopulism and Modernization: The Debate on Theory and Tactics in the Socialist Revolutionary Party. 1905–1914," *Russian Review* 34 (1975); and Maureen Perrie's "The Social Composition and Structure of the Socialist Revolutionary Party before 1917," *Soviet Studies* 24 (October 1972). There are, in addition, three articles dealing specifically with SR-perpetrated terror: Maureen Perrie, "Political and Economic Terror in the Tactics of the Russian Socialist Revolutionary Party before 1914," in Mommsen and Hirschfeld, *Social Protest, Violence and Terror*; Hildermeier, "Terrorist Strategies of the Socialist-Revolutionary Party"; and Manfred Hildermeier, "Zur Sozialstruktur der Führungsgruppen und zur terroristischen Kampfmethode der Sozialrevolutionären Partei Russlands," *Jahrbücher für Geschichte Osteuropas* 20 (1972). Also of interest are two biographies of major SR figures: Boris Nikolajewsky's rather

outdated *Aseff the Spy. Russian Terrorist and Police Stool* (New York, 1934); and the recent *Boris Savinkov. Renegade on the Left* (New York, 1991), by Richard B. Spence. The only published scholarly attempt to deal specifically with the Maximalists is D. Pavlov's *Esery-maksimalisty v pervoi Rossiiskoi revoliutsii* (Moscow, 1989).

4. "Neotlozhnye zadachi," *Revoliutsionnaia Rossiia* 3 (1902); also cited in Levanov, *Iz istorii bor'by bol'shevistskoi partii protiv eserov*, 94.

5. See, for example, 20 February (5 March) 1910 police report, Okhrana XVIb(3)-4; and an unsigned manuscript on V. L. Burtsev, probably written by Chernov, p. 10, Nic. 384–5.

6. Perrie, "Political and Economic Terror," 64–65; "Terror i sotsialisty-revoliutsionery," *Revoliutsionnoe slovo* 2 (1906): 1, PSR 3-171.

7. Iu. Gardenin (Victor Chernov), "Terroristicheskii element v nashei programme," in *Sbornik "Revoliutsionnaia Rossiia,"* vyp. 2: 79, PSR 9-788.

8. Ibid., 84. For similar statements, see a 16 (29) June 1909 report to DPD, Okhrana XVIb(3)-7.

9. Iu. Gardenin (Victor Chernov), "Terror i massovoe dvizhenie" in *Sbornik "Revoliutsionnaia Rossiia,"* 122, PSR 9-788.

10. Cited in Hildermeier, "Terrorist Strategies of the Socialist-Revolutionary Party," 83; see also Gardenin, "Terroristicheskii element," 73, 77, PSR 9-788.

11. Cited in McDaniel, "Political Assassination and Mass Execution," 110.

12. Gardenin, "Terroristicheskii element," 74, PSR 9-788; Hildermeier, "Terrorist Strategies of the Socialist-Revolutionary Party," 83.

13. Cited in M. Pavlovich, "Lenin i es-ery," *Pod znamenem marksizma* 10 (1923): 157.

14. Cited in ibid., 159–60.

15. Hildermeier, "Terrorist Strategies of the Socialist-Revolutionary Party," 84.

16. *Zakliuchenie sudebno-sledstvennoi komissii po delu Azefa* (n.p., 1911) 26.

17. For the full text of the quasi-formal charter adopted by the Combat Organization in August 1904, which reveals the near autonomy of the terrorists from central party leadership, see ibid., 28.

18. Laqueur, *Terrorism*, 84.

19. Knight, "Female Terrorists," 147. As is generally true in other countries for terrorist groups resembling religious cults as much as ideological organizations, the "spirit of a religious order" prevailed among the Russian terrorists (Martha Crenshaw, "Theories of Terrorism: Instrumental and Organizational Approaches," in Rapoport, *Inside Terrorist Organizations*, 20; Zeev Ivianski, "Fathers and Sons: A Study of Jewish Involvement in the Revolutionary Movement and Terrorism in Tsarist Russia," *Terrorism and Political Violence* 2 [2] [1989]: 154).

20. Undated letter from V. M. Chernov to B. I. Nicolaevsky, Nic. 206–6.

21. *Zakliuchenie sudebno-sledstvennoi komissii po delu Azefa*, 12.

22. Hildermeier, "Terrorist Strategies of the Socialist-Revolutionary Party," 85; see also Savinkov, *Vospominaniia terrorista*, 74–76.

23. Chernov, *Pered burei*, 177, 228; see also Radkey, *Agrarian Foes of Bolshevism*, 73.

24. Savinkov, *Vospominaniia terrorista*, 40, 92, 194–96.

25. GARF f. 5831 (B. V. Savinkov), op. 1, d. 559: 5; "Iz pisem E. Sazonova," letter dated May 1906, pp. 4–5, Nic. 12–1.

26. Walter Reich, ed., *Origins of Terrorism* (Cambridge, England, 1990), 31, 33.

27. Savinkov, *Vospominaniia terrorista*, 68.

28. Hildermeier, "Terrorist Strategies of the Socialist-Revolutionary Party," 85.

29. Naimark, "Terrorism and the Fall of Imperial Russia," 16; see also *Telegramma Rossiiskogo Telegrafnogo Agentstva* 5 (2 April 1902), PSR 2-126. Balmashev was sentenced to death by a military court and hanged in the Schlisselburg prison on 16 May 1902.

30. Spiridovich, *Partiia sotsialistov-revoliutsionerov*, 125–27.

31. "K delu Fomy Kochury," *Byloe* 6 (1906): 102–3.

32. "Ko vsei soznatel'noi i trudovoi Rossii," (n.p., n.d.); and a leaflet issued in 1903 by the PSR Central Committee following the assassination of Governor Bogdanovich, both in PSR 3-168.

33. "Pis'mo S. V. Zubatova A. I. Spiridovichu po povodu vykhoda v svet ego knigi 'Partiia s.-r. i ee predshestvenniki,'" *KA* 2 (1922): 281; Gerasimov, *Na lezvii s terroristami*, 195.

34. Spiridovich, *Partiia sotsialistov-revoliutsionerov*, 123–24; cited in an unsigned and undated manuscript probably written by Chernov, Nic. 12–2.

35. Nikolajewsky, *Aseff the Spy*, 54. Other people also noted Gershuni's ability to "hypnotize" (see, e.g., a 26 February 1904 letter with an illegible signature addressed to Emiliia Kaufman in Geneva, written from St. Petersburg, Okhrana XVIIn-2A).

36. "Pamiati S. V. Sikorskogo," *KS* 41 (1928): 147; and Nestroev, *Iz dnevnika maksimalista*, 8; see also M. Spiridonova, "Iz zhizni na Nerchinskoi katorge," *KS* 15 (1925): 171.

37. Spiridovich, *Partiia sotsialistov-revoliutsionerov*, 125–26. Nicolaevsky claims that Pobedonostsev was simply "prudent enough not to attend the funeral" (Nikolajewsky, *Aseff the Spy*, 50).

38. Savinkov, *Vospominaniia terrorista*, 22; A. I. Spiridovich, *Zapiski zhandarma* (Moscow, 1991), 122; see also the unsigned and undated manuscript probably written by Chernov in Nic. 12–2.

39. Gershuni also planned to write an agitational letter for Grigor'ev. See the indictment of Gershuni and his associates implicated in terrorist plots in 1902: *Obvinitel'nyi akt*, 12, 38–39, PSR 3-170I. Gershuni was not alone in this practice, for after recruiting perpetrators for terrorist acts other revolutionaries sometimes composed propagandistic farewell notes on their behalf (see, for example, newspaper clipping entitled, "Delo Polkova," *Revoliutsionnaia Rossiia* [July 1905], PSR 8-650).

40. After Mel'nikov's arrest and conviction, he violated the traditional revolutionary code of behavior by appealing to the tsar for pardon. His fellow revolutionaries were especially outraged when, following revocation of his death sentence, Mel'nikov appealed again, this time to Plehve, against whom he had plotted, and managed to exchange his prison term for exile in Siberia (*Shlisselburg prisoners' collective statement. Re. Mel'nikov* [n.p., n.d.], Nic. 11–23; see also 2 [15] March 1904 report to DPD, Okhrana XVIb[3]-4).

41. Spiridovich claims that at the time of his previous arrest, Gershuni avoided administrative exile and bought himself freedom by providing the investigation with detailed information about the radicals (Spiridovich, *Zapiski zhandarma*, 49). There is evidence that in 1903 the authorities spared the lives of Mel'nikov and Gershuni precisely to demonstrate their insignificance (2 [15] March 1904 report to DPD, Okhrana XVIb[3]-4).

42. Another combatant, Mariia Benevskaia, lost a hand defusing a bomb (Savinkov, *Vospominaniia terrorista*, 124–26, 209–10; Chernov, *Pered burei*, 175).

43. Crenshaw, "Theories of Terrorism," 19.

44. M. Gorbunov, "Savinkov, kak memuarist," *KS* 5 (42) (1928): 175–77; Naimark, "Terrorism and the Fall of Imperial Russia," 2. Chernov depicts Savinkov as a fellow traveller in the party, filled with "great disdain for the people," and lacking any solid ideological position. At one point Savinkov claimed to be a supporter of the People's Will but subsequently, following a visit to Petr Kropotkin, pronounced himself an anarchist, and for a while also leaned toward "spiritual-religious revolutionism" (Victor Chernov, "Savinkov v riadakh P.S.-R," 157–58, Nic. 616–9; Nurit Schleifman, *Undercover Agents in the Russian Revolutionary Movement, The SR Party, 1902–1914* [New York, 1988], 174).

45. For many years Savinkov denied the autobiographical character of his novels, acknowledging it only in a 1924 letter to his sister; see also Spence, *Boris Savinkov*, 92; and Gorbunov, "Savinkov, kak memuarist," *KS* 3 (40) (1928): 174n–75.

46. Gorbunov, "Savinkov, kak memuarist," *KS* 3 (40) (1928): 173; 28 March 1912 report to DPD, Okhrana XVIb(3)–4; reports to DPD dated 9 (22) November 1912, and 10 (23) January 1913, Okhrana XVIIi-1; Nic. 290–9. On the other hand, some terrorists declared that if Savinkov were expelled from the PSR, they too would leave the party (14 [27] January 1913 report to DPD, Okhrana XVIIi-1).

47. Spence, *Boris Savinkov*, 92; Gorbunov, "Savinkov kak memuarist," *KS* 4 (41) (1928): 171; Aileen Kelly, "Self-Censorship and the Russian Intelligentsia, 1905–1914," *Slavic Review* 46 (2) (Summer, 1987): 201.

48. V. Ropshin, *Kon' blednyi* (Nice, 1913), 11–12, 134, 137, 143.

49. Ibid., 32.

50. Critics have noted the marked influence of Dostoevsky on Savinkov's fiction, and Feliks Kon, in his introduction to Savinkov's memoirs, remarked that a Dostoevskian mentality (*dostoevshchina*) was characteristic of this notorious terrorist (Savinkov, *Vospominaniia terrorista*, 5; see also Spence, *Boris Savinkov*, 93; and Kelly, "Self-Censorship and the Russian Intelligentsia," 201–3).

51. Kelly, "Self-Censorship and the Russian Intelligentsia," 201–2.

52. For a personal account of this act, see Savinkov, *Vospominaniia terrorista*, 55–58. For the SR public explanation of Plehve's assassination, see the leaflet *15-oe iiulia 1904 g.* (St. Petersburg, July 1904), PSR 3-168. E. S. Sazonov was subsequently tried and, thanks to the new liberal course taken by the government, and the outstanding talents of his eminent lawyer Karabchevskii, avoided the death penalty and was sentenced to hard labor. On 27 November 1910 he committed suicide in the Zerentui prison in protest against penal repressions (V. Pirogov, "Smert' E. S. Sazonova," *KS* 3 [1922]: 71–74; Spiridovich, *Zapiski zhandarma*, 252).

53. Many local SR groups considered the assassination of Plehve their primary objective and made preparations for this act independently from the Combat Organization (2 [15] March 1904 report to DPD, Okhrana XVIb[3]-4). The minister of the interior was himself convinced that it was only a matter of time before he fell victim to a terrorist attack, and in a notable exchange replied to a suggestion to have the black bunting that had been hung for Sipiagin's funeral removed from the staircase of his home, "No, you'd better save it; you can still use it for me" (cited in Edward H. Judge, *Plehve. Repression and Reform in Imperial Russia 1902–1904* [Syracuse, NY, 1983], 234).

54. Savinkov, *Vospominaniia terrorista*, 89.

55. Ibid., 88–89; *Zakliuchenie sudebno-sledstvennoi komissii po delu Azefa*, 32.

56. Savinkov, *Vospominaniia terrorista*, 102. Soon after this terrorist act, the following poem, entitled "His Excellency's Driver," circulated in the capitals:

Saddened by the past examples,
A driver to a powerful lord
Tries to soften SR terrorists
With lamenting, pleading word.

"Worthy terrorists, I toast you,
And wish you a speedy victory!
But I beg you to take measures
For my personal safety.

I'm concerned about the future,
Fear cuts me like a knife;
Can you find a type of bomb
That would spare the driver's life?

(*Signal*, vyp. 3 [27 November 1905], Nic. 436–3).

57. According to police sources, at the end of 1905 the PSR Central Committee had in its treasury approximately four hundred thousand rubles (Gerasimov, *Na lezvii*, 55). Savinkov recalled that "the Combat Organization at the time had significant funds at its disposal: following the assassination of Plehve, donations came to many tens of thousands of rubles." The terrorists even gave a certain percentage of this money to the party for its general expenses (Savinkov, *Vospominaniia terrorista*, 129–31, 78). As for the membership of the Combat Organization, in the words of Osip Minor, a prominent SR Central Committee member, there were so many combatants that the leaders "did not know what to do with them" (7 [20] February 1906 report to DPD, Okhrana XXVa-1).

58. "25 let nazad. Iz dnevnika L. Tikhomirova," *KA* 1 (38) (1930): 59–60.

59. Savinkov, *Vospominaniia terrorista*, 129. On the March 1905 arrests, see also a 28 April 1905 police report, p. 6, Okhrana XIIIc(2)-6B.

60. According to Petr Struve, "Trepov's role immediately following the events of 9 January and then in the October [1905] days, with [his famous slogan] 'Do not spare the bullets,' created the legend that he was a reactionary, powerful in his influence, . . . a certain monster of reaction. He was nothing of the kind" (P. Struve, *Patriotica* [St. Petersburg, 1911], 49, 51). That the general public viewed Trepov as an opponent of reform is also reflected in a police report to P. I. Rachkovskii dated 25 October (7 November) 1905, Okhrana XVIb(3)-4; see also V. A. Posse, *Moi zhiznennyi put'* (Moscow-Leningrad, 1929), 390. Several other unsuccessful plots to kill Trepov were initiated by SR terrorists outside the Combat Organization. During the most famous attempt on his life, which took place in Peterhof on 1 July 1906, an SR *boevik* killed General Kozlov by accident, mistaking him for Trepov (P. Vitiazev, M. Isakovich, S. Kallistov, "Iz vospominanii o N. D. Shishmareve," *KS* 6 [1923]: 252).

61. Savinkov, *Vospominaniia terrorista*, 176.

62. Ibid., 184.

63. *Protokoly pervogo s'ezda Partii Sotsialistov-Revoliutsionerov* (n.p., 1906), 314.

64. Kseniia Pamfilova-Zil'berberg, "'Sasha' (A. Savost'ianova)" (unpublished typescript, 1914), p. 24, ACh 40.

65. *Zerkalo* 1 (1906): 11, Nic. 436–19.

66. For a description of this act, see Gerasimov, *Na lezvii s terroristami*, 15.

67. "Sudebnaia khronika. Pokushenie na zhizn' general-gubernatora Dubasova," *Russkie vedomosti* 266 (1 November 1906), PSR 8-650.

68. *Sprut* 15 (26 April 1906): 6, Nic. 436–5.

69. While the first Duma was in session the SR leaders ceased their terrorist operations only half-heartedly, leaving open the option of resuming political assassinations at the first sign of conflict between the government and the Duma (29 May [11 June] 1906 report to DPD, Okhrana XIIc[1]-1A). Having chosen to send deputies to the Second Duma, ostensibly for peaceful legislative work, the SRs nevertheless continued to stage terrorist acts, openly sanctioned by their Central Committee, against the government (Perrie, "Political and Economic Terror," 66). According to police information, F. M. Onipko, an SR deputy to the Third Duma, proposed to the Central Committee that he use his position to make an attempt on the tsar's life during an official reception at the Winter Palace. Party leaders declined the offer (31 May [13 June] 1908 report to DPD, Okhrana XVIb[4]-1).

70. Savinkov, *Vospominaniia terrorista*, 249.

71. Ibid., 278–81.

72. Ibid., 280–85. There were several attempts to revive the old Combat Organization, as in mid- and late 1907 when the SRs planned the assassination of the tsar. These efforts proved short-lived and ultimately futile; the *boeviki* were unable to carry out a single terrorist act (Spiridovitch, *Histoire du terrorisme Russe*, 484–88).

73. For a draft of a combat detachment charter, see *Primernyi ustav Boevoi Druzhiny* (Moscow, October 1906), pp. 1–3, PSR 8-722.

74. By January-February 1907, only two of the group's ten members were "ideologically motivated SRs" (Schleifman, *Undercover Agents*, 77; "K kharakteristike Letuchego otriada Sev. obl.," p. 1, Nic. 287–18; Gerasimov, *Na lezvii s terroristami*, 118).

75. General Min's prominent part in suppressing the December 1905 uprising in Moscow earned him a reputation as a reactionary and elicited vicious attacks in the antigovernment press: "Reliable sources inform us that . . . Min has been promoted to Zululand admiral by the late Zulu king. . . . He was awarded the medal of 'Voracious Alligator' 1st Rank, bearing the inscription: 'For special services against humanity'" ("Khronika," *Zabiiaka* 1 [6 January 1906]: 10, Nic. 436–13). For the official records of the trial of Konopliannikova, see "Delo Zinaidy Konopliannikovoi," *Byloe* 1 (23) (1917): 258–74.

76. Gerasimov, *Na lezvii s terroristami*, 118–19.

77. Ibid., 119.

78. "Obvinitel'nyi akt po delu o pisariakh," 22 September 1907, pp. 1–2, 5, PSR 3-170I. Members of the Northern Flying Combat Detachment planned and executed a number of other terrorist undertakings (see "Obvinitel'nyi akt po delu ob Al'berte Trauberge, Elene Ivanovoi, Al'vine Shiamberg, Fedore Masokine, i drugikh, predannykh Peterburgskomu voenno-okruzhnomu sudu pomoshnikom glavnokomanduiushchego voiskami gvardii i Peterburgskogo voennogo okruga," in PSR 1-77).

79. "Obvinitel'nyi akt po delu ob Anne Rasputinoi, Lidii Sture, Sergee Baranove, Mario-Kal'vino i dr., predannykh sudu Pomoshnikom Glavnokomanduiushchego voiskami Gvardii SPB. voennogo okruga," in PSR 9-778, reprinted in *Byloe* 9–10 (1909): 153–57.

80. For the details, see "K arestam 7-go fevralia," newspaper clipping, title of publication illegible, dated 8 (21) February 1908, PSR 7-602; Gerasimov, *Na lezvii s terroristami*, 121–22.

81. See a copy of the document entitled "Obvinitel'nyi akt po delu ob Anne Rasputinoi," PSR 9-778; also in *Byloe* 9–10 (1909).

82. Gerasimov, *Na lezvii s terroristami*, 122–23, 146.

83. Ibid., 95–96, 101–5; Spiridovitch, *Histoire du terrorisme russe*, 451–52; "Obvinitel'nyi akt po delu ob otstavnom leitenante Borise Nikitenke, syne Kollezhskogo Sovetnika Vladimire Naumove . . . i dr. predannykh Peterburgskomu voenno-okruzhnomu sudu Vr. i. d. Pomoshnika Glavnokomanduiushchego voiskami gvardii i Peterburgskogo voennogo okruga," PSR 9-778.

84. Cited in Gusev, *Partiia eserov*, 66; "Zaiavlenie Tsentral'nogo Komiteta" (St. Petersburg, 31 July 1907), PSR 3-168. A PSR deputy to the Second Duma, Shirskii, also affirmed that his party had nothing to do with the plot (*GD* 1907, 34–2:229).

85. K. Markelov, "Pokushenie na tsareubiistvo v 1907 g.," *Byloe* 3 (31) (1925): 164–74.

86. Ibid., 157–59, 175–76; Gerasimov, *Na lezvii s terroristami*, 105–7; report no. 1429 (1912) to DPD, Okhrana XIIc(1)-1C; and *Tovarishch* 349(19 August [1 September] 1907): 2, PSR 8-650.

87. P. Rutenberg, "Delo Gapona," *Byloe* 11–12 (1909): 113, 115.

88. Savinkov, *Vospominaniia terrorista*, 241, 246.

89. Rutenberg, however, subsequently insisted that while the Central Committee had ordered him to assassinate both Gapon and Rachkovskii, he was implicitly permitted to proceed with the act against Gapon alone in case it proved impossible to kill Rachkovskii as well (ibid., 248; see also Rutenberg, "Delo Gapona," *Byloe* 11–12 (1909): 95–96; see also letters from L. E. Shishko to I. A. Rubanovich and M. A. Natanson dated April 1908, Nic. 194–12).

90. Gerasimov, *Na lezvii s terroristami*, 66; see also "Dokumenty o smerti Gapona," *KL* 2 (13) (1925): 244–46.

91. Rutenberg, "Delo Gapona," *Byloe* 11–12 (1909): 93, 99. Members of the Central Committee also tried to cover up the fact that Rutenberg was a member of the Combat Organization (Popova, "Dinamitnye masterskie," *KS* 4 [33] [1927]: 66; letter from Nicolaevsky to Chernov dated 15 October 1931).

92. Chernov later admitted that the SRs "overestimated Gapon's remaining popularity in workers' circles" (letter from Chernov to Nicolaevsky dated 7 October 1931).

93. Rutenberg, "Delo Gapona," *Byloe* 11–12 (1909): 95, 115.

94. Savinkov, *Vospominaniia terrorista*, 248–49.

95. "Obvinitel'nyi akt po delu o pisariakh," 1, PSR 3-170I.

96. Perrie, "Political and Economic Terror," 69.

97. Ibid.

98. M. Ivich, ed., "Statistika terroristicheskikh aktov" *Pamiatnaia knizhka sotsialista-revoliutsionera*, vyp. 2 (n.p., 1914). In 1912, the SR newspaper *Znamia truda* (*Banner of Labor*) raised this figure to 218 (cited in Levanov, *Iz istorii bor'by*, 100). The acknowledged victims of the SR terror were: 2 ministers; 33 governors, governors-general, and vice-governors; 16 city governors, heads of Okhrana sections, chiefs of city police, procurators and their deputies, and heads of criminal investigation departments; 24 prison and hard labor chiefs, heads of prison departments, police inspectors

and chief wardens; 26 police officers and deputies; 7 generals and admirals; 15 colonels; 8 barristers; and 26 spies and provocateurs (Gusev, *Partiia eserov*, 75).

99. There were numerous cases not recorded in the SR statistics published by Ivich in 1914. See, for example, *Obzor revoliutsionnogo dvizheniia v okruge Irkutskoi sudebnoi palaty za 1897–1907 gg.* (St. Petersburg, 1908), pp. 82, 110, Nic. 197–2; and Krasnoiarskii Komitet Partii S-R, "Izveshchenie," (n.p., n.d.), PSR 3-171.

100. E. Vagner-Dzvonkevich, "Pokushenie na nachal'nika kievskoi okhranki polkovnika Spiridovicha," *KS* 13 (1924): 136–38. This was not the only instance when the SRs claimed credit for a terrorist act they had not committed. See, for example, N. M. Rostov, "Eshche o vzryve traktira 'Tver'" v 1906 godu," *KL* 1 (40) (1931): 246; and 24 May (6 June) 1911 police report, Okhrana XVIb(3)-7.

101. Izmailovich was killed at the scene of the crime by angry sailors (Nestroev, *Iz dnevnika maksimalista*, 43; Knight, "Female Terrorists," 153–54).

102. For examples, see: Gusev, *Partiia eserov*, 61; Ivich, "Statistika terroristicheskikh aktov," 9–11; Knight, "Female Terrorists," 153. The SR leaders were well aware of this situation, and privately many of them felt that local terrorists were justified in breaking the official party resolution on terror. Osip Minor and Il'ia Rubanovich declared that "The terrorist activity of the Party of Socialists-Revolutionaries will not stop until the State Duma is able to satisfy all demands" presented by the PSR to the government (16 May [3 June] 1906 report to DPD, p. 6, Okhrana XIc[5]-1).

103. Ivich, "Statistika terroristicheskikh aktov," 11–12; Savinkov, *Vospominaniia terrorista*, 255; *Biulleten' Ts.K.P.S.-R.* 1 (March 1906): 7.

104. V. Zenzinov, "G. A. Gershuni—glava Boevoi Organizatsii" (unpublished article dated December 1932), 34, Nic. 12–2.

105. Similarly, Boris Vnorovskii, who threw a bomb at Dubasov, declared in advance that he would postpone the attempt if the admiral's wife were in the carriage with him. As leader of the Combat Organization, Savinkov approved this decision, and Kaliaev's (Savinkov, *Vospominaniia terrorista*, 95–96, 205).

106. Zenzinov, "G. A. Gershuni," 34, Nic. 12–2.

107. Savinkov, *Vospominaniia terrorista*, 255, 274–75. According to other sources eight people were killed and fifty-four wounded (*VE* 6 [1906], 783).

108. See, for example, 4 August 1905 police report, pp. 24–25, Okhrana XIIIc(2)-6B.

109. "Obvinitel'nyi akt po delu o syne kollezhskogo sovetnika Sergee Il'inskom, potomstvennom dvorianine Aleksandre Tsavlovskom i potomstvennom pochetnom grazhdanine Fedore Serebrennikove," PSR 3-170II. In an official leaflet, the PSR acknowledged that in the last years of his life Ignat'ev did not hold a single important administrative post, but at the same time they claimed, "to his final breath he did not stop serving the government of Nicholas II by his instructions, advice, and directions in domestic, as well as foreign policy" ("Po povodu kazni dvukh pravitel'stvennykh lits," [unpublished article, n.p., n.d.], PSR 3-171).

110. *Golos revoliutsii. Izdanie Krasnoiarskogo Komiteta Partii Sotsialistov Revoliutsionerov* 3 (November 1906), PSR 3-171; see also a leaflet issued by the Tambov PSR Committee, 10 April 1907, PSR 7-541.

111. "Rezoliutsiia priniataia Severokavkazskim Soiuznym S"ezdom," p. 7, PSR 9-759. For only a few examples, see a 7 April 1905 police report, p. 17, Okhrana XIIIc(2)-6A; N. Komarov, "Ocherki po istorii mestnykh i oblastnykh boevykh organizatsii partii sots.-rev. 1905–1909 gg.," *KS* 25 (1926): 79; leaflets issued by the Kishinev Combat

Detachment and the Kishinev PSR Group, 15 July, and September 1905, PSR 4-481; leaflet issued by the Briansk PSR Committee, 3 May 1907, PSR 4-321; leaflet issued by the Odessa PSR Committee, April 1905, PSR 5-427; *Trud* 7 (1906): 2, PSR 5-444; *Novgorodskii vechevoi kolokol* 5 (8 October 1907): 9, PSR 7-543; *Obzor revoliutsion-nogo dvizheniia v okruge Irkutskoi sudebnoi palaty za 1908 god* (St. Petersburg, 1909), 25, Nic. 197–3.

112. 20 September 1906 police report, Okhrana XIIId(1)-9; the same document may be found in Okhrana XXIVa-5C.

113. Ibid. A similar resolution to begin killing minor state officials and policemen was adopted at the congress of representatives of the SR Peasant Union in Finland on 8–13 September 1906 (18 September 1906 police report, Okhrana XIIId[1], folder 9).

114. Ivich, "Statistika terroristicheskih aktov," 8–9; see also a leaflet issued by the Minsk PSR Committee, 5 August 1905, PSR 5-435.

115. *Obzor revoliutsionnogo dvizheniia v okruge Irkutskoi sudebnoi palaty za 1897–1907 gg.*, 141, Nic. 197–2.

116. Nestorev, *Iz dnevnika maksimalista*, 47.

117. There is evidence that Shishmarev undertook this act without the sanction of the local SR committee (I. Genkin, "Tobol'skii tsentral," *KS* 10 [1924]: 176; Vitiazev, Isa-kovich, and Kallistov, "Iz vospominanii o N. D. Shishmareve," *KS* 6 [1923]: 259, 261).

118. Grigorii Frolov, "Terroristicheskii akt nad samarskim gubernatorom," *KS* 1 (8) (1924): 117.

119. Ibid.

120. "Obvinitel'nyi akt po delu o pisariakh," 4, PSR 3-170I.

121. 18 September 1906 police report, Okhrana XIIId(1)-9.

122. P. Kobozev, "Moi vospominaniia o 1905 g. v gor. Rige," *KL* 5 (1922): 295–96.

123. PSR 1-49.

124. "Listovka Boevogo komiteta pri Bakinskoi Organizatsii PSR," dated 25 May 1907, PSR 7-553I.

125. Perrie, "Political and Economic Terror," 69–70, 72; see also Pavlov, *Esery-Maksimalisty*, 21.

126. Perrie, "Political and Economic Terror," 70.

127. *Protokoly pervogo s"ezda Partii Sotsialistov-Revoliutsionerov*, 332.

128. Perrie, "Political and Economic Terror," 70.

129. Cited in Levanov, *Iz istorii bor'by*, 107.

130. *Protokoly pervogo s"ezda Partii Sotsialistov-Revoliutsionerov*, 333; see also Gusev, *Partiia eserov*, 54.

131. Levanov, *Iz istorii bor'by*, 108.

132. Cited in Perrie, "Political and Economic Terror," 71; and in Pavlov, *Esery-maksimalisty*, 41.

133. Perrie, "Political and Economic Terror," 71.

134. Ibid.

135. Cited in ibid., 72; see also Levanov, *Iz istorii bor'by*, 111.

136. A majority at the First Congress of the PSR resolved not to incorporate agrarian terror into the party program, or to advocate it, but at the same time not to declare themselves against it (Pavlov, *Esery-maksimalisty*, 53). In practice, however, leaders of the PSR officially renounced agrarian and factory terror on numerous occasions. See, for example, *Pamiatnaia knizhka sotsialista-revoliutsionera* (n.p., 1911), 48–50; "Re-

zoliutsiia priniataia na pervoi konferentsii Severnoi Oblasti partii S-R.," 6, PSR 3-208; *Izveshchenie o III-m Oblastnom S'ezde Sibirskogo Soiuza Partii Sotsialistov-revoliutsionerov* (n.p., 1907), p. 6, PSR 3-201; *Izveshchenie Tsentral'nogo Komiteta o IV s'ezde Soveta Partii i obshchepartiinoi konferentsii* (n.p., September 1908), p. 12, PSR 3-168; and an untitled pamphlet issued by the Organizatsionnoe Biuro pri Ts.K.P.S.-R. dated May 1908, pp. 10, 13, Nic. 194–15 (for the same document, see PSR 3-168). Still, many SR leaders sympathized with these aspects of economic terror (see, for example, a leaflet issued by the Geneva Group of the PSR, *Rezoliutsiia o boevykh druzhinakh v derevne v sviazi s agrarnym terrorom* [n.p., 1904], PSR 2-126 [for the same document, see 8–650]; and *Protokoly pervogo s'ezda Partii Sotsialistov-Revoliutsionerov*, 334, 136). Occasionally, the SRs could not resist the temptation to incite violence against the property of exploiters (see, for example, Pavlov, *Esery-maksimalisty*, 55; and an untitled article by A. S. Martynov [Vasil'ev] in *Krasnoe znamia* 2 [n.d.], Nic. 169–5).

137. Gerasimov, *Na lezvii s terroristami*, 87.

138. Pavlov, *Esery-maksimalisty*, 85. A number of Maximalist groups continued to operate throughout the empire until the fall of 1907, by which time, according to a police report, multiple "arrests destroyed their organizations totally" (5 October [22 September] 1907 report to DPD, Okhrana XVIa-2).

139. Cited in Naimark, "Terrorism and the Fall of Imperial Russia," 17; Nestroev, *Iz dnevnika maksimalista*, 64.

140. Nestroev, *Iz dnevnika maksimalista*, 112.

141. "Vzryv na Aptekarskom ostrove," *Byloe* 5–6 (27–28) (1917): 212; see also GARF f. 102, OO, op. 1906, d. 305, 305a.

142. Gerasimov, *Na lezvii s terroristami*, 89.

143. Count V. H. Kokovtsev, *Iz moego proshlogo*, vol. 1 (Paris, 1933), 230.

144. Serebrennikov, *Ubiistvo Stolypina*, 40. Six more people died of their wounds the next day (S. S. Ol'denburg, *Tsarstvovanie imperatora Nikolaia II [25 let pered revoliutsiei]* [Washington, 1981], 365). Society was shocked and horrified by this act, but although the SR Central Committee officially denied any responsibility for this Maximalist undertaking, and even declared its opposition to such brutality, some SR leaders, including Mikhail Gots and Savinkov, remained reluctant to condemn the terrorists (Pavlov, *Esery-maksimalisty*, 175–76; Spiridovich, *Partiia Sotsialistov-revoliutsionerov*, 290–91; Savinkov, *Vospominaniia terrorista*, 276).

145. Gerasimov, *Na lezvii s terroristami*, 146.

146. 11 June (29 May) 1906 report to DPD, Okhrana XIIc(1)-1A; and 4 (17) January 1907 report to DPD, Okhrana XIIIb(1)-1A, Outgoing Dispatches (1907), doc. 3.

147. P. L'vov-Marsiianin, "Rabochii druzhinnik Nikita Deev," *KS* 8 (1924): 234–35.

148. For descriptions of a few of the numerous local Maximalist terrorist acts, see *Obzor revoliutsionnogo dvizheniia v okruge Irkutskoi sudebnoi palaty za 1908 god*, 19, Nic. 197–2.

149. According to Pavlov there were 2,000–2,500 active Maximalists in Russia in 1907. The typical group consisted of approximately thirty members, although some included more than one hundred people (Pavlov, *Esery-maksimalisty*, 194, 196).

150. For example, according to a financial report prepared by the Vladimir provincial SR organization, of income totaling 1,720 rubles and 95 kopeks, 1,120 rubles had been obtained by expropriation (PSR 2-127).

151. Zakharova-Tsederbaum, "V gody reaktsii," *KS* 60 (1929): 73.

152. See, for example, a 24 December 1905 (6 January 1906) police report to P. I. Rachkovskii, Okhrana XXIVh-1; 12 August 1906 police report, Okhrana XXVc-1; *Obzor revoliutsionnogo dvizheniia v okruge Irkutskoi sudebnoi palaty za 1897–1907 gg.*, 32, Nic. 197–2; unaddressed letter from the Zakavkazskii Regional Committee of the PSR signed by Z. O. Konstantinov (25 May 1907), PSR 7-550; *Izvestiia Kurskogo komiteta Partii Sotsialistov-Revoliutsionerov*, 1 (1 February 1907), p. 2, PSR 4-324.

153. Gershuni, "Ob ekspropriatsiiakh," 7–8, Nic. 12–1.

154. Ibid., 5–8.

155. Ibid., 8. For Gershuni's speech, see also *Protokoly Vtorogo (Ekstrennogo) S'ezda Partii Sotsialistov-Revoliutsionerov* (New York, 1986), 149–53.

156. *Rezoliutsii Soveta partii S.-R.* (n.p., 1906), p. 4, PSR 3-168.

157. See, for example, "Postanovleniia konferentsii Vostochnogo Zagranichnogo Avtonomnogo Komiteta s predstaviteliami Nikol'sk-Ussuriiskoi i Khabarovskoi Grupp P.S.-R., 7–14 November 1907. Ob eskpropriatsiiakh," *Materialy Dal'nevostochnogo komiteta P.S.-R. (1907 g.)*: 3, PSR 3-200; "Izdaniia Iuzhnogo Oblastnogo Komiteta PSR," PSR 5-424; and "Chitinskii gubernskii komitet. Otchet dlia Sibirskogo oblastnogo s'ezda," (Tomsk, 1907), 2–3, PSR 3-171.

158. *Protokoly Vtorogo (Ekstrennogo) S'ezda Partii Sotsialistov-Revoliutsionerov*, 160; see also Okhrana XVIb(3)-1A.

159. Perrie, "Political and Economic Terror," 76.

160. See, for example, Kobozev, "Moi vospominaniia o 1905 g. v gor. Rige," *KL* 5 (1922): 296; *Obzor revoliutsionnogo dvizheniia v okruge Irkutskoi sudebnoi palaty za 1908 god*, 24, Nic. 197–2; "Kazanskie maksimalisty," *Birzhevye vedomosti* 11905 (7 September 1910): 4, PSR 3-219.

161. Gershuni, "Ob ekspropriatsiiakh," 2, Nic. 12–1; Komarov, "Ocherki po istorii mestnykh i oblastnykh boevykh organizatsii," *KS* 25 (1926): 79.

162. "Rezoliutsiia priniataia Severokavkazskim Soiuznym S'ezdom," p. 5, PSR 9-759; "Sovet Partii o boevykh druzhinakh" (n.p., n.d.), p. 5, PSR 3-202; leaflet issued by the Orel PSR Provincial Committee, October 1906, PSR 5-433; *Russkie vedomosti* 200 (1 September 1907), PSR 8-650; SR leaflet from the town of Kozlov, 12 March 1907, PSR 7-541; "Zaiavlenie bakinskogo komiteta PSR," n.d., PSR 7-553I.

163. R. Kantor, "Smertniki v tiur'me," *KS* 6 (1923): 129.

164. PSR 5-443.

165. Kantor, "Smertniki v tiur'me," *KS* 6 (1923): 120. One of the largest expropriations undertaken on the personal initiative of the leader of a local SR combat group was an attack on the International Bank in Odessa, from which nearly eighty-three thousand rubles were stolen and distributed among the participants (Vitiazev, Isakovich, and Kallistov, "Iz vospominanii o N. D. Shishmareve," *KS* 6 [1923]: 253).

166. "Kazanskie maksimalisty," 4, PSR 3-219.

167. Kantor, "Smertniki v tiur'me," *KS* 6 (1923): 127n.

168. See, for example, Kobozev, "Moi vospominaniia o 1905 g. v gor. Rige," *KL* 5 (1922): 296.

169. According to Gerasimov, the Maximalists stole more than 800,000 rubles (Gerasimov, *Na lezvii s terroristami*, 87); a Maximalist source claims 775,000 rubles ("Ekspropriatsiia ekspropriatorov," *Maksimalist* 6 [2 April 1920]); other sources give the figure of 875,000 rubles (Valentinov, *Maloznakomyi Lenin*, 89). Obviously indiffer-

ent to questions of dogma, Mazurin, "a born rebel" and a man of "desperate courage," called himself an anarchist; behind his expropriation practices was the conviction that "confiscation of private capital—this is what the revolution is" (Pavlov, *Esery-maksimalisty*, 73–74; V. M. Chernov, "Maksimalisty" [undated typescript], p. 20, Nic. 391–10; cited in Hildermeier, *Die Sozialrevolutionäre Partei Russlands*, 138).

170. "Obvinitel'nyi akt o Mikhaile Alekseeve Mikhailove, Sergee Aleksandrove Siniavskom . . . i drugikh, chisle 83 chel.," p. 14, PSR 9-778; Spiridovich, *Partiia Sotsialistov-revoliutsionerov*, 285–86. Although the SRs protested the Maximalist practice of expropriation, they readily accepted and used Maximalist donations of profits from these exploits (Pavlov, *Esery-maksimalisty*, 77n.).

171. According to Gerasimov, the Maximalists took nearly all of the six hundred thousand rubles being transported (Gerasimov, *Na lezvii s terroristami*, 92). During this expropriation, several Maximalists were killed; according to one revolutionary, two of them were shot down by their own comrades when they started to run away without waiting for a signal (copy of a letter written by "Akakii" in St. Petersburg to Dmitriev in Geneva, 14 March 1907, Okhrana XXIVi-1B). Ten Maximalists were captured by the police, and seven of them were subsequently sentenced to death and hanged (Spiridovich, *Partiia Sotsialistov-revoliutsionerov*, 292–93). The initiator of this expropriation, Mikhail Sokolov, was arrested in St. Petersburg a month later, tried by court-martial, and hanged on 2 December 1906 (Savinkov, *Vospominaniia terrorista*, 201).

172. Spiridovich, *Partiia Sotsialistov-revoliutsionerov*, 307; Nestroev, *Iz dnevnika maksimalista*, 80–82.

173. For a sample extortion letter, see *Obzor revoliutsionnogo dvizheniia v okruge Irkutskoi sudebnoi palaty za 1908 god*, 19, Nic. 197–3.

174. I. Pavlov, *Ochistka chelovechestva* (Moscow, 1907), 9, 15.

175. Ibid., 9.

176. Ibid., 14, 17–18, 23, 30.

177. Posse, *Moi zhiznennyi put'*, 407. Some SRs fully approved of the mass extermination of their opponents in the government camp, with one prominent party member, Count Khilkov, declaring that he "thought nothing of sacrificing thousands of heads in order to accomplish an established goal" (20 February [7 March] 1905 report to DPD, Okhrana XIc[5]-1).

178. Spiridovich, *Partiia Sotsialistov-revoliutsionerov*, 311.

179. According to prominent SR N. V. Chaikovskii, "The sins of Maximalism" lay on the SRs (letter from N. V. Chaikovskii written from the United States and dated 2 July 1907, Nic. 183–9, p. 6).

CHAPTER THREE
THE SOCIAL DEMOCRATS AND TERROR

1. Rostov, "Eshche o vzryve traktira 'Tver','" *KL* 1 (40) (1931): 246.

2. Burenin, *Pamiatnye gody*, 85.

3. Although several scholars do focus their attention on the Bolshevik policy of expropriation, they neglect the faction's participation in political murders (Abdurakhman Avtorkhanov, *Proiskhozhdenie partokratii*, v. 1 [Frankfurt/Main, 1981]; Souvarine, *Stalin*; Robert C. Williams, *The Other Bolsheviks: Lenin and His Critics* [Bloomington, Indiana, 1986]). Historians studying the SD movement for the most part ignore

its members' involvement in terrorist activities, although J.L.H. Keep mentions it in *The Rise of Social Democracy in Russia* (Oxford, 1963), and Henry J. Tobias discusses the official policy of the Bund toward terrorism briefly in *The Jewish Bund in Russia from Its Origins to 1905* (Stanford, 1972), without, however, touching upon practical aspects of the problem, and following the party only to 1905. David Allen Newell is the only historian who addresses the issue in detail, although his dissertation, "The Russian Marxist Response to Terrorism: 1878–1917" (Stanford, 1981) is also devoted primarily to the SDs' theoretical stand, rather than their practical policies.

4. In 1878, for example, S. M. Stepniak-Kravchinskii, acting on the party's orders, fatally stabbed gendarme chief General Mezentsev. In February of the following year Grigorii Gol'denberg killed Khar'kov's Governor Kropotkin, a cousin of the famous anarchist, who had a reputation of his own as a liberal. In March, Drenteln, head of the secret police, was fired upon in at central St. Petersburg street, with the Executive Committee of the Land and Freedom organization accepting responsibility for the act; it also claimed credit for the assassinations of several alleged police spies. From 31 October 1878 to 14 August 1879, Land and Freedom spent nearly six thousand rubles, with a quarter of that sum used in support of terrorist activities (Venturi, *Roots of Revolution*, 629–30, 655; and Deborah Hardy, *Land and Freedom. The Origins of Russian Terrorism*, 1876–1879 [Westport, Conn., 1987], 70, 84).

5. Deich and his associates had no proof of Gorinovich's guilt, and based their attack on suspicions, guesses, and rumors. Gorinovich survived, blind and permanently disfigured (Jay Bergman, *Vera Zasulich* [Stanford, 1983], 27–28; and Hardy, *Land and Freedom*, 55; AM 5).

6. Cited in Lev Trotsky, *Dnevniki i pis'ma* (Tenafly, New Jersey, 1986), 190.

7. Cited in *Sbornik "Revoliutsionnaia Rossiia,"* 99, PSR 9-788. By 1887, however, in the group's second program, the Liberation of Labor leaders put less emphasis on terror as a necessary aspect of the antigovernment struggle, but still asserted that they would not hesitate to resort to it in case of need (Trotsky, *Dnevniki i pis'ma*, 190).

8. For example, Marx cited in Ianson (Braun), "Latviia v pervoi polovine 1905 goda," *PR* 12 (1922): 48.

9. Both sides acknowledged that "the essential disagreements between the two factions, the Social Democratic and the Socialist-Revolutionary, [were] in their attitude toward the peasantry and toward terrorism" *(Sbornik "Revoliutsionnaia Rossiia,"* 94, PSR 9-788).

10. One SR publicist asserted that many early SDs, "not having at the time the need to concur with the narrow-minded calculations of faction politics, recognized the necessity of terrorism" (ibid., 100).

11. Newell, "Russian Marxist Response to Terrorism," 308; V. V. Vitiuk, "K analizu i otsenke evoliutsii terrorizma," *Sotsiologicheskie issledovaniia* 2 (April-May-June, 1979): 143.

12. Vitiuk, "K analizu i otsenke evoliutsii terrorizma," 144. On another occasion Zasulich went even further, proclaiming that the SDs were "against terror for the very reason that it is not revolutionary" (ibid., 148).

13. Cited in Burtsev, "Za terror," *Narodovolets* 4 (1903): 31, PSR 1-19.

14. Cited in M. Pavlovich, "Lenin i es-ery," *Pod znamenem marksizma* 10 (1923): 155.

15. Cited in Vitiuk, "K analizu i otsenke evoliutsii terrorizma," 146, 145; see also V. I. Lenin, *PSS*, V. 6 (Moscow, 1959), 375. On another occasion, Lenin wrote: "We are convinced that to sacrifice one revolutionary for even ten rascals means only to disorganize our own ranks," already too thin for the most important work among the proletariat (cited in Pavlovich, "Lenin i es-ery," 161).

16. Cited in *Sbornik "Revoliutsionnaia Rossiia,"* 99 PSR 9-788.

17. Cited in Burtsev, "Za terror," *Narodovolets* 4 (1903): 34, PSR 1-19.

18. Nic. 70–3; also cited in Burtsev, "Za terror," *Narodovolets* 4 (1903): 33, PSR 1–19.

19. For other examples of antiterrorist statements by various groups and committees of the RSDRP, see Levanov, *Iz istorii bor'by bol'shevistskoi partii protiv eserov*, 100–102.

20. Many former terrorists joined the RSDRP (see, for example, "Obzor Kavkazskikh revoliutsionnykh partii," 33, Okhrana XXa-1B; and Lenin, *PSS*, 6:180). A familiar assertion by Lenin's sister Mariia Ul'ianova that her brother renounced terror and took "another road" as early as 1887, requires reconsideration, for Isaak Lalaiants, a prominent Social Democrat who was close to Lenin in 1893, noted the future Bolshevik leader's attraction to terror as it was practiced by the People's Will organization. Trotsky, too, observed these early sympathies in Lenin (Trotsky, *Dnevniki i pis'ma*, 191; see also a letter from B. I. Nicolaevsky to N. V. Valentinov dated 9 December 1955, in Nic. 508–1).

21. See, for example, Genkin, "Tobol'skii tsentral," *KS* 10 (1924): 163.

22. Leonid Krasin, a Bolshevik active in Baku in the early stages of his revolutionary career, was critical of the *Iskra* campaign against the SRs, considering it "very harmful for the work on the local sites, where much had to be done in cooperation" (*Leonid Borisovich Krasin ["Nikitich"]*, 159). Another Bolshevik recalled that he and his comrades "could not stand polemics," and were always willing to join memebers of other parties in joint actions (A. Martsinkovskii, "Vospominaniia o 1905 g. v g. Rige," *PR* 12 [1922]: 328).

23. As Lenin himself put it, "Marxism rejects all abstract thinking and doctrinaire prescriptions about the types of struggle. . . . Marxism will never reject any particular combat method, let alone reject it forever" (Stefan T. Possony, *Lenin Reader* [Chicago, 1966], 475–76).

24. Cited in Pavlovich, "Lenin i es-ery," 155; see also Lenin, *PSS*, 6:375.

25. V. I. Lenin, *PSS*, v. 5 (Moscow, 1959), 7; see also Possony, *Lenin Reader*, 468. Trotsky later also denounced the "eunuchs and pharisees" who opposed terrorism on principle, although he thought capitalism too strong an enemy to be defeated by individual actions (Laqueur, *Terrorism*, 68). In his attacks on the SRs, Lenin was deliberately searching for fine points of disagreement, arguing on one occasion that for the SDs, "terror appears to be one of [many] possible auxiliary means, not a special tactical method," as he alleged it was for the SRs (Lenin, *PSS*, 6:371).

26. Lenin, *PSS*, 5:7.

27. Ibid., v. 4 (Moscow, 1959), 223.

28. Many Social Democrats shared these opinions. See, for example, R. Arskii, "Epokha reaktsii v Petrograde (1907–1910 gg.)," *KL* 9 (1923): 65, 67.

29. Lenin also warned, "It is not guerrilla actions which disorganize the movement, but the weakness of a party which is incapable of taking such actions under its control"

(Laqueur, *Guerrilla Reader*, 175; see also Lenin, *PSS*, 4:223; and V. I. Lenin, *PSS*, v. 11 [Moscow, 1960], 342).

30. Possony, *Lenin Reader*, 478.

31. Cited in Vitiuk, "K analizu i otsenke evoliutsii terrorizma," 147.

32. Cited in Pavlovich, "Lenin i es-ery," 156; see also Newell, "Russian Marxist Response to Terrorism," 391.

33. Lenin, *PSS*, 11:339; cited also in Arskii, "Epokha reaktsii v Petrograde," *KL* 9 (1923): 65.

34. Lenin, *PSS*, 11:341; cited also in N. Chuzhak, "Lenin i 'tekhnika' vosstaniia. Dva momenta v istorii partii," *KS* 12 (73) (1931): 78.

35. Laqueur, *Guerrilla Reader*, 173.

36. Cited in Chuzhak, "Lenin i 'tekhnika' vosstaniia," *KS* 12 (73) (1931): 78.

37. 5 March (20 February) 1906 report to DPD, Okhrana XXI-2.

38. Lenin, *PSS*, 11:340–343.

39. Cited in Chuzhak, "Lenin i 'tekhnika' vosstaniia," *KS* 12 (73) (1931): 77.

40. Cited in Avtorkhanov, *Proiskhozhdenie partokratii*, 1: 169; see also Laqueur, *Guerrilla Reader*, 176.

41. Cited in Spiridovich, *Istoriia bol'shevizma v Rossii*, 138.

42. N. Burenin, "Memoirs of an Old Revolutionist" (typescript in English), pt. 1: "1901–1906 in Finland," p. 26, AK; and T. I. Vulikh, "Bol'sheviki v Baku (1908)," p. 6, Nic. 207–9.

43. *Leonid Borisovich Krasin ("Nikitich")*, 252. For a similar episode, see Mark Buzanskii, *Budni podpol'ia* (Moscow, 1932), 82–85.

44. In one case, two Bolsheviks encountered a spy by chance and seized the initiative to strangle him to death (Myzgin, *So vzvedennym kurkom*, 92). For other examples, see Ida Peder-Sermus, "Kak i pochemu ia perestala byt' bol'shevichkoi," 1, Nic. 27–5; Aleksandr Sokolov-Novoselov, *Vooruzhennoe podpol'e* (Ufa, 1958), 68–70; L. Rogov, "Iz zhizni Bakinskoi tiur'my," *KS* 37 (1927): 127–28; and Dubinskii-Mukhadze, *Kamo*, 62.

45. T. S. Krivov, *V leninskom stroiu* (Cheboksary, 1969), 57–58.

46. See, for example, M. Gordeev-Bitner, "Boevaia druzhina v 1905 g. za Nevskoi zastavoi," *KL* 5 (20) (1926): 104; and Peder-Sermus, "Kak i pochemu ia perestala byt' bol'shevichkoi," 1, Nic. 27–5. In some instances, the Bolsheviks announced openly that their motive for an assassination was revenge (Myzgin, *So vzvedennym kurkom*, 142; see also S. Sulimov, "K istorii boevykh organizatsii na Urale," *PR* 7 [42] [1925]: 107).

47. For further details, see Pozner, *Boevaia gruppa pri TsK RSDRP(b)*, 180–84; and Rostov, "S pervoi volnoi," *KS* 20 (1925): 52–53; see also Obninskii, *Polgoda russkoi revoliutsii*, 163. In the first half of 1906 the Bolshevik regional combat detachment in the St. Petersburg area also executed several local right-wing leaders who had evaded death in the bombing of the Tver' tavern (Gordeev-Bitner, "Boevaia druzhina," *KL* 5 [20] [1926]: 108).

48. Myzgin, *So vzvedennym kurkom*, 14; see also L. S., "Moisei Georgievich Tskhoidze," *KS* 34 (1927): 195; and *Pervyi shturm samoderzhaviia* (Moscow, 1989), 358–60.

49. Gordeev-Bitner, "Boevaia druzhina," *KL* 5 (20) (1926): 108; Pozner, *Boevaia gruppa pri TsK RSDRP(b)*, 181; and S. Z. Lakoba, *Abkhaziia v gody pervoi rossiiskoi revoliutsii* (Tbilisi, 1985), 39.

50. Pozner, *Boevaia gruppa pri TsK RSDRP(b)*, 92.

51. Ibid., 122.

52. O. Varentsova, "Mikhail Vasil'evich Frunze v Ivanovo-Voznesenskom raione," *PR* 12 (47) (1925): 209. The attempt was a failure, and the two Bolsheviks were condemned to death, but their sentences were commuted to six years of hard labor for Frunze and eight for Gusev. For the full transcript of the court proceedings, official reports, and the sentence, see: Varentsova, "Mikhail Vasil'evich Frunze, PR 12 (47) (1925): 212–24; "Desiat' let so dnia smerti M. V. Frunze," *KA* 5 (72) (1935): 49–50; "Iz revoliutsionnoi deiatel'nosti M. V. Frunze," *KA* 6 (73) (1935): 84–90; and P. Berezov, *Mikhail Vasil'evich Frunze* (Moscow, 1947), 33–36.

53. Pozner, *Boevaia gruppa pri TsK RSDRP(b)*, 103.

54. Rostov, "S pervoi volnoi," *KS* 20 (1925): 53–54.

55. Before attempting to execute his plan, Ignat'ev sought Lenin's approval, but Lenin categorically forbade the venture (Burenin, *Pamiatnye gody*, 266–69).

56. With Lenin absent, only A. V. Lunacharskii, another Bolshevik leader and a future Soviet Commissar of Enlightenment, agreed with Bonch-Bruevich's proposal, while other comrades "were not up to this . . . risky measure" (V. Bonch-Bruevich, "Moi vospominaniia o P. A. Kropotkine," *Zvezda* 6 [1930]: 196). Lunacharskii also demonstrated his terrorist sympathies on other occasions (see 3 [16] October 1912 report to DPD, Okhrana XVIIs-3).

57. 3 (16) October 1912 report to DPD, Okhrana XVIIs-3. For a description of this operation, see Pozner, *Boevaia gruppa pri TsK RSDRP(b)*, 99.

58. *Leonid Borisovich Krasin ("Nikitich")*, 244–45.

59. A. Beloborodov, "Iz istorii partizanskogo dvizheniia na Urale," *KL* 1 (16) (1926): 93, 97.

60. See, for example, L. S., "Moisei Georgievich Tskhoidze," *KS* 34 (1927): 194; and Martsinkovskii, "Vospominaniia o 1905 g. v g. Rige," *PR* 12 (1922): 329.

61. Martsinkovskii, "Vospominaniia o 1905 g. v g. Rige," *PR* 12 (1922): 329.

62. Basalygo, "Revoliutsionnoe dvizhenie v Khar'kove," *Letopis' revoliutsii* 1 (6) (Gos. izd. Ukrainy, 1924): 133–34.

63. See, for example, Okhrana XVIIn-4B; P. Nikiforov, *Murav'i revoliutsii* (Moscow, 1932), 120.

64. See, for example, Pozner, *Boevaia gruppa pri TsK RSDRP(b)*, 99.

65. Police Department doc. no. 8610, 6 June 1906, Okhrana XIIId(1)-9.

66. Letter from B. I. Nicolaevsky to V. S. Voitisnkii, 15 July 1956, VC 5–2e; see also V. M. Zenzinov, "Stranichka iz istorii rannego bol'shevizma" (undated manuscript), p. 11, Nic. 392–4.

67. *Leonid Borisovich Krasin ("Nikitich")*, 232. In Williams' opinion, "Krasin, not Lenin, initiated Bolshevik plans for armed units capable of striking against the Russian government in 1905. In January he set up under the Central Committee a 'Military Technical Group' . . . to supervise the illegal tasks of the party," including the purchase and assembly of explosives. "At one point Krasin even designed a bomb, although most of the work was carried out by two chemists code-named Alpha and Omega (Williams, *Other Bolsheviks*, 62; see also Burenin, *Pamiatnye gody*, 85, 114). Krasin's dream was to devise a portable bomb as small as a walnut (Trotsky, *Dnevniki i pis'ma*, 194; see also B. Kremnev, *Krasin* [Moscow, 1968], 33).

68. 15 (28) May 1906 report to DPD, Okhrana XVIb(6)-2; 26 (13) February 1907 police report, Okhrana XXb-1; 31 October (13 November) 1907 report to DPD, p. 2, Okhrana XXb-2; see also Hugh Phillips, "From a Bolshevik to a British Subject: The Early Years of Maksim M. Litvinov," *Slavic Review* 48 (3) (Fall, 1989): 395–96.

69. V. M. Gurgenidze, "Ubiistvo Il'i Chavchavadze po arkhivnym dannym," (1987 manuscript), p. 11, AS.

70. Ibid., 4.

71. The Bolsheviks charged Chavchavadze with all imaginable crimes, calling him "bourgeois," "an exploiter of the peasantry," "an enemy of the workers," "a docile slave of the government," a "spy," a "reactionary," a "misanthrope," and so on (ibid., 6, 31; *Rech'* 303 [10 December 1908], PSR 4-346).

72. Gurgenidze, "Ubiistvo Il'i Chavchavadze," 8, 12, AS. To mislead the investigation and conceal the true motives behind the attack, the assassins tried to lend their act the appearance of an ordinary robbery by stealing Chavchavadze's watch and tearing off his wife's earrings (*Rech'* 303, [10 December 1908]). Among the participants in the murder were Social Democrats known for their previous involvement in revolutionary banditry, and therefore unlikely to have reservations about expropriating valuables from their enemies (Gurgenidze, "Ubiistvo Il'i Chavchavadze," 23, AS).

73. Gurgenidze, "Ubiistvo Il'i Chavchavadze," 24, 7–8, AS.

74. For Gurgenidze's argument, see especially ibid., 13–14, 16–17, 31–32; and "Ob odnom iz ubiits I. Chavchavadze, ob 'imeretime' (Gazeta 'Isari' ['Strela'], 13 fevralia 1908 goda. 'Opiat' ob ubiistve I. Chavchavadze')," 1–2, AS.

75. Kremnev, *Krasin*, 148–49.

76. 28 June (11 July) 1908 report to DPD, Okhrana XIIIb(1)-1B, doc. 244.

77. Cited in Levanov, *Iz istorii bor'by bol'shevistskoi partii protiv eserov*, 99.

78. Bonch-Bruevich, "Moi vospominaniia o Kropotkine," 196.

79. See P. A. Garvi, "Peterburg 1906" (typescript), p. 144, Nic. 56–2; and Dubinskii-Mukhadze, *Kamo*, 82.

80. The SDs even asserted that at the time of the assassination the Combat Organization was a myth subsequently made real by the SRs (2 [15] March 1904 report to DPD, Okhrana XVIb[3]-4; and Zenzinov, "G. A. Gershuni—glava Boevoi Organizatsii," 17–19, Nic. 12–2).

81. In a personal letter one revolutionary wrote: "Even if the SDs do not recognize systematic terror, they would not say that Balmashev acted foolishly by killing Sipiagin since everyone would only be glad that Sipiagin, like Obolenskii and the others, had been killed" (Okhrana XVId-4).

82. *Pamiati Grigoriia Andreevicha Gershuni* (Paris, 1908), 45.

83. One SD representative to the State Duma argued that "terrorist acts are a result of the criminal policies carried out by the government" (*GD* 1907, 8–1:419; for similar statements, see *GD* 1907, 34–2:230–31).

84. Laqueur, *Terrorism*, 66.

85. Laqueur acknowledges that after the assassination of Plehve, Plekhanov "was prepared to justify such operations under certain circumstances and suggested cooperation with the Social Revolutionaries. It was only after leading Social Democrats such as Axelrod and Martov threatened to leave the party that he withdrew his suggestion of cooperation" (ibid., 41; see also Souvarine, *Stalin*, 90).

86. Posse, *Moi zhiznennyi put'*, 321. At the same time, Plekhanov denounced the Bolshevik leaders for their expropriation practices (B. I. Nicolaevsky, "Bol'shevistskii Tsentr" [unfinished manuscript], introduction: "K istorii 'bol'shevistskogo Tsentra,'" 75, Nic. 544–11).

87. Tobias, *Jewish Bund*, 156.

88. Iu. Martov, "Tol'ko mertvye ne vozvrashchaiutsia," (1905 typescript), Nic. 52–6.

89. Newell, "Russian Marxist Response to Terrorism," 438.

90. See, for example, 9 (22) January 1910 report to DPD, Okhrana XIIIb(1)-1A, Outgoing Dispatches, doc. 35.

91. In at least one case, the Mensheviks even asked their organization outside the prison to help the SRs and anarchists assassinate the head of the prison (Vitiazev, Isakovich, and Kallistov, "Iz vospominanii o N. D. Shishmareve," *KS* 6 [1923]: 257).

92. N. Rostov, "Iuzhnoe Voenno-Tekhnicheskoe Biuro pri Tsentral'nom Komitete RS-DRP," *KS* 22 (1926): 98.

93. Ibid.

94. See, for example, 15 September 1905 police report, p. 9, Okhrana XIIIc(2)-6C.

95. L. S., "Ivan Vasil'evich Savin," *KS* 41 (1928): 160.

96. Rostov, "Iuzhnoe Voenno-Tekhnicheskoe Biuro," *KS* 22 (1926): 105–6.

97. A. Sukhov, "Tri mesiatsa raboty v Shendrikovskoi gruppe," *PR* 10 (45) (1925): 118. This, however, did not prevent the Social Democrats from issuing public protests against the anarchist tactic of economic terror ("Iupiter serditsia," *Anarkhist* 1 [10 October 1907], 17).

98. Sukhov, "Tri mesiatsa raboty v Shendrikovskoi gruppe," *PR* 10 (45) (1925): 118.

99. Ibid., 118–19.

100. One revolutionary described the tradition of violence in the Caucasus that she encountered upon her arrival in Baku: "The population remained armed, and a revolver or dagger was used on any pretext. To carry arms was considered so natural that when a guard was placed at the post office after an attempted robbery there, he asked every entering customer to leave his weapon at the door. Revolvers and huge daggers were piled in one heap, and each person picked up his weapon when leaving the building" (Zakharova-Tsederbaum, "V gody reaktsii," *KS* 60 [1929]: 77).

101. I. V. Shaurov, *1905 god* (Moscow, 1965), 201.

102. Grigorii Uratadze, *Vospominaniia gruzinskogo sotsial-demokrata* (Stanford, 1968), 130.

103. Noi [Noah] Zhordaniia, *Moia zhizn'* (Stanford, 1968), 44.

104. Okhrana XVIIn-5A.

105. Baron (Bibineishvili), *Za chetvert' veka*, 145.

106. Rozhdestvenskii, "Desiat' let sluzhby," 49(b)-50, AR; S. Maglakelidze and A. Iovidze, eds., *Revoliutsiia 1905–1907 gg. v Gruzii. Sbornik dokumentov* (Tbilisi, 1956), 588, 635; Obninskii, *Polgoda russkoi revoliutsii*, 49–50; Uratadze, *Vospominaniia gruzinskogo sotsial-demokrata*, 130–32; Zhordaniia, *Moia zhizn'*, 45.

107. Souvarine, *Stalin*, 74.

108. Ibid.

109. Rozhdestvenskii, "Desiat' let sluzhby," 49, AR. In a number of areas, such as Georgia's western Guriia district, "the Social Democratic Party ruled alone," and was so strong that one of its groups participated in a battle with as many as one hundred

Cossacks and a detachment of constables, killing many of them and mutilating the dead and wounded (Baron [Bibineishvili], *Za chetvert' veka*, 123, 125–26.)

110. Maglakelidze and Iovidze, *Revoliutsiia 1905–1907 gg. v Gruzii*, 277–78. The Social Democrats in Guriia officially renounced terrorism as early as May 1903 (V. Kalandadze and V. Mkheidze, *Ocherki revoliutsionnogo dvizheniia v Gurii* [St. Petersburg, 1906], 26). As the SDs later admitted, however, even though "the Social Democratic Party rejected terror in principle, fought against it [and] forbade its members to resort to it, not infrequently small groups or individual members of the party committed such acts for one reason or another without the knowledge of the leading organs of the SD organizations. But . . . there were also times when terror was practiced (often unofficially) by one organization of the Social Democratic Party or another" (S. Arkomed, "Krasnyi terror na Kavkaze i okhrannoe otdelenie," *KS* 13 [1924]: 71–72).

111. For a partial list of the numerous terrorist acts perpetrated by members of the RSDRP in the Caucasus, see Baron (Bibineishvili), *Za chetvert' veka*, 122–46; and Gurgenidze, "Ubiistvo Il'i Chavchavadze," 22, AS. The victims ranged from a street policeman by the name of Gegeliia to Lieutenant Colonel Khodetskii of the Kurinskii regiment. In the city of Aleksandropol' the party also authorized the execution of the provisional governor-general, Alikhanov-Avarskii (Maglakelidze and Iovidze, *Revoliutsiia 1905–1907 gg. v Gruzii*, 377, 435; Rozhdestvenskii, "Desiat' let sluzhby," 49[b], AR; see also 27 [14] July 1907 report to DPD, Okhrana XXVc-1; and S. Alliluev, "Moi vospominaniia," *KL* 8 [1923], 159–60). For a description of the murder of Alekhanov and the four other victims of this act, see the SR newspaper published in Novgorod, *Novgorodskii vechevoi kolokol* 3–4 (1 August 1907): 6, PSR 7-543.

112. Baron (Bibineishvili), *Za chetvert' veka*, p. 124; Gurgenidze, "Ubiistvo Il'i Chavchavadze," 23, AS; Maglakelidze and Iovidze, *Revoliutsiia 1905–1907 gg. v Gruzii*, 108; Nikiforov, *Murav'i revoliutsii*, 175.

113. Some of his fellow revolutionaries were upset by the brutality of the act (Arkomed, "Krasnyi terror na Kavkaze," *KS* 13 [1924]: 72).

114. See, for example, *Khronika revoliutsionnykh sobytii na Odesshchine v gody pervoi russkoi revoliutsii [1905–1907 gg.]* (Odessa, 1976), 96.

115. 13 October 1905 police report, p. 2, Okhrana XIIIc(2)-6C. In December 1905, SDs in Ekaterinoslav killed secret police agent Samuil Chertkov (G. Novopolin, "V mire predatel'stva," *Letopis'revoliutsii* 4 [Gos. Izdatel'stvo Ukrainy, 1923]: 37–38), and in December 1908 they made an unsuccessful attempt to assassinate a worker in Moscow who had turned out to be a police employee (Okhrana XXIVa-5q). "I shall never forget the enthusiasm with which each . . . [revolutionary] demanded to be the one to avenge the arrest of . . . [a comrade] and to execute the provocateur," wrote one former SD (B. Futorian, "Miron Konstantinovich Vladimirov," *KS* 17 [1925]: 236–37). For other cases, see: Ia. Kornil'ev, "Piat' predatelei (Iz tiuremnykh vstrech)," *KS* 37 (1927): 107; E. Levitskaia, "Stranichki vospominanii (1905 god)," *PR* 6 (1922): 156; and Voitinskii, *Gody pobed i porazhenii*, 2:271.

116. 3 March 1905 police report, p. 8, Okhrana XIIIc(2)-6A; and V. Voitinskii, *Gody pobed i porazhenii*, bk. 2 (Berlin, 1924), 272–73.

117. According to one source, "There were quite a number of registered cases of murder and attempted murder carried out by Social Democratic workers against indi-

vidual representatives of the police in the course of 1905" (Kirzhnits, *Evreiskoe rabo-chee dvizhenie*, 97); see also K., "Ivan Timenkov," *Byloe* 14 [1912]: 46; and G. Kotov, "Vtoroi raz v tiur'me," *PR* 4 [1922], 197).

118. The bombs fell into deep snow and failed to explode (V. Iakubov, "Aleksandr Dmitrievich Kuznetsov," *KS* 3 [112] [1934]: 134; see also 21 July 1905 police report, pp. 18–19, Okhrana XIIIc[2]-6B; and "Iz istorii rabochego dvizheniia na Ukraine v 1905 g.," *KA* 5 [102] [1940]: 87). In the words of one revolutionary, among the SDs, "there were, of course, enough volunteers to participate in the assassination" of a policeman (A. Gambarov, "Ocherk po istorii revoliutsionnogo dvizheniia v Luganske [1901–1921 gg.]," *Letopis' revoliutsii* 4 [Gos. izd. Ukrainy, 1923]: 76–77.

119. Gambarov, "Ocherki po istorii revoliutsionnogo dvizheniia v Luganske," *Letopis' revoliutsiia* 4 (Gos. izd. Ukrainy, 1923): 71–72.

120. Iurenev, "Rabota R.S.-D.R.P. v Severo-Zapadnom krae," *PR* 8–9 [31–32] [1924]: 190; see also Z. Chikviladze, "Afrasion Merkviladze i ego krasnaia sotnia," *KS* 17 (1925): 97.

121. Chikviladze, "Afrasion Merkviladze," *KS* 17 (1925): 97.

122. Liadov, *Iz zhizni partii*, 191.

123. Iurenev, "Rabota R.S.-D.R.P. v Severo-Zapadnom krae," *PR* 8–9 [31–32] [1924]: 190.

124. Burtsev, "Za terror," *Narodovolets* 4 (1903): 35, PSR 1-19.

125. Cited in ibid., 34; and in Tobias, *Jewish Bund*, 100. For a similar statement, see Kirzhnits, *Evreiskoe rabochee dvizhenie*, 400.

126. Nic. 70–3; see also Tobias, *Jewish Bund*, 148.

127. For a discussion of the controversy among the Bund central leadership on the question of political violence, see Tobias, *Jewish Bund*, 147–48, 150–52, 154. Significantly, an item in *Arbeiter Stimme* stated explicitly that the party was struggling "against terrorism as a system and *not* against individual personalities" (Newell, "Russian Marxist Response to Terrorism," 314).

128. Burtsev, "Za terror," *Narodovolets* 4 (1903): 35, PSR 1-19.

129. Nic. 68–8.

130. Keep, *Rise of Social Democracy*, 79.

131. "F. M. Koigen (Ionov)," *PR* 11 (23) (1923): 6; see also Tobias, *Jewish Bund*, 152–53.

132. Cited in Okhrana XVIc-7; see also Tobias, *Jewish Bund*, 155.

133. Genkin, "Sredi preemnikov Bakunina," *KL* 1 (22) (1927): 200.

134. 17 (4) February 1906 report to DPD, Okhrana XXIVh-1.

135. Kirzhnits, *Evreiskoe rabochee dvizhenie*, 249. The revenge was often of the cruelest nature, as when a member of a "local Jewish revolutionary organization" (presumably the Bund) in the town of Kremenchug threw sulfuric acid in a policeman's face (Okhrana XIIIc[2]-4B; see also 19 August [1 September] 1911 police report, Okhrana XVIIIa-3t and XIIIc[2]-6C, p. 29).

136. For more information and official documents concerning this assassination attempt, see "Girsh Lekert i ego pokushenie," *KA* 15 (1926), 87–103; and Tobias, *Jewish Bund*, 150–51.

137. The Bund committee in Minsk echoed this call for revenge: "Let not a single wild measure of the tsarist satraps be left without an answer!" (cited in *Sbornik "Revoliutsionnaia Rossiia,"* 144, PSR 9-788).

138. Tobias, *Jewish Bund*, 151; and cited in *Sbornik "Revoliutsionnaia Rossiia,"* 144–45, PSR 9-788.

139. In Lodz, for example, two members of a Bundist combat unit fired shots at *dvorniki* who tried to stop them (R. Arskii, "Iz istorii revoliutsionnogo dvizheniia v Pol'she," *KL* 4 [15] [1925]: 209). Bundists also attacked police to free arrested comrades (Tobias, *Jewish Bund*, 226).

140. Kirzhnits, *Evreiskoe rabochee dvizhenie*, 274. For examples, see Nestroev, *Iz dnevnika Maksimalista*, 38, 42; see also Avrich, *Russian Anarchists*, 18.

141. 11 August 1905 police report, Okhrana XIIIc(2)-6C.

142. Kirzhnits, *Evreiskoe rabochee dvizhenie*, 97, 202, 204.

143. 28 July 1905 police report, Okhrana XIIIc(2)-6B.

144. Kirzhnits, *Evreiskoe rabochee dvizhenie*, 400.

145. "Girsh Lekert i ego pokushenie," *KA* 15 (1926): 89.

146. Ibid., 89–90.

147. Cited in Tobias, *Jewish Bund*, 315.

148. Ibid., 311; "Khronika vooruzhennoi bor'by," *KA* 4–5 (11–12) (1925): 169.

149. P. Iagudin, "Na Chernigovshchine," *KS* 57–58 (1929): 294.

150. Kirzhnits, *Evreiskoe rabochee dvizhenie*, 280; see also Tobias, *Jewish Bund*, 321, 325.

151. Kirzhnits, *Evreiskoe rabochee dvizhenie*, 280; see also a letter from B. I. Nicolaevsky to N. Fisher dated 26 March 1937, p. 3a, Nic. 479–16.

152. For a description of the formation of these units, see Tobias, *Jewish Bund*, 226–27. According to one source, "The initiative to form self-defense units almost everywhere came from the Bundist organizations" (N. A. Bukhbinder, "Evreiskoe rabochee dvizhenie v 1905 g. Pervoe maia," *KL* 7 [1923]: 9). For one of the many proclamations calling for Jewish self-defense, see "K evreiskomu narodu!" February 1905, Nic. 737–14.

153. Police authorities also noted several incidents in which members of the self-defense units shot at pedestrians from inside carriages (10 November 1905 police report, p. 13, Okhrana XIIIc[2]-6C).

154. Ibid.

155. Kirzhnits, *Evreiskoe rabochee dvizhenie*, 258. A former revolutionary acknowledged the existence of bourgeois self-defense organizations in Vil'na that consistently refused to cooperate with the radical socialist self-defense units (Iurenev, "Rabota R.S.-D.R.P. v Severo-Zapadnom krae," *PR* 8–9 [31–32] [1924]: 188–89).

156. Kirzhnits, *Evreiskoe rabochee dvizhenie*, 297, 355–56; see also 4 August 1905 police report, pp. 12, 16, Okhrana XIIIc(2)-6B.

157. Kirzhnits, *Evreiskoe rabochee dvizhenie*, 355–56; and Obninskii, *Polgoda russkoi revoliutsii*, 161.

158. "Obzor partii, primykaiushchikh k RSDRP," 1910, p. 8, Okhrana XVIb(6)-1C; also cited in Kirzhnits, *Evreiskoe rabochee dvizhenie*, 400.

159. "Pokushenie na ubiistvo g.-m. Kosheleva, predsedatelia Rizhskogo voennogo suda," p. 1, Nic. 199–7.

160. "Obzor partii, primykaiushchikh k RSDRP," p. 39, Okhrana XVIb(6)-1C.

161. Among the SD terrorists, and even among their leaders, were a number of school-age youths who were quite willing to sacrifice theoretical principles for real action (see "Krasnaia gvardiia' v Rige v 1906 g.," *KA* 4–5 [41–42] [1930]: 213).

162. Years later a former member of the SD Party admitted that there were people

in their ranks who "used the revolutionary mask for their own self-interests" (Ianson [Braun], "Latviia v pervoi polovine 1905 goda," *PR* 12 [1922]: 49; see also "Pribaltii-skii krai," *KA* 4–5 [11–12] [1925], 269).

163. "Krasnaia gvardiia' v Rige," *KA* 405 (41–42) (1930): 213.

164. The Latvian Social Democrats proclaimed as their goals national self-determination and the "revival of the Latvian land" ("Pribaltiiskii krai," *KA* 4–5 [11–12] [1925]: 266). The SDs in the Caucasus frequently expressed their nationalistic feelings (see, e.g., Baron [Bibineishvili], *Za chetvert' veka*, 86). The Bund, while warning against "arousing national feelings, which can only befog the class consciousness of the proletariat and lead to chauvinism," in fact also sought national autonomy for the Jews (cited in a 26 March 1937 letter from Nicolaevsky to Fisher, p. 3).

165. They did concede, "It was no secret that in 1905 there were cases of terrorist attacks, not at all permissible from the Social Democratic standpoint," asserting, however, that these acts were not sanctioned by the SD Party and were perpetrated on the personal initiative of individual radicals (Ianson [Braun], "Latviia v pervoi polovine 1905 goda," *PR* 12 [1922]: 34, 49).

166. "Pokushenie na ubiistvo g.-m. Kosheleva," 1, Nic. 199–7.

167. Ianson (Braun), "Latviia v pervoi polovine 1905 goda," *PR* 12 (1922): 35.

168. *Ianis Luter Bobis*, 167.

169. "Obzor partii, primykaiushchikh k RSDRP," 30, Okhrana XVIb(6)-1C; and *Ianis Luter Bobis*, 80.

170. *Ianis Luter Bobis*, 131.

171. Ianson (Braun), "Latviia v pervoi polovine 1905 goda," *PR* 12 (1922): 48.

172. "Obzor partii, primykaiushchikh k RSDRP," 40, Okhrana XVIb(6)-1C.

173. "Pokushenie na ubiistvo g.-m. Kosheleva," 1, Nic. 199–7.

174. Ibid.

175. For a description of a particularly bloody attack on the dragoon barracks in Riga, see *Ianis Luter Bobis*, 280–81; see also "Pribaltiiskii krai," *KA* 4–5 (11–12) (1925): 269–71, 273n. For an account of an assault by several Latvian terrorists on a police department in Riga, and the liberation of their comrades from the custody of 160 policemen and soldiers, see Burenin, *Pamiatnye gody*, 246–47; and *Ianis Luter Bobis*, 121–22, 266–71.

176. "Obzor partii, primykaiushchikh k RSDRP," 31, Okhrana XVIb(6)-1C; see also Ames, *Revolution in the Baltic Provinces*, 97.

177. "Review of Beika's *God leznykh brat'ev*," 12, Nic. 121–5.

178. Pozner, *Boevaia gruppa pri TsK RSDRP(b)*, 13, 196.

179. *Ianis Luter Bobis*, 147.

180. "Review of Beika's *God lesnykh brat'ev*," 2, Nic. 121–5.

181. "Obzor partii, primykaiushchikh k RSDRP," 32–33, Okhrana XVIb(6)-1C.

182. Ibid., 33. That terror continued on a rather large scale was also evident from the party's ongoing need to issue other antiterrorist resolutions as late as June 1907, when the Latvian SD Central Committee required all party organizations "to conduct the most energetic struggle against instances of individual terror" (Levanov, *Iz istorii bor'by bol'shevistskoi partii protiv eserov*, 101).

183. "Obzor deiatel'nosti i nastoiashchego polozheniia Pol'skoi Sotsialisticheskoi Partii (P.P.S) i Sotsial-Demokratii Pol'shi i Litvy (P.S.-D.)," (Paris, 17 [30] January 1911), pp. 11–12, Okhrana XIX-12A.

184. Cited in *Sbornik "Revoliutsionnaia Rossiia,"* 143, PSR 9-788.

185. Pestkovskii, "Bor'ba partii v rabochem dvizhenii v Pol'she v 1905–1907 gg.," *PR* 11 (1922), 42.

186. "Obzor partii, primykaiushchikh k RSDRP," 2, Okhrana XVIb(6)-1C.

187. Moshinskii (Iuz. Konarskii), "F. E. Dzerzhinskii i varshavskoe podpol'e 1906 g.," *KS* 50 (1928): 21.

188. Ibid., 20–21.

189. Ibid., 21–22.

190. "Pol'skie revoliutsionnye i natsionalisticheskie oranizatsii," September 1909, Okhrana XIX-12A, p. 36.

191. "Obzor deiatel'nosti Litovskoi sotsial-demokraticheskoi partii," 1909, p. 14, Okhrana XXII-2.

192. See copy of 5 February 1910 police report, Okhrana XXII-1A.

193. Ibid; see also 13 January 1910 police report, Okhrana XIIId(2)-49.

194. "Obzor Kavkazskikh revoliutsionnykh partii," 30, Okhrana XXa-1B; excerpt from an unsigned letter written in Kiev to Charlotte Abramson in Geneva, 22 October 1903, Okhrana XXa-1A.

195. For other terrorist plans of the Gnchakisty, see 4 September 1903 police report, pp. 1–2, Okhrana XIIIc(2)-2C.

196. Okhrana XXa-1A; see also "Obzor Kavkazskikh revoliutsionnykh partii," 33, Okhrana XXa-1B.

197. Okhrana XXa-1A.

198. See, for example, "Krasnaia gvardiia' v Rige v 1906 g.," KA 4–5 (41–42) (1930): 214.

199. Cited in Williams, *Other Bolsheviks*, 108; see also "Rezoliutsiia na IV (Stokgol'mskom) S"ezde (May, 1906)," p. 26, Okhrana XVIb(6)-1C; and Krivov, *V leninskom stroiu*, 67.

200. "Rezoliutsiia na IV (Stokgol'mskom) S"ezde," p. 26, Okhrana XVIb(6)-1C.

201. See Valentinov, *Maloznakomyi Lenin*, 89.

202. Lenin, *PSS*, 11:341–342.

203. Cited in Spiridovich, *Istoriia bol'shevizma v Rossii*, 137.

204. The very name of the Bolshevik Center was known only to selected members of that faction; in the press it was referred to only as "an extended editorial board of the newspaper *Proletariat*" (3 [16] July 1909 report to DPD, Okhrana XVIb[6]-1a). According to a police source, "The true governing body of the Party" was "not the Central Committee, but the secret Bolshevik Center" (13 [26] June 1909 police report, Okhrana XVIb[6]-1a).

205. Cited in Spiridovich, *Istoriia bol'shevizma v Rossii*, 137. By August 1908 the Board of Three had split, with Krasin and Bogdanov no longer playing prominent roles in the Bolshevik Center, where the leading positions were now occupied by Lenin, Grigorii Zinov'ev, Lev Kamenev, and Viktor Taratuta (Nicolaevsky, "Bol'shevistskii Tsentr," 118, Nic. 544–11).

206. Souvarine, *Stalin*, 102. That Lenin and his followers were extremely short on funds is evident from one of Litvinov's letters: "Where do we get the money? I am ready to sell my soul to the devil for the filthy lucre" (cited in B. Mogilevskii, *Nikitich [Leonid Borisovich Krasin]* [Moscow, 1963], 68).

207. Bibineishvili, *Kamo*, 98–100; Williams, *Other Bolsheviks*, 113; Dubinskii-Mukhadze, *Kamo*, 58; see also R. Karpova, *L. B. Krasin. Sovetskii diplomat* (Moscow, 1962), 35.

208. For a description of the Tiflis expropriation (also known as the expropriation in Erevan Square), see Williams, *Other Bolsheviks*, 114; Bibineishvili, *Kamo*, 118–30; and S. Medvedeva-Ter-Petrosian, "Tovarishch Kamo," *PR* 8–9 (31–32) (1924): 127–30. Avtorkhanov indicates that Kamo's combatants expropriated as much as 340,000 rubles (Avtorkhanov, *Proiskhozhdenie partokratii*, 1:182).

209. Uratadze, *Vospominaniia gruzinskogo sotsial-demokrata*, 163, 164.

210. Vulikh notes that the Georgian terrorists and expropriators considered Stalin "the second person in the party after Lenin" (Vulikh, "Bol'sheviki v Baku," 5, Nic. 207–9; and T. I. Vulikh, "Osnovnoe iadro kavkazskoi boevoi organizatsii," 1, Nic. 207–11). Souvarine also suggests that Stalin "did not himself execute operations, but directed those who did." The Regional Congress of Transcaucasian SD Organizations resolved to expel him from the party for his involvement in the Tiflis expropriation (Souvarine, *Stalin*, 99–100). Nicolaevsky concurred on this point, although he felt that Stalin's role was somewhat exaggerated. He also asserted that the Bolsheviks abroad were able to force the Central Committee to revoke the decision of the Transcaucasian SDs (letters from B. I. Nicolaevsky to I. I. Zhordaniia, dated 5 February 1957, and I. I. Tsereteli, dated 9 September 1956, p. 1, Nic. 144–9; and Nicolaevsky, introduction to "Bol'shevistskii Tsentr": "K istorii 'bol'shevistskogo Tsentra,'" 71–72, Nic. 544–11; see also R. Arsenidze, "Iz vospominanii o Staline," *Novyi zhurnal* 72 [New York, 1963]: 232; N. Blinov, "Ekspropriatsii i revoliutsiia," *Argumenty i fakty* 30 [1989]: 6; and Alexander Rabinowitch, Janet Rabinowitch, and Ladis K. D. Kristof, eds. *Revolution and Politics in Russia. Essays in Memory of B. I. Nicolaevsky* [Bloomington, 1972], 165).

211. There is evidence that it was Lenin who in 1906 or 1907 proposed organizing a group of Caucasian *boeviki*, and suggested to Stalin that the members of the band formally leave the party, because in case of failure, "the Mensheviks would chew us up (*nas s'ediat*)" (letters from D. Shub to P. A. Garvi dated 16 June, 1 November 1947, and 1 December 1947, Nic. 438–19). In other areas of the Russian Empire SD committees took the same precautions, ordering their combatants to leave the party "on paper" (G. A. Aleksinskii, "Vospominaniia. Konets 1905 i 1906–1910 gody," [undated typescript], 107, Nic. 302–3).

212. Souvarine, *Stalin*, 96.

213. Pozner, *Boevaia gruppa pri TsK RSDRP(b)*, 79.

214. Vulikh, "Osnovnoe iadro kavkazskoi boevoi organizatsii," 3, Nic. 207–11.

215. The *boeviki* were very poor; Kamo himself "lived on fifty kopecks a day and gave them [his fellow combatants] no more" (Souvarine, *Stalin*, 96). Vulikh relates that seven people lived in a two-room apartment; two of them were once forced to stay in bed because their comrades had borrowed their only trousers. In 1905–1906 many of these revolutionaries were already manifesting symptoms of the tuberculosis that subsequently killed them (Vulikh, "Osnovnoe iadro kavkazskoi boevoi organizatsii," 3–4, Nic. 207–11; and Vulikh, "Vstrecha s gruppoi bol'shevikov-eksistov," 1, Nic. 207–10).

216. Vulikh, "Osnovnoe iadro kavkazskoi boevoi organizatsii," 4–5, Nic. 207–11. Sources vary on the exact sum stolen, with figures ranging from 2,500 to 10,000 rubles (Uratadze, *Vospominaniia gruzinskogo sotsial-demokrata*, 164–65). Other robberies included the November 1906 expropriation of 21,000 rubles from a post office railway car at the Chiaturi junction (Souvarine, *Stalin*, 100). The total acquired by Kamo's group as a result of all expropriations was in the range of 325,000–350,000 rubles (Nicolaevsky, introduction to "Bol'shevistskii Tsentr": "K istorii 'bol'shevistskogo Tsentra,'" 32, Nic. 544–11).

217. Vulikh, "Bol'sheviki v Baku (1908)," 5–6, Nic. 207–9. According to Nicolaevsky, when a Bolshevik worker protested these extortions, Stalin accused him of being a provocateur; the man was sentenced to death but managed to escape severely wounded (letter from B. I. Nicolaevsky to T. I. Vulikh dated 8 August 1949, Nic. 207–15).

218. 31 October (13 November) 1907 report to DPD, pp. 3, 5, Okhrana XXb-2.

219. Nicolaevsky, introduction to "Bol'shevistskii Tsentr": "K istorii 'bol'shevistskogo Tsentra,'" 54, Nic. 544–11.

220. 31 October (13 November) 1907 report to DPD, p. 4, Okhrana XXb-2; and 4 November (22 October) 1907 report to DPD, Okhrana XXVIIc, folder 1.

221. Telegram to the director of the Police Department, Trusevich, dated 4 November (22 October) 1907, Okhrana XXVIIc-1. A number of Bolsheviks were arrested in Europe attempting to exchange money from the Tiflis holdup (see, for example, copy of a Munich police report dated 18 January 1908, Okhrana XXb-2). Although the Bolsheviks managed to forge the serial numbers on some of the stolen 500-ruble notes, they could not exchange many of them. Only 100,000 of the expropriated 250,000 rubles were in such large bills; the other 150,000 were in smaller notes and could thus be more easily exchanged abroad (Nicolaevsky, introduction to "Bol'shevistskii Tsentr": "K istorii 'bol'shevistskogo Tsentra,'" 33, Nic. 544–11). Kamo (under the name of Dmitrii Mirskii) was also taken into custody in Berlin with concealed dynamite. Although no stolen money was found on him, he was imprisoned in Germany. For a detailed description of this police operation, see Williams, *Other Bolsheviks*, 114–16.

222. Sulimov, "K istorii boevykh organizatsii na Urale," *PR* 7 (42) (1925): 109.

223. Sokolov-Novoselov, *Vooruzhennoe podpol'e*, 65; Kh. I. Muratov and A. G. Lipkina, *Timofei Stepanovich Krivov*, (Ufa, 1968), 36.

224. According to a radical acquaintance of Mikhail Kadomtsev, the combatant "considered himself an orthodox Marxist, but in his sympathies in tactical questions and in a number of his other qualities he remained . . . a radical-minded SR of the old 'heroic' times, a Maximalist . . . and even an anarchist, but least of all a Social Democrat of the 1905–1914 period" (Genkin, "Tobol'skii tsentral," *KS* 10 [1924]: 161).

225. Krivov, *V leninskom stroiu*, 35–36; Myzgin, *So vzvedennym kurkom*, 12, 21, 23.

226. Myzgin, *So vzvedennym kurkom*, 48; S. Zalkind, "Vospominaniia ob Urale. (1903–1906 gg.)," *PR* 4 (16) (1923): 135–36; Muratov and Lipkina, *Krivov*, 36. The Bolsheviks also assaulted government printing houses (Sokolov-Novoselov, *Vooruzhennoe podpol'e*, 63–64).

227. Beloborodov, "Iz istorii partizanskogo dvizheniia na Urale," *KL* 1 (16) (1926): 93. Among the most notorious cases were two robberies on the Samara-Zlatoust railroad line, in the Voronki and Dema train stations in August and September of 1906, respectively. In the first assault the Bolsheviks expropriated 25,000 rubles, and in the second 163,000 rubles (Krivov, *V leninskom stroiu*, 91; Sokolov-Novoselov, *Vooruzhennoe podpol'e*, 61; F. P. Bystrykh, *Bol'shevistskie organizatsii Urala v revoliutsii 1905–1907 godov* [Sverdlovsk, 1959], 294). Nicolaevsky claims that the Bolsheviks acquired 200,000 rubles in the Dema station expropriation; Myzgin asserts that they got away with nearly 250,000 rubles (Nicolaevsky, introduction to "Bol'shevistskii Tsentr": "K istorii 'bol'shevistskogo Tsentra,'" 33, Nic. 544–11; Myzgin, *So vzvedennym kurkom*, 16).

228. Krivov, *V leninskom stroiu*, 67–68; Muratov and Lipkina, *Krivov*, 54. According to another source, the expropriation took place on 29 August 1909 (4 August 1911

police report, Okhrana XXIVj-1). This and other sources also mention an earlier Bolshevik expropriation at the Miass station, in 1908. According to official estimates, the *boeviki* collected more than 86,000 rubles on that occasion, and killed a number of guards and railway employees (see Nicolaevsky, "Bol'shevistskii Tsentr," pt. 1, Notes to Documents 1–14, 28, n. 68, Nic. 545–1).

229. At that time Kerensky was an attorney building his reputation by specializing in political and terrorist cases (see, e.g., Frolov, "Terroristicheskii akt nad samarskim gubernatorom," *KS* 1 [8] [1924]: 119). Kerensky's involvement in terrorist practices was not limited to his professional legal activities, however, In December 1905 he is said to have volunteered to join the SR Combat Organization, intending to assassinate Nicholas II, but was not accepted (Richard Abraham, *Alexander Kerensky: The First Love of the Revolution* [New York, 1987], 32–33). According to Gerasimov Kerensky persisted, and became head of an SR combat detachment in the Aleksandro-Nevskii district of St. Petersburg, only to be immediately arrested by the Okhrana (Gerasimov, *Na lezvii s terroristami*, 51).

230. Krivov, *V leninskom stroiu*, 70–71.

231. For example, in 1907 the Bolsheviks expropriated in excess of one thousand rubles from a zemstvo near the town of Dvinsk and, on another occasion, seized several hundred unused passport forms and seals (I. Iurenev, "Dvinsk [1907–1908 g.]," *PR* 3 [15] [1923]: 209). In February of 1906 the Bolsheviks attempted to rob a St. Petersburg savings bank, but succeeded only in killing a police officer who happened to be there by coincidence. They also looted several state liquor stores (Rostov, "S pervoi volnoi," *KS* 20 [1925]: 53–54). Bolshevik confiscation of weapons in Riga is described in Martsinkovskii, "Vospominaniia o 1905 g. v g. Rige," *PR* 12 (1922): 328.

232. Medvedeva-Ter-Petrosian, "Tovarishch Kamo," *PR* 8–9 (31–32) (1924): 117.

233. Pozner, *Boevaia gruppa pri TsK RSDRP(b)*, 102–3; and Nicolaevsky, "Bol'shevistskii Tsentr," Notes to Documents 1–14, 15, n. 32, Nic. 544–11.

234. Cited in Trotsky, *Stalin*, 97. Similar cases are mentioned in "Sostoianie RSDRP s 30 iiunia po nachalo noiabria 1909 g.," Okhrana XVIb(6)-2.

235. *KPSS v rezoliutsiiakh i resheniiakh s'ezdov, konferentsii i Plenumov TsK*, v. 1, 9th ed. (Moscow, 1983), 242.

236. Williams, *Other Bolsheviks*, 106; and 27 March (9 April) 1910 police report, Okhrana XVIb(6)(b)-1. When the Bolsheviks demanded that Martov be tried by the party, he announced that he "would have nothing to do with bandits, counterfeiters, and thieves" (Okhrana XVId-1, 1908).

237. *Byvshie liudi, Al'manakh I* (n.p., n.d.), 9, Nic. 757–5.

238. For example, the Swiss Federal Attorney General complained that "there exist a mass of Russians who are strongly suspected of participating in common crimes" inside Russia, such as bank robberies (Williams, *Other Bolsheviks*, 106). Even European socialists were irritated by the apparently criminal activity of the Russian Social Democrats (see Nicolaevsky, introduction to "Bol'shevistskii Tsentr": "K istorii 'bol'-shevistskogo Tsentra,'" 66, Nic. 544–11).

239. Nicolaevsky, introduction to "Bol'shevistskii Tsentr": "K istorii 'bol'shevist-skogo Tsentra,'" 119, Nic. 544–11; see also Souvarine, *Stalin*, 126.

240. Letter from B. I. Nicolaevsky to N. V. Valentinov dated 17 January 1959, p. 2, Nic. 508–2. Valentinov, who knew Lenin intimately before 1917, concurred on this point (letter from N. V. Valentinov to B. I. Nicolaevsky dated 10 January 1959, p. 1, Nic. 508–2).

241. Cited in Nicolaevsky, introduction to "Bol'shevistskii Tsentr": "K istorii 'bol'-shevistskogo Tsentra,'" 13, Nic. 544–11. Bogdanov claimed that Lenin also imposed financial repressions against party organizations that refused to support his views, and that he purposely delayed the usual transfer of funds to them, even though this sometimes interfered with their ability to protect themselves from the police (see Nicolaevsky, introduction to "Bol'shevistskii Tsentr": "K istorii 'bol'shevistskogo Tsentra,'" 132, Nic. 544–11).

242. According to Bogdanov, the Bolshevik Center spent hundreds of thousands of rubles in just two years; Nicolaevsky thought this estimate correct, considering the substantial sums the Bolsheviks acquired in 1907 (ibid., 13, 33).

243. Souvarine, *Stalin*, 106; see also 31 October (13 November) 1907 report to DPD, p. 3, Okhrana XXb-2; Okhrana XVId-1, 1908. At times, the St. Petersburg Bolshevik committee received not less than 2,000–3,000 rubles per month (Nicolaevsky, introduction to "Bol'shevistskii Tsentr": "K istorii 'bol'shevistskogo Tsentra,'" 54n, Nic. 544–11). According to Grigorii Zinov'ev, among the overwhelming Menshevik majority in the Central Committee following the Stockholm Congress, there were several Bolshevik "hostages" (cited in Nicolaevsky, introduction to "Bol'shevistskii Tsentr": "K istorii 'bol'shevistskogo Tsentra,'" 3, Nic. 544–11).

244. Dubinskii-Mukhadze, *Kamo*, 68.

245. Souvarine, *Stalin*, 106. Even the proceeds from expropriations proved insufficient to satisfy Bolshevik requirements, and after the Fifth RSDRP Congress in London the delegates could not afford to return home until the party leaders borrowed a substantial sum from a British businessman (letter from N. V. Valentinov to B. I. Nicolaevsky dated 10 January 1959, pp. 4–5, Nic. 508–2). A prominent Bolshevik described the situation in Ekaterinburg in the Urals: "Of course we had no money . . . but we did have a good combat detachment. A successful expropriation of a mail train . . . gave us enough funds for the entire [election] campaign." They were extremely short of printing supplies, but were able to fill their needs in a single assault on a provincial printing house. The writer recalled that "three or four newspapers were established this way" (Liadov, *Iz zhizni partii*, 194).

246. Sulimov, "K istorii boevykh organizatsii na Urale," *PR* 7 (42) (1925): 111. For a description of the bomb school in Lemberg, see Myzgin, *So vzvedennym kurkom*, 67–71. Throughout the empire, there were a number of similar schools, including one in the Finnish village of Kuokkala. This school, established for the purpose of "teaching fighting techniques to *boeviki*," belonged to the combat organization of the Bolshevik-controlled St. Petersburg RSDRP Committee, and also operated an explosives laboratory. In its theoretical and practical program, the school was an establishment for graduating terrorists little different from those of the People's Will or the SR trend (see Pozner, *Boevaia gruppa pri TsK RSDRP[b]*, 267, 254–55).

247. Sokolov-Novoselov, *Vooruzhennoe podpol'e*, 61; Bystrykh, *Bol'shevistskie organizatsii Urala*, 294; Muratov and Lipkina, *Krivov*, 54; Valentinov, *Maloznakomyi Lenin*, 89. According to Okhrana sources, members of the Vpered group organized and maintained the school on funds from the 1908 and 1909 Miass robberies; of the sums expropriated at this train station, seventeen thousand rubles went to the school. Although officially the school was set up to train party propagandists, it actually graduated combat instructors, that is, officers for the combat detachments. Several expropriators from the Urals traveled to Italy to attend this school (4 August 1911 police report,

Okhrana XXIVj-1; 2 [15] December 1910 police report, Okhrana XXIVj-2g; G. Z. Ioffe, *Krakh rossiiskoi monarkhicheskoi kontrrevoliutsii* (Moscow, 1977), 149; Nicolaevsky, "Bol'shevistskii Tsentr," Notes to Documents 1–14, n. 68, p. 28, Nic. 544–11). Soviet sources claim that more than eighty thousand rubles expropriated at the Miass station were sent to Italy to subsidize the school (*Lenin ob Urale*, 387). The decision to start a school to train combat instructors was made in May 1906 at an SD combat unit confer-ence, where the revolutionaries resolved "to see that the means necessary for the estab-lishment of such a school be raised" (4 June 1906 police report, Okhrana XIIId[1]-9).

248. Cited in Chuzhak, "Lenin i 'tekhnika' vosstaniia," *KS* 12 (73) (1931): 104.

249. Cited in Williams, *Other Bolsheviks*, 83; Newell, "Russian Marxist Response to Terrorism," 447–50. The vote on this resolution demonstrated that the overwhelming majority of RSDRP leaders, including several Bolsheviks, wished to halt the criminal activity conducted under the guise of partisan actions; only 13.6 percent of the delegates (primarily Bolsheviks and Latvians) wished to continue it. More than 20 percent of the delegates present abstained from the vote (Nicolaevsky, introduction to "Bol'shevist-skii Tsentr": "K istorii 'bol'shevistskogo Tsentra,'" 37, Nic. 544–11).

250. Spiridovich, *Istoriia bol'shevizma v Rossii*, 169. The Bolsheviks in the Urals, with Lenin's approval, agreed to demobilize the combat organizations gradually, but to try to preserve the best detachments (Myzgin, *So vzvedennym kurkom*, 99). Terrorist acts continued against managers opposed to revolutionary agitation at their factories, and also, "From time to time a death sentence was issued for one exposed provocateur or another" (A. Rogov, "Na revoliutsionnoi rabote v Baku," *KS* 35 [1927]: 103–4).

251. Murashev, "Stolitsa Urala v 1905–1908 gg.," *KS* 4 (65) (1930): 50–51.

252. The intricate case of the Schmidt inheritance was notorious. The son of a wealthy factory owner, Nikolai Schmidt, imprisoned for participation in the December 1905 uprising in Moscow, died suddenly in his cell in February 1907 without having written a formal will. His lawyer claimed authorization to transfer his entire estate to the RSDRP. The Bolshevik Center immediately seized the opportunity and announced that the fortune that Schmidt had inherited from his grandfather, millionaire Vikula Morozov, belonged to the Bolshevik faction alone. Acting with the utmost secrecy, the Bolsheviks forced the legal heir, Schmidt's younger brother Aleksei, to relinquish all rights to the legacy in favor of his two sisters, Ekaterina and Elizaveta, so that each would then receive nearly 129,000 rubles (Nicolaevsky, introduction to "Bol'shevist-skii Tsentr": "K istorii 'bol'shevistskogo Tsentra,'" 25, 27, 126–27, Nic. 544–11). It was this money, as well as the sisters' own shares of the Morozov inheritance, that Lenin and Krasin were determined to get their hands on. They initially assigned a member of their faction, the lawyer N. A. Andrikanis, to procure Ekaterina's portion, and when the emissary betrayed their trust by marrying her and agreeing to transfer only one-third to the Bolsheviks, they threatened to kill him if he did not turn over the entire sum (12 December [29 November] 1907 report to DPD, Okhrana XXVb-2C, 2–3; and Nicolaevsky, introduction to "Bol'shevistskii Tsentr": "K istorii 'bol'shevistskogo Tsentra,'" 25–26, Nic. 544–11). After many complications, conflicting claims, and eventually the mediation of a committee of SRs, the Bolsheviks and Adrikanis reached a compromise in 1908, with the latter relinquishing half of Ekaterina's share, or eighty-five thousand rubles (31 May [13 June] 1908 report to DPD, Okhrana XXVb-2C; and Spiridovich, *Istoriia bol'shevizma v Rossii*, 165n). To secure the second half of the inheritance, Lenin forced A. M. Ignat'ev to enter against his will into a fictitious mar-

riage with Elizaveta Schmidt, who as a minor could not legally give up her share of the money and needed a husband to do so for her. Matters were further complicated by the duplicitous role played by the notorious Viktor Taratuta, a suspected police agent and, in the opinion of his fellow Bolsheviks, an inveterate rogue, who had been a key figure in extracting the funds from Aleksei and Ekaterina Schmidt. Lenin had initially commissioned him to obtain Elizaveta's share of the inheritance, and following Andrikanis's example, Taratuta quickly became her lover while Ignat'ev was still wooing her. As an outlaw Taratuta could not marry Elizaveta, but he did everything he could to prevent her marriage to Ignat'ev, clearly working against Lenin's wishes. At the same time, Taratuta "threatened her pro-Menshevik relatives with energetic action by the Caucasian *boeviki* if the whole sum was not paid over" (28 June [11 July] 1908 report to DPD, Okhrana XIIIb[1]-1B, doc. 244; Nicolaevsky, introduction to "Bol'shevistskii Tsentr": "K istorii 'bol'shevistskogo Tsentra,'" 46, Nic. 544–11; Burenin, *Pamiatnye gody*, 263; Souvarine, *Stalin*, 126). By June 1908, the Bolshevik Center had finally acquired a larger portion of Elizaveta's share (Williams, *Other Bolsheviks*, 118). The Mensheviks, and especially Martov, were outraged by the affair from the outset, demanding that the entire sum be transferred to the Central Committee. As late as 1915, portions of Schmidt's inheritance were still the object of contention between the Mensheviks and the Bolsheviks. When the "last slice of the booty," entrusted pending final settlement to three German SDs—Karl Kautsky, Clara Zetkin, and Franz Mehring, eventually fell into the hands of the Bolsheviks, they had accumulated a total of approximately 280,000 rubles of the Schmidt inheritance (Nicolaevsky, introduction to "Bol'shevistskii Tsentr": "K istorii 'bol'shevistskogo Tsentra,'" 23, 33, Nic. 544–11; Souvarine, *Stalin*, 126; Williams, *Other Bolsheviks*, 119). The police referred to the affair of the Schmidt inheritance, from which Lenin and his group benefited by a combination of extortion, threats, and lies, as "a bloodless expropriation," and Trotsky subsequently labeled the Bolshevik methods "an expropriation within the Party" (16 [3] December 1907 report to DPD, Okhrana XIc[4]-1; and Souvarine, *Stalin*, 126). For the Soviet version of this affair, see Andrikanis, *Khoziain "chertova gnezda."*

253. According to their agreement with a British businessman at the time of the Fifth RSDRP Congress, the Bolsheviks were to return the money borrowed from him by 1 January 1908. When this date arrived, Lenin declared that because of many recent Bolshevik expenses, "to demand the money now is unthinkable and would be equal to usury" (cited in a letter from V. N. Valentinov to B. I. Nicolaevsky dated 10 January 1959, p. 5, Nic. 508–2). At Krasin's insistence, the Bolsheviks finally repaid the debt in 1923 (letter from V. N. Valentinov to B. I. Nicolaevsky dated 10 January 1959, p. 6, Nic. 508–2). In addition, in 1909 Lenin and his supporters in the Bolshevik Center refused to return three thousand rubles that Krasin had borrowed for the faction from a wealthy St. Petersburg widow, A. I. Umnova. Krasin, indignant at the refusal, paid Lenin in kind: according to police sources, he seized twenty-five thousand rubles remaining after the Tiflis expropriation, forcing the Bolshevik Center to reconsider its decision (3 [16] July 1909 report to DPD, Okhrana XVIb[6]-1a; see also B. I. Nicolaevsky, introduction to "Bol'shevistskii Tsentr": "K istorii 'bol'shevistskogo Tsentra,'" 115–116, Nic. 544–11).

254. 27 March (9 April) 1910 report to DPD, Okhrana XVIb(6)(b)-1.

255. Chuzhak, "Lenin i 'tekhnika' vosstaniia," *KS* 12 (73) (1931): 104.

256. Aleksinskii, "Vospominaniia. Konets 1905 i 1906–1910 gody," 74, Nic. 302–3; undated draft of a police report, Okhrana XVIa-1.

257. Rostov, "Iuzhnoe Voenno-Tekhnicheskoe Biuro," *KS* 22 (1926): 94–95; and A. Trofimenko, "K istorii voenno-tekhnicheskogo biuro iuga Rossii v 1905–1906 gg.," *Letopis' revoliutsii* 5–6 (14–15) (Gos. izd. Ukrainy, 1925): 103.

258. Trofimenko, "K istorii voenno-tekhnicheskogo biuro," *Letopis' revoliutsii* 5–6 (14–15) (Gos. izd. Ukrainy, 1925): 103, 105.

259. As a result of his disagreements with the Menshevik antiterrorist resolutions at the Fifth Party Congress, Al'bin broke his ties with them (Shaurov, *1905 god*, 178–79, 235, 239).

260. Blinov, "Ekspropriatsii i revoliutsiia," 6; see also Dubinskii-Mukhadze, *Kamo*, 68–69. A Latvian Social Democrat, Azis, argued at the London Congress that if the party were to vote to expel expropriators from its ranks, "then it would be forced to expel the entire Central Committee" (cited in Chuzhak, "Lenin i 'tekhnika' vosstaniia," *KS* 12 [73] [1931]: 111).

261. See, for example, Kantor, "Smertniki v tiur'me," *KS* 6 (1923): 123–24; and S. L. Gel'zin (Babadzhan), "Iuzhnoe Voenno-Tekhnicheskoe Biuro pri TsK RS-DRP," *KS* 61 (1929): 31.

262. 31 October (13 November) 1907 report to DPD, p. 2, Okhrana XXb-2; and Bibineishvili, *Kamo*, 106–7. Valentinov asserts that the SDs obtained only one hundred thousand rubles from this expropriation (Valentinov, *Maloznakomyi Lenin*, 89 n.).

263. Baron (Bibineishvili), *Za chetvert' veka*, 123, 130.

264. Nikiforov, *Murav'i revoliutsii*, 175.

265. Aleksinskii, "Vospominaniia. Konets 1905 i 1906–1910 gody," 105–7, Nic. 302–3; Baron (Bibineishvili), *Za chetvert' veka*, 127.

266. Gurgenidze, "Ubiistvo Il'i Chavchavadze," 22–23, AS.

267. 3 (16) July 1909 report to DPD, Okhrana XVIb(6)-1a.

268. Avrich, *Russian Anarchists*, 18.

269. Iagudin, "Na Chernigovshchine," *KS* 57–58 (1929): 301.

270. Letter from P. A. Kropotkin to M. I. Gol'dsmit dated 22 February 1906, Nic. 81–4.

271. "Ko vsem," leaflet published by the Grodnenskii SD Committee of the Bund, September 1905, Nic. 68–8.

272. Peters, "1905 god v Libave," *PR* 11 (46) (1925): 201.

273. Laqueur, *Guerrilla Reader*, 173; Souvarine, *Stalin*, 90.

274. Pozner, *Boevaia gruppa pri TsK RSDRP(b)*, 176–77.

275. This expropriation was undertaken on the initiative of two RSDRP Central Committee members in Finland, one of whom was the Menshevik A. Bushevich (Rybak). The leader of the raid was Ianis Luter (Bobis), the notorious Latvian terrorist. According to Bruno Kalnin, after getting away with 162,243 rubles in cash, the combatants spent part of the money on personal needs, and then Bushevich transferred the rest to the RSDRP Central Committee (letter from Kalnin to Nicolaevsky dated 11 August 1965, Nic. 485–16; *Ianis Luter Bobis*, 283–85, 294; see also E. Stasova, "Iz vospominanii o partiinoi rabote do revoliutsii 1917 g.," *PR* 12 [71] [1927]: 192).

276. Chuzhak, "Lenin i 'tekhnika' vosstaniia," *KS* 12 (73) (1931): 107.

277. Souvarine, *Stalin*, 105. While opposing the participation of Polish SDs in revolutionary robberies, Tyshko took Lenin's side in the party scandal over the Tiflis expropriation in the summer and fall of 1908. Nicolaevsky convincingly argues that Tyshko did so for one reason only: out of the funds expropriated from the party as a result of the

Schmidt affair, the leaders of the Bolshevik Center continuously paid Tyshko's group substantial sums for its support against the Mensheviks. Thanks to this alliance, in which Tyshko played the role of a mercenary, Lenin was able to silence most voices of protest against the Bolsheviks' illegal actions and even to obtain control over the central organizations of the RSDRP, demonstrating once again that his fund-raising activities were undertaken primarily for these goals (Nicolaevsky, introduction to "Bol'shevistskii Tsentr": "K istorii 'bol'shevistskogo Tsentra,'" 127–29, Nic. 544–11; see also a letter from B. I. Nicolaevsky to Bruno Kalnin dated 15 October 1956, Nic. 485–16; and Aleksinskii, "Vospominaniia. Konets 1905 in 1906–1910 gody," p. 68, Nic. 302–3).

278. See, for example, "Obzor deiatel'nosti Litovskoi sotsial-demokraticheskoi partii," 14; 4 December 1903 police report, p. 1, Okhrana XIIIc(2)-2C.

CHAPTER FOUR
TERRORISTS OF A NEW TYPE

1. *Khleb i volia* 19–20 (July 1905), 11.

2. Kropotkin, *Russkaia revoliutsiia i anarkhizm*, 3; 11 July 1910 police report, Okhrana XVIb(5)-5B. In accordance with their general belief that "the spirit of destruction is a creative spirit," the anarchists set forth little in the way of a positive program. Still, they did propose that special schools be established to educate children as future proponents of independent protest, so that they would be "prepared from childhood to hate all obedience and prejudice" (Kropotkin, *Russkaia revoliutsiia i anarkhizm*, 3; see also: "Anarkhizm," 1, Okhrana XVIb[5]-5A).

3. Avrich, *Russian Anarchists*, 34. Avrich's book remains the most thorough scholarly study of anarchism in Russia.

4. Grossman-Roshchin, "Dumy o bylom," *Byloe* 27–28 (1924): 176.

5. Avrich, *Russian Anarchists*, 43.

6. *Al'manakh. Sbornik po istorii anarkhicheskogo dvizheniia v Rossii*, 181. According to the anarchist creed, man is naturally good and humane and therefore does not need to comply with norms established by compulsory institutions such as law and government (Genkin, "Anarkhisty," *Byloe* 3 [31] [1918]: 163).

7. Genkin, "Anarkhisty," *Byloe* 3 [31] [1918]: 164; unpublished and undated police brochure, "Anarkhizm i dvizhenie anarkhizma v Rossii," 87–88, Nic. 80–4 (for the same source, see Okhrana XVIb[5]-5A).

8. *Al'manakh. Sbornik po istorii anarkhicheskogo dvizheniia v Rossii*, 46.

9. Avrich, *Russian Anarchists*, 34.

10. See, for example, P. Kochetov, "Vologodskaia ssylka 1907–1910 godov," *KS* 4 (89) (1932): 87.

11. According to Avrich, there were approximately five thousand active anarchists in the Russian Empire at the peak of the movement, 1905–1907 (Avrich, *Russian Anarchists*, 34, 69n.).

12. Ibid., 34.

13. Cited in Laqueur, *Terrorism*, 42.

14. A. Dobrovol'skii, ed., *Anarkhizm. Sotsialism. Rabochii i agrarnyi voprosy* (St. Petersburg, 1908), 14. During the anarchist congress in London in late 1904, Kropotkin demanded a "thoughtful and careful approach toward terrorist methods," and rejected the practice of expropriation (L. Lipotkin, "Russkoe anarkhicheskoe dvizhenie v sever-

noi Amerike. Istoricheskie ocherki" [undated manuscript], 98, Arkhiv L. Lipotkina, International Institute of Social History, Amsterdam). In 1905, however, Kropotkin expressed a modified stand on terrorism in a letter to a friend, Mariia Gol'dsmit, stating that it is better to allow "thoughtless and harmful acts . . . than to paralyze the spontaneous activity" of the terrorists (Nic. 81–4).

15. Kropotkin, *Russkaia revoliutsiia i anarkhizm*, 7, 9, 52.

16. Avrich, *Russian Anarchists*, 59–60; "K tovarishcham anarkhistam-kommunistam" (St. Petersburg, September 1906), Nic. 3–3.

17. Kropotkin provided money out of his private funds to anarchists returning to Russia from abroad to implement terrorist projects (10 [23] May 1907 report to DPD, Okhrana Vf-2).

18. Kropotkin, *Russkaia revoliutsiia i anarkhizm*, 9. While the Anarchists-Communists supported the SRs in their use of terror as a disorganizing tool, they disagreed with the SR use of violence to win concessions from the tsarist regime, insisting that the struggle should continue to the final destruction of the establishment ("K tovarishcham anarkhistam-kommunistam," Nic., 3–3).

19. Kropotkin, *Russkaia revoliutsiia i anarkhizm*, 52–54.

20. Avrich, *Russian Anarchists*, 60.

21. Kropotkin, *Russkaia revoliutsiia i anarkhizm*, 55.

22. "Anarkhizm i dvizhenie anarkhizma v Rossii," 55, Nic. 80–4; "Anarkhizm," 55, 92, Okhrana XVIb[5]-5A. This view was fairly representative of most anarchists-syndicalists, who denounced conspiratorial tactics and argued, in the words of their leader in Western Europe, Maksim Raevskii (L. Fishelev), that only the labor movement could provide the organized army of freedom fighters required for a successful social revolution (Avrich, *Russian Anarchists*, 61–63).

23. P. Katenin, *Ocherki russkikh politicheskikh techenii* (Berlin, 1906), 100.

24. Lokerman, "Po tsarskim tiur'mam," *KS* 25 (1926): 187.

25. For a justification of motiveless terror by the leader of a small anarchist group in Moscow, see Zavarzin, *Zhandarmy i revoliutsionery*, 177.

26. Genkin, "Anarkhisty," *Byloe* 3 [31] [1918]: 164.

27. Avrich, *Russian Anarchists*, 44, 48.

28. "K tovarishcham anarkhistam-kommunistam," Nic. 3–3.

29. "Anarkhizm i dvizhenie anarkhizma v Rossii," 25, Nic. 80–4.

30. See, for example, S. Anisimov, "Sud i rasprava nad anarkhistami-kommunistami," *KS* 10 (95) (1932): 138.

31. Unaddressed letter written by A. A. Lopukhin dated 6 December 1904, p. 7, Nic. 205–13.

32. Ibid.

33. Genkin, "Anarkhisty," *Byloe* 3 [31] [1918]: 164.

34. Ibid.

35. Avrich, *Russian Anarchists*, 49–51.

36. Arshinov, *Dva pobega*, 5.

37. See, for example, *Al'manakh. Sbornik po istorii anarkhicheskogo dvizheniia v Rossii*, 27–28, 42, 69; newspaper clippings from *Tovarishch* (25 July 1907), and *Russkoe slovo* (23 June 1907) in PSR 8-650. Like other revolutionaries, the anarchists rarely conducted serious investigations, and expeditiously executed anyone suspected of being a police informer, occasionally taking mistaken vengeance on comrades who

had no dealings with the authorities (see, for example, 3 [16] January 1907 report to DPD, Okhrana XIIIb[1]-1A, Outgoing Dispatches, doc. 2; Genkin, "Anarkhisty," *Byloe* 3 [31] [1918]: 175n; and "Sudebnye vesti," newspaper clipping from *Novoe vremia* 11233 [22 February 1907], PSR 8-650).

38. See, for example, Arshinov, *Dva pobega*, 11, 18; Genkin, "Sredi preemnikov Bakunina," *KL* 1 (22) (1927): 199. Dvorniks were frequent targets for terrorist attacks because their duties included assisting the authorities in searches, arrests, and surveillance operations (see, for example, *Al'manakh. Sbornik po istorii anarkhicheskogo dvizheniia v Rossii*, 10–11, 35).

39. See, for example, 21 July 1905 police report, p. 25, Okhrana XIIIc(2)-6B; 15 September 1907 police report, Okhrana XIIIc(1)-1B, Incoming Dispatches, doc. 499; 8 (21) July 1911 police report, Okhrana XXVc-1; reference 27, Okhrana XVIIn-8–2; newspaper clipping from *Tovarishch* 349 (19 August [1 September] 1907), PSR 8-650; "Ben'iamin Fridman (Nemka Malen'kii). (Nekrolog)," p. 4, Okhrana XXIVe-2d; Tashkentets, "Pervaia viselitsa v g. Penze," *KS* 50 (1928): 93; Genkin, "Sredi preemnikov Bakunina," *KL* 1 (22) (1927): 177, 199; Anisimov, "Sud i rasprava," *KS* 10 (95) (1932): 144; leaflet "Tiranam palacham i nasil'nikam—smert'" (January 1907), Nic. 3–2; "Fedosei Zubar' (Nekrolog)," p. 1, Okhrana XXIVe-2d; newspaper clipping from *Rech'* 212 (8 September 1907), PSR 8-650; *Obzor revoliutsionnogo dvizheniia v okruge Irkutskoi sudebnoi palaty za 1908 god*, 34, Nic. 197–3. There were many occasions when terrorists were killed by their own bombs along with their targets. For example, on 14 March 1909, in the small town of Smela, after a long and bloody shoot-out with the police, anarchist Makarii Miroshnik placed dynamite in his mouth and blew himself up; his comrade, Aris, threw a hand grenade under his own feet (*Al'manakh. Sbornik po istorii anarkhicheskogo dvizheniia v Rossii*, 188).

40. Arshinov, *Dva pobega*, 46; see also V. Simanovich, "Vospominaniia proletariia," *KS* 6 (79) (1931): 99; and "Tiranam palacham i nasil'nikam—smert'," Nic. 3–2.

41. See, for example, "Ubiistva, napadeniia, grabezhi," newspaper clipping from *Russkoe slovo* 102 (5 June 1907), PSR 8-653; *Obzor revoliutsionnogo dvizheniia v okruge Irkutskoi sudebnoi palaty za 1897–1907 gg.*, 201–202, Nic. 197–2; "Fedosei Zubar' (Nekrolog)," 4, Okhrana XXIVe-2d.

42. See, for example, police telegram no. 1306 dated 13 (26) November 1910, Okhrana XIIIa-9; 17 (30) December 1907 report to DPD, Okhrana XXVc-2K; 8 (21) February 1906 report to DPD, Okhrana XXIVi-1A; 3 (16) January 1909 report to DPD, Okhrana XIIIb(1)-1A, Outgoing Dispatches, doc. 7; police telegram no. 870 from St. Petersburg dated 21 May (7 June) 1908, Okhrana XIIIc(3)-27; Grossman-Roshchin, "Dumy o bylom," *Byloe* 27–28 (1924): 182; Genkin, "Sredi preemnikov Bakunina," *KL* 1 (22) (1927): 182; "Anarkhizm," 78, Okhrana XVIb[5]-5A. According to police information, an anarchist group in Warsaw also planned a series of terrorist assaults on foreign consulates in that city, "in order to bring about the interference of European states in internal Russian affairs" (13 [26] July 1906 report to DPD, Okhrana XVIb[4] folder 1).

43. For examples, see newspaper clipping from *Anarkhist* 3 (May 1909): 28, PSR 7-558; "Ben'iamin Fridman," 4, Okhrana XXIVe-2d; "Tiranam palacham i nasil'nikam—smert'," Okhrana XIIIb(1)-1C, Outgoing Dispatches (1906), doc. 235; reports to DPD dated 24 October (6 November) 1907, and 17 (30) December 1907, Okhrana XIIIb(1)-1C, Outgoing Dispatches, docs. 485 and 568; *Al'manakh. Sbornik po istorii*

anarkhicheskogo dvizheniia v Rossii, 6–7, 27, 32, 44, 64, 59, 69, 187; Vitiazev, Isakovich, and Kallistov, "Iz vospominanii o N. D. Shishmareve," *KS* 6 (1923): 257; Avrich, *Russian Anarchists*, 66.

44. *Al'manakh. Sbornik po istorii anarkhicheskogo dvizheniia v Rossii*, 44.

45. Ibid., 11, 28, 35; "Iz Rossii," *Anarkhist* 4 (September 1909): 29; "Fedosei Zubar' (Nekrolog)," 5, Okhrana XXIVe-2d.

46. 28 April 1905 police report, p. 20, Okhrana XIIIc(2)-6B.

47. See, for example, "Fedosei Zubar' (Nekrolog)," 5, Okhrana XXIVe-2d.

48. Fuller, *Civil-Military Conflict*, photograph 5 between pp. 164 and 165, and pp. 150–52; see also police reference note dated 12 November 1906, p. 10, Nic. 179–1; Ames, *Revolution in the Baltic Provinces*, 31 and 47, photographs.

49. Cited in Genkin, "Sredi preemnikov Bakunina," *KL* 1 (22) (1927): 198.

50. *Al'manakh. Sbornik po istorii anarkhicheskogo dvizheniia v Rossii*, 26.

51. Ibid., 8, 15.

52. See, for example, ibid., 36, 39, 58, 125, 166, 179; unaddressed letter written by A. A. Lopukhin, 6 December 1904, p. 7, Nic. 205–13; Arshinov, *Dva pobega*, 15–16, 75.

53. *Al'manakh. Sbornik po istorii anarkhicheskogo dvizheniia v Rossii*, 181.

54. "Ben'iamin Fridman," 2, Okhrana XXIVe-2d; Simanovich, "Vospominaniia proletariia," *KS* 6 (79) (1931): 94.

55. See, for example, Kirzhnits, *Evreiskoe rabochee dvizhenie*, 174; "Dekabr'skie dni v Donbasse," *KA* 6 (73) (1935): 102, 115–16, 121.

56. Genkin, "Sredi preemnikov Bakunina," *KL* 1 (22) (1927): 198; "Fedosei Zubar' (Nekrolog)," 5, Okhrana XXIVe-2d.

57. Genkin, "Sredi preemnikov Bakunina," *KL* 1 (22) (1927): 197; newspaper clipping from "Sudebnaia khronika," *Russkie vedomosti* 111 (1908), PSR 2-150; "Anarkhizm i dvizhenie anarkhizma v Rossii," 56, Nic. 80–4.

58. See, for example, 19 November 1913 police report, Okhrana XXII-1B; Simanovich, "Vospominaniia proletariia," *KS* 6 (79) (1931): 91; "Dekabr'skie dni v Donbasse," *KA* 6 (73) (1935): 120; "Ekaterinoslav," unpublished leaflet, undated, pp. 1–2, Okhrana XXIVe-2d; 17 (30) December 1907 report to DPD, Okhrana XIIIb(1)-1C, Outgoing Dispatches, doc. 568; *Al'manakh. Sbornik po istorii anarkhicheskogo dvizheniia v Rossii*, 24, 27–28, 63, 69, 167, 179, 187, 189; "Anarkhizm," 45–46, Okhrana XVIb[5]-5A.

59. Naimark, "Terrorism and the Fall of Imperial Russia," 18.

60. *Obzor revoliutsionnogo dvizheniia v okruge Irkutskoi sudebnoi palaty za 1908 god*, 33, Nic. 197–3.

61. "Anarkhizm," 31, 25, Okhrana XVIb[5]-5A; Genkin, "Sredi preemnikov Bakunina," *KL* 1 (22) (1927): 198. For similar resolutions, see a 17 (30) December 1907 report to DPD, Okhrana XXVc-2K.

62. Genkin, "Sredi preemnikov Bakunina," *KL* 1 (22) (1927): 198; see also "Fedosei Zubar' (Nekrolog)," 5, Okhrana XXIVe-2d.

63. Laqueur, *Terrorism*, 42; GARF f. 102, DPOO, op. 1905, d. 2605:122.

64. See, for example, Simanovich, "Vospominaniia proletariia," *KS* 6 (79) (1931): 95.

65. Genkin, "Anarkhisty," *Byloe* 3 [31] [1918]: 176.

66. *Al'manakh. Sbornik po istorii anarkhicheskogo dvizheniia v Rossii*, 37.

67. "Fedosei Zubar' (Nekrolog)," 15, Okhrana XXIVe-2d.

68. *Al'manakh. Sbornik po istorii anarkhicheskogo dvizheniia v Rossii*, 115.

69. Ibid., 45.

70. Naimark, "Terrorism and the Fall of Imperial Russia," 18.

71. Ibid.; Genkin, "Sredi preemnikov Bakunina," *KL* 1 (22) (1927): 199; "Pamiati Moishe Kirshenbaum ('Tokar' ')," *Anarkhist* 5 (March, 1910): 2–3; "Fedosei Zubar' (Nekrolog)," 2, Okhrana XXIVe-2d.

72. *Al'manakh. Sbornik po istorii anarkhicheskogo dvizheniia v Rossii*, 7, 38, 17, 151; "Anarkhizm," 55, Okhrana XVIb[5]-5A; Okhrana XVIIn-8, 2.

73. *Al'manakh. Sbornik po istorii anarkhicheskogo dvizheniia v Rossii*, 26.

74. Avrich, *Russian Anarchists*, 44, 63.

75. Cited in M. Slonim, *Russkie predtechi bol'shevizma* (Berlin, 1922), 47.

76. Criminal members of anarchist groups testified that their leaders did much to convince them that their banditry was socially progressive (see, for example, Zavarzin, *Zhandarmy i revoliutsionery*, 180).

77. Laqueur, *Terrorism*, 102; see also Naimark, "Terrorism and the Fall of Imperial Russia," 18.

78. Avrich, *Russian Anarchists*, 51, 63; *Al'manakh. Sbornik po istorii anarkhicheskogo dvizheniia v Rossii*, 45.

79. *Al'manakh. Sbornik po istorii anarkhicheskogo dvizheniia v Rossii*, 46; see also Genkin, "Anarkhisty," *Byloe* 3 [31] [1918]: 181.

80. *Al'manakh. Sbornik po istorii anarkhicheskogo dvizheniia v Rossii*, 6.

81. Kochetov, "Vologodskaia ssylka," *KS* 4 (89) (1932): 86–88.

82. For a description of a former criminal who joined the anarchist movement, see Simanovich, "Vospominaniia proletariia," *KS* 6 (79) (1931): 96–97.

83. Laqueur, *Terrorism*, 102.

84. "Anarkhizm," 81–82, Okhrana XVIb[5]-5A.

85. "Dopros Gerasimova. 26 aprelia 1917 goda," 3.

86. Zavarzin, *Zhandarmy i revoliutsionery*, 180–181, 185.

87. Genkin, "Sredi preemnikov Bakunina," *KL* 1 (22) (1927): 200. For a description of terrorist acts perpetrated by the Black Ravens, see a newspaper clipping from *Russkoe slovo* 2 (November 1907), PSR 8-650.

88. Newspaper clipping from *Tovarishch* (20 October 1907), PSR 8-650.

89. 20 February (5 March) 1906 report to DPD, Okhrana XXI-2; see also Kirzhnits, *Evreiskoe rabochee dvizhenie*, 175.

90. "Fedosei Zubar' (Nekrolog)," 3–4, Okhrana XXIVe-2d.

91. *Al'manakh. Sbornik po istorii anarkhicheskogo dvizheniia v Rossii*, 63.

92. See, for example, 27 September 1907 police report, Okhrana IXd-1; 23 August (5 September) 1907 report to DPD, Okhrana XIIIb(1)-1B, Outgoing Dispatches, doc. 366.

93. Grossman-Roshchin, "Dumy o bylom," *Byloe* 27–28 (1924): 179.

94. *Al'manakh. Sbornik po istorii anarkhicheskogo dvizheniia v Rossii*, 162–163.

95. For the similar biography of a Baku anarchist, L. Domogatskii, see GARF f. 102, DPOO, op. 1915, d. 12, ch. 6: 1–2. Domogatskii claimed to have murdered sixteen people and wounded eight himself, and to have been involved with comrades in the deaths of another fifty men, primarily low-ranking police officers, in addition to committing fourteen robberies. Before he became an anarchist, Domogatskii served time in prison for murder.

96. Ravich-Cherkasskii, "Moi vospominaniia o 1905 gode," *Letopis' revoliutsii* 5–6 (14–15) (Khar'kov, 1925): 319.

97. Zavarzin, *Zhandarmy i revoliutsionery*, 188.

98. Ibid., 188–189. For a similar description, see "Anarkhizm i dvizhenie anarkhizma v Rossii," 37, Nic. 80–4.

99. Genkin, "Sredi preemnikov Bakunina," *KL* 1 (22) (1927): 174.

100. Arshinov, *Dva pobega*, 74.

101. K., "Ivan Timenkov," *Byloe* 14 (1912): 47–49. For similar examples of former SRs in 1907–1909 uniting into small groups of five to seven men to engage in uncontrolled violence, see Beloborodov, "Iz istorii partizanskogo dvizheniia na Urale," *KL* 1 (16) (1926): 99. One such group, the Union of Extremist Terrorists (Soiuz krainikh terroristov), incorporated the program of the PSR into its by-laws (GARF f. 102, OO, op. 1901, d. 187: 1, 32). Members of local SR organizations occasionally combined forces with defectors from their own ranks for joint terrorist attacks (see, for example, Nestroev, *Iz dnevnika Maksimalista*, 42).

102. Reference 27, Okhrana XVIIn-8, p. 1; see also "Anarkhizm," 49, Okhrana XVIb[5]-5A; and 22 April 1904 police report, p. 4, Okhrana XIIIc(2)-4A.

103. Paul H. Avrich, "The Last Maximalist: An Interview with Klara Klebanova," *Russian Review* 32 (4) (October, 1973): 416.

104. For a description of terrorist acts and expropriations carried out under the direction of Savitskii against local conservatives and the bourgeoisie, see Iagudin, "Na Chernigovshchine," *KS* 57–58 (1929): 298.

105. S. Sibiriakov, "Pamiati Petra Sheffera," *KS* 22 (1926): 239.

106. Beloborodov, "Iz istorii partizanskogo dvizheniia na Urale," *KL* 1 (16) (1926): 93–94.

107. Ibid., 95.

108. Lbov's detachment continued to operate until 1908 when the terrorists, constantly pursued by the police, began to disperse. Their leader finally fell into the hands of the authorities, was tried, and hanged (ibid., 93, 96–98).

109. "Pribaltiiskii krai v 1905 g.," *KL* 1 (16) (1926): 266–67; " 'Krasnaia gvardiia' v Rige v 1906 g.," *KA* 4–5 (41–42) (1930): 213. For other examples of obscure SD groups in Latvia that demonstrated clear anarchist tendencies, see GARF f. 102, DPOO, op. 1911, d. 23, ch. 40 B, "Latyshskaia SDRP": 276 ob.; and Rabinowitch, Rabinowitch, and Kristof, *Revolution and Politics in Russia. Essays in Memory of B. I. Nicolaevsky*, 143.

110. "Anarkhizm," 61, Okhrana XVIb[5]-5A.

111. 27 (14) July 1907 report to DPD, Okhrana XXVc-1; Okhrana VIj-16B.

112. Police report from Paris dated 14 September 1906, Okhrana VIj-15C. Another autonomous group formed in 1909 with the primary goal of assassinating Nicholas II (GARF f. 102, DPOO, op. 1909, d. 80, ch. 52).

113. "Sudebnaiia khronika. Delo o predpolagavshemsia vzryve okhrannogo otdeleniia," newspaper clipping from *Tovarishch* (19 October 1907), PSR 8-650.

114. "Sudebnaia khronika," newspaper clipping from *Kolokol* 852 (3 January 1909), PSR 7-602. For a description of a similar group in Sevastopol', see GARF f. 102, op. 1914, d. 340: 23.

115. Newspaper clipping from *Tovarishch* 349 (19 August [1 September] 1907), PSR 8-650; newspaper clipping from *Rus'* 143 (25 May 1908), PSR 8-653. References to the so-called Non-Party Union of Terrorists (Bespartiinyi soiuz terroristov) may be

found in GARF f. 102, op. 1912, d. 88: 1, 7–7 ob.; see also a reference to a combat detachment called Freedom Is Inside Us (Svoboda vnutri nas) operating in Sevastopol' in 1906, in GARF f. 102, op. 1914, d. 340: 22 ob.-23.

116. Okhrana XIIIa-10B, I.

117. Fishman, *East End Jewish Radicals*, 272.

118. "Ustav partii 'Nezavisimykh'," March 1909, Okhrana XVIa-2.

119. Ibid.

120. See, for example, Nikiforov, *Murav'i revoliutsii*, 263.

121. "Vospominaniia byvsh. okhrannika," *Bessarabskoe slovo*, 1930, Nic. 203–25; M. Barsukov, "Kommunist-buntar'," 200–201, Nic. 747–10.

122. Ibid., 202–3; and *G. I. Kotovskii. Dokumenty i materialy* (Kishinev, 1956), 12, 29.

123. *G. I. Kotovskii. Dokumenty in materialy*, 12, 30, 34. Many women, including some in the highest social circles, demonstrated their fascination with this legendary revolutionary rogue by sending him flowers, candies, and admiring notes during his imprisonment ("Vospominaniia byvsh. okhrannika," Nic. 203–25).

124. *G. I. Kotovskii. Dokumenty i materialy*, 50; Barsukov, "Kommunist-buntar'," 207, Nic. 747–10.

125. Sukhomlin, "Iz tiuremnykh skitanii," *KS* 55 [1929]: 103.

126. Kirzhnits, *Evreiskoe rabochee dvizhenie*, 178n; *Al'manakh. Sbornik po istorii anarkhicheskogo dvizheniia v Rossii*, 58.

127. Genkin, "Sredi preemnikov Bakunina," *KL* 1 (22) (1927): 193–94.

128. 22 April 1904 police report, p. 4, Okhrana XIIIc(2)-4A; Reference 27, Okhrana XVIIn-8, 1–2; "K tovarishcham anarkhistam-kommunistam," Nic. 3–3.

129. Anisimov, "Sud i rasprava," *KS* 10 (95) (1932): 136–137; "Anarkhizm i dvizhenie anarkhizma v Rossii," 73, Nic. 80–4; 17 (30) December 1907 report to DPD, Okhrana XXVc-2K; Okhrana XVIIn-8. For descriptions of similar large-scale expropriations of state money and property, with damages in the thousands of rubles, see: newspaper clippings from *Tovarisch* (3 August 1907), and "Sudebnaia khronika," *Tovarishch* 374 (18 September 1907), both in PSR 8-650; 8 (21) September 1907 report to DPD, Okhrana XXVc-1; 21 May (3 June) 1909 report to DPD, Okhrana XIIIb(1)-1B, Outgoing Dispatches, doc. 296; 25 September (8 October) 1909 report to DPD, Okhrana XIIIb(1)-1C, Outgoing Dispatches, doc. 468; newspaper clipping from *Russkoe slovo* (7 November 1907), PSR 8-650; newspaper clipping from *Rech'* (24 November 1907), PSR 8-650; "Fedosei Zubar' (Nekrolog)," 7, Okhrana XXIVe-2d.

130. See, for example, 31 December 1911 (12 January 1912) report to DPD, Okhrana XIIIb(1)-1J, Outgoing Dispatches (1911), doc. 1727; Avrich, *Russian Anarchists*, 46.

131. Okhrana XIIIa-13B; Anisimov, "Sud i rasprava," *KS* 10 (95) (1932): 143; see also *Al'manakh. Sbornik po istorii anarkhicheskogo dvizheniia v Rossii*, 70.

132. Anisimov, "Sud i rasprava," *KS* 10 (95) (1932): 135. The anarchists also planned a number of unsuccessful large-scale robberies; one was to have taken place on board the commercial ship *Rumiantsev* in Odessa, but the plot was discovered by the police (newspaper clipping from *Russkie vedomosti* [25 March 1908], PSR 3-227).

133. See, for example, a newspaper clipping from "Sudebnaia khronika" in *Russkie vedomosti* 111 (13 May 1908), PSR 2-150; newspaper clipping from "Iz zala suda," *Russkoe slovo* (14 May 1908), PSR 2-150; *Al'manakh. Sbornik po istorii anarkhich-*

eskogo dvizheniia v Rossii, 57, 61, 63; *Obzor revoliutsionnogo dvizheniia v okruge Irkutskoi sudebnoi palaty za 1908 god*, 35, Nic. 197–3.

134. Reference 66, Okhrana XVIIn-8.

135. "Pamiati Kirshenbaum," *Anarkhist* 5 (March 1910): 3.

136. Zavarzin, *Zhandarmy i revoliutsionery*, 179.

137. See, for example, a newspaper clipping from "Sudebnaia khronika" in *Russkie vedomosti* 149 (1 July 1907), PSR 8-650; newspaper clipping from *Russkie vedomosti* (16 October 1907), PSR 8-653; newspaper clipping from *Russkoe slovo* 127 (5 June 1907), PSR 8-653; *Al'manakh. Sbornik po istorii anarkhicheskogo dvizheniia v Rossii*, 61, 70; *Obzor revoliutsionnogo dvizheniia v okruge Irkutskoi sudebnoi palaty za 1897–1907 gg.*, 202, Nic. 197–2; *Obzor revoliutsionnogo dvizheniia v okruge Irkutskoi sudebnoi palaty za 1908 god*, 11, 17, 33–34, Nic. 197–3; Obninskii, *Polgoda russkoi revoliutsii*, 82; Andrei Sobol', "Otryvki iz vospominanii," *KS* 13 (1924): 154.

138. Newspaper clipping from "Sudebnaia khronika" in *Tovarishch* 374 (18 September 1907), PSR 8-650.

139. Gershuni, "Ob ekspropriatsiiakh" (undated letter to comrades), 4, Nic. 12–1.

140. Newspaper clipping from "Sudebnaia khronika" in *Tovarishch* 375 (19 September 1907), PSR 8-650.

141. *Obzor revoliutsionnogo dvizheniia v okruge Irkutskoi sudebnoi palaty za 1908 god*, 11, Nic. 197–3.

142. Ibid., 11–13. For an account of another band of fugitive political convicts, see GARF f. 102, DPOO, op. 1915, d. 167, ch. 15: 40 ob.-41. When similar groups formed the same year in Cheliabinsk, another destination for administrative deportees, the local authorities soon complained to the court about the unbearable impact of the resulting crime wave on life in the area. They requested that the political exiles be relocated, and that future deportees never be send to their region (newspaper clipping from *Russkie vedomosti*, 25 October 1908, PSR 3-227; see also Nestroev, *Iz dnevnika maksimalista*, 222).

143. For the testimony of a former police agent who claimed to have been tortured by anarchists, see a newspaper clipping from the *New York Tribune* (28 September 1911), AM 2-G.

144. For samples of extortion letters, see GARF f. 102, OO, op. 1912, d. 98: 37, 42, 44, 57, 96; a copy of a report from the governor of Moscow to the Police Department dated 17 October 1906, no. 5396, Okhrana XXVd-2C; and Okhrana XXVd-2G; see also "Anarkhizm," 79, Okhrana XVIb[5]-5A; 18 March 1906 police report, Okhrana XXVb-1; 28 December 1905 (10 January 1906) police report, Okhrana XXIVh-4g; Okhrana XVIIn-8; newspaper clipping from *Tovarishch* (16 May 1907), PSR 4-346; newspaper clipping from *Nasha gazeta* (4 March 1909), PSR 8-653; L. Rogov, "Iz zhizni Bakinskoi tiur'my," *KS* 35 (1927): 127; GARF f. 102, OO, op. 1914, d. 340.

145. "Anarkhizm," 51–52, Okhrana XVIb[5]-5A.

146. For examples of such behavior, see a newspaper clipping from *Russkoe slovo* 9 (13 January 1909), PSR 8-653; *Al'manakh. Sbornik po istorii anarkhicheskogo dvizheniia v Rossii*, 35.

147. *Al'manakh. Sbornik po istorii anarkhicheskogo dvizheniia v Rossii*, 69–70; newspaper clipping from *Russkoe slovo* 9 (13 January 1909), PSR 8-653.

148. See, for example, Genkin, "Sredi preemnikov Bakunina," *KL* 1 (22) (1927): 199; newspaper clipping from *Tovarishch* (13 June 1907), PSR 8-653; newspaper clip-

ping from *Russkoe slovo* 126 (3 June 1907), PSR 8-653; *Al'manakh. Sbornik po istorii anarkhicheskogo dvizheniia v Rossii*, 115–16; Obninskii, *Polgoda russkoi revoliutsii*, 166; GARF f. 102, DPOO, op. 1912, d. 98, ch. 3: 1–20.

149. Newspaper clipping from *Novoe vremia* (16 May 1907), PSR 4-346.

150. Nestroev, *Iz dnevnika Maksimalista*, 41.

151. Newspaper clipping from *Russkoe slovo* (15 June 1908), PSR 8-653.

152. *Al'manakh. Sbornik po istorii anarkhicheskogo dvizheniia v Rossii*, 104.

153. Ibid.

154. Ibid., 97, 149.

155. *Obzor revoliutsionnogo dvizheniia v okruge Irkutskoi sudebnoi palaty za 1908 god*, 17, Nic. 197–3; Genkin, "Sredi preemnikov Bakunina," *KL* 1 (22) (1927): 200.

156. Okhrana XVIIn-8, p. 2; *Al'manakh. Sbornik po istorii anarkhicheskogo dvizheniia v Rossii*, 104. While opposed to indiscriminate robberies and revolutionary banditry, Kropotkin thought it unwise for the movement to condemn the perpetrators publicly since, he feared, it would then appear that the anarchists supported the authorities on this issue (copy of a letter from Petr Kropotkin in London to Mariia Gol'dsmit in Paris dated 17 [30] September 1906, Okhrana XVIb[5]-3).

157. "Anarkhizm," 64, Okhrana XVIb[5]-5A; see a newspaper clipping from "Delo anarkhistov-ekspropriatorov," in *Tovarishch* 379 (23 September 1907), PSR 8-650;

158. *Al'manakh. Sbornik po istorii anarkhicheskogo dvizheniia v Rossii*, 151, 93, 104; Genkin, "Sredi Preemnikov Bakunina," *KL* 1 (22) (1927): 201.

159. *Al'manakh. Sbornik po istorii anarkhicheskogo dvizheniia v Rossii*, 152; "Anarkhizm," 90, Okhrana XVIb[5]-5A.

160. Avrich, *Russian Anarchists*, 34.

CHAPTER FIVE
THE "SEAMY SIDE" OF THE REVOLUTION

1. Cited by V. Zenzinov in an unpublished manuscript, "Stranichka iz istorii rannego bol'shevizma," (n.d.), 11, Nic. 392–4.

2. See, for example, "Iz obshchestvennoi khroniki," *VE* 8 (1907): 844.

3. According to one memoirist, "It was impossible to speak of party loyalty (*partiinost'*)" within the milieu from which many terrorists were recruited. A large number of them were "green youths, absolute babes in the political sense, sympathizing with radical tactics . . . with an extremely obscure perception of the revolution, the revolutionaries, party programs, and the fundamentals of theory" (Moskvich, "K istorii odnogo pokusheniia," *Byloe* 14 [1912]: 38–39).

4. "Bolkhov. Derevenskie anarkhisty," newspaper clipping from *Russkoe slovo*, 23 October 1907, PSR 8-650. For a similar illustration of the lack of ideological discrimination among extremists who were barely acquainted prior to their joint act of expropriation, see "Materialy o provokatorakh," an undated letter from an anonymous revolutionary, in PSR 5-518.

5. "Girsh Lekert i ego pokushenie," *KA* 15 (26): 89, 91. Bolshevik terrorist and expropriator Kamo was thrown out of school at the age of fourteen, but even prior to his formal expulsion he apparently paid little attention to his studies, judging from the fact that he mastered basic Russian grammar and the four elementary operations of

arithmetic only after the 1917 revolution (A. Zonin, "Primechaniia k st. Medvedevoi 'Tovarishch Kamo,'" *PR* 8–9 [31–32] [1924]: 144; Dubinskii-Mukhadze, *Kamo*, 186–87).

6. See, for example, 27 October 1911 police report, Okhrana XVIIc-1; Kantor, "Smertniki v tiur'me," *KS* 6 (1923): 135. For numerous references to assassination attempts motivated by revenge, usually against police collaborators, see: 10 March 1905 police report, p. 3, Okhrana XIIIc(2)-6A; 7 July 1905 police report, p. 24, Okhrana XIIIc(2)-6B; and AM 10-CC, pp. 550–51. It was, incidentally, not unusual for representatives of the new generation of extremists to make assertions such as, "I would kill my own father if I knew he was a provocateur" (Okhrana XVIc-2).

7. G. A. Aleksinskii, "I. G. Tsereteli (vospominaniia i razmyshleniia)," unpublished and undated manuscript, Nic. 302–2.

8. 19 May 1905 police report, p. 4, Okhrana XIIIc(2)-6B; 4 August 1905 police report, p. 29, Okhrana XIIIc(2)-6B. For a similar case, see 2 June 1905 police report, p. 4, Okhrana XIIIc(2)-folder 6B.

9. 14 (27) October 1909 report to DPD, Okhrana XIIIb(1)-1C, Outgoing Dispatches (1909), doc. 498.

10. "Avtobiografiia V. Bushueva," PSR 1-28.

11. Copy of a letter with illegible signature written in Paris to Lala Rabinovitch in Geneva, 9 June 1906, Okhrana XVIIn-5A.

12. See, for example, Anisimov, "Sud i rasprava," *KS* 10 (95) (1932): 138; and 29 November 1903 police report, Okhrana XVIb(4)-1. In Rostov-on-Don a thirteen-year-old girl threw carbolic acid in the face of a local police official in revenge for her brother's arrest (*Russkoe Slovo* 129 [6 June 1907], PSR 8-650).

13. See, for example, GARF f. 102, DPOO, op. 1912, d. 20, ch. 86A: 1–4. While the act is generally considered politically motivated, the true impetus behind the much-discussed January 1906 murder of Gavrila Luzhenovskii, chief advisor to the governor of Tambov, by Mariia Spiridonova, may have been something other than revolutionary sentiments. This assassination is particularly noteworthy because it was widely publicized and caused a great outcry in liberal society. According to antigovernment publications, Spiridonova, then a nineteen-year-old schoolgirl, killed Luzhenovskii to avenge his cruel treatment of peasants during the suppression of agrarian disorders in the Tambov province. According to a recent hypothesis, however, she was in fact originally motivated exclusively by personal considerations, and only subsequently couched her defense in revolutionary language on the advice of her liberal lawyer, in order to transform her case from a criminal matter to a political one (see E. Breitbart, "'Okrasilsia mesiats bagriantsem . . . ' ili podvig sviatogo terrora," *Kontinent* 28 [1981]: 321–42; for the traditional view of this case, see I. Steinberg, *Spiridonova. Revolutionary Terrorist* [London, 1935]). Many mysteries still surround Spiridonova's act and its motives, but whatever hypothesis is considered closest to the truth, much of what was stated about this case in the antigovernment press and by Spiridonova herself was deliberate misrepresentation of reality. For example, she admitted that she "could have been, but was not" raped by Cossack officers after her arrest, as was asserted by many liberal and left-wing newspapers. These newspapers also published letters allegedly written by Spiridonova that she later renounced as forgeries. Similarly, the evidence does not support Spiridonova's claims that before her assassination attempt she was pursued by

PSR members to join the central Combat Organization (an undated letter, and a letter dated 6 March [1906] from Spiridonova, PSR 4-351; excerpt from a letter written by G. A. Gershuni to L. S. dated 3 September 1906, p. 2, Nic. 12–1). Interestingly, according to Oliver Radkey, as late as 1917, Spiridonova, by this time a leader of the Left SR Party, "had the mental attitude of a high-school girl"; she has also been accused of "feminine hysteria" (Knight, "Female Terrorists," 159).

14. 9 (22) August and 17 (30) May 1907 reports to DPD, Okhrana XXIVi-1B.

15. An undated confessional letter from Lidiia Pavlovna Ezerskaia, PSR 1-2. Decades later, a former Maximalist still felt her own involvement in extremist activity was the sole justification for her existence: "They were wonderful years . . . without those few years, my life would have no real meaning" (Avrich, "Last Maximalist," 420).

16. Knight, "Female Terrorists," 153.

17. "Materialy o provokatorakh," PSR 5-518.

18. Copy of a 14 March 1907 letter from a revolutionary in St. Petersburg to Dmitriev in Geneva, Okhrana XXIVi-1B. In some cases, individuals suffering from incurable illnesses offered their services to terrorist organizations. A certain "R . . ." allegedly wrote to an SR leader in Paris informing him that at the present stage of his consumption he had no more than two or three months to live, and was therefore volunteering to kill former Chairman of the Council of Ministers Count Witte (who at the time no longer held any official post, and was traveling abroad), if it would promote the goals of the revolution and the party (newspaper clipping from *Kievskaia mysl'*, 24 April 1909, PSR 4-346). Revolutionary leaders sometimes took the initiative and deliberately recruited followers suffering from major medical conditions to perform terrorist acts. According to police sources, Mikhail Gots tried to persuade a former Odessa student named Ivanov, also seriously ill with consumption, to become a political assassin (4 [17] December 1904 report to DPD, Okhrana XVIIh-2G).

19. 28 June (11 July) 1913 report to DPD, Okhrana XXII-1B; Nestroev, *Iz dnevnika maksimalista*, 218.

20. "Ko vsem!" and "Opoveshchenie," undated leaflets issued by the Elizavetgrad PSR Committee, PSR 9-747; see also GARF f. 102, OO, op. 1911, d. 302: 20.

21. See, for example, "Postanovlenie s"ezda 'Estonskogo Soiuza RSDR Partii,'" Okhrana XXII-1A.

22. 21 January (3 February) 1913 report to DPD, Okhrana XVIIi-1.

23. 3 (16) May 1906 report to DPD, Okhrana XIc(5)-1.

24. "Redaktsiia 'Znam. Truda,'" document from the editorial staff archives of *Znamia Truda*, PSR 3-238; see also "Materialy o provokatorakh," PSR 5-518.

25. 16 (29) January 1909 report to DPD, Okhrana XXVc-1.

26. See, for example, PSR 7-623I; "'Zil'berman,' 'Sasha,'" Nic. 88–31; 7 (20) January 1908 report to DPD, Okhrana XXVc-1; Pavlov, *Esery-maksimalisty*, 81n.

27. Gerasimov, *Na lezvii s terroristami*, 91.

28. Nestroev, *Iz dnevnika maksimalista*, 75–76.

29. Spiridovich, *Partiia Sotsialistov-revoliutsionerov*, 310. According to Nestroev, group leader Mikhail Sokolov put up only ten thousand rubles for Ryss's release (Nestroev, *Iz dnevnika maksimalista*, 65). Ryss's biography is noteworthy in itself. Early in his career he fled abroad because he was wanted in Rostov for forging gymnasium diplomas, claiming that he used profits for revolutionary work. In Europe he was implicated in other crimes, including stealing and selling rare library books.

After his return to Russia he was arrested in June 1906 in Kiev during an attempted robbery targeting an artel. At that point he offered his services to the police and for several months supplied them with a combination of facts and misinformation regarding the affairs of the Maximalists. At the same time, Ryss assured the revolutionaries that he was feeding the Okhrana false information, and some of his comrades considered his activities of great value. The game did not last long, however, and police suspicions forced Ryss to flee once more. He was arrested in April 1907, sentenced to death, and hanged in February 1908 (P. Berline, "Stranitsa proshlogo. O dvukh poveshennykh," *Novoe russkoe slovo*, 7 September 1952, Nic. 438–28; Gerasimov, *Na lezvii s terroristami*, 88, 91–93; Pavlov, *Esery-maksimalisty*, 14n., 169–72, 179–80, 183).

30. Copy of a letter from a revolutionary in St. Petersburg to Dmitriev in Geneva, Okhrana XXIVi-1B; 17 (30) March 1907 report to DPD, Okhrana XIIIb(1)-1A, Outgoing Dispatches (1907), doc. 109.

31. Pozner, *Boevaia gruppa pri TsK RSDRP(b)*, 103.

32. V. M. Sivilev, "Staryi bol'shevik, rabochii Motovilikhinskogo zavoda, Aleksandr Petrovich Kalganov," *KS* 25 (1926): 238, 242.

33. See, for example, police reports dated 17 August 1906 and May 1907, Okhrana XXVc-2C.

34. "Postanovlenie s'ezda 'Estonskogo Soiuza RSDR Partii,'" Okhrana XXII-1A.

35. Pozner, *Boevaia gruppa pri TsK RSDRP(b)*, 103.

36. "Iz vospominanii M. Sotnikova," *Byloe* 14 (1912): 114.

37. Some anarchist leaders thought that after so many petty expropriations and acts of indiscriminate terror carried out by the anarchists and various obscure groups throughout the country, in which victims were blown to bits for refusing to donate one hundred rubles or less to the extremists, the revolutionaries were "terribly discredited" (Genkin, "Sredi preemnikov Bakunina," *KL* 1 [22] [1927]: 200). To cleanse their movement in the eyes of the public, some anarchists proposed a series of large-scale combat operations (copy of a 2 October 1907 letter from Samuil Beilin in Grodno to Nikolai Muzil', Okhrana XIIIb[1]-1C, Outgoing Dispatches [1907], doc. 450).

38. See, for example, Okhrana VIj-17B; reference note 7, Okhrana XVIIn-8; Zavarzin, *Zhandarmy i revoliutsionery*, 179; Nestroev, *Iz dnevnika Maksimalista*, 221; 22 April (5 May) 1908 report to DPD, Okhrana XXVc-1; 30 April 1916 police report, p. 2, Okhrana XVIb(5)-3. In one case, a revolutionary named Rogal'skii demanded two thousand francs from a fellow Maximalist, threatening to report him as a provocateur if he refused to comply (6 [19] August 1912 report to DPD, Okhrana XXVb-1).

39. Copy of a 24 July 1907 letter to Katia in Paris, written from Switzerland and signed "Aleks.," Okhrana XVIIn-3.

40. Zavarzin, *Zhandarmy i revoliutsionery*, 115.

41. 4 (17) August 1907 report to DPD, Okhrana XXVc-2M. Evidence suggests that the Dushet expropriators were motivated from the start not by party interests, but exclusively by desire for personal enrichment. Furthermore, the Georgian Socialist-Federalist leadership was forced to concede that the behavior of the combat detachment under the authority of the party's Central Committee was "revolting," because its members had implicated themselves not only in embezzlement, but also in other "unseemly deeds" ("Revoliutsionnaia Partiia Sotsialistov-Federalistov Gruzii," 9, 15–16, Nic. 80–7).

42. GARF f. 102, DPOO, op. 1912, d. 13, ch. 60 B: 40.

43. Perrie, "Political and Economic Terror," 75.

44. Nestroev, *Iz dnevnika Maksimalista*, 218.

45. Ibid.

46. 18 (31) October 1907 report to DPD, Okhrana XXVc-2H.

47. See, for example, "'Zil'berman,' 'Sasha,'" Nic. 88–31. The revolutionaries were well aware of this tendency, and having found their comrades guilty of embezzlement also suspected them of police connections (copy of a letter signed "Aleks." to Katia, Okhrana XVIIn-3).

48. 7 (20) November 1914 report to DPD, Okhrana XXIVa-5q; see also "Redaktsiia 'Znam. Truda,'" PSR 3-238; and a confidential report from the Secretary of the SR Regional Committee Abroad (November 1908, Paris), PSR 5-496.

49. 26 August 1909 memorandum from the acting vice-director of the Police Department to the directors of the provincial gendarme departments and Okhrana sections, Okhrana XIIId(1)-10. According to an explanation given to the SRs by the exposed police spy Metal'nikov, he had accepted this employment in order to earn six thousand rubles from the authorities, a sum essential, as he put it, for financing an expropriation planned in the city of Kazan', which, in turn, was to supply the SR terrorists with funds required for a major political assassination (24 February [8 March] 1912 report to DPD, Okhrana XXIVa-1A).

50. 23 February (8 March) 1905 report to DPD, Okhrana XXIVi-1A; Radkey, *Agrarian Foes of Bolshevism*, 75; letter from B. I. Nicolaevsky to V. M. Chernov, 15 October 1931, Nic. 206–6. The revolutionaries sometimes established direct contacts with highly placed representatives of hostile foreign powers, such as the Turkish minister of the interior. In 1912, he not only assisted Kamo (who represented himself as a Georgian Socialist-Federalist in order not to compromise the Bolshevik faction) in his travels, but also promised, "If you and your organization will demonstrate [your strength] by some action, we will provide you with various types of secret aid that you may need" (Dubinskii-Mukhadze, *Kamo*, 162; Zonin, "Primechaniia k st. Medvedevoi 'Tovarishch Kamo,'" PR 8–9 [31–32]: 147–48).

51. See, for example, Radkey, *Agrarian Foes of Bolshevism*, 75; 5 (18) April 1910 report to DPD, Okhrana XXVb-2K; and 2 (15) March 1911 report to DPD, Okhrana XIX-12A.

52. 20 December 1914 (2 January 1915) report to DPD, Okhrana VIIIb-1A.

53. 4 (17) July 1915 report to DPD, Okhrana XXIVh-2.

54. Copy of 30 January 1909 official letter no. 122907, from P. Kurlov to A. P. Izvol'skii, Okhrana Va-3.

55. 14 (27) February 1912 report to DPD, Okhrana XIX-12B.

56. 10 June 1904 police report, Okhrana XIIIc(2)-4B. For other cases of revolutionary cadres recruited in return for direct financial compensation, see a 1907 report filed by police agent Krauso, Okhrana XXIVh-4K; "Obvinitel'nyi akt po delu o pisariakh," 5, PSR 3-170I; and "Iz dnevnika A. N. Kuropatkina," KA 1 (8) (1925): 97. For examples of combatants receiving regular salaries, see "Dashnaktsutiun. Obvinitel'nyi akt," 248, Nic. 256–5.

57. See, for example, *Obzor vazhneishikh doznanii, proizvodivshikhsia v Zhandarmskikh Upravleniiakh za 1897 god*, 113, Nic. 196–9.

58. Zavarzin, *Rabota tainoi politsii*, 111–12.

59. See, for example, a 17 (30) December 1907 report to DPD, Okhrana XXVc-2K.

In one case, an individual living under the alias "Ivan Ivanovich" received a monthly subsidy of seventy-five francs from the PSR Foreign Delegation (Zagranichnaia delegatsia) in 1913, even though he was not a party member and was known only to its leaders. Police sources seem to connect this information with the fact that Ivan Ivanovich had previously served as a guard in the Tashkent Provincial Treasury, from which he had helped the revolutionaries expropriate eight hundred thousand rubles in 1906 before escaping abroad (25 July [7 August] 1913 report to DPD, Okhrana XXVc-1). For a similar case, in which a participant in a revolutionary robbery, then living in Paris, ironically also under the pseudonym "Ivan Ivanovich," was subsidized by the PSR Central Committee, see a 6 November 1909 police report, Okhrana XXVc-1.

60. 10 June 1904 police report, Okhrana XIIIc(2)-4B.

61. Copy of a 10 October 1909 letter translated from Yiddish into Russian, from "Ios'ka Shvarts" in Warsaw to "Gal'd" in Paris, Okhrana XXVIId-7.

62. Copy of 4 October 1907 Police Department order no. 1363 to the directors of the regional gendarme and security police sections, PSR 1-26; copy of a letter from Kurlov to Izvol'skii, Okhrana Va-3; see also 1909 "Otchet o partiiakh," Okhrana XVId-1; "Iz obshchestvennoi khroniki," *VE* 8 (1907): 844.

63. Unaddressed letter from G. Gershuni dated 23 February 1906, p. 4, Nic. 12–1. Similarly, other left-wing publications, as well as individual radicals, were forced to concede that revolutionary robberies after 1905 "most often . . . took the form of ordinary robberies" (*Volia* 89 [10 {23} December 1906]: 26, PSR 7-592). According to one revolutionary, on a superficial level expropriations "appeared to be 'revolutionary guerrilla activities,' but in reality they deteriorated more and more into banditry, and only the incredible cruelty of the courts-martial helped to maintain a certain aureole around them" (Voitinskii, *Gody pobed i porazhenii*, bk. 2: 94). For his part, Lenin acknowledged that the proceeds of the smaller expropriations—and the majority of "ex's" in Russia were in fact petty robberies—went "mostly, and sometimes entirely, to the maintenance of the 'expropriators'" (Lenin, "Guerrilla Warfare," Walter Laqueur, ed., *The Guerrilla Reader. A Historical Anthology* [Philadelphia, 1977], 172). This generalization appears quite accurate. See, for example, Nic. 11–22, p. 6.

64. Undated letter from "Sasha" to V. L. Burtsev, pp. 6–7, Nic. 150–11.

65. See, for example, August 1909 gendarme report no. 5504 to the Police Department, Okhrana XXII-2.

66. 9 (22) February 1913 report to DPD, Okhrana XXVd-1.

67. Letter from "Sasha" to Burtsev, p. 6, Nic. 150–11. In a number of cases, revolutionaries who found themselves in financial need resorted to writing extortion letters over the names of various extremist organizations (some of which, such as the Anarchist-Communist group Karma, or the SR Kazan' Beatles [Kazanskie zhuchki], existed only in their authors' imaginations), demanding large payments from private citizens under threat of immediate reprisal (report 10981 from the governor of Moscow to the Police Department, dated 16 October 1907, Okhrana XXVd-2D; GARF f. 102, OO, op. 1911, d. 302: 20).

68. 3 (16) September 1910 police report, Okhrana XVIb(5)-5B.

69. PSR 1-94.

70. Gel'zin (Babadzhan), "Iuzhnoe Voenno-Tekhnicheskoe Biuro," *KS* 61:42; 10 (23) December 1910 report to DPD, Okhrana XIIIb(1)-1F, Outgoing Dispatches (1910), doc. 1141.

71. Based on past experience, the police authorities considered it entirely possible that Russian revolutionaries abroad would be willing to assist Makharashvili in representing himself as a political victim of the tsarist regime (30 March [12 April] 1915 report to DPD, Okhrana XXVc-1). In another case, an expropriator by the name of Aleksandr Belentsov, who disappeared with some of the proceeds following an expropriation at a Moscow bank (thus robbing his comrades as well as the bank), and who was subsequently imprisoned in Switzerland, threatened his fellow revolutionaries with disclosure of their role in the robbery if they did not act to prevent his extradition to the Russian authorities. After discussing the situation, the radicals came up with three options: liberate Belentsov from the Swiss jail, poison him in prison, or kill him with a bomb on his way to Russia if he were indeed extradited (15 [28] April 1906 report to DPD; 26 June 1906 police report, Okhrana XXVc-2B).

72. GARF f. 102, DPOO, op. 1913, d. 304: 33, 35 ob.; Gel'zin (Babadzhan), "Iuzhnoe Voenno-Tekhnicheskoe Biuro," *KS* 61 (1929): 42; see also PSR 2-127; and two leaflets issued by the Saratov PSR Committee, one dated 1 January 1907, the other undated, Arkhiv PSR 5-521I.

73. Handwritten copy of an article by Peskel, "S-ry i anarkhisty na Litve," PSR 3-269.

74. See, for example, excerpt from a 27 February 1908 letter signed "Leon" to V. I. Malchina in Nice, Okhrana XIIIc(1)-1B, Incoming Dispatches (1908), doc. 377; "Postanovlenie s"ezda 'Estonskogo Soiuza RSDR Partii,'" Okhrana XXII-1A.

75. GARF f. 102, DPOO, op. 1912, d. 13, ch. 60B: 40; V. O. Levitskii, "A. D. Pokotilov," *KS* 3 (1922): 159, 171; Spence, *Savinkov*, 47. On Bartol'd as a "superfluous person," a braggart, and a heavy drinker with symptoms of mental illness, see 21 January (3 February) 1913 report to DPD, Okhrana XXIVi-3I; 22 October (4 November) 1912 report to DPD, Okhrana XVIc-2; Okhrana XIIIa-1, p. 4; 9 (22) December 1910 report to DPD, Okhrana XVIIi-2V; 12 (25) April 1912 report to DPD, and an attached letter from Savinkov to "Vasilii Viktorovich" (Leonovich-Kobyzev) dated 23 April 1912, Okhrana XVIIi-1.

76. See, for example, an excerpt from a letter signed "Leon" to Malchina, Okhrana XIIIc(1)-1B, Incoming Dispatches (1908), doc. 377; copy of a letter from Kurlov to Izvol'skii, Okhrana Va-3; Nikiforov, *Murav'i revoliutsii*, 266. Occasionally, however, local combatants expelled drunkards without waiting for official sanction from higher party authorities (Pozner, *Boevaia gruppa pri TsK RSDRP[b]*, 103).

77. "Redaktsiia 'Znam. Truda,'" PSR 3-238.

78. Excerpt from a letter signed "Leon" to Malchina, Okhrana XIIIc(1)-1B, Incoming Dispatches (1908), doc. 377.

79. Excerpt from a letter signed "Aleksandr" in Switzerland, to E. V. Trofimenko in Kiev, dated 6 October 1908, Okhrana XVId-4; see also 15 January 1911 police report, Okhrana XVIb(3)-4; 21 November (4 December) 1911 report to DPD, Okhrana XXVb-2P; and a report from Agent Dmitriev dated 5 November 1907, pp. 64–65, Okhrana IIb-2 (Switzerland).

80. Copy of a letter with an illegible signature to A. I. Eramasov, Okhrana XVIIo-1. For a similar example, see 30 June (13 July) 1914 report to DPD, Okhrana XVIb(5)-4.

81. Nestroev, *Iz dnevnika Maksimalista*, 221.

82. Lenin, "Guerrilla Warfare," 177; Aleksinskii, "I. G. Tsereteli," Nic. 302–2; "Iz zapisnoi knizhki arkhivista. Presnia v dekabre 1905 g.," *KA* 6 (73) (1935): 205.

83. Iu. Kizhmer, "Bor'ba s 'podavantsami' v rizhskikh tiur'makh," *KS* 20 (1925): 236; V. N. Zalezhskii, "V gody reaktsii," *PR* 2 (14) (1923): 368; Nestroev, *Iz dnevnika Maksimalista*, 219.

84. For a vivid description of prison life for these "politicals," see Nestroev, *Iz dnevnika Maksimalista*, 219–22; Iu. Krasnyi, "Tov. Dzerzhinskii v tiur'me," *KS* 27 (1926): 195–96.

85. Lokerman, "Po tsarskim tiur'mam," *KS* 25 (1926): 187. Other sources describe how individuals calling themselves revolutionaries begged police authorities for money (Nestroev, *Iz dnevnika Maksimalista*, 222).

86. *Al'manakh. Sbornik po istorii anarkhicheskogo dvizheniia v Rossii*, 152. While the criminal prisoners rarely expressed sympathy for the theoretically inclined Social Democrats, they were more tolerant of the SRs, and often expressed admiration for the anarchists, occasionally even claiming to be anarchists themselves. For a description of cooperation and joint undertakings between political and criminal prisoners, including preparations for a mass escape, see Sukhomlin, "Iz tiuremnykh skitanii," *KS* 55 (1929): 102, 106–7. Some revolutionaries affirmed that it was not unusual for a criminal gang leader in prison to operate on the assumption that the politicals were their friends (Nestroev, *Iz dnevnika Maksimalista*, 183). Significantly, following the execution of SR expropriator Nikolai Kozyrev, his friends among the criminal prisoners ended a note to his fellow radicals: "Long live his party" (R. Kantor, "Smertniki v tiur'me," *KS* 6 [1923]: 136). It is also noteworthy that in the eyes of his fellow prisoners, the Bolshevik Kamo was simply another gang leader (Medvedeva-Ter-Petrosian, "Tovarishch Kamo," *PR* 8–9 [31–32] [1924]: 140).

87. Koval'skaia, "Po povedu stat'i Orlova," *KS* 52 (1929): 165; Shaurov, *1905 god*, 235; see also Nestroev, *Iz dnevnika Maksimalista*, 220.

88. Lokerman, "Po tsarskim tiur'mam," *KS* 25 (1926): 185.

89. D. Nadel'shtein, "Butyrskie ocherki," *KS* 45–46 (1928): 199.

90. Vitiazev, Isakovich, and Kallistov, "Iz vospominanii o N. D. Shishmareve," *KS* 6 (1923): 257–58; see also G. Kramarov, "Neudavsheesia ubiistvo na etape," *KS* 3 (64) (1930): 122–26.

91. 7 (20) November 1914 report to DPD, Okhrana XXIVa-5q; 20 February 1910 police report, Okhrana XXII-1A. Among the revolutionaries, the use of fists and even mass beatings to settle disagreements was as common as the implementation of physical means in the interrogation of suspected police agents (see, for example, excerpt from a 13 March 1904 letter signed "Lenia" in Paris to P. I. Nechaev in Moscow, Okhrana XVId-3; Iurenev, "Rabota R.S.-D.R.P. v Severo-Zapadnom krae," *PR* 8–9 [31–32] [1924]: 176; 27 March [9 April] 1910 report to DPD, Okhrana XVIb[6][b]-1; M. Mishin, "Tiumenskaia organizatsiia RSDRP v 1905–1917 gg.," *KS* 4 [113] [1934]: 56; 7 [20] February 1914 report to DPD, Okhrana XXVIId-7).

92. AM 10-BB, pp. 1–2. For a similar incident involving a female victim who was mutilated and shot as a suspected spy, see a clipping from the newspaper *Parus* 96 (7 June 1907), PSR 8-653.

93. Dubinskii-Mukhadze, *Kamo*, 156.

94. See Laqueur, *Terrorism*, 133.

95. Cited in McDaniel, "Political Assassination and Mass Execution," 97.

96. Numerous examples justify the assertion that mental illness often led individuals to terrorism, and occasionally to contemplating a particular assassination even against

the recommendations of other radicals. See, for instance, an undated police report, Okhrana XXIVi-3U; undated police report, Okhrana XIIIa-12; "Delo o predpolagav-shemsia vzryve okhrannogo otdeleniia," newspaper clipping from *Tovarishch*, 19 November 1907, PSR 8-650; Okhrana XIIIa-8; copy of a 24 July 1913 police report in French, Okhrana XIIIa-15. Medical experts stated that many mentally unbalanced extremists were not accountable for their actions (see, for example, newspaper clipping from *Russkie vedomosti* 168 [24 July 1907], PSR 8-650; 15 September 1907 police report, Okhrana XIIIc[1]-1B, Incoming Dispatches [1907], doc. 499; "Delo o pokushe-nii 16 lits na zhizn' generala Trepova v 1905 godu," *Byloe* 10 [22] [1907]: 305; Fuller, *Civil-Military Conflict*, 179; see also newspaper clipping from *Novaia Rus'*, 24 February 1909, PSR 7-602).

97. Post, "Terrorist Psycho-logic," Reich, ed., *Origins of Terrorism*, 25.

98. For example, Mariia Seliuk, a terrorist who played a leading role in a 1904 PSR-sponsored conspiracy against Plehve, "suffered from a mental disorder," and was "psychologically deranged" (14 [27] December 1904 report to DPD, Okhrana XIIIb[1]-1C, Outgoing Dispatches [1904], doc. 322); Men'shchikov, "Secrets of the Russian Safety," 20, Nic. 179–25; 1 (14) December 1908 unsigned letter to Olia, PSR 3-269; leaflet issued by the Penza PSR Committee, 26 February 1908, PSR 5-471; see also Knight, "Female Terrorists," 148.

99. While residing in Berlin in 1907, Kamo sought medical assistance and underwent certain treatments, although the sources do not reveal whether he was treated for mental illness as well as medical problems, including an eye injury sustained in an explosion (report by Ia. A. Zhitomirskii ["Ottsov"] on the Kamo case, pp. 1–2, Nic. 662–15; "Kamo, Semen A., Interrogation by Komissiia po issledovaniiu . . . provokat-sii" [4 February 1912] Ms Coll. Aleksinskii, Bakhmeteff Archive, Columbia University Libraries).

100. In the history of modern medicine, there are examples of individuals—some with specialized medical training and experience—who feigned mental illness successfully for short periods, but in the overwhelming majority of cases an imposter was ultimately forced to admit failure in trying to fool the experts. Even the most determined and knowledgeable of these pretenders found themselves unable to maintain the charade for more than a few months. According to the Bolsheviks, Kamo "performed a . . . miracle of impersonation: he posed successfully for two years" (Baron [Bibineish-vili], *Za chetvert' veka*, 96–97).

To determine whether Kamo was feigning madness, the German psychiatrists used rather sophisticated procedures, including pain tolerance tests. Kamo reacted with complete indifference, later recalling only that "the burned flesh stung terribly." The doctors had never encountered such tolerance for pain in normal patients, either in their own practices or in the medical literature (Baron [Bibineishvili], *Za chetvert' veka*, 101). The Bolsheviks later claimed that Kamo was able to withstand torture because of his enormous will power and was thus fully capable of misleading his doctors in their diagnosis.

Nevertheless, the revolutionaries were unable to explain how a mentally stable individual could deny himself sleep for four months. They also could not account for his two suicide attempts while in medical custody, which he survived only because of timely intervention by medical personnel (Baron [Bibineishvili], *Za chetvert' veka*, 98–99). Nor could the Bolsheviks disprove the physicians' assertions that "such physical phenomena as increased palpitation [and] trembling eyelids could not be simulated at all." Medical experts stated that Kamo "easily loses mental equilibrium and then enters a state of obvious insanity . . . deliberate simulation or exaggeration of the symptoms of the illness is out of the question." Agreeing that Kamo's behavior could not be faked for any considerable period of time, the doctors concluded: "Only a truly ill patient in a state of madness behaves this way. . . . In this case, we are dealing with a type of mental disorder, which most accurately is attributable to a form of hysteria" (Zonin, "Primechaniia k st. Medvedevoi 'Tovarishch Kamo,'" *PR* 8–9 [31–32] [1924]: 146).

Despite the findings of the German medical experts, the Russian police authorities abroad continued to claim that Kamo was faking insanity in order to escape appropriate punishment under Russian law, and insisted on his return to Russia (19 May [1 June] 1908 report to DPD, Okhrana XXVIIc-1). However, following his extradition in October of 1909, a special committee of Russian medical experts, taking into consideration Kamo's indifference to pain and various other symptoms, including his trembling hands and tongue, concluded that it was absolutely impossible for any patient to simulate them (Dubinskii-Mukhadze, *Kamo*, 122, 136, 138). The Russian doctors thus fully agreed with their German colleagues (for a report on the results of the medical investigation of Kamo's physical state, see Baron [Bibineishvili], *Za chetvert' veka*, 106).

The two attempts Kamo made on his own life while in German custody were not his only encounters with suicide. Throughout his revolutionary career his impulsive and hysterical personality apparently gave him little protection against these recurring urges to kill himself. One such impulse struck him, according to his sister, soon after the revolution of 1917 (Medvedeva-Ter-Petrosian, "Tovarishch Kamo," *PR* 8–9 [31–32] [1924]: 141). Ironically, Kamo survived the Bolshevik takeover only to be struck by a car and killed while riding a bicycle on the streets of Tiflis on the evening of 14 July 1922. Autorkhanov speculates that the accident was actually an assassination ordered by Stalin, by then rising through the ranks of the new Soviet government, to silence Kamo's bragging about their past shady exploits together (Avtorkhanov, *Proiskhozhdenie partokratii*, 203–4).

101. Among other well-known revolutionaries, Vladimir Burtsev, with whom Kamo became acquainted in Europe, also concluded that the Georgian *boevik* was a victim of "complete mental derangement" (31 December 1911 [13 January 1912] report to DPD, Okhrana XXVIIc-1; 1912 report from Ia. A. Zhitomirskii, Okhrana IIIf-36). Furthermore, there are indications that following Kamo's escape abroad in 1911, A. A. Bogdanov, a leading member of the Bolshevik faction who was a medical doctor by profession, found it appropriate to place him in a mental clinic in Belgium for treatment (1912 report from Ia. A. Zhitomirskii, Okhrana IIIf-36).

102. Cited in Roberta Ann Kaplan, "'A Total Negation of Russia,' Russian Intellectual Perceptions of Suicide, 1900–1914" (unpublished paper, Harvard University 1988), 32.

103. Cited in Laqueur, *Terrorism*, 127.

104. Ibid., 135; Knight, "Female Terrorists," 150.

105. Ariel Merari, "The Readiness to Kill and Die: Suicidal Terrorism in the Middle East," *Origins of Terrorism*, Walter Reich, ed., 193.

106. P. G. Kurlov, *Gibel' imperatorskoi Rossii* (Moscow, 1991), 90–91; Naimark, "Terrorism and the Fall of Imperial Russia," 18. SR Lidiia Sture repeatedly stated that

if she could not enter a combat organization, she would kill herself (I. Zhukovskii-Zhuk, "Pamiati Lidii Petrovny Sture," *KS* 19 [1925]: 253).

107. See, for example, an agent's 1910 report translated from German, Okhrana XVIb(4)-2.

108. See, for example, Nadel'shtein, "Butyrskie ocherki," *KS* 45–46 (1928): 198–99. As early as 1901, some revolutionaries recognized that many young men and women, if presented with an "all-powerful means of destruction, would enthusiastically go for a heroic deed, rather than end their lives by suicide" (22 December 1901 report to DPD, Okhrana XIIIb[1]-1, Outgoing Dispatches [1901], doc. 11).

109. Radkey, *Agrarian Foes of Bolshevism*, 70.

110. See, for example, 20 November 1909 police report, Okhrana XIIIc(1)-1H, Incoming Dispatches (1909), doc. 1377.

111. Cited in Knight, "Female Terrorists," 150. In the same spirit, Spiridonova wrote to her comrades, "I want them to kill me; I cannot imagine the grief that will be in my heart if they do not kill me. . . . My death now will have a tremendous revolutionizing significance. . . . It would be a brilliant act of agitation" (undated letter from M. A. Spiridonova, PSR 4-351; see also E. Roizman, "Vospominaniia o Frume Frumkinoi," *KS* 28–29 [1926]: 302).

112. For some terrorists, participation in political murder was justified only by the sacrifice of their own lives, as in the case of SR combatant Dora Brilliant. An obvious introvert known for her tendency toward depression and hysteria, this young woman was reportedly deeply tormented by her inability to resolve the "disharmony between consciousness and feeling." She became increasingly unstable, especially following her arrest in 1905 and subsequent imprisonment in the Peter and Paul Fortress in St. Petersburg. While in prison in October 1907 she apparently suffered a nervous breakdown and died shortly thereafter at the age of twenty-seven. Another female terrorist, Rashel' Lur'e, was seemingly unable to overcome similar inner conflicts, and after leaving the Combat Organization and emigrating abroad, committed suicide in 1908 at the age of twenty-four (Knight, "Female Terrorists," 149–50; Savinkov, *Vospominaniia terrorista*, 186). In a revealing case, a revolutionary who developed serious heart problems in prison realized following his release that because of his physical condition he could no longer be "either a terrorist, or a rebel." Finding himself "unable to live without the cause [and] the struggle," he saw no alternative but to take his own life (undated letter from P. Polivanov to his comrades, PSR 1-63).

113. Undated police report, Okhrana XVIIn-5A; 14 (27) December 1904 report to DPD, Okhrana XIIIb(1)-1C, Outgoing Dispatches (1904), doc. 322; Men'shchikov, "Secrets of the Russian Safety," 20, Nic. 179–25. For a similar example, see *Spisok lits*, 507, Okhrana XIIId(1)-4.

114. Knight, "Female Terrorists," 152.

115. Fruma Frumkina echoed Shkol'nik: "For me nothing except revolutionary work exists" (cited in ibid., 152–53).

116. Hildermeier, "Terrorist Strategies of the Socialist-Revolutionary Party," 86.

117. Knight, "Female Terrorists," 151, 153.

118. Ibid.; Naimark, "Terrorism and the Fall of Imperial Russia," 17–18; Spiridovich, *Zapiski zhandarma*, 134–35. One of Frumkina's prison comrades recalled that during her initial days at hard labor she attacked literally every jailer (Roizman, "Vospominaniia o Frumkinoi," *KS* 28–29 [1926]: 383). Following one of her failed

terrorist schemes, Frumkina was tried before a military court. Her behavior led the judges to question her competency and assign a medical expert to determine whether she was as psychologically unbalanced as she appeared. After the experts declared Frumkina sane, she was sentenced to be hanged, and was executed shortly thereafter (a collection of newspaper clippings on Frumkina's terrorist activities can be found in PSR 3-186).

119. Knight, "Female Terrorists," 152; "Delo o pokushenii 16 lits na zhizn' Trepova," *Byloe* 10 (22) (1907): 305, 307; Savinkov, *Vospominaniia terrorista*, 133–34. Gerasimov notes 1 September 1906 as the day of Leont'eva's act (Gerasimov, *Na lezvii s terroristami*, 14–15).

120. Roizman, "Vospominaniia o Frumkinoi," *KS* 28–29 [1926]: 302; A. V. Pribylev, *Zinaida Zhuchenko* (n.p., 1919), 15; Genkin, "Anarkhisty," *Byloe* 3 (31) (1918): 166–67; "Redaktsiia 'Znam. Truda,'" document from the *Znamia Truda* editorial staff archives, PSR 3-238; Radkey, *Agrarian Foes of Bolshevism*, 70n; Savinkov, *Vospominaniia terrorista*, 131–32; see also *Al'manakh. Sbornik po istorii anarkhicheskogo dvizheniia v Rossii*, 59; Pozner, *Boevaia gruppa pri TsK RSDRP(b)*, 13. The mental state of Tat'iana Leont'eva visibly deteriorated after her terrorist act and imprisonment in Switzerland, forcing prison authorities to transfer her to a mental institution in Bern (newspaper clipping from *Parus* 71 [6 May 1907], PSR 3-198). The extremists themselves recognized the instability of certain of their comrades, assigning them nicknames such as "Leibele the crazy" ("Anarkhizm i dvizhenie anarkhizma v Rossii" [n.d.]: 47, Nic. 80–4).

121. Koval'skaia, "Po povedu stat'i Orlova," *KS* 52 (1929): 165.

122. Knight, "Female Terrorists," 150. For other examples, see L. Prozorov, "Samoubiistva v tiur'makh i okolo tiurem po dannym 1906 i 1907 goda," *Meditsinskoe obozrenie* 12 (1908): 69–72; and I Minaev, "Pamiati Serezhi Il'inskogo," *KS* 18 (1925): 305–6.

123. D. Venediktov-Beziuk, "Sukhaia gil'otina," *KS* 8–9 (93–94) (1932): 158.

124. Knight, "Female Terrorists," 150.

125. Vulikh, "Osnovnoe iadro kavkazskoi boevoi organizatsii," 8–9, Nic. 207-11.

126. Obninskii, *Polgoda russkoi revoliutsii*, 161. The terrorists of this era were not the first Russian radicals to use hanging as a punishment; late nineteenth-century revolutionaries occasionally employed it against suspected (though not necessarily actual) traitors (see, for example, Nic. 150–15).

127. *Volia* 54 (25 August 1906): 4, PSR 7-569.

128. "Pribaltiiskii krai v 1905 g.," *KA* 4–5 (11–12) (1925): 283.

129. Vulikh, "Osnovnoe iadro kavkazskoi boevoi organizatsii," 8, Nic. 207–11.

130. 21 April 1905 police report, p. 4, Okhrana XIIIc(2)-6B.

131. 2 April 1909 police report, Okhrana XIX-6; Zavarzin, *Rabota tainoi politsii*, 131–36.

132. Zavarzin, *Rabota tainoi politsii*, 128–29.

133. Ibid., 111.

134. Levitskii, "A. D. Pokotilov," *KS* 3 (1922): 159; Spiridovich, *Zapiski zhandarma*, 133–134; GARF f. 102, OO, op. 1916, d. 122: 54, 132–33; E. D. Nikitina, "Nash pobeg," *KS* 56 (1929): 124, 127n.

135. According to Laqueur, "That their members have been young is the only feature common to all terrorist movements." He explains this by the fact that the "latest calls

to action don't usually fire the middle-aged and elderly with enthusiasm, and daring attacks also necessitate speed of movement" (Laqueur, *Terrorism*, 120).

136. *Sekira* 12 (1906): 7, Nic. 436–2; see also *Gudok* 4 (March 1906): 5, Nic. 435–15; and *Nagaechka* 4:9, Nic. 435–27.

137. Myzgin, *So vzvedennym kurkom*, 91.

138. Ibid., 6, 22, 89; S. Sulimov, "K istorii boevykh organizatsii na Urale," *PR* 7 (42): 106.

139. Perrie, "Social Composition and Structure," 231; see also Perrie, "Political and Economic Terror," 68, 78n.

140. "Obvinitel'nyi akt o meshchanakh Movshe Arone Davidove Zakgeime i Tsirle Khaimovoi Shkol'nik," 1, PSR 9-778.

141. Nadel'shtein, "Butyrskie ocherki," *KS* 45–46 (1928): 197.

142. "Pamiati S. V. Sikorskogo," *KS* 41 (1928): 146; Tashkentets, "Pervaia viselitsa v g. Penze," *KS* 50 (1928): 93; newspaper clipping from *Russkoe slovo*, 21 October 1907, PSR 8-650.

143. Genkin, "Sredi preemnikov Bakunina," *KL* 1 (22) (1927): 181.

144. Avrich, *Russian Anarchists*, 44; see also *Al'manakh. Sbornik po istorii anarkhicheskogo dvizheniia v Rossii*, 31, 44, 46, 167, 182; Genkin, "Sredi preemnikov Bakunina," *KL* 1 (22) (1927): 181.

145. Riabkov-"Pchela," "Kak ia popal na rabotu pri nashem podpol'nom pravitel'stve," *PR* 3 (1921): 221.

146. Trotsky, *Stalin*, 96.

147. Vera Figner quoted in McDaniel, "Political Assassination and Mass Execution," 97.

148. Perrie, "Social Composition and Structure," 229.

149. An especially vivid illustration of this is the assassination in 1905 of an elderly gendarme, Lieutenant Colonel Ivanov, in Rostov-on-Don. For twenty-five years Ivanov served as a gendarme on the railroad; he did not like or understand politics, and cherished dreams of settling in a village after his retirement. His plans were not destined to be realized: he was shot and killed by two teenagers who had heard at revolutionary meetings that all gendarmes were enemies of the people, and decided on their own to assassinate Ivanov (Zavarzin, *Zhandarmy i revoliutsionery*, 98). In another incident, a local gang of hooligans, excited by an armed demonstration organized by students in the town of Gori on 14 March 1905, raided an estate and then attacked a group of soldiers. Three people, including a child, were killed, and six were wounded (police report dated 17 March 1905, p. 11, Okhrana XIIIc[2]-6A).

150. Excerpt from an unsigned letter from Kiev dated 2 March 1904, to N. Shpitsman in Berlin, Okhrana XXIVl-1.

151. *Volia* 71 (4 October 1906), 4, PSR 7-569.

152. G. Novopolin, "Delo ob ubiistve general-gubernatora V. P. Zheltonovskogo," *KS* 31 (1927): 26–39.

153. Cited in Kaplan, "'Total Negation of Russia,'" 39. This was not a unique case of passion for Spiridonova aroused by publicity. While in prison she received love letters from a number of admirers (undated letter from Spiridonova, no. 11, PSR 4-351).

154. Frolov, "Terroristicheskii akt nad samarskim gubernatorom," *KS* 1 (8) (1924): 120.

155. Many teenage terrorists claimed that personal economic hardship was the major factor motivating their joining the extremists. One stated at his trial that he could not afford new pants and had to wear a pair handed down by his brother because he "looked like a ragamuffin" in his old ones; another complained bitterly that he was always starving and had to "flop anywhere," because no one offered him a place to sleep (*Al'manakh. Sbornik po istorii anarkhicheskogo dvizheniia v Rossii*, 182).

156. See, for example, a clipping from *Russkoe slovo* 126 (3 June 1907), PSR 8-653.

157. V. Kniazev, "1905," *Zvezda* 6 (1930): 249–50, 237; see also S. Sibiriakov, "Boris Berkov," *KS* 31 (1927): 248.

158. The most common forms of struggle against school authorities were protest meetings and strikes, in which pupils as young as twelve were active participants (see, for example, Obninskii, *Polgoda russkoi revoliutsii*, 78, 89.

159. For examples, see: ibid., 86, 155, 163–68; newspaper clippings: "Seminarist—razboinik," *Kolokol* 897 (28 February 1909), *Novaia Rus'* 18 (19 January 1909), *Russkoe slovo* 21 (27 January 1909), and *Nasha gazeta* 48 (27 February 1909), all in PSR 7-602; *Novoe vremia* 11213 (1 June 1907), PSR 8-650; 8 September 1905 police report, p. 13, Okhrana XIIIc(2)-6C; AM 10-CC, p. 558; 11 September 1903 police report, p. 13, and 25 December 1903 police report, both in Okhrana XIIIc(2)-2C; 4 March 1904 police report, p. 6, Okhrana XIIIc(2)-4A; 3 June 1904 police report, p. 10, and 10 June 1904 police report, p. 5, Okhrana XIIIc(2)-4B; 24 June 1904 police report, pp. 1–2, Okhrana XIIIc(2)-4B; 11 November 1904 police report, p. 5, and 16 December 1904 police report, p. 6, Okhrana XIIIc(2)-4B; 24 February 1905 police report, p. 6, and 10 March 1905 police report, p. 15, Okhrana XIIIc(2)-6A; 17 March 1905 police report, p. 8, and 31 March 1905 police report, p. 15, Okhrana XIIIc(2)-6A; 20 October 1905 police report, p. 9, Okhrana XIIIc(2)-6C; 6 May 1909 police report, Okhrana XIIIc(1)-1C, Incoming Dispatches (1909), doc. 496; newspaper clippings from *Tiflisskie vedomosti*, 20 June 1908, and *Stolichnaia pochta*, 5 November 1906, PSR 4-346; police reference no. 69, Okhrana XVIIn-2B.

160. Police reference no. 69, Okhrana XVIIn-2B.

161. See, for example, ibid.; 14 (27) May 1909 report to DPD, Okhrana XVIb(4)-1.

162. Clippings from *Novoe vremia*, 24 December 1907 and 30 March 1908, PSR 4-346; 17 March 1905 police report, pp. 12–13, Okhrana XIIIc(2)-6A.

163. 15 September 1905 police report, p. 5, Okhrana XIIIc(2)-6C.

164. Clipping from *Russkoe slovo* 94 (25 April 1909), PSR 4-346.

165. Kniazev, "1905," *Zvezda* 6 (1930): 235, 241, 243.

166. Kaplan, "A Total Negation of Russia," 42. Like their adult counterparts, a considerable number of extremist youngsters took their own lives rather than fall into the hands of the authorities (see, for example, 24 June 1904 police report, p. 2, Okhrana XIIIc[2]-4B; Arshinov, *Dva pobega*, 10; 29 September 1905 police report, p. 7, Okhrana XIIIc[2]-6C; undated handwritten manuscript, "Ben'iamin Fridman [Nemka Malen'kii]. [Nekrolog]," 1, Okhrana XXIVe-2D).

167. Nestroev, *Iz dnevnika Maksimalista*, 78.

168. See, for example, Simanovich, "Vospominaniia proletariia," *KS* 6 (79) (1931): 94; *Obzor revoliutsionnogo dvizheniia v okruge irkutskoi sudebnoi palaty*, 36–37, Nic. 197–2; Zavarzin, *Zhandarmy i revoliutsionery*, 142–45, 148–49; Myzgin, *So vzvedennym kurkom*, 6, 22; Arshinov, *Dva pobega*, 10–11, 47; Baron (Bibineishvili), *Za chetvert' veka*, 86–87; Kniazev, "1905," *Zvezda* 6 (1930): 245–46; police reference no.

68, Okhrana XVIIn-5B; newspaper clipping from *Tovarishch*, 3 July 1907, PSR 8-650; clippings from *Rech'*, 6 January 1909, and *Slovo* 670 (7 [20] January 1909), PSR 4-346; clipping from *Nasha gazeta*, 7 January 1909, PSR 4-346; 18 September 1903 police report, p. 8, Okhrana XIIIc(2)-2C; police report dated 28 July 1905, p. 8, Okhrana XIIIc(2)-6B; clipping from *Vek* 62 (5 December 1906), PSR 4-346; Sulimov, "K istorii boevykh organizatsii na Urale," *PR* 7 (42) (1925): 110; Zavarzin, *Rabota tainoi politsii*, 112. In one notable case, a homeowner informed police authorities that his daughter, a gymnasium student, had crafted a bomb and hidden it in his yard (Obninskii, *Polgoda russkoi revoliutsii*, 85, 167).

169. Sulimov, "K istorii boevykh organizatsii na Urale," *PR* 7 (42) (1925): 106; Sokolov-Novoselov, *Vooruzhennoe podpol'e*, 36, 43–44, 70; Myzgin, *So vzvedennym kurkom*, 6.

170. Frolov, "Terroristicheskii akt nad samarskim gubernatorom," *KS* 1 (8) (1924): 117; see also newspaper clipping from *Volia* 64 (18 September 1906), PSR 7-569; and L. Starr, "P. I. Pakerman," *KS* 4 (113) (1934): 141.

171. Sulimov, "K istorii boevykh organizatsii na Urale," *PR* 7 (42) (1925): 106; Sokolov-Novoselov, *Vooruzhennoe podpol'e*, 43–44.

172. Following adult examples, juveniles made frequent attempts to disarm street policemen, occasionally employing creative subterfuges. One adolescent carved a browning pistol out of soap, painted it black, and used the toy weapon to confiscate six real ones (Liadov, *Iz zhizni partii*, 135).

173. Nestroev, *Iz dnevnika Maksimalista*, 78. In one episode, a group of adolescents from a Bolshevik combat group, planning an expropriation, seemed to treat the enterprise as an amusing play in which they were actors enthusiastically assuming new roles that required them to change their appearances by using makeup, black masks, and fake beards (Myzgin, *So vzvedennym kurkom*, 6–7). Some teenagers devoted a great deal of time and energy to developing sophisticated, and largely useless, passwords; others were passionately eager for a few moments of glory carrying a red flag in an antigovernment demonstration. Among one youngster's notes instructions explaining how to make simple explosives were found next to a recipe for homemade candies (Kniazev, "1905," *Zvezda* 6 [1930]: 230–32, 234, 239, 241, 247).

174. Zavarzin, *Zhandarmy i revoliutsionery*, 149.

175. *Al'manakh. Sbornik po istorii anarkhicheskogo dvizheniia v Rossii*, 44. For a description of one underage terrorist's plans to set off an explosive device at a gendarme office in the town of Lomzh in October of 1905, see a 13 October 1905 police report, p. 7, Okhrana XIIIc(2)-6C. During the revolutionary events of 1905 youngsters frequently joined combat detachments en route to various targets, and took part in such undertakings as disrupting communication lines and building barricades ("Iz zapisnoi knizhki arkhivista," *KA* 6 [73] [1935]: 205; "Dekabr'skie dni v Donbasse," *KA* 6 [73] [1935]: 121). Similarly, during student disturbances at gymnasiums and seminaries, teenagers attacked police officers, cossacks, and guards with knives, daggers, and other weapons (see, for example, 17 February 1905 police report, p. 12, Okhrana XIIIc[2]-6A; 17 March 1905 police report, p. 13, Okhrana XIIIc[2]-6A).

176. For examples, see: clipping from an unidentified newspaper, no. 155 (5 July 1908), PSR 3-227; clipping from an unidentified newspaper dated July 1908, PSR 4-346; clipping from *Russkie vedomosti*, 16 March 1908, PSR 3-227; *Rus'*, 3 November 1907, and *Novoe vremia*, 16 November 1907, PSR 8-650; B. Nicolaevsky, "Novoe o

proshlom," *Byloe* 15 (1920): 169; 10 November 1905 police report, p. 18, Okhrana XIIIc(2)-6C; Obninskii, *Polgoda russkoi revoliutsii*, 74, 112, 114, 117, 121, 155–56; Savinkov, *Vospominaniia terrorista*, 275; "Obvinitel'nyi akt po delu o syne kollezhskogo sovetnika Sergee Il'inskom," PSR 3-170II; 6 January 1905 police report, p. 7, Okhrana XIIIc(2)-6A; leaflet issued by the Odessa Committee of the PSR, May 1905, PSR 5-427; Moskvich, "K istorii odnogo pokusheniia," *Byloe* 14 (1912): 38–43.

177. Frolov, "Terroristicheskii akt nad samarskim gubernatorom," *KS* 1 (8) (1924): 114.

178. See, for example, newspaper clippings from *Tovarishch*, April 1907, and *Russkoe slovo* 58 (9 March 1908), PSR 4-346; newspaper clipping from *Sibir'*, 13 March 1909, PSR 7-602; *Volia* 35 (12 July 1906): 3, PSR 7-569; 29 September 1905 police report, p. 7, Okhrana XIIIc(2)-6C; 30 December (year is missing) police report, p. 7, Okhrana XIIIc(2)-4B.

179. Police Department materials, protocol dated 17 September 1901, St. Petersburg, PSR 8-675; clippings from several unidentified newspapers collected under the heading, "Vzryv v Znamenskom monastyre v Kurske," PSR 3-293. For a description of sacrilegious acts performed by students, see also Kniazev, "1905," 238.

180. GARF f. 102, DPOO, op. 1905, d. 2605: 58; 31 March 1905 police report, p. 15, Okhrana XIIIc(2)-6A; undated newspaper clippings from *Journal* and *Matin*, Okhrana, box 84(1905), p. 107.

181. See, for example, GARF f. 102, DPOO, op. 1905, d. 2605: 1, 7, 10, 123 ob., 128, 141–141 ob.

182. 1 July 1904 police report, p. 6, Okhrana XIIIc(2)-4B.

183. Zavarzin, *Zhandarmy i revoliutsionery*, 145, 148; Pozner, *Boevaia gruppa pri TsK RSDRP(b)*, 33.

184. Kantor, "Smertniki v tiur'me," *KS* 6 (1923): 125. As the youngsters themselves acknowledged, alcohol was often an important factor in their decisions to participate in hazardous operations (Kniazev, "1905," *Zvezda* 6 [1930]: 247).

185. Sukhomlin, "Iz tiuremnykh skitanii," *KS* 55 (1929): 103; copy of a letter from Beilin to Muzil', Okhrana XIIIb(1)-1C, Outgoing Dispatches (1907), doc. 450. It was also a simple matter for youngsters involved in expropriations of private property to claim that they had acted in the name of anarchism (clipping from *Russkoe slovo*, 22 January 1910, PSR 8-653).

186. See Tagantsev, *Smertnaia kazn'*, 163.

CHAPTER SIX
THE UNITED FRONT

1. Burtsev, *Doloi tsaria!*, 22, PSR 1-19.

2. M. Aldanov, "Azef," *Poslednie novosti* (1924), Nic. 205–19.

3. Naimark, *Terrorists and Social Democrats*, 244.

4. Michael Melancon, " 'Marching Together!': Left Block Activities in the Russian Revolutionary Movement, 1900 to February 1917," *Slavic Review* 49 (2) (Summer, 1990): 239.

5. 12 (25) November 1911 police report, Okhrana XVIb(3)-4; 28 October (10 November) 1910 report to DPD, Okhrana XVIc-4.

6. *Protokoly pervogo s'ezda Partii Sotsialistov-Revoliutsionerov*, 342; *Pamiatnaia*

knizhka sotsialista-revoliutsionera, 25; "Izveshchenie o V-m S"ezde Soveta PSR," Okhrana XVIb(3)-1A.

7. Savinkov, *Vospominaiia terrorista*, 201; Nestroev, *Iz dnevnika maksimalista*, 71. Although nothing came of the negotiations between the Combat Organization and the Maximalists, at various points in his career as a terrorist Savinkov entertained schemes for political assassinations in conjunction with the Maximalists, as well as several anarchists and obscure independent revolutionaries (see, for example, Police Department report dated 20 April 1910, Okhrana XXIVh-2; 29 May [11 June] 1909 report to DPD, Okhrana XVIb[4]-1; "Otchet o partiiakh. 1909. Sotsialistov-Revoliutsionerov-Maksimalistov," Okhrana XVId-1; 4 [17] May 1912 report to DPD, Okhrana XXVa-1; March 1911 police report, Okhrana VIL-1).

8. *Obvinitel'nyi akt o Mikhaile Alekseeve Mikhailove, Sergee Aleksandrove Siniavskom . . . i drugikh, v chisle 83 chel.*, PSR 9-778, p. 14; Nestroev, *Iz dnevnika maksimalista*, 84–85; "Ekspropriatsiia ekspropriatorov," *Maksimalist* 6 (2 April 1920).

9. Letter from N. V. Chaikovskii written from the United States, dated 2 July 1907, pp. 6–7, Nic. 183–9.

10. Letter from B. I. Nicolaevsky to M. A. Aldanov dated 5 February 1928, Nic. 471–19.

11. 11 (24) May 1906 report to DPD, Okhrana XIc(5)-1. For a description of another SR-anarchist scheme, see GARF f. 102, DPOO, op. 1912, d. 113: 1.

12. 26 December 1910 report to DPD, Okhrana XIIIb(1)-1F, Outgoing Dispatches (1910), doc. 1160; Okhrana XXII-2; biographical note 2, Okhrana XVIIn-8; Gambarov, "Ocherk po istorii revoliutsionnogo dvizheniia v Luganske," *Letopis' revoliutsii* 4 (Gos. izd. Ukrainy, 1923): 72; 20 February (5 March) 1906 report to DPD, Okhrana XXI-2; March 1905 report to DPD, Okhrana XIIIb(1)-1A, Outgoing Dispatches (1905), doc. 40b; 6 (19) October 1908 report to DPD, Okhrana XIIIb(1)-1B, Outgoing Dispatches (1908), doc. 378; *Al'manakh. Sbornik po istorii anarkhicheskogo dvizheniia v Rossii*, 35, 41, 46; "Pamiati S. V. Sikorskogo," *KS* 41 (1928): 145; Arshinov, *Dva pobega*, 26.

13. *Al'manakh. Sbornik po istorii anarkhicheskogo dvizheniia v Rossii*, 40; Gambarov, "Ocherk po istorii revoliutsionnogo dvizheniia v Luganske," *Letopis' revoliutsii* 4 (Gos. izd. Ukrainy, 1923): 73; copy of an unsigned letter from St. Petersburg to Dmitriev in Geneva dated 14 March 1907, Okhrana XXIVi-1B.

14. 20 February (5 March) 1906 report to DPD, Okhrana XXI-2.

15. This tendency was evident among several political organizations (see, for example, Zavarzin, *Rabota tainoi politsii*, 113).

16. 15 January 1911 police report, Okhrana XVIb(3)-4; see also 24 February 1916 police report, Okhrana XVIc-4. In Baku, the SR Party committee considered unification with the Droshakisty, local Armenian revolutionaries (23 February [8 March] 1905 report to DPD, Okhrana XXIV-1A).

17. See, for example, 18 February (2 March) 1912 report to DPD, Okhrana XXIVi-1B; 12 (25) February 1911 report to DPD, Okhrana XVIb(3)-5C.

18. 30 August (12 September) 1907 report to DPD, Okhrana XXIVi-1B. For other instances of anarchist-Maximalist cooperation, see Nic. 101–7.

19. *Al'manakh. Sbornik po istorii anarkhicheskogo dvizheniia v Rossii*, 61. For a description of preparations for another joint anarchist-Maximalist expropriation, see a police agent's report dated 1 July 1907, Okhrana VIj-16A.

20. Avrich, *Russian Anarchists*, 55, 62.

21. "Anarkhizm i dvizhenie anarkhizma v Rossii," (n.d.), 23, Nic. 80–4; see also Okhrana XVIb(5)-5A.

22. Tobias, *Jewish Bund*, 329. For a description of revolutionary robberies carried out by the SRs in concert with anarchists in Belostok, see *Al'manakh. Sbornik po istorii anarkhicheskogo dvizheniia v Rossii*, 8–9, and in other locations, 59.

23. *Bol'sheviki Ekaterinburga vo glave mass* (Sverdlovsk, 1962), 101.

24. Newspaper clipping from *Tovarishch*, 19 October 1907, PSR 8-650.

25. Nestroev, *Iz dnevnika maksimalista*, 73.

26. *Al'manakh. Sbornik po istorii anarkhicheskogo dvizheniia v Rossii*, 91.

27. Copies of both proclamations are found in PSR 7-623II. For other instances of cooperation between members of the PSR and Dashnaktsutiun in terrorist activities, see 4 August 1905 police report, p. 26, Okhrana XIIIc(2)-6B.

28. Okhrana XVIIn-6.

29. 18 April (1 May) 1907 report to DPD, Okhrana XIX-13.

30. Report to the director of the Okhrana section in Warsaw dated 10 (23) February 1909, Okhrana XXIVa-1A.

31. Undated letter signed "tov. Amerikanets," PSR 3-295.

32. 7 September 1906 police report, Okhrana XIIIc(1)-1E, Incoming Dispatches (1906), doc. 579; 23 January 1907 police report, Okhrana XIIId(2)-43.

33. Copy of a decoded telegram from St. Petersburg dated 7 (20) June 1909, Okhrana XIIIc(3)-28.

34. *Leonid Borisovich Krasin ("Nikitich")*, 254.

35. Letter from E. E. Lazarev to comrades, dated 13 October 1908, Nic. 11–12.

36. 19 November 1913 police report, Okhrana XXII-1B.

37. 30 August (12 September) 1907 report to DPD, Okhrana XXIVi-1B. In November and December 1907, the SRs also made plans to kill Stolypin by detonating a bomb inside the Russian Parliament hall. They reportedly considered the anticipated massacre justified because there were "few leftists in the [Third] Duma," and there was "no need to feel sorry about the Kadets." The Duma would be dispersed in the panic, and then the SRs "would see what to do" (26 November [9 December] 1907 report to DPD, Okhrana XXIVi-1B; Pavlov, *Esery-maksimalisty*, 203–4).

38. Lenin himself occasionally sanctioned the arms deals (Pozner, *Boevaia gruppa pri TsK RSDRP[b]*, 60, 62, 66, 167–68).

39. Ibid., 167n., 171.

40. Ibid., 165.

41. P. S. Shuvalov, "Iz bor'by za khleb i voliu (iz vospominanii rabochego)," *KL* 5 (1922): 279; Liadov, *Iz zhizni partii*, 163.

42. I. Iurenev, "Dvinsk (1904–1906 gg.)," *PR* 12 (1922): 136. In an offhand remark the author of these memoirs assures his readers that for a while, until the authorities collected their strength and began their offensive against the revolution, the SD combatants in Dvinsk were "quite disciplined; 'ex's' [and] terrorist acts began to take place only after December" of 1905 (Iurenev, "Dvinsk, [1904–1906 gg.]," *PR* 12 [1922]: 136).

43. For a description of the terrorist activities of this composite group, see Iurenev, "Rabota R.S.-D.R.P. v Severo-Zapadnom krae," *PR* 8–9 (31–32) (1924): 188–91.

44. Kobozev, "Moi vospominaniia o 1905 g. v gor. Rige," *KL* 5 (1922): 298; "Obzor partii, primykaiushchikh k RSDRP," 1910, p. 30, Okhrana XVIb(6)-1C; see also Poz-

ner, *Boevaia gruppa pri TsK RSDRP(b)*, 171–72; I. Torf, "K istorii napadeniia na rizhskuiu tsentral'nuiu tiur'mu v 1905 g.," *KS* 74 (1931): 190.

45. Pozner, *Boevaia gruppa pri TsK RSDRP(b)*, 171.

46. Ibid.; Torf, "K istorii napadeniia na rizhskuiu tsentral'nuiu tiur'mu v 1905 g.,"
KS 74 (1931): 190.

47. "Obzor partii, primykaiushchikh k RSDRP," 31–32, Okhrana XVIb(6)-1C.

48. "Doneseniia Evno Azefa," *Byloe* 1 (23) (1917): 221; 23 February (8 March)
1905 report to DPD, Okhrana XXIVi-1A.

49. See, for example, 17 (30) August 1906 report to DPD, Okhrana XIIc(2)-2B; and
Mishin, "Tiumenskaia organizatsiia RSDRP," *KS* 4 (113) (1934): 54–55.

50. Mishin, "Tiumenskaia organizatsiia RSDRP," *KS* 4 (113) (1934): 54–55; Alliluev, "Moi vospominaniia," *KL* 8 (1923): 159.

51. 27 February (12 March) 1905 report to DPD, Okhrana XXIVi-1A.

52. See, for example, 30 October 1909 police report, Okhrana XXIVi-1B.

53. See, for example, GARF f. 102, DPOO, op. 1911, d. 330: 1, 8 ob., 14; 27
May 1905 report to DPD, Okhrana XIIIc(1)-1A, Incoming Dispatches (1905), doc. 14;
G. G. Sushkin, "D. K. Bochkov," *KS* 74 (1931): 226; Kochetov, "Vologodskaia ssylka
1907–1910 godov," *KS* 4 (89) (1932): 87; Melancon, "'Marching Together!,'" 240,
247.

54. B. Nicolaevsky, "Novoe o proshlom," *Byloe* 15 (1920): 168; see also GARF f.
102, DPOO, op. 1908, d. 123: 5–5 ob.; Melancon, "'Marching Together!,'" 242; Nikiforov, *Murav'i revoliutsii*, 266; and P. Nikiforov, "V gody reaktsii v Irkutskoi tiur'me,"
KS 8–9 (93–94) (1932): 236–237.

55. *Al'manakh. Sbornik po istorii anarkhicheskogo dvizheniia v Rossii*, 91.

56. Levanov, *Iz istorii bor'by bol'shevistskoi partii protiv eserov*, 121.

57. Ibid., 121, 123. During the first Russian revolution Lenin frequently urged his
supporters to enter into cooperation with any outsiders determined to fight the government (see, for example, Chuzhak, "Lenin i 'tekhnika' vosstaniia," *KS* 12 [73] [1931]: 77).

58. Tashkentets, "Petr Danilovich Romanov," *KS* 27 (1926): 235.

59. See, for example, 11 December 1913 police report, Okhrana XVIb(3)-1A.

60. Melancon, "'Marching Together!,'" 247.

61. *Leonid Borisovich Krasin ("Nikitich")*, 245–46.

62. At one point, Karl Trauberg, leader of the SR Northern Flying Combat Detachment, attempted to persuade the Bolsheviks to share the details concerning fabrication
of a certain bomb with the SR terrorists in exchange for two tons of rifle bullets. Contrary to the general spirit of cooperation among revolutionaries, however, the deal fell
through (Pozner, *Boevaia gruppa pri TsK RSDRP(b)*, 176).

63. See, for example, ibid., 118.

64. Pozner, *Boevaia gruppa pri TsK RSDRP(b)*, 118; *Leonid Borisovich Krasin
("Nikitich")*, 232; see also Aleksinskii, "Vospominaniia," 51n, Nic. 302–3; and Shaurov, *1905 god*, 236–37.

65. Pozner, *Boevaia gruppa pri TsK RSDRP(b)*, 103.

66. Riabkov-"Pchela," "Kak ia popal na rabotu pri nashem podpol'nom pravitel'stve," *PR* 3 (1921): 234.

67. Pozner, *Boevaia gruppa pri TsK RSDRP(b)*, 188–89 nn.

68. For a discussion of joint ventures between Bolsheviks and anarchists in the periphery, see Myzgin, *So vzvedennym kurkom*, 77.

69. 29 November (12 December) 1907 report to DPD, Okhrana XXVc-1.

70. Pozner, *Boevaia gruppa pri TsK RSDRP(b)*, 167.

71. *Leonid Borisovich Krasin ("Nikitich")*, 254.

72. Ibid., 255. On Finnish assistance to the Bolsheviks, see also Pozner, *Boevaia gruppa pri TsK RSDRP(b)*, 40–41.

73. Williams, *Other Bolsheviks*, 123–24; see also Souvarine, *Stalin*, 125; and a letter from B. I. Nicolaevsky to T. I. Vulich dated 15 May 1956, Nic. 207–16. During their collaboration, Lbov and his associates reportedly transferred approximately thirty thousand rubles to the Bolsheviks (Nic. 511–48).

74. E. A. Anan'in, "Iz vospominanii revoliutsionera 1905–1923 gg.," Inter-University Project on the History of the Menshevik Movement, paper 7 (New York, October 1961), 34.

75. Burenin, *Pamiatnye gody*, 256.

76. Myzgin, *So vzvedennym kurkom*, 81, 84–88.

77. The sailor had to give up his scheme because of security precautions on the yacht (Pozner, *Boevaia gruppa pri TsK RSDRP[b]*, 143–44).

78. See, for example, 8 (21) February 1906 report to DPD, Okhrana XXIVi-1A; undated report to DPD, Okhrana XIIIb(1)-1G, Outgoing Dispatches (1911), doc. 1106.

79. See, for example, *Anarkhist* 1 (10 October 1907): 17.

80. Tobias, *Jewish Bund*, 328.

81. A mixed committee for self-defense operating in Minsk included representatives of the Bund, the PSR, the local Workers' Party, the Jewish organization Poalei-Zion, and a group of Zionists-Socialists (Bukhbinder, "Evreiskoe rabochee dvizhenie v 1905 g.," *KL* 7 [1923]: 9). The Bundists also took part in joint efforts with other revolutionary organizations, such as the SRs and the PPS, to form federated strike committees. Many of these committees exhibited militant tendencies during labor disputes after 1903, a phenomenon particularly widespread in Belorussia and the Western Ukraine (see, for example, Melancon, "'Marching Together!,'" 241).

82. *Al'manakh. Sbornik po istorii anarkhicheskogo dvizheniia v Rossii*, 8.

83. Kirzhnits, *Evreiskoe rabochee dvizhenie*, 172.

84. 29 May (11 June) 1905 report to DPD, Okhrana XVIb(4)-3.

85. Martsinkovskii, "Vospominaniia o 1905 g. v g. Rige," *PR* 12 (1922): 327–328.

86. "Pokushenie na ubiistvo g.-m. Kosheleva predsedatelia Rizhskogo voennogo suda," 1–3, 5, 7, Nic. 199–7.

87. 20 February 1910 police report, Okhrana XXII-1A.

88. 24 August 1908 police report, Okhrana XXII-1A.

89. Pozner, *Boevaia gruppa pri TsK RSDRP(b)*, 179; Pal'vadre, *Revoliutsiia 1905–7 gg. v Estonii*, 155, 160–61.

90. One disagreement among various participants in the anarchist movement was reflected in a resolution adopted by a conference in Vil'na in which representatives of local Bread and Liberty groups denounced the practice of small-scale expropriations against private property on the part of the Black Banner organizations, and prohibited the Chernoznamentsy from formally joining the Bread and Liberty circles (Anarkhizm, [1909?] [*sic*], pp. 1, 41, Okhrana XVIb[5]-5A; for the same document, see Nic. 80–4; "Pamiati Moishe Kirshenbaum," *Anarkhist* 5 [March 1910]: 2–3).

91. Letter from P. Kropotkin to a "dear comrade" dated 10 May 1904, Nic. 81–9.

92. 1907 letter from P. Kropotkin to M. I. Gol'dsmit, Nic. 81–5.

93. 7 (20) February 1914 report to DPD, Okhrana XXVIId-7.

94. Savinkov, *Vospominaniia terrorista*, 285–86.

95. See, for example, Ravich-Cherkasskii, "Moi vospominaniia o 1905 gode," *Letopis' revoliutsii* 5–6 (14–15) (Gos. izd. Ukrainy, 1925): 319; Iurenev, "Rabota R.S.-D.R.P. v Severo-Zapadnom krae," *PR* 8–9 (31–32) (1924): 176; Kochetov, "Vologodskaia ssylka 1907–1910 godov," *KS* 4 (89) (1932): 87–88; *Al'manakh. Sbornik po istorii anarkhicheskogo dvizheniia v Rossii*, 89, 93–94, 103.

96. See, for example, *Al'manakh. Sbornik po istorii anarkhicheskogo dvizheniia v Rossii*, 7.

97. Rostov, "Eshche o vzryve traktira 'Tver'," *KL* 1 (40) (1931): 247.

98. 7 (20) September 1906 report to DPD, Okhrana XVIIr(1)-7B.

99. *Leonid Borisovich Krasin ("Nikitich")*, 136. Representatives of the Polish Socialist Party and several Armenian Droshakisty were also present at this conference (Pozner, *Boevaia gruppa pri TsK RSDRP[b]*, 52).

100. One well-publicized episode was the purchase by representatives of the PSR, assisted by Georgii Gapon and his followers, and Finnish activists led by Konni Zilliacus, of a steamboat, the *John Grafton*, which carried a supply of weapons and explosives intended for the SRs, the Finnish radicals, and the Polish and Georgian Socialists in Russia. The radicals received a substantial financial contribution for this venture from representatives of the Japanese diplomatic corps, and specifically from Akashi, the Japanese Military Attaché in Switzerland. After arranging for transportation of the weapons, the SRs appealed to the Bolshevik Central Committee for assistance once the steamboat reached Russian territory. Maxim Litvinov of the Bolshevik Center was assigned the task of concealing the weapons, but the *John Grafton* hit submerged rocks near the Gulf of Finland on 26 August (8 September) 1905, and the revolutionaries sank the vessel to prevent the weapons from falling into the hands of the authorities. While everyone on board escaped safely, the radicals lost a large portion of their supply of weapons and explosives (see Pozner, *Boevaia gruppa pri TsK RSDRP[b]*, 220–47; also see Riabkov, "Pchela," "Kak ia popal na rabotu pri nashem podpol'nom pravitel'stve," *PR* 3 (1921): 236; police report to P. I. Rachkovskii dated 24 December 1905 [6 January 1906], Okhrana XXIVh-1).

101. 6 (19) June 1911 report to DPD, Okhrana XXIVi-3D.

102. Savinkov, *Vospominaniia terrorista*, 184.

103. In 1906–1908 an entire network of these organizations emerged in roughly thirty cities throughout the empire (Melancon, "'Marching Together!,'" 246).

104. S. Mstislavskii, "Iz istorii voennogo dvizheniia. 'Ofitserskii' i 'Boevoi' Soiuzy 1906–1908 gg.," *KS* 55 (1929): 12.

105. This time Snesarev managed to escape unharmed, but after a subsequent confrontation with revolutionary workers, was shot and killed by an unknown assassin (ibid., 13–14).

106. Ibid., 14–16.

107. Pozner, *Boevaia gruppa pri TsK RSDRP(b)*, 46–47, 53.

108. Due to the authorities' immediate interference, nothing came of these deliberations (A. V. Sokolinskii, "Fidlerovskoe delo. [Vospominaniia uchastnika]," *KS* 31 [1927]: 10).

109. Melancon, "'Marching Together!,'" 243.

110. V. A. Sobolev, "Vospominaniia buntaria o 1905 g.," *KS* 74 (1931): 138–40.

111. Melancon, "'Marching Together!,'" 246.

112. *Biulleten' TsK P. S.-R.* 1 (March 1906): 7.

113. Nadel'shtein, "Butyrskie ocherki," *KS* 45–46 (1928): 197–98.

114. 30 June (13 July) 1914 report to DPD, Okhrana XVIb(5)-4.

115. 22 September (5 October) 1907 report to DPD, Okhrana XVIa-2.

116. Copy of a 5 September 1909 report to DPD, Okhrana XIIIc(1)-1G, Incoming Dispatches (1909), doc. 1093.

117. Indeed, the Union proved incapable of staging a single terrorist attempt and soon disintegrated (ibid.).

118. Cited in "Otrazhenie sobytii 1905 g. za granitsei," *KA* 2 (9) (1925): 40; Burtsev, *Doloi tsaria!*, 40–41, PSR 1-19.

119. Okhrana XVIc-2; "Letuchii liarok," no. 3, Izdanie Parizhskoi Gruppy Sodeistviia P. S.-R. (18 February 1908), PSR 1-88a.

120. Cited in "Delo tovarishcha Vasil'eva," *Izvestiia oblastnogo komiteta zagranich. organizatsii* 7 (1908): 8. For similar statements from the German SDs, see "Terror i sotsialisty-revoliutsionery," *Revoliutsionnoe slovo* 2 (July 1906): 1. The legitimacy of SR terrorism against the Russian autocracy was recognized by most European socialists, and in 1903, in a *cause célèbre* of its day, the leaders of the Second International launched a successful campaign to prevent the extradition of Mikhail Gots, one of the chief emigré organizers of the SR Combat Organization, from Italy to Russia (Perrie, "Political and Economic Terror," 63).

121. Burtsev, *Doloi tsaria!*, 41, PSR 1-19; cited in Dubinskii-Mukhadze, *Kamo*, 83.

122. Excerpt from a letter written by Dr. L. Gutman in Berlin to Dr. M. O. Gurevich in Moscow, dated 29 July 1904, Okhrana XVIIs-4.

123. Avrich notes, for example, that "the courtroom statements of the Russian terrorists often resembled the famous trial speech of the French 'propagandist by deed,' Emile Henry, which had been translated into Russian by the Geneva Group of Anarchists and published . . . in 1898." Another translation of the same speech appeared in the anarchist publication *Free Will* (*Vol'naia Volia*) in 1903 (Avrich, *Russian Anarchists*, 68n.).

124. The initial attempts to organize joint terrorist ventures between Russian and Bulgarian terrorists took place as early as April 1895 (June 1895 police report, Okhrana XXIVi-1A).

125. Several Combat Technical Group chemists were able to adapt the Macedonian bombs to the requirements of the Russian situation by turning them into hand grenades. In the revolutionary days of 1905 the Russian authorities were surprised to discover that some bombs used in combat operations in St. Petersburg and other cities were based on the Macedonian model, but were unable to determine how the Bulgarian explosives made their way into Russia (Pozner, *Boevaia gruppa pri TsK RSDRP[b]*, 43n.-44).

126. 13 (26) May 1905 report to DPD, Okhrana XIc(5)-1; Okhrana XVIIn-6.

127. Okhrana XXIVi-1A.

128. "Telegrammy," *Ezh* 1 (n.d.): 13, Nic. 435–12.

129. See, for example, Dubinskii-Mukhadze, *Kamo*, 90; 14 (27) November 1907 report to DPD, Okhrana XXIVi-1B; 11 April 1907 police report, Okhrana XVIc-5; "Svedeniia o vvoze oruzhiia v Rossiiu, snosheniia s komitetami v Rossii i svedeniia o deiatel'nosti revoliutsionnykh organizatsii" (n.d.), 1–2, Okhrana XXIVh-5n.

130. "Svedeniia o vvoze oruzhiia v Rossiiu, snosheniia s komitetami v Rossii i svedeniia o deiatel'nosti revoliutsionnykh organizatsii," 1, Okhrana XXIVh-5n; excerpt from a letter from Gagman to Gurevich, Okhrana XVIIs-4.

131. 28 December 1905 (10 January 1906) police report, Okhrana XXIVh-4G; 31 July 1913 police report, Okhrana XXII-1B; 13 (26) December 1905 police report, Okhrana XXIVh-4C; see also 21 June 1913 police report, Okhrana XXII-1B.

132. Dubinskii-Mukhadze, *Kamo*, 98.

133. 8 (21) March 1914 report to DPD, Okhrana XXIVl-2g.

134. 13 (26) December 1905 police report, Okhrana XXIVh-4C.

135. 7 August 1906 police report, Okhrana VIj-15C; 7 August 1908 police report, Okhrana XVIIs-1.

136. 6 (19) September 1907 report to DPD, Okhrana XVIc-3.

137. 22 March (4 April) 1910 police report, Okhrana XVIb(5)-5b.

138. 12 (25) May 1911 report to DPD, Okhrana XVIb(5)-2. For other instances of cooperation between Russian and Austrian anarchists, see Zavarzin, *Zhandarmy i revoliutsionery*, 178.

139. See, for example, "Otrazhenie sobytii 1905 g. za granitsei," *KA* 2 (9) (1925): 40.

140. 14 (27) May 1916 report to DPD, Okhrana XXIVi-1B. Perhaps because embezzlement had provided a large portion of the group's funds, the leaders did not wish to inform their followers of the exact source of the money, causing a major conflict among the anarchists, some of whom threatened not only to leave the conspiracy, but also to report its plans to the authorities (30 April 1916 police report, Okhrana XVIb[5]-3).

141. 8 (21) October 1907 report to DPD, Okhrana XXIVh-1; police reports dated 12 and 16 October 1907, Okhrana VIj-16B.

142. Police report to P. I. Rachkovskii dated 16 October 1901, Okhrana XIX-12A.

143. 1 September 1895 police report, Okhrana XXa-1A.

144. Rataev, "Evno Azef," *Byloe* 2 (24) (1917): 189; "Doneseniia Evno Azefa," *Byloe* 1 (23) (1917): 218. In 1904 several Polish revolutionary nationalists residing in Paris sent a telegram to the father of the Finnish terrorist Shauman, congratulating him for his son's heroic deed, the recent assassination of Governor-general Bobrikov, a leading representative of the Russian administration in Helsinki (6 [19] July 1904 report to DPD, Okhrana XXI-1).

145. "Anarkhizm," 97, Okhrana XVIb(5)-5A.

146. June 1905 police report, Okhrana XVIb(6)-2; 25 October (7 November) 1905 police report, Okhrana XVIb(3)-4; translated letter from Tonetti in Lausanne to Lidia Gogeliia in Geneva, dated 5 November 1905, Okhrana XVIb(3)-4.

147. Copy of a telegram from D.S.S. Zhdanov in Smirna to the Russian Ambassador in Constantinople dated 15 January 1906, Okhrana XXIVf-1A.

148. A decoded police telegram from Odessa dated 17 January 1906, Okhrana XIIIc(3)-20.

149. 24 August 1908 police report, Okhrana XXII-1A.

150. 4 December 1903 police report, Okhrana XIIIc(2)-2C.

151. In September 1908 the Military District Court of Warsaw sentenced Vaterlos to fifteen years of hard labor (police reference no. 41, Okhrana XVIIn-8; "Anarkhizm i dvizhenie anarkhizma v Rossii," p. 47, Nic. 80–4; Genkin, "Sredi preemnikov Bakunina," *KL* 1 [22] [1927]: 182–83; Genkin, "Anarkhisty," *Byloe* 3 [31] [1918]: 166).

152. *Al'manakh. Sbornik po istorii anarkhicheskogo dvizheniia v Rossii*, 126.

153. 12 November 1909 police report, Okhrana XXI-1.

154. 15 March 1914 police report, Okhrana XVIIs-3.

155. The aims of the Black Hand were internationalist, transcending strictly Serbian interests. In 1911, for example, the group planned the assassination of the king of Greece (Laqueur, *Terrorism*, 113).

156. "Obzor kavkazskikh revoliutsionnykh partii," 1 September 1901, 39, 42, 44, Okhrana XXa-1B.

157. "Iranskaia revoliutsiia 1905–1911 gg. i bol'sheviki Zakavkaz'ia," *KA* 2 (105) (1941): 63–66.

158. Cited in Laqueur, *Terrorism*, 44.

159. Ibid., 44–45, 113.

160. Melancon, "'Marching Together!,'" 251–52.

CHAPTER SEVEN
THE KADETS AND TERROR

A substantial portion of this chapter appeared as an article entitled, "The Kadets and Terrorism, 1905–1907," in *Jahrbücher für Geschichte Osteuropas* 36 (1988), pp. 248–67, published by Franz Steiner Verlag Wiesbaden GmbH, Sitz Stuttgart.

1. Lenin, *PSS*, 6:76.

2. For a discussion of Popular Socialist cooperation with the SRs, see N. D. Erofeev, *Narodnye sotsialisty v pervoi russkoi revoliutsii* (Moscow, 1979); and Terrence Emmons, *The Formation of Political Parties and the First National Elections in Russia* (Cambridge, Mass., 1983), 82–87.

3. *GD* 1907, 40–2:747–48; and *GD* 1906, 4–1:118.

4. Trotsky, *Stalin*, 98.

5. *GD* 1907, 23–1:1686; 38:2, 600.

6. *GD* 1907, 23–1:503.

7. A. A. Kizevetter, *Napadki na partiiu Narodnoi Svobody (vospominaniia 1881–1914)* (Prague, 1929), 53.

8. The secondary literature dealing directly with the Kadets is limited, and no comprehensive published history of the Party of People's Freedom in the prerevolutionary period exists. Still, the extensive literature on the 1905–1907 period in general is useful in determining the Kadet position on the issue of terrorism, as are numerous unpublished and primary sources, which include documents and publications issued by the Kadets and other political parties, as well as memoirs and historical accounts written by contemporaries of the first Russian revolution.

9. P. Miliukov, *God bor'by* (St. Petersburg, 1907), 118; see also V. V. Shelokhaev, *Kadety—glavnaia partiia liberal'noi burzhuazii v bor'be s revoliutsiei 1905–1907 gg.* (Moscow, 1983), 310–21.

10. See, for example, V. A. Maklakov, *Rechi* (Paris, 1949), 51.

11. Nestroev, *Iz dnevnika Maksimalista*, 78.

12. *GD* 1907, 9–1:491. One SR deputy, a priest, maintained, "It is possible to find justification for terror even in the Gospels" (Tyrkova-Vil'iams, *Na putiakh k svobode*, 344).

13. In the words of Grigorii Aronson, "Broad public opinion had little interest in liberalism" (Grigorii Aronson, *Rossiia nakanune revoliutsii* [Madrid, 1986], 144).

14. Thomas Riha, *A Russian European: Paul Miliukov in Russian Politics* (London, 1969), 78.

15. Cited in ibid., 78.

16. P. Miliukov, *Russia and Its Crisis* (Chicago and London, 1906), 524; copy of a letter from B. I. Nicolaevsky to P. N. Miliukov dated 13 May 1931; copy of a letter from P. N. Miliukov to B. I. Nicolaevsky dated 18 May 1931, Nic. 492–26. On the conference in Paris and subsequent collaboration between the liberals and the SRs, see Galai, *Liberation Movement*, 214–21.

17. Cited in Riha, *Russian European*, 83.

18. Cited in Galai, *Liberation Movement*, 220.

19. Aronson, *Rossiia nakanune revoliutsii*, 159.

20. See the discussion in K. F. Shatsillo, *Russkii liberalizm nakanune revoliutsii 1905–1907 gg.* (Moscow, 1985), 254–55, 300.

21. See, for example, Vagner-Dzvonkevich, "Pokushenie na nachal'nika kievskoi okhranki polkovnika Spiridovicha," *KS* 12 (1924): 137.

22. L. Men'shchikov, *Okhrana i revoliutsiia*, pt. 3 (Moscow, 1932): 170–71; excerpt from a letter written by Evgenii Vashakidze in Paris to Sof'ia Shavdiia in Odessa dated 30 March 1909, Okhrana XIIIc(1)-1C, Incoming Dispatches, doc. 400; see also Gerasimov, *Na lezvii s terroristami*, 55; and a reference in Z.A.B. Zeman, ed., *Germany and the Revolution in Russia, 1915–1918* (London, 1958), 21. According to police sources, the revolutionaries suddenly found themselves short on funds when a number of liberal organizations began to be formed in Russia that needed money for their own purposes (20 February [5 March] 1906 report to DPD, Okhrana XXI-2).

23. Cited in Riha, *Russian European*, 83. Some time before Plehve was assassinated, another prominent member of the Union, Prince Dmitrii Shakhovskoi, who was soon to join the Kadet Central Committee and become secretary of the First State Duma, was so outraged by the minister's behavior that he repeatedly insisted in a conversation with a friend, "Plehve ought to be killed. . . . It is time for Plehve to be killed" (Tyrkova-Vil'iams, *Na putiakh k svobode*, 166).

24. Shatsillo, *Russkii liberaliszm nakanune revoliutsii 1905–1907 gg.*, 300. Similarly, word of Plehve's assassination by the SRs produced in Struve's household "jubilation as if this were news about a victory over an enemy" (Tyrkova-Vil'iams, *Na putiakh k svobode*, 176).

25. 11 August 1905 police report, p. 9, Okhrana XIIIc(2)-6C.

26. Cited in Riha, *Russian European*, 78. This position on the part of the Union of Liberation turned it into a truly radical organization in the eyes of the authorities. They took information from one of their agents in Berlin very seriously when he reported that a small group of left-wing members of the Union of Liberation in St. Petersburg were plotting the assassination of Nicholas II, and in mid-January of 1905 had approached the leaders of the PSR abroad to obtain their cooperation (29 January [11 February] 1905 report to DPD, Okhrana XXIVi-2A).

27. See Shelokhaev, *Kadety*, 145.

28. Cited in Michael Karpovich, "The Two Types of Russian Liberalism: Maklakov and Miliukov," *Continuity and Change in Russian and Soviet Thought*, E. J. Simmons, ed. (Cambridge, Mass., 1955), 136.

29. *Konstitutsionno-demokraticheskaia partiia. S'ezd 7–18 oktiabria 1905 g.* (n.p., n.d.), 7.

30. I. V. Gessen, "V dvukh vekakh," *Arkhiv russkoi revoliutsii* 22 (1937): 226; "Dnevnik A. A. Polovtseva," *KA* 4 (1923): 104. Tyrkova-Vil'iams describes the same incident in her memoirs, although she mistakenly assumes Count Ignat'ev to have been the victim of this assassination attempt (Tyrkova-Vil'iams, *Na putiakh k svobode*, 259).

31. "Klub partii Narodnoi svobody (iz neizdannykh vospominanii kn. D. I. Bebutova)," undated manuscript, pp. 15–16, Nic. 779–2.

32. 11 May 1906 report from a police agent in Paris, Okhrana VIj-15C. For similar activities of Mandel'shtam, and other aspects of the Kadet-SR collaboration in Paris in the same period, such as their joint campaign in April 1906 against a proposed French loan to the tsarist government, see an 18 April (1 May) 1906 report to DPD, Okhrana XIIIb(1)-1B, Outgoing Dispatches, doc. 119.

33. 9 (22) June 1906 report to DPD, Okhrana XVIIg-2D.

34. Although the Kadets did insist on the forcible confiscation of landowners' property, they did not demand nationalization of the means of production—the common slogan of all socialists.

35. Emmons, *Formation of Political Parties*, 414 n.; "Kadety v 1905–1906 gg. (Materialy TsK partii 'Narodnoi Svobody')," *KA* 3 (46) (1931): 53; see also "Spor o revoliutsii: dva pis'ma V. A. Maklakova Kn. V. A. Obolenskomu," *Vestnik russkogo khristianskogo dvizheniia* 146 (1986): 272; and Ascher, *Revolution of 1905*, 294.

36. V. A. Maklakov, *Iz vospominanii* (New York, 1954), 351.

37. Excerpt from a letter written by Vashakidze to Shavdiia, Okhrana XIIIc(1)-1C, Incoming Dispatches, doc. 400.

38. The Kadets expressed this goal on many occasions. See, for example, Kizevetter, *Napadki*, 61–65; V. A. Maklakov, *Pervaia Gosudarstvennaia Duma* (Paris, 1939), 197; and Miliukov, *God bor'by*, 492–95.

39. See Judith Elin Zimmerman, "Between Revolution and Reaction: The Russian Constitutional Democratic Party, October, 1905–June, 1907," Ph.D. diss. (Columbia University, 1967), 58.

40. See, for example, items in *Rech'*, issues 173 (7 October 1906): 2; and 1 (14 January 1907): 2; see also *Pervaia Gosudarstvennaia Duma* (St. Petersburg, 1907), 94.

41. Gusev, *Partiia eserov*, 60.

42. See Gerasimov, *Na lezvii s terroristami*, 78; and Maklakov, *Iz vospominanii*, 351. Many prominent members of the PSR were prepared to enter into a temporary alliance with the Constitutional Democrats, with Gershuni arguing during the Second PSR Congress in February 1907: "For the present, the Kadets are not our enemies and are no threat to us. . . . There is no need to fight against them" (cited in Levanov, *Iz istorii bor'by bol'shevistskoi partii protiv eserov*, 117).

43. Tyrkova-Vil'iams, *Na putiakh k svobode*, 345.

44. Pipes, *Struve*, 56.

45. See *Konstitutsionno-demokraticheskaia partiia. S"ezd 17–18 oktiabria 1905 g.*, 26, 25; *GD* 1906, 1–1:3; and *Rech'* 60 (11 May 1906): 1.

46. *GD* 1906, 2–1:35, 37.

47. Ibid., 2–1:24–25.

48. For the terms of the amnesty, see "Khronika-Akty," *VE* 6 (1905): 346–48.

49. Even the terrorists "whose behavior during their terms of imprisonment recommended them for mercy" should, in the Council's view, have been subject to amnesty (see P. N. Shipov, *Vospominaniia i dumy o perezhitom* [Moscow, 1918], 434–36, 440–41).

50. This was emphasized by a prominent Kadet representative in the Duma, F. I. Rodichev: "Gentlemen, I invite you: let us be unanimous, let us not raise the argument about the limitation of the amnesty, let us state one common wish: the amnesty must be general, without exceptions" (*GD* 1906, 2–1:24; see also *Rech'* 66 [19 May 1906]: 2).

51. P. N. Miliukov, *Tri popytki* (Paris, n.d.), 47. Significantly, Miliukov was well aware at the time that amnesty could be arranged, but "not for the bombists" (cited in Riha, *Russian European*, 125).

52. *GD* 1906, 4–1:74, 76, 75.

53. Ibid., 4–1:137.

54. Cited in Gerasimov, *Na lezvii s terroristami*, 78. Subsequently, Miliukov denied that he had ever made such a statement (see Pavel Nikolaevich Miliukov, "K stat'e M. V. Vishniaka," p. 1, Bakhmeteff Archive Ms. Coll. Savchenko, Columbia University Libraries).

55. See, for example, *GD* 1906, 4–1:231.

56. According to Minister of Justice Shcheglovitov, "The abolition of capital punishment for political crimes . . . would have been equal to the refusal of the State to defend . . . its loyal servants" (*GD* 1906, 29–2:1479–80).

57. Venozhinskii, *Smertnaia kazn' i terror*, 32. The conservatives generally shared this opinion, with some, such as Lev Tikhomirov, a prominent former member of the People's Will who converted to the government's side, holding the authorities responsible for this situation, for they appeared ready to make concessions to society only out of fear of the bomb-throwing terrorists ("25 let nazad. Iz dnevnika L. Tikhomirova," *KA* 2 [39] [1930]: 73). It is noteworthy that Lenin seemed to concur on this point, arguing, "If autocracy were to crush the revolution decisively and finally, the Kadets would become powerless, since their strength derives from the revolution" (cited in Shelokhaev, *Kadety—glavnaia partiia liberal'noi burzhuazii*, 159).

58. *GD* 1906, 3–1:45. For similar statements, see *Rech'* 77 (1 June 1906): 1.

59. *GD* 1906, 4–1:231; see also *Rech'* 62 (13 May 1906): 1.

60. *GD* 1906, 3–1:44–45.

61. Miliukov, *God bor'by*, 354; *Rech'* 77 (1 June 1906): 1; Kizevetter, *Napadki na partiiu Narodnoi Svobody*, 54.

62. *GD* 1906, 15–1:642; see also *GD* 1907, 8–1:410.

63. Miliukov, *God bor'by*, 353; see also *Rech'*, issues 36 (13 April 1906): 5; and 77 (1 June 1906): 1.

64. *GD* 1906, 4–1:231; see also *Rech'*, issues 20 (27 March 1906): 4; 62 (13 May 1906): 1; and 71 (25 May 1906): 1.

65. *GD* 1906, 29–2:1496.

66. Grigorii Frolov, "Terroristicheskii akt nad samarskim gubernatorom," *KS* 1 (8) (1924): 114.

67. *Rech'* 149 (9 September 1906): 2.

68. "Sovremennaia letopis'," *Byloe* 10 (1906): 342.

69. *GD* 1907, 9–1:485–86; for details, see Obninskii, *Polgoda russkoi revoliutsii*, 157.

70. *GD* 1907, 38–2:607–8. The Kadets possessed information about many terrorist acts of a strictly criminal nature. See, for example, Obninskii, *Polgoda russkoi revoliutsii*, 156, 158–59, 162–64.

71. *GD* 1906, 29–2:1496.

72. Ibid., 29–2:1487.

73. Ibid., 29–2:1496. For similar statements, see Obninskii, *Polgoda russkoi revoliutsii*, 153.

74. Ivan Turgenev, "Porog," *Novyi sbornik revoliutsionnykh pesen i stikhotvorenii* (Paris, 1899), 61–62.

75. *GD* 1906, 29–2:1495–96. The Kadets were not alone in using this image for political purposes; the SRs also found it convenient for their propaganda of terrorism (see B. Savinkov, "Revoliutsionnye siluety. Dora Brilliant," *Znamia truda* 8:10).

76. *Rech'* 18 (25 March 1906): 2. "Marusia" is the affectionate diminutive form of Mariia. Many common people were very receptive to the hidden suggestions in Kadet writings, as is evident, for example, in the confession of a sailor: "She is a saint, I pray to her" (Zalezhskii, "V gody reaktsii," *PR* 2 [14] [1923]: 338). Conversely, the antigovernment press, in its attacks on two police officers named Zhdanov and Abramov who reportedly mistreated Spiridonova physically after her arrest, often did not mince words, portraying the officers as savage beasts in one popular anecdote: "Schoolteacher: 'Dear children, what do you know about Abramov?' Children: 'Teacher, we haven't studied wild animals yet'" (*Sprut* 13 [21 March 1906]: 6, Nic. 436–5). The notoriety of the two police officers predetermined their fate, for both Zhdanov and Abramov were killed in May 1906 by unidentified terrorists (Tambov PSR Committee leaflet dated 5 May 1906, PSR 4-351; and *Volia* 7 [9 May 1906]: 3, Arkhiv PSR 7-569).

77. *GD* 1906, 11–1:442.

78. *Rech'* 13 (20 March 1906): 1; and *GD* 1906, 15–1:643.

79. See: *GD* 1907, 8–1:396; and *GD* 1906, 16–1:738.

80. See, for example, discussions in *GD* 1907, 8–1:400; *Rech'*, issues 79 (3 June 1906): 5; and 82 (7 June 1906): 2; and especially numerous cases of juvenile terrorist attempts in Obninskii, *Polgoda russkoi revoliutsii*, 155–56, 163–67.

81. See, for example, the following issues and pages of *Rech'*: 47 (26 April 1906): 1–2; 62 (13 May 1906): 2; 72 (9 April 1907): 2; 43 (22 April 1906): 1; 46 (25 April 1906): 2; and 47 (26 April 1906): 1–2.

82. Tyrkova-Vil'iams, *Na putiakh k svobode*, 343.

83. See V. V. Leontovich, *Istoriia liberalizma v Rossii 1762–1914* (Paris, 1980), 478; and *GD* 1906, 4–1:138.

84. The Kadets even compiled and published statistics on political assassinations from October 1905 to October 1906. The underlying purpose of this publication, however, was to demonstrate the insignificance of terrorist activity in comparison with the repressive measures of the government (Dvoikh, "Pogibshie 17 Oktiabria 1905 g.-17 Oktiabria 1906 g.," *Vestnik Partii Narodnoi Svobody* 33–35 [Moscow, 1906]: 1808–15, 1725–36).

85. See, for example, the following issues and pages of *Rech'* for 1906: 32:2; 36:5; 38:4; 39:3; 65:3; 71:3; 73:4; 74:3; 79:5; 80:2; 82:2; 90:1; 120:2; 137:1; 138:2; 139:2; 161:3; 164:3; and for 1907: 14:4; 50:4; 53:3; 108:2. Most of these articles and editorials were unsigned, representing the opinion of the newspaper and not of individual contributors. Out of fairness it should be noted that one particularly severe instance of terrorism did evoke a mild condemnation from *Rech'*. Following the Bloody Wednesday massacre in Warsaw in August 1906, the rampage led by the PPS against police and military forces "to bolster the revolutionary mood of the proletariat" that resulted in more than one hundred civilian casualties, *Rech'* did remark, "There is no excuse for anarchist [*sic*] terror" (cited in Trotsky, *Stalin*, 96; *Rech'* 133 [22 August 1906]: 1).

86. See, for example, *Rech'* issues for 23 February 1906: 1; and 137 (26 August 1906): 1; and Miliukov, *God bor'by*, 260–64.

87. Riha, "*Riech'*, A Portrait of a Russian Newspaper," *Slavic Review* 22 (4) (December 1963): 663.

88. Several of these assassinations are described in Gerasimov, *Na lezvii s terroris-tami*, 150–55; and Pipes, *Russian Revolution*, 170. Top officials in the tsarist adminis-tration expressed their concern over the activities of several conspiratorial right-wing groups, considering them potentially no less dangerous for the security of the country than the clandestine antigovernment organizations (Police Department circular dated 15 April 1905, Okhrana XIIId[1]-9). For the most part, however, the extremists on the right were responsible for outbreaks of mob violence directed against the revolution, including spontaneous and organized armed demonstrations and especially the po-groms, rather than individual political assassinations (Keep, *Rise of Social Democracy*, 227, 243; and Pestkovskii, "Bor'ba partii v rabochem dvizhenii v Pol'she v 1905–1907 gg.," *PR* 11 [1922]: 47).

89. *Rech'* 148 (8 September 1906): 1.

90. A. Kaminka, "Mikhail Iakovlevich Gertsenshtein," *Vestnik Partii Narodnoi Svobody* 19–20 (July 1906): 1220; and "K smerti M. Ia. Gertsenshtein," *Vestnik Partii Narodnoi Svobody* 21–22 (August 1906): 1313–15; see also the following issues and pages of *Rech'* for 1906: 131:2; 132:1; 148:1; and for 1907: 8:1, 2, 3; 10:1; 12:1; 17:1; 20:1; 22:1; 33:4; 34:2, 3; 35:1; 38:1; 45:3; 55:2; 62:1; 66:1; 80:4; 137:2; 138:2.

91. See *Rech'* 119 (5 June 1907): 1; and 117 (2 June 1907): 3. No denunciation of the third terrorist act followed (see *Rech'* 120 [6 June 1907]: 2). This attitude toward polit-ical murders was described effectively by a former Kadet, Prince E. N. Trubetskoi, who pointed out that many who expressed indignation and horror at the assassination of Gertsenshtein did so "only because this was murder inflicted from the right; a murder from the *left* would have been met with justification and even sympathy from the same persons." Needless to say, the Kadets objected strongly to this accusation (*Rech'* 134 [23 August 1906]: 1).

92. See a newspaper clipping from *Russkie vedomosti* (21 March 1907), PSR 4-346.

93. *GD* 1907, 9–1:445, 477.

94. Ibid., 9–1:479, and 8–1:392; see also the following issues and pages of *Rech'*: (23 February 1906): 1; 6 (13 March 1906): 1; 10 (17 March 1906): 4; 75 (30 May 1906): 1. One Duma episode is particularly revealing. When Chief Military Prosecutor Pavlov appeared before the audience to respond to interrogation about the use of military courts against the revolutionaries, the Kadets, along with the socialists, prevented this repre-sentative of the administration from completing a sentence with their continuous shouts: "Get out! Get out! Executioner! Murderer! You have blood on your hands!" Pavlov was forced to leave the floor. Several days later he was assassinated by the SRs, and in the eyes of the government the Duma opposition was partly responsible for his death, for its insults and accusations were likely to have encouraged the terrorists to act (Tyrkova-Vil'iams, *Na putiakh k svobode*, 298, 300).

95. In the words of Tyrkova-Vil'iams, "Despite the fact that their numbers were few in the [Second] Duma, the Kadets enjoyed a great deal of prestige in the country. Their moral condemnation of terror could have sobered many who were helping the revolu-tionaries without giving it much thought" (Tyrkova-Vil'iams, *Na putiakh k svobode*, 345).

96. *GD* 1907, 8–1:374–75.

97. *Rech'* 81 (19 April 1907): 1.

98. They did so on numerous occasions. See, for example, *GD* 1907, 8–1:373, 402, 433, 445; also: 9–1:445, 476; zas. 18, 1:1275; 40–2:737.

99. *GD* 1907, 8–1:433; and 9–1:475.

100. Pipes, *Struve*, 56.

101. Significantly, while protesting these accusations, the Kadets mentioned nothing of political murders (*Rech'* 113 [29 May 1907]: 1; see also A. A. Kizevetter, *Na rubezhe dvukh stoletii [Vospominaniia 1881–1914]*, [Moscow, 1906], 461).

102. *GD* 1907, 9–1:477; see also: *GD* 1907, 9–1:529; and *Rech'* 42 (21 April 1906): 1.

103. *GD* 1906, 15–1:643.

104. On many occasions Golovin demonstrated that his allegiance to the Kadet Party and his obvious sympathy for the Duma's left dominated his decisions as chairman (see, for example, *GD* 1906, 34–2:237–39, 287; and especially the case in which he used a formal pretext not to allow a moment of respect for government officials assassinated by terrorists, in *GD* 1906, 18–1:1275–78, 1373–76). Even some Kadets agreed that Golovin was not a good chairman (see Gessen, "V dvukh vekakh," 241; and Tyrkova-Vil'iams, *Na putiakh k svobode*, 339).

105. *GD* 1907 20–1:1533.

106. Ibid., 24–1:1833; see also ibid., 38–2:608–10.

107. See V. A. Maklakov, *Vtoraia Gosudarstvennaia Duma* (Paris, n.d.), 216.

108. *GD* 1907, 34–2:286–87.

109. Ibid., 38–2:608–9.

110. Ibid., 26–1:1928. The question of condemning political assassination came up in the Second Duma indirectly once more, on 17 May. The Kadets once again refused to issue a direct statement, but out of fear of government dissolution of the Duma, decided to offer a resolution in which, according to Maklakov, "they concealed [the denunciation] so well that it could only be found with a magnifying glass" (Maklakov, *Vtoraia Gosudarstvennaia Duma*, 218–19, 220; see also *GD* 1907, 40–2:759; for an excerpt from this resolution, see *VE* 6 [1907]: 763). It was only on 8 February 1908 that a coalition of moderate and conservative representatives in the Third Duma was finally able to obtain enough votes to issue a formal condemnation of terrorist practices (*Tret'ia Gosudarstvennaia Duma. Materialy dlia otsenki ee deiatel'nosti* [St. Petersburg, 1912], 108–9).

111. Cited in V. D. Nabokov, "Sprava i sleva," *Vestnik Partii Narodnoi Svobody* 37 (1906): 1935; see also *Rech'* 82 (20 April 1907): 1. Interestingly, the Kadets admitted that they could not deny the truth of such arguments (*Rech'* 72 [1 June 1906]: 1).

112. Venozhinskii, *Smertnaia kazn' i terror*, 32; see also Miliukov, *God bor'by*, 496.

113. Cited in Nabokov, "Sprava i sleva," 1935.

114. *VE* 1 (1907): 355; see also *VE* 3 (1907): 333–34.

115. Shipov, *Vospominaniia*, 399.

116. Tyrkova-Vil'iams, *Na putiakh k svobode*, 283; Miliukov, *God bor'by*, 117–128; Riha, *Russian European*, 83.

117. On 15 May 1907 Struve and Bulgakov, for example, voted against the refusal of the Kadet faction to discuss the Duma resolution against terrorism (*VE* 6:762 n; see also Maklakov, *Vtoraia Gosudarstvennaia Duma*, 216). Even leftist Kadet O. Ia. Pergament at one point directly declared his personal opposition to terrorist tactics. This, however, was the only instance in which a Kadet Duma deputy went against the decision of the group (*GD* 1907, 40–2:763).

118. Pipes, *Struve*, 56.

119. Riha, *Russian European*, 140; *VE* 8 (1907): 841.

120. Maklakov, *Pervaia Gosudarstvennaia Duma*, 207.

121. Shipov, *Vospominaniia i dumy o perezhitom*, 450.

122. See Maklakov, *Pervaia Gosudarstvennaia Duma*, 207; and Miliukov, *Tri popytki*, 47.

123. See Shipov, *Vospominaniia*, 457–60.

124. Tyrkova-Vil'iams, *Na putiakh k svobode*, 283; see also Shipov, *Vospominaniia*, 460; and Miliukov, *Tri popytki*, 47.

125. See Emmons, *Formation of Political Parties*, 366; and Hans Rogger, *Russia in the Age of Modernization and Revolution, 1881–1917* (London-New York, 1983), 223.

126. Cited in Shelokhaev, *Kadety*, 160.

127. The Kadets, for example, unlike the parties to their left, voted on 7 May 1907 in favor of a Duma declaration expressing satisfaction that Nicholas II had escaped a terrorist attempt on his life planned by a group of SR conspirators led by Nikitenko, Naumov, and Siniavskii (*GD* 1907, 34–2:197–99). They also changed their tactics and no longer pressured the tsar for total political amnesty (see *GD* 1907, 46–2:1148; and *GD* 1907, 49–2:1301–2). This did not improve their position in the eyes of their conservative opponents, who observed, "Having seen that a direct revolution is lost for the moment," the Kadets put on the "mask of 'misunderstood and loyal constitutionalists'" (Venozhinskii, *Smertnaia kazn' i terror*, 31). Maklakov subsequently expressed the same opinion (Maklakov, *Vtoraia Gosudarstvennaia Duma*, 244–45).

128. *GD* 1907, 40–2:756.

129. Pipes, *Struve*, 56. In his manifesto announcing the dissolution of the Second Duma the tsar proclaimed: "Having avoided denouncing murders and violence, the Duma has not shown cooperation with the government in restoring order" (cited in Tyrkova-Vil'iams, *Na putiakh k svobode*, 364). For the full text of the official statement, see "Vnutrennee obozrenie," *VE* 7 (1907): 334–35.

130. Von Borcke, "Violence and Terror in Russian Revolutionary Populism," 60.

131. Cooperation between the Kadets and various extremist groups continued through the outbreak of the 1917 revolution. Descriptions of their behind-the-scenes dealings may be found in: 28 January (10 February) 1909 report to DPD, Okhrana XVIId-1A; 17 (30) 1909 report to DPD, Okhrana XXVb-2G; and 13 (26) April 1913 report to DPD, Okhrana XXVb-3C.

CHAPTER EIGHT
THE END OF REVOLUTIONARY TERRORISM IN RUSSIA

1. Cited in Serebrennikov, *Ubiistvo Stolypina*, 42.

2. Some high officials in Nicholas II's administration were equally worried about the possibility of losing financial credit abroad as a result of reactionary domestic policies (Shatsillo, *Russkii liberalizm nakanune revoliutsii 1905–1907 gg.*, 307).

3. Many police and military officers suffered the pangs of guilty consciences as a result of their participation in suppression of the revolution; some began to drink heavily and even went insane or committed suicide, unable to overcome their shame. In a number of cases, children of state servants in charge of operations against the radicals

also killed themselves (Prozorov, "Samoubiistva v tiur'makh," 74–75; Koval'skaia, "Po povodu stat'i Orlova," *KS* 52 [1929]: 165). Stepan Balmashev was not altogether incorrect when, after his arrest following the assassination of Minister of the Interior Sipiagin, he mocked Durnovo, who implored him to petition the tsar to revoke his death sentence: "I see that it is harder for you to hang me than it is for me to die" (Chernov, *Pered burei*, 166).

4. Chernov, *Pered burei*, 222; Myzgin, *So vzvedennym kurkom*, 141. While handling the case of Kamo, a prosecutor by the name of Golitsinskii, who considered the Bolshevik terrorist a remarkable person and wished to help him avoid execution, deliberately delayed issuance of the indictment until the announcement on 13 (26) February 1913 of a general amnesty in connection with the three hundredth anniversary of the Romanov dynasty (Stasova, "Iz vospominanii o partiinoi rabote," *PR* 12 [71] [1927]: 196). In 1905, public prosecutors in Kiev took up a collection and gathered two hundred rubles to help a terrorist escape abroad (E. Vagner-Dzvonkevich, "Pokushenie na nachal'nika kievskoi okhranki polkovnika Spiridovicha," *KS* 13 [1924]: 135–36; see also Spiridovich, *Zapiski zhandarma*, 75). According to William Fuller, "Some military judges were so renowned for clemency and even judicial misconduct in favor of the accused that attorneys sought to have their clients' cases heard by them. Col. A. A. Adrianov, a judge of the Moscow Military District Court from 1907 to 1909, especially distinguished himself in this regard. At various points in his astonishing career, he advised defendants to sham illness to delay trials, and warned acquitted prisoners that the police intended to re-arrest them" (Fuller, *Civil-Military Conflict*, 184). Even more surprising, according to General Gerasimov a certain high official in the Ministry of Transportation went so far as to provide the SR terrorists with information about the tsar's movements (Gerasimov, *Na lezvii s terroristami*, 126, 130).

5. Obninskii, *Polgoda russkoi revoliutsii*, 109–10.

6. 5 (18) April 1905 report from L. Rataev to the Director of the Police Department, Okhrana XIc(5)-1. For illustrations of this situation, see "Bor'ba s revoliutsionnym dvizheniem na Kavkaze," *KA* 3 (34) (1929): 193, 197; and *Volia* 71 (4 October 1906): 4, PSR 7-569.

7. Chernov, *Zapiski*, 227, 219.

8. Phillips, "From a Bolshevik to a British Subject," 390.

9. Spiridonova, "Iz zhizni na Nerchinskoi katorge," *KS* 14, 192–93.

10. Phillips, "From a Bolshevik to a British Subject," 390.

11. Rataev, "Evno Azef," *Byloe* 2 (24): 189.

12. Cited in "Iz obshchestvennoi khroniki," *VE* 10 (1906): 866.

13. Ivan Bunin, *Okaiannye dni* (Leningrad, 1991), 65.

14. Prison officials often exerted little effort to prevent escapes. Maxim Litvinov recalled that during one successful mass breakout by revolutionaries, "the guard had been more or less sympathetic and had only resisted halfheartedly (Phillips, "From a Bolshevik to a British Subject," 391).

15. Spiridonova, "Iz zhizni na Nerchinskoi katorge," *KS* 14 (1925): 192.

16. Rataev, "Evno Azef," *Byloe* 2 (24) (1917): 189.

17. For only a few of the numerous examples of such escapes, and pertinent partial statistics, see "Bor'ba s revoliutsionnym dvizheniem na Kavkaze," *KA* 3 (34) (1929): 193, 198.

18. 26 August (8 September) 1906 report to DPD, Okhrana XIX-13.

19. "Bor'ba s revoliutsionnym dvizheniem na Kavkaze," *KA* 3 (34) (1929): 215–16; circular issued over Stolypin's signature to all governors, governors-general, and city mayors (1906), p. 8, Nic. 80–2.

20. "Slukhi," *Sprut* 13 (21 March 1906): 4, Nic. 436–5.

21. Pipes, *Russian Revolution*, 170.

22. Fuller, *Civil-Military Conflict*, 173.

23. Pipes, *Russian Revolution*, 169–70.

24. Ibid., 170.

25. According to Article 87, these emergency decrees lapsed unless approved by the Duma within sixty days of reconvening (ibid., 160, 170). An excerpt from the government's declaration introducing the field courts-martial is included in Faleev, "Shest'-mesiatsev voenno-polevoi iustitsii," *Byloe* 2 (14) (1907): 46–47. Pal'vadre cites later official clarifications of the law in *Revoliutsiia 1905–7 gg. v Estonii*, 138–40. Nicholas II subsequently justified implementation of the field courts system: "This is painful and difficult, but it is true that, to our grief and shame, only the execution of a few will prevent oceans of blood" ("Pis'mo Nikolaia II k Dubasovu," *KA* 4–5 [11–12] [1925]: 442).

26. Faleev, "Shest' mesiatsev voenno-polevoi iustitsii," *Byloe* 2 (14) (1907): 47, 49–50; Pipes, *Russian Revolution*, 170; Fuller, *Civil-Military Conflict*, 174–75.

27. Fuller, *Civil-Military Conflict*, 174; "Vnutrennee obozrenie," *VE* 4 (1907): 755–58.

28. For examples, see: Faleev, "Shest' mesiatsev voenno-polevoi iustitsii," *Byloe* 2 (14) (1907): 64–65; "Sovremennaia Letopis'," *Byloe* 3 (1906): 317, and *Byloe* 11 (1906): 338; see also Fuller, *Civil-Military Conflict*, 175. One conservative author also argued that the system was useless and unfair, for while the "fools"—the perpetrators of terrorist acts—were executed, the leaders who had incited them to act remained unpunished (Venozhinskii, *Smertnaia kazn' i terror*, 26–27).

29. An overwhelming majority of the death sentences issued were for terrorist acts and armed assaults. With the exception of a few isolated cases, revolutionaries accused of the manufacture and possession of explosives received up to fifteen years of hard labor (Rostov, "S pervoi volnoi," *KS* 20 [1925]: 54).

30. The abolition of the field courts-martial system is discussed by Golubev in *Vtoraia Gosudarstvennaia Duma*, 23–25. Golubev's claim that as many as 1,000 people were put to death by the field courts in five months is somewhat exaggerated. On the other hand, the figure of 683 prisoners sentenced to death, and supposedly executed between August 1906 and April 1907, seems an understatement ("V gody reaktsii," *KA* 1 [8] [1925]: 242; McCauley, *Octobrists to Bolsheviks*, 46). Ol'shanskii estimates that in the first six months of their existence, these courts issued 1,042 death sentences, and according to Fuller, they were responsible for the execution of at least 950 persons (N. Ol'shanskii, "Iustitsiia krovi," *KL* 2 [13] [1925]: 143; Fuller, *Civil-Military Conflict*, 175). According to other estimates, the field courts-martial issued as many as 1,000 death sentences (see, for example, Pipes, *Russian Revolution*, 170); still other sources claim that altogether 1,144 persons were executed under this system (A. B. Ventin, "Iz itogov sudebnykh repressii po politicheskim delam v Rossii za dva goda 'konstitutsii,'" *Tovarishch*, n.d., PSR 2-132; Rogger, *Russia in the Age of Modernization*, 223; Naimark, "Terrorism and the Fall of Imperial Russia," 19).

31. Repressive measures employed by the military in the Baltic provinces are described in "Pribaltiiskii krai," *KA* 4–5 (11–12) (1925): 281–88.

32. Fuller, *Civil-Military Conflict*, 150; V. A. Starosel'skii, "'Dni svobod' v Kutaisskoi gubernii," *Byloe* 7 (19) (1907): 302; Faleev, "Shest' mesiatsev voenno-polevoi iustitsii," *Byloe* 2 (14) (1907): 69–70; "Sovremennaia Letopis'" in several issues of *Byloe* from 1906: 2:308–10, 3:316–17, 10:352, and 12:309; *Volia* 87 (26 November [9 December] 1906): 26, PSR 7-592; and "Iz zapisok A. F. Redigera," *KA* 5 (60) (1933): 127.

33. See, for example, "Sovremennaia Letopis'" in several issues of *Byloe* from 1906: 3:314, 4:319 and 325, 5:301, and 11:336; Faleev, "Shest' mesiatsev voenno-polevoi iustitsii," *Byloe* 2 (14) (1907): 66–67; Obninskii, *Polgoda russkoi revoliutsii*, 112, 114, 117; a clipping from *Russie vedomsti*, 16 March 1908, and a clipping from an unidentified newspaper, no. 155 (5 July 1908), both in PSR 3-227.

34. Tagantsev, *Smertnaia Kazn'*, 91; "Smertnaia kazn' v Rossii ostaetsia?," *Novoe vremia*, 22 January 1910? (*sic*), PSR 4-346; S. K. Viktorskii, *Istoriia smertnoi kazni v Rossii i sovremennoe ee sostoianie* (Moscow, 1912), 354.

35. Fuller, *Civil-Military Conflict*, 169, 176, 181.

36. Cited in Pipes, *Russian Revolution*, 170.

37. Fuller, *Civil-Military Conflict*, 182; F. Kon, "Voennye sudy v Tsarstve Pol'skom," *KS* 20 (1925): 147; Ventin, "Iz itogov sudebnykh repressii;" A. B. Ventin, "K statistike sudebnykh repressii po politicheskim delam v Rossii za 1907 g.," *Tovarishch* 366 (8 September 1907), and "K statistike sudebnykh repressii po politicheskim delam v Rossii za 1908 g.," *Tovarishch* 6 (22 March [4 April] 1908), both in PSR 2-132.

38. Gerasimov, *Na lezvii s terroristami*, 8. Spiridovich complained, for example, that although the Police Department was fully informed about efforts to unite the SR forces into a larger party in 1901, and in possession of adequate means, it failed to prevent the consolidation (Spiridovich, *Zapiski zhandarma*, 80–81).

39. *Satiricheskoe obozrenie* 1 (1906): 2, Nic. 436–1.

40. Arkomed, "Krasnyi terror na Kavkaze," *KS* 13 (1924): 78–81; *Volia* 96 (28 January [10 February] 1907): 35, PSR 7-592; Obninskii, *Polgoda russkoi revoliutsii*, 126, 129; "Zapros o gen. Dumbadze," *Rech* (28 March 1908), PSR 2-150. For a vivid, if much exaggerated and only partially reliable picture of government atrocities presented by contemporary left-wing sources, see also Kirzhnits, *Evreiskoe rabochee dvizhenie*, 268–69.

41. Myzgin, *So vzvedennym kurkom*, 140–41; see also N. Zalezhskii, "V gody reaktsii," *PR* 2 (14) (1923): 339; and Voitinksii, *Gody pobed i porazhenii*, 304–5.

42. According to official statistics, whereas in 1905 detainees numbered 85,000, by 1906 this figure had risen to 111,000, and it reached 125,000 in 1907. By April 1908 the enormous total stood at more than 167,500 (cited in Prozorov, "Samoubiistva v tiur'makh," 78).

43. L. Lipotkin, "Russkoe anarkhicheskoe dvizhenie v severnoi Amerike. Istoricheskie ocherki" (undated manuscript), 152–53, Arkhiv L. Lipotkina, International Institute of Social History, Amsterdam; Zalezhskii, "V gody reaktsii," *PR* 2 (14) (1923): 339, 369; "Sovremennaia Letopis'," *Byloe* 6 (1906): 316; Voitinksii, *Gody pobed i porazhenii*, 304–5; Kropotkin, *Terror in Russia*, 16–18, 20–25; "Novye pravila o soderzhanii katorzhnykh," *Tovarishch* (11 July 1907), PSR 2-132; I. Genkin, *Iz vospominanii*

politicheskogo katorzhanina (1908–1914 gg.) (Petrograd, 1919), 67, 85, 87. Baron Taube, head of the St. Petersburg gendarme corps, even ordered his subordinates to refer to expropriations and other terrorist acts "by their true names: 'robberies' [and] 'murders'" (cited in *Tovarishch*, 23 December 1907, PSR 2-132).

44. "Zapros o gen. Dumbadze," *Rech* (28 March 1908), PSR 2-150; Gerasimov, *Na lezvii s terroristami*, 147; Ames, *Revolution in the Baltic Provinces*, 33–35.

45. See, for example, "Iz obshchestvennoi khroniki," *VE* 10 (1906): 869. For descriptions of illegal and arbitrary uses of military justice, see: Faleev, "Shest' mesiatsev voenno-polevoi iustitsii," *Byloe* 2 (14) (1907): 48–49, 55, 69; "Sovremennaia Letopis'," *Byloe* 11 (1906): 338; and Fuller, *Civil-Military Conflict*, 150.

46. *Zarnitsy* 6 (1906): 2, Nic. 436–17.

47. PSR 3-216. Parts of this poem may also be found in S. Isakov, *1905 god v satire i karikature*, (n.p., 1928), 171–72.

48. *Anchar* 1 (March 1906): 3, Nic. 435–2.

49. Fuller, *Civil-Military Conflict*, 185.

50. *Al'manakh. Sbornik po istorii anarkhicheskogo dvizheniia v Rossii*, 181–182; Faleev, "Shest' mesiatsev voenno-polevoi iustitsii," *Byloe* 2 (14) (1907): 67; "Sovremennaia Letopis'," *Byloe* 11 (1906): 335.

51. For such claims, see, for example, "Vnutrennee obozrenie," *VE* 4 (1907): 757–58.

52. Pipes, *Russian Revolution*, 170–71; see also Ascher, *Revolution of 1905*, 295.

53. A tongue-in-cheek fictional newspaper advertisement announcing employment opportunities is one of the many verbal attacks on the brutality of the government: "A slaughterhouse has thirty-six openings for former governors" (Isakov, *1905 god v satire i karikature*, 179).

54. See, for example, an excerpt from an intercepted letter signed by "Sema" in Odessa, written to Iakov Akbroit in Berlin, 12 January 1906, Okhrana XIIIc(1)-1A, Incoming Dispatches (1906), doc. 57; 25 November (8 December) 1906 report to DPD, Okhrana XXb-1.

55. Pal'vadre, *Revoliutsiia 1905–7 gg. v Estonii*, 72–73.

56. Outraged, Stolypin challenged Rodichev to a duel; the latter chose to apologize (see V. Maevskii, *Borets za blago Rossii* [Madrid, 1962], 69–70).

57. "Vnutrennee obozrenie," *VE* 4 (1907): 757. According to a contemporary, "The assassinations in August [1906] represented the acme in the wave of terror. After September, assassinations were on the wane." This, however, could not be said of the expropriations, which multiplied daily (Voitinksii, *Gody pobed i porazhenii*, 94).

58. See, for example, Pal'vadre, *Revoliutsiia 1905–7 gg. v Estonii*, 73.

59. See, for example, Levanov, *Iz istorii bor'by bol'shevistskoi partii protiv eserov*, 144; and Povolzhskii, "Nekotorye vnutrennie prichiny partiinogo krisisa," *Izvestiia Oblastnogo Zagranichnogo Komiteta* 9 (February 1909): 4, PSR 1-88. The connection between the decline of the revolutionary process throughout the empire and the diminishing intensity of the terrorists' efforts was particularly evident in border areas such as Poland. The overwhelming majority of the local extremists were first and foremost radical nationalists, and their morale suffered not only from the government's increasing effectiveness in combating the revolution, but also from the tendency of the Polish bourgeois and moderate forces to curtail their previous demands for complete independence for the sake of obtaining at least autonomous status for the country, as well as the stabilization of public life in the region. Such attitudes had a profound impact on the

PPS, which in the postrevolutionary period demonstrated a tendency to collaborate with ultranationalist nonsocialist forces, and whose isolated combat operations were no longer comparable in scope to its widespread practice of violence in 1904–1907 ("Obzor deiatel'nosti i nastoiashchego polozheniia Pol'skoi Sotsialisticheskoi Partii," and "Pol'skie revoliutsionnye i natsionalisticheskie organizatsii," pp. 28–30, both in Okhrana XIX-12A; undated police report [1912], Okhrana XIX-12B).

60. Excerpt from a 31 January 1908 letter signed "yours V," in Iaroslavl', addressed to Iakov Zhitomirskii in Paris, Okhrana XIIIc(1)-1A, Incoming Dispatches (1908), doc. 172.

61. Pipes, *Russian Revolution*, 191; 25 November (8 December) 1906 report to DPD, Okhrana XXb-1; excerpt from an intercepted unsigned letter dated 28 February 1909, written from Paris to K. V. Guma, Okhrana XVIb(3)-10.

62. Cited in Schleifman, *Undercover Agents*, 88.

63. According to Nicolaevski, Azef offered his services to the police in April of 1893 (Nikolajewsky, *Aseff the Spy*, 24–25, 30). In his Duma speech concerning the Azef affair, Prime Minister Stolypin asserted that Azef had become a police agent as early as 1892 (P. A. Stolypin, *Polnoe sobranie rechei predsedatelei Soveta ministrov P. A. Stolypina v Gosudarstvennoi dume i Gosudarstvennom sovete [1907–1911gg.]* [New York, 1990], 160; for corroboration of the date, see also *Delo A. A. Lopukhina v osobom prisutstvii pravitel'stvuiushchego Senata. Stenograficheskii otchet* [St. Petersburg]).

64. Nikolajewsky, *Aseff the Spy*, 41–42; see also Rataev, "Evno Azef," *Byloe* 2 (24) (1917): 195.

65. Nikolajewsky, *Aseff the Spy*, 56.

66. For a detailed and largely revisionist discussion of Azef's activities as a police agent, see Geifman, "Political Parties and Revolutionary Terrorism in Russia, 1900–1917," Ph.D. diss. (Harvard, 1990), 69–87.

67. Stolypin, *Polnoe sobranie rechei*, 160.

68. Gerasimov, *Na lezvii s terroristami*, 131; see also a 22 October (4 November) 1912 report to DPD, Okhrana XVIc-2.

69. "Izveshchenie Tsentral'nogo Komiteta o provokatsii E. F. Azeva," (7 [20] January 1909), p. 2, PSR 3-168; Nikolajewsky, *Aseff the Spy*, 29; see also a letter from E. Kolosov to Valentina Kolari written in Paris 21 October 1912, Okhrana XVIb(3)-10. Many SRs also noted with surprise how exceptionally fortunate Azef was in avoiding arrest for so many years (Okhrana XIIIb[1]-1B, doc. no. 123, 1906).

70. In March 1906, for example, Nikolai Tatarov informed Savinkov that the police spy within the PSR was Tolstyi. The SR leaders, however, believed this assertion to be an attempt on Tatarov's part to acquit himself at the expense of an innocent man. According to Savinkov, some members of the Central Committee interpreted the information pertaining to Azef's alleged police ties as part of an elaborate government intrigue originated by the Police Department to stain the reputation of a prominent revolutionary and end his activity (Savinkov, *Vospominaniia*, 227, 323).

71. On Burtsev's personal involvement in terrorist plots, see: 9 (22) March 1904 report to DPD, Okhrana XVIId-1A; 8 (21) May 1907 report to DPD, Okhrana XVIb(1)-1; Okhrana XVIId-1A; and Okhrana XXVIIb-1. For a long time Burtsev believed that the primary goal of every revolutionary organization was to assassinate the tsar, and even criticized the SRs for choosing governors and ministers as their targets instead of

striking at the very heart of the autocracy (Posse, *Moi zhiznennyi put'*, 311; V. Burtsev, "Sotsialisty-revoliutsionery i narodovol'tsy," *Narodovolets* 4 [London, 1903]: 20, PSR 1-19).

72. "Izveshchenie Tsentral'nogo Komiteta o provokatsii E. F. Azeva," 1, PSR 3-168.

73. Clipping from the *New York Times*, 7 January 1910; "Azeff's Career, Told by Vladimir Bourtzeff," *New York Tribune*, 31 August 1912; and "Russian Spy Admits Guilt," *Sun*, 15 September 1912, all in PSR 1-19; Gerasimov, *Na lezvii s terroristami*, 136.

74. M. Aldanov, "Azef," *Poslednie novosti* (1924), Nic. 205–19; *Otchet o sostoiav-shemsia 1/14 ianvaria 1909 g. v Parizhe sekretnom zasedanii iskliuchitel'no chlenov "pravoi" gruppy partii sotsialistov-revoliutsionerov po delu Azefa*, in a 6 (19) January 1909 report to DPD, Okhrana XVIc-9; V. Zenzinov, "Razoblachenie provokatsii Azeva" (New York, 1924), 9, Nic. 205–18.

75. According to Mikhail Aldanov, a contemporary and student of the Azef affair, Azef "was not killed because everybody was totally confused" (M. Aldanov, "Azef," Nic. 205–19). On the other hand, Burtsev suggested that the SR leaders purposely allowed Azef to flee because they did not want to kill him in Paris—an act that would undoubtedly have resulted in the arrest and deportation of many Russian political emigrés (30 December 1908 [12 January 1909] report to DPD, Okhrana XIIc[1]-2a). A thorough party investigation, with interrogation of the accused, could therefore not be held. For its part, the government, while denying the use of provocation in combatting the revolution, sought primarily to establish the true role of Lopukhin, who was tried at a special session of the Senate held in February of 1909, and convicted of abusing his former official position and collaborating with the revolutionaries. He was initially sentenced to five years of hard labor, but the sentence was reduced to life in Siberian exile. In 1913, as a result of the general amnesty, Lopukhin was allowed to return to St. Petersburg after four years of exile (*Delo Lopukhina*, 4, 6; Gerasimov, *Na lezvii s terroristami*, 135). The full story of the Azef affair thus never fully unfolded, leaving ample room for rumor, legend, and historical distortion.

76. Chernov, *Pered burei*, 285.

77. Schleifman, *Undercover Agents*, 88.

78. Cited in Levanov, *Iz istorii bor'by bol'shevistskoi partii protiv eserov*, 144.

79. Cited in Aldanov, "Azef," Nic. 205–19.

80. Gerasimov, *Na lezvii s terroristami*, 145; 13 September 1909 police report, Okhrana XIIId(1)-10; 22 October (4 November) 1912 report to DPD, Okhrana XVIc-2; Povolzhskii, "Nekotorye vnutrennie prichiny," 7, PSR 1-88; cited in Hildermeier, "Neopopulism and Modernization," 466; 18 November (1 December) 1913 report to DPD, Okhrana XXIVa-1B; "Oblastnoi zagranichnyi komitet Sots.-Rev." (Paris, 30 June 1909), PSR 1-31; Radkey, *Agrarian Foes of Bolshevism*, 79. In 1909 even Savinkov was suspected of having served the tsarist police as an agent provocateur, and some Russian newspapers did not discard the same possibility regarding Burtsev (4 [17] June 1909 report to DPD, Okhrana XVIb[3]-7; newspaper clipping from *Kievskaia mysl'*, 15 [28] February 1909, PSR 1-106). For a description of a pamphlet entitled, "The Conclusions of the Judicial Commission of Inquiry into the Azef Affair," published in 1911, see Schleifman, *Undercover Agents*, 107–10.

81. Cited in Levanov, *Iz istorii bor'by bol'shevistskoi partii protiv eserov*, 106.

82. See, for example, 4 (17) June 1909 report to DPD, Okhrana XVIb(3)-7; 30 December 1909 (12 January 1910) report to DPD, Okhrana XVIb(2)-7; agent's report from Paris dated 16 October 1909, Okhrana XVIb(3)-1A; 20 February (5 March) 1910 police report, Okhrana XVIb(3)-4; 13 September 1909 police report, Okhrana XIIId(1)-10; 23 November (6 December) 1910 report to DPD, Okhrana XVIb(3)-1A; Laqueur, *Terrorism*, 42; "Bol'nye voprosy," *Izvestiia Oblastnogo Zagranichnogo Komiteta* 12 (November, 1910): 1, PSR 1-88; Schleifman, *Undercover Agents*, 105.

83. The words "provocateur" and "provocation" were frequently abused in radical circles, their meanings distorted to refer to common police agents and their activities among the revolutionaries. The Russian government, in contrast, conformed to the standard definition of the term "provocateur," for according to both the classic definition and Russian and Western legal usage of the term, "provocation" implies first and foremost instigation to an act, with "agent provocateur" defined as someone who "incites another person to a criminal act." A provocateur is thus "an individual who takes upon himself the initiative for a crime, involving in it other persons who choose this path at . . . [his] instigation" (Vladimir Nabokov, "Ugolovnaiia otvetstvennost' agenta-provokatora" [manuscript for an article published in *Pravo* in 1909], Nic. 205–20; Stolypin, *Polnoe sobranie rechei*, 158). Contrary to the accepted assumption, the label of "agent provocateur" is not appropriate in Azef's case; there is no evidence that as a police spy he instigated any of the PSR's terrorist acts. For a detailed discussion, see Geifman, "Political Parties and Revolutionary Terrorism," 65–68.

84. Radkey, *Agrarian Foes of Bolshevism*, 79.

85. Gusev, *Partiia eserov*, 74, 76; V. Dal'nii, "Terror i delo Azeva," *Izvestiia Oblastnogo Zagranichnogo Komiteta* 9 (February, 1909): 11, PSR 1-88; Schleifman, *Undercover Agents*, 89–90, 94–95; Hildermeier, "Neopopulism and Modernization," 457–58; N. R., "'Bankrotstvo terrora' i delo Azeva," *Burevestnik* 15 (March, 1909), 13, Nic. 205–21.

86. 30 December 1908 (12 January 1909) report to DPD, Okhrana XIIc(1)-2A; 20 February (5 March) 1910 police report, Okhrana XVIb(3)-4; Schleifman, *Undercover Agents*, 56, 86. See also 14 (27) December 1909 report to DPD, Okhrana XIIIb(1)-1D, Outgoing Dispatches (1909), doc. 708; and 24 January (6 February) 1909 report to DPD, Okhrana XXVIIb-1.

87. See, for example, N. R., "'Bankrotstvo terrora,'" 13–14, Nic. 205–21; "Delo Azeva i zagranichnaia sotsialisticheskaia pechat'," *Izvestiia Oblastnogo Zagranichnogo Komiteta* 9 (February, 1909): 12–15, PSR 1-88; Schleifman, *Undercover Agents*, 115.

88. See, for example, an official SR announcement, dated 14 (27) August 1909, concerning the police activities of Zinaida Zhuchenko, secretary of the Moscow PSR Regional Committee ("Prilozhenie k #21–22 'Znameni Truda'," PSR 8-650).

89. "K ubiistvu polkovnika Karpova," reprint from *Znamia Truda* 25, PSR 3-219; see also Gerasimov, *Na lezvii s terroristami*, 166–70, 172–76.

90. Dal'nii, "Terror i delo Azeva," 12, PSR 1-88.

91. 21 July 1908 police report, PSR 1-26; Gusev, *Partiia eserov*, 74; 31 October 1910 police report, Okhrana XVIb(3)-1A; 23 October (5 November) 1913 report to DPD, Okhrana XVIb(4)-1.

92. Savinkov, *Vospominaniia terrorista*, 373; Schleifman, *Undercover Agents*, 106; 14 (27) December 1909 report to DPD, Okhrana XIIIb(1)-1D, Outgoing Dispatches (1909), doc. 708; 23 October (5 November) 1910 police report, Okhrana XVIIi-2S; 14 (27) May 1909 report to DPD, Okhrana XVIb(4)-1; 18 April 1909 police report to A. M. Garting, Okhrana XXIVa-5F; 23 November (6 December) 1910 report to DPD, Okhrana XVIb(3)-1A.

93. M. Gorbunov, "Savinkov, kak memuarist," *KS*, 4 (41) (1928): 169–70; 18 November (1 December) 1910 report to DPD, Okhrana XXIVi-2P.

94. 31 October 1910 police report, Okhrana XVIb(3)-1A; 23 July 1910 police report, Okhrana XXIVi-2O; 6 (19) April 1910 report to DPD, Okhrana XXVb-1; 3 (16) December 1910 report to DPD, Okhrana XVIb(3)-1B; 31 January 1913 police report, and 1 (14) February 1911 report to DPD, both in Okhrana XXIVi-1B.

95. 27 April (10 May) 1911 report to DPD, Okhrana XXIVi-1B; *Pamiatnaia knizhka sotsialista-revoliutsionera*, 17; "Izveshchenie Ts. K. P. S.-R.," PSR 8-650; Gusev, *Partiia eserov*, 74; Spiridovitch, *Histoire du terrorisme russe*, 627–28.

96. 8 (21) June 1911 report to DPD, Okhrana XXVIId-7; "Obzor deiatel'nosti i nastoiashchego polozheniia Pol'skoi Sotsialisticheskoi Partii," Okhrana XIX-12A; A. Sergeev, "Zapros o napadeniiakh na chinov politsii," *Russkoe slovo*, 1911, PSR 8-716.

97. Cited in Serebrennikov, *Ubiistvo Stolypina*, 37. Preparations for the assassination of Stolypin are mentioned in: 5 (18) May 1911 report to DPD, Okhrana XXIVi-1B; 30 December 1909 (12 January 1910) report to DPD, Okhrana XVIb(2)-7; 14 (27) May 1909 report to DPD, Okhrana XVIb(4)-1; and 18 November (1 December) 1910 report to DPD, Okhrana XXIVi-2P.

98. Serebrennikov, *Ubiistvo Stolypina*, 79, 85, 87, 92–93, 105.

99. Ibid., 96.

100. Ibid., 81, 90–91, 221; testimony of S. I. Demediuk, Nic. 101–7; Pipes, *Russian Revolution*, 188.

101. Alexander Solzhenitsyn, *August 1914. The Red Wheel-I* (New York, 1989), 489.

102. Pipes, *Russian Revolution*, 188. In a famous precedent, provocateur Sergei Degaev was offered a similar choice by the People's Will. On the story of Degaev, who assassinated his superior, Col. G. D. Sudeikin, head of the secret police in St. Petersburg at the time, see Naimark, *Terrorists and Social Democrats*, 53–58. Zavarzin, *Rabota tainoi politsii*, 17; Serebrennikov, *Ubiistvo Stolypina*, 94, 225–26. This assessment of Stolypin's significance was common among the revolutionaries, many of whom believed that his "elimination . . . is even more important than the removal of the Tsar himself" (cited in a 7 [20] July 1907 report to DPD, Okhrana XIIIb[1]-1B, Outgoing Dispatches [1907], doc. 296).

103. Serebrennikov, *Ubiistvo Stolypina*, 190–91; Pipes, *Russian Revolution*, 187–189; Kurlov, *Gibel' imperatorskoi Rossii*, 140–41.

104. Serebrennikov, *Ubiistvo Stolypina*, 84, 130, 139.

105. Ibid., 130, 129; Izgoev cited in N. V., "Ob A. Petrove," *Budushchee* 18 (18 February 1912), Nic. 101–15.

106. Serebrennikov, *Ubiistvo Stolypina*, 130.

107. Prior to his assassination of Stolypin, Bogrov approached prominent SR Egor Lazarev to request that the party claim responsibility for the proposed act after the fact. When Lazarev questioned the feasibility of the proposal, Bogrov responded, "Then let

the party name any other person. I put myself fully at the party's disposal." When asked, "Do you clearly understand that in making this offer to us you are condemning yourself to death?" Bogrov replied, "If I did not understand that, I would not have come to you. I came to ask not for material or technical help from the party, but for ideological and moral help. I want to make sure that after my death there will still be people and an entire party who will interpret my behavior correctly, explaining it by social and not personal motives" (ibid., 146–47).

108. Ibid., 97.

109. See PSR 1-82.

110. For example, the SR Central Committee, fearing another Azef affair, hastened to put an end to the rumors that Bogrov had acted on orders from the PSR ("Zaiavlenie Tsentral'nogo Komiteta Partii Sots.-Rev.," PSR 2-151).

111. GARF f. 102, OO, op. 1912, d. 98: 103.

112. 22 December 1912 (4 January 1913) report to DPD, Okhrana XXIVi-1B; 23 October (5 November) 1913 report to DPD, Okhrana XVIb(4)-1.

113. 14 September 1911 police report, Okhrana XVIb(3)-1A.

114. 16 (29) May 1912 report to DPD, Okhrana XVIc-2; 23 April (6 May) 1911 report to DPD, Okhrana XVIIi-3B(h); V. K. Agafonov, *Zagranichnaia Okhranka* (n.p., 1918), 142–43; 23 October (5 November) 1913 report to DPD, Okhrana XVIb(4)-1; 26 March (8 April) 1913 report to DPD, and 27 September 1913 police report, both in Okhrana XVIb(3)-1A; police note dated 28 March 1912, Okhrana XVIb(3)-4; 28 September (11 October) 1913 report to DPD, Okhrana XXIVi-3K; 20 January 1913 agent's report signed "W," Okhrana XXVIId-5; Gusev, *Partiia eserov*, 81.

115. 18 November (1 December) 1913 report to DPD, Okhrana XXIVa-1B.

116. Gusev, *Partiia eserov*, 81; 28 April 1911 police report, Okhrana XVIb(3)-1A.

117. 23 October (5 November), and 24 October (6 November) 1913 reports to DPD, and 5 April 1913 police report, Okhrana XVIb(4)-1; police directive dated 22 February 1914, Okhrana XVIb(3)-1A; 24 December 1912 police report, Okhrana XXVb-3A; 5 (18) June 1913 report to DPD, Okhrana XXVb-3F; 14 January 1912 police report, Okhrana XXI-1; 21 January (3 February) 1913 report to DPD, Okhrana XXIVi-3I; 14 (27) October 1913 report to DPD, Okhrana XXIVi-1B.

118. 8 November 1913 police report, Okhrana XXVc-1.

119. GARF f. 102, OO, op. 1914, d. 9, ch. 55B: 7-7 ob., 14.

120. Souvarine, *Stalin*, 102; *Leonid Borisovich Krasin ("Nikitich")*, 234; Dubinskii-Mukhadze, *Kamo*, 165–66.

121. 11 December 1913 police report, Okhrana XVIb(3)-1A; 1912 police report, Okhrana XIIIa-12; see also 14 (27) October 1913 report to DPD, Okhrana XXIVa-1B; 27 August (9 September) 1912 report to DPD, Okhrana XVIb(4)-1. Prospects of collaboration between the SRs and the free socialists reportedly collapsed because the independent radicals refused membership to an SR Central Committee representative. Although the total financial base of this group consisted of seventy francs, and its leader was so poor that he had to make a living selling crèpes on the street, the free socialists attributed their decision to "not wishing to have a provocateur in their midst," an assertion that illustrates the repercussions of the Azef affair for the reputation of the PSR in the revolutionary community (26 March [8 April] 1913 report to DPD, Okhrana XVIb[3]-1A).

122. See, for example, police circular dated 6 April 1912, Okhrana Vf-2; 14 (27)

January 1914 police report, Okhrana XIIIa-16A; 7 (20) February 1914 report to DPD, Okhrana XXVIId-7; "Une bande de vendeurs de platine surveillée par la police bèlge," *Le Matin*, 10 October 1913, Okhrana XXVc-1; copy of a 14 August 1912 note from the Head of St. Petersburg Okhrana to DPD, Okhrana XXIVi-1B.

123. GARF f. 109, DPOO, op. 1912, d. 113: 1; 18 February (2 March) 1912 report to DPD, Okhrana XXIVi-1B.

124. 17 September 1913 police report, Okhrana XIIIa-15.

125. See, for example, GARF f. 102, DPOO, op. 1912, d. 98, ch. 25B: 1–4; op. 1913, d. 98, ch. 27: 17 ob.-18, 39, 55, 71.

126. 14 (27) February 1912 report to DPD, Okhrana XIX-12B; GARF f. 102, DPOO, op. 1912, d. 13, ch. 60B: 35, and d. 161; 9 (22) November 1912 report to DPD and 1912 police report, both in Okhrana XIX-12B; 1912 police report, Okhrana XIIIa-12.

127. GARF f. 102, DPOO, op. 1912, d. 13, ch. 60B: 35; and d. 62, ch. 9B: 8, 9 ob. 13 ob. Members of the PPS prone to drunkenness and corruption considered the Revolutionaries-Avengers common bandits (GARF f. 102, DPOO, op. 1912, d. 12, ch. 1B: 9 ob.).

128. 24 July 1913 police report, Okhrana XIIIa-15; 19 February (4 March) 1914 report to DPD, Okhrana XXII-1B; 14 January 1912 police report, Okhrana XXI-1; 28 January 1914 agent's report signed "W," Okhrana XIIIa-16A; 17 (30) January 1914 report to DPD, Okhrana XXa-1B; 18 February 1914 agent's report signed "W," Okhrana XIIIa-16B; 15 April 1914 agent's report signed "W," Okhrana XIIIa-17B.

129. See, for example, police report written sometime after January 1915, Okhrana XIIIa-17B.

130. GARF f. 102, DPOO, op. 1916, d. 122: 55.

131. 7 (20) January 1915 report to DPD, Okhrana XVId-1; 4 (17) June 1915 report to DPD, Okhrana XXIVi-1B; 24 February 1916 police report, Okhrana XVIc-4; 29 February (13 March) 1916 report to DPD, Okhrana XXIVa-1B.

132. Unsigned reports from Paris to Count A. A. Ignat'ev dated 13 (26) November 1915 and 28 December 1915 (10 January 1916), Okhrana VIIIb-1A. For supplementary documents on this group, see Okhrana XVIb(5)-3; and undated police note in French, Okhrana XXVa-2U. For an account of anarchist activities in the United States in 1916, see GARF f. 102, OO, op. 1916, d. 122: 31–32ob.

133. *G. I. Kotovskii. Dokumenty i materialy*, 14.

134. GARF f. 102, DP, op. 1912, d. 25, ch. 101: 6. For a reference to another instance of teenage terrorism, this time in Dvinsk, see a clipping from an unidentified newspaper, 2 November 1912, in PSR 8-688.

135. GARF f. 102, DP, op. 1916, d. 79: 7, 9.

136. Ibid., op. 1916, d. 122: 186.

137. Ibid., OO, op. 1916, d. 122: 122.

138. Newell, "Russian Marxist Response to Terrorism," 461.

139. GARF f. 102, DPOO, op. 1912, d. 346: 3; and d. 274(I): 1.

140. Sivilev, "Staryi bol'shevik," 242.

141. Cited in Levanov, *Iz istorii bor'by bol'shevistskoi partii protiv eserov*, 105; see also 25 February (10 March) 1917 report to DPD, Okhrana XVIIa-5L; Newell, "Russian Marxist Response to Terrorism," 464; and Laqueur, *Terrorism*, 67.

142. 23 December 1916 police report, Okhrana XVIIa-4W.

EPILOGUE

1. Ford, "Reflections on Political Murder," 7. According to one estimate, during a single decade beginning in 1968, terrorist groups worldwide killed approximately ten thousand people (Meltzer, *Terrorists*, 192).

2. Meltzer, *Terrorists*, 7.

3. Martha Crenshaw, "Theories of Terrorism," 19.

4. Hildermeier, "Terrorist Strategies," 82.

5. Von Borcke, "Violence and Terror in Russian Revolutionary Populism," 58. At least in the early phase of the party's history the Kadet leaders seemed to concur on this point, with Miliukov asserting that his party stood "closest to those groups among the Western intellectuals who are known under the name of 'social reformers,'" with its program "undoubtedly the most Leftist of all those advanced by similar political groups in Western Europe" (cited in Karpovich, "Two Types of Russian Liberalism," 138).

6. Laqueur, *Terrorism*, 119; Weinberg and Eubank, "Political Parties and the Formation of Terrorist Groups," 126.

7. Von Borcke, "Violence and Terror in Russian Revolutionary Populism," 60.

8. Robert K. Massie, *Nicholas and Alexandra* (New York, 1967), 395.

9. Laqueur, *Terrorism*, 129.

10. 15 March 1949 letter from Archimandrite Vladimir in Teheran to V. M. Chernov in New York, Nic. 391–38.

11. Aleksinskii, "Vospominaniia," 15, Nic. 302–3; George Leggett, *The Cheka: Lenin's Political Police* (Oxford, 1986), 269.

12. For examples of former terrorists of various ideological trends using their past experience for the benefit of the Soviet organs of repression, see: Vulikh, "Osnovnoe iadro kavkazskoi boevoi organizatsii," 7, Nic. 207–11; Pozner, *Boevaia gruppa pri TsK RSDRP(b)*, 170n; Sokolov-Novoselov, *Vooruzhennoe podpol'e*, 39n; Muratov and Lipkina, *Krivov*, 111; V. Iakubov, "Aleksandr Dmitrievich Kuznetsov," *KS* 3 (112) (Moscow, 1934), 134, 138; *Soldaty leninskoi gvardii* (Gor'kii, 1974), 201, 204; *Soldaty leninskoi gvardii (kniga vtoraia)* (Gor'kii, 1977), 310, 313, 316–17; G. Shidlovskii, "O. G. Ellek (Pamiati starogo bol'shevika)," *KS* 9 (106) (Moscow, 1933): 143–44; Fishman, *East End Jewish Radicals*, 291; Tobias, *Jewish Bund*, 348; R. M. Aslanova-Gol'tsman, "Svetloi pamiati I. Ia. Bartkovskogo," *KS* 48 (Moscow, 1928), 158–59; "Vospominaniia byvsh. okhrannika," *Bessarabskoe slovo* (1930), Nic. 203–25; Zavarzin, *Rabota tainoi politsii*, 157.

13. Krivov, *V leninskom stroiu*, 110–12, 128; Pozner, "Rabota boevykh bol'shevistskikh organizatsii 1905–1907 gg.," *PR* 7 (42): 85; Myzgin, *So vzvedennym kurkom*, 21; Ioffe, *Krakh rossiiskoi monarkhicheskoi kontrrevoliutsii*, 150.

14. "Kommentarii B. I. Nikolaevskogo k knige L. Shapiro, *The Communist Party of the Soviet Union*" (1958 manuscript), p. 4, Nic. 519–30B.

15. Letter from B. I. Nicolaevsky to T. I. Vulikh dated 25 May 1956, Nic. 207–16. Ioffe, *Krakh rossiiskoi monarkhicheskoi kontrrevoliutsii*, 149–51.

16. Nikolai Ross, ed., *Gibel' tsarskoi sem'i. Materialy sledstviia ob ubiistva tsarskoi sem'i (avgust 1918-fevral' 1920)* (Frankfurt, 1987), 586; Richard Halliburton, *Seven League Boots* (Indianapolis, Indiana, 1935), 120, 140.

17. V. I. Shishkin, "Krasnyi banditizm v sovetskoi Sibiri," *Sovetskaia istoriia: problemy i uroki* (Novosibirsk, 1992).

18. Pipes, *Russian Revolution*, 528.

19. Dubinskii-Mukhadze, *Kamo*, 5, 195–96; Medvedeva-Ter-Petrosian, "Tovarishch Kamo," *PR* 8–9 (31–32), 141–42.

20. Iurii Fel'shtinskii, *Krushenie mirovoi revoliutsii* (London, 1991), 330n.

21. Avtorkhanov, *Proiskhozhdenie partokratii*, v. 1, pp. 181–82.

22. Shishkin, "Krasnyi banditizm," 76.

BIBLIOGRAPHY

This selected bibliography includes only works cited in the notes, and excludes separate references for archival documents, and for memoirs published as articles in frequently cited journals.

ARCHIVES

Arkhiv Samizdata, Radio Liberty, Munich
Columbia University Libraries, New York:
   Bakhmeteff Archive, Ms. Coll. Aleksinskii and Savchenko
Gosudartsvennyi Arkhiv Rossiiskoi Federatsii, Moscow, Russia
Hoover Institution Archives, Stanford University, Stanford, California:
   Arkhiv Zagranichnoi Agentury Departamenta Politsii (Okhrana Collection) Boris I.
     Nicolaevsky Collection
   Vladimir L. Burtsev Collection
International Institute of Social History, Amsterdam:
   Aleksandr Rozhdestvenskii Collection
   Arkhiv L. Lipotkina
   Arkhiv L. P. Men'shchikova
   Arkhiv Partii Sotsialistov-Revoliutsiuonerov
   Arkhiv V. M. Chernova
   Arkhiv V. P. Zhuka
   L. B. Krasin Collection
   V. S. Voitinskii Collection

PUBLISHED DOCUMENTS AND PERIODICALS

Al'manakh. Sbornik po istorii anarkhicheskogo dvizheniia v Rossii. Paris, 1909.
Anarkhist.
Biulleten' Ts.K.P.S.-R. 1. N.p., March, 1906.
Byloe.
Daily Chronicle (1 February 1901).
Delo A. A. Lopukhina v osobom prisutstvii pravitel'stvuiushchego Senata. Stenografi-cheskii otchet. St. Petersburg, 1910.
Dobrovol'skii, A., ed. *Anarkhizm. Sotsialism. Rabochii i agrarnyi voprosy.* St. Petersburg, 1908.
"Dopros A. I. Spiridovicha 28 aprelia 1917 goda." *Padenie tsarskogo rezhima*, v. 3. Leningrad, 1925.
"Dopros Gerasimova 26 aprelia 1917 goda." *Padenie tsarskogo rezhima*, v. 3. Leningrad, 1925.
"Dopros M. I. Trusevicha 4 maia 1917 goda." *Padenie tsarskogo rezhima*, v. 3. Leningrad, 1925.
G. I. Kotovskii. Dokumenty i materialy. Kishinev, 1956.

Gosudarstvennaia Duma. Stenograficheskie otchety, sessiia pervaia, 1906, zasedaniia 1–38. St. Petersburg, 1906; sessiia vtoraia, 1907, zasedaniia 1–53. St. Petersburg, 1907.

Ivich, M., ed. "Statistika terroristicheskikh aktov." *Pamiatnaia knizhka sotsialista-revoliutsionera*, vyp. 2. N.p., 1914.

Izvestiia oblastnogo komiteta zagranich. organizatsii.

Katorga i ssylka.

Khleb i volia 19–20 (July 1905).

Khronika revoliutsionnykh sobytii na Odesshchine v gody pervoi russkoi revoliutsii (1905–1907 gg.). Odessa, 1976.

Kirzhnits, A. D., ed. *Evreiskoe rabochee dvizhenie.* Moscow, 1928.

Konstitutsionno-demokraticheskaia partiia. S'ezd 17–18 oktiabria 1905 g. N.p., n.d.

Koz'min, B. P., ed. *Zubatov i ego korrespondenty.* Moscow-Leningrad, 1928.

KPSS v rezoliutsiiakh i resheniiakh s'ezdov, konferentsii in Plenumov Tsk, v. 1, 9th ed. Moscow, 1983.

Krasnaia letopis'.

Krasnyi arkhiv.

Kropotkin, Petr, ed. *Russkaia revoliutsiia i anarkhizm. Doklady chitannye na s'ezde Kommunistov-Anarkhistov v oktiabre 1906 goda.* London, 1907.

Laqueur, Walter, ed. *The Guerrilla Reader. A Historical Anthology.* Philadelphia, 1977.

Letopis' revoliutsii. (Gos. izd. Ukrainy).

Letopis' revoliutsii. (Khar'kov).

Maglakelidze, S., and A. Iovidze, eds. *Revoliutsiia 1905–1907 gg. v Gruzii. Sbornik dokumentov.* Tbilisi, 1956.

Maklakov, V. A. *Rechi.* Paris, 1949.

"Neotlozhnye zadachi." *Revoliutsionnaia Rossiia* 3 (Geneva, January 1902).

Novoe vremia. St. Petersburg, April–May, 1909.

Obninskii, Viktor P., ed. *Polgoda russkoi revoliutsii.* Moscow, 1906.

Obzor vazhneishikh doznanii, proizvodivshikhsia v Zhandarmskikh Upravleniiakh za 1897 god. St. Petersburg, 1902.

Pamiati Grigoriia Andreevicha Gershuni. Paris, 1908.

Pamiatnaia knizhka sotsialista-revoliutsionera, vyp. 1. N.p., 1911.

Pis'mo Vladimira Lapidusa. N.p., 1907.

"Pokazaniia V. L. Burtseva 1 aprelia 1917 g." *Padenie tsarskogo rezhima*, v. 1. Leningrad, 1925.

Possony, Stefan T., ed. *Lenin Reader.* Chicago, 1966.

Proletarskaia revoliutsiia.

Protokoly pervogo s'ezda Partii Sotsialistov-Revoliutsionerov. N. p., 1906.

Protokoly Vtorogo (Ekstrennogo) S'ezda Partii Sotsialistov-Revoliutsionerov. C. J. Rice, ed. New York, 1986.

Rech'. St. Petersburg, 1906–1908.

Ross, Nikolai, ed. *Gibel' tsarskoi sem'i. Materialy sledstviia ob ubiistva tsarskoi sem'i (avgust 1918–fevral' 1920).* Frankfurt, 1987.

Russkoe slovo.

Serebrennikov, A., ed. *Ubiistvo Stolypina. Svidetel'stva i dokumenty.* New York, 1986.

Sotsialist-Revoliutsioner.

"Spor o revoliutsii: dva pis'ma V. A. Maklakova Kn. V. A. Obolenskomu." *Vestnik russkogo khristianskogo dvizheniia* 146 (1986).

Stolypin, P. A. *Polnoe sobranie rechei predsedatelia Soveta ministrov P. A. Stolypina v Gosudarstvennoi dume i Gosudarstvennom sovete (1907–1911 gg.).* New York, 1990.

Tret'ia Gosudarstvennaia Duma. Materialy dlia otsenki ee deiatel'nosti. St. Petersburg, 1912.

Trotsky, Lev. *Dnevniki i pis'ma.* Tenafly, New Jersey, 1986.

Vestnik Evropy.

Zakliuchenie sudebno-sledstvennoi komissii po delu Azefa. Izdanie Tsentral'nogo Komiteta P. S.-R.: n.p., 1911.

Zeman, Z.A.B., ed. *Germany and the Revolution in Russia, 1915–1918.* London, 1958.

Znamia truda.

Zvezda.

MEMOIRS

Anan'in, E. A. "Iz vospominanii revoliutsionera 1905–1923 g.g." Paper 7, Inter-University Project on the History of the Menshevik Movement. New York, October 1961.

Arsenidze, R. "Iz vospominanii o Staline." *Novyi zhurnal* 72 (New York, 1963).

Arshinov, P. *Dva pobega. (Iz vospominanii anarkhista 1906–9 gg.).* Paris, 1929.

Avrich, Paul H. "The Last Maximalist: An Interview with Klara Klebanova." *Russian Review* 32 (4) (October 1973).

Baron (Bibineishvili). *Za chetvert' veka.* Moscow-Leningrad, 1931.

Bonch-Bruevich, V. "Moi vospominaniia o P. A. Kropotkine." *Zvezda* 6 (Moscow-Leningrad, 1930).

Bunin, Ivan. *Okaiannye dni.* Leningrad, 1991.

Burenin, N. E. *Pamiatnye gody. Vospominaniia.* Leningrad, 1967.

Buzanskii, Mark. *Budni podpol'ia.* Moscow, 1932.

Chernov, V. M. *Pered Burei.* New York, 1953.

———. *Zapiski Sotsialista-Revoliutsionera.* Berlin, 1922.

Genkin, I. *Iz vospominanii politicheskogo katorzhanina (1908–1914 gg.).* Petrograd, 1919.

Gerasimov, A. B. *Na lezvii s terroristami.* Paris, 1985.

Gessen, I. V. "V dvukh vekakh." *Arkhiv russkoi revoliutsii* 22 (Berlin, 1937).

Ianis Luter Bobis. Stranitsy zhizni revoliutsionera-podpol'shchika. Sbornik statei i vospominanii. Riga, 1962.

Kizevetter, A. A. *Na rubezhe dvukh stoletii (vospominaniia 1881–1914).* Prague, 1929.

Kokovtsev, Count V. H. *Iz moego proshlogo,* v. 1. Paris, 1933.

Krivov, T. S. *V leninskom stroiu.* Cheboksary, 1969.

Kryzhanovskii, S. E. *Vospominaniia.* Petropolis, n.d.

Kurlov, P. G. *Gibel' imperatorskoi Rossii.* Moscow, 1991.

Leonid Borisovich Krasin ("Nikitich"). Gody podpol'ia. Moscow-Leningrad, 1928.

Liadov, M. *Iz zhizni partii v 1903–1907 godakh.* Moscow, 1956.

Maklakov, V. A. *Iz vospominanii.* New York, 1954.

Myzgin, Ivan. *So vzvedennym kurkom.* Moscow, 1964.

Nestroev, G. *Iz dnevnika maksimalista*. Paris, 1910.

Nikiforov, P. *Murav'i revoliutsii*. Moscow, 1932.

Piatnitskii, O. *Zapiski bol'shevika*. Moscow, 1956.

Posse, V. A. *Moi zhiznennyi put'*. Moscow-Leningrad, 1929.

Pozner, S. M., ed. *Boevaia gruppa pri TsK RSDRP(b) (1905–1907 g.g.) Stat'i i vospominaniia*. Moscow-Leningrad, 1927.

Savinkov, B. "Revoliutsionnye siluety. Dora Brilliant." *Znamia truda* 8.

———. *Vospominaniia terrorista*. Khar'kov, 1926.

Shipov, D. N. *Vospominaniia i dumy o perezhitom*. Moscow, 1918.

Shul'gin, V. *Dni*. N.p., 1925.

Sokolov-Novoselov, Aleksandr. *Vooruzhennoe podpol'e*. Ufa, 1958.

Spiridovich, A. *Zapiski zhandarma*. Moscow, 1991.

Tyrkova-Vil'iams, A. *Na putiakh k svobode*. New York, 1952.

Uratadze, Grigorii. *Vospominaniia gruzinskogo sotsial-demokrata*. Stanford, 1968.

Voitinskii, V. *Gody pobed i porazhenii*, bk. 2. Berlin, 1924.

Zavarzin, P. P. *Rabota tainoi politsii*. Paris, 1924.

———. *Zhandarmy i revoliutsionery*. Paris, 1930.

Zhordaniia, Noi [Noah]. *Moia zhizn'*. Stanford, 1968.

SECONDARY WORKS

Abraham, Richard. *Alexander Kerensky: The First Love of the Revolution*. New York, 1987.

Agafonov, V. K. *Zagranichnaia okhranka*. N.p., 1918.

Ames, Ernest O. F., ed. *The Revolution in the Baltic Provinces of Russia*. London, 1907.

Andrikanis, E. N. *Khoziain "chertova gnezda"*. Moscow, 1960.

Aronson, Grigorii. *Rossiia nakanune revoliutsii*. Madrid, 1986.

Ascher, Abraham. *The Revolution of 1905: Russia in Disarray*. Stanford, 1988.

Avrich, Paul. *The Russian Anarchists*. Princeton, New Jersey, 1967.

Avtorkhanov, Abdurakhman. *Proiskhozhdenie partokratii*, v. 1. Frankfurt/Main, 1981.

Berdiaev, Nikolai. *Smysl istorii*. Paris, 1969.

Berezov, P. *Mikhail Vasil'evich Frunze*. Moscow, 1947.

Bergman, Jay. *Vera Zasulich: A Biography*. Stanford, 1983.

Bibineishvili, B. *Kamo*. Staryi bol'shevik: n.p., 1934.

Blinov, N. "Ekspropriatsii i revoliutsiia." *Argumenty i fakty* 30 (1989).

Blok, Alexander. "The People and the Intelligentsia." Marc Raeff, ed., *Russian Intellectual History: An Anthology*. New Jersey, 1978.

Bol'sheviki Ekaterinburga vo glave mass. Sverdlovsk, 1962.

Breitbart, E. "'Okrasilsia mesiats bagriantsem . . . ' ili podvig sviatogo terrora." *Kontinent* 28 (1981).

Burtsev, V., ed. *Za sto let, 1800–1896*. London, 1897.

Bushnell, John. *Mutineers and Revolutionaries: Military Revolution in Russia, 1905–1907*. Bloomington, Indiana, 1985.

Bystrykh, F. P. *Bol'shevistskie organizatsii Urala v revoliutsii 1905–1907 godov*. Sverdlovsk, 1959.

Crenshaw, Martha. "Theories of Terrorism: Instrumental and Organizational Approaches." Rapoport, David C., ed. *Inside Terrorist Organizations*. London, 1988.

Dubinskii-Mukhadze, I. *Kamo*. Moscow, 1974.

Dvoikh. "Pogibshie 17 Oktiabria 1905 g.-17 Oktiabria 1906 g." *Vestnik Partii Narodnoi Svobody* 33–35 (Moscow, 1906).

"Ekspropriatsiia ekspropriatorov." *Maksimalist* 6 (2 April 1920).

Emmons, Terence. *The Formation of Political Parties and the First National Elections in Russia*. Cambridge, Mass., 1983.

Emmons, T., and W. S. Vucinich, eds. *The Zemstvo in Russia*. Cambridge, Mass., 1982.

Erofeev, N. D. *Narodnye sotsialisty v pervoi russkoi revoliutsii*. Moscow, 1979.

Fel'shtinskii, Iurii. *Krushenie mirovoi revoliutsii*. London, 1991.

Fishman, William J. *East End Jewish Radicals, 1875–1914*. London, 1975.

Ford, Franklin L. "Reflections on Political Murder: Europe in the Nineteenth and Twentieth Centuries." Mommsen, Wolfgang J., and Gerhard Hirschfeld, eds. *Social Protest, Violence and Terror in Nineteenth- and Twentieth-Century Europe*. New York, 1982.

Fuller, William C., Jr. *Civil-Military Conflict in Imperial Russia 1881–1914*. Princeton, New Jersey, 1985.

Galai, Shmuel. *The Liberation Movement in Russia 1900–1905*. Cambridge, England, 1973.

Geifman, Anna. "Aspects of Early Twentieth-Century Russian Terrorism: The Socialist-Revolutionary Combat Organization." *Terrorism and Political Violence* 4 (2) (1992).

———. "The Kadets and Terrorism, 1905–1907." *Jahrbücher für geschichte Osteuropas* 36 (1988).

———. "Political Parties and Revolutionary Terrorism in Russia, 1900–1917." Ph.D. dissertation. Harvard University, 1990.

Gul', Roman. *General B. O.* London, 1930.

Gusev, K. V. *Partiia eserov: Ot melkoburzhuaznogo revoliutsionarizma k kontrrevoliutsii*. Moscow, 1975.

Haimson, Leopold. *The Russian Marxists and the Origins of Bolshevism*. Cambridge, Mass., 1955.

Halliburton, Richard. *Seven League Boots*. Indianapolis, Indiana, 1935.

Harcave, Sidney. *First Blood: The Russian Revolution of 1905*. New York, 1964.

Hardy, Deborah. *Land and Freedom: The Origins of Russian Terrorism, 1876–1879*. Westport, Conn., 1987.

Hildermeier, Manfred. "Neopopulism and Modernization: The Debate on Theory and Tactics in the Socialist Revolutionary Party. 1905–1914." *Russian Review* 34 (1975).

———. *Die Sozialrevolutionäre Partei Russlands: Agrarsozialismus und Modernisierung in Zarenreich (1900–1914)*. Cologne, 1978.

———. "Zur Sozialstruktur der Führungsgruppen und zur terroristischen Kampfmethode der Sozialrevolutionären Partei Russlands." *Jahrbücher für Geschichte Osteuropas* 20 (1972).

———. "The Terrorist Strategies of the Socialist-Revolutionary Party in Russia, 1900–1914." Mommsen, Wolfgang J., and Gerhard Hirschfeld, eds. *Social Protest, Violence and Terror in Nineteenth- and Twentieth-Century Europe*. New York, 1982.

Iakovlev, Ia. *Russkii anarkhizm v velikoi russkoi revoliutsii*. Moscow, 1921.

Ioffe, G. Z. *Krakh rossiiskoi monarkhicheskoi kontrrevoliutsii*. Moscow, 1977.

Isakov, S. *1905 g. v satire i karikature*. N.p., 1928.

"Iupiter serditsia." *Anarkhist* 1 (10 October 1907).

Ivianski, Zeev. "Fathers and Sons: A Study of Jewish Involvement in the Revolutionary Movement and Terrorism in Tsarist Russia." *Terrorism and Political Violence* 2 (2) (1989).

————. "The Terrorist Revolution: Roots of Modern Terrorism." Rapoport, David C., ed. *Inside Terrorist Organizations*. London, 1988.

Judge, Edward H. *Plehve. Repression and Reform in Imperial Russia 1902–1904*. Syracuse, New York, 1983.

Kalandadze, V., and V. Mkheidze. *Ocherki revoliutsionnogo dvizheniia v Gurii*. St. Petersburg, 1906.

Kaminka, A. "Mikhail Iakovlevich Gertsenshtein." *Vestnik Partii Narodnoi Svobody* 19–20 (July 1906).

Kaplan, Roberta Ann. "Russian Intellectual Perceptions of Suicide, 1900–1914." Unpublished paper. Harvard University, 1988.

Karpova, R. *L. B. Krasin. Sovetskii diplomat*. Moscow, 1962.

Karpovich, Michael. "The Two Types of Russian Liberalism: Maklakov and Miliukov." Simmons, E. J., ed., *Continuity and Change in Russian and Soviet Thought*. Cambridge, Mass., 1955.

Katenin, P. *Ocherki russkikh politicheskikh techenii*. Berlin, 1906.

Keep, J.L.H. *The Rise of Social Democracy in Russia*. Oxford, 1963.

Kelly, Aileen. "Self-Censorship and the Russian Intelligentsia, 1905–1914." *Slavic Review* 46 (2) (Summer 1987).

Kizevetter, A. A., ed. *Napadki na partiiu Narodnoi Svobody i vozrazheniia na nikh*. Moscow, 1906.

Knight, Amy. "Female Terrorists in the Russian Socialist Revolutionary Party." *Russian Review* 38 (2) (April 1979).

Kremnev, B. *Krasin*. Moscow, 1968.

Kropotkin, Petr. *The Terror in Russia. An Appeal to the British Nation*. London, 1909.

"K smerti M. Ia. Gertsenshtein." *Vestnik Partii Narodnoi Svobody* 21–22 (August 1906).

Lakoba, S. Z. *Abkhaziia v gody pervoi rossiiskoi revoliutsii*. Tbilisi, 1985.

Laqueur, Walter. *Terrorism*. Boston-Toronto, 1977.

Leggett, George. *The Cheka: Lenin's Political Police*. Oxford, 1986.

Lenin, V. I. *Lenin ob Urale*. Sverdlovsk, 1984.

————. *Polnoe sobranie sochinenii*, 5th ed., vols. 4–6, 11. Moscow, 1959–1960.

Leontovich, V. V. *Istoriia liberalizma v Rossii, 1762–1914*. Paris, 1980.

Levanov, B. V. *Iz istorii bor'by bol'shevistskoi partii protiv eserov v gody pervoi russkoi revoliutsii*. Leningrad, 1974.

Levin, Alfred. *The Second Duma; A Study of the Social-Democratic Party and the Russian Constitutional Experiment*. New Haven, Conn., 1940.

Lincoln, William Bruce. *In War's Dark Shadow: The Russians before the Great War*. New York, 1983.

Lunacharskii, A. V. *Byvshie liudi. Ocherki partii es-erov*. Moscow, 1922.

McCauley, Martin. *Octobrists to Bolsheviks. Imperial Russia 1905–1917*. London, 1984.

McDaniel, James Frank. "Political Assassination and Mass Execution: Terrorism in Revolutionary Russia, 1878–1938." Ph.D. dissertation. University of Michigan, 1976.

Maevskii, V. *Borets za blago Rossii*. Madrid, 1962.

Maklakov, V. A. *Pervaia Gosudarstvennaia Duma*. Paris, 1939.

―――. *Vtoraia Gosudarstvennaia Duma*. Paris, n.d.

Massie, Robert K. *Nicholas and Alexandra*. New York, 1967.

Melancon, Michael. "'Marching Together!': Left Block Activities in the Russian Revolutionary Movement, 1900–February 1917." *Slavic Review* 49 (2) (Summer 1990).

―――. *The Socialist Revolutionaries and the Russian Anti-War Movement, 1914–1917*. Columbus, Ohio, 1990.

Meltzer, Milton. *The Terrorists*. New York, 1983.

Men'shchikov, L. *Okhrana i revoliutsiia*, pt. 3. Moscow, 1932.

Merari, Ariel. "The Readiness to Kill and Die: Suicidal Terrorism in the Middle East." Walter Reich, ed., *Origins of Terrorism*. Cambridge, 1990.

Miliukov, P. *God bor'by*. St. Petersburg, 1907.

―――. *Russia and Its Crisis*. Chicago and London, 1906.

―――. *Tri popytki*. Paris, n.d.

Mogilevskii, B. *Nikitich (Leonid Borisovich Krasin)*. Moscow, 1963.

Muratov, Kh. I., and A. G. Lipkina. *Timofei Stepanovich Krivov*. Ufa, 1968.

Nabokov, V. D. "Sprava i sleva." *Vestnik Partii Narodnoi Svobody* 37 (November 1906).

Naimark, Norman M. "Terrorism and the Fall of Imperial Russia." Lecture, Boston University (14 April 1986).

―――. *Terrorists and Social Democrats: The Russian Revolutionary Movement under Alexander III*. Cambridge, Mass., 1983.

Newell, David Allen. "The Russian Marxist Response to Terrorism: 1878–1917." Ph.D. dissertation. Stanford University, 1981.

Nikolajewsky, Boris. *Azeff the Spy. Russian Terrorist and Police Stool*. New York, 1934.

"Ob ekspropriatsiakh." *Nastuplenie* 12 (25 September [8 October] 1907).

Ol'denburg, S.S. *Tsarstvovanie imperatora Nikolaia II (25 let pered revoliutsiei)*. Washington, 1981.

Pal'vadre, Ia. K. *Revoliutsiia 1905–7 g.g. v Estonii*. Leningrad, 1932.

"Pamiati Moishe Kirshenbaum ('Tokar')." *Anarkhist* 5 (March 1910).

Pavlov, D. *Esery-maksimalisty v pervoi Rossiiskoi revoliutsii*. Moscow, 1989.

Pavlov, I. *Ochistka chelovechestva*. Moscow, 1907.

Pavlovich, M. "Lenin i es-ery." *Pod znamenem marksizma* 10 (October 1923).

Perrie, Maureen. *The Agrarian Policy of the Russian Socialist Revolutionary Party from Its Origins through the Revolution of 1905–1907*. Cambridge, England, 1976.

―――. "Political and Economic Terror in the Tactics of the Russian Socialist Revolutionary Party before 1914." Mommsen, Wolfgang J. and Gerhard Hirschfeld, eds., *Social Protest, Violence and Terror in Nineteenth- and Twentieth-Century Europe*. New York, 1982.

―――. "The Social Composition and Structure of the Socialist Revolutionary Party before 1917." *Soviet Studies* 24 (October 1972).

Pervaia Gosudarstvennaia Duma. St. Petersburg, 1907.

Pervaia russkaia revoliutsiia 1905–1907 gg. i mezhdunarodnoe revoliutsionnoe dvizhenie, pt. 1. Moscow, 1955.

Pervyi shturm samoderzhaviia. Moscow, 1989.

Phillips, Hugh. "From a Bolshevik to a British Subject: The Early Years of Maksim M. Litvinov." *Slavic Review* 48 (3) (Fall 1989).

Pipes, Richard. *The Russian Revolution*. New York, 1990.

———. *Struve: Liberal on the Right, 1905–1944*. Cambridge, Mass., 1980.

Platonov, A. *Stranichka iz istorii eserovskoi kontrrevoliutsii*. Moscow, 1923.

Pomper, Philip. *Sergei Nechaev*. New Brunswick, New Jersey, 1979.

Post, Jerrold M. "Terrorist Psycho-Logic: Terrorist Behavior as a Product of Psychological Forces." Reich, Walter, ed., *Origins of Terrorism*. Cambridge, England, 1990.

Pribylev, A. V. *Zinaida Zhuchenko*. N.p., 1919.

Prozorov, L. "Samoubiistva v tiur'makh i okolo tiurem po dannym 1906 i 1907 goda." *Meditsinskoe obozrenie* 12 (1908).

Rabinowitch, Aleksander and Janet, and Ladis K. D. Kristof, eds. *Revolution and Politics in Russia. Essays in Memory of B. I. Nicolaevsky*. Bloomington, Indiana, 1972.

Radkey, O. H. *The Agrarian Foes of Bolshevism: Promise and Default of the Russian Socialist Revolutionaries, February–October 1917*. New York, 1958.

Randall, Francis Ballard. "The Major Prophets of Russian Peasant Socialism: A Study in the Social Thought of N. K. Mikhailovskii and V. M. Chernov." Ph.D. dissertation. Columbia University, 1961.

Reich, Walter, ed. *Origins of Terrorism*. Cambridge, England, 1990.

Rice, C. *Russian Workers and the Socialist-Revolutionary Party through the Revolution of 1905–1907*. New York, 1988.

Riha, Thomas. *"Riech'*, A Portrait of a Russian Newspaper." *Slavic Review* 22 (4) (December 1963).

———. *A Russian European: Paul Miliukov in Russian Politics*. London, 1969.

Robbins, Jr., Richard G. *Famine in Russia, 1891–1892*. New York, 1975.

Rogger, Hans. *Russia in the Age of Modernization and Revolution, 1881–1917*. London-New York, 1983.

Ropshin, V. (Savinkov). *Kon' blednyi* (Nice, 1913).

———. *To, chego ne bylo*. N.p., 1912.

Sablinsky, Walter. *The Road to Bloody Sunday*. Princeton, New Jersey, 1976.

Schapiro, Leonard. *Russian Studies*. New York, 1988.

Schleifman, Nurit. *Undercover Agents in the Russian Revolutionary Movement. The SR Party, 1902–1914*. New York, 1988.

Shatsillo, F. *Russkii liberalizm nakanune revoliutsii 1905–1907 gg*. Moscow, 1985.

Shaurov, I. V. *1905 god*. Moscow, 1965.

Shelokhaev, V. V. *Kadety—glavnaia partiia liberal'noi burzhuazii v bor'be s revoliutsiei 1905–1907 gg*. Moscow, 1983.

Shirokova, V. V. *Partiia "Narodnogo Prava."* Saratov, 1972.

Shishkin, V. I. "Krasnyi banditizm v sovetskoi Sibiri." *Sovetskaia istoriia: problemy i uroki*. Novosibirsk, 1992.

Sletov, S. N. *K istorii vozniknoveniia Partii Sotsialistov-Revoliutsionerov*. Petrograd, 1917.

Slonim, M. *Russkie predtechi bol'shevizma*. Berlin, 1922.

Soldaty leninskoi gvardii. Gor'kii, 1974.

Soldaty leninskoi gvardii (kniga vtoraia). Gor'kii, 1977.

Solzhenitsyn, Alexander. *August 1914. The Red Wheel-I*. New York, 1989.

Souvarine, Boris. *Stalin (A Critical Survey of Bolshevism)*. New York, 1939.

Spence, Richard B. *Boris Savinkov: Renegade on the Left*. New York, 1991.

Spiridovich, A. *Istoriia bol'shevizma v Rossii*. Paris, 1922; reprinted New York, 1986.

————. *Partiia sotsialistov-revoliutsionerov i ee predshestvenniki (1886–1916)*. Petrograd, 1918.

Spiridovitch, A. *Histoire du terrorisme Russe, 1886–1917*. Paris, 1930.

Steinberg, I. *Spiridonova. Revolutionary Terrorist*. London, 1935.

Steklov, Iu. *Partiia sotsialistov-revoliutsionerov*. Moscow, 1922.

Strakhovsky, Leonid I. "The Statesmanship of Peter Stolypin: A Reappraisal." *Slavonic and East European Review* 37 (1958–1959).

Struve, P. "Nashi neprimirimye terroristy i ikh glavnyi shtab." *Osvobozhdenie* 55 (2 September 1904).

————. *Patriotica*. St. Petersburg, 1911.

Tagantsev, N. S. *Smertnaia kazn'*. St. Petersburg, 1913.

Tobias, Henry J. *The Jewish Bund in Russia from Its Origins to 1905*. Stanford, 1972.

Troitskii, N. A. *"Narodnaia volia" pered tsarskim sudom*. Saratov, 1971.

Trotsky, Leon. *Stalin*. New York, 1967.

Turgenev, I. "Porog." *Novyi sbornik revoliutsionnykh pesen i stikhotvorenii*. Paris, 1899.

Ulam, Adam B. *In the Name of the People: Prophets and Conspirators in Prerevolutionary Russia*. New York, 1977.

Valentinov, V. *Maloznakomyi Lenin*. Paris, 1972.

Venozhinskii, Viacheslav. *Smertnaia kazn' i terror*. St. Petersburg, 1908.

Venturi, Franco. *Roots of Revolution: A History of the Populist and Socialist Movement in Nineteenth-Century Russia*. New York, 1970.

Viktorskii, S. K. *Istoriia smertnoi kazni v Rossii i sovremennoe ee sostoianie*. Moscow, 1912.

Vitiuk, V. V. "K analizu i otsenke evoliutsii terrorizma." *Sotsiologicheskie issledovaniia* 2 (April–May–June 1979).

Volk, S. S. *Narodnaia volia, 1879–1982*. Moscow-Leningrad, 1966.

Von Borcke, Astrid. "Violence and Terror in Russian Revolutionary Populism: The *Narodnaya Volya*, 1879–83." Mommsen, Wolfgang J., and Gerhard Hirschfeld, eds. *Social Protest, Violence and Terror in Nineteenth- and Twentieth-Century Europe*. New York, 1982.

Walkin, Jacob. *The Rise of Democracy in Pre-Revolutionary Russia*. New York, 1962.

Weinberg, Leonard, and William Eubank. "Political Parties and the Formation of Terrorist Groups." *Terrorism and Political Violence* 2 (2) (Summer, 1990).

Weinberg, Robert. "Workers, Pogroms, and the 1905 Revolution in Odessa." *Russian Review* 46 (1987).

Williams, Robert C. *The Other Bolsheviks: Lenin and His Critics*. Bloomington, Indiana, 1986.

Zalezhskii, V. *Anarkhisty v Rossii*. Moscow, 1930.

Zhordaniia, N. *Bol'shevizm*. Germany, 1922.

Zimmerman, Judith Elin. "Between Revolution and Reaction: The Russian Constitutional Democratic Party, October, 1905–June, 1907." Ph.D. dissertation. Columbia University, 1967.

INDEX